Understanding and Assessing

Trauma

in Children and Adolescents

ROUTLEDGE PSYCHOSOCIAL STRESS SERIES
Charles R. Figley, Ph.D., Series Editor

Editorial Board

UNDERSTANDING AND ASSESSING
TRAUMA
IN CHILDREN AND ADOLESCENTS

MEASURES, METHODS, AND YOUTH IN CONTEXT

KATHLEEN NADER

Routledge
Taylor & Francis Group
New York   London

Routledge
Taylor & Francis Group
270 Madison Avenue
New York, NY 10016

Routledge
Taylor & Francis Group
2 Park Square
Milton Park, Abingdon
Oxon OX14 4RN

Routledge is an imprint of Taylor & Francis Group, an Informa business

Printed in the United States of America on acid-free paper
10 9 8 7 6 5 4 3 2 1

International Standard Book Number-10: 0-415-96073-8 (Hardcover)
International Standard Book Number-13: 978-0-415-96073-1 (Hardcover)

Library of Congress Cataloging-in-Publication Data

Nader, Kathleen.
    Understanding and assessing trauma in children and adolescents : measures, methods, and youth in context / Kathleen O. Nader.
      p. ; cm. -- (Routledge psychosocial stress series ; 35)
    Includes bibliographical references and indexes.
    ISBN 978-0-415-96073-1 (hardcover : alk. paper)
    1. Post-traumatic stress disorder in children--Diagnosis. 2. Post-traumatic stress disorder in adolescence--Diagnosis. 3. Psychic trauma in children--Diagnosis. 4. Psychic trauma in adolescence--Diagnosis. I. Title. II. Series.
    [DNLM: 1. Stress Disorders, Post-Traumatic--diagnosis. 2. Adolescent. 3. Child. 4. Interview, Psychological. 5. Psychological Tests. 6. Stress Disorders, Post-Traumatic--psychology. WM 170 N135u 2007]

RJ506.P55N33 2007
618.92'8521--dc22
          2007005561

Visit the Taylor & Francis Web site at
http://www.taylorandfrancis.com

and the Routledge Web site at
http://www.routledge.com

With appreciation for their beautiful uniqueness,
this book is dedicated to
Andrea, Breaux, Casey, Chappell, Christian,
John Ryan, Lauren, Maresa, Matthew,
Nathan, Nixon, Noah, Wallis,
and all of our dear children.
My soul honors yours.

Contents

Part III Methods and Measures for Assessing Trauma in Youths

Part IV Assessing Additional Trauma Symptoms

Part V Pulling it All Together

Foreword

The Routledge Series in Psychosocial Stress is proud to welcome another stellar book of critical importance that is the first of its kind. Practitioners rarely receive sufficient education and training about children and youth, even fewer about assessment, and a very small but fortunate percentage of practitioners receive sufficient training and guidance to assess young people who have been traumatized. In a single volume, this book provides practitioners and parents the information and tools they need.

The author, Dr. Kathleen Nader, is well-known among her colleagues in traumatology worldwide. She is an accomplished scholar who has published in some of the most respected and widely read journals in psychiatry and psychology over a 20-year period. She was the longtime director of evaluation at the UCLA Trauma, Violence, and Sudden Bereavement Program, where she collaborated with Dr. Robert Pynoos and others. Dr. Nader has helped to produce some of the most widely used and referenced scales in the world that focus on children and adolescents.

In the preface to this remarkable book, Dr. Nader traces her career-long interest and work with traumatized children and adolescents to the failure of traditional methods with two little girls whose mother had been murdered. Dr. Nader was two weeks into her second clinical internship at the University of Southern California Child Psychiatry Department when she was called upon to help following the 1984 incident, now known as the 49th Street School shooting, one of the first of its kind, in south-central Los Angeles. A sniper fired repeatedly into a crowded schoolyard, killing a 10-year-old girl and a passerby. Thirteen other children and a teacher were shot. Many other children were pinned down on the playground under heavy gunfire. Since then, her work has focused on understanding and helping children exposed to traumatic events throughout the world. She has constantly reminded us through her lectures, video presentations, publications, and this book that we are all affected when children are traumatized, in part because the effects can be so pervasive and long-lasting.

She has responded to calls for help from Kuwaiti children exposed to the terror of invading and occupying Iraqi forces; helped children caught in the battles in the Balkans; helped children who survived the bombing of a Wyoming grade school after children were held hostage there; assisted other schools across the United States after the September 11th terrorist attacks; and others. In addition to these deployments, she has applied her knowledge about the assessment and treatment of children and adolescents through practical articles and videotapes aimed at the busy practitioner and the general public.

This book is a trailblazer in many ways. Books on traumatized children are far outnumbered by those that focus on adults. No book available today focuses on understanding, assessing, and treating both children and adolescents. This gap in the literature is particularly problematic because, as Dr. Nader notes in her book, "traumatic experiences compound the struggle with developmental tasks." Moreover, a large percentage of adults who are troubled and dangerous have histories of traumatic experiences from childhood. The following questions are addressed:

- How are children and teens affected by trauma?
- How are children's and teens' brains affected by trauma?
- How do trauma symptoms interact in traumatized children and adolescents?
- What factors enable children and adolescents to be resilient in the face of trauma?
- What is the nature of assessing children and youth who are suspected of being traumatized?
- What traits and symptoms are especially important to the assessment and treatment of children and adolescents?

The Series Editorial Board joins me in congratulating Dr. Nader on her significant achievement with the publication of this groundbreaking book. We expect that it will quickly become one of the most widely referenced among scholars and recognized as a valued resource for practitioners responsible for helping traumatized children and adolescents.

Charles R. Figley, Ph.D.
Series Editor
Tallahassee, Florida

Preface

The genesis of this book dates to the early 1980s, when two young girls were brought to Tulane University child psychiatry clinic for treatment after their mother was murdered. For another doctoral intern and me and our trainers, the girls were not responding to traditional treatment methods. My search for information to learn how to help these little girls later resulted in a second internship at the University of Southern California Child Psychiatry Department. Two weeks after the internship began, a man began shooting at children on an elementary school playground in south-central Los Angeles. When we began on-site assessments and initial interventions with these children, no scales were available that directly measured children's traumatic reactions. We had to create them. Many scales have been subsequently developed. Much has been learned since then, and much needs elaboration. When I began to update a chapter on assessing traumatized children (Nader, 1997), it became clear that a single chapter could not sufficiently capture all of the information relevant to assessing traumatized youths. This book combines years of assessments, treatments, and study with a look at current measures and recent findings. It covers topics key to assessment and treatment of youths with trauma or other disorders.

This book explores issues related to understanding and assessing youths' symptoms and reactions and the many factors that affect their reactions such as their traits, abilities, backgrounds, and circumstances. Methods and measures of assessment are available for the many variables that may influence a youth's reactions to extreme experiences. Scale descriptions are presented in the book after a discussion of each identified variable. To follow are a discussion of important topics related to assessment and a summary of the materials presented in the book's chapters.

THE AFFECTS OF TRAUMA

Childhood traumas affect all of us. Traumatic events may damage children's personal lives, development, health, mental health, and abilities to perform life-tasks adequately. Furthermore, children and adults with childhood traumas are numerous in our prisons and on lists of the notorious. In addition to nonproductive, self-destructive, or other undesirable posttrauma symptoms and behaviors, some unresolved traumatized individuals have committed mass violence, serial crimes, and terrorist acts. Effective treatments for childhood traumatic reactions are imperative. Correct assessments are essential to appropriate treatment planning.

GAPS IN KNOWLEDGE

Although much has been learned in the last 30 to 40 years about trauma in youths, many gaps remain in our learning. Evidence now suggests variations in traumatic response among age groups. Early systematic assessments of youths were based upon the symptoms found for adults. Basing assessments of youths' reactions on adult findings has, in some ways, resulted in misconceptions about the nature of traumatic response at varying ages. Moreover, earlier research had not taken into account all of the variables that may affect youths' reactions. When the symptoms, conditions, traits, and subgroups that are examined are too limited, variations and aspects of youths' reactions are missed. Failing to group youths by their personality types, pubertal stage, or reactivity patterns, for example, or measuring one point in time instead of patterns of change across time may fail to capture important traumatic effects.

GATHERING INFORMATION

A considerable body of research has now demonstrated the substantial importance that traits and conditions such as early child-caregiver attachments, personality traits, and economic conditions can have on mental health. In an ideal research world, all youths would be assessed from birth for their early attachment styles, parents' attachment styles, and other characteristics as well as their ongoing biases in attention and reaction, ongoing interactive styles, personalities, neurochemical levels, and other qualities and behaviors that may affect their resilience, vulnerability, risk, and reactions. Routine assessments of this kind would necessitate legislation and other protections that *fully* guard confidentiality and prevent the misuse of information.

As will be discussed in chapter 3, studies have suggested that, among youths, relational aggression is most often used by females. Among adults and youths, however, it is used by both genders, for example, in the form of racial or other discrimination and as a method of diminishing others with an objective of increasing the aggressor's power. Our goals in assessing youths include identifying and understanding their symptoms, other reactions, and disorders as well as protecting youths and assisting their healing. It is essential that the assessment information we gather about youths be prevented from inflicting harm, such as creating vulnerability to any form of misuse or aggression.

ACCURACY

Accurate intervention planning requires accurate assessments of youths following their traumatic experiences. To correctly assess youths, scales and methods that cover their range of immediate and long-term reactions must be available. The transmutation of symptoms over time and complex transactions among variables have yet to be discovered. Although research suggests, for example, that particular personalities are more vulnerable to traumatic symptoms following catastrophic events, it may be that different personalities have different vulnerabilities following traumas. Not all of these possible vulnerabilities or their relationships to personality traits and styles have been measured. Youths with differences in traits, attachment styles, cultural heritages, or economic and family circumstances may have varying needs in treatment and for recovery. Cognizance of these complexities and collaboration among specialties is needed to discover the many truths about single, repeated, and prolonged traumas and their effects on infants, toddlers, and youths in early and late childhood or adolescence.

PART I. UNDERSTANDING TRAUMA IN YOUTHS AND THE ISSUES RELATED TO ITS ASSESSMENT

The effects of traumatic experiences on youths of varying ages are, in some ways, similar to those of adults and yet, in other important ways, different. The dissimilarities reflect aspects of the developing body and brain and of cognitive processing, skill levels, and emotional regulation. Traumas can have dramatic effects on youths' ongoing development and life-course. Researchers have begun to examine in more depth the number of ways that trauma may affect youths of varying ages initially and over time. Part I includes a look at the ways that trauma may affect youths and issues related to the assessment of posttrauma reactions. Chapter 1 presents the American Psychiatric Association's diagnostic criteria and research findings for posttraumatic stress disorder (PTSD), acute stress disorder (ASD), and associated symptoms as well as additional childhood reactions and complex traumatic reactions. Research has demonstrated differences for children in the effects of trauma on the brain, its processes, and its development. Chapter 2 explores the neurobiology of trauma in children, describing the effects of trauma on neurochemistry and brain development as well as their assessment.

More than one route may lead to the same set of symptoms. Trauma alone or in combination with other variables creates one of those pathways. Multiple variables can be complexly interrelated in their contributions to the outcomes of trauma. Chapter 3 examines the complexity of associations between variables through the examination of a single possible outcome variable (aggression) and the variable's multiple associations.

Traits or symptoms (possible outcomes) that follow traumatic events may be a result of trauma, other variables, or a combination of variables. Multiple methods, sources, and locations of assessment as well as an understanding of an outcome variable and its associated variables are essential to accurate assessments. Many aspects of evaluation—methods of evaluation, training, briefing/preparation, locations of assessment, translations of scales, symptom ratings, question order, and reliability and validity of measures—affect the results of study. Chapter 4 explores these aspects of assessment. A number of factors (mediating and moderating variables) influence the levels and nature of symptoms and reactions. Resilience factors or their absence may mediate or moderate traumatic response. Chapter 5 discusses youths' resilience in the face of adversity. It examines risk and protective factors for children exposed to trauma as well as providing a description of the resilient child.

PART II. ASPECTS OF YOUTH AND ENVIRONMENT: THEIR INFLUENCE ON THE ASSESSMENT OF TRAUMA

Traumatic reactions can vary by gender, age and developmental issues, and personality factors as well as by culture and other family circumstances and background issues. Each of these variables may affect the assessment process and findings as well. Chapter 6 looks at the nature of the child who has been affected by trauma. Personality theories, traits, types, and findings are examined. Chapter 7 provides a discussion of the youth's background, including family and cultural issues that are relevant to childhood traumatic response and its assessment.

A wealth of research has now demonstrated the importance of the child–caregiver attachment relationship to a youth's growth, development, and mental health. Chapter 8 includes a summary of theories and findings regarding childhood attachment (e.g., attachment bonds, attachment styles, parenting, and family patterns of attachment). It demonstrates the influence of attachment on trauma as well as the influence of trauma on attachment.

PART III. METHODS AND MEASURES FOR ASSESSING TRAUMA IN YOUTHS

Improper interviews following traumatic experiences have sometimes worsened symptoms. Chapter 9 presents the general principles of interviewing traumatized youths. It provides examples of introductions and discusses other issues such as special methods of interview, creating a safe environment, wording of questions, and closure. A section on forensic interviews provides issues important to interviewing youths whose circumstances may result in court cases.

Youths may respond to traumas with *simple* PTSD, more complex reactions, or other symptoms and disorders. Failure to assess the possible range of reactions and the complications that occur, for example when there is a traumatic death, may result in poor intervention planning and treatment failures. Chapter 10 focuses on the nature of the traumatic event including its intensity and duration, timing and phase of response, and events with deaths. Controversy remains over whether some events may be traumatic for youths that may not be traumatic for adults. This chapter discusses the applicability of DSM Criterion A to children.

The importance of interviewing youths directly about their traumatic reactions has been well-demonstrated. Chapter 11 delineates issues and measures appropriate for school-age children's and adolescents' self-reports of PTSD and other symptoms. This book describes measures that assess more than a simple PTSD diagnosis because youths often present with symptoms in addition to PTSD. Controversy exists over applicability of DSM IV criteria B through D to children. For example, some symptoms are more difficult for children to report than adults. DSM IV does not take into account the developmental impacts of traumas on youths. Chapter 12 presents a number of projective tests used to assess trauma and its symptoms. Cautions are relevant when using such tests.

Caregivers and teachers are also important sources of information when evaluating youths. Chapter 13 discusses adult reports (parent, teacher, and clinician) in the assessments of traumatic reactions. Caregiver measures of trauma symptoms for children younger than 6 as well as for youths older than 6, and clinical assessment scales and methods (e.g., observational), are provided.

PART IV. ASSESSING ADDITIONAL TRAUMA SYMPTOMS

Youths often present with symptoms in addition to those specified in the DSM diagnosis of PTSD. Traumatic experiences may slightly or dramatically affect the youth's processing and integration of information. Chapter 14 details the concepts, symptoms, and research findings related to posttrauma information processing and to dissociation.

In addition to the behavioral and other symptoms that may occur after traumas, comorbid disorders often occur for traumatized youths and adults. Chapter 15 examines the symptoms in addition to PTSD and syndromes (comorbid or sole) that may follow trauma. Measures to assess these other symptoms and syndromes include those that measure sexualized behaviors, attitudes toward life, child behaviors, and children's psychiatric disorders.

PART V. PULLING IT ALL TOGETHER

Referral sources, other agencies, or courts may request reports following traumatic events. Chapter 16 demonstrates aspects of report writing for the clinic or the court. Case examples illustrate the sections of a report.

Chapter 17 provides a very brief set of conclusions. One of the case examples has been followed through much of the book. This chapter provides an update on the case example of Mathew. Table 17 compares his reactions when treated in adolescence to his current status.

Acknowledgments

I am very thankful for those who assisted the process of my writing this book. Sincere appreciation is extended to the esteemed colleagues who reviewed the chapters of this book: Martha Alcock, Linda Berens, Yael Danieli, Kenneth Fletcher, Robert Geffner, Robert D. Laird, Mary K. Rothbart, Thomas J. Scheff, Joyanna Silberg, Terry Trepper, Mary Beth Williams, and John P. Wilson. My thanks to the many authors found in this book who provided copies of their scales, measures, and interviews for my review. Many of these authors provided some of the articles about their measures and reviewed the descriptions of their measures. I am grateful to John P. Wilson, Kenneth Fletcher, Allison Spencer, and Marilee Conant for their encouragement and for the articles that they gathered for me. Ken, Allison, and Marilee were kind enough to copy edit many of the chapters. Allison is responsible for the author index and assisted with the subject index. Many thanks to Liz Hahn, Larry Martin, Sherry Moore, Carol Nader, and LeeAnn Pothast for their help with putting page numbers to index terms. Sincere appreciation is extended to all of those who had a part in bringing this book to final publication: to Mark Holbrook for his excellent advice regarding the early phases of the publication process, and to Dana Bliss, Charles Figley, Charlotte Roh, Prudence Board, and all of those at Routledge and Taylor and Francis whose efforts and assistance were invaluable. A number of students and typists helped with gathering articles and typing as the book evolved. I am especially thankful for the efforts of Chelsea Oldroyd, Sheena Staff, and the late Jackie George, whose gracious presence is missed by many of us.

Part I

Understanding Trauma in Youths and the Issues Related to Its Assessment

1

How Children and Adolescents
Are Affected by Trauma

Because of rapid access to information, children in many nations are exposed, daily, to the world's multiple stresses. In addition to media exposure, every year millions of children in and outside of the United States are exposed to mass or individual violence (e.g., child abuse, school and community violence, war, terrorist attacks), natural and human-made disasters, severe deprivation, animal attacks, and severe accidents. These experiences may occur when the child is alone or among strangers (e.g., hiking, crossing the street, biking), with family (e.g., car accidents, hostage or war experiences), or in a group (e.g., terrorist attacks, sniper shootings, natural disasters). They may occur once or repeatedly, in less than a day or over a prolonged period. Research has contradicted the notion that young children are more resilient following trauma (Scheeringa, Zeanah, Myers, & Putnam, 2005). Following traumatic experiences, a significant number of children react in ways that substantially disrupt or impair their and their family's daily lives, their growth and development, and their abilities to function normally (Box 1.1; Fletcher, 2003; La Greca, Silverman, Vernberg, & Roberts, 2002a; Webb, 2004; Wilson, Friedman, & Lindy, 2001). Unresolved traumatic reactions may seriously derail a youth's life path; task, work, or academic performance; and well-being. Much more information is needed to achieve a full understanding of the manner in which catastrophic experiences affect children over time. Researchers are finding that multimethod and multimeasure assessments increase understanding of the nature of childhood posttraumatic reactions.

Accurate assessment of trauma in children and adolescents as well as in adults requires examination of psychological, biophysiological, sociocultural, and spiritual dimensions of response (Boehnlein, 2001). This book addresses the many issues that are important to evaluating children and adolescents. A youth's reaction to a stressful event and the symptoms

BOX 1.1
Case Examples[1]

a. *Mathew.* Mathew was a happy 12-year-old boy with no history of behavior problems. During a lunch out with his best friend's family, a man in army fatigues entered the restaurant and for more than an hour walked around the room shooting people. Mathew's best friend, John, and his best friend's mother were killed. His best friend's father, Joe, was shot eight times but survived. Joe's body shielded Mathew. During the long siege, every time Mathew lifted himself up to try to see what was happening, the shooter shot Joe. Mathew was wounded twice in the arms. He witnessed the deaths, mutilation, and injury of many other individuals. He lay under the table thinking how much he wanted to get up and beat up the shooter. After the shooter was shot and killed, the S.W.A.T. team, which were also dressed in army fatigues, entered the restaurant, kicking over bodies. Mathew thought they were more shooters. When one SWAT member reached down to pull him up from under the table, Mathew tried to punch him. Then Mathew tried to awaken his best friend by poking him in the thigh, shaking him, and calling to him. In the ambulance, he saw a mutilated woman and a man "screaming like a girl."

Mathew began to behave violently and self-destructively. He provoked fights or carried weapons into areas frequented by aggressive weapon-carrying adolescents. He became violent in response to specific traumatic reminders: whenever he wore boots like the shooter, whenever anyone poked him in the thigh (as he had poked his friend), or whenever anyone grabbed him on the arm (as the SWAT member had). After a teacher grabbed Mathew's arm, Mathew hit him. He anesthetized himself from the emotional pain with alcohol and marijuana. Mathew was hospitalized twice. He later stated that he learned to be a criminal and a drug addict in the hospital and when he went AWOL with other "inmates." Mathew's mother took him to other clinicians before she finally found a childhood trauma specialist during his second hospitalization. By then, he was taking hard drugs and frequently fighting violently with others. He poked at the sites of his wounds with pencils and other objects and later found pleasure in drawing blood into the needle before injecting drugs (see Table 17.1 for a comparison of early and current symptoms).

The trauma program psychiatrist who conducted Mathew's initial intake evaluation told the ongoing therapist not to get her hopes up. "We will be lucky to keep him alive through high school," he said. At age 15, Mathew began each treatment session disavowing the need for therapy. Mathew then readily described his experiences and often engaged in spontaneous play that re-created the shooter endangering others, his feelings of helplessness, the need to fight back without being shot, and his desire to protect the friend who was shot to death. For a few weeks, he moved to the floor and regressed to the play and toys of a very young child. During a period of time that he refused to go to therapy, Mathew served as rescuer for his troubled friends and allowed himself to be endangered during his rescue efforts. He was stabbed during one friend's rescue. *(Case example continued in other chapters.)*

b. *Tony.* An earthquake of 5.6 magnitude partially collapsed an elementary school gymnasium during third-period gym class. Twenty-three children and two teachers were injured. Five children were killed. Tony (age 8) was in the gym when the earthquake collapsed the two outer walls. He sustained multiple injuries. His leg was broken in three places, and his hip was fractured. Tony was hospitalized for 3 weeks and required a period of physical recuperation after he returned home. Before the gym collapsed, Tony was a good student, well-behaved, and well-liked by his peers and by adults. Following the earthquake, he was nervous and jumpy. He became anxiously attached to his mother and refused to go back to school. To her distress, he would not let his mother leave his physical proximity. At first, he told the story of the earthquake over and over. Later, he had periods of nervous quiet or of expressing fears of disaster recurrence. Tony was easily distracted by sounds or movement. He became frightened when the windows rattled. When his peers visited, he began to scream and cover his ears if they hovered or more than one of them talked at the same time. He couldn't stand for them to touch him. Tony had difficulty concentrating and frequently engaged in angry outbursts. He startled easily, cried out in his sleep nightly, and complained of stomachaches. (Case example continued in other chapters.)

c. *Laticia.* When she was 17, Laticia's best friend was injured fatally when the two girls were robbed. Laticia sat next to Tanya's bed while she lingered near death for days before dying. Laticia became preoccupied with thoughts of what Tanya must have been feeling while she was dying. Although Tanya was unconscious, she seemed to react to Laticia's presence. Laticia engaged in repeated risky activities such as driving at excessive speeds on the freeway and running across tracks when trains were coming.

d. *Lonnie and David.* Following a long series of hospital procedures, a 3-year-old girl described elaborate dreams of trying to get away from the "cutters" coming to cut her. A 5-year-old boy with relapsed leukemia dreamed repeatedly of spacemen coming to take him to their planet. In his early dreams, he was afraid of them. He died a few months after he developed a comfortable relationship with them in his dreams.

e. *Joanie.* Until Joanie was age 12, her father and his friends repeatedly molested her. Her mother failed to protect or validate her. At age 12, Joanie threatened to go to the police, and the molestation stopped. After that, she felt empowered regarding men. She convinced herself that she was the user and not the used during her multiple relationships. She later realized that it was a false sense of control. Also as an adult, Joanie was very punishing to her female friends for any perceived betrayal, even if they only disagreed with one of her creative opinions. (Case example continued in other chapters.)

f. *Sheila.* Sheila's mother had wanted a son. The mother had neglected Sheila, who was repeatedly injured, was molested as a child, and was raped as an adolescent. When she felt helpless and unlovable for any reason, it re-evoked the distress of her earlier traumas. As a youth and as an adult, she wore her "boy boots" and dressed like a young boy when she was feeling very helpless and unlovable. She said that it made her feel safer.

g. *Laurie.* Molested as a child by her mother's boyfriend, Laurie, a competent executive, often, when fatigued or stressed, felt helpless and became childlike in her speech and mannerisms. In treatment, she expressed concern about undermining her own authority by seeking the opinions of supportive (young and old) employees about simple matters she would normally handle herself.

[1] *For protection of the youths described and their confidentiality, the names and other identifying details have been changed in all case examples. Cases may be composites of two or more cases.*

© *Nader, 2006.*

he/she exhibits can be related to many different factors such as aspects of the event (e.g., type and intensity of the trauma, chapter 10), qualities of the child (e.g., age, developmental issues, temperament, gender; chapter 6), facets of the child's background (e.g., family circumstances, culture, history, support systems, attachment relationships, parenting; chapters 7, 8), and the phase of the youth's response (e.g., initial or later; stunned or numb vs. grieving or extremely aroused) (Fletcher, 2003; Nader, 2001b; Webb, 2004). Examining the effects of any single element is complicated by the interrelationships of elements (chapter 3; Fletcher, 2003; Nader, 2001b).

Multiple factors also contribute to the accuracy or inaccuracy of scale development and of assessment of the differences among groups of youths. Among these factors are the method of selection of subjects (e.g., random, matched, self-), preparation for assessment (e.g., training, briefing regarding the event, community preparation, sample selection; chapter 4), the interview or other method of scale completion (e.g., interviewers, interview style; sources of information; the circumstances of measure completion, observation, or interview; chapters 4, 9 through 13), and the scales and measures used (e.g., their adaptation for children and cultures; validity and reliability; comprehensiveness; chapters 4, 7, 11, 13).

The History of Assessing Trauma in Youths

Prior to 1980[*], the assessment of childhood traumatic response was accomplished primarily through clinical case examination (Carey-Trefzer, 1949; Bloch, Silber, & Perry, 1956; Newman, 1976) and/or review of case records (Levy, 1945). Terr's examination of children following a school bus kidnapping (Terr, 1979, 1981b, 1983a) and other studies of children exposed to violence and disaster (Eth & Pynoos, 1985a) demonstrated the effectiveness of directly interviewing children regarding their experiences and responses. The need for a more systematic statistical analysis of children's traumatic reactions resulted in the application of a number of research instruments. These instruments included measures of depression (e.g., Birleson, 1981), anxiety (e.g., Reynolds & Richmond, 1978), fear (e.g., Ollendick, 1983), and "caseness" (Rutter & Graham, 1967; Elander & Rutter, 1996), as well as applying adult trauma scales to children (e.g., Horowitz, Wilner, & Alvarez, 1979). After a sniper opened fire on a crowded elementary school playground in south-central Los Angeles in 1984, the necessity for an emergency revision of Frederick's (1985) 16-item Adult Posttraumatic Stress Reaction Index marked the emergence of trauma scales for children (Nader, Pynoos, Fairbanks, & Frederick, 1990; Pynoos et al., 1987). Over the past 2 decades, a number of measures have been developed and revised to reflect a growing knowledge of children's posttraumatic reactions.

It has become clear that reliance on just one type of assessment is not the most accurate approach to assessing youths' posttrauma reactions. Accuracy increases as assessments are made using more than one method (e.g., scales, observations, interviews) and measuring more than one aspect of

---

[*] The first paragraph and some of the contents interspersed throughout portions of this work can be found in Nader, K. (1997c), published by Guilford Press.

the youth's experience (e.g., perceptions of the traumatic experience, reactions to it, support received from others during and after). A more accurate understanding of the course of youths' traumatic reactions also relies on repeated measurement over time with many of the same measures (see Caspi, 1998; Rothbart & Bates, 1998; Shiner, Tellegen, & Masten, 2001). The traumatic experience needs to be understood in context, as an experience embedded in a child's life, as one experience in a network of other experiences, and as a set of circumstances that can be experienced differently by different people. Some researchers have begun to explore the wider context of the traumatic experience, attempting to identify important mediating and moderating factors associated with children's traumatic reactions and symptoms, examining the success of alternate treatments, and assessing the long-term effects of the traumatic experience over time (Greenwald, 2002b; La Greca et al., 2002a; Nader, 2001b). Nevertheless, current understanding of childhood traumatic reactions has been limited or confused by (1) the lack of detailed information about children's lives prior to their traumatic experiences, (2) mixed methods and study results (sometimes based on small sample sizes), (3) unidentified mediating and moderating variables, (4) inadequate information about grouping or outcome variables; (5) the need to identify the changing nature of symptoms over time, and (6) the lack of detailed studies of children before and after traumas and at intervals across the life span.

Current Assessment Tools

Over the last several years, measures for school-age youths' self-reports of posttraumatic stress disorder (PTSD) and other symptoms have been created and revised (chapter 11; Table 11.1). A number of measures, interviews, and methods have been developed to assess other aspects of trauma in youths and to address specific types of traumatic experience (chapters 10 through 15). Scales, tests, and interviews for assessing neurobiological responses (chapter 2), exposure rates and levels (chapter 10), complicated trauma and traumatic grief reactions (chapter 10), adult reports (chapter 13), observational methods (chapter 12), information processing and dissociation (chapter 13), comorbid disorders (chapter 15), and associated symptoms (chapters 14, 15) are discussed in this book. Measures of child attributes such as temperament, attachment style, personality type, self-esteem, coping, life satisfaction, and trait anxiety are discussed as well (chapters 5 through 9, 15).

The Need for Accurate Assessment

The potential early and long-term negative consequences of unresolved traumatic response underscore the need for accurate assessment of child-

TABLE 1.1
DSM-IV Child PTSD

Criterion	Symptoms
A. Exposure (both[1])	1. Experienced, witnessed, or confronted with an event(s) involving actual or threatened death or serious injury or threat to the physical integrity of self or others AND 2. A response of intense fear, helplessness, horror, or disorganized or agitated behavior
B. Reexperiencing (1)	1. Recurrent, intrusive distressing recollections of aspects of the event (images, thoughts, or perceptions); repetitive play with traumatic themes 2. Recurrent distressing dreams 3. Acting/feeling as though reliving the experience; reenactment of aspects of the experience 4. Intense psychological distress in response to reminders 5. Physiological reactivity to reminders
C. The persistent avoidance or appearance of numbing of responsiveness (3)	1. Efforts to avoid thoughts, feelings, or conversations associated with trauma 2. Efforts to avoid activities, places, or people that arouse recollections of the trauma 3. Inability to recall an important aspect of the trauma 4. Markedly diminished interest or participation in significant activities 5. Feeling detached or estranged from others 6. Restricted range of affect (e.g., unable to have loving feelings) 7. Sense of foreshortened future (e.g., does not expect a career, marriage, children, or normal life span)
D. Increased arousal (2)	1. Sleep disturbance 2. Irritability or outbursts of anger 3. Difficulty concentrating 4. Hypervigilance 5. Exaggerated startle response
E. Duration	More than 1 month
F. Functioning	Clinically significant distress or impairment in social, academic, occupational, or other important areas of functioning

Adapted from APA (1994, 2001). *Diagnostic and Statistical Manual of Mental Disorders Fourth Edition (DSM-IV)*, pp. 424–428.
[1]*Numbers in parentheses are the minimum number of symptoms required for a DSM-IV diagnosis of PTSD.*

hood trauma (Table 1.2). Failure to resolve moderate to severe traumatic reactions or specific symptoms may lead to long-term consequences that interfere, over time, with the child's ability to engage in productive behaviors and to function adequately socially, academically, professionally, and personally (La Greca et al., 2002a, 2002b; Nader, 2001b; Silverman, Reinherz, & Giaconia, 1996). A number of initial and long-term disturbances and disorders have been associated with childhood traumatic experience: psychiatric disorders; physical problems and disorders; academic difficulty; emotional and behavioral problems; relationship difficulties; and suicidal ideation and attempts (Boney-McCoy & Finkelhor, 1995; Silverman et al.; van der Kolk, 2003; chapters 8, 14, 15).

The survivors of traumatic experiences may not be the only ones to suffer as a consequence of their exposures to these events. A growing body of evidence suggests that individuals who experience traumas are more likely to have children who experience traumas or who are more vulnerable when exposed to extreme stressors (Danieli, 1998; Perry, 1997). As detailed in chapter 8, adults' unresolved traumas have been linked to their children's disorganized/disoriented attachment patterns (Hesse, Main, Abrams, & Rifkin, 2003). In turn, disorganized/disoriented attachments have been associated with dissociative-like behaviors, aggression, and other psychopathology as well as increased risk of PTSD (Hesse et al.; Schore, 2003).

The prevention of many violent and destructive acts may depend on the accurate assessment and effective treatment of children. Trauma or unresolved traumatic grief frequently has been a part of the psychological histories of perpetrators of traumatic events such as school shootings (Hough, Vega, Valle, Kolody, del Castillo, & Tarke, 1989; Nader & Mello, 2002; Pynoos et al., 1987; Seals & Young, 2003), inner-city violence (Garbarino, 1999; Parson, 1997), child abuse (Dodge, Bates, Pettit, & Valente, 1995), and domestic violence (Davies, 1991). School snipers and mass murderers in the 1970s and 1980s were frequently witnesses or victims of intrafamilial or extrafamilial violence. For example, the 1984 Los Angeles 49th Street School sniper had relatives who died in the Jonestown Guyana massacre. The 1989 Stockton, CA school sniper witnessed the spousal abuse of his mother. Victims of overt aggression (e.g., assaults) or relational aggression (e.g., bullying, exclusion) have been among those who committed multiple shootings at their schools (Seals & Young). Small studies of incarcerated adolescents suggest that these violent adolescents significantly more often than not have histories of violent traumas (Ford, 2002). Traumas other than interpersonal violence can lead to further violence, as well. Individual and intrafamilial violence have also been found to follow natural disasters such as flooding in the Midwestern United States (Kohly, 1994). Thus, violence may be an indirect, if not direct, result of natural disasters (see Buchanan, 1998; Simmons & Johnson, 1998).

TABLE 1.2
Possible Results of Unresolved Trauma

Results	Some Examples
Influenced life	Reasonably normal life influenced by experience—influence on expectations, attitudes, interactions, cautions, choices, and behaviors; may create vulnerabilities
Changes in personal traits	Changes in cognitive ability, morality, and/or normal mood; reduced confidence; inhibitions; increased risk-taking; increased aggression; lower self-esteem; loss of a sense of personal control; a victim coping style
Disturbances in interpersonal functioning	Loss of friends; choosing friends who have been or feel victimized; irritability, bullying, fear or suspiciousness, victimization coping, or other personality changes may be aversive to others; withdrawal; changes in self-esteem, sense of control, and trust as well as symptoms may affect relationships and interactional style
Cognitive dysfunction	Memory and concentration problems; inhibited imagination; confusion; delayed processing of information; faulty information processing; difficulties reading others' emotions or purpose
Mental health disturbances or disorders	Chronic or complicated Posttraumatic Stress Disorder, Acute Stress Disorder; substance-related disorders; conduct, mood, anxiety, somatoform, eating, sleep, impulse control, personality, and/or dissociative disorders or problems
Attempts at numbing emotions or avoidance	Substance or medication abuse; varying levels of dissociation; a style of confusion, self-distraction, or distracting others
Compulsive repetition of traumatic behaviors and sequences	Trauma engendered script-like reenactments of trauma-related roles or aspects of the personal traumatic experience such as promiscuity or prostitution after molestation; aggressive acts when dressed like an assailant; frozen watchfulness when feeling threatened; feeling choked and exhausted anytime adrenalin increases; provoking attacks; dangerous risk-taking; repeated poor choices with problematic results; panic when there are certain noises, sensations, or smells
Distancing or warding off behaviors	Self-isolation; over-reactive anticipation of loss or injury with steps to protect oneself; rituals of self-protection; self-punishment
Self-punishment or disruption of numbing/dissociation	Provoking attacks; otherwise eliciting punishment or abuse from others; poor self-care; self-mutilation
Somatic complaints	Aches and pains such as stomachaches, body aches, headaches; deficient immune response; ill health; adult health disorders

©Nader, 2001, 2005.

Using Adult Criteria for Children

Even when the available empirical literature essentially supports commonalities between disturbances in youths and in adults, disorders can be expressed in different ways at different stages of development (House, 2002). For example, although older adolescents' reactions may be similar to those of adults following traumatic exposure, youths can have a decidedly different presentation and reporting style. As discussed in chapters 11 and 13, the applicability to children of *DSM-IV* diagnostic criteria continues to be debated. Some experiences, such as death of a parent, that may not be traumatic for most adults are potentially traumatic for young children. Children appear to exhibit a wider range of associated symptoms than adults in their traumatic reactions (House). Moreover, for young children, trauma can have more complicated long-term consequences (chapter 5; "Beyond PTSD," below). Traumatic events may disrupt a youth's developmental processes. More study is needed to identify and assess symptoms; patterns of behavior, emotion, and thought; and symptom combinations in addition to those listed in *DSM* or ICD to determine their applicability to different age groups: infants, toddlers, young children, preadolescents, early adolescents, and late adolescents.

Determining the trauma-related presence of specific symptoms may be more difficult for children than for adults. Some symptoms, such as avoidance symptoms, can be more difficult for children to recognize and describe (La Greca & Prinstein, 2002). Particular behavioral or emotional patterns, such as fearful inhibition, appear in normal children with specific personality styles and/or at certain developmental phases (chapter 6). Some confusion exists because of the synergistic nature of trauma symptoms (see Wilson, 2004b). For example, reexperiencing and arousal symptoms often occur in combination. Distressing thoughts can contribute to sleep disturbance. Traumatic memories and physiological arousal often occur in combination.

Types of Trauma

A number of clinicians and researchers have attempted to distinguish between the types of events that lead to variations in traumatic reactions (Nader & Stuber, 1992; Terr, 1991; van der Kolk, Roth, Pelcovitz, & Mandel, 1992; chapter 10). For example, Terr described Type I traumas as isolated traumatic events of short duration and Type II traumas as ongoing or chronic traumas (chapter 10). *Simple PTSD* is assumed to be the most likely form of trauma to follow one or more isolated traumatic episodes of relatively short duration (Terr; Tinnen, Bills, & Gantt, 2002). Other researchers have suggested that the tendency toward specific symptoms or disorders is related primarily to personality style rather than to experience (Dalton, Aubuchon, Tom, Pederson, & McFarland, 1993; Otis & Louks, 1997). It is likely that a combination of factors contribute to the nature of traumatic response in youths.

For adults, Tinnen et al. (2002) distinguished between types of traumatic reactions as they relate to dissociative symptoms. Among symptoms that differentiate *Simple PTSD* from other forms of PTSD are the absence of hallucinations, mild victim mythology/coping (see "Complex PTSD," below), and only mild dissociative experiences (adults' Dissociative Experiences Scale [DES] scores of 20 to 30). Dissociation is a primary symptom of *acute stress disorder* (ASD; see below). *Dissociative PTSD* may follow the most severe Type I traumas, such as rape, combat, or particular disaster experiences, or Type II traumas with a sadistic perpetrator. Dissociative PTSD includes hallucinations and dissociative symptoms (DES score of 30 or more). Tinnen et al. suggest that dissociative PTSD may be a subset of complex PTSD. *Complex PTSD*, most often associated with severe or multiple traumas, is differentiated from dissociative PTSD by the absence of hallucinations and marked personality changes (DES scores, 20 to 50).

PTSD, ACUTE STRESS, AND COMPLEX TRAUMA

The widely assessed *DSM* diagnostic and associated symptom groups of PTSD and acute stress disorder, and the symptoms of complex trauma, are described here. Additional assessment information is provided in other chapters of this book. Although *DSM* and complex trauma criteria provide a useful method of assessment and diagnosis, it is important to remember that symptoms of one syndrome often occur in combination with symptoms of other syndromes; one symptom may trigger another symptom or a set of related symptoms, as well. Other factors affect the manner in which symptoms are presented. Moreover, children's symptoms may evolve, affect their interactions with others, disrupt their personal development, and complicate other aspects of their lives over time.

DSM Posttraumatic Stress Disorder

Although some individuals may be more vulnerable than others to the effects of catastrophic events and developmental age may dictate which events are overwhelmingly stressful, traumatization is among the normal responses to extremely stressful life experiences (Fenichel, 1945; Wilson, 2004b). For a diagnosis of PTSD (Table 1.1), *DSM-IV* requires exposure to possible death or serious injury to self or others (A1); a response involving intense fear, helplessness, horror, or, for children, disorganized or agitated behavior (A2; APA, 1994; chapter 13); and symptoms that persist for more than 1 month. Adult or child reports of youths' posttrauma reactions have included symptoms from each of the three main PTSD symptom clusters described below (reexperiencing, avoidance/numbing, and hyperarousal) and functional impairment (chapters 11 through 15). Although some researchers have found that children report more re-experiencing than arousal symptoms, these findings may reflect problems in reporting and measurement (Fletcher, 2003; La Greca & Prinstein, 2002; Terr, 1979; see chapter 4). Survivor guilt, phobic avoidance of reminders of the event, or more complex symptoms may accompany PTSD (APA). Individuals with PTSD may be at greater risk of developing other types of anxiety, such as panic or phobias, as well as at greater risk for other disorders such as depression, somatization, and substance-related disorders (chapter 15).

Reexperiencing Symptoms

Since the mid-20th century, reexperiencing symptoms have been well documented for children following a variety of traumatic events (Bloch et. al., 1956; Galente & Foa, 1986; La Greca & Prinstein, 2002; McFarlane, Policansky, & Irwin, 1987). Widely varying aspects of the traumatic experience, such as particular sensory impressions, strongly felt desires, attempts to understand, a sense of injustice, a sense of betrayal, condemnation of one's self or actions, or changes in attentional focus may become deeply ingrained in children's traumatic memory representations (Nader, 1997c; Nader & Mello, 2002; chapter 3). Traumatic memories often recur accompanied by extreme psychological and physiological distress (see Table 1.1, B1, 4, 5) and sometimes by emotional numbing usually without physiological arousal (van der Kolk, 2003).

Recurrent, Distressing Recollections. Repetitively intruding memories of traumatic perceptions (B1) may include sensory, cognitive, biological, and emotional memories of, for example, blood, mutilation, death, danger, analyses of what is happening, frightened or frightening eyes, fast heartbeat, flying bullets, or shattering glass. Thoughts of experiences that occurred during (e.g., episodes of action, inaction, waiting, witnessing, searching, being injured, intense fear), before (e.g., the last or an important contact with deceased victims), and after the event (e.g., the look on a parent's face, rescue efforts, bodies, destruction, smells) are etched into memory and may replay themselves repeatedly (Nader & Mello, 2001; Pynoos & Nader, 1988; Terr, 1991). After an earthquake, Galente and Foa (1986) reported that children's memories were dominated by the precise moments when they last heard from each buried victim who was not rescued. Children's drawings were filled with menacing images. After the terrorist attacks of September 11, 2001, New York children reported repeated thoughts of injured people running to find safety and others jumping from the towers (Webb, 2002b). Children recalled unresolved misunderstandings, things that were promised but left undone, or harsh words between themselves and someone who died on September 11.

Repetitive Play, Reliving, and Reenactment. Most children do not report full-blown dissociative flashbacks (B3; Pynoos & Nader, 1988; Terr, 1983a). Children may, however, act or feel as though aspects of an event are recurring (B3) or may reenact portions of the event in their play (B1), activities (B3), or reactions to reminders of their experiences. Youths may react by fighting, fleeing, trying to rescue, or acting like a frozen witness in a manner like that experienced during the event. For example, children who have been in war zones or school shootings have run for cover or hit the ground when they heard a car backfire. Children exposed to tornadoes or earthquakes have panicked when the wind rattled the windows or a passing semitruck made the building shake. More subtle reminders such as increased stress or fast heartbeat have elicited fear or panic as though a threat were recurring. For example, in third grade, a boy's school was hit by a natural disaster, and 10 of his classmates were killed. When taking his Scholastic Achievement Test in his senior year of high school, he had a panic attack after reading a question about the same kind of natural disaster.

Traumatic play may replicate aspects of the event (Terr, 1989; see chapter 13, Box 13.1b). Bloch et al. (1956) described children's tornado games. For children exposed to a bushfire (McFarlane et al. 1987), playing games about the fire appeared to be related to the mother's failure to cope with the fire or overprotective behaviors. Traumatic play may increase anxiety or provide a measure of relief for youths (Nader & Pynoos, 1991). Its ability to promote adaptation rather than elevate anxiety may depend upon the youth's ability to freely express and rework traumatic emotions and episodes (chapter 13). Traumatized youths may indulge in play at older ages than nontraumatized youths (Terr; Webb, 2002a; Box 1.1a). Adolescents may replay their traumatic experiences in their activities or in regressed play (Box 1.1a, 1.1c). Traumatic play may not be event-specific. Children's play may include a variety of disasters or types of endangerment in addition to the event experienced. An 8-year-old boy (after a sniper attack) and a 6-year-old girl (after her father was stabbed) played out repeated disasters, fires, earthquakes, shootings, and knifings that were followed by rescue efforts.

From their personal symbolism, history, and individual traumatic experiences, youths (and adults traumatized as children) may repeatedly include, in their actions, drawings, or writing, symbolic representations of trauma segments (Box 1.1a, 1.1e). In addition to the memory segments of their external experiences and perceptions before, during, and after a traumatic event, youths' repetitive enactments (and thoughts) may include their intense desires to intervene (e.g., to rescue a victim, undermine an assailant), be rescued, or retaliate (e.g., to punish those responsible or those who failed to protect), and aspects of their traumatic role identifications or trauma induced script-like patterns of behavior (chapter 14). Youths may reenact, singly or phasically, these *trauma-related roles* or *desires to act* that intensely registered during and after an event. In addition to the trauma-related roles of perpetrator, rescuer, victim, or witness, traumatic roles may include many more roles engendered by intense peritraumatic fears, desires, and other experiences (see chapter 14). After a shooting at his school, 8-year-old Mohammed played repeated superhero games in which he rescued numerous individuals in succession. A traumatized youth may change roles or identifications over the course of time (in and out of treatment) (Box 1.1a 14.1a). Remaining in one of the roles without resolution or unconsciously and repeatedly re-enacting intense traumatic desires may lead to dangerous or troublesome behaviors (Nader, 1997c; Box 1.1a, 1.1g).

Distressing Dreams. In addition to or in place of distressing dreams or nightmares (B2) about their trauma experiences, children's posttrauma dreams may include other disasters and threats or more generalized scary features such as monsters or an unrecognizable threat (Lacey, 1972; McFarlane et al., 1987; Nader, 1996; Newman, 1976; Terr, 1983b). Although young children may not remember night terrors, they have sometimes enacted aspects of an event in them such as running for safety from a sniper or screaming with eyes wide open as though seeing something horrifying. Elaborate dreams are one of the ways that accelerated development (indicated by precocious knowledge or behavior) may follow traumatic experiences (Nader). Research suggests that between ages 3 and 7, children normally report few dreams upon being awakened from REM sleep. Their dreams contain few human characters but more often include animals (Foulkes, 1990; Foulkes, Hollifield, Sullivan, Bradley, & Terry, 1990). Between ages 11 and 12, dreaming begins to approximate that of adulthood, and children are able to construct a dream narrative (Westerlund & Johnson, 1989). Traumatized preschool children may have dreams more like those described for older children (Box 1.1d).

Reactivity to Reminders. Traumatic reminders—internal or external cues that symbolize or resemble some aspect of the traumatic event (APA, 2001; see Table 1.3)—may trigger physiological arousal (B5) and psychological distress (B4) for youths and for adults. Physiological arousal such as activation of the neurochemicals related to extreme threat may occur as other possible side effects of distress such as stomachaches, headaches, fatigue, sluggish immune response, and increased illness (chapter 2). As described above, symbolic reminders of the trauma or traumatic response also may elicit re-enactments or script-like behaviors that become a part of a youth's (and later the adult's) repertoire of behaviors (Box 1.1f).

TABLE 1.3
Sample of General and Specific Traumatic Reminders

Event	Reminders
General (may occur for many types of events)	News stories; specific locations (e.g., where there was harm, destruction, or blood; the place the child was during the event); talking about it; specific persons (e.g., who look, act, or talk a certain way); concrete items (e.g., items present at the site of a horrible experience); blood or specific red liquids; bleeding; sounds (e.g., those mimicking the trauma: screaming, yelling for help, moaning); atmospheric conditions; smells; behaviors; being touched in certain ways; potentially dangerous situations; certain emotions; certain sensations (e.g., stickiness; light-headedness; tension in the stomach; headaches; other pain; pressure to the body); a certain look (e.g., paleness; anger; wide eyes); certain people or reminders of them (e.g., injured, dead, those who endangered others or rescued someone); someone dying; injuries (e.g., broken limbs, wounds); media images (e.g., of violence, weapons, crumbling buildings, strong winds, images that resemble some aspect of the event); certain foods (e.g., what the child was eating during the event; what was smelled cooking or on the breath of the offender); vehicles like the ones near the event; clothes (e.g., those worn during the event by self or others)
Tornado	Rain, wind, gray skies; green or other haze seen during the experience; rattling windows or shaking buildings (the feel or sound of them); things falling or flying (sights or sounds of falling/flying items); sounds of tornado and winds (e.g., train sounds); being hit with something; specific or general debris; media images such as flying window glass, breaking glass, tornadoes, the aftermath of disasters
Earthquake	Shaking or rattling buildings (e.g., when truck passes or wind makes things rattle); things falling or crashing; crashing or rumbling sounds; dust flying; certain sensations of motion (e.g., sense of things bouncing, rocking, or swirling); enclosed spaces; being hit with something; specific or general debris; demolished buildings or buildings falling
Shooting or knifing	People who resemble the assailant in some way; sounds (e.g., gun violence: popping noises; loud bangs; a car backfiring; knifing: scrape of a blade; what assailant said or noises made); weapons; places (e.g., with bullet holes or holes that resemble bullet holes; that look like where the violence occurred); wounds or injuries; locations that seem unsafe or resemble the location of the violence; clothing (e.g., uniforms for war; assailant's clothes)
Bombing	People who resemble the assailant in some way; sounds (e.g., exploding sounds; loud bangs; rumbling, crashing noises; screams; moans); weapons (e.g., if assailant carried bomb and weapons); places or media images (e.g., demolished buildings); wounds (e.g., burns, broken bones, crushing injuries); burnt things
Fire	Fire/flame; heat; smoke; sunburn; burning smells; feeling trapped; feeling like it is difficult to breathe; crowds running or shoving; things crashing or crackling

TABLE 1.3 (continued)
Sample of General and Specific Traumatic Reminders

Event	Reminders
Sexual abuse/rape	People who resemble the abuser in some way; situations that resemble the abuse situation; smells (e.g., of the abuser, odors present during the abuse; his or her breath, perfume/cologne, alcohol; bodily fluids; certain food smells); weapons or other items (e.g., used to coerce, molest, or rape); sounds (e.g., like the abuser's voice; specific words); sensations (e.g., a heavy body or pressure, pain); certain kinds of pain or pleasure; particular body sensations such as in the mouth, anus, or vagina); certain facial expressions; certain emotions (e.g., feeling threatened, combinations of emotions); things that seemed to trigger the abuse episode; being pushed against something; consistencies of liquid
Physical abuse/assault	People who resemble the abuser in some way; situations that resemble the abuse situation; smells (e.g., of the abuser, odors present during the abuse; that precede or accompany abuse such as alcohol); weapons or other items (e.g., used to beat or restrain); sensations (e.g., of being hit or pushed, certain kinds of pain); bruises or injuries; certain facial expressions (e.g., anger, grinning, sadistic); certain emotions (e.g., feeling threatened, combinations of emotions); things that seemed to trigger the abuse episode; certain gestures; facial expressions

Reprinted with permission from Nader, 1993b, 1995.

Numbing and Avoidance Symptoms

Children and observers have reported youths' posttrauma numbing and avoidance behaviors and experiences. Avoidance of traumatic reminders, numbing, detachment, and emotional blunting often coexist with the reexperiencing features of trauma (van der Kolk, 2003). Numbing and avoidance have been described both as symptoms and as coping mechanisms following catastrophic events (see chapter 5). Some researchers have found that youths' emotional numbing (loss of interest, detachment, and restricted affect) is distinct from the avoidance/numbing criterion of adult PTSD (Sack, Seeley, & Clarke, 1997; Scheeringa et al., 2005). Over time, numbing and avoidance symptoms, which are associated with an inability to experience pleasure and joy and with general withdrawal from engagement with life, may become the dominant symptoms of PTSD (van der Kolk).

Efforts to Avoid. Although children do not always have the option of avoiding reminders, they often report the desire to avoid traumatic reminders (C1, C2; Nader et al., 1990; Pynoos et al., 1987). Avoidance can be active (e.g., distraction or resistance techniques) or less overt. Following a tornado (Nader, 1997c), children's rowdy efforts to distract themselves and each other made concentration and a normal school routine impossible. Avoidance of play or activities may be intermittent for children.

Amnesia. Although children have reported amnesia for portions of an experience, such as right after a bomb went off or when the youth's head hit a barrier after being struck by a car and propelled against it, clinicians have reported children's recall of a forgotten segment in treatment during repeated review of the event (Nader, 2001b).

Lack of Engagement. Lack of engagement with others, following traumas, may reflect avoidance of reminders (C2) or a sense of estrangement (C5). It may also indicate irritability (D2) or an altered view of self (chapter 5). Youths may have difficulty with the noise and activities of others after traumas (Box 1.1b). Younger school-age children may cling or stay close to adults yet feel emotionally detached. After a shooting at a church parking lot, children expressed feelings of estrangement from family and friends even when parents reported their children's increased clinging. Children who had not reported a sense of detachment from their families have described feeling alone with their feelings about what happened to them (Nader et al., 1990). Engagement may be intermittent, altered, or lacking for young traumatized children.

Restricted or Blunted Affect. Shock, bewilderment, partial loss of temporal and spatial orientation, loss of energy, and withdrawal behavior are among expectable reactions to the overwhelming aspects of traumatic experiences (Ayalon, 1983; Kinzie, Sack, Angell, Manson, & Rath, 1986). Klein (1974) explained that, for Holocaust children, suppression of affects not in the direct service of survival in combination with concentration camp experiences resulted in "numbness of feeling." In addition to affective constriction, Eth and Pynoos (1985a) observed subdued natures or mute behaviors and unemotional or third-person attitudes. Youths may feel perpetually sad, guilty, or frightened and either rarely able or unable to feel positive emotions such as joy.

Worldview. After severe or repeated traumas, youths may begin to expect an altered future. Children become more aware that bad things can happen in their lives. They may feel pessimistic, unlucky, undeserving, unlikely to have a normal life, or concerned about bringing children into the world (Fletcher, 2003; Nader, 1997c; Terr, 1983a; see "Complex PTSD," below). After war, for example, adolescents have expressed concerns about having a family (Nader, Pynoos, Fairbanks, Al-Ajeel, & Al-Asfour, 1993).

Hyperarousal Symptoms

Threat or danger activates a state of hyperarousal (see chapter 2). Under normal conditions, arousal decreases, and the system returns to its baseline function or homeostasis (Wilson, 2004b). Following traumatic stress experiences (especially prolonged or repetitive ones), homeostasis may not be reestablished. The system continues to function as if the trauma were ongoing. Hyperarousal causes the traumatized to become easily distressed in response to unexpected stimuli (van der Kolk, 2003). As a consequence of the involuntary search for similarities between the trauma and the present, otherwise neutral experiences are interpreted as being associated with trauma. Children have reported symptoms of increased arousal as ongoing occurrences, as episodic incidents (e.g., in response to perceived threat or intense stress), and in combination with re-experiencing symptoms. A few studies of children and of adults have indicated a pattern that chronic hyperarousal predicts subsequent emotional numbing: loss of interest, detachment, and restricted affect (Scheeringa et al., 2005; Weems, Saltzman, & Reiss, 2003). Scheeringa et al. did not find this pattern in 124 children ages 20 months to 6 years of age. Instead, they found that re-experiencing symptoms decreased and avoidance/numbing symptoms increased with time.

Sleep Disturbance. Difficulties falling asleep (D1) have sometimes resulted from the recurrent intrusions of distressing traumatic memories (Wolfe & Birt, 2002b), fears (e.g., of bad dreams or harm while sleeping), increased sensitivity to stimuli (e.g., sounds, sensations, itchy skin like during the shooting), or states of arousal (e.g., fast heartbeat, adrenalin pumping). In addition to difficulties falling and staying asleep, youths may cry, walk, or talk in their sleep. Sleep disturbances may lead to a variety of other problems such as clumsiness, irritability, lack of concentration, fatigue, or other physical symptoms of lack of sleep. Following treatment for nightmares, adults experienced a reduction of other trauma symptoms (Krakow, Hollifield et al., 2001); similar treatment for nightmares did not diminish concurrent symptoms for a small group of adolescents (Krakow, Sandoval et al., 2001). More study is needed to separate the effects of poor sleep from the other ongoing effects of trauma.

Irritability and Outbursts of Anger (D2). Trauma may result in increased readiness to arousal or reactivity (van der Kolk & Sapporta, 1991). Increased biochemical reactivity may combine with changes in information processing (e.g., attributional biases; Dodge et al., 1995) that contribute to outbursts of anger (chapters 2, 3, 14). Irritability is a common expression of distress in youths who are depressed as well as those who are traumatized (Hammen & Rudolph, 2003). For some trauma survivors, hypersensitivity to stimuli, such as sounds, may lend to irritability (Bloch et al., 1956; Kardiner, 1941; Williams, in press; see "Temperament," chapter 6).

Difficulty Concentrating. Youths report or demonstrate behaviors associated with poor concentration (D3) following traumatic events. McFarlane et al. (1987) reported high distractibility and restlessness scores for bushfire disaster-affected children. Disturbed sleep, intrusive reexperiencing symptoms, and neurochemical changes may contribute to youths' posttrauma difficulties with concentration (Pynoos & Eth, 1985; Pynoos et al., 1987). For example, youths have described being unable to concentrate because of thoughts of the event or of a deceased victim, distraction by reminders of the event (e.g., rattling windows, popping noises, sirens, screaming children), or just not being able to listen (e.g., too nervous, mind wanders).

Hypervigilance and Exaggerated Startle Response. Hypervigilance (D4) and exaggerated startle response (D5) reflect psychobiological changes (hyperarousal of the sympathetic nervous system; Wilson, 2004b). After traumas, youths may become extremely vigilant or alert to possible signs of threat or danger. Sudden unexpected sounds or surprise approaches may elicit a startle response or other signs of distress (Carrion, Weems, Ray, & Reiss, 2002; Nader & Fairbanks, 1994). Children vary in how general or specific the worrisome stimuli must be to trigger arousal. Some children respond to information, sights, or sounds that specifically resemble those from the trauma, such as popping or banging sounds after a shooting or tornado warnings rather than any rainy conditions. Other youths respond to more general stimuli such as the tick of a wall clock.

Functional Impairment

Traumatic experiences and resulting symptoms may undermine a youth's ability to function normally (adequately or successfully). Research has demonstrated the negative impact of anxiety on a broad range of children's psychosocial functioning, the high levels of comorbidity among anxiety disorders, and the long-term implications of childhood anxiety for adult functioning (Albano, Chorpita, & Barlow, 2003; see chapter 15). Youths may continue to operate well in one or more areas of living or may perform slightly to significantly less well in all arenas: social, familial, emotional, occupational, academic (chapter 11). The degree of impairment from exposure to trauma is affected by many factors such as the nature of the child and the event as well as age at occurrence, length and degree of exposure, support received afterward, and comorbidity (Albano et al.; Nader, 2001b; van der Kolk, 2003; Webb, 2004).

Associated and Other Symptoms

Traumatized children have reported other symptoms in addition to those listed in *DSM-IV* PTSD Criteria B through F. Early studies of childhood trauma (prior to the development of PTSD measures to assess children) revealed the presence of symptoms such as regressions, changes in temperament and personality, aggression, revenge fantasies, somatic complaints, enuresis and encopresis, helplessness and hopelessness, changes in values, altered grief responses, belief in omens, memory distortions, changes in future outlook, and a need for compensation (Bloch et al., 1956; Burgess, 1975; Eth & Pynoos, 1985b; Fields, 1979; Freud & Burlingham, 1943; Gislason & Call, 1982; Kinzie et al., 1986; Klein, 1974; McFarlane et al., 1987; Mercier & Despert, 1943; Terr, 1979). Research has confirmed trauma's association with *guilt* as a result of being unable to provide aid, being safe when others were harmed or killed, or believing personal actions endangered others; *dissociative reactions*; increased general *fears* such as fears of the dark, being alone, a recurrence of events, or fears specifically related to aspects of the experience such as people dressed like the assailant, sounds similar to those in the event, confined spaces or open spaces (depending on where the experience occurred); *worries* about others or personal safety; *anxiety* (e.g., regarding separation from caretakers or others, when alone or in general); *grief; depression; low self-esteem;* and *externalizing problems* (Ayalon, 1983; Fletcher, 2003; Ford, 2002; Greenwald, 2002b; Nader et al., 1990; Pynoos et al., 1987; Terr, 1983a). Although less often reported, children or their observers have also described youths' somnambulism, warped time perspective, eating disturbances, panic attacks, or self-destructive behaviors (Fletcher; Nader et al.; Terr, 1979). Not all studies inquire about all of these symptoms. Some of these and other symptoms omitted from most studies of trauma may occur under certain circumstances such as the increased intensity or duration of traumatic reactions. The report of guilt or grief has been associated with increased trauma symptoms initially as well as over a year after exposure to violence (Lacey, 1972; Nader et al.; Pynoos et al.). Moreover, traumatic grief is more complicated than normal bereavement; trauma symptoms may interfere with the grieving process and resolution (Eth & Pynoos; Nader, 1997b; chapter 10).

DSM Acute Stress Disorder

DSM-IV acute stress disorder (APA, 1994) may follow an event described in PTSD Criterion A. It occurs within 1 month of the traumatic event and lasts a minimum of 2 days and a maximum of 4 weeks (APA). The diagnosis requires only one symptom from each of *DSM-IV* PTSD Criteria B, C, and D; impaired functioning (social, occupational, pursuit of a task); and at least three dissociative symptoms: "(1) a subjective sense of numbing, detachment, or absence of emotional responsiveness; (2) a reduction in awareness of surroundings (e.g., 'being in a daze'); (3) derealization; (4) depersonalization; and (5) dissociative amnesia (i.e., inability to recall an important aspect of the trauma" (APA, p. 432; chapter 14). Symptoms of survivor guilt, despair and hopelessness, self-neglect, and increased impulsiveness or risk-taking may accompany ASD. Saxe (2005) found ASD in 31% of 72 children hospitalized for a burn. Risk factors for ASD among this population included high resting heart rate, lowered body image, and parents' acute stress symptoms. Meiser-Stedman, Yule, Smith, Glucksman, and Dalgleish (2005) found no difference in the prevalence of ASD for assault and traffic accident victims. Hamlin, Jonker, and Scahill (2004) discovered that gunshot-injured youth were 18.6 times more likely to have ASD symptoms than medically ill children. Studies have demonstrated that adults with ASD are at greater risk of developing PTSD (APA; Brock, 2002; Wilson, 2004b). For adults and children, dissociative symptoms appear to add little to ASD's predictive power (Kassam-Adams & Winston, 2004; Meiser-Stedman et al.).

Complex PTSD

Understanding and assessing PTSD in a holistic framework includes a sensitive understanding of how the inner self processes of the person are affected by trauma. Traumatic events, especially those involving acts of interpersonal assault, violence, abuse, or prolonged coercive internment under degrading conditions, attack the bases of the self and systems of personal meaning. The results of traumatic injury to the self and person-hood are deleterious, diverse, and in some cases, pathologically lethal. (Wilson, 2004b, p. 32)

Complex PTSD, Disorders of Extreme Stress Not Otherwise Specified (DESNOS), or developmental trauma (Table 1.4), proposed for *DSM-V*, refers to a group of symptoms most commonly associated with interpersonal, early, extreme, or prolonged stressors (e.g., neglect, abuse, or other violence; APA, 1994; Pearlman, 2001; chapter 10). The earlier the onset of trauma and the longer its duration, the greater the likelihood of suffering complex trauma symptoms (Roth, Newman, Pelcovitz, van der Kolk, & Mandel, 1997; van der Kolk, 2003). Nevertheless, research evidence suggests that a percentage of individuals exposed to childhood single nonviolent traumas such as natural disasters also experience complicated PTSD (van der Kolk, Roth, Pelcovitz, Sunday, & Spinazzola, 2005). In addition to the symptoms of PTSD, complex trauma may include feeling permanently damaged; hostility; depersonalization and other dissociative symptoms; relationship difficulties; revictimization; somatization; self-harm, self-destructive behavior, and impulsive behaviors; feelings of ineffectiveness, shame, despair, or hopelessness; putting others at risk; affect dysregulations; loss of previously held beliefs; social withdrawal; personality or character changes; feeling constantly threatened; and/or disruptions in identity (APA; Herman, 1992a; Pearlman; van der Kolk; Williams & Sommer, 2002; Wilson, 2004b). Clinicians have categorized symptoms of the complicated traumatic reactions (Table 1.4). Complex trauma primarily has been studied in adults. More study is needed to determine characteristics of the child, the experience, and other factors that lead to youths' more complex traumatic reactions.

As a result of traumatic information processing (chapters 3, 14) and dysregulation of emotions, "victim coping" or a "victim mythology" may develop (Ford, 2002; Tinnen et al., 2002). Tinnen et al. suggest that "a patient with complex PTSD is usually a victim of childhood trauma who feels small, weak, and inadequate in a world that seems increasingly unmanageable and overwhelming" (p. 104; see "Shame and Guilt," chapter 15). In addition to feeling weak and vulnerable, the victim feels unacceptable, unworthy of love, and easily crushed by "an indifferent, cold, and essentially hostile world" (p. 104). He or she develops a basic belief (worldview) of him- or herself as "a damaged victim in a dangerous world" (p. 105). Victim coping or mythology is characterized by an attitude of "safety first" and the belief that, in order to be safe from harm,

TABLE 1.4
Conceptualizations of Complex Trauma, Complex PTSD, or Disorders of Extreme Stress Not Otherwise Specified.

Conceptualization	Categories	Description/Examples
Complex PTSD or DESNOS Herman, 1992; van der Kolk, Roth, Pelcovitz, Sunday, & Spinazzola, 2005	(1) Dysregulation of affect and impulses	• Difficulties with affect regulation, excessive risk-taking, modulation of anger, self-destructive behaviors, suicidal preoccupations, difficulty modulating sexual involvement
	(2) Alterations in attention and consciousness	• Amnesia, transient dissociative episodes
	(3) Alterations in self-perception	• Guilt/responsibility, shame, minimizing, feeling that nobody can understand, sense of ineffectiveness, feeling permanently damaged
	(4) Distorted perception of the perpetrator	• Distorted beliefs about the perpetrator, idealization of the perpetrator, preoccupation with hurting the perpetrator
	(5) Alterations in relationships with others	• Inability to trust, revictimization, victimizing others
	(6) Somatization	• Chronic pain, conversion symptoms, sexual symptoms, digestive or cardiopulmonary symptoms (e.g., increased resting heart rate)
	(7) Alterations in systems of meaning	• Hopelessness or despair, loss of previously held belief systems
Complicated traumatic reactions and the complexity continuum Briere & Spinazzola, 2005	(1) Altered self-capacities	• Dysfunctions in identity, affect regulation, and interpersonal relatedness
	(2) Cognitive disturbances	• Altered information processing or schemata associated with, e.g., low self-esteem, self-blame, helplessness, hopelessness, pessimistic expectations of loss, rejection, and danger
	(3) Mood disturbances	• Affective symptoms or disorders—anxiety, depression, anger, or aggression
	(4) Overdeveloped avoidance reactions	• Dissociation, substance abuse, tension reduction behaviors such as binging-purging, self-mutilation, suicidality that distract or invoke stress-incompatible affect
	(5) Posttraumatic stress	• PTSD reexperiencing, avoidance/numbing, and arousal

Sources: APA, 1994; Briere & Spinazzola, 2005; Herman, 1992c; van der Kolk & Courtois, 2005; van der Kolk, Roth, Pelcovitz, Sunday, & Spinazzola, 2005.

distrust and defiance are necessary (Ford; Tinnen et al.). Such a youth may defend him- or herself, for example, by putting on a front of being fierce or by presenting him- or herself as weak and harmless ("wouldn't hurt a fly"). Victim coping may include feeling emotionally numb or empty, disoriented (or spaced out), and unable to think logically or clearly (Ford; Nijenhuis, Spinhoven, Vanderlinden, van Dyck, & van der Hart, 1998). Tinnen et al. describe how the person with victim mythology does not live in the present but engages in continuous inner flight from the woes of today. He or she may have a sense of entitlement to future reward because of past and present suffering. Ford explains that this kind of coping is emotionally and mentally exhausting and is demoralizing (e.g., it may seem like *an inescapable life sentence*, p. 40).

Wilson (2004b) describes how severe traumas (e.g., rape, war, repeated abuse, concentration camp experiences) damage the inner self or "soul" of a person (see also Kalsched, 1996; Knox, 2004b). Wilson goes on to say that a "broken spirit" is an injury that affects critical dimensions of existence: a sense of connection to self, others, and nature; vision of and hopes for the future; spiritual sources of meaning; and the sacred, innermost personal core. In addition to disrupting meaning and hope, Pearlman (2001) suggests that trauma's damage to spirituality may include devastating impacts on openness to all aspects of life, transcendence, and a person's relationship to nonmaterial facets of life. Consequently, cynicism or despair; a narrow focus on self and victimhood; inability to experience joy, love, wonder, awe, passion, gratitude, or community; and irreverence for life, nature, and humanity may result.

BEYOND PTSD

Because children may respond to traumas with disorders, symptoms, and patterns of thought and behavior other than those described in the diagnostic criteria of PTSD, assessing the results of childhood trauma is not as simple as measuring the presence or absence of *DSM-IV* PTSD. Children's reactions (including PTSD) may appear later or may evolve or change over time (Nader, 1997a; Briere & Elliott, 1997). Single-incident and repeated traumas can activate or exacerbate vulnerabilities, induce risk, amplify preexisting symptoms or conditions, and create sensitivities. Transitions from one developmental stage to another (e.g., the move into adolescence for sexually abused children) can trigger old or new responses. Trauma may completely derail a youth from a life path in progress. Because children take into future situations and challenges the biological, cognitive, social, and emotional knowledge, skills, and other resources gained in earlier phases (Geiger & Crick, 2001; Price & Lento, 2001), trauma can have a cascading and cumulative effect on youths (Cicchetti, 2003b). We have become fairly adept at assessing the symptoms of PTSD in children (Carlson, 1997; Nader). Methods of accurately measuring the other possible short- and long-term reactions that follow youths' traumatic experiences are either missing altogether or are only just beginning to emerge.

The Deeper Wound

In addition to PTSD, clinicians and researchers have observed disturbances in identity, judgment, development, and ego resources (Nader, 1997c; Pearlman, 2001; Wilson, 2004b). For example, a child may identify him- or herself as a victim, an aggressor, or a slut; as lonely, painfully different, or damaged. Researchers have confirmed changes in youths' information processing (e.g., attributional biases; changed expectations; negative self-talk in stressful or challenging situations) and automatic reactions (e.g., aggressive self-protection; failure to protect oneself; watchful freezing under certain conditions) (Dalgleish, Taghavi, Neshat-Doost, Moradi, Canterbury & Yule, 2003; Dodge, Bates, & Pettit, 1990; Pearlman; chapters 2, 3, 5, 14). The significant number of traumatized youths among those who have been incarcerated may be linked to these attitudinal and behavioral changes as well as to other variables (chapter 3).

Developmental Interruption

Trauma can interrupt and disrupt brain development in a way that may distort experience and disturb cognition and social interaction (Cicchetti, 2003b; chapter 2). Reductions in hippocampus brain volume and neurochemical changes may have a dramatic impact on the rest of a child's life (Bremner, 2003; De Bellis, Keshavan et al., 1999; Sapolsky, 2000). A single traumatic experience is enough to alter brain functioning (Stein & Kendall, 2004). Traumas such as abuse or neglect may induce chaotic biochemical changes that impede maturation of the brain's coping systems (Schore, 2001; Stein & Kendall). Structural limitations in the developing right brain, from early traumas or traumatic attachments, may be expressed as a number of enduring functional deficits (Schore, 2003; chapter 2).

At each phase of development, youths must use internal and external resources to adapt to developmental demands: to learn to regulate emotions and to establish desirable peer relationships, for example. Successful adaptation to these demands is likely to result in a normative life trajectory. Development is an integrative process: Each stage of development is partially contingent upon the achievement of the preceding stages. As Yates, Egeland, and Sroufe (2003) explain, "Earlier patterns of adaptation provide a framework for, and are transformed by, later experiences to yield increasing complexity, flexibility, and organization . . ." (pp. 246-247). Competence in one developmental period provides a foundation for success with subsequent developmental issues. Disruptions to emerging skills, such as intelligence, coping and problem-solving skills, self-regulation, self-esteem, and trust, may undo resilience, create risk and vulnerabilities, and send the youth on a trajectory toward problem behaviors or psychopathology. Although failure at negotiating important developmental issues and tasks does not always precede pathology, it may indicate a deviant trajectory or an elevated risk for maladaptive behavior. The level of difficulty to return to a normal developmental progression increases the longer an individual stays on a deviant pathway (Geiger & Crick, 2001; Yates et al.). Major or minor life events that disrupt emotion, physiology, and cognition present a strain on an individual's adaptive capability and may interrupt habitual functioning (Ingram & Price, 2001). Thus, stress may bring to realization a vulnerability to maladaption or pathology.

The Core Self

Trauma can wound the personal spirit by interrupting the life that would have been and the self that was, distorting and undermining self-confidence and self-concept, and altering the youth's relationships to others and the environment. Kalsched (1996) defines the *self* as "a core of the individual's imperishable personal spirit" (p. 3). Kalsched suggests that when the individual suffers severe trauma, the *self* is riddled with anxiety, becomes increasingly fragile, and becomes embroiled in a constant struggle to survive. Traumatized individuals live in a constant state of dread that the original traumatic state will return. Hypervigilance replaces play, and the *survival self* replaces the *individuating self* (see also Ford, 2002).

Sense of Self

At any stage, strong challenges to self-concept and disruptions to the development of important life skills may have a major adverse impact on a person's life. Issues of trust, self-concept, sense of control, autonomy, and cognitive processing, among others, may significantly affect the ensuing course of development (see chapter 5). Negative life events may reduce a child's sense of personal control, perhaps by inducing feelings of helplessness or impairing relationships. Negative life events may lead to diminished self-esteem by directly devaluing the child, exposing the child to some stigma, or decreasing opportunities to engage in esteem-enhancing activities (Haine, Ayers, Sandler, Wolchik, & Weyer, 2003). In turn, reduced qualities such as self-esteem, trust, and sense of control may affect many other aspects of life, increasing the risk of developing mental-health problems (chapter 5).

Life Trajectory

In addition to disruptions to development and self-view, posttrauma alterations in interactional style, confidence, or academic performance can have important consequences for many aspects of life. Posttrauma changes may diminish or alter the opportunities the youth is offered and the choices the youth makes. Because of changes such as increased reticence, irritability, or hypervigilance, for example, adults and other youths may no longer offer the youth social, academic, or career opportunities. Trauma symptoms may impede successful actions and alter the youth's reactions to failures. The posttraumatic self may impair relationships, including those with members of a youth's previously established support systems. For adults and youths, trauma may affect all levels of functioning including psychological, social, physical, interpersonal, spiritual, and other belief systems (e.g., ideology, values; Wilson, 2004b).

When all goes well, a youth takes forward through life qualities that have become prominent and then have undergone maturation during the phases of his or her development (Nader, 2001b). In addition to relationship skills and self-concept, a youth's normal development of curiosity, playfulness, conscience, imagination, and independence evolve over time. An ability to play may become a part of a well-rounded life. A well-chosen profession may depend upon a healthy curiosity, imagination, or the youthful joy of creative play. Qualities such as an adolescent's sense that anything is possible can be very useful in accomplishing the seemingly impossible. When this quality has evolved, it will likely include a realistic understanding of one's vulnerability. Trauma can disrupt the normal maturation of traits, may polarize behaviors, and may render thinking more concrete and less imaginative. It may, for example, induce inhibition related to a heightened sense of vulnerability or may result in dangerous risk-taking.

Flow: Skill in Action

Milton Erikson has explained that a hypnotic state occurs when all of the senses are gathered on a particular focus and conscious awareness of the outer world fades (Rossi, 1993). Csikszentmihalyi (1990, 1997a, 1997b) has used the term *flow* to describe a similar state that occurs during optimal experience. Flow (also known as *the zone* or *groove* or *a Zen experience*) may occur when meditating, resting, playing, interacting socially, and working as well as when the mind is stretched to its limits in order to accomplish something challenging and worthwhile (Csikszentmihalyi, 1997b). This spontaneous self-hypnotic state is characterized by involvement so deeply in something that nothing else seems to matter; action and awareness are merged (Csikszentmihalyi, 1997a). Concentration is intensely focused in the moment such that time, fears, depression, worries about self or failure, and anxiety are out of consciousness (Csikszentmihalyi, 1997b; Stein & Kendall 2004). Some skilled activities, such as an excellent tennis backhand, occur in a state of flow. When conscious awareness is focused on *automatic* procedural efforts, their automatic accurate nature or *flow* is disrupted (Sapolsky, 1998). An individual's normal flow may be interrupted, for example, if someone focuses attention on how to make his or her excellent backhand stroke work. Traumatic states and symptoms can interrupt the ability to attain a state of flow.

INTERPRETATION OF FINDINGS

Theories help to drive efforts to understand psychopathology more fully. If the focus on a theory or theories becomes too narrow, important aspects of reactions, precipitants, and protections may not be sought or found. Narrowing the focus of inquiry to exclude unrecognized or important variables (or variable combinations) may lead to inadequate or inaccurate beliefs and assumptions about the nature of childhood traumatic response. Using only one method of assessment also may lead to error (Crick, Nelson, Morales, Cullerton-Sen, Casas, & Hickman, 2001; chapter 4). Crick and Dodge (1996) suggest that video-recorded stimuli and individual interviews may be more effective than questionnaires in eliciting attributional biases, for example.

Interpreting Data

Although this volume is not intended to serve as an in-depth text on the statistical analysis and interpretation of research findings, a few issues regarding interpretation of data are important to mention. Determining exactly what is being measured by an assessment task or measure can be obscured by the invalidity of a scale, the lack of access to contrary findings (negative findings often are not published), or the need for comparison to an unidentified appropriate comparison group (Vasey, Dalgleish, & Silverman, 2003). For example, researchers have found information processing biases, such as selective attention, associated with trauma in youths. In tests of adults' information processing, anxious adults evidenced significant interference with color naming for threat words. The fact that a similarly strong interference was found in ornithologists for bird words suggests that the assessment task may have been measuring attentional bias for personally significant stimuli rather than for threatening stimuli (Vasey et al.). People may selectively attend to things that currently have meaning for them.

Association does not necessarily equate to causality. The statistical association of one variable with another does not guarantee that one caused the other. The relationship between variables may be indirect or the result of another or other variables. When causality can be inferred, the directionality of causation may be difficult to assess (Boehnlein, 2001; Caspi, 1998). Given the lack of pretrauma information, questions frequently arise about what came first (temporal ordering). "Did the [e.g., lack of social support, negative personality traits, perception of racism] precede or follow the trauma?" (see Pole, Best, Metzler, & Marmar, 2005). Does trauma lead to specific television watching, or does specific television watching lead to trauma symptoms (e.g., after the September 11 terrorist attacks; Schlenger et al., 2002). Disordered mental states can lead to disturbances in bodily functions, and disturbed bodily functions can lead to disordered mental states (Boehnlein). Differences in siblings' internalizing symptoms may lead to differential treatment from mothers, or differential treatment from mothers may lead to internalizing (Caspi). For most studies of trauma in youths, information about personality characteristics, information processing biases, and other variables is available only in retrospect and may be subject to bias, inaccuracy, or selectively focused attention. Prospective studies that assess relevant variables and changes over time are needed.

The focus of analyses and the assumptions made about the nature of variables (e.g., temporal ordering) affect results of analyses. In a study of New York police officers following the September 11 terrorist attacks (Pole et al., 2005), when the analysis included assumptions about the temporal ordering of predictors (e.g., that, for Hispanic officers, the perception of racism and attempts toward social desirability preceded the trauma and, so, was controlled for on the first step of analysis), increased symptoms in Hispanic officers was fully explained by (1) greater social desirability (the tendency to endorse self-report items in ways that avoid controversy and elicit the approval of others), (2) greater perceived racism in the workplace, (3) greater peritraumatic dissociation, and (4) greater wishful thinking and self-blame coping. When, for the purposes of analysis, no assumptions were made about temporal ordering, the increased symptoms were best explained by (1) greater social desirability, (2) greater somatization, (3) greater wishful thinking and self-blame coping, and (4) lower social support.

Whether the focus of study is variation within or between individuals, researchers must contend with normal daily variability (Nesselroade, 2002). Domains studied in individual differences such as creativity, locus of control, memory, mood, school performance, self-concept, aggression, talents, temperament, and work values have shown considerable, systematic change over time. Methods are now available to examine individual pathways to these outcomes and differences in these pathways among groups (Aber, Brown, & Jones, 2003; Nesselroade; see chapter 3, 4).

Caspi (1998) advised that it may be statistically inconceivable to expect enormous effect sizes when assessing behavioral outcomes. When a correlational analysis reveals that an intervention program explains only 9% of the total variation in outcome for children at risk for behavior problems, Caspi explains such a correlation (.3) suggests that whereas 65% of control-group children would develop behavior problems, only 35% of treated children would (a 30% reduction). In a 1989 simulation study, when a behavioral outcome was totally determined by three traits working additively, the upper-bound trait-behavior correlation was approximately .5 (Caspi).

A diagnosis of PTSD requires symptoms that persist for at least 1 month following the trauma (APA, 2001). Information about early responses may assist the discovery of the nature of traumatic reactions (North & Pfefferbaum, 2002). A measure asking a few questions of children and their caretakers 1 month following traffic-related injuries has predicted children with posttraumatic stress 3 months after the accidents (Winston, Kassam-Adams, Garcia-Espana, Ittenbach, & Cnaan, 2003). In addition to the need for replication of the measure's effectiveness, mental-health findings across groups exposed to different types of traumas and different populations have differed considerably (North & Pfefferbaum). Moreover, children have had significant and long-lasting delayed reactions to their traumatic experiences (Yule, Udwin, & Bolton, 2002; see chapter 2). Basing predictions on a few early indicators, or (worse still) basing the use of resources on them, may be a disservice to the children with delayed responses and to traumatized children with symptoms not among the specified few.

CONCLUSIONS

Children may respond to traumatic experiences with disorders, symptoms, and changed patterns of thought and behavior that seriously derail normal development; task, work, or academic performance; and well-being. Trauma may injure a child's personal spirit or core self by derailing the youth's life trajectory, distorting and undermining his or her sense of self, and disrupting the youth's relationships. In addition to PTSD, clinicians and researchers have observed disturbances in identity, spirituality, judgment, and ego resources following severe or prolonged traumas. Because children take into future situations and challenges the biological, cognitive, social, and emotional knowledge, skills, and other resources gained in earlier phases, trauma can have a cascading and cumulative effect on youths. New and revised methods, measures, and interviews are available to explore the many aspects of traumatic exposure and response. Because of developmental variables, assessing children's traumatic reactions is different from assessing adults' reactions. Aspects of the child, his or her circumstances, the traumatic event, the rater, the assessment measures, the context, and the methods of interview all affect the accuracy and completeness of assessment, findings, and their interpretations. Multiple methods, measures, and sources of information in a variety of contexts over time are important to accurately assess children.

Understanding childhood traumatic reactions has been limited or confused by (1) the lack of detailed information about children prior to their traumatic experiences, (2) mixed methods and study results (and sometimes small sample sizes), (3) unidentified mediating and moderating variables, (4) inadequate information about grouping and outcome variables, (5) the need to identify the changing nature of symptoms over time, and (6) the lack of detailed studies of children before and after traumas and at intervals across the life span. More information is needed regarding risk factors; the interactions of specific risk factors, symptoms, and other variables; differences in symptoms and syndromes by gender and age group; the manner in which trauma-related symptoms may manifest or remain dormant as time passes; and the effectiveness of interventions over time. Routine and intermittent school assessments of a number of child characteristics, large samples, long-term studies, and better identification of all of the outcomes of childhood traumatic experience would improve knowledge and benefit the affected children.

2

How Children and Adolescents' Brains Are Affected by Trauma

Among the important functions of the human nervous system are the capacity to recognize and avoid danger, form attachments, learn from experience, be self-aware, recognize and express emotions, cooperate, withhold or delay a response, generate and choose among strategies for action, and communicate socially (Mash & Dozois, 2003). Impairment of the developing brain and neural networks can hinder any or all of these realms. Studies show that altered neurobiological and brain functions may be a long-term consequence of trauma (De Bellis, Baum et al., 1999; De Bellis, Keshavan et al., 1999). Trauma is one of the methods by which an individual is "no longer himself" but is a product of "the biology that is distorting him" (Sapolsky, 1998). A single traumatic experience is enough to alter brain functioning (Stein & Kendall, 2004). Chaotic biochemical changes may impede maturation of the brain's coping systems (Schore, 2001; Stein & Kendall). Early traumas including severe traumatic attachments result in structural limitations in the developing right brain. These limitations are expressed in a number of enduring functional deficits including dysregulation of emotions under stress and increased risk of psychopathology (Schore, 2003). Research suggests a neurobiological basis for many childhood disorders.

Because the brain is most receptive (most plastic) to environmental input in early childhood, the young child is most vulnerable to variances of experience (Perry, Pollard, Blakely, Baker & Vigilante, 1995). Each brain section or structure has been linked to specific functions (e.g., understanding language, processing visual stimuli, analyzing, and planning) (Stein & Kendall, 2004). Collaboration between the areas of the brain is critical to healthy brain functioning. The ability to coordinate the functions of various brain areas is not inborn but must develop. In addition its to deleterious effects on the developing brain, trauma can disrupt the usual collaboration between the emotional (limbic system) and cognitive (neocortex) parts of the brain. Chronic stress especially can alter psychobiological maturation, induce increases in hypothalamic-pituitary-adrenal axis (HPA) activation, and result in poorer recovery from stress (Gilbert, Cheung, Grandfield, Campey, & Irons, 2003). Biological changes in the brain can result in an emotion-based style of coping that attempts to manage overwhelming feelings rather than thoughtfully respond to challenges (Stein & Kendall). This chapter describes youths' neurobiological responses to threat and, then, looks at brain growth and development and trauma's affect on them.

Disparate Findings

Perhaps because they are small, limited, and include differences in methodology, timing, and focus, studies of traumatized youths and neurochemical mechanisms have had conflicting results. The association of neurobiological changes and trauma must be distinguished from association with other factors such as injuries, substance abuse, other disorders, illness, pre- and postbirth conditions, socioeconomic status (SES), and heredity (De Bellis, Keshavan et al., 1999). Outcomes have been affected by a number of additional child and assessment variables such as pubertal stage, IQ, age, gender, height, weight, personality, trauma history, time of day, time since the event, and assessment method (De Bellis, Baum et al., 1999; Lipschitz, Morgan, & Southwick, 2002). For example, human cortisol and essentially all catecholamines (epinephrine, norepinephrine, and dopamine) and their metabolites are excreted into urine on a 24-hour diurnal rhythm (De Bellis, Baum et al.). Cortisol and catecholamines have been assessed using 2-, 6-, or 24-hour urine samples (Lipschitz et al.). Discrepancies in findings regarding cortisol levels also may be related to factors such as the prevalence of numbing versus intrusiveness, personal traits, or which of a dissociative patient's personalities is in control (Nijenhuis, van der Hart, & Steele, 2002). Rapid changes occur as a result of natural maturation across childhood and adolescence (Dahl, Dorn, & Ryan, 1999). These changes affect the assessment of neuroendocrine function. Brain alterations involved in pubertal maturation may occur years before any visible signs of puberty. It is essential that biological measures be carefully controlled for age and pubertal maturation, among other relevant variables. As will be discussed, the high comorbidity of anxiety and depression make distinguishing between them essential as well (Heller, Schmidtke, Nitschke, Koven, & Miller, 2002).

Cicchetti (2003a) points out the likelihood that intervening mechanisms (chapter 5) inhibit the expression of genes or neurochemical processes. These genetic and neurochemical processes would otherwise be likely to result in maladaptive developmental outcomes and psychopathology.

Suomi (2002) found, for example, that a defect in the serotonin transporter gene does not convey detectable liability, such as distractibility or impulsivity, for rhesus monkeys raised by nurturant foster mothers.

THE RESPONSE TO THREAT: FIGHT-FLIGHT AND BEYOND

The body's neurophysiological hyperarousal reaction exists to promote survival (Perry et al., 1995). When sensory information registers in the brain, it is matched, in the brain stem and midbrain, against previously stored patterns of activation (Perry, 1999). Unknown input or input associated with previous threat sets off an initial alarm response. The initial experience of intense stress normally triggers the release of stress-responsive neurochemicals: cortisol, epinephrine, norepinephrine, vasopressin, oxytocin, and endogenous opioids (van der Kolk, 2003). Utilizing these neurotransmitters, neuromodulators, and neuropeptides, the alarm response begins a wave of neuronal activation that moves from brain stem through midbrain to thalamic, limbic, and cortical brain areas (Perry). The sensation of anxiety occurs at the level of the thalamus and the limbic areas. Often, the brain's response to incoming sensory information takes place well before the signals reach the higher, cortical regions for "interpretation" (Box 2.1a).

During stress reactions, the sympathetic and parasympathetic branches of the autonomic nervous system generally produce coordinated and opposite physiologic reactions. The sympathetic nervous system (SNS) responds to emergency and arousal: fear, flight, fight, and sex (Sapolsky, 1998). The parasympathetic nervous system is calming. The sympathetic and parasympathetic nervous systems do not function simultaneously; one shuts off the other. As SNS activity increases, parasympathetic activity decreases. Sapolsky explains that, when there is a threat (e.g., a lion), the SNS increases heart rate, blood pressure, and glucose and diverts energy from (shuts down) digestion, in order to send energy to the legs so that they can run. If threat is insignificant, the parasympathetic system calms and reactivates digestion and immune function. Chronically turning on the SNS is what would happen if a person or animal was starving or a lion was chasing every day. Humans can turn on the SNS chronically with thoughts.

Beyond Fight-Flight

The body's *stress response* mobilizes reactions to danger that may include freeze (immobilization), fight (aggression), flight (withdrawal), or submission (appeasement) (Stein & Kendall, 2004). Response patterns vary at different stages of development and in the face of different stressors (Perry et al., 1995). Perry et al. explain that the well-known *fight-flight* response is

---

BOX 2.1
CASE EXAMPLES: THE WAY THE BRAIN FUNCTIONS

a. *Yolanda*. Traffic was moving at about 70 miles per hour (the tolerated 5 miles per hour over the posted speed limit). When it suddenly began to rain, a large fuel truck skidded diagonally across the freeway. Yolanda was in the far right lane. Although the cars to her left were able to swerve left to avoid a collision, she had no time to follow them. The cars on the right shoulder prevented Yolanda's escape in that direction. She was clearly going to hit the fuel truck. The impact would kill her even if the truck did not explode. Suddenly, she found herself sitting in her car with her hands tightly clutching the steering wheel and her foot hard down on the brake. Her car was wedged between two other cars on the freeway shoulder. The cars were so close together that she would have needed the capacity to move directly sideways to get out of the space. Yolanda did not know how she got into the space.

b. *Johnny*. Johnny was working on his art project under the table when a deranged woman with a gun took his kindergarten class hostage. Johnny watched helplessly while several of his classmates were shot, one fatally. The woman shot a child who tried to run to the teacher. He watched the woman with the gun carefully and determined that she looked at children who moved and caught her attention and that she looked intently at a child before shooting him. Johnny held his breath and watched in terror when a boy reached out to pick up a paper he had dropped. As expected, the woman shot the boy. The young children became tired, waiting motionless. Wearily, the boy next to Johnny began to slide down. When she turned her focus in Johnny's direction, he promptly ran for cover and slid like a pro baseball player behind the teacher's file cabinet, effectively saving his own life. Posttrauma, he experienced a greatly diminished self-image until he recognized the competence with which he had saved his own life. He decided he should become a baseball player because of this successful action.

c. *Jalal*. When he was 5, Jalal heard his mother screaming for him from the living room. He ran into the room and found a man on top of his mother, raping and strangling her. Jalal hurried into the kitchen to get a knife. He tried to stab the man but the knife would not go in. The man picked him up and threw him against the wall. The man then ordered Jalal to go to bed and go to sleep. Jalal obeyed. When his father returned from the late shift, he found Jalal's mother dead on the living room floor.

---

commonly seen in adult, male mammals. Infants and children are much less likely to use a classic fight-flight response. A hyperarousal continuum and a dissociative continuum are more likely for a traumatized child.

Fight-Flight

The body's alarm reaction includes increased SNS activity, resulting in elevated heart rate, blood pressure, respiration, muscle tone, hyper-vigilance; release of stored sugar; and tuning out of all noncritical information (De Bellis, Baum et al., 1999; Perry et al., 1995; Sapolsky, 1998). These processes prepare the body for defense or flight (Perry et al.). If the threat materializes, a full fight-or-flight response may be activated. The hyperarousal alarm reaction triggers specific neurochemical response: norepinephrine, dopamine, gamma amino butyric acid (GABA), and serotonin. Because young children are not well-equipped to fight or flee, they may vocalize (cry, yell, or scream) to elicit a caretaker's assistance or protection. When threat persists, the child will attempt to fight or flee or will move into the dissociative continuum (Box 2.1c, 5.1b).

The "Sensitized" Hyperarousal Response

Brain regions involved in the fight-flight or hyperarousal response to threat are critically involved in regulating arousal, attention, the response to stress, vigilance, affect, behavioral irritability, locomotion, sleep, and the startle response (Perry et al., 1995). These brain systems are reactivated when the child is exposed to a specific reminder of the traumatic event. With the sensitization of brain stem and midbrain neurotransmitter systems, other critical physiological, cognitive, emotional, and behavioral functions mediated by these systems become sensitized. Repetitive re-experiencing of a traumatic event leads to dysregulation of these functions (Perry et al.; van der Kolk, 2003). Consequently, a traumatized child may, over time, exhibit anxiety, behavioral impulsivity, motor hyperactivity, sleep disturbances, tachycardia, hypertension, and a variety of neuroendocrine abnormalities. Following numerous types of traumas, for instance, researchers have found increased heart rate (decreased heart period) with exposure to trauma stimuli even in very young children (Scheeringa, Zeanah, Myers, & Putnam, 2004). Everyday stressors, which previously may not have elicited any response, may now elicit an exaggerated reaction (Box 1.1). Traumatized children can be hyperreactive and overly sensitive. Perry et al. explain that the child's now-persistent fear state has become a trait.

Freeze

Schore (2003) explains that the simultaneous activation of hyperexcitation and hyperinhibition (like slamming on the brakes and flooring the gas at the same time) results in the *freeze response*. Freezing allows better sound localization, keener visual observation and environmental scanning for potential threat, and time to organize and plan (Perry et al., 1995). Lack of movement has been used by animals and humans as a form of camouflage, reducing the chance of attracting a predator. During a sniper attack on a school playground and a hostage-taking at another elementary school, children protected themselves by becoming immobile (Box 2.1b).

Perry et al. (1995) explain that traumatized children who have developed a "sensitized" hyperarousal or "sensitized" dissociative pattern often physically and/or cognitively freeze when they feel anxious. Such behaviors, which may include nonresponsiveness to an adult's directives, are often labeled oppositional-defiant behavior. Adults may then give the child another set of directives, typically involving more threat and increasing the child's anxiety. The child may escalate into dissociation.

The Dissociative Continuum

Dissociation involves disengaging from stimuli in the external world and attending to an "internal" world (Perry et al., 1995;

Schore, 2003; chapter 14). It permits various levels of withdrawal from intolerable stimuli. Some people dissociate early in the arousal continuum, whereas others dissociate only in states of complete terror (Perry et al.). Traumatized children use a variety of dissociative techniques such as mentally going to a different place, assuming the persona of a hero or an animal, or witness consciousness (e.g., floating, watching from the outside). Dissociative responses may become predominant if the experience includes immobilization, inability to escape, or pain.

Like the hyperarousal/fight-or-flight response, dissociation involves brain stem-mediated increases in circulating epinephrine and associated stress steroids (Perry et al., 1995). In contrast to the hyperarousal state, dissociative states include (1) elevations in the pain numbing and blunting opiates and the behavior-inhibiting stress hormones such as cortisol (Schore, 2003), (2) increased vagal tone, decreasing blood pressure and heart rate despite increases in circulating epinephrine (Perry et al.), and (3) an increased relative importance of dopaminergic systems, which are intimately involved in the reward systems and affect modulation. Endogenous opioids mediating pain and other sensory processing are clearly involved in altering perception of painful stimuli, time, place, and reality. Most opiate agonists can induce dissociative responses and are of primary importance in mediating the freeze or surrender dissociative responses. Neuropeptide Y (NPY) deficits found after chronic stress exposure may promote anxiety and distress (Nijenhuis et al., 2002). NPY is one of the neurochemicals associated with dissociative symptoms (Nijenhuis et al.).

Memory and Associations

Under normal circumstances, the capacity for association enables the brain to rapidly identify threat-associated sensory information and to act rapidly to promote long-term survival (Perry, 1999; Schore, 2003). Thus combat veterans or youths who live in war zones can respond automatically to the sounds of gunfire. A pattern of incoming sensory information may be interpreted as danger and acted upon in the brain stem, midbrain, and thalamus milliseconds before the cortex interprets the information as harmless (Perry). Youths who live in war zones such as Ireland or the Middle East may run for cover in response to a car backfiring or a firecracker exploding.

Although semantic memory representations may coexist with sensory flashbacks, traumatic memories are primarily imprinted in sensory and emotional modes (van der Kolk, 2003). The sensory imprintations remain stable over time and may recur in all of their original vividness when triggered by reminders. According to McCleery and Harvey (2004), "Peritraumatic noradrenergic hyperactivity leads to a strongly consolidated but fragmented memory, focusing on the most threatening and horrific aspects of the traumatic situation," which promotes continuing hyperarousal when aspects of the event are recalled (pp. 490–491). Reexperiencing thus increases the likelihood of negative appraisals, which in turn maintain a sense of threat. Specific trauma-related reminders or intense neutral stimuli such as a loud noise (indicating loss of stimulus discrimination) may serve as triggers. The brain's capacity to generalize specific events may engender "false" associations between specific aspects of a traumatic event and other nonthreatening situations (Nader, 1997c; Perry, 1999). Accordingly, a simple rise in heart rate or a queasy feeling induced by a nonthreatening experience but similar to that experienced during the traumatic event can trigger a brain stem-mediated alarm response.

Enhanced memory of emotionally arousing stimuli has been well-documented in humans and animals (McCleery & Harvey, 2004). Studies have demonstrated that, administered in the concentrations produced during significant stressors, stress hormones such as adrenalin and glucocorticoids enhance memory. Opioids and GABA or benzodiazepine receptor agonists impair memory. Although the basolateral nucleus of the amygdala does not itself store long-term memory, it influences memory processes of other brain locations. Individuals with a damaged amygdala exhibit deficits in the emotional enhancement of memory but have intact declarative memory for neutral material. Beta-adrenergic blockers inhibit the usual memory enhancement of emotional elements, whereas yohimbine (a stimulant of noradrenergic activity) facilitates memory.

THE RESPONSE TO THREAT: NEUROCHEMICAL REACTIONS

As indicated earlier, an initial experience of intense stress normally triggers the release of stress-responsive neurochemicals (e.g., epinephrine, norepinephrine, dopamine, and their metabolites) (Lipschitz et al., 2002; van der Kolk, 2003; Table 2.1). Endorphins, the benzodiazepines, and the inhibitory neurotransmitters help to quiet the brain and to restore it to its natural balance (Stein & Kendall, 2004). A homeostasis exists, within limits, in the neurotransmitter system such that hyperstimulation leads to downregulation and hypostimulation to upregulation of neurotransmitter systems (Grigorenko, 2002). When a sound is continuous, the listener may begin to "tune it out." According to Sapolsky (1998), *downregulation* (the reduction of neurological receptors and the resultant diminished response to the same level of a neurotransmitter) is a similar process. Early experience affects receptor numbers (Cicchetti, 2003b).

Similar factors produce variable outcomes (McBurnett, King, & Scarpa, 2003). Chronic and persistent stress may increase the stress response or inhibit it and precipitate desensitization (McBurnett et al.; van der Kolk, 2003). Research suggests that differences in responses may be related to the type and length of trauma, genetics, personality, the responsiveness of the SNS and HPA axis, and other factors as well (Cicchetti, 2003b; McBurnett et al.; Sapolsky, 1998). Studies of rats bred as *novelty seeking* (behav-

TABLE 2.1
Neurochemicals Activated during Stress

Neurochemical	During Stress or Brain Development
Epinephrine (i.e., adrenalin) and norepinephrine (i.e., noradrenaline, NA)	Increase SNS activity: heart rate, blood pressure, respiration, conversion of glycogen to glucose, lypolysis (conversion of fats to fatty acids), muscle tone, alertness; attention narrows and neurons become more sensitive to stimuli related to danger; heightened NA may directly enhance memory for the traumatic event; contribute to hyperarousal, flashbacks, intrusive memories, and nightmares.
Cortisol	Converts fats to glucose, inhibits the immune response, suppresses inflammation, and assists a return to a calm state; shuts off aspects of stress response that may be harmful if continued (e.g., SNS activation). The hippocampus has receptors for cortisol; when acutely administered, cortisol has been found to cause memory and attention problems; is elevated during dissociative states.
Vasopressin	Is a hypothalamic neuropeptide associated with SNS activation; it potentiates immobilization reactions via SNS activation behaviorally expressed as fear; heightened levels are associated with nausea.
Dopamine (DA)	Is an intermediate in the synthesis of epinephrine; instigates growth spurts in neurons, glia, and blood vessels; involved in the reward systems and affect modulation; is an endogenous opiate that is elevated during dissociative states; is diminished with ADHD and hyperactive with schizophrenia.
Serotonin/ 5-hydroxytryptamine	Inhibits activation of the HPA axis; involved in mediating fear, anxiety, mood, and appetite; serotonin reuptake inhibitors decrease aggression, ameliorate anxiety, and induce secure attachment phenomena; essential to higher mental functioning such as learning and consciousness; excess causes relaxation and sedation; deficiency associated with low mood, lack of will power, poor appetite control, and the dysregulation of aggression.
Monoamine oxidase (MAO)	Catalyzes key neurotransmitters: serotonin, norepinephrine, and dopamine; low MAO activity in platelets associated with suicidal behavior, bipolar disorder, and alcoholism and with monotony avoidance, sensation seeking, and impulsiveness and impulsive aggression; smoking inhibits MAO.
Gamma amino butyric acid (GABA)	Conductor of the complex process of inhibition; induced cortical malformations result in dysregulation of GABA; plays an important role in some of the anxiolytic and hypnotic drugs and in the pathophysiology of stress, epilepsy, and anxiety.
Benzodiazepines	Have an antianxiety influence.
Endorphins	Endogenous opioids; have natural analgesic properties; contribute to insensitivity to pain during extreme stress or shock; may be triggered by certain foods (e.g., chocolate, chili peppers) or activities (e.g., prolonged continuous exercise, massage, laughter, sex, meditation, acupuncture) as well as by great stress; believed to enhance the immune system, relieve pain, reduce stress, and postpone the aging process.

References: Altman, 2002; Byrnes, 2001; Columbia Encyclopedia, 2005; Davidson, 2004; De Bellis, Baum et al., 1999; Grigorenko, 2002; McCleery & Harvey, 2004; Neborsky, 2003; Price & Lento, 2001; Sahelian, 2005; Sapolsky, 1998; Schore, 2003; Stein & Kendall, 2004.

ioral activation), *harm avoidant* (behavioral inhibition), and *short latency to aggress* have demonstrated that the same early environments can result in directionally opposite effects on hormones related to genetic strain. Limbic system impairments and impairments in dopamine, noradrenaline, and serotonin receptors have been implicated in the dysregulation of aggression (Schore, 2003). An efficient mature orbitofrontal system can adaptively regulate both the sympathoadrenomedullary catecholamine (hyperarousal) and the corticosteroid (hypoarousal) levels.

Gonzalez and Isaacs (2005) suggest that neurochemical levels are influenced by the predominance of alkalinity versus acidity that can be measured in an individual's blood or hair. For example, individuals who are predominantly alkaline-prone tend to overproduce serotonin and underproduce epinephrine and norepinephrine. Gonzalez and Isaacs state that serotonin predominance or excess corresponds to personality characteristics such as hyperreactivity and hypersensitivity. These and other group differences are important to assessment, diagnosis, intervention, and medication issues.

Neurotransmitters and Traits

Individuals differ because of differences in their levels of chemical messengers (neurochemicals and hormones), numbers and brain distribution of neurons, the patterns of connections between neurons, the numbers of receptors for particular chemical messengers, their sensitivity, and other aspects of the brain and its neurobiology (Sapolsky, 1998). How readily a person speaks his or her mind, for example, may be related to the number of neurons in his or her frontal cortex. According to Sapolsky, the closest thing humans have to a superego is the frontal cortex. When this brain region is injured by disease or head trauma, an individual becomes *frontally uninhibited*. Even if formerly quiet and taciturn, the individual is likely to become loud and aggressive. In contrast, after an episode of temporal lobe epilepsy, which involves the limbic system, a person becomes extremely humorless, neophobic (dislikes change), hypergraphic (writes all of the time), and more interested in religion. Cicchetti (2003b) points out that, especially in a "temperamentally sensitive brain," "less severe forms of psychological insult may create emotional sensitizations that ripple through the developmental process with effects that . . . compound themselves into relatively enduring forms of psychopathology" (p. 347).

Neurotransmitters are excitatory or inhibitory to varying degrees (Sapolsky, 1998). If there are no receptors for benzodiazepines, for example, the result is an anxious person. Preschoolers' cortisol reactivity has correlated positively with social competence and negatively with shyness/internalizing (Hart, Gunnar, & Cicchetti, 1995 is cited in Cicchetti, 2003b). Maltreated youths measured lower on cortisol reactivity, lower in social competence, and higher in externalizing behaviors. Serotonin involvement has been established in anxiety and withdrawal and has been implicated in shyness, depression, hypersensitivity, and hyperreactivity (Gonzalez & Isaacs; Schmidt & Fox, 2002). Adults who score high on neuroticism have reduced efficiency of serotonin transportation (Schmidt & Fox). Sapolsky indicates that insufficient serotonin and norepinephrine or a chronically activated sympathetic nervous system may contribute to the occurrence of depression or depressive disorders. Serotonin appears to inhibit or regulate activation of the HPA system. The lack of serotonin may result in the overactivation of the HPA system and the release of increased cortisol. Eysenck (1967) found that *introverts* were more physiologically reactive than extraverts. Similarly, infants with *inhibited* temperaments are more reactive to stress (Kagan, Snidman, & Arcus, 1995; Lipschitz et al., 2002; Stein & Kendall, 2004). Nachmias and Gunnar (1996) found that these infants exhibited elevations in cortisol levels in response to stressful situations only if they were a part of the insecurely attached group.

The HPA Axis

The physiological reactions to threat are coordinated by the SNS rapid response as well as by the slower, longer response of the hypothalamus, pituitary gland, and outer cortex of the adrenal glands (HPA axis; McBurnett et al.; Sapolsky, 1998). Corticotropin-releasing factor (CRF), released by the hypothalamus, causes the pituitary to release adrenalcorticotrophic hormone (ACTH) (Stein & Kendall, 2004). After moving through the bloodstream to the adrenal glands, ACTH instigates the release of cortisol. Cortisol is a glucocorticoid (steroid) hormone that converts fats to glucose, inhibits the immune response, suppresses inflammation, and assists a return to a calm state (Lipschitz et al., 2002; Stein & Kendall). The ability to elevate cortisol during traumas is essential to survival (Cicchetti, 2003b). Chronic HPA hyperactivity can cause brain damage. Studies suggest that adults with PTSD exhibit an increased HPA axis reactivity. Overreaction may be upward or downward (i.e., hypocortisolism or hypercortisolism; McCleery & Harvey, 2004). Studies of cortisol levels in youths have yielded mixed findings (Lipschitz et al.). Results are likely to be influenced by the age of the child during assessment and when traumatized. *Stress inoculation* may be a factor in reactivity levels. Rat studies have shown that mild stress stimulation during a critical period can be adaptive in contrast to prenatal stress, which has been associated with attention deficits, hyperanxiety, and disturbed social behavior. Developmental changes in the HPA axis as well as variables listed in the preceding section may explain differences in findings. Studies of neurochemicals, in general, have yielded mixed and contradictory findings (Grigorenko, 2002). Much is yet to be learned about the way in which they act, combine, interact, and vary under different conditions.

Assessment of Cortisol

HPA axis abnormalities have been evaluated through assessments of basal cortisol secretion and the dexamethasone suppression test (DST) (Garber & Flynn, 2001). A number of conditions can affect cortisol levels such as dietary intake, anticipation of a stressful event, or exposure to a pathogen (McBurnett et al., 2003). Prolonged HPA activation may lead to sensitization or desensitization. Like a thermostat, HPA acts to release cortisol until levels rise and then shuts off until circulating levels fall off. Although variable, the classic diurnal rhythm includes a rise in early morning cortisol, a steady decline throughout the day, and a nadir before sleep (Cicchetti, 2003b; McBurnett et al.). It is, therefore, essential to hold the hour of collection constant across subjects. Morning is the best time of collection for youths hypothesized to have low cortisol levels, and the afternoon best for capturing high reactivity. McBurnett et al. recommend repeated samples (two to five) across time. Evidence suggests that hypocortisolism measured directly after car accidents (but not 1 week later) is associated with increased risk of PTSD (McCleery & Harvey, 2004). Because one role of cortisol is to terminate aspects of the stress response that could be harmful if continued (e.g., SNS activation), a relatively low cortisol response may permit sympathetic arousal to continue, thus amplifying a vicious circle.

Cortisol and Depression

Research has found a consistent association between minor and major stressful life events and depression (especially chronic or cumulative stressors) (Garber & Flynn, 2001). Most studies have found no differences in cortisol levels between normal and depressed youths. A few studies have found cortisol elevations near sleep onset in severely depressed and suicidal adolescents. These elevations have predicted recurrence of depression. Although findings have been mixed, research has found an association between DST nonsuppression and suicidal behavior or completion, endogenous subtypes of depression, and prior history of major depression.

Neurobiology and Aggression

Among a variety of factors that may contribute to aggression in youths (chapter 3) are changes in levels of hormones, changes in reactivity to chemical messengers, specific brain injury, and activation of the flight-fight neurochemistry (Sapolsky, 1998). Cortisol reactivity is associated with aggression and with dominance-subordinance roles as well. Studies of same-sized fish revealed that low-cortisol responders clearly dominated high-responders within 3 hours of pairing (McBurnett et al., 2003). Sapolsky states that testosterone exaggerates pre-existing patterns of aggression by rendering one more readily provoked. The levels of neurohormones such as estrogen and progesterone that occur in premenstrual syndrome (PMS) also may affect the amygdala in a way that results in aggression, as evidenced by the disproportionate numbers of incarcerated women who had PMS prior to committing a violent crime.

Youths with childhood-onset and adolescent-onset conduct disorder (CD) have emerged as distinctly different groups. Although findings have been mixed, a number of studies have shown a link between low cortisol and high aggression (McBurnett et al., 2003). Low cortisol has been found for childhood-onset aggressive CD rather than later-onset CD. However, anxiety moderates the relationship between conduct disturbance and cortisol. Youths with CD and comorbid anxiety disorder have had higher cortisol levels. Mean cortisol levels decrease in socially stressful situations for boys with high externalizing and low internalizing problems. Low cortisol has also been associated with persistent ADHD. McBurnett et al. have demonstrated that the link between cortisol and CD or hyperactivity is due to a strong association between aggression and cortisol rather than a direct association between the two disorders and cortisol. The key variable is early-onset aggression, and the link has now been replicated for girls.

Violent Traumas

Some studies have shown a relationship between violent traumas and increased HPA reactivity (summarized in McBurnett et al., 2003). Cicchetti (2003b) cautions that the affect is not uniform. Youths with different types of abuse, with different problems (internalizing vs. externalizing), and with different disorder combinations have exhibited differences in morning and daytime cortisol levels (Cicchetti; De Bellis, Baum et al., 1999). For example, youths with physical, emotional, and neglect abuse but no sexual abuse had high morning and afternoon cortisol levels (akin to hypercortisolism). Unlike children with major depressive disorder (MDD) alone but like youths with both PTSD and MDD and depressed adults with childhood abuse (De Bellis, Baum et al.), maltreated youths with *internalizing* problems displayed higher morning cortisol levels and average across-the-day levels compared to other maltreated and non-maltreated youths (akin to hypercortisolism). Not all maltreated youths display HPA axis dysregulation, and changes in the environment may result in improvement.

The Quieting Effect

One role of cortisol and a function of endorphins (internally produced painkillers), benzodiazepines (with an antianxiety effect), and inhibitory neurotransmitters serotonin and GABA is to quiet the brain and to restore it to its natural balance (McCleery & Harvey, 2004; Stein & Kendall, 2004). The calming or inhibiting neurochemicals are described here and in Table 2.1.

Dopamine

Dopamine systems play a central role in hormone release, cognition, motor control, emotional balance, and reward (Schneider, Moore, & Kraemer, 2003). Dopamine rapidly increases under stress (Schore, 2003). In the developing brain, it can induce DNA mutations and cell death. Perinatal distress has been linked to dopamine hypofunction and a blunting of the right (not left) prefrontal cortex's stress regulating response. The dopaminergic system is implicated in a number of personality disorders and in personality traits associated with antisocial behaviors and neuropsychiatric conditions (Grigorenko, 2002). Among the problems and disorders are Tourette's syndrome, ADHD, schizoid/avoidant behavior, conduct disorder, and schizophrenia (Grigorenko; Price & Lento, 2001; Sapolsky, 1998).

Serotonin

Serotonin is a modulatory neurotransmitter with inhibitory effects involved in mediating fear, anxiety, mood, and appetite (Lipschitz et al., 2002). Serotonergic signaling seems to play a key role in the generation and modulation of behaviors such as affect, addition, aggression, locomotion, feeding, sexual activity, and vomiting (Grigorenko, 2002). Serotonin has been implicated in psychiatric conditions such as anxiety disorders, depression, obsessive-compulsive disorders, eating disorders, hypertension, and substance abuse/dependence (Garber & Flynn, 2001; Grigorenko). The metabolites of serotonin have predicted suicidal and aggressive behavior in adults and have been linked to aggression in youths (Lahey et al., 1998; Lipschitz et al.; Price & Lento, 2001).

GABA

Gamma amino butyric acid provides a major inhibitory system in the brain (Siegel, 2003). GABA decreases excitability of individual neurons and limits excessive neuronal activity (Grigorenko, 2002). Septohippocampal GABA combined with the cholinergic pathway, rather than the cholinergic pathway alone, is key to learning. Child abuse may result in a damaged cerebellar vermis, rendering it unable to support GABA input to hypothalamic nuclei in the brain stem or GABA's soothing function on the limbic structures (Siegel, 2003). GABA has been implicated in the aggression heightening effects of alcohol, stress, anxiety, and epilepsy (Grigorenko).

Assessment of Neurochemicals

A number of factors affect the evaluation of neurochemical differences (McBurnett et al., 2003). Child, environment, event, ethnicity, measurement, and analysis characteristics are among them. In some cases, less noticeable influences, such as interviewer gender and issues of social struggle and hierarchy, have made a difference, for example, in the study of aggression. Failure to distinguish between types of a variable, such as different forms of behavioral disorders or of anxiety, may result in the canceling of effects.

Samples of blood, saliva, and urine have been used to assess neuro-chemicals in youths exposed to traumas (Table 2.2). Each method has its benefits and limitations. The expertise of laboratory personnel, of course, is important (Dahl et al., 1999). The study of cortisol, adrenocorticotropic hormone, and other neurochemicals may require frequent sampling across the circadian cycle in order to best characterize the underlying pattern of peaks, nadirs, and quiescence. Tables 2.2 and 2.3 present methods of collection.

BRAIN DEVELOPMENT

The brain contains two broad classes of cells: glial cells and neurons (Byrnes, 2001). The more numerous *glial cells* do not appear to play a direct role in the processing of information. They provide firmness and struc-

---

TABLE 2.2
Methods of Sampling Neurochemicals

Type Of Test	Methods	Cautions
Blood samples	• Venipuncture	• Anticipatory anxiety about blood draw may confound stress hormone measurements.
	• Intravenous (IV) catheter	• Adaptation to IV is possible if it permits normal activities and free range of motion. May require explanations, reassurance, and the control to stop the procedure at any time.
Salivary methods	• Spitting into a tube • Inserting a sialistic capsule into the mouth • Soaking cotton rolls inserted in the side of the mouth	• Correlations between serum and saliva cortisol are moderate to high. • Significant rises in cortisol are generally apparent in salivary measures. The cortisol nadir has not been reflected accurately in salivary measures. • Food and drink intake affect results.
Urine measures	• 2-hour collection • 4-hour collection • 24-hour collection	• Difficulties collecting, storing, and handling large samples of urine. • Samples lost due to bedwetting. • Missed samples. • Comparisons may be inaccurate related to differences in time of collection. • Collection time is relevant for certain symptoms or disorders.

References: Dahl, Dorn, & Ryan, 1999; De Bellis, Keshavan et al., 1999; Lipschitz, Morgan, & Southwick, 2002.

TABLE 2.3
Common Brain and Neurochemical Tests

Brain size	Neuroimaging techniques: magnetic resonance imaging (MRI), functional MRI, positron emission tomography (PET), and single photon emission computed tomography (SPECT); electroencephalography (EEG).
Catecholamines	Assessment of urine or cerebral spinal fluid (e.g., analyzed by solid phase extraction with a calibrator and control [Bio-Rad] and determined by high pressure liquid chromatography with electrochemical detection).
Cortisol	Assessed in urine samples (2-, 6-, or 24-hour); e.g., using radioimmunoassay (RIA), MAGIC COR RIA kit (Ciba Corning), saliva samples (e.g., using RIA kits).
Serotonin	Metabolite levels in cerebral spinal fluid; whole blood serotonin.

References: Dahl, Dorn, & Ryan, 1999; De Bellis, Baum et al., 1999; De Bellis, Keshavan et al., 1999; Lipschitz, Morgan, & Southwick, 2002; Nijenhuis, Van der Hart, & Steele, 2002.

ture to the brain, form the myelin sheath that surrounds the axons of long neurons, provide scaffolding for neuron migration, and take up and remove some of the neurotransmitters released during synaptic transmission. *Neurons* do play a role in information processing. In addition to growing in size, neurons also sprout new dendrites (arborization) and gain a myelin sheath. A dendrite is the branching portion of a neuron that receives neurotransmitters. Myelination is the process of adding a fatty acid coating (myelin) to an axon to speed up firing. The most dramatic increases in myelination occur between the ages of 6 months and 3 years (De Bellis, Keshavan et al., 1999).

Neural connections throughout the brain are built as a result of repeated patterns: Desire and emotion are transformed into action, stimulating and reinforcing pathways that link the cognitive, emotional, and motor systems (Stein & Kendall, 2004). Purposeful action (motor planning and sequencing) is also necessary to brain development. The infant learns about cause and effect: Behaviors/actions lead to consequences. In addition, infants learn from attachment relationships patterns that serve as right hemispheric coping strategies for dealing with environmental stressors and for affect regulation (Schore, 2003). The chaotic biochemical changes induced by trauma that interfere with maturation of the brain's coping systems can lead to difficulties with identity formation, emotion regulation, and relationships (Schore, 2001; Stein & Kendall).

The Progression of Brain Development

Brain systems develop sequentially and hierarchically from less complex (brain stem) to more complex (limbic, cortical areas) (Perry et al.,

TABLE 2.4
Brain Systems

System	Involved in
Brain Stem	Regulating internal homeostasis; regulating heart rate, blood pressure, level of arousal, and some reflexes; first stop for internal and external sensory input; perception is nonconscious.
Cerebellum	Coordination of motor, social, emotional, and several cognitive functions; balance (initially controlled movement).
Limbic	Maintaining the balance between internal and external reality; urges, appetites; attachment, affect regulation, and aspects of emotion; self-preservation; evaluating experience for its emotional significance; links sensation (pleasure or pain) to context; the hub of memory.
Hypothalamus	Maintaining homeostasis by regulating functions such as temperature, blood pressure, and glucose levels; exchanging information between brain and body.
Amygdala	Conditioned learning; ability to learn by association; storage of fearful memories; monitoring incoming stimuli for threat; instigates fight-flight response when danger is detected.
Hippocampus	Processing of all conscious memories; conditioned learning; learning by association; linking stimuli to context (pain, sustenance, pleasure).
Thalamus	Relaying information to other systems; permitting use of senses in combination.
Corpus callosum	Connecting cortical areas of right and left hemisphere, allowing exchange of conscious information between the two.
Anterior commissure	Carrying unconscious, emotional information between the hemispheres.
Cortex	Analyzing and interacting with the external world; abstract cognition, complex language, reasoning, planning, judgment, problem solving, working memory.
Neocortex	Cognition and metacognition (thoughts about thoughts, emotions, and behaviors).
Dorsolateral prefrontal cortex	Mediating language and cognition.
Medial prefrontal cortex	Fear-responding and emotional dysregulation; the interface between the lower subcortical areas that generate emotional states and the higher cortical areas that regulate these states; receiving multimodal sensory input.
Orbitofrontal cortex (the right region)	Self-regulation, moral guidance.

References: Bremner, 2003; Byrne, 2001; Perry, Pollard, Blakely, Baker, & Vigilante, 1995; Schore, 2003; Stein & Kendall, 2004; van der Kolk, 2003.

1995; Table 2.4). Different areas develop, organize, and become fully functional at varying periods during childhood. Disruptions of experience-dependent neurochemical signals during these periods—lack of sensory experience during critical periods, and atypical or abnormal patterns of neuronal activation due to extreme experiences such as trauma—may lead to major abnormalities or deficits in neurodevelopment. Stress response systems originate in the lower parts of the brain. The lower brain helps to regulate and organize the higher brain (Perry, 2006). If the lower parts of the brain are poorly organized or regulated, the higher parts of the brain will disorganize and dysregulate. Animal studies have shown that the more highly enriched the environment, the more developed and dense are the cortices, synapses, and dendritic growth in the cortex (Cicchetti, 2003b; Stein & Kendall, 2004). Extensive dendritic growth facilitates behavioral task performance; decreased dendritic arborization is linked to a decline in performance. Mental functioning correlates directly with the number of both neurons and synapses (connections betweens neurons) in the brain (Stein & Kendall). Because a child's brain is rapidly making new synapses, it has increased plasticity or potential for change. This means that the impact of experiences on the brain is greater and that the recovery of the brain is greater.

Age. Nervous system development begins before birth; neurons develop and complete migration to their final locations shortly after birth (Stein & Kendall, 2004). In the first 2 years of life, the human brain grows faster than at any other stage. In the first year, the brain expands approximately 2 1/2 times its birth size. Newborns' positron-emission tomography (PET) scans show no activity in the prefrontal cortex and minimal activity in sensory and motor areas of the cortex. Lower centers (e.g., brain stem, thalamus, amygdala) are active; infants can use all of their senses to respond to stimuli with emotions. When the brain has matured in adolescence, it weighs 4 times what it did at birth (Byrnes, 2001).

Prenatal Stress. In the developing prenatal and infant brain, undifferentiated neural systems are critically dependent upon sets of environmental and microenvironmental cues to appropriately differentiate, divide, migrate, and create synaptogenesis (Cicchetti, 2003b; Perry et al., 1995). Too little arousal does not contribute to brain organization; too much, and the neurons become overly excited and the system disorganizes (Stein & Kendall, 2004). For humans and animal primates, prenatal stress has been linked to dysregulation of the HPA axis and alterations in neurochemical activity (Schneider et al., 2003). Prenatally distressed monkeys have exhibited decreased exploration and locomotion, increased freezing behavior, and increased adrenal hormone and cortisol reactivity to stress. Animal studies have demonstrated that the offspring of mothers stressed during pregnancy were less able to regulate the stress response (Maestripieri & Wallen, 2003; Schneider et al.; Stein & Kendall). Prenatal stress can result in increased fearfulness, irritability, sleep disturbances, aggressiveness, neuromotor difficulties, and attention problems; diminished cognitive abilities; and reduced interest in play. Retrospective studies of humans have linked prenatal stress to ADHD, severe emotional disturbances, anxiety, social withdrawal, schizophrenia, and criminality.

Brain Growth. A pattern of organization, disorganization, and reorganization characterizes early brain development (Stein & Kendall, 2004). Periods of rapid growth of neuronal connections are followed by selective elimination (pruning) (Schore, 2003; Siegel, 2003; Stein & Kendall). That is, the overproduction of synapses is followed by pruning of unused connections and the emergence of new neural networks. This pattern permits the brain to adapt to the needs of the environment. The right and left hemispheres alternate periods of rapid growth. The brain's right hemisphere is dominant in its growth during the first 3 years of life (Siegel). Synapses proliferate in association with disorganization in the child's brain and behavior (Stein & Kendall). New skills emerge, are reinforced, and stabilize. Growth spurts generally occur in early infancy, age 3 to 3 1/2, between 6 and 10, at prepuberty, and in mid-adolescence.

Critical Periods of Brain Development

Animal studies have confirmed that a very narrow window (critical period) in brain development exists, during which specific sensory experience is necessary for optimal organization and development of the brain region mediating a related specific function (Allen, Bruss, & Damasio, 2004). When an animal's sensory input was blocked by covering an eye, for example, the brain structures that normally receive the related projections failed to develop (Allen et al.). Studies of congenitally deaf and matched controls suggest similar phenomena in humans (Allen et al.; Perry et al., 1995). Allen et al. reported that the gray:white matter ratio was significantly higher in deaf versus nondeaf subjects related to a reduction in white matter. Auditory deprivation from birth may have resulted in less myelination, fewer connections with the auditory cortex, and the decay over time of unused axonal fibers. Perry et al. suggest that deprivation of experiences or overactivation of important neural systems during critical periods may be the most destructive result of early child maltreatment.

Attachment and Brain Development

Interactions between children and caregivers shape the ultimate architecture of the brain (Schore, 2003; Siegel, 2003; Stein & Kendall, 2004; chapter 8). Secure attachments produce growth-facilitating environments that enhance neuronal connections and help to strengthen and integrate key brain structures and the connections between groups of neurons. Reciprocal caregiver-infant interactions trigger increases in dopamine, the neurotransmitter that instigates growth spurts in neurons, glia, and blood vessels in the prefrontal cortex, especially in the right hemisphere (Stein & Kendall).

Through interactively regulating the infant's positive and negative states, the sensitive parent directly influences development of the infant brain's stress response system. The mother must be psychobiologically attuned to her infant (Schore, 2003; Siegel, 1999). Indifference or rejection from a caregiver will obstruct cognitive and emotional development. The caregiver synchronizes to the rhythmic structure of the infant's affect, communications, gestures, and play, and modifies his or her own behavior to fit that structure. Thus the caregiver "facilitates the infant's unique information-processing capacities by adjusting the mode, amount, variability, and timing of the onset and offset of stimulation to the infant's actual\integrative capacities . . ." (Schore, p. 116). Recognition of style differences is essential to a caregiver's ability to individualize interactions with infants in order to best facilitate their mastery of each stage and skill. The child and caregiver re-create inner psychophysiological states similar to each other's. Schore explains that, when the "good-enough" primary caregiver induces a stress response in her infant through a misattunement, she rapidly reinvokes a reattunement. This reattunement is critical to enabling a shift from the negative affective states to reestablish a state of positive affect. The reestablished synchrony permits coping and recovery from stress. As the dyadic regulation of emotion, the attachment mechanism thus psychobiologically modulates positive states, such as joy and excitement, as well as negative states, such as aggression and fear.

In disorganized attachments, the caregiver is inaccessible, reacts to the infant's distress inappropriately or rejectingly, and/or participates minimally or unpredictably in affect regulation (Hesse, Main, Abrams, & Rifkin, 2003; Schore, 2003). Rather than modulating affective states, he or she induces extreme levels of arousal and stimulation without providing interactive repair. The amount, intensity, and timing of the caregiver's stimuli surpass the infant's tolerance, triggering an alarm state. As occurs in pain states, brain levels of adrenalin, noradrenaline, and dopamine are elevated (Cicchetti, 2003b; Schore; Table 2.1). Repeated stress triggers the persistent activation of the catecholamines. In these "kindling" states activated when the environment is deemed unsafe and challenging, high levels of the excitatory neurotransmitter *glutamate* and the immobilization potentiating neuropeptide *vasopressin* are released. Dissociation, a hypometabolic regulatory process, may result.

Trauma and Brain Development

Neglect, starvation, and other traumas can create unrelenting fear and discomfort (Cicchetti, 2003b; Sapolsky, 1998). Stress that overwhelms the organism appears to affect a wide range of brain structures and neurobiological systems (Lipschitz et al., 2002; van der Kolk, 2003). Chronic hyperactivity of the HPA axis can result in hippocampal neuronal loss, inhibited neurogenesis, slowed myelination, abnormalities in synaptic pruning, and cognitive and affective functional impairment (Cicchetti; Sapolsky, 2000). Some research suggests that the degree of impairment is determined by the severity of the trauma, the age at which the trauma occurred, the duration of trauma, and the level of social support received (Lipschitz et al.; van der Kolk). Other studies have not found such associations (Sapolsky, 2000). Early childhood trauma or maltreatment has a greater capacity to inflict significant and *cascading* dysfunction than a similar experience in adolescence or adulthood (Perry, 2006).

For veterans and for adults with a history of child abuse, symptom provocation studies have produced functional magnetic resonance imaging (fMRI) consistent with dysfunction in the medial prefrontal cortex, dorsolateral prefrontal cortex, hippocampus, and amygdala (Bremner, 2003). Dorsolateral prefrontal cortex dysfunction may mediate language and cognition problems. Medial prefrontal cortex dysfunction may correspond to failure of extinction to fear-responding and emotional dysregulation. Decreased benzodiazepine receptor binding in the medial prefrontal cortex may contribute to elevated anxiety and other pathological PTSD-related emotions. Cortisol release at the time of the stressor, differences in glucocorticoid receptor sensitivity, or decreased brain-derived neurotrophic factor may lead to hippocampal damage and reduction (Bremner; Sapolsky, 1998).

Computing Brain Volume

The volumes of brain *regions of interest* are generally summed to obtain an overall brain volume value (Allen et al., 2004). MRI has replaced computed tomography (CT or CAT scans) as the method of choice for assessing brain volume (Allen et al.). The MRI briefly uses powerful magnets to align hydrogen nuclei in the body tissues and uses the subsequent emission of radio waves to clearly delineate gray matter, white matter, and cerebral spinal fluid (CSF). Separate contiguous images are stacked to form a three-dimensional scan.

Brain Volume

Adult brain studies have shown that human cranial volume is largely inherited (Allen et al., 2004). Although genetics may strongly influence the overall volumes of major brain sectors, environmental influences may have a strong effect on smaller regions.

Gender. Between the sexes, there is considerable overlap; men, however, generally have larger brains than women. Some of the variation can be attributed to body dimensions. Peters and his colleagues found that the difference in brain volume dropped by two thirds when height was included as a covariate (cited in Allen et al., 2004). The proportions of men and women's major lobes are similar. Men and women both usually have larger right hemispheres. Women have a greater ratio of gray matter (predominantly neuronal cell bodies) to white matter (predominantly nerve fibers insulated by fatty myelin, and supporting cells) than men because they have less white matter. Men have more nonaxonal components (glia, blood vessels). The belief that women have greater communication between their "emotional" right brains and their "analytic" left brains and the belief that greater brain size means greater cognitive ability have not been substantiated (Allen et al.; Byrnes, 2001).

Hippocampus. High levels of glutamate and cortisol alter growth of the developing limbic system (Schore, 2003). Sapolsky (1998) explains that when there is lack of oxygen due to such experiences as epileptic seizures, strokes, or long-term exposure to hormones such as glucocorticoids that require a great deal of oxygen and energy, the hippocampal neurons are among the first to die. The hippocampus directs learning and memory. All conscious memories are processed in the hippocampus (Stein & Kendall, 2004). Hippocampal dysfunction may underlie PTSD memory deficits. Decreases in hippocampal volume and explicit memory deficits have been demonstrated for Cushing's syndrome, depression, and PTSD (Bremner, 2003; Sapolsky, 2000). Investigators suggest a lateralization of effects: Right hippocampal atrophy predominates from adult PTSD, and left hippocampal atrophy from childhood PTSD. Explicit memory deficits occurred for the greatest degrees of atrophy but not for minimal atrophy. Severe atrophy has predicted severe dissociative symptoms. Studies have been small and need replication. The hippocampus is one of the few brain regions that produces new neurons from birth into old age. For adult patients with hippocampal disorders, a reduction in cortisol has reversed atrophy (Starkman, Giodani, Gebarski, Berent, Schork, & Schteingart, 1999, cited in Byrnes, 2001). Because of the plasticity of their brains, Byrnes suggests that regeneration is likely to be especially true for children.

Other Brain Regions. Although studies suggest that trauma or aversive dyadic caregiver-infant interactions may lead to brain cell death in the limbic system as a result of elevated corticosteroid levels (Fosha, 2003; Schore, 2003), De Bellis, Keshavan et al. (1999) did not find in traumatized youths the predicted decrease in hippocampal volume found in adults with PTSD. They examined 44 chronically maltreated (primarily sexually abused) children and adolescents with chronic PTSD and 61 nonabused children and adolescents matched for age, gender, height, weight, Tanner Stage (pubertal stage), race, and, in most cases, handedness. Youths with PTSD had smaller intracranial and cerebral volumes—cerebral and prefrontal cortex, cerebral and prefrontal cortical gray matter and cortical white matter, right and left amygdala and associated gray matter, right and left temporal lobes, and the corpus callosum and its regions 4 through 7—than matched controls. Adolescent twins with a history of moderate to severe major depression have also had reduced subgenual prefrontal cortical volume compared to controls (Garber & Flynn, 2001).

In the De Bellis, Keshavan et al. study, brain volume positively and robustly correlated with age at onset and negatively correlated with duration of abuse. Smaller intracranial and cerebral volumes may also be a product of chronically stressful and impoverished environments. PTSD intrusive symptoms correlated negatively with intracranial volume and corpus callosum region 7. Childhood dissociation and PTSD correlated negatively with total corpus callosum and specific regions. Abused youths did not exhibit a reversal of the right-left brain asymmetry suggested by studies of electroencephalogram (EEG) coherence. De Bellis, Baum et al. (1999) found that duration of maltreatment correlated significantly with urinary free cortisol and catecholamine concentrations. These increased neurochemicals may adversely affect brain development. Increased steroid hormones and catecholaminergic neurotransmitter activity have been found to modulate the developmental processes of neuronal migration, differentiation, and synaptic proliferation. A traumatized youth may be functioning at a developmental age somewhat to far below his or her actual age (see chapter 9).

Rhythm, Repetition, and Recovery

As pointed out in chapter 1, the sequencing of interventions can be important to a youth's recovery and to the success of treatment methods. Perry (2006) indicates that healing is from the bottom up: brain stem first. A child must feel safe in order to begin to heal. Children can begin to benefit from more traditional therapies such as talk therapies after state-regulation has improved. Brain stem-mediated anxiety, hypervigilance, and impulsivity necessitate appropriately timed, patterned repetitive sensory input. Activities such as dance, drumming, music, or massage provide repetitive rhythmic brain stem stimulation that can help to modulate brain stem dysregulation (Field, Seligman, Scafidi, & Schanberg, 1996; Perry). Perry indicates that treatments such as music, movement, and eye movement desensitization and reprocessing (EMDR) tap into the powerful brain stem memory association of the mother's soothing heartbeat ($\approx$80 beats per minute or subrhythms of 40 or 60 beats per minute). Some Asian religions match to an individual's heartbeat the rhythm of personalized chants/mantras aimed at soothing and spiritually healing alterations in consciousness. Ancient cultural practices such as aboriginal healing and grief rituals also enlist this repetitive rhythmic activity. Perry points out that, because traumatized youths may be functioning at developmental levels below normal age level, reparative experiences must be developmentally appropriate rather than age appropriate. Reparative attachment relationships may begin with a pet. A dog, for example, can provide repetitively nurturing and unconditionally accepting experiences for a child.

THE ORGANIZATION OF THE BRAIN

PET scans demonstrate that, normally, most tasks activate multiple brain areas (Stein & Kendall, 2004). Communication between the areas of the brain is essential to higher-order thinking, problem-solving, creativity, and emotional processing. Current conceptualizations of the organization of the brain describe three major areas: brain stem, limbic system, and cortical regions (see Table 2.4). By 12 months of age, the entire prefrontal cortex is active (Stein & Kendall). The prefrontal cortex (especially the orbitofrontal cortex) is central to integrating information from all areas of the brain. The prefrontal cortex is mediated by the neurotransmitters dopamine and norepinephrine. Dopamine increases blood flow and stimulates glial cell and neuron growth, thereby enhancing prefrontal cortex development. At 14 to 18 months, with increased demands from parents for impulse control, norepinephrine (associated with stress response) increases. Schore (1994) postulates that norepinephrine helps to mature an efficient inhibitory system—the ability of the cortex to override emotions (Stein & Kendall). Before 18 months, urges that arise in the limbic system and relay to the cortex lead to action. Between 18 and 24 months, thinking and language become prominent. The ability to conceptualize is demonstrated in imaginative play. The continuing development of the prefrontal cortex between ages 3 and 5 underlies development of the self-monitoring capacities. The orbitofrontal and ventromedial cortices are responsible for processing and regulating emotion. The anterior cingulate is the last stop before consciousness; it recruits areas of the cortex to process emotions and urges from the limbic system and decides which information to pass on to the cortex (Stein & Kendall).

Assessment of Brain Activity

Damasio (2002) notes, "Researchers can now directly record the activity of a single neuron or group of neurons and relate that activity to aspects of a specific mental state, such as the perception of the color red or of a curved line" (p. 72). Brain-imaging techniques such as PET scans and fMRI scans reveal how different brain regions are engaged by a specific mental effort (Damasio; Sapolsky, 1998; Table 2.3).

Traits and Brain Activity

Research has linked differences in brain functioning with different temperamental traits (Caspi, 1998; Rothbart & Bates, 1998; chapter 6; see "The Right and Left Hemispheres," below). EEG and fMRI have demonstrated that personality traits can predict patterns of regional brain activity (Heller et al., 2002). Infants, youths, and adults exhibit individual and neurological differences in their reactivity to and tolerance for stimuli, organization of behavior, processing of information, attunement to specific sensory modalities (e.g., visual, auditory), and their preferences for sounds or tones (e.g., low vs. high tones) or levels of touch (e.g., soft or firm) (Ayers, 1978; Chess & Thomas, 1991; Grinder & Bandler, 1976; Lichtenberg & Moffitt, 1994; Stein & Kendall, 2004).

Frontal Asymmetry. Asymmetry demonstrated in increased right frontal electroencephalogram activity has been associated with infants' negative affects, emotional reactivity, and vulnerability to psychopathology. Schmidt & Fox (2002) suggest the involvement of serotonin in frontal EEG activity. Dawson, Frey, Panagiotides, Osterling, & Hessel (1997) found that infants of depressed mothers exhibited this asymmetry as well as higher levels of emotional dysregulation (evidenced in heart rate, vagal tone, cortisol levels), immune system changes, and behavioral changes such as problems with eating, sleeping, affect, and activity level (cited in Stein & Kendall, 2004). Fox, Henderson, Rubin, Calkins, and Schmidt (2001) found that young children who remained continuously temperamentally inhibited from 4 months to 4 years of age also displayed right frontal EEG asymmetry as early as 9 months from birth. Those who changed from inhibited to noninhibited did not display this asymmetry. Schmidt and Fox found, in response to unfamiliar social situations, undergraduates who were both highly shy and highly social had significantly faster and more stable heart rates than those who were highly shy but low social. At baseline, the two groups had comparable right frontal EEG activity, but the high shy-high social group exhibited greater left frontal EEG activity. Similar EEG findings occurred for 6 year olds.

Brain Activity, Affect, and Assessment

Heller et al. (2002) have described findings regarding affect and brain activity. Data has generally supported that *activated pleasant affect* (e.g., euphoria or elation) is associated with increased left rather than right frontal brain activity and increased right posterior activity. *Activated unpleasant affect* (e.g., fear or anxiety) corresponds to increased right frontal and right posterior activity. *Unactivated pleasant affect* (e.g., calm or relaxation) is associated with increased left frontal and decreased right posterior activity. *Unactivated unpleasant affect* (e.g., boredom or depression) corresponds to increased right frontal and decreased right posterior activity. These findings emerge only when the variance for anxiety is removed when measuring depression and vice versa. Heller et al. underscore that it is, therefore, essential to separate depression and anxiety, experimentally or statistically, in the study of psychopathology. In addition, two different types of anxiety with very different neural networks have been identified. *Anxious apprehension* (worry) focuses on the future, includes rumination about potentially negative outcomes of events, and includes higher left than right frontal activity. *Anxious arousal* (panic), on the other hand, is a more immediate fear reaction that involves autonomic arousal and more right frontal activity. Heller et al. found that trait apprehensive adults were more likely to respond to a stressful task with anxious arousal than controls. Although there are some similarities among them, anxious arousal and anxious apprehension were clearly distinguishable from each other as well as from positive affect, negative affect, and depression. Worry, then, is not merely a subcategory of negative affect or depression. Failure to identify the type of anxiety or to separate anxiety and depression can lead to disparate findings. Although anxious arousal has been more strongly associated with PTSD, anxious apprehension has accounted for unique variance in its study.

The Right and Left Hemispheres

Each brain hemisphere is associated with a unique style of thinking, behavior, and motivational patterns (Stein & Kendall, 2004). The *left hemisphere* includes positive and optimistic emotions; the tendency to approach, explore, and take action; and the processing of verbal communication, numbers, and words. It analyzes, problem-solves, processes information sequentially, provides a detailed perspective, and permits elaboration (Schore, 2003; Stein & Kendall). The *right hemisphere* includes the negative and pessimistic emotions; the tendency to avoid and withdraw; processing of nonverbal, emotional communication, imagery, and visual-spatial information; and limited analytic capabilities (Stein & Kendall). It is involved with visual and metaphorical thinking and provides a global rather than a detailed perspective. The right brain hemisphere is dominant for the regulation of bodily states, the processing of unconscious socioemotional information, the unconscious fast-acting regulatory operations, the capacity to cope with emotional stress, and the corporeal and emotional self (Schore, 2003). Prefrontal right brain areas have been found central to affect regulation and to the ability to understand the emotional states of others (empathy). Impairments in right orbitofrontal functioning are considered important to a predisposition to violence. If either hemisphere is damaged, a distortion of reality may result.

Siegel (2003) has described the function of the brain in the processing of traumas. The right hemisphere experiences more intensely emotionally arousing states, mediates retrieval of autobiographical memories, and registers and regulates body states. Traumatic memories appear to be stored in the right hemisphere of the brain. Left hemisphere processing uses syllogistic reasoning—cause-and-effect relationships that can explain the right- and wrongness of things. A coherent story (driven by the left hemisphere) is the logical, linear telling of a sequence of events using words or other modalities, such as drawings. A coherent narrative is achieved when neural integration across the hemispheres is achieved. The deeper healing process is the procurement of neural integration. "Trauma induces separation of the hemispheres that impairs the capacity to achieve these complex, adaptive, self-regulatory states as revealed in incoherent narratives" (Siegel, p. 15). Telling of coherent narratives is one method of acquiring integration and is an indicator of integration.

Communication between Hemispheres

Nerve pathways such as the corpus callosum and the cingulum integrate brain systems by connecting and transmitting communications between the two hemispheres (Perry et al., 1995; Stein & Kendall, 2004). The corpus callosum joins the left and right hemispheres. The cingulum delivers information from the limbic system to the neocortex. Most frequently, the verbal left hemisphere dominates in speaking for unconscious parts of the brain. The mind and body are constantly processing emotions even without conscious awareness of what is going on. The senses deliver information to the thalamus, where information is simultaneously relayed to the amygdala and the cortex. The route from the thalamus directly to the amygdala permits instantaneous response (LeDoux, 1996; Stein & Kendall; Box 2.1a). The information is delivered to the cortex for a more thorough analysis. When researchers flash an image of a fearful, angry face for a few milliseconds, followed by a neutral or happy face, subjects report only seeing the happy or neutral face (Mlot, 1998; Stein & Kendall). Nevertheless, their heart rates increase as though they have seen the angry or fearful face. Activity in the amygdala (the limbic structure that detects danger) increases in response to the subliminal image of the fearful face and quiets in response to the happy face.

Split-Brain Studies. Split-brain studies examine patients whose corpus callosum was cut in order to remedy uncontrollable seizures (Stein & Kendall, 2004). After these commissurotomies, the exchange of cognitive information between the hemispheres is prevented. Emotional information, however, is able to cross via a lower route, the anterior commissure, which connects the unconscious limbic structures in both hemispheres. This communication may result in action out of conscious awareness. In split-brain cases, "alien hand" refers to the tendency of the left hand to act independently and in opposition to left hemisphere decisions regarding actions. For example, the right hand might reach for a traditional work blouse or shirt, and the left hand might put it back and grab a more colorful one. When a split-brain youth answers a written question, he or she may answer differently depending upon in front of which eye (i.e., which hemisphere's visual field) the question is placed (Stein & Kendall).

Trauma and Brain Functioning

Most child studies of the brain and trauma have focused on maltreatment: abuse, neglect, and sexual molestation. Such early traumatic attachments inhibit the growth and maturation of the right hemisphere, which is in a critical period of growth for the infant's first year and is dominant for the first 3 years (Schore, 2003). Abuse is likely to result in an overactive stress-response system and an underdeveloped cortex (Perry, 1999; Stein & Kendall, 2004; van der Kolk, 2003). Extreme stress disrupts the functioning of the cortex, particularly the prefrontal cortex, which is critically involved in inhibiting the stress response (Stein & Kendall). Impairment in the first 18 months of life is associated with abnormal social and moral development and a later syndrome resembling psychopathy (Schore). Orbitofrontal cortex impairment is central in the behavioral expression of violence.

Both fear and stress involve the amygdala, the hippocampus, and the adrenal glands (Byrnes, 2001). As discussed, prolonged stress may cause atrophy or death of neurons in the hippocampus or alterations in neurochemistry and the growth of other brain regions (Byrnes; Sapolsky, 1998). Persistent overactivation of the stress response also affects subsequent stress sensitivity (Cicchetti, 2003a). These changes, in turn, impact physiological systems including immune response. Consequently, study of systemic immune system and other health functioning as well as long-term structural and functional changes in the brain are important to the investigation of extreme stress.

CONCLUSIONS

Studies of trauma and neurobiology have yielded mixed results for youths, adults, and animals. Differences in findings may be related to measurement issues or to failure to take into account relevant variables or subtypes of variables and conditions. It is essential, for example, to separate anxiety and depression, to define the types of anxiety, and to recognize the child, event, and environmental characteristics that may influence findings. The neurobiological changes related to traumas must be distinguished from those related to factors such as injuries, substance abuse, environment, other disorders, illness, pre- and postbirth conditions, SES, and heredity. Neurobiology may vary with differences in pubertal stage, IQ, age, gender, handedness, height, weight, personality, trauma history, time of day, time since the event, and assessment method.

Variations in brain structure correspond to differences in traits and functioning. Strong evidence reveals brain and neurochemical changes as a result of prolonged or severe traumas including attachment traumas. Neurochemical changes affect personality, skill development, and reactivity. Early disruptions to brain development and neurochemistry may color the way youths greet the world, function in it, interact with others, cope with adversity, and respond to life's challenges. Like the other effects of trauma, altered neurobiology can have a cascading effect on a youth's life.

3

Are There Different Pathways to a Symptom or Set of Symptoms?

Variables associated with emotional and behavioral disturbances can be complexly interrelated. Many of the outcome variables associated with trauma have been associated with other risk or vulnerability factors that can be brought to fruition by nontraumatic adversity or multiple adversities (see chapter 5). In addition to the possible involvement of multiple factors, the assessment of youths' traumatic reactions is complicated by the transactional nature of variables. Mixed findings regarding the role of a number of variables (e.g., age, gender, ethnicity) may be related to these complex interrelationships as well as to methodological, sample, and event issues. Rutter (2003) suggests that it is unlikely that individual risk factors can be reduced to a single temperamental, behavioral, or environmental characteristic. Although, for example, incarcerated youths often have histories of trauma, they usually have multiple risk factors (Wood, Foy, Goguen, Pynoos, & James, 2002). The prediction and understanding of symptom outcomes may require the identification of constellations of factors (Huesmann, Moise-Titus, Podolski, & Eron, 2003; Rutter). Among synergistic traumatic reactions, for example, may be the combination of information processing biases (e.g., the assumption of threat) with hyperarousal (e.g., stress hormones aimed at self-protection) and intense emotional reactivity. In addition to the interactions among risk factors and symptoms are the possible bidirectional and transactional effects between youths and their environments (Caspi, 1998; Rutter). For example, expectations lead to behaviors that may elicit reactions that perpetuate the expectations. Wilson (2004a) suggests that, after traumas, symptoms may occur tridirectionally. That is, one symptom may trigger a second that triggers a third. Re-experiencing symptoms (e.g., reactions to reminders) may activate arousal (e.g., increased heart rate, HPA system response) that in turn may lead to avoidance or to aggression.

Economics, time, and other practical matters impact study design. As a result, studies sometimes examine specific results or associations of youths' traumatic experiences without adequately examining the other risk, vulnerability, and associated factors that may contribute to the observed outcomes. Without a full understanding of an outcome variable, however, results may be misleading or inaccurate. In order to demonstrate the complexity of assessing the association between two variables, this chapter examines one possible outcome of trauma and the other factors linked to its occurrence. Exposure to violent traumas has been associated with youths' conduct disturbances, including aggression (Ford, 2002; Greenwald, 2002b; Schore, 2003). The following discussion of aggression and its relationship to trauma and to other variables is provided to demonstrate the complexity of associations.

Outcomes are Multidetermined

Aggression, like many of the other possible outcomes of traumatic exposure, is multidetermined (Dodge, Bates, Pettit, & Valente, 1995). Focusing on one potential result of traumatization (aggression) demonstrates that there are multiple possible pathways to the same outcome and that multiple considerations are necessary for accurate assessment and interpretation of data (Box 3.1a, 3.1b, 3.1c). When assessing trauma or other risk factors, in order to effectively evaluate an outcome variable, it is essential to define its subtypes and variations—by stage, age, or gender, for example. As will be demonstrated in the discussion of aggression, girls sometimes express symptoms differently than do boys. Proneness or risk for particular reactions may vary by age or by age and gender. The examination of aggression as an outcome helps to elucidate assessment issues, such as the importance to outcomes of the quality of early attachments, peer relationships, parenting, child attributes, and comorbidity or symptom combinations. The discussion of aggression that follows helps to explain, for example, why after a school sniper attack and after a suicide in front of students at a school, youths with previous conduct disturbances were found to report few if any trauma symptoms but showed a subsequent increase in aggressive behaviors (Nader, 1998; Pynoos et al., 1987).

After providing information about the association between trauma and aggression, this chapter gives a detailed examination of aggression (a possible outcome of trauma) in relationship to its associated variables. Some of these same variables have been associated with a number of outcomes that are also linked to trauma. A discussion of aggression illustrates how complex analysis and interpretation can be. It demonstrates the

BOX 3.1
Aggression Case Examples

a. *John*. John, a fifth grader, was on the playground at his elementary school when a sniper began shooting. He ran for cover and found safety. When he looked back, his friend was sprawled on the playground, bleeding. It was the last time he saw his classmate. In high school, John became a member of a violent gang. They terrorized and assaulted other neighborhood youths and their families. Did John become aggressive because he was predisposed to it by his temperament, traumatic experience, family environment, inner-city neighborhood, information processing biases, neurobiology, or other possible determinants? Did he join a gang because of peer pressure or rejection? Because he feared they would kill him if he did not? To be a part of the perpetrator rather than the victim group? To counteract a sense of helplessness? To desensitize himself to bloody images? To remedy a poor attachment relationship with his parents and a need to belong? In response to societal circumstances that include the neglect of busy working parents, strong demands on youths, and the glorification of violence? Did his post-sniper attack symptoms include behaviors, such as irritability, rage, or impulsivity, that resulted in responses from peers and adults that exacerbated his behaviors? Would he have become aggressive if he had not had a traumatic experience?

b. *An Elementary School Disaster*. Following a natural disaster that caused the collapse of part of a school building and multiple deaths, numerous children and adults were traumatized. Youths became disruptive and sometimes aggressive in the classrooms, hallways, and schoolyard. When admonished in the hall to behave, one child said, "Why should we behave? Bad things happen anyway!" Other children echoed, "Yeah!"

c. *Tish*. Eleven-year-old Tish started to run when the building began to shake. Her friend grabbed her foot to pull her under the bleachers for safety. The bleachers collapsed under falling wall bricks, and Tish's ankle was broken in three places. Her friend had a fractured vertebra, a fractured collar bone, and a broken arm. Tish was previously well-adjusted and mild-mannered. After the earthquake, she remained well-liked by her peers. She reported PTSD symptoms such as nightmares, avoidance of reminders, and anxiety with thoughts about the earthquake or when a building shook. She became aggressive toward her mother. It was only after a treatment session in which she thoroughly reviewed the experience of her friend pulling her back under the bleachers that she stopped her aggression. She finally expressed, in the privacy of the treatment session, her anger at her friend for pulling her back. She could not express her anger to the friend because her friend was injured and because she did not want to lose the friendship.

importance of assessing multiple variables using multiple methods and sources of information to determine the meaning of an outcome.

TRAUMA AND AGGRESSION

Evidence suggests a bidirectional relationship between trauma and aggression. Aggression may induce trauma or other behavioral and emotional disturbances. In addition, antisocial behavior in childhood increases the risk of later exposure to major negative life events and psychosocial adversities (Rutter, 2003). From the other direction, trauma has been associated with subsequent aggressive behavior. Specific life choices such as a particular marital partner and certain experiences such as success may attenuate risk factors for aggression or other undesirable life outcomes. Other choices and other experiences such as trauma may increase risk.

Greenwald (2002a) has pointed out that traumatic experiences may lead to aggression in a number of ways including by (1) disrupting attachment, violating basic trust, and interfering with empathy; (2) leading to a perpetual state of alertness (with increased sensitivity to threat); (3) producing hostile attribution biases (and reduced social competence); (4) engendering anger and/or other affect dysregulation with acting out; and (5) leading to substance abuse or other high-risk activities (e.g., to dampen intolerable emotions). Trauma may also lead to brain damage that interferes with the regulation of impulses, emotions, and behaviors (Schore, 2003). Conduct disturbances are among the comorbid disorders identified for traumatized youths (see chapter 15). Externalizing behaviors have co-occurred with trauma and with aggression. Trauma exposure has been linked to aggressive/criminal acting out, juvenile incarceration, antisocial behavior, and disruptive behavior disorders (e.g., oppositional defiant disorder [ODD], attention-deficit/hyperactivity disorder [ADHD], conduct disorder [CD]; Chamberlain & Moore, 2002; Ford, 2002; Greenwald; Wood et al., 2002). Studies of antisocial youths have shown that 70 to 92% had histories of trauma exposure (Greenwald).

Different types of aggression, different personality characteristics, and different histories suggest variations in the factors that must be considered in assessment as well as in the types of interventions that will be most effective (Barry, Frick, & Killain, 2003; Crick, 1995; de Castro, Slot, Bosch, Koops, & Veerman, 2003). Future research must distinguish the effects of variables or variable combinations (e.g., single or repeated traumatic exposure, conflicted family life, genetics, temperament), determine which factors may have created a risk of or vulnerability to the development of aggressive behavior, and ascertain the interplay of factors.

AGGRESSION AND ITS ASSOCIATIONS

Theoretical Perspectives

A number of theoretical perspectives have been applied to youths' aggressive behaviors (Crick et al., 1998; Ford, 2002; Laird, Jordan, Dodge, Pettit, & Bates, 2001). These perspectives include social learning theory, coercion theory, cognitive conceptual framework, and victimization model among others. A belief that multiple pathways lead to aggression allows for the contributions of peer rejection, child traits, peer influence, and other aspects of youth and life.

Huesmann et al. (2003) have described several of the theories that attempt to explain the long-term relationship between exposure to violence (direct or via the media) and aggression. Among them are social-cognitive, desensitization, aggressive behavior stimulating exposure, third-variable, priming and arousal, excitation transfer, and general arousal theories. *Social-cognitive theory* attributes the link between exposure to violence and aggression through the learning of schemas about a hostile world, aggressive scripts for social problem solving, and beliefs that aggression is acceptable. *Desensitization theory* suggests that, with repeated exposure to violence, the normal negative emotional response (e.g., elevated heart rate, perspiration, discomfort) to observing violence, blood, and gore habituates and the observer becomes desensitized. This in turn may result in a flat response to planning or thinking about violence. Another theory is that aggressive behavior or its correlate *stimulates exposure* to violence and thus engenders the relationship between them. The *third-variable theory* proposes that, because a wide variety of demographic, family, and personal characteristics (e.g., parenting factors, socioeconomic status [SES]) have correlated with aggression and with specific other variables (e.g., trauma, violent TV watching), the long-term positive relations between aggression and any one of the other variables may be derived from their joint association with one or more of these "third variables." *Priming and arousal theories* observe that stimuli previously paired with exposure to violence or items that inherently suggest violence (e.g., weapons) activate memory traces for aggressive scripts, schemas, and beliefs. These priming stimuli, coupled with a provoking situation, are more likely to result in aggression. *Excitation transfer* explains that, after an initial exposure to violence (via media or in person), a subsequent provocation may be perceived as more severe than it is because the emotional response to the previously observed/experienced violence is attributed to the later provocation. Alternatively, the *general arousal theory* suggests that arousal after observed or experienced violence may simply reach a peak that reduces any inhibiting mechanism's (e.g., normative beliefs, previous self-control) ability to restrain aggression. These theories are not mutually exclusive (Huesmann et al.).

Researchers also have theorized a relationship between aggression and temperament or personality. Functionally similar to the mechanism in most social animals for controlling aggression, Blair, Jones, Clark, and Smith (1997) suggest the existence of a violence inhibition/control mechanism (VIM) in humans. Blair and his colleagues posit that the normally developing child's VIM initiates a withdrawal response when activated by distress cues. Deficits in the VIM at an early age disrupt the normal developmental trajectory, resulting in failure of moral distinctions and the reduced suppression of anger. When coupled with cognitive impairments or a maladaptive social environment, VIM deficits may result in psychopathy. Rothbart and Bates (1998) note that specific dimensions of temperament are associated in differential manners with internalizing and externalizing behaviors. Although a *continuity model* (the persistence of behavior over time) might apply, they favor a vulnerability or predisposition model. That is, specific youth characteristics may make a child more vulnerable or prone to particular specific types of development.

Ford (2002) has described a preliminary model for conceptualizing the relationship between violent traumatization and conduct disturbances such as oppositional defiance and aggression. Recognizing that not all violent victimization leads to conduct or other disturbances, Ford postulates that, when it does, violent victimization is followed by dysregulation of both emotion and information processing followed by severe and persistent problems with OD and covert or overt aggression. Trauma symptoms such as information processing biases and impulsiveness then compound posttrauma reactions.

Youth, Environmental, and Experiential Characteristics

Aggressive behavioral development has been linked statistically to a number of factors in youths including genetic predispositions, social cognitions or information processing patterns, neighborhood quality (including ongoing war or inner-city violence), domestic conflict or family instability, propaganda, group regression, neurobiology, mental-health problems, modeling and imitation of others' behaviors, harsh physical experiences in early life, exposure to other violent traumas, watching violent television, coercive discipline, rejection by peers, chronic goal-blocking, unacknowledged shame leading to increased frustration and anger, early conflict-ridden or insecure attachments, high levels of specific narcissistic traits combined with low self-esteem, early physical aggression, failure to succeed in school, relations with deviant peers, and specific temperament traits (Aber, Brown, & Jones, 2003; Barry, Frick, & Killain, 2003; Chamberlain & Moore, 2002; de Castro et al., 2003; Dodge et al., 1995; Klain, 1998; Laird et al., 2001; Rutter, 2003; Scheff, 1997; Volkan, 2001). In addition to the specific youth characteristics, histories, and experiences that have been associated with aggression, cultural and countrywide conditions are as important as, if not more important than, individual differences. For example, the current crime rate in the United States is much higher than the rate in 1950 (Garbarino, 2002; Rutter). Some of these conditions and characteristics may lead to a number of vulnerabilities or symptoms.

Manifestations of aggression vary across age. For example, simple forms of aggression peak in early childhood, major conduct disturbances tend to appear at a later age, and major crime peaks later still (Rutter, 2003). Aber et al. (2003) found that a general shift in children approximately between the ages of 8 and 9 included self-reported increasing levels of cognitive processing that placed youths at risk for future aggression and violence. Research has distinguished between the profiles of early-childhood-onset (early emerging life course, persistent and stable trajectory) and adolescent-onset antisocial behavior (Laird et al., 2001). Early starters are at greater risk for a number of child and adult problems (e.g., maladjustment, criminal behavior) (Laird et al.; McBurnett, King, & Scarpa, 2003). Effectively examining the relationship of aggression to other variables requires

TABLE 3.1
Types of Aggression

Types of Aggression	Reactive or Hostile Aggression	Proactive or Instrumental Aggression
	Retaliatory or defensive responses to provocation or frustration	Deliberate, goal-directed behavior governed by external reinforcements Instrumental: aimed at an outcome such as acquisition of a position or an object Bullying: aims to dominate or intimidate a peer
Overt aggression	Uses threat of physical injury or actual physical damage in response to frustration or perceived offense or threat	Without provocation, harms others through the threat of physical injury or through actual physical damage for personal gain
Relational aggression	Harms others through the threat of or actual damage to their peer relationships as a defensive measure	Harms others through the threat of or actual damage to their peer relationships for personal gain

understanding differences in the types of aggression as well as its manifestations at various ages.

Types of Aggression

Study results on the magnitude of gender differences in aggression depend in part on the way aggression is defined (Chamberlain & Moore, 2002; Crick, 1995). Studies have identified a number of types of aggression including reactive or proactive, social, indirect, physical, relational, and verbal aggression (Crick et al., 1998; Table 3.1). There is some variation in the way that forms of aggression are defined. Recent studies have focused on two main categorizations of aggression (reactive or hostile and proactive or instrumental). *Reactive aggression* is characterized by retaliatory or defensive responses to provocation or frustration (Crick & Dodge, 1996; Crick et al.). *Proactive aggression* is deliberate, goal-directed behavior governed by external reinforcements (e.g., obtaining a desired goal). Crick and Dodge found that proactive aggressive children (ages 9 to 12) evaluated verbal and physical aggressive acts more positively than reactive aggressive or nonaggressive youths. They were more likely to endorse instrumental and self-enhancing goals than relationship-enhancing goals. Reactive aggressive youths (fifth and sixth graders), on the other hand, attributed hostile intent to peers (even when none was intended) more often than nonaggressive youths. They were less likely to give peers the benefit of the doubt. Dodge, Bates, and Pettit (1990) found that hostile attributional biases predicted later aggressive acts. Using ambiguous situations and probe detection tasks with boys and girls ages 11 to 16, Schippell, Vasey, Cravens-Brown, and Bretveld (2003) found that reactive aggression but not proactive aggression was associated with biased attention to ridicule, rejection, and failure cues. The bias was in the direction of suppression of these cues, however. The authors suggest that this suppression may insulate youths from recognizing information that would correct their erroneous interpretations, from becoming aware of the inappropriateness of their behaviors, and from altering their self-concepts.

Dodge and Coie (1987) and Dodge, Coie, Pettit, and Price (1990) subdivided proactive aggression into two categories (see also Schwartz, Dodge, & Coie, 1993). *Instrumental aggression* is aimed at a nonsocial outcome such as the acquisition of a position or an object. *Bullying aggression* aims to dominate or intimidate a peer. Schwartz et al. studied the transactional behaviors of victims and aggressors (see "Aggressor and Aggressee," below).

The study of childhood aggression has focused primarily on overt aggression, which harms others through the threat of physical injury or through actual physical damage (e.g., pushing, hitting, kicking, or assault) (Crick, 1995). Recent studies have shown that a relationally oriented form of aggression is more characteristic of girls (Chamberlain & Moore, 2002; Crick; Crick, Nelson, Morales, Cullerton-Sen, Casas, & Hickman, 2001; Greenwald, 2002b; Simmons, 2002). Relational aggression harms others through the threat of or actual damage to their peer relationships (e.g., exclusion, withdrawal of friendship or acceptance, gossip) (Crick; Crick et al., 2001). Both forms of aggression can be either reactive or proactive. In most countries and at different age levels, overt aggression is more common for boys than for girls, and relational aggression is more common for girls than for boys (Chamberlain & Moore; Crick et al., 1998). Relationship aggression is more common for adolescent girls than for younger girls (Chamberlain & Moore). In ambiguous situations, both overtly aggressive and relationally aggressive youths more often attribute malicious intent to peers than nonaggressive youths (Crick; see "Information Processing," below; chapter 14). Girls have been more distressed than boys by relational aggression (Crick; Crick et al., 2001).

Comorbid Disorders/Symptoms and Aggression

Similar to findings for physically aggressive youths, teachers report that relationally aggressive youths exhibit, in middle childhood, more externalizing behaviors (e.g., impulsivity, oppositional behavior) and, in adolescence, more conduct problems (e.g., delinquency, antisocial personality features) than peers (Crick et al., 1998). Victims of relational aggression especially girls, are at risk for internalizing problems (e.g., depression, loneliness) and anxiety symptoms or disorders (Box 5.1a). Males who have described their own exposure to relational aggression (e.g. bullying) have been among those who have committed mass violence at schools such as the Columbine shooters in 1999 and the Virginia Tech shooter in 2007.

Symptoms such as aggressive behavior may vary in relationship to specific comorbid disorders. Using a peer provocation task, Waschbusch, Pelham, Jennings, Greiner, Tarter, & Moss (2002) examined reactive aggression in 9- to 13-year-old boys with attention-deficit/hyperactivity disorder only, oppositional defiant disorder/conduct disorder (ODD/CD) only, both ADHD and ODD/CD, and controls. Results showed no differences among the four groups following high levels of provocation, but found significantly different behavioral (more aggression), physiological (more accelerated heart rates), and affective (angrier affect) responses immediately following low provocation for children with comorbid ADHD/ODD/CD. Boys with comorbid ADHD/ODD/CD showed a slower dissipation of reactive aggression across time and demonstrated a hostile attribution bias. Waschbusch and his colleagues suggest that this study demonstrates that conclusions about some disorders (e.g., ADHD) that do not account for comorbidity (e.g., with ODD/CD) are of questionable validity.

More about Gender

Research suggests that girls tend to emphasize communal concerns in their interactions with peers. Compared to boys, girls report more intimacy, emotional closeness, and support in their friendships; their peer networks are more likely to consist of dyads and triads (Crick et al., 1998). Increasing evidence suggests that girls are more likely to commit physical aggression in close relationships than in the community (Chamberlain & Moore, 2002). In contrast, boys' same-gender interactions tend to be aimed toward status enhancement in larger, less tightly knit networks (Crick et al.). Aggression's link to previous aggression may differ by gender as well as by type of aggression. Studies of incarcerated youths suggest that boys with severe and chronic delinquency have histories of antisocial and aggressive behavior, whereas overt aggression in seriously delinquent girls emerges in adolescence (Aber et al., 2003; Chamberlain & Moore).

Aspects of social and cognitive information processing have different developmental trajectories in males than in females. In a longitudinal study of 11,160 youths, Aber et al. (2003) found that although girls were generally at lower risk levels for aggression between ages 6.0 and 12.5, by age 12.5 risk levels were almost equivalent to those of boys for both aggressive and competent interpersonal negotiation strategies and for conduct problems. Risk was slightly greater for girls than boys for hostile attribution bias and aggressive fantasies. For teacher-reported prosocial behavior, however, girls increased steadily from ages 6.0 to 12.5.

Youths who engage in types of aggression that are not generally expected of their gender may have additional difficulties (Crick & Werner, 1998; see "Information Processing," below). For example, in comparison to relationally aggressive girls or physically aggressive boys, relationally aggressive boys were likely to have fewer friends and to be more socially and emotionally maladjusted (Crick et al., 1998).

Relationships between Youths

Youths' behavioral natures influence the types of friends with whom they choose to associate, the individuals who are available to them as friends, and the reactions they elicit from others. Youths help to shape one another. Studies have examined peer relationships and their associations with aggression.

Peer Relationships

For aggressive and nonaggressive children, there are multiple pathways to adolescent externalizing behavior problems (Dodge et al., 1995; Laird et al., 2001). Peer experiences are among the relevant guiding factors. Laird et al. found that more than half of youths with high externalizing problems in early childhood continued to exhibit such problem behaviors in adolescence. Nearly two thirds of those who continued to show externalizing behavior problems had experienced peer rejection in childhood, and over one third were highly involved with antisocial peers. Peer rejection and antisocial peers were less likely among those who did not remain high externalizers. For adolescents with late-onset externalizing problems, both antisocial peer involvement and (even more strongly) peer rejection served as onramps to externalizing behavior problems. Even after controlling for the stability of externalizing problems (from early childhood into adolescence), peer rejection but not antisocial peer involvement predicted later externalizing problems.

Evidence suggests that youths select friends who are similar to them (Caspi, 1998; Laird et al., 2001). Existent or altered personalities may attract or repel specific peers. For example, alterations in confidence levels, behaviors, attitudes, and interactional styles following trauma may estrange some relationships and result in new ones. Aggressive and non-aggressive youths are equally likely to have friends (Crick et al., 1998). Physically aggressive youths, however, tend to associate with similarly aggressive youths. Research suggests that, over time, youths who affiliate with antisocial peers tend to engage in higher levels of antisocial behavior. Peer relationships may serve to maintain maladaptive behavior patterns including aggression (e.g., with early-childhood-onset aggression, following traumas) or to promote these behavior patterns (e.g., with adolescent-onset antisocial behavior) (Laird et al.; see "Aggressor and Aggressee," below). For example, Mathew (Box 1.1a), who at age 12 witnessed the murders of his best friend and numerous others, began to react violently to any reminders of his experience and to associate with other rageful and aggressive youths. They, in turn, encouraged him to engage in additional aggressive behaviors such as fighting with rival peer groups.

Friendships may provide a supportive function (e.g., companionship, validation, caring) for both aggressive and nonaggressive youths (Crick et al., 1998). Relationally aggressive youths' dyadic friendships have included relatively high levels of jealousy, intimacy, and desires to keep friendships exclusive. Lower levels of intimacy and coalitional aggression against other youths have typified physically aggressive youths' friend- ships. Physical aggression is highly correlated among siblings. Frequent and intense coercive exchanges occur within aggressive sibling dyads more often than among peer dyads. Most often, the older sibling initiates the aggression (Crick et al.).

Aggressor and Aggressee

In their 1990 study, Dodge, Coie and their colleagues found that each boy's behavior was influenced by that of his peers. Similarly, aggressors and victims help to shape each other's behaviors (Schwartz et al., 1993). In a longitudinal study, Schwartz et al. found that boys shaped the future behaviors of attackers by reinforcing aggressive behaviors (e.g., permit- ting domination, giving up objects). Although aggressive boys may target youths who are not well-regarded, the peer-group environment fostered chronic victimization by offering positive regard to aggressors for ago- nistic behaviors toward boys who became victims but not for aggression toward nonvictims. Although in early study sessions peer responses to persuasion attempts did not differ between groups, in the final sessions, peers rarely rewarded and frequently refused persuasion attempts by vic- tim boys. Behavioral differences between victims (boys who initiated con- siderably less aggression than they received) and contrasts (nonaggressive nonvictims) increased over time. Differences in how well boys were liked by their peers appeared to develop after the emergence in differences in victimization.

Aggressive and nonaggressive victims are behaviorally distinct (Schwartz et al., 1993). In a study of 155 lower- to lower-middle-class Afri- can American nonaggressive male victims, Schwartz et al. found that, in general, victims rarely initiated assertive behavior such as persuasion or social conversation, spent more time in passive play, and received lower leadership ratings than other boys. Even though low social preference by peers did not appear to precede chronic victimization, nonassertive behavior did precede it. Although frequently targeted for *proactive* aggres- sion, victims did not differ from contrasts in their initiation and receipt of *reactive* aggression. For example, chronically victimized boys have been among those who have committed school shootings or suicides (Seals & Young, 2003).

Some of the characteristics of a victim (e.g., slow to initiate conversation) may be characteristic of particular personality traits (e.g., introversion) (see chapter 6). Correlates may vary across contexts, however (Schwartz et al., 1993). Although some behavioral styles (e.g., nonassertiveness) may be stable across settings, peer reactions to these styles may be context specific.

HISTORY, CIRCUMSTANCES, THE ENVIRONMENT

A number of variables in a youth's history, circumstances, and environment (e.g., cultural history/propaganda, insecure attachment, group regression, unresolved rage) may lead to a proneness to aggression or vulnerability to being led into the enactment of violence. Some of these factors are intertwined with traumatic events.

Creating an Aggressive Society

A number of researchers and theoreticians have suggested that war and ongoing terrorism can create a culture of death, terror, and violence (Bar-On, 1999; Lira, 2001). Repeated wars or violent conflicts, such as those in Ireland, Yugoslavia, Israel, and inner cities in the United States, lend to a major theme in society of retaliation as well as of death and dying (Bar-On; Garbarino, 1999). Klain (1998) has described the transmission of a warlike tradition that began to develop in former Yugoslavia after World War II and was reinforced by subsequent wars and conflicts. Songs, literature, and oral traditions handed down stories of the idealization of their own authoritarian figures, projections of danger and hostility onto those from rival countries, atrocities by rivals (sometimes fabricated or distorted), reservoirs of hatred and rage, the sanctity of revenge, and the value of killing the most individuals from rival nations.

Volkan (2001) suggests that large-group regression—a return to fears, wishes, expectations, and defense mechanisms from an earlier stage of development—follow massive traumas, humiliation, or the impositions of a regressed, paranoid leader, who may either reinforce group symptoms and encourage members to remain regressed or encourage them to progress. This regression includes attempts to repair, maintain, or protect the large-group identity and to separate it from an "enemy's" identity. A regressed society imposes rigid obligations that must be obeyed at all times while permitting what normally would be considered antisocial or antihuman behaviors. The world is perceived as a place of lurking dangers. Fears and other internal demons (e.g., rage) are projected onto "the enemy" or other external receiver. "They" (the demonized others) are all bad; "we" (their own ethnic/cultural group) are all good. "They" are associated with things foul, made less human, and ultimately dehumanized, thus justifying their killing or torture. Chosen historical traumas are reactivated, folklore (e.g., myths, songs) is created, and parts of history may be erased in order to confirm these beliefs and to fuel aggression or a sense of victimhood (Volkan; see Klain, 1998).

Some of the same methods used to destroy cultures are a part of creating a compliant culture geared to retaliation against a defined foe. Alvarez (1997) and Sykes and Matza (1957) described techniques used to neutralize the norms that oppose crime and violence and to provide a cultural foundation for violence (cited in Scheff, 1997): (1) denial of responsibility (e.g., "sanctioned by God"; "only carrying out orders"); (2) denial of injuring (e.g., "ethnic cleansing" or "extermination"); (3) denial of victimization (e.g., "the victim brought it on himself or herself"; "they started it/are the aggressors"); (4) condemning the targets of violence (e.g., "they posed a threat against us", "are guilty of worse crimes" such as mistreatment of native inhabitants or of specific races); (5) appeal to higher loyalties (e.g., patriotic, religious); (6) denial of humanity (e.g., portrayal of the Jews by the Nazis, Bosnians by the Serbs, the United States by Al-Qaeda, Al-Qaeda by the United States). These methods may be relevant to gang wars as well as to international wars.

Fear and rage following traumatic events (e.g., September 11, 2001) also have contributed to aggression against those who resemble the perpetrators of the terror (e.g., Arabs, Muslims). Posttrauma cultures are often characterized by fear, hatred, and rage. Scheff (1997) suggests that unacknowledged emotions (hatred and rage) are generated by alienation and by cultural scripts for demonizing purported enemies. When anger's source is feelings of rejection or inadequacy, rage and aggression may mask a resulting shame. This composite of shame and anger result in the rage that generates violence. Scheff offers that any steps that decrease mass alienation (e.g., genuine regret/sorrow/shame for directly or indirectly inflicting harm, providing welcomed postdisaster assistance, desired reconstruction) automatically lessen pressure toward conflict.

Humiliation

After 35 years of interviewing incarcerated men, Gilligan (2003) concluded that the fastest way of provoking someone to violence is to shame him. Moreover, people resort to violence when they feel that the only way to wipe out shame or humiliation is by shaming those who they feel shamed them. The most powerful way to shame someone is to commit violence toward him or her. Childhood experiences such as severe assaults, abuse, relational aggression, and neglect often include repeated humiliation and intense helplessness. Knox (2004) states that it is unbearable to feel that one is of no value, unlovable, or the object of hatred (see also Gilligan). The traumatic fear, humiliation, and profound sense of helplessness that result (Crick et al., 2001; Knox) are intense emotions that may result in lashing out or lashing inward. Researchers have found among murderers, for example, frequent histories of repeated humiliations such as occur in violent or other intense traumatic experiences. Biblical stories,

Homeric epics, war historians, and current analytic and forensic psychologists have recognized the path from rejection, slighting, disrespect, or embarrassment to shame and humiliation followed by anger or rage, then aggression (Gilligan). Gilligan points out that shame alone is not sufficient for the result of violence. He suggests that the following conditions enhance the possibility of violence after shame: (1) the individual has not developed the capacity for emotions that inhibit violence (e.g., remorse, guilt, empathy) or the situation has diminished these emotions; (2) the intensity of the shame and humiliation is so overwhelming that it threatens the viability and cohesion of the self; (3) the person believes that he does not have sufficient nonviolent means to save or restore his self-esteem; and (4) cultural conditioning that to maintain masculinity, certain situations call for violence.

Home and Community Environment

In addition to cultural and societal factors, the family and community environments may contribute to aggression. These conditions may be as general as SES and as specific as the parent-youth relationship.

Family and Community

McBurnett et al. (2003) have summarized the findings regarding the environment and disruptive behavior disorders (DBDs) including aggressive disorders. Studies suggest that rates for DBD youths are higher than average for (1) parental police contacts, substance abuse, and domestic violence; (2) mothers with depressive disorders; (3) low SES and multiple environmental stressors (possible exposure to violence); (4) pre- and post-natal exposure to brain chemistry-altering drugs (illicit and legal) such as mothers who smoke; and (5) the annoyance of adults and youths in response to their rule-breaking and a corresponding reduction in positive social interaction. If youths have attention and motivation deficits, academic work may be more difficult, contributing to negative self-worth. Youths with conduct disorders often have been exposed to less consistent, harsh physical punishment that is difficult to predict and exposed to a hostile and pessimistic environment.

Relationships with Parents: Attachment

Researchers have found a relationship between disturbed attachments and a number of other variables such as temperament, trauma, aggression, psychopathology, and cortisol elevations (Greenberg, DeKlyen, Speltz, & Endriga, 1997; James, 1994; Lyons-Ruth & Jacobvitz, 1999; Rothbart & Bates, 1998; Schore, 2003; Weinfield, Sroufe, Egeland, & Carlson, 1999). Evidence suggests a correlation between specific parental behaviors and the behaviors of a targeted child (Fonagy et al., 1997). The level of conflict-negativity versus warmth-support directed to a specific child correlated with that child's level of antisocial behavior. Additionally, a high level of conflict with one child was associated with lower levels of antisocial behavior in that child's siblings.

Both temperament and attachment have been statistically related to the ways youths regulate affect and cope with stress (Rothbart & Bates, 1998). Child abuse traumas may be a part of or may contribute to disturbed attachments. Child abuse traumas also may cause brain injury or interrupted brain development (Schore, 2003). Schore suggests that the result may be inefficient capacities to regulate rage. He also suggests that even a single, timely positive relationship may alter a trajectory toward violence.

Creating a disturbed attachment with parents is among the techniques used to perpetuate an environment that in turn perpetuates violent aggression. Traumatized caretakers (e.g., in Palestinian orphanages) and parents functioning in a "regressed-group identity" (e.g., in Nazi Germany) may knowingly or unknowingly maintain a large-group identity that leads to suicide killings (Volkan, 2001). In Nazi Germany, mothers were directed to ignore their children's dependency needs, thus injuring their sense of basic trust and creating an insecure attachment. Subsequently, their identity formation was filled with Nazi propaganda. Posttrauma group regression with its real or fantasized humiliation or victimization is fertile ground for the creation of suicide bombers and other terrorists (Scheff, 1997; Volkan). Volkan defines the two essentials for creating suicide bombers: (1) a youth whose personal identity is already disturbed and who is seeking an outside source to stabilize this disturbed inner world and (2) a training method that forces a large-group identity to fill the damaged or subjugated individual identity. Youths who have endured concrete traumas (e.g., actual humiliation such as loss of a parent, beating, or torture by an enemy, e.g., in the Gaza Strip, Afghanistan) are the best candidates to become suicide bombers/killers. Their education is most easily accomplished when a religious element of group identity provides a solution for a personal sense of shame, humiliation, or helplessness. Sanctioned by God, they may feel a sense of omnipotence in carrying out their acts of destruction. The killings are ritualized and made psychologically easy (Volkan).

Research suggests that, compared to other children, parent-child relationships for both physically and relationally aggressive children include low levels of warmth (Crick et al., 1998). *Relationally aggressive* youths' relationships with their mothers are characterized by high levels of physical aggression directed at the mother by the child, higher levels of exclusivity in the relationship with both parents, and greater closeness to mothers into the preadolescent years. In contrast, mother-child relationships for *physically aggressive* youths are characterized by conflict resolution problems, higher relational aggression directed to the child by the mother, and lower levels of closeness and intimacy.

Parenting

Particular parenting styles vary with circumstances such as cultural norms, educational levels, child characteristics, and the constraints or advantages of SES and family marital status. A number of parenting practices have been associated with aggressive, delinquent, and antisocial behaviors (Laird, Pettit, Dodge, & Bates, 2003; Pettit, Laird, Dodge, Bates, & Criss, 2001). Research suggests that proactive planning and anticipatory guidance have been effective socialization tools with preschool children and (added to other supportive and positive parenting) for early childhood (Pettit et al.). Harsh discipline has been consistently associated with externalizing problems. Buss, Block, and Block (1980) found that highly active 5 year olds whose parents responded with impatience, hostility, and frequent power struggles were described at age 7 by teachers as aggressive, manipulative, and noncompliant (Caspi, 1998).

Baumrind (1989) distinguished between authoritative and authoritarian parents (Pettit et al., 2001). *Authoritative* parents are warm and accepting and firm in establishing behavioral guidelines while generally promoting psychological autonomy. *Authoritarian* parents, however, are highly demanding and low in warmth and encouragement of autonomy. Other researchers have contrasted the use of psychological forms of control (e.g., guilt induction, love withdrawal) with the use of behavioral regulation (monitoring, regulation, supervision, and behavioral management) or parental monitoring (awareness and regulation of youths' whereabouts, activities, and companions) (Barber, Olsen, & Shagle, 1994). Pettit et al. state that emotional manipulation, intrusiveness, demandingness, constraining the youth's communication, and hostility figure prominently in the assessment of psychological control. Parental monitoring that focuses on the child's behavior and provides guidance and supervision includes tracking skills for all ages and additional skills (e.g., communication, active listening) for older youths. In a longitudinal multi-informant and multitrait study of youths ages 8–10 and then 13–14, Pettit et al. demonstrated that the absence of monitoring was associated more strongly with delinquency behavior problems than with anxiety/depression. On the other hand, psychological control correlated both with anxiety/depression and delinquency behavior problems. Monitoring did not predict anxiety/depression. Rather, it was linked to lower levels of delinquent behavior (for children with high and low earlier levels of behavior problems) and was associated with fewer mother-reported behavior problems for girls than for boys (after controlling for preadolescent delinquent problems). Girls were more highly monitored than boys, and their reports of mothers' psychological control correlated with anxiety and delinquent behaviors. It may be that, for girls, mothers' psychological control behaviors escalate as behavior problems increase or vice versa.

As with other interpersonal transactions, the parent and the youth may evoke or reinforce behaviors from the other. For example, Patterson (1982) found that children's coercive behaviors led to punitive and angry responses often escalating until adults withdrew (Caspi, 1998). Early coercive family interactions in which family members alternate in the roles of aggressors and victims portend deteriorated family management practices.

When antisocial children reach adolescence, the parents are less likely to supervise and monitor their offspring. Inept disciplinary strategies, in turn, foreshadow persistent and progressively more serious delinquency.

Moral Socialization

Moral socialization includes the inhibition of violence and antisocial behaviors (Blair et al., 1997). By 42 months of age, normally developing children recognize that it is wrong to victimize another. Although gentle discipline may not have an adverse effect on moral socialization, studies suggest that harsh authoritarian and power-assertive parenting practices (relying on punishment) are less effective than the induction and fostering of empathy. For normally developing children, Blair et al. suggest that power-assertive (fear-inducing punishment) techniques may be better for socialization of conventional rules (e.g., quiet in class), and that fostering empathy may be better for moral transgressions (those that involve a victim, e.g., stealing or aggression).

Trauma can interrupt moral development or contribute to a changed morality that in turn contributes to aggression (Garbarino, 1999; Nader, 2001b; Box 3.1b). Noting that most people justify "necessary" killing (e.g., in war, to protect someone from death or severe injury), Garbarino suggests that inner-city youths exposed to ongoing violence may kill based on a moral code dominated by a troubled emotional life, an intense personal need for justice, and a different idea of what is necessary for survival. For example, after retrieving his own chain from another boy who had stolen it but posed no immediate threat to him, Calvin shot the boy in the head. He later explained that he shot the boy to avoid being in danger from him in the future (Garbarino).

Personality factors have also been associated with a faulty moral development. Research suggests that more fearful children show stronger development of a conscience. In the development of a conscience, Kochanska (1997) found that more fearful children benefit from a caregiver's gentle reasoning, whereas less fearful youths benefit from positive attachment relationships (see also Rothbart, Ahadi, Hershey, & Fisher, 2001). Children exhibit differences in their susceptibility to reward and punishment. Some youths are more likely to stop a prohibited activity when punishment is likely; others are more motivated when a reward is anticipated (see "Types of Aggression," above; chapter 6).

CHARACTERISTICS OF YOUTHS

Many aspects of youths are relevant to aggressive behavior. Among them are personality characteristics and information processing styles discussed here and emotional health issues and moral development discussed above. Some child characteristics (alone or in combination) may be predictive of later aggression. Others may serve as mediators of its development.

Personality

As has been true with many variables in the study of trauma and of aggression, the results have been mixed for their association with aspects of personality as well as aspects of neurobiology (Shoal, Giancola, & Kirillova, 2003; chapter 6). "Which came first?" also has been a topic of discussion. For example, child abuse has correlated with resistance to control tendencies in infancy and to externalizing problems in the pre-school period (Dodge et al., 1995). Studies of aggressive children suggest that they provoke others who tend to respond aggressively to them (Hues-mann et al., 2003).

Studies suggest correlations between some traits and conduct distur-bances such as aggression and between other traits and nonaggression. In a review of findings on temperament and behavior, Rothbart and Bates (1998) observed that early inhibition is related to later internalizing; early resistance to control versus early manageability was related to later exter-nalizing; and early negative affect to both dimensions of behavior. Caspi and Silva (1995) found that adults who were undercontrolled as children tended to be low on harm avoidance and high on social alienation. In con-trast, inhibited children were, as adults, high on harm avoidance, low on aggression, and low on social potency. Among other traits and behaviors, the negative affect composite behaviors have been linked to aggression (Rothbart, Ahadi et al., 2001; Rothbart & Bates).

Psychopathic individuals are said to lack remorse, guilt, and empathy (Blair et al., 1997). Studies of adult psychopaths have found primary defi-cits in anxiety and fear. Although, in a study by Blair and colleagues, the responses of psychopathic men and nonpsychopathic men to threatening stimuli and to anger were similar, psychopathic men were less responsive (but not nonresponsive) to distress cues of individuals shown in slides. This suggests that empathy may be an important factor in the occurrence and treatment of some aggressors. For children, using the parent-reported Child Behavior Questionnaire (chapter 6), both empathy and guilt/shame were positively related to effortful control, which includes inhibitory and atten-tional control, and related to the internalizing aspects of negative affectiv-ity (NA) (Rothbart, Ahadi et al., 2001). Aggression was positively correlated with the externalizing aspects (e.g., anger) of NA and negatively correlated with its internalizing aspects (e.g., sadness).

Cortisol, Trauma, Personality, and Aggression. Aggression appears to be reg-ulated by multiple neurochemical systems (Rothbart & Bates, 1998). Limbic system impairments and impairments in dopamine, noradrenaline, and serotonin receptors have been implicated in the dysregulation of aggression (Schore, 2003). Altered levels of cortisol (a behavior-inhibiting stress hormone that is secreted by the adrenal glands during stress reactions) have been associated with trauma and with aggression (Byrnes, 2001; Schore; chapter 2).

Some studies have established a preliminary link between low resting cortisol and aggressive behavior (Shoal et al., 2003). A number of studies have found low resting cortisol levels in youths with childhood-onset aggression (McBurnett et al., 2003). Although effects between cortisol level and aggressive behavior are likely bidirectional, the heritability of resting cortisol level suggests that its influence largely may be manifested before the occurrence of aggression. In addition, studies have shown that cortisol levels vary with risk or occurrence of several disorders such as risk of substance use disorder, major depression, or PTSD.

Although results have been mixed, a growing number of studies indicate a relationship between cortisol level and personality, attachment security, and aggression (Rothbart & Bates, 1998; Shoal et al., 2003). Shoal et al. reported that resting cortisol levels were positively related to children's fearful attachment to their mothers and reluctance to approach unfamiliar individuals or events; negatively related to adolescents' self-reported irritability; and positively related to college students' anxiety and openness to the values and ideas of others. Resting cortisol levels have been positively associated with the personality characteristics of harm avoidance (a continuum of avoidance of excitement and danger) and self-control (a continuum of reflectiveness, caution, and carefulness) (Shoal et al.). Highly aggressive individuals have reported low harm avoidance and low self-control. Cortisol also has correlated with aspects of negative emotionality (a continuum of predisposition to states of distress, fear, anger, and hostility). Caspi et al. (1997) found that low harm avoidance, low self-control, and high negative emotionality in 18 year olds predicted conviction for violent crimes by age 21. Shoal and his colleagues suggest that personality traits might serve to mediate the relation between low cortisol levels and increased aggressive behavior. They found that low cortisol in preadolescence is predictive of aggressive behavior 5 years later (in middle adolescence). Of the personality traits measured, only self-control accounted for significant amounts of variance in aggressive behavior.

Shoal et al. (2003) suggest that low resting salivary cortisol levels appear to predict characterological impulsivity and insensitivity to punishment (see also Rothbart & Bates, 1998). Cortisol's link to physically and verbally aggressive actions may be through its associations with these personality traits. High resting cortisol levels predicted later reflectiveness and caution, whereas low levels predicted impulsiveness and carelessness and the aggressive behavior associated with them. Preadolescent cortisol levels were not associated with adolescent trait aggression (i.e., lower resting cortisol is not linked specifically to an "aggressive disposition" during adolescence) but rather to more aggressive behavior through increased impulsivity and general behavioral dysregulation. Behavioral and emotional dysregulation also have been identified as byproducts of trauma (Schore, 2003).

Information Processing

Early temperamental characteristics as well as early experiences may set up anticipatory attitudes that affect interactions and relationships (Caspi, 1998; chapter 14). Information processing research has consistently shown that aggressive youths exhibit attributional biases (Crick & Dodge, 1996; de Castro et al., 2003; Schippell et al., 2003). That is, they perceive, interpret, and make decisions about social interactions that increase the likelihood of their aggressive acts. Crick (1995) points out that aggressive acts are likely to lead to increased actual hostility and rejection from peers, thereby reinforcing the bias. Youths' evaluations of their own social behaviors include their moral assessments (response evaluation), outcome expectations, confidence in their ability to perform a response, and assessment of their frequency of engaging in a response. Studies have demonstrated that overtly aggressive youths evaluate overt aggression more positively, expect more positive outcomes from its use, feel more confident about enacting aggression, and make more response decisions that favor overtly aggressive behaviors (Crick & Werner, 1998). Quiggle, Garber, Panak, and Dodge (1992, cited in Caspi) found that, compared to depressive youths, aggressive youths search the situation for fewer cues before making an attributional decision, tend to make more hostile attributions, generate more aggressive responses, and more frequently expect rewards from aggressive problem solving.

Dodge et al. (1995) found an association between childhood abuse and conduct disturbances. Their findings also suggested that abused youths become defensively attuned to hostile cues and inattentive to relevant nonhostile cues. Moreover, among the mental mechanisms that may be factors in their aggressive behavior are an acquired repertoire of aggressive responses, the belief that aggression may lead to positive outcomes for the aggressor, and a sense of self-efficacy for aggressing. Similarly, Ford (2002) has described a kind of "victim coping" (e.g., defensive attitudes, numbing and emptiness, spaced out/disoriented, "brain fog") used by violently traumatized youths. The youths adopt a generalized expectation of danger and betrayal and an unspoken belief that distrust and defiance are essential for self-protection or for coping with unmanageable emotions.

Even in ambiguous provocation situations, aggressive youths attribute malicious intent more often than their peers (Crick & Dodge, 1996). In a study of third- to sixth-grade children (Crick, 1995), relationally aggressive youths (in contrast to their nonaggressive peers) exhibited a hostile attributional bias specifically toward assessed relational provocation situations rather than toward overt aggressive situations. Neither the relationally aggressive nor the both relationally and overtly aggressive group was likely to give the benefit of the doubt to peers even when no hostility was intended. More study is needed to determine if individual youth biases are consistently directed toward specific types of aggression.

Assessment of Aggression

Numerous approaches have been used to assess aggression. Among them are observation and peer-, self-, parent-, and teacher-report methods (Crick et al., 1998). A self-report hypothetical situation instrument has been used to assess youths' evaluations of using specific forms of aggression. Videotapes have assisted the use of child observational methods as well as methods enlisting youths' responses to situations (Crick & Dodge, 1996). Peer nomination methods have been endorsed as a cross-situationally applicable measure to distinguish between relationally and overtly aggressive youths and to indicate social preferences, that is, how well-liked or disliked a youth is (Crick et al.; Laird et al., 2001). Risk for aggression has been measured through examining parent, teacher, and youth reports of cognitive and behavioral patterns such as hostile attribution biases, aggressive fantasies, aggressive and competent interpersonal negotiation strategies, aggressive or competent intervention strategies, conduct problems, depressive symptoms, aggressive behavior, and prosocial behavior (Aber et al., 2003). Crick and her colleagues recommend using a composite score averaged over multiple contexts (home, school, work) and informants (peer, self, parent, teacher, researcher). Youths may engage in certain aggressive behaviors only in certain contexts.

In the study of aggression and its relationship to other variables, research suggests the need to delineate the type of aggression (relational or overt; proactive or reactive), the context (e.g., type of provocation), gender differences, age and developmental differences, social-cognitive biases, and emotional states (Crick et al., 1998; Crick & Werner, 1998). Experimental evidence indicates an increasing ability with age to distinguish between relational and overt aggression. Moreover, aggression reflects changing needs and the acquisition of additional developmental skills at different ages (Crick et al.; see "Cortisol, Trauma, Personality, and Aggression," above). For example, across the age span, relationally aggressive youths use the tactics of ignoring and exclusion. With age, they become more adept at employing subtle, complex, and nonverbal relationally aggressive behaviors such as building coalitions against someone.

A number of biases may affect the accuracy of reporting on aggressive behaviors. A youth's extreme physical aggression may bias some observers toward reporting increased relational aggression for the youth as well (Crick et al., 1998). For example, teacher but not peer reports have suggested a significant correlation between boys' overt and relational aggression. The need for social acceptance may be a factor in reporting. For example, studies suggest that relationally aggressive girls underreport their use of relational aggression (Crick & Werner, 1998).

CONCLUSIONS

Validly linking symptoms or disorders such as aggression, depression, conduct disorder, or changes in self-esteem to traumatic experiences requires an investigation of all of the possible contributing factors. Multiple factors are likely to contribute to youths' traumatic reactions. Variables can be complexly interrelated. Associations may be bi- or tridirectional. Outcomes may be related to multiple or combined factors or to a shared link with an outside variable(s) ("the third variable"). For example, violence/aggression may result in traumatization. Traumatization may be the main factor or a factor in subsequent violence/aggression. Common variables (e.g., temperament, attachment, parenting styles, peer relationships, biochemical factors, information processing, morality, environmental influences) may be a part of the variation in trauma levels and in other symptomatic reactions such as anxiety disorders and conduct disturbances.

4

The Nature of Assessing Traumatized Children and Adolescents

Among the many factors that affect the accuracy of youth assessments are the comprehensiveness of, nature of, and preparation for assessment as well as the reliability and validity of measures used. Comprehensive assessment of children includes collecting information from multiple sources and in multiple contexts. In addition to employing assessment scales or interviews with parents, children, and other sources, direct observation of children at school or daycare, with caregivers, and in clinical settings has assisted in obtaining accurate information regarding youths' symptoms and reactions (Reynolds & Kamphaus, 1998; Scheeringa, Peebles, Cook, & Zeanah, 2001). Identifying the subtypes and characteristics of children, the traumatic experience, and the child's history that affect outcomes may prevent the canceling out of effects. In the process of establishing the reliability and validity of measures, items are sometimes excluded before establishment of important information such as (1) rare items that may give important information about the course and duration of reactions, (2) the manner in which symptoms may change and manifest over time, and (3) specific risk and protective factors that may alter the nature of traumatic response.

THE NEED FOR MULTIMEASURE ASSESSMENT

Assessment of childhood traumatic response must include examination of multiple interrelated issues in addition to those frequently measured (La Greca, Silverman, Vernberg, & Roberts, 2002b). No single variable explains all of the effects of an experience. For example, information processing patterns do not account for all of the effects of early abuse; therefore, additional mechanisms also are a part of the outcomes of abuse (Dodge, Bates, Pettit, & Valente, 1995). Recognizing the variables that affect response is essential to accurate assessment. Moreover, multiple issues, such as genetics, temperament, economic and cultural adversities, parent-child fit, personal resources, and family psychopathology and conflict, must be taken into account when designing and when evaluating intervention programs for at-risk youths. Future research would be improved by the use of multiple measures as well as multiple assessment sessions to evaluate constructs relevant to youths' traumatic reactions (see Rothbart & Bates, 1998; Vasey, Dalgleish, & Silverman, 2003).

A variety of issues and circumstances must be taken into account when assessing children and interpreting data. For example, some of the symptoms on the dissociation scales (e.g., feeling dizzy, forgetting things, having trouble remembering things, feeling like he or she is not in his or her body) may be common to other disorders (e.g., painful catastrophic ailment) or to specific cultural practices. Similarly, the number and nature of symptoms endorsed may be influenced by life experiences, family, and cultural norms. Symptoms reported, for example, on a sexual behavior inventory may reflect family nudity, children's witnessing of household sexual behaviors, types of television shows watched, children's access to magazines with nude pictures, and children's exposure to sexually re-enacting traumatized children (see Friedrich, 1993a). Gender differences may require new definitions of traumagenic events. Boys who suffered violence directed against their genitals with a primarily violent intent, for example, had symptomatology equivalent to sexually abused boys (Boney-McCoy and Finkelhor, 1995). Girls often differ from boys in their expressions of aggression (Wood, Foy, Goguen, Pynoos, & James, 2002; Simmons, 2002).

Research findings reflect researchers' theoretical perspectives, the population studied, and the combination of instruments used. In many cases, a considerable amount of the variance remains unexplained by the variables studied. De Castro, Slot, Bosch, Koops, & Veerman (2003) found a hostile attribution effect only when certain combinations of measures and participants were considered. They concluded that participants with similar aggression scores may differ in the kinds of aggression expressed, the context in which aggression occurs, or their emotional states during participation. Pinderhughes (1998) described how family secrets and aspects of African American heritage, such as slavery, racism, and Black elitism, influenced emotional health, over the course of her life, from youth. She suggested, in order to understand and effect genuine change in victim status, it is essential to bear witness in therapy to narratives of personal, family, and cultural history. Only then is it possible to assess the true impact of traumatic experiences on a person's life.

Identifying Variables

Nesselroade (1995) observed that "complexly determined outcomes cannot be predicted with high precision from only one or a few antecedents" (p. 345). There are dangers associated with assessing either too many or too few variables. If too many variables are assessed, trivial variables might need to be combined with overly elaborate relationships in order to make them theoretically interesting. On the other hand, if too few are assessed, variables will be defined so inclusively that important relationships can be concealed or neglected (Nesselroade). In a large representative study of the trajectories of youths toward aggressive behaviors, only a few demographic (SES, cultural background, gender) and intervention variables were considered (Aber, Brown, & Jones, 2003). The authors suggest that the variance in growth and change not explained could have been accounted for by variables that were not assessed in the study such as temperament, neighborhood environment, and family dynamics.

Exposure to trauma alone does not shape traumatic reactions (Kroll, 2003). In order to fully and accurately understand symptom endorsement and scale scores, it is essential to examine the appropriate (pre-, post-, and during the event) variables that may contribute to specific posttraumatic reactions. Differences or levels of traumatic reactions may not be statistically or clinically significant until the effects of variables such as cultural attitudes, brain dominance, personality traits, weight subgroup, or pubertal stage are identified (De Bellis, Keshavan et al., 1999). Some symptoms may appear only after prolonged or intense exposure. For example, dissociation has been related to age, gender, duration, and severity of sexual abuse (Friedrich, Jaworski, Huxsahl, & Bengtson, 1997; Friedrich, Gerber et al., 2001). Because symptoms (e.g., dissociation) have also been found in other than identified populations (e.g., nonabused psychiatric patients), the other variables contributing to these symptoms must be identified. Some symptoms may occur for most people at some point in time. North and Pfefferbaum (2002) point out that sleeplessness affects many people at one time or another.

Variations in Experience

Specific types of experiences that a youth endures before, during, or after a traumatic event may affect the rate of occurrence and intensity of symptoms such as intrusive, distressing memories or reduced impulse control (Nader, 1997a; chapter 10). After the Gulf War, Kuwaiti youths who had committed aggression against another person during the war reported higher postwar levels of arousal and less impulse control than other youths exposed to the war (Nader & Fairbanks, 1994). Studies of war and terrorism suggest that, with or without direct exposure, children who were very worried about someone or feared someone they cared for was endangered during an event may have increased symptoms after seeing graphic media images of the event (Nader, Pynoos, Fairbanks, Al-Ajeel,

& Al-Asfour, 1993; Pfefferbaum et al., 1999). The person who helplessly witnessed an assault or accident when a person was hit from behind may have more symptoms than the injured person who did not anticipate the injury or know what hit them.

It may be necessary, at times, to determine the nature of specific symptomatic behavior (Nader, 1997a). For example, are the symptoms related to loss or to trauma (e.g., trauma vs. grief dreams, trauma vs. grief play)? Are they associated with the fear or sleeplessness that may initially affect the broader population, or are they a part of traumatic response? Stallard, Velleman, Langsford, & Baldwin (2001) pointed out a conceptual confusion between some coping strategies and symptoms of PTSD. Social withdrawal, for example, can be a coping strategy or a symptom of avoidance (Fletcher, 2003).

Course

A number of factors may affect the accuracy of assessment over time. Symptoms, such as fear or poor concentration, may reduce when other symptoms, such as sleep disturbance, diminish (Krakow, Hollifield et al., 2001). Over time, some symptoms may change into behavioral patterns such as impulsive reactivity, specific interactional styles, selective attention, attributional biases, emotional and behavioral scripts as well as vulnerabilities, inhibitions, or styles of assessment and decision-making. Consequently, the ongoing effects of trauma may go unnoticed if only traditional scales and measures are used.

The Child's Characteristics and Needs

When important personal variables are excluded from an analysis, effects may be attributed to trauma that are, in fact, a result of other variables or variable combinations. To determine the differences among traumatized children related to some characteristics (e.g., gender) or experiences (e.g., exposure to violence), it is essential to control for the effects of personality traits and types (see chapter 6). Particular characteristics are more prevalent in one than the other gender. Early traits such as inhibition and lack of control have been associated with later low and high levels of aggression or externalizing symptoms, respectively (Biederman et al., 1990; Caspi, Henry, McGee, Moffitt, & Silva, 1995). Lipschitz, Morgan, and Southwick (2002) described two biological subtypes of traumatized youths: those with high and those with reduced autonomic responsiveness. The former is anxious, hypervigilant, fearful, and on guard; the latter withdraws, dissociates, and becomes numb and depressed.

The quality and congruence of relationships, such as those between parent and child, therapist and patient, and even treatment modality and help-seeker personality, can play an important role in symptomatology and in the effectiveness of treatment. The presence or lack of compatibility between an adult or method and a youth's personality and needs may explain child traits, symptoms, and recovery rates. Kochanska and Clark (1997) found, for example, that the goodness of fit between child temperament and parent responsiveness had a major effect on the development of the child's conscience. Fearful children whose parents used gentle discipline as well as fearless children with a secure attachment to their parents scored higher on conscience composite scores. Similarly, in our study of young children undergoing bone-marrow transplants (Lee, Cohen, Stuber, & Nader, 1994), when parents applied a comforting style that matched the child's preferred method of being comforted (e.g., to be distracted with activity, provided information, or held and verbally soothed), the child's distress was more likely to decrease visibly, whereas it clearly increased when there was no such match.

Normative Data

The concept of normative data for a measure needs to be considered in the context of factors that may affect those norms. Norms based on the responses of one culture may not apply to other cultures (Lee, Lei, & Sue, 2001; Rousseau & Drapeau, 1998). Norms are frequently established separately for males and females, for different ethnicities, for distinct age groups, and even for differing SES. Other less frequently considered factors may play an important part in the etiology and prognosis of symptoms among traumatized children and adolescents. Very young and cognitively delayed children may be less able to provide detailed accounts of their symptoms and/or experiences (Elliott & Briere, 1994b). Inquiry about a child's previous experiences, using such instruments as life events scales and exposure questionnaires, has proven useful in some studies attempting to develop norms for trauma measures. If exposure and pre-existing conditions have not been measured, the sample used for norming a trauma measure may include traumatized individuals, which could result in means that are higher than actually found among the truly nontraumatized population. The variance of the measure is also likely to be artificially enlarged by the inclusion of unsuspected trauma victims among a sample of supposedly nontraumatized children. Children from larger urban areas report higher exposure rates and symptom levels than do children from smaller towns and rural areas (Briere, 1996; Richters & Martinez, 1991; Singer, Anglen, Song, & Lunghofer, 1995). Elliott and Briere (1994a) found lower reported symptom levels among children who deny the event or their symptoms. Samples of children used for establishing normative data that include a substantial number of youths who deny the trauma or underreport their symptoms could potentially bias the norms toward lower means, while at the same time increasing the variation. Thus, unless careful consideration is given to sampling issues, normative samples may be compromised by unknown biases. Reliance on simple random sampling may be inadequate to address these potential problems.

Trauma and Life Course

Assessing the impact of traumas across a youth's life course is not as simple as assessing *DSM* PTSD. Especially in children, traumatic reactions may have cascading or additive effects, just as childhood ill-temperedness, for example, has been found to lead to cumulative consequences: difficulties with school authorities, negative school experiences, lower occupational status (Caspi, 1998). Disruptions to academic and interpersonal functioning as well as disturbed developmental processes (e.g., the normal development of conscience; brain development) may drastically alter a youth's life course. A youth on a successful path among peers and toward a career may be undermined in a progressive fashion (Box 4.1a). When loved ones are killed or injured in traumatic events, the trauma may have additional cumulative effects.

Individual Styles

The different ways that individuals interact with their environments can influence and be influenced by traumatic reactions. Caspi (1998) has summarized three of the ways through which individuals interact with their environments: (1) *reactive* transactions (individuals experience, interpret, and react to the same environment differently); (2) *evocative*

BOX 4.1

Case Examples: Life Changes and Parent-Youth Relationships

a. *Life Changes.* After injury in a natural disaster, Tony (age 8), formerly a friendly and well-liked boy, became more irritable and overwhelmed by noise and people. His outbursts and moods changed his school functioning and distanced peer relationships. Sandy (age 11) refused therapy after traumatization in a natural disaster and never resolved her anger and feelings that she had not been protected. As an adolescent, she joined antisocial groups in defiant and illegal activities. Jane's repeated child abuse experiences (ages 8 to 16) so disrupted her trust of people that relationships were impaired, choices were hindered, and opportunities were missed throughout her life.

After the rest of her family was murdered while she was restrained nearby, the formerly dynamic and popular Charlene dropped from an A to a C student. Her friends seemed superficial and petty in their complaints. None of her relatives could provide a relationship based on trust and discipline such as the one her parents had developed with her over the years. Her longing for the closeness and comfort of that original relationship influenced all of her life choices. Her academic and career goals faded as she became more dependent upon her boyfriend for the support and emotional nourishment that her family had once provided.

b. *Parent-Youth Relationships.* Samples of parents' concerned remarks months after their children were traumatized illustrate possible changes in attitudes toward their children: "He is angry and verbally abusive towards me all of the time now." "She wants me near her every minute. I have little privacy; no time to myself. I am so tired and irritable." "My bright, confident, cheerful son is now depressed, pouty, hesitant ... needy. I feel like I lost my son. Who is this boy who came home that day?" One year after a sniper attack, a mother who had reported a year earlier that her child was well-adjusted and easygoing before the trauma stated, "He is irritable, angry, and defiant, but he has always been like that."

transactions (an individual's personality evokes distinctive responses from others); and (3) *proactive* transactions (individuals differentially select or create environments of their own). Individuals are selectively responsive to information that is consistent with their self-views and expectations, for instance (Caspi; Crick & Dodge, 1994; Dalgleish, Taghavi, Neshat-Doost, Moradi, Canterbury, & Yule, 2003). In a *reactive* world, interpretation biases may create corresponding facts (Caspi; Crick, 1995; chapters 3, 14).

Very early in life, children *evoke* consistent responses from others. A child's behavior, expressions, and characteristics affect interactions with adults and with peers. Research suggests that personality differences are represented in facial expressions (Caspi, 1998). A youth may have mannerisms or behaviors that elicit different types of discipline, degrees of validation, and levels of nurturance from others. Conduct-disordered boys evoke more negative responses than nonproblem boys from mothers of nonproblem boys and mothers of conduct-disturbed boys (Anderson, Lytton, & Romney, 1986, cited in Caspi). An extravert's positive emotions may elicit more positive emotions in others, thereby reinforcing the extraverted personality. Youths with negative emotional styles may create situations that lead to rejection or reciprocation and thus add to negative emotionality. Therefore, when negative emotionality follows traumatic experience, youths may rouse more negativity from others. Evoked responses may increase as a result of expectations by adults and peers who have interacted with an agreeable or disagreeable youth. Parents have described how their relationships and responses to their children changed following traumatic events (Nader, Pynoos, Fairbanks & Frederick, 1990); Box 4.1b).

Youths' *proactive* interactions are most evident in their choices of friends and later in mate and job selection. Across the lifespan, associations with like others (in dyads and groups) occur through a process of selection (choosing to associate with similar others; selecting activities compatible with their dispositions), influence (of others to become like them), and deselection (of peers with behaviors different from their own) (Caspi, 1998). Youths and adults shape their lives and environments through selection. Research confirms that friends tend to resemble each other in attitudes, values, behaviors, and physical characteristics (Caspi; Laird, Jordan, Dodge, Pettit, & Bates, 2001). Traumatic life experiences shape subsequent behavior and attitudes and the selection of friends and circumstances. Youths may begin to associate with other traumatized or troubled youths or develop attachments to those who endured the traumatic event with them (Stuber & Nader, 1995).

Continuity versus Change

Many variations exist in the demonstrated continuity or change in specific disorders (House, 2002). Some problems or disorders, such as autism, are quite stable over time. Others, such as many mood disorders, may be chronic but intermittent. Some disorders have demonstrated both high levels of stability and of instability such as ADHD and learning disabilities. Still other disorders, such as enuresis, disappear with time.

Studies of youths following traumatic events intend to measure changes in traits, behaviors, and functioning. Especially for children, some characteristics are in an ongoing state of change (Caspi & Roberts, 2001; Putnam, Ellis, & Rothbart, 2001). Although it becomes increasingly consistent with age, personality continues to develop (Roberts & Del Vecchio, 2000). In a sample of over 3,000 individuals, Roberts & Del Vecchio found that estimates of personality consistency were lowest in childhood (.31), increased at age 30 (to .64), and plateaued between ages 50 and 70 (.74).

From childhood to adolescence, youths vary widely in the amount of continuity or change they exhibit (Aber et al., 2003; Caspi & Roberts, 2001). Change is affected by environmental, biosocial, genetic, and historical factors as well as experiential factors (Caspi & Roberts). Bellah, Madsen, Sullivan, Swidler, and Tipton (1985) and Roberts and Helson (1997) identified alterations in secular trends in the United States between 1950 and 1985. Individualistic and self-centered attitudes increased in samples of students and adults (cited in Caspi & Roberts). Research has established the fading influence of parenting over time (Caspi, 1998). As studies of twins have demonstrated, genetic influence on change and development may decline after young adulthood, and the effects of nonshared environments may increase.

More than one type of *continuity (versus change)* in traits can be measured in the assessment of youths: *differential* (a youth's relative placement in a group over time), *absolute* (the quantity or amount of an attribute over time, usually assessed by examining a group), *structural* (the persistence in correlational patterns among a set of variables across time), and *ipsative* (continuity at the individual level rather than as a part of a sample) (Caspi & Roberts, 2001). The child who has daily temper tantrums at age 2 but only weekly temper tantrums at age 9 may rank first in tantrums among his peers at both ages. If, in adulthood, he or she is irritable and moody, "we may grant that the phenotype has changed but claim that the underlying genotype has not" (Caspi & Roberts, p. 52).

Assessing change requires recognition that the nature of traits and behaviors may change over time, that levels of change may have different significance, and that an ensemble of characteristics and variables may be complexly interrelated. Change can be multidirectional, and a youth may experience simultaneous losses and gains (Nesselroade & McCollam, 2000). The predictive value of variables may alter when subsequent events or new developmental challenges that also affect the predicted outcomes intervene (Thompson, 1999). Change from different initial levels can have different meanings. The difference between 1 and 2 may have a different significance from the difference between 7 and 8. The difference between none and mild dissociative experiences such as daydreaming or spacing out may be less important than the difference between flashbacks and episodes of altered identity (Nesselroade & McCollam; Putnam, 1997).

The Process of Change

Nesselroade (2002) noted three fundamental kinds of comparisons used to identify differences: (1) qualitative and quantitative differences among kinds of entities, (2) entities of the same kind (interindividual differences), and (3) within the same entity over different occasions (intraindividual differences). Differential psychology emphasizes the second kind of comparisons. Further analysis of interindividual differences yields information about typical outcomes of developmental processes for sets of similar entities. Although these analyses reveal similarity and differences of states among the same kind of entities, they do not provide direct information about the change (developmental) process itself.

Change in a sample's attributes is inferred when a mean difference is sustained across a series of comparisons (Nesselroade, 2002; Schwartz, Dodge, & Coie, 1993). Only comparisons of an individual to him- or herself (intraindividual differences) across occasions, however, provide information about the processes of change. Same-age youths vary widely in their developmental or biological age (Caspi, 1998). Although developmental curves may follow the same pattern, individual differences in the onset of growth may alter the nature of correlational findings across specified time periods. Methods are being developed that focus on identifying change processes (e.g., rates of change and changes in rates of change; Nesselroade). The traditionally dominant focus of differential psychology is *differences among persons*; the alternative focus is *differences in changes among persons*. That is, interindividual differences in intraindividual changes in some variables are contrasted with interindividual differences in the initial, final, or average level of those variables (Nesselroade).

Longitudinal research permits direct identification of (1) intraindividual change and (2) interindividual differences and similarities in intraindividual change and allows the analysis of (1) interrelationships in behavioral change, (2) determinants of intraindividual change, and (3) determinants of interindividual differences in intraindividual change (Nesselroade, 2002). Aber et al. (2003) employed an accelerated longitudinal (cross-sequential) design and a hierarchical linear model to create synthetic growth curves for a highly representative sample of youths. These methods permitted the delineation of *patterns of growth* across measures and groups. Youths defined by their genders, SES (i.e., eligibility for free school lunch), and race or ethnicity had almost identical trajectories over 2 years in their risk factors for aggressive behaviors. Their three sequential patterns of growth were characterized as (1) positive linear, (2) late acceleration, and (3) gradual deceleration. Youths showed first, a steady increase in hostile attribution biases, aggressive interpersonal negotiation strategies, competent interpersonal negotiation strategies, conduct problems, depressive symptoms, aggressive behavior, and prosocial behavior, then had a late acceleration in hostile attribution biases, aggressive intervention strategies, and teacher-rated prosocial behavior. Finally, they had a gradual deceleration in competent interpersonal negotiation strategies, teacher reports of aggressive behavior, and child reports of aggressive fantasies and depressive symptoms. Youth subgroups (boys, low SES, and minorities) who were previously reported to score higher on measures of aggression demonstrated initial higher risk and higher rates of linear growth between ages 6 and 12. Lower risk youths (girls and Whites) caught up to them, however, by age 12. Aber et al. suggested extending research on specific differences to include differences in rates of growth or change. Individual trajectories over time include acceleration as well as velocity of change. When only variable-centered (rather than person-centered) approaches are used to assess outcomes, the multiple pathways to that outcome are indistinguishable (Laird et al., 2001).

Identifying Contexts

In addition to examining children's and adolescent's functioning at school, home, and work, Crick points out the importance of assessing youths in dyadic or group contexts (Crick et al., 1998). The nature and quality of peer support is an important mediator of reactions to and recovery from traumatic experiences. A few studies have emphasized the positive functions of having friends. The quality of a youth's friendships (e.g., level of support, symmetry) and the nature of the friends (e.g., traits and popularity levels) have an impact on developmental outcomes (Crick et al.). It may also be important to consider family dyads. Caspi (1998) suggests that, from infancy to adolescence, transforming the between- and within-family focus to between and within sibling pairs is appropriate. When children are followed across time into adulthood, the emphasis changes from family of origin to marital family.

METHOD AND PREPARATION FOR MEASUREMENT

Children's posttrauma screening instruments have been administered (1) in direct interviews with children; (2) by mail or other distribution for completion and return; and (3) by distribution to groups of children to complete while a researcher reads the questions and explains their meaning when needed. Angold and her colleagues (1995) identified two basic types of structured diagnostic interview for use by clinicians and researchers with children and adolescents: (1) respondent-based or *fully structured* and (2) interviewer-based or *semistructured* interviews (Angold, Prendergast, Cox, Harrington, Simonoff & Rutter). In *fully structured* interviews, the interviewer directs a series of carefully phrased, age-appropriate questions verbatim to the interviewee. Thus, when the interview is properly conducted, variability due to differences in the phrasing of questions, coding, and "clinical judgment" is reduced or eliminated by the format of the interview. The interviewers need relatively little training or clinical experience. This type of interview makes no distinction, however, between variations in subjects' definitions of words, personal concepts of severity levels, understanding of the questions, or rapport with or trust of the interviewer (Angold et al.). For example, perhaps as a result of personal meaning and normal levels of specific symptoms, children's responses to the original version of the Diagnostic Interview Schedule for Children (DISC; Costello, Edelbrock, Kalas, Kessler, & Klaric, 1982) inflated estimates of the prevalence of rare phenomena (such as manic, obsessive-compulsive, and psychotic symptoms) (Breslau, 1987). Clinical practice suggests that careful cross-questioning and the elicitation of detailed descriptions of the phenomena are required in order to determine symptom frequency and intensity (Angold et al.).

During *semistructured* interviews, the interviewer pursues questioning until she or he has determined whether or not a particular symptom or behavior is present (Angold et al., 1995). Symptom definitions and detailed questions are usually available on the interview schedule. In an attempt to avoid clinician biases and variability, the semistructured clinical interview ensures detailed coverage of prespecified content areas and operationalizes symptom constructs being measured. The latter requires a greater level of interviewer training. Currently, there is no real evidence that one interviewing strategy is superior to the other (Angold et al.). Some researchers have combined the two methods (Angold et al.; Nader, Newman, Weathers, Kaloupek, Kriegler, & Blake, 2004).

Using a *semistructured* interview method rather than having the child complete and return the instrument seems to increase the sensitivity of the measurement (Jones & Ribbe, 1991). In general, children and adolescents tend to answer more accurately when they can ask questions and when a skilled interviewer asks the appropriate probing questions. Follow-up or probing questions have sometimes helped to determine whether a behavior is appropriately endorsed as a symptom (Scheeringa et al., 2001). No matter what format is used for the interview, children's responses may be subject to conscious and unconscious distortions primarily in the direction of greater social desirability (Piers & Herzberg, 2002). When questioned in a group, children tend to answer in the way they think that their peers will answer. During a study of children exposed to a disaster, it was observed that children filling out self-esteem questionnaires in a group tended to minimize their symptoms in order to look more normal. In a 1994 study of children exposed to the Northridge, CA earthquake, Kelly Johnson (2006), her colleagues, and this author conducted interviews of randomly selected children and, then, of the whole classroom group. It was apparent that it was popular among children to have symptoms as a result of the earthquake. Despite efforts to keep the children at a distance from one another and to have them answer honestly and without paying attention to their peers, children who had appeared to answer thoughtfully and accurately in the one-to-one interviews increased the numbers and/or intensity of symptoms in the subsequent group situation. In order to minimize socially acceptable responding, Harter (1982) used a two-choice format, inferring that some children are one way and others are another way with the option of saying the chosen way is really true or sort of true for the child.

Kappa levels for two different administrative techniques of the Diagnostic Interview for Children and Adolescents (DICA) suggest greater effectiveness of direct interview in comparison to the self-administered questionnaire. For a computerized self-administered DICA, kappas were generally lower than for "in-person" interviews (Reich & Kaplan, 1994). When the Horowitz's Impact of Event Scale for Children (HIES-C), a self-report measure, and the DICA-6R-A, a semistructured interview, were used to assess PTSD among children exposed to fires with low levels of life threat, the DICA-6R-A demonstrated greater differences between groups (Jones & Ribbe, 1991). When both measures were used in semi-structured interviews, the HIES-C revealed greater differences between groups (Jones, Ribbe, & Cunningham, 1994).

Interviewing children or adolescents by telephone is another method of conducting clinician-administered ratings of children's symptoms. Reich and Earls (1990) found interviewing children by phone to be economical, saving both time and money, and permitting continued contact with respondents at a distance. However, when matched groups of children interviewed by phone or in person were compared using the DICA, the telephone group as a whole reported fewer symptoms than the in-person group. In a study (Todd, Joyner, Heath, Neuman, & Reich, 2003) using the Missouri Assessment of Genetics Interview for Children (MAGIC, a revision of the DICA; Reich & Todd, 2002a), the differences in phone and in-person interviews for parents and adolescents were not significant (none were conducted for younger children). It may be that certain cultures (e.g., Asian) as well as certain personality styles (e.g., introverts) will be less willing to give accurate or detailed descriptions of their symptoms over the phone. One month after 9/11, a quick telephone survey was completed. Even though Asians were in closer proximity to the event, more exposed, and observed by community workers to be symptomatic, the survey results suggested that Asians had the least anxiety followed by Blacks and then Latinos (Yee, Pierce, Ptacek, & Modzelesky, 2003). Yee et al. explained that Asian people were not willing to discuss their anxiety on the phone or to someone who was not speaking their language.

Web-based surveys have also been used for data collection (Schlenger et al., 2002). Such surveys limit assessment to brief self-report methods (North & Pfefferbaum, 2002). Much of the inadvisability of using Internet surveys with youths is obvious. In addition to the problems noted for telephone surveys and problems with consent, Web-based surveys may pose additional difficulties such as problems with available population and selection, identity confirmation, confidentiality, security, accuracy of reporting, coaching by other parties, peer group faked responses, site failures, unauthorized copying, difficulties changing answers or completing the measure, and inability to ask clarifying questions (Naglieri, McNeish, & Bardos, 2004).

Training

Following traumatic events, interviewer and clinician training is important to the safety of the children, adolescents, and adults who are interviewed (chapter 9; Box 9.1a). Most assessment-scale authors recommend or require an understanding of childhood traumatic response and methods of interviewing traumatized children. Although varying amounts of training have been recommended for the different instruments, in general, greater accuracy, better concordance with clinical diagnoses and other raters, as well as better therapeutic results have been reported for trained interviewers. Scheeringa et al. (2001) found that trained raters were better able than parents to identify some symptoms in children (e.g., reactivity to reminders and restricted range of affect).

More study is needed to determine the kinds and amounts of training and the characteristics of trainees that yield the best results. A trainee's posttraining comfort with using and applying a method may be important to outcomes. Aber et al. (2003) examined the amount of training associated with better results for a classroom curriculum in conflict resolution and intergroup understanding (to reduce the risk of aggression). Lower levels of teacher training and coaching and higher levels of instruction of children were associated with reduced risk of aggression. The authors suggest that teachers with lower levels of training were more successful because they were implementing the program more frequently. Teachers who were executing the curriculum less frequently were perceived by trainers to need additional training and consequently received it.

Preliminary Briefing

Preliminary briefing is an essential part of preparation for assessment and/or intervention with children following traumatic events. Knowing the details of the traumatic event—including those identified by police, news, and eyewitness reports of the event—enables the researcher to recognize aspects of symptomatic response and variables that might affect response. Following a school hostage-taking in which the assailant dictated a suicide note and then killed herself, children's most severe responses were associated with their worry about the safety of their peers. Before killing herself, the woman had waved her guns and accidentally fired a shot that narrowly missed a child (Nader, 1997c). Exposure questions regarding the child's sense of life threat and fear for the safety of others were based on knowledge of these behaviors. Similarly, following a tornado that knocked down a cafeteria wall, killing nine children, surviving children were capable of discussing their need to avoid reminders of the disaster when asked by interviewers about specific reminders (e.g., rattling windows, sitting next to walls, and lasagna—the lunch served that day) (see Nader & Pynoos, 1993; Table 1.3).

Having a clear understanding of the sequence and nature of the event allows the clinician to evaluate the child's accuracy of recall. When interviewed following a sniper attack, those children who had been closest to the danger attempted to place distance between themselves and the danger in their *initial* recall, whereas children who had been absent from school that day sometimes tried to bring themselves closer to the event in their initial recall. After asking for and hearing a description of the child's experience, the clinician took the child through the described experience step by step, eliciting more detail. In their more thorough retelling of the event, children were able to describe their experiences accurately (Pynoos & Nader, 1989).

As mentioned above, understanding cultural issues related to the affected population is essential to ensure an accurate and ethical data collection process. Specific procedures before, during, and after data collection may not only contribute to greater accuracy, but they may also help to honor the beliefs of the affected population and assist the recovery process at the same time (Box 7.1). In order to work effectively with a large Southeast Asian population in her school, Pat Busher, principal of Cleveland Elementary School In Stockton, California, engaged in formal and informal cross-cultural education, including making contacts in the community and bringing in experts to train her school staff. In 1989, a young man opened fire on children on the school grounds, killing 5 and injuring 29 children and one teacher. Busher invited local clergy—Cambodian and Vietnamese Buddhist monks, a Vietnamese Catholic priest, and Protestant ministers—to perform a blessing ceremony upon the school and school grounds. This included the exorcism of dead spirits who, it was believed, might grab the children and take them into the next world. Children were given chants to use when frightened. Children and adults were provided factual information to dispel rumors and unfounded fears (P. Busher, personal communication, January 24 and 30, 1995). Performing valued cultural or religious practices effectively and appropriately can assist in separating transient fear-related arousal symptoms from ongoing traumatic reactions.

Preparing the Environment for Assessment

Before researchers or assessors enter a postdisaster area, survivors will need to attend to vital activities (North & Pfefferbaum, 2002). For adults, these activities may include maintaining or finding safety, attending to injuries, securing housing, burying the dead, and applying for resources. Making certain that youths *are* safe is a first priority; helping youths to feel safe and nurtured is also essential (Nader, 1999d). Establishing relationships with affected family or community members and leaders is part of preparing an effective assessment and intervention process (Stamm & Stamm, 1999; Yee et al., 2003). Addressing the traumatic reactions of traumatized adults may be a necessary prelude to assessment and treatment of youths (Nader & Muni, 2002; Nader & Pynoos, 1993). In addition to attention to cultural, general, and individual needs, parent, family, group, or classroom meetings may help to reduce anxiety and educate caregivers and teachers about normal reactions and effective treatment of children (Nader & Muni).

Mass Traumas

Schools, organizations, or communities will have engaged in varying levels of preparedness for mass traumatic events such as natural disasters, sniper or terrorist attacks, or large-scale accidents. Many schools and communities now have crisis teams. The level and nature of preparedness and immediate response to the crisis may influence the levels and nature of traumatic reactions. Efforts like preparing absent relatives prior to their reunion with students can prevent looks of fear or horror and frightening outbursts that may exacerbate youths' reactions (Nader, 1997c; Nader & Pynoos, 1993). Sanction by community religious, church, business, school, and familial leaders of the training programs, assessments, and interventions of experts and researchers from inside and outside of a community may determine whether accurate assessment and effective interventions are possible. Following September 11 and other mass traumatic events, participation of local leaders in outreach and treatment programs has enhanced the effectiveness of the programs (Waizer, Dorin, Stoller, & Laird, 2005; Yee et al., 2003).

Fang and Chen (2004) have described the benefits of working with area schools, newspapers, and radio stations to prepare and educate a populace. After mass traumatic events, youths assessments and interventions may be most effectively pursued within the school environment (Nader & Muni, 2002; Pynoos & Nader, 1988; Shaw, 1997; Williams, 1994). School is a familiar, safe setting for youths and provides easy access to them. The aid of peers, teachers, and administrators can be enlisted to enhance evaluation and treatment of students. Media may provide education and can aid by announcing intervention programs and preparing parents and children for the course of assessment and treatment events.

Individual or Family Traumas

When children may be traumatized, establishing a rapport with caregivers as well as with the children is important to assessment and intervention. In addition to information from the reports of firefighters, police officers, or others who responded to a crisis, nonoffending parents may be able to provide information about a youth's traumatic experience and initial response as well as about the child's history and pretrauma personality. Measures are available to elicit detailed information about the child's personality and behavior before and after the event (chapters 6, 13, 15). When parents may also be traumatized, attention must be given to their needs and symptomatic reactions as well.

The Source of Information

Documentation of the presence or absence of a symptom or trait for clinical or research purposes may be based on information from a single source or by using the "either–or" rule common in clinical practice (i.e., a symptom is counted as present if reported by either parent or child) (Costello, Angold, March, & Fairbank, 1998). Because no single source (e.g., children, peers, parents, teachers, clinicians) can provide complete and accurate data and because youths behave and respond differently in different contexts (i.e., to different settings and amid different individuals), comprehensive assessment requires multiple sources of data (Achenbach & Rescorla, 2001; Briere, 1996; Ferdinand et al., 2003; Friedrich et al., 1997; Reich & Earls, 1987; Reynolds & Kamphaus, 1998; Sternberg et al., 1993; Weissman et al., 1987). Not only are certain behaviors situation-specific, but also different observers may perceive and interpret behaviors differently (Ferdinand et al.; Reynolds & Kamphaus). Expectations of what is normal may contribute to a disparity between child or parent and teacher reports of behavior problems (Aber et al., 2003). In the event that one group must be chosen, Weissman et al. recommended interviewing the children. In order to fully understand the nature of childhood traumatic response, however, multiple sources of information must be examined and collected over time.

Issues regarding the concordance or discordance between parent and child reports of children's psychiatric symptoms have varied according to the nature of the symptoms and the disorder. Children generally report more symptoms for themselves than others report for them. Adult raters and scale agreement have generally been lowest for internalizing symptoms and highest for the more observable externalizing symptoms (Reynolds & Kamphaus, 1998). Children have often reported fewer behavioral problems for themselves than adults have reported for them (Ferdinand et al., 2003).

ADAPTING MEASURES FOR CHILDREN AND CULTURES

In order to make a measure appropriate for use with youths and specific cultures, a number of adaptations are necessary. For children of all cultures, the appropriateness of rating scales, wording, definitions of impairment, and question order must be considered. For cultures, attention must be given to translations, including the meaning of words, concepts, and behavioral/verbal expressions for each age group within the culture that will be assessed.

Cultural Adaptation

Cultural issues in the assessment of trauma in youths are discussed in chapter 7. To follow are issues related to the translation of scales and measures.

Translation of Measures

Most of the millions of refugees in the United States and other parts of the world have had significant traumatic experiences as well as multiple stressful events (Hollifield et al., 2002). Translations of instruments may be necessary for cultural adaptation even when the individual speaks the original language of the measure or the consultant. Failing to use appropriate translations may affect study and diagnostic results. For example, Spanish-speaking adults have scored higher on levels of pathology when interviewed in English rather than in Spanish (Canive, Castillo, & Tuason, 2001).

Severe anxiety, despair, or cognitive slippage can impair a person's usually adept ability to speak in a second language (Westermeyer, 1990). Poor communication in an interview with a traumatized individual can lead to a variety of clinical misadventures, including preventable suicides (Nader, 1997a; Swiss & Giller, 1993; Westermeyer). Although a bilingual person may regain second-language skills with treatment, until then it is advisable to use an interpreter or interviewers proficient in the language of the questionee. Interpreters should be reasonably fluent in both languages, be experienced in interpreting, be able to exchange words from one language to the next without losing meaning, have the ability to present the connotative as well as the denotative meaning, understand trauma and psychological terminology, recognize the importance of nonverbal communication, be able to communicate questions that do not come up in normal conversation (e.g., suicidal plans, hallucinations, conflicts), understand interviewing techniques with distraught patients, be trusted by the patient, be willing to share all information with the clinician, and be trustworthy with confidential information (Kirmayer, Young, & Hayton, 1995; Phan & Silove, 1997; Westermeyer).

Canino & Bravo (1999) suggest that instruments be tested for cultural equivalence on five dimensions: semantic (the meaning of questions), content (relevance of the content to the target population), technical (e.g., applicability of the assessment format), conceptual (construct validity; e.g., whether scores relate to measurable dysfunction), and criterion (similar interpretation of results in relation to established cultural norms). It does not work to ask a child if he or she has become afraid of sleeping alone in a culture or family in which children always share a bedroom (Ahadi, Rothbart, & Ye, 1993) or to assess seasonal depression in locations where sunlight hours are similar throughout the year (Canino & Bravo). Similarly, using self-report measures read by children may be technically problematic in less literate cultures (Canino & Bravo).

Cultural Meanings

Culture influences informal labeling practices as well as diagnostic practices (Mash & Dozois, 2003). The form, frequency, and predictive significance of different child behaviors vary across cultures. For example, in Western cultures, shyness and oversensitivity in children have been associated with vulnerability, peer rejection, and social maladjustment. Conversely, these same traits seen in Shanghai Chinese children are associated with leadership, school competence, and academic achievement (Ahadi et al., 1993; Chen, Rubin, & Li, 1995; Mash & Barkley, 2003; Mills, 2001). Cultural translations of rating scales add an additional potential for inaccuracy or confusion. For example, the Vietnamese translations for "quite a bit" and "extremely" have little distinction between them (Phan & Silove, 1997).

Words used in assessing posttraumatic reactions or exposures may have different or more inclusive meanings in one culture than another. For Philippine Ilongot people, *liget* is the only concept at all similar to the Western concept of *anger* (Mills, 2001). Similar to *anger, liget* implies energy and irritation as well as a sense of violent action and intentional show of force. Unlike *anger,* it includes a competitive character and is related to envy and ambition. It does not require the belief that the person toward whom it is directed has done anything wrong, nor does it necessarily involve bad feelings towards anyone or anything. It spurs people to action resulting in achievements and triumphs. Terms describing physical, mental, and emotional reactions may differ for individuals from the same country (e.g., Vietnam) but from different regions (e.g., central, north, or south province) or different spiritual backgrounds (e.g., Buddhist, Confucian) (Phan & Silove, 1997). Literal translations may give completely misleading results outside of the country. The literal translation of the Vietnamese words *rau qua* is "terribly sad" but refers to "a lot of worries" rather than to depression. The Buddhist term *duhkha* (Vietnamese: *kho/rau/sau*), literally "suffering," for Buddhists has a potentially positive aspect in that it is an essential part of the quest for enlightenment. Translations may misconstrue this term as meaning depressive symptoms (Phan & Silove). Concepts that combine ideas in one region may represent separate ideas or meanings for another. In some cultures, the idea of thought and emotion or of thought and will are combined. Malaysian aboriginal Chewong have no words for "think" or "feel" (Mills).

Back Translations

Karno, Burnam, Escobar, Hough, & Eaton (1983) recommend a system of translation and "back translation" to the original language for accuracy. Several back and retranslations may be necessary. The accuracy of a translation is, then, best confirmed by subsequent use of the instrument with children. Thus, to use an interview with a child to test an English instrument translated into German, (1) a local German translator interprets both a German interviewer and the German child interviewee to a listening qualified member of the translating team whose primary language is English, and (2) the translation team member makes note of any mismatches between the child's answers and the questions asked, other discrepancies, or the child's or interviewer's confusion about a question. Moreover, having a translator who matches the target population's understanding of terminology, rather than a mental-health professional, is more informative in the back translation process. In the translation process for an instrument described in chapter 11, a single question in the third back translation still did not match the original item. A local psychologist dismissed this lack of match. She said that the problem was not with the question but with the translator, who was a schoolteacher and not psychologically sophisticated. The general population, however, especially youths, are also unlikely to be sophisticated in psychological terminology (Nader, 1997a).

Symptom Ratings

Measures of children's traumatic reactions vary in their rating systems. Measures may ask for the onset and duration of each symptom or of symptoms in general. A few scales include both a current and a lifetime rating (e.g., Clinician-Administered PTSD Scale for Children and Adolescents, or CAPS-CA, Child and Adolescent Psychiatric Assessment, or CAPA) in order to distinguish a more intense earlier reaction from the current level of symptoms. Usually, one of the following scoring systems is used: (1) the presence or absence (e.g., DISC) or the degree of presence of symptoms (e.g., Child Dissociative Checklist); (2) frequency of occurrence (e.g., Child Posttraumatic Stress-Reaction Index, DICA); or (3) both frequency and intensity ratings (e.g., CAPS-CA, CAPA). Jones, Ribbe, and Cunningham (1994) found that children reported fewer PTSD symptoms on the DICA-R than on the HIES-C. They suggest that the measurement of intensity on the HIES-C versus the measurement of presence or absence of symptoms on an earlier version of the DICA-R may have accounted for the greater symptom report on the former. Carrion, Weems, Ray, and Reiss (2002) found that, independent of frequency, the intensity of some symptoms (e.g., avoidance, distress in response to cues, difficulty concentrating, feelings of recurrence) predicted a PTSD diagnosis or a child's functional impairment when frequency did not. For some symptoms (e.g., restricted range of affect, sense of foreshortened future), frequency was predictive of impairment. Thus, using both frequency and intensity ratings may promote rating accuracy and provide useful assessment information. Recall of frequency and duration can be most difficult for younger children. For recall of a nontraumatic situation, McKenna, Foster, and Page (2004) found that identifying landmarks (special times or dates like holidays) assists the determination of frequency and duration of occurrences.

Defining Levels of Impairment

A number of issues contribute to consistency between assessors in endorsing symptoms. In addition to the need for clearly specified terms, definitions, and formulas for endorsing assessment items, it is essential to define (1) age-appropriate developmental expectations (the boundary between normal developmental changes in behavior and psychopathology); (2) thresholds of impairment (between mild perturbations and symptom-level impairments; Scheeringa et al., 2001); and (3) the degree to which specific symptoms occur in children even in a healthy state or as a healthy temporary response (or coping strategy) to certain experiences. Clinically significant levels of impairment can be difficult to define because of the compounding effects of some functional impairments over time and the delayed onset of some symptoms and impairments. For example, will mild social or scholastic impairment worsen when relationships or academic progress are disrupted? An additional difficulty exists for very young children who may have been exposed to traumatic events since early infancy (e.g., to domestic violence, physical or sexual abuse). For these children, it is difficult to pinpoint onset of symptoms or to observe changes in behaviors (Scheeringa et al.).

The manner in which children tend to answer questions may complicate the method by which "intensity" is measured. There may be great variations in what "a lot" or "extremely" means to different children and for different circumstances. Moreover, young children have learned to say "a lot" or "this big" with arms spread wide open as a fun response to adult inquiry. When using hand measurements for preschool children to rate intensity of feelings, it has been apparent that, if having the hands all the way out was an option, most of the children would joyfully make that choice and giggle as though asked about something fun instead of about the trauma (Stuber, Nader, & Pynoos, 1997). Additionally, some rating scales may be difficult for different cultures (Ahadi et al., 1993). Cut-off points for the presence or levels of a disorder may vary as well (Manson, Ackerson, Dick, Baron, & Fleming, 1990).

Qualitative differences in the meaning of scale ratings for different children and different cultures again become relevant when determining which events are valid trauma precipitators. *DSM-IV* (APA, 1994) Criterion A excludes events such as nonviolent divorce or being bullied at school without real threat of physical harm. Although children with exposures to a variety of events may meet Criteria B through D requirements, when presence or absence of symptoms is measured, there are qualitative differences, for example, between the responses of children exposed to a sniper attack and those of children whose parents have divorced without preceding or current violence (Berna, 1993; Goldwater, 1993; Kohr, 1995). Disparate experiences and similar experiences with different intensities may elicit important variations in children's symptomatic presentation and course. For example, children exposed to violence for which the life threat is external, visible, and menacing differ from those children who have life-threatening ailments and undergo bone-marrow transplantation (BMT), for which the life threat is a result of an invisible internal foe and the catastrophic attempts at cure (e.g., bone-marrow extractions, lumbar punctures, chemotherapy; Nader & Stuber, 1992). For accurate identification of the differences in children's responses to a variety of events, it is essential that scales measure qualitative differences in response and that scale ratings include clearly delineated definitions (e.g., of "A lot").

Using Icons

Although icons or picture representations have been used successfully in depicting symptoms for children, the use of some icons in standard rating scales may be ill-advised for several reasons. First, it is important for children to feel that it is okay to say or feel anything. For some children, icons may set a more playful, less serious tone and may subtly suggest that a lighter atmosphere is sought (Nader, 1997a). Second, children below a certain age tend to take things literally and concretely; increased concreteness has been observed in trauma victims of all ages (Punamaki, Quota, & El-Sarraj, 2001). If the pictures locate stress in the head or stomach or place the occurrence of symptoms on specific days, these rating scales may elicit falsely low ratings for children who do not experience stress in the head or stomach or on those days. Moreover, young children (and sometimes older traumatized children) may be easily focused upon one train of thought or emotion. Pictures may narrow the focus or distract the child from the question asked.

Question Order

The order of items may be particularly significant for youths. Children have sometimes been found to be better at reporting their subjective symptoms than their overt, objectionable symptoms. Youths also exhibit concerns regarding how peers will judge them, about the implications of having symptoms, and about how their symptom levels compare to everyone else's. Therefore, opening an endorsement list with questions or statements about anger, impulsive acts, or other potentially socially undesirable feelings or behaviors may result in resistance. It may assist accurate reporting to first ask the child about subjective symptoms that do not elicit defensiveness such as the intensity of the event or frequency of intrusive thoughts. This also permits the child to discover that the interviewer is nonjudgmental about his or her answers before answering questions for which he or she fears judgment. When clarifying questions precede a more general initial probe question, a child may provide a falsely low rating. Asking the child for specific dates of onset or specific symptom descriptions, such as asking what the child avoids before asking if the child avoids reminders in general, for example, may be problematic. Elementary school-age children have often been able to say that they want to stay away from reminders or they have repeated thoughts/images of the event on a daily basis. When asked to describe the things they want to avoid or the thoughts/images and are unable to think of any, they sometimes decide that they may not have these symptoms after all.

Reliability and Validity of Scales and Interviews

Interviews and questionnaires are considered "works in progress" until they are field-tested (Shaffer, Fisher, & Lucas, 1999). Psychometric tests are used to determine the validity and reliability of a measure and its individual scales and items when used with a targeted population. Developmental level, culture, information processing, personality, and cognitive ability may influence understanding and the appropriateness of specific measures. Because behaviors and symptoms manifest differently at different ages, scale content must also vary. Measures that have been consistently validated for use with adults and adolescents may be consistently invalid when used with children (Vasey et al., 2003).

As discussed earlier in this chapter, the predominant methods used in the last few decades to assess traits and change have not provided much direct information regarding the nature of the change process. Information processing models are tied to process; psychometric models are not. Nesselroade (2002) suggests that current methods of assessment should be strengthened and extended by applying them to the change process. He points out (p. 551) that intraindividual variability concepts have "(a) captured important sources of variance including erroneously interpreted individual differences as when asynchronous intraindividual variability is confounded with interindividual differences at a given time point, (b) formalized the identification of occasion-specific sources of variance among persons, (c) provided one possible explanation for such phenomena as increasing interindividual variability with increasing age to the extent that it is observed, and (d) provided a source of 'predictors' of other behaviors." Statistics such as test-retest correlations often begin, are spaced, and end arbitrarily (Nesselroade & McCollam, 2000). Nesselroade & McCollam purport that, for developmentalists, sound descriptions should apply to process rather than simply to a sequence of measurements.

A few common issues are important when interpreting the results of psychometric assessments. Psychometric values or statistics are generally higher for larger samples. Scales and subscales with more items fare better than those with fewer items. Scores commonly decline over brief test-retest intervals (Achenbach & Rescorla, 2001; Shaffer et al., 1999). Measures usually show greater differences between trauma and nontrauma groups than between trauma and other clinical groups. Reliability for categorical data (but not for continuous data) is believed to be the greatest when patients have no symptoms or have a severe disorder

(Shaffer et al.). Cultural biases or values may be present in measures' rating scales, interpretations of findings, and labeling practices (Ahadi et al., 1993; chapter 7).

Many factors, such as small sample size, may contribute to unreliability in a measure (Shaffer et al., 1999). Cognitive factors such as difficulties with comprehension, information retrieval, and estimation or confusion because of age, intelligence, education, or question structure may hinder reliability. The timing of assessment may be a factor in ratings; occasions of increased distress like anniversaries or life stresses may amplify symptoms. Between the beginning and ending of a test or by the time of retesting, the respondent may experience changes in beliefs about what information is being sought. Some interviewees may fail to endorse a symptom to avoid having to answer probe questions that would follow or because of embarrassment or social desirability issues. Mood and disposition toward symptoms may influence symptom endorsement. Moods may differ at different assessment periods; the testing process itself may reduce distress or elevate distress or otherwise change the mood (chapter 9). Recall may be better at an initial interview or closer to the time of an experience. Small changes near the time of the interview may have a disproportionate effect (Shaffer et al.).

Reliability

Reliability assessments determine whether test scores are consistent (Weathers, Keane, King, & King, 1997). Three measures of the reliability of an instrument are widely used: interrater reliability (rating agreement between raters), test-retest reliability (stability over time), and internal consistency (Costello et al., 1998). Test-retest methods take into account variability due to changes in the respondents or testing conditions (Weathers et al.). Internal consistency and split-half methods primarily address variability due to item content.

Interrater reliability tests determine whether raters are using similar procedures, methods of eliciting information, and/or interpretations of the same responses (Shaffer et al., 1999). Test-retest reliability examines whether respondents answer questions in the same way after an interval long enough to reduce memory and practice effects and brief enough so that scores are not affected by actual changes in symptoms levels (Weathers et al., 1997). Pearson or Spearman rho correlation (r) coefficients are often used to assess interrater and test-retest reliability. Pearson r may be used with ordinal or continuous scores. Spearman r is appropriate for categorical scores. For continuous data, intraclass correlations (ICCs) (Bartko, 1976) are considered the more correct measure of test-retest and interrater reliability (Cicchetti & Sparrow, 1981). ICCs control for the possibility of chance agreement (Bartko & Carpenter, 1976; Costello et al., 1998). ICC can be affected by differences in the rank ordering as well as in the magnitude of the correlated scores. In contrast, Pearson r mainly reflects differences in rank ordering even if correlated scores differ markedly in magnitude (e.g., if one rater rates all of the scores 5 points lower than the other, r = 1.0; Achenbach & Rescorla, 2001). For categorical or dichotomous (e.g., presence-absence) data, Cohen's kappa (κ) (Cohen, 1960) corrects for chance agreement (Weathers et al., 1997; see Table 4.1). Paired t-tests are also computed for test-retest reliability for ordinal/continuous measures. Cicchetti & Sparrow have shown that the number of categories of classification dictate the minimal sample size needed.

Internal consistency reliability refers to the extent to which a scale measures a common underlying characteristic and is usually assessed by a correlational statistic (Costello et al., 1998; Cronbach, 1951; Kuder & Richardson, 1937). A high internal consistency score suggests that all items in a scale are largely a function of the same underlying construct (Reynolds & Kamphaus, 1998; see Table 4.1). To assess internal consistency, coefficient alpha (Cronbach, 1988) or, if the items are dichotomous, Kuder-Richardson Formula 20 (KR-20; Kuder & Richardson) measure the average intercorrelations among items in a test (Piers & Herzberg, 2002). Cronbach's alpha is affected by the number of items: the more items, the greater the α. Another method for assessing the consistency of content is split-half reliability, in which the test is split into equivalent halves for each individual, and the relevant statistic is the Pearson correlation between the two halves (Piers & Herzberg).

Validity

Validity refers to the appropriateness, usefulness, and meaningfulness of specific inferences made from measure scores (Weathers et al., 1997). Measures of validity may include face validity, construct validity, content validity, convergent validity, discriminant validity, and criterion validity (Piers & Herzberg, 2002; Weathers et al.). Face validity alludes to whether the scale appears to measure what it is intended to measure. Construct validity refers to whether the measure accurately reflects a theoretical construct or concept. Content validity points to whether the test items measure the appropriate behavior. Convergent validity examines whether

TABLE 4.1
Psychometric Reliability Statistics

Statistic	Poor	Fair or Acceptable	Good or Acceptable	Excellent or Desirable	References
Cohen's κ: Correlation	≤ .39	.40–.60	.60–.75	.75–1.00	Cohen, 1960; Fleiss, 1981; Costello, Angold, March, & Fairbank, 1998
Cronbach's ∝: Internal Consistency			≥ .70	≥ .80	Cronbach, 1951, 1988

there is correlation with measures of characteristics similar to but not the same as those measured by the scale. Discriminant validity means that the measure is not measuring something that it is not supposed to be measuring; therefore, it would have nonsignificant or very low correlations with measures of unrelated items. Criterion validity refers to the measure's ability to accurately predict an outcome variable such as PTSD.

Factor Analyses

Factor analyses explore interrelationships among and between variables (Putnam, Ellis, & Rothbart, 2001). Factor analytic methods are used to identify patterns of co-occurring items whose scores are mutually associated with each other (Achenbach & Rescorla, 2001). Factor analyses are used to reveal simple clusters of variables that are structure-discrete and define a dimension (e.g., PTSD dimensions of re-experiencing, avoidance, and arousal) (McCrae & John, 1992). Important symptoms or traits (e.g., hostility or fear), however, may represent blends of two or more dimensions (e.g., the personality dimensions of low emotional stability and low agreeability; McCrae & John) or a complex relationship between aspects of an individual (e.g., temperament, neurophysiology, and learned behaviors).

In a factor analysis, a different selection of variables can result in a different set of dimensions within the same factor (McCrae & John, 1992). That is, the set of dimensions yielded by a factor analysis depends on the set of descriptors entered into the data matrix (Rothbart & Bates, 1998). How factors are rotated as well as how they are derived affect the results of analyses (Caspi, 1998). Separate factor analyses (e.g., of parent, child, and teacher reports) may provide multiple ways of operationally defining a construct (e.g., a syndrome or subscale) (Achenbach & Rescorla, 2001). In adult studies of depression, different factor structures have been found for different cultures and different genders (Bolton, 2001). The number and nature of factors also may vary by age group: infants, toddlers, children, preadolescents, early or late adolescents, (Putnam et al., 2001).

CONCLUSIONS

Accurate assessment of youths and interpretation of findings requires measuring variables and trajectories across time, using multiple sources, contexts, and methods. Although exposure to traumatic events has proven a potent predictor of trauma, exposure alone does not shape traumatic reactions or the course of response and recovery. Numerous factors must be considered in the design of assessments and of treatment methods. In addition to considering the nature of the event and the youth's personal exposures, researchers must consider the importance of issues such as processes of change, child traits, child and family circumstances, and the complexity of reactions.

Accuracy of youth assessments is influenced by the comprehensiveness of, nature of, and preparation for assessment as well as the reliability and validity of measures used. Findings regarding children's responses to trauma have sometimes been contradictory. Failure to identify all appropriate mediating variables may be a factor in these mixed results. Accurate long-term assessment will necessitate delineating the changing nature of children's symptoms over time as well as the symptoms not currently listed for a diagnosis of PTSD. For example, methods are needed for assessing whether and how initial childhood reactions translate into behavioral patterns, life choices, vulnerabilities, reactivity, and inhibitions.

5

Risk and Resilience Factors
Trauma's Mediator, Moderator, or Outcome Variables

Many variables affect the outcomes of childhood adversity. Researchers and theorists agree to some measure that youths who are able to adapt to the demands of each phase of development are likely to have a normal developmental trajectory, whereas those who fail or have difficulties in negotiating these demands may enter a trajectory toward psychopathology (Price & Lento, 2001). Not all youths exposed to adversity develop problems or psychopathology, whereas some youths with little apparent life difficulty do develop problems (Yates, Egeland, & Sroufe, 2003). These findings have contributed to the study of risk and resilience factors (Price & Lento). Risk factors are variables that are empirically associated with a disorder and predict its *increased probability* of occurrence, whereas vulnerability factors are a subset of risk factors, endogenous to the individual, that may serve as *causal mechanisms* in the development of a disorder (Ingram and Price, 2001; Price & Lento). Risk and vulnerability may interact or operate in concert. Resilience, on the other hand, refers to reduced vulnerability and the presence of protective factors such as increased competence. Resilience, risk, and protective factors, such as self-esteem (SE), locus of control, trust, and coping skills, are not always assessed when evaluating youths exposed to traumas. Their levels are important to trauma outcomes and to treatment planning.

Mediating and Moderating Variables
Single characteristics rarely exclusively predict vulnerability or resilience; instead, they combine with each other and with psychological and

environmental mediators (Punamaki, Quota, & El-Sarraj, 2001). Mediating and moderating variables are variables that influence the relationship between a predictor variable and an outcome variable (Lindley & Walker, 1993; Table 5.1). A variable that serves as a link or an intervening variable between two processes or events is a *mediating* variable (Haine, Ayers, Sandler, Wolchik, & Weyer, 2003). Circumstances or processes influence the mediator, which in turn influences an outcome such as mental-health status or achievement. Mediating variables include such qualities as group and personal motivation, interpersonal relationships, and the youth's (and parents') cognitive and emotional styles. Trauma may affect self-esteem, and self-esteem may affect competence. Under those circumstances, self-esteem is a mediating or intervening variable between trauma and competence. Conduct disturbances, such as antisocial behavior, appear to undermine academic achievement, which, in turn, may contribute to later problems in multiple domains of competence and internal well-being (Masten & Powell, 2003). Whether intellectual competence or creativity leads, in adverse living conditions, to outcomes such as optimal development or delinquency depends on mediators such as the youth's attentional style or emotional regulation and parental attitudes and behaviors toward the child (Punamaki et al.). The highly creative child's capacities may not translate into emotional well-being if the youth feels rejected and alienated, for example.

A *moderating* variable is one that may change the magnitude or the direction of the relationship between a predictor variable such as trauma and an outcome variable such as symptoms or changed attitudes (Lindley & Walker, 1993). Moderators can act as stress-buffers or stress-exacerbators (Haine et al., 2003). Such variables serve to alter the impact or outcome of risk or adversity factors either by increasing or decreasing individual susceptibility to the harmful effects of the stressor or by, in some way, protecting the child from the full effects of the threat (Masten & Powell, 2003). Secure infant attachments and supportive care in the first 2 years of life and the competence these experiences engender, thus, increase the capacity to rebound from maladaptive behavior patterns (Yates et al., 2003). Some variables are associated with resilience under particular circumstances. Cambodian war refugee youths, for example, fared better if they learned to speak English (Masten & Powell).

RESILIENCE, RISK, AND VULNERABILITY DEFINED

Resilience reflects evidence of positive adaptation despite significant life adversity (Cicchetti, 2003a). It is inferred when one manifests competent functioning in spite of significant hardship. Competent functioning includes effective performance in the developmental tasks salient for a given age, society/culture or context, and time (Masten & Powell, 2003).

TABLE 5.1
Mediating and Moderating Variables

Variable	Mediating	Moderating
Definition	A variable (M) that accounts for the relationship between the predictor variable (T) and an outcome variable (O). M explains how or why T influences O.	A variable (M) that may change the magnitude or the direction of the relationship between a predictor (T) and an outcome variable (O). M explains the circumstances under which T influences O.
Type	Categorical or continuous	Categorical or continuous
Relationship to outcome variable	M is a consequence of T and an antecedent of O. M is the intervening variable (i.e., the process or mechanism) through which T influences O. M may have additive or suppressive influences on the relationship between T and O.	T and M are antecedents of O, when O is assessed. (If O = mental-health status, a level of mental-health status precedes and follows a predictor variable such as trauma.)
Examples	• Accurate assessment of locus of control over health (T) may lead to increased healthful activities (M), such as exercise, healthy diet, and check-ups, which in turn lead to better health (O). • Level of social support influences level of self-esteem, which in turn is associated with the helpfulness of coping.	• The greater the level of social support (M), the greater the relationship between resilience (T) and mental health (O). • Assuming the absence of other exacerbating variables, the greater the level of social support, the lower the level of PTSD.
Statistical evidence	(1) O is regressed on the predictor variable. (2) If step 1 is significant, then M is regressed on the predictor variable. (3) O is simultaneously regressed on the predictor and M variables. The mediator function is substantiated when steps 1 and 2 are significant, and in step 3 (controlling for steps 1 and 2), the relationship between T and O becomes nonsignificant.	Main effects may or may not be significant. The interaction effect is significant. Ideally, M is not correlated with T or O.
Consider assessing when . . .	The relationship of T and O is strong.	The relationship of T and O is strong, weak, or inconsistent.

Primary Source: Lindley, P., & Walker, S. N. (1993); Theoretical and methodological differentiation of moderation and mediation. *Nursing Research,* 42(5), 276–279. With permission. Other Sources: Haine, et al., 2003, Lipschitz et al., 2002; Ozolins and Stenstrom, 2003, Pole et al., 2005. Mediating and moderating variables are variables that influence the relationship between a predictor variable and an outcome variable. In this table, T = the predictor variable, M = a third or other variable, and O = the outcome variable.

For youths in the United States, this includes academic competence, social competence, autonomous functioning, and the ability to follow rules of conduct in different settings (behavioral and emotional self-regulation) as well as internal adaptation represented in well-being and levels of distress (Masten & Powell; Yates et al., 2003). Resilience does not require outstanding achievements but, instead, average or above behavior for a normative cohort. Two types of resilience factors have been identified (Fergusson & Horwood, 2003): *Protective processes* are beneficial to those exposed to a risk factor but are not or are of less benefit for those not exposed to the risk. There is an interactive relationship between the risk and the protective factor. *Compensatory processes* are equally beneficial to those exposed and those not exposed to the adversity. Such processes show up in a main effects model.

Studies have identified secure attachments (chapter 8), effective parenting, intellectual skills, and socioeconomic advantages in association with competence in major developmental tasks (Fergusson & Horwood, 2003; Masten & Powell, 2003; Table 5.2). In contrast, the trait of negative emotionality (chapter 6) and the adverse experiences of premature birth, poverty, parental mental illness, divorce, war, and maltreatment have had higher rates of negative and undesirable outcomes (Luthar, 2003; Yates et al., 2003). Competencies that serve as resilience develop through transactional exchanges between infants and their environments (Yates et al.). Youths who have internalized representations of available protection, self-worth, and sensitive care may be more responsive to the positive features of their environments and better able to benefit from environmental resources. Those who develop the capacity to trust from their early relationships may create or select environments that sustain their positive beliefs. Data has consistently shown that supportive, responsive, structured, and affectively stimulating environments contribute to children's self-worth, social competence, empathic involvement with others, self-confidence, curiosity, and positive affective expression (Yates et al.). Available care and positive self-regard foster the development of flexible problem-solving skills, emotion-regulation patterns, and an expectation of success in the face of adversity.

The Vulnerability and Resilience Continuum

Vulnerability, a latent trait rather than a state, is a predisposition (diathesis) to illness or pathology (Ingram & Price, 2001). Although alterable, it is stable and resistant to change. Vulnerability processes influence and are influenced by the environment (Price & Lento, 2001). Whether stemming from inborn or learned, environmental, or genetic characteristics, vulnerability is endogenous (within the individual) and must be activated by triggering (stressful) events in order to produce a disorder. Major or minor life events that disrupt the mechanisms maintaining stability in a person's physical, emotional, and cognitive functioning strain the person's

TABLE 5.2
General Risk and Protective Factors

	Protective Factors	Risk Factors
Child	Intelligence; academic achievement; positive self-esteem; internal or accurate locus of control with the ability to attribute negative experiences to external factors; positive restructuring of life between youth and adulthood; adaptability/ flexible coping strategies; self-regulations skills; sociability; positive outlook	Prenatal stress; more stressful choices; negative emotionality; antisocial behavior or other conduct disturbances; poor response to challenges; fewer/ lower cognitive skills; external locus of control; low self-esteem
Family	Better socioeconomic status; more resources; consistent, responsive parenting; high parenting quality; high warmth, structure and monitoring, involvement, and expectations	Single-parent household; foster placement; maltreatment; lower socioeconomic status; parental psychopathology; parental conflict; insecure or disorganized attachments
Resources	Social support: friendships, adults who are supportive and good models, nurturant kinship networks, and social networks such as religions or clubs; good health care; good and safe neighborhood; good school	Fewer social and community resources; unsafe neighborhood; poor health care and social services

adaptive capabilities (Ingram & Price). The strain may interrupt functioning and interfere with physiological and psychological homeostasis. Because competencies acquired or not developed at one phase affect each subsequent phase of development, the interruption may have cascading and cumulative effects (see Luthar, 2003).

Resilience, in contrast, suggests that it is difficult to experience psychopathology. Research reveals, for example, that children with secure attachments are more resistant to stress and more likely to rebound toward adequate functioning following a period of troubled behavior (Weinfield, Sroufe, Egeland, & Carlson, 1999). Ingram and Price (2001) place vulnerability and resilience on opposite ends of a continuum. This continuum interacts with stress in order to produce the possibility of a disordered state. Extreme vulnerability and little life stress may result in a disorder. With high levels of resilience, a great deal of stress is needed to cause psychopathology.

Cumulative Risk

Risk factors typically co-occur with other risk factors and usually include a sequence of stressful events. Consequently, research often focuses on *cumulative risk* (Masten & Powell, 2003). Stressful events related to a person's own behavior, *nonindependent events,* such as breaking up with a romantic partner or being expelled from school, are distinguished from *independent* events such as the death of a parent. Nonindependent stressors tend to accumulate with age. Maladaptive youths have displayed a larger increase than adaptive youths in nonindependent stressors over time (Masten & Powell). Fergusson and Horwood (2003) studied over time the impact on youths of multiple independent stressors. They found that youths exposed to six or more adverse factors had 2.4 times more externalizing and 1.8 times more internalizing disorders than youths with low adversity.

SELF-SYSTEM PROCESSES

Self-system processes (organized constructions about the self in relation to the social context), such as self-esteem, locus of control, threat appraisal, and world assumptions, can serve either as a source of distress or as personal resources or protective factors (Haine et al., 2003). Safety and trust, esteem and self-efficacy, and power and control are all self-schemas that may enhance recovery from traumatic experiences (Regehr, 2001). These processes are often interrelated. High self-esteem has been significantly but modestly linked, for example, to an internal locus of control (Ozolins & Stenstrom, 2003). Interpersonal trust has been strongly related to an internal or accurately assessed locus of control (Rotenberg & Cerda, 1994). Self-esteem and an internal or accurately assessed locus of control are presumed to be associated with parental practices and characteristics such as warmth, supportiveness, and encouragement of independence. Both have correlated with healthful behaviors and resilience in youths. The ability to trust has been attributed to trust in early attachment relationships. Early attachments (chapter 8) assist the child to develop self-confidence, self-control, self-awareness, and awareness of the emotions of others, and they set the stage for later relationships. These self-system processes may influence a youth's adjustment following trauma or loss, or they themselves may be altered by trauma. Among the relevant questions to ask in the assessment of self-systems are (1) whether the child can accurately assess self, (2) if traits and behaviors preceded or followed trauma, (3) if they preceded trauma, do they serve as risk factors for increased trauma, (4) have the patterns of self-system development been normal, and (5) are there gender differences in the pace or pattern of their development?

Trust

The ability to trust is essential to all aspects of life and functioning. *Trust* denotes an individual's expectations and beliefs about the reliability of self or others (Hardin, 2001; King, 2002; Rosenbloom & Williams, 2002).

For accurate assessment, trauma's role in faulty development of trust must be separated from the effects of long-term environmental conditions (Mitchell, 1990). The following environmental conditions may undermine the ability to trust: emotionally distant, inconsistent, or abusive parenting; economic deprivation or conflict over needed resources; repeated disappointment by others who fail to behave in an anticipated positive manner; embarrassment over having trusted unwisely; learning from parents and others who speak of people's unreliability; projection onto others one's own untrustworthiness; low self-concept and doubt about one's ability to survive disappointment; an overall negative and pessimistic attitude about others' trustworthiness (and the satisfaction of being right); experiences of discrimination and prejudice; and rigidity and the need for control, especially when there is the perception of a lack of control (King; Mitchell; Rotenberg & Cerda, 1994).

Lack of trust interferes with effective interpersonal functioning (King, 2002; Mitchell, 1990; Rotenberg & Morgan, 1995). Individuals low in interpersonal trust are less confident, less popular with others, less satisfied with relationships, more lonely, more isolated, and less happy, and have a negative self-concept (King; Mitchell). Verbal or nonverbal behavior may communicate lack of trust and may elicit untrustworthy behaviors from others. Andreou (2004) found that girls who scored high on *distrust* also scored high on *victimization*. Youths who were classified as both bullies and victims had low faith in human nature and high expectations in others' untrustworthiness, and believed others are manipulable in interpersonal situations.

Interpersonal trust is important in the workplace (Mitchell, 1990; Box 5.1a). Changes in workplace circumstances require adjustment in interpersonal alliances and thus the need for new, continued, or stronger trust in others. Delegation of tasks is an act of trust. Trusting others—especially while exuding strength and the ability to do well with or without the others' trustworthiness—elicits good will from them and encourages consistent trustworthiness. The perception of vulnerability may increase vulnerability. Trusting others emphasizes their capabilities and desirability and may increase support from them or better performance in the workplace.

Trauma and Trust

Trauma can disrupt or undermine attachments, trust, empathy, and relationship styles. Following traumatic experiences, lack of trust may include fear of others as well as a lack of critical judgment of others (Regehr, 2001). For young children, trauma may undermine a normal progression from believing in the protection, knowledge, and skill of adults (Stilwell, Galvin & Kopta, 1991) to increased self- or peer-reliance. After a broad range of traumas (natural disasters as well as violence), children can have trouble trusting those who are supposed to know best and to protect them. The capacity to trust can be seriously undermined by intra-

---

BOX 5.1
Case Examples: Trust and Coping

a. *Brandy*. In high school, Brandy began to experience ongoing relational aggression (see chapter 3) from her peers instigated by a former good friend. Girls who were her friends in elementary and middle school gossiped about her. Their stories were often fabricated. They played tricks on Brandy, used the personal information they knew about her against her, and excluded her from activities. They would make her feel like she was going to be included and then all would laugh and walk away. Brandy was depressed, cried frequently, and lost faith in herself, her lovability, and her competence. Years later, in her first position after college, her old fears returned. She worked with other intelligent, ambitious young adults. A strong competition for position resulted in some gossip and exclusionary behaviors among the group. Brandy did not know whom to trust and suspected every offered opportunity. She became cautious and began to worry about sharing information and about delegating tasks when teamwork was required. In response to her behaviors, her coworkers were wary of her and began to withdraw from her.

b. *Mathew* (continued). The massacre experience was unbearable for Mathew. During the long siege, he began to wish for escape and tried to will himself to sleep. Either because of the loss of blood or the desire for escape, he did lose consciousness for a while. He described it, "I finally fell asleep." Later, Mathew described how, following the massacre, in addition to being able to hide his emotions, he could "just not feel." He shut down. When he was unable to avoid stress, he went to sleep or took drugs.

---

or extrafamilial violence or other human-perpetrated traumatic experiences (Putnam, 1997). When the individuals a youth expects to rely upon the most are not trustworthy, when their goodwill cannot be counted upon, or worse still, when they inflict or allow injury, then it may become difficult to know whom or how to trust. When trust is damaged, basic assumptions about the world and other fundamental aspects of relationships are altered (Mitchell, 1990; Putnam; Schiraldi, 2000). The inability to trust parents or a supreme being to provide protection may make it difficult to regain a sense of safety following traumatic experiences. Damaged trust following traumas may lead to confused or biased expectations of others (Ford, 2002; chapter 3, 14). Expectations may then affect behaviors, interactions, and choices.

Self-Esteem

Self-esteem is the overarching concept in a hierarchy of subdomains that tap general satisfaction with oneself as a person (Harter, Waters, & Whitesell, 1998). Piers and Harris (1964) state that self-concept is a relatively stable set of personal attitudes reflecting both description and evaluation of personal behavior and attributes. Harter et al. suggest that the core self-portrait tends to fluctuate across situations and times. Harter and Pike (1984) identified six domains of self-perception that youths as young as age 8 are able to identify: scholastic competence, athletic competence, physical appearance, peer acceptance, conduct/behavior, and self-worth. Self-perception domains may influence one another. Peer acceptance, for example, may be attributable to other domains such as appearance or specific competence.

Self-Esteem and Adjustment

SE is related to a broad area of adjustment and well-being, including social relationships, school achievement, and resilience to stressful life events (Harter et al., 1998; Table 5.3). People with high SE have been found to be more satisfied with life and experience more positive emotions, and are less likely to be anxious or depressed (Twenge & Campbell, 2001). In contrast, certain forms of SE have been linked to aggression under conditions of threat (chapter 3).

The emotions and attitudes characteristic of low SE may make it difficult for youths to get what they want out of life (Martin, 2003). Low SE has been associated with psychopathology such as suicidality, substance abuse, personality disorders, posttraumatic stress disorders, childhood social withdrawal, and eating disorders (Fletcher, 2003; Heinonen, Räikönnen, & Keltikangas-Järvinen, 2003; Rubin, Burgess, Kennedy, & Stewart, 2003). Low SE has resulted in vulnerability to criticism, self-destructive behaviors, negative feelings about self and others, and interference with relationships (Rosenbloom & Williams, 2002).

Self-Assessments

Self-evaluations begin to develop in early childhood. Theories of SE suggest that SE develops either through (1) one's feelings of competence, which may reflect the discrepancy between one's goal or ideal and one's performance; (2) social interactions and relationships, especially mother-

TABLE 5.3
Self-Esteem

Level of Esteem	Associated Background Variables	Associated Characteristics
Low self-esteem	Insecure attachments, divorce, parental unemployment, inflation, economic hard times, high crime rates, culture that devalues children, trauma	Psychopathology, vulnerability to criticism, self-destructive behaviors, negative feelings about self and others, interference with relationships, negative emotionality, social withdrawal
High self-esteem	Secure attachments, culture that values children	Positive emotions; life satisfaction; aggression under threat; adjustment and well-being in social relationships and school achievement; resilience to stressful life events; reduced likelihood of anxiety or depression

child attachment relationships; (3) more or less unconscious incorpora-
tion of the way others are perceived to see one; or (4) a culture directly or
indirectly promoting a focus on the self (Harter et al., 1998; Heinonen et
al., 2003; Twenge & Campbell, 2001). Research has revealed a stronger relationship between self-appraisal and the perceptions of others' appraisals
than with others' actual appraisals. Self-concept may mirror parents' self-
concepts as well (Geiger & Crick, 2001).

Competence. What constitutes competence and social acceptance varies greatly across the ages from preschool to high school (Harter & Pike,
1984). Moreover, young and mentally retarded children do not have the
cognitive capacity to assess themselves in the manner that older youths
do. Young children may confuse the wish to be competent with actual
competence, confuse the ideal with the real self. They do not make a clear
distinction between cognitive and physical competence. Consequently, at
young ages, competence scores are likely to be inflated. It is especially
important to use additional sources of information in the assessment of
young children's competence and social acceptance. Children become
increasingly better able to realistically assess their own competence levels
in elementary school years (Hammen & Rudolph, 2003). By the third or
fourth grade, behavioral patterns emerge that are associated with extreme
tendencies to overrate or underrate cognitive competence. Children whose
self-assessments tend to fall within either of these extremes have a greater
tendency to avoid challenge than do youths who accurately rate their own
competence. By seventh grade, children more often acknowledge difficulty in understanding why things happen to them. Ten- to 12-year-old
youths' perceptions of personal competence—academic, acceptance, and
social skills—have predicted their levels of resilience (Wyman, 2003).

Relationships. Parents shape their children's views of self, others, and the
world through their interpretations of experiences, modeling of behaviors, and the quality of care they provide (Thompson, 1999). Studies suggest that children learn to imitate and also internalize maternal cognitive
styles, aversive interactions, and stressful events (Hammen & Rudolph,
2003). Thus, children learn self-blaming cognitive styles, negative attitudes about their adequacy and worth, and a sense of hopelessness or
uncertainty about future outcomes. Parental role dissatisfaction is linked
to difficult temperaments in children and is associated with less effective parenting. Parental negativity, such as hostility and lack of empathy,
increases difficult temperament in children (Heinonen et al., 2003). Different aspects of a youth's mental representations (working models) have different developmental timetables and, perhaps, different periods of critical
influence (Thompson, 1999). Secure attachment at age 6, for example, may
be of significance to the emerging self-image. The self-representational
systems are becoming expanded and refined during this age.

Early sensitive or insensitive caregiving contributes beliefs that guide
future relational expectations, related self-appraisals, and behaviors
toward others (Bowlby, 1980, 1988; Thompson, 1999; chapter 8). Individ-

uals with *secure working models* of relationships tend to seek and expect supportive, satisfying encounters with others and tend to behave in a positive, open manner that elicits the expected relationships. Youths (and adults) with *insecure working models* may expect less support from others, and their expectations may engender a distrust and uncertainty that deter supportive relationships. In turn, people's negative responses to their hostility and distrust confirm and reinforce their expectations. Depressive symptoms have been linked to negative interpersonal expectations and perceptions, biased information processing regarding interpersonal interactions, and maladaptive relationship-oriented beliefs (Hammen & Rudolph, 2003).

Others' Appraisals. The opinions of others form an important initial basis on which children judge themselves (Harter et al., 1998). In early childhood, the parents' hopes and aspirations usually form the basis for what are perceived to be ideal self-representations (Heinonen et al., 2003). Harter and colleagues suggest that ordinarily, youths come to internalize these early evaluations of others as their own. Directionality has not been determined: External approval may influence self-esteem; one's self-regard may influence others' approval levels. Negative competence-related feedback is internalized by youths in the form of negative self-perceptions that increase the risk of depression and other symptoms and disorders (Hammen & Rudolph, 2003). Reduced reinforcement may also lead to increased withdrawal or functional impairment. These reactions may in turn worsen the problem by provoking aversive interpersonal reactions and rejection.

Adolescents who believe that self-esteem results from the validation of others tend to be more preoccupied with approval and to report lower levels of approval and global self-worth as well as more fluctuating approval and self-worth. As interpersonal understanding, perspective-taking ability, and differentiation of role-related selves increase in adolescence, self-worth and the perception of support from significant others also become more differentiated; multiple selves that vary in different social contexts proliferate (Harter et al., 1998). At all ages, individuals may internalize others' support or approval. Although parents' approval remains important to them, adolescents seek support and approval from other adults and from peers as well. Peer approval has been more predictive of SE than support from close friends. Harter et al. found that *validation support* (e.g., interest and respect in what the adolescent thinks, says, and feels) perceived within a specific context (e.g., parent, classmate) was predictive of self-worth in that context and was less predictive of global self-worth or of self-worth in other contexts. That is, validation from a specific group of significant others is most strongly associated with one's sense of self-worth with those particular others.

Small to large differences in adolescents' SE have been found in their peer (male, female, and romantic relationships) and adult (parents, teachers, and counselors) relational contexts (Harter et al., 1998). For the vast majority of adolescents, *global self-worth* or overall self-worth is more highly correlated with one of these individual contexts. For some youths, for example, global self-worth is more highly correlated with female peer approval or with parent approval. Thus treatment may be more effective when support from a particular group is enhanced or when attention is refocused to other contexts. Subgroups of adolescents are identifiable on the basis that their global self-worth is more highly correlated with one context than with the others (Harter et al.). Females have reported greater relational self-worth than males.

Birth Cohort and Culture. Birth cohort has explained more of the variance in SE scores than family environment in most studies. SE scores for U.S. college students showed an increase in scores between the 1960s and the 1990s, with scores peaking in the 1980s. Twenge and Campbell (2001) attribute this change to increased individualism, acceptance of expressing high SE, and cultural emphasis on self-fulfillment and on increasing SE. Among college students, African Americans usually reported higher SE than Whites, and Asian Americans reported lower SE than Whites.

Patterns of Change in Self-Esteem

Although beliefs about oneself are revised and updated throughout development (Thompson, 1999), changes in SE, from one age to the next, generally have been small to moderate in studies (Twenge & Campbell, 2001). Mental age is more highly related to the self-structure than chronological age (Harter & Pike, 1984). Normally, children's self-concepts become more negative or less unrealistically positive in middle childhood (ages 7–8) and again in early adolescence (followed by a slow increase in SE in later adolescence) (Geiger & Crick, 2001; Twenge & Campbell). Deviations in this normal pattern of development may indicate an increased risk for distorted personality patterns and self-concepts characteristic of the adult personality disorders (Geiger & Crick).

A meta-analysis of studies of SE by Twenge & Campbell (2001) shows that a scale written for children (Coopersmith Self-Esteem Inventory, SEI; see below) confirmed decreasing SE from elementary to middle school and increasing SE into high school and college. SEI scores did not recover to above their elementary school levels until college for all female and mixed-sex groups. A scale originally written for use with adolescents (Rosenberg Self-Esteem Scale, RSE) did not find this pattern, but reported that SE steadily increased with age. The normal drop in SE in early adolescence may reflect changes in roles and relationships with parents and peers, and less personal attention from teachers. In later adolescence, as these issues resolve or become better established, or as competence is gained, SE generally improves. The SE of older youths is less likely than that of younger youths to be affected by such experiences as divorce or changes in the cultural value of children.

Gender. Gender has explained a portion of the variance in studies of the determinants of SE (Twenge & Campbell, 2001). RSE found girls' scores to be always lower than boys'. Both boys' and girls' SEI scores revealed a small setback in adolescence; the RSE did not. The SEI demonstrated a dip comparable for both sexes in junior high but a greater increase in scores for boys over time. Boys recovered SE during high school, and girls, during college. As a consequence, in some studies, a large gender gap in SE is apparent in high school.

Self-Esteem and Temperament

Temperament characteristics of negative mood, withdrawal and rigidity, low adaptability, reactivity to the environment, and high distractibility have been related to low SE among youths (Heinonen et al., 2003). The path between temperament and SE may be indirect. Specific temperamental characteristics of a child elicit different parenting and peer responses. Sociocultural expectations and socialization practices may dictate gender differences in the development of SE. Cultures differently define traits such as high activity and low sociability as more or less accepted in girls than in boys (Ahadi, Rothbart, & Ye, 1993; Heinonen et al.; chapters 6, 7).

Self-Esteem and Traumatic Stress

High SE may buffer the effects of negative life events by allowing children to appraise stressful events in ways that are less threatening to their self-worth. It may make children better able to integrate stressful experiences with less negative arousal by using adaptive coping mechanisms (Haine et al., 2003). Researchers have found an association between poor self-concept and traumatic experiences (Lanclos, 2001; Rubin et al., 2003; Whealin & Jackson, 2002). Traumatic experiences can devastate how survivors feel about themselves including the ways they view, interpret, and judge themselves (Rosenbloom & Williams, 2002). Negative life events may lead to diminished SE by directly devaluing the child, stigmatizing the child, or decreasing opportunities to engage in esteem-enhancing activities (Haine et al.). Traumatic events that lead to demoralization and degradation (e.g., torture, violence, relationship aggression) are particularly damaging to SE. For example, Bolger and Patterson (2003) found that, compared to other youths, maltreated children had significantly lower SE as well as more difficulties developing SE, autonomy, emotional and behavioral self-regulation, and good peer relationships. Maltreated youths were more likely to be rejected by peers, less popular, and less likely to have a best friend. High-quality friendships, however, were associated with greater increases in SE over time.

Measures of Self-Concept

Children's reports regarding their self-concepts may be subject to conscious and unconscious distortion, usually in the direction of greater social desirability (Piers & Herzberg, 2002). Piers and Herzberg suggest that a comprehensive evaluation of a child's self-concept requires clinical sensitivity, familiarity with applicable research, and the integration of other sources of data (e.g., clinical observations, interactions, and therapy session data as well as tests, referral sources, school records, prior history, classroom observations, other psychological tests). Studies are needed that include assessment of self-concept before and after exposure to events.

Measures of SE include important differences. Twenge and Campbell (2001) suggest that RSE (Rosenberg, 1965) and SEI (Coopersmith, 1967) are the two most popular self-esteem measures. The RSE items are more self-referent, measuring the respondent's view of self rather than the social environment, whereas the SEI items are more other-referent. SEI was developed using a sample of fifth and sixth graders and is most popular for measuring child and early adolescent self-esteem. RSE was written for middle to late adolescents and has been used primarily with college students (Twenge & Campbell). The SEI, Harter, and Piers-Harris scales are described here.

The Coopersmith Self-Esteem Inventory
Age range: 8–13
Format: Youth self-report

The Coopersmith SEI (Coopersmith, 1989) was designed to measure children's (ages 8 to 13) and young adults' self-appraisals of the extent to which they regard themselves competent, successful, significant, and worthy. Its brevity (50 items plus 8) and simplicity have made it one of the most popular youth self-report measures of self-esteem (Bolton, 2003). The total scale includes eight items each for *general* (personal self), *social* (self-peer), *home* (parents), and *school* (academic) plus an eight-item *lie* scale. Items include those regarding social relations ("I'm popular with kids my own age"; "My parents and I have a lot of fun together"), aspects of the social environment not entirely under the child's control ("My parents usually consider my feelings"; "My teacher makes me feel I'm not good enough"), affect ("I often get upset at school"; "I'm pretty happy"), and self-descriptions ("I'm a failure"; "I have a low opinion of myself") (Twenge & Campbell, 2001). An abbreviated scale (the school short form) consists of 25 items that have had the highest correlations with the total self-score on the school form. The scale manual provides norms for children ages 9 to 13 and for college students. Chapman and Mullis (2002) found a gender bias in 6 of the 25 items on the short form of the inventory.

The Perceived Competence Scales for Children (PSC-C)
Age range: 4–7, mid- to late-childhood, adolescence, college years, adults
Format: Multisource and -format

Perceived Competence Scales for Children (Harter, 1982, 1985, 1988) assess youths' self-perceptions of competence in multiple domains. The pictorial scale for early childhood (ages 4 to 7) assesses *cognitive, physical appearance, physical competence, peer acceptance,* and *behavioral conduct* domains (Harter, 1999). The middle- to late-childhood scale measures *scholastic* and *athletic* competence, *physical appearance, peer acceptance, behavioral conduct*, and *global self-worth* (GSW). The GSW subscale examines the youth's general feelings of worth and SE independent of any skill domain (McInerney, Lillemyr, & Sobstad, 2004). It determines if a child likes or dislikes who he or she is (Harter et al., 1998). The adolescent scale adds three domains: *close friendships, romantic relationships*, and *job competence* (Harter, 1999). Each scale includes seven items measured on a four-point scale (McInerney et al.). To study self-worth in different contexts, Harter has used a Relational Self-Worth (RSW) subscale that includes GSW items and five items for each of four separate relationship contexts (parents, teachers, male classmates, female classmates; Harter et al.). The child is presented with contrasting descriptive statements (e.g., "Some kids like the kind of person they are but other kids often wish they were someone else.") and asked two questions regarding the statements: (1) which of the two statements is most like him or her, and (2) whether the statement the child has selected is "really true for me" or "sort of true for me."

The Piers-Harris Children's Self-Concept Scale (Piers-Harris 2)
Age range: 7–18
Format: Child completion

The Piers-Harris Children's Self-Concept Scale (Piers, 1977) has been used for more than 500 journal articles and books in psychology, education, and the health sciences. The current Piers-Harris 2 is a 60-item self-report questionnaire (subtitled *The Way I Feel About Myself*). The self-concept scales comprise a total score (overall self-concept) (Piers & Herzberg, 2002). Six domain scales assess *behavioral adjustment* (problematic specific behaviors and general problem situations at home or school, such as "I do many bad things"), *intellectual and school status* (intellectual abilities, academic tasks, and general satisfaction and future expectations about school achievement), *physical appearance and attributes* (physical appearance, leadership skills, and ability to express ideas), *freedom from anxiety* (anxiety, dysphoric mood, worry, nervousness, fear, sadness, shyness, and feeling left out), *popularity* (popularity, ability to make friends, and social inclusion), and *happiness and satisfaction*. A higher score indicates a more positive self-evaluation. Two validity scales include the *inconsistent responding index* (INC; random response patterns) and the *response bias index* (RES; tendency to respond Yes or No irrespective of item content). Piers-Harris 2 provides new, representative nationally normative data for students, ages 7 to 18. Respondents indicate whether each statement is true for them by circling Yes or No. Computer analysis is possible through a PC program or by submitting data to Western Psychological Services in Los Angeles.

Locus of Control

Belief that control over events, outcomes, behaviors, or emotions is internal (within the person) has been labeled an *internal locus of control* in contrast to the belief that control is outside of the person's control (*external locus of control*). Youths with high levels of perceived internal control tend to think that their own actions or attributes bring about their successes and failures (Bolger & Patterson, 2003). Findings about control beliefs have varied somewhat across studies, perhaps, in part, because control beliefs have been defined in a number of ways (Hawley & Little, 2002). Assessment of control beliefs and their association with trauma requires delineating types and contexts of control and other influences on its variability.

The importance of control may reflect specific qualities of goals (Grob, Little, & Wanner, 1999, cited in Hawley & Little, 2002). Perceived control over goals may be related to (1) general expectancy of control over goals, (2) personal importance of the goals, (3) persistence of striving for goals over time, and (4) comparative control relative to peers. Grob et al. examined 600 Swiss adolescents' personal, social, and societal control beliefs. Across time, beliefs about control over social and personal goals produced a rainbow curve (apex at age 45): Adolescents and "old" individuals rated their control as less than that of other age groups. Perceptions of control over societal events started low and decreased across time. Social goals such as maintaining a harmonious relationship with a significant other were rated the highest across the lifespan.

The value of external versus internal control also may vary across contexts (Jackson, Frick, & Dravage-Bush, 2000; Ozolins & Stenstrom, 2003; see "Measures of Locus of Control," below). For youths with empathy, belief in personal control over a detrimental outcome, such as victimization of self or others, may result in guilt feelings and increased helplessness. Believing in both internal and external control may be beneficial in some cases. Ozolins and Stenstrom found that youths with a combination of strong beliefs in internal control of health, high degree of belief that powerful others such as health-care professionals and parents determine health, and low degree of belief that health is a function of chance or luck had significantly higher self-esteem than those with high or low belief in internal control combined with a high belief in chance. A high belief in the power of others may increase support seeking.

Maladaptive coping styles, depression, pessimism, anxiety, poor health habits, substance abuse, less involvement in school activities, and a high degree of societal estrangement have been linked to low levels of internal locus of control, strong belief in chance, and low self-esteem in adolescents (Haine et al., 2003). Nowicki and colleagues have found that an internal locus of control is positively correlated with academic achievement and negatively associated with anxiety and aggressiveness (Haine et al.; Nowicki & Strickland, 1973). Children with an internal locus of control may use more appropriate coping strategies or be less likely to appraise stressors as threatening, leading to a reduced negative impact of events.

Types of Control Beliefs

Among the types of control beliefs that have been delineated are primary versus secondary control and goal-specific issues of control. *Primary* control beliefs include beliefs about one's ability to change a situation, whereas *secondary* control beliefs include beliefs that one can adapt to uncontrollable situations (Deardorff, Gonzales, & Sandler, 2003). Secondary control has more than one form such as *interpretive* control (developing a healthy understanding of events) and *vicarious* control (trusting in powerful or authoritative others). Some research has shown that *primary* control beliefs are less adaptive when youths are confronted with truly uncontrollable stressors (Bulman & Brickman, 1980, cited in Deardorff et al.), such as the ongoing threat of violence experienced by inner-city children. Under these conditions, rather than trying to change the situation, strategies of altering the self, or *secondary* control such as managing emotions or controlling autonomic arousal, may be more adaptive. Gonzales, Tein, Sandler, & Friedman (2001) found that active coping strategies, including directly trying to change problem situations, do not relate to the mental-health problems of inner-city adolescents who experience high levels of stress.

Accurate Control Beliefs. The Rochester Child Resilience Project (Wyman, 2003) studied whether or not youths' realistic control attributions about the abilities of their age group to control events and problems were more adaptive than undifferentiated beliefs about internal control. They found that youths classified as stress resilient were more likely to have low control expectations for uncontrollable events (e.g., parental divorce or substance abuse) and high control expectations for controllable events (e.g., academic problems or personal substance abuse) than youths classified as stress affected. Children as young as age 7 were able to differentiate the *degree of controllability* of family problems as well as their abilities to influence them.

Positivity Bias. A *self-serving* or *positivity bias* is an individual's inclination to view things such that a positive self-image is maintained (Mezulis, Abramson, Hyde, & Hankin, 2004). Accordingly, individuals attribute successes and good outcomes to self and assign negative or failure events to things that are changeable. Positive outcomes are attributed to internal, stable, and global dimensions such as ability and traits, whereas negative outcomes are assigned to internal, unstable, and specific causes such as lack of effort. Such attributions suggest that negative outcomes can be avoided in the future. In a meta-analysis of 266 studies, Mezulis et al. found a *self-serving* or *positivity bias* across diverse age, gender, and cultural groups. Within the United States, levels of the bias were remarkably consistent across ethnic groups. Worldwide, the bias was very large in *Western* cultures (effect size (d) = .75 to 1.29) and significantly smaller in

Asian cultures (d = .30) except for Chinese and Koreans (d = 1. 04). Lower levels of the self-serving bias compared to cultural peers are associated with increased levels of psychopathology.

Trauma and Locus of Control

Researchers have found an association between maladaptive control-related beliefs and some of the symptoms and disorders associated with trauma (Hammen & Rudolph, 2003). During traumatic events, control is undermined or is taken away (Schiraldi, 2000). Feeling personally helpless is a part of a traumatic experience (APA, 1994). Especially for young children, feeling that adults are in control following a catastrophic event may prevent symptoms from escalating (La Greca, Silverman, Vernberg, & Roberts, 2002b). The efforts of adults to control the aftermath of the trauma may reduce youths' feelings of being overwhelmed and the sense that things are out of control.

Negative life events may reduce a child's internal locus of control by inducing feelings of helplessness or impairing relationships (Haine et al., 2003). Experience with uncontrollable events may lead to the expectation that nothing a person does can control future outcomes (Deardorff et al., 2003). Seligman's "learned helplessness" model posits that depression stems from experiencing uncontrollable, noncontingent events (Hammen & Rudolph, 2003). The revised model attributes depression to the interaction between a "depressive attributional style" and exposure to negative events. A *depressive attributional style* includes a tendency to attribute negative outcomes to internal, global, and stable factors and to ascribe positive outcomes to external, specific, and unstable factors. Repeated experiences may result in biased information processing such as resistance to evidence of control (Malcarne & Hansdottir, 2001). Bolger and Patterson (2003) found that youths who were either neglected or sexually abused and neglected perceived higher levels of external control than other maltreated youths. Perceived external control accounted substantially for the link of combined neglect and sexual abuse with internalizing symptoms.

Trauma may induce an obsessive need to be in control (Stein & Kendall, 2004). Stein and Kendall suggest that abused youths may become oppositional and fight against authority figures in order to gain an illusory sense of control. Intimacy can be difficult for such children because closeness leads to feelings of vulnerability and loss of control (James, 1994). The need and longing for intimacy and connection combined with fears may result in a pattern of moving closer, becoming frightened, and then pulling away (Stein & Kendall).

Protection. A personal experience of mastery, control, or self-efficacy can attenuate some of the negative effects of traumatic experiences (Fletcher, 2003; Hammen & Rudolph, 2003; Nader, 1997c). Moran and Eckenrode (1992) found that maltreated girls with high external locus of control and low self-esteem reported greater levels of depression than comparison or maltreated girls with internal locus of control and high self-esteem (Fletcher). Similarly, Bolger and Patterson's (2003) study of maltreated youths supports the protective nature of an internal locus of control against internalizing symptoms. Studies have demonstrated that control beliefs mediate the relationship between stress and depressive symptoms in ethnically diverse, inner-city adolescents as well (Deardorff et al., 2003).

Context. The effects of control beliefs may differ for different stressful contexts (Haine et al., 2003). Control beliefs have been shown to mediate the effects of negative life events in some stressed youth populations (children of divorce, inner-city adolescents), but not others (children of alcoholics, bereaved children) (Deardorff et al., 2003; Haine et al.).

Ethnicity. At higher levels of stress or within certain ethnic groups, primary control beliefs may not prove adaptive. Primary control beliefs may not be consistent with "familism," certain religious beliefs, or collectivist beliefs that are emphasized in some non-European American cultures (Freeberg & Stein, 1996). Although Cowen, Work, Wyman, Parker, Wannon, and Gribble (1992) found that primary control beliefs differentiated stress-affected and stress-resilient youths, Magnus, Cowen, Wyman, Fagen, and Work (1999) later showed these findings were not true for the African American children in the sample.

Measures of Locus of Control

Measures of locus of control include the Nowicki-Strickland Internal-External control scales (NSIE; Nowicki & Strickland, 1973) and the Multidimensional Measure of Children's Perceptions of Control (MMCPC; Connell, 1985). Some researchers believe that youths' answers to items related to locus of control may depend on the context of the question (Connell; Jackson et al., 2000). Researchers have found group differences in locus of control scale results for social class, ethnic/cultural groups, academic achievement levels, personality factors, parenting practices, psychological adjustment, and deaf adolescents (Nowicki-Strickland, 2005). Jackson et al. suggest that disparate findings in studies of locus of control may reflect a failure to delineate group membership, such as distinguishing youths with purely externalizing problems from those with both internalizing and externalizing problems. They found that, when *internal*, *external*, and *unknown* control domains were assessed as dependent variables and group status (externalizing and mixed behavior) as independent variables, the externalizing behavior group demonstrated a higher *unknown* locus of control than the group with mixed problems.

NSIE includes scales for preschoolers, children (C), adults (college and noncollege forms), and geriatric adults, permitting family assessment (Nowicki, 2005). CNSIE is a 40-item scale that can be completed by fifth graders and above by themselves. The authors recommend rater administration of the scales in order to ensure that subjects understand the items and work at a similar pace (Nowicki). Items/questions (e.g., "Do you believe that some kids are just born lucky?") are answered with Yes or No responses (Haine et al., 2003).

MMCPC (Connell, 1985) is a 48-item self-report measure designed to identify a youth's understanding of the *source* (internal, powerful other, or unknown) and *outcome* (success or failure) of experiences in four domains (social, cognitive, physical, and general) (Bolger & Patterson, 2003; Jackson et al., 2000). The scale provides a domain-specific and multidimensional alternative to existing youth assessments of locus of control. For each item (e.g., "When I do well in school, it's because the teacher likes me."), the youth is provided a statement and asked to circle one of four responses using a Likert format (from 1 = Not at all true to 4 = Very true).

COPING STRATEGIES

Coping strategies are among the skills attained in the course of normal development. They are important during and after traumatic experiences. In 1984, Lazarus and Folkman described coping as "continually changing behavioral and cognitive efforts to manage external and/or internal demands that are appraised as exceeding the individual's resources" (cited in Stallard, Velleman, Langsford, & Baldwin, 2001). Kardiner (1941) suggested that trauma is an alteration in the environment for which an individual's habitual adaptive strategies are inadequate; the failure of adaptation leads to symptoms (de Silva, 1999). Youths' coping may differ from adults'.

Youth Coping. According to Compas (1998), there is no clear consensus on what dimensions constitute coping in young people. He defines coping as a subset of the ways that individuals respond to stress, including both the effortful and volitional responses as well as the involuntary responses. Involuntary responses are either based in individual differences in temperament or are learned as a result of repeated practice so that they no longer require conscious, volitional control. Stallard et al. (2001) posit that more complex methods of assessing youth coping using a developmental perspective are needed. Children may use a combination of methods rather than individual methods to cope with specific symptoms or emotions. A youth may, for example, use both withdrawal and distraction when feeling angry.

Types of Coping. Stallard et al. (2001) summarize two types of coping strategies: *problem-focused* (e.g., approach-focused coping, primary control, or monitoring) and *emotion-focused* (e.g., managing and regulating the emotional consequences that accompany the stressor through avoidance, secondary control coping, or blunting). A Web-based survey of adults following the September 11, 2001 terrorist attacks at three assessment phases (original within first month, at 2 months, at 6 months) found that coping strategies used in the immediate aftermath of the attacks consistently, significantly predicted outcomes over time (Silver, Holman, McIntosh,

Poulin, & Gil-Rivas, 2002). *Active coping* (e.g., planning, support seeking) served as a protective factor. Quickly abandoning coping efforts (e.g., "giving up," denial, self-distraction) increased the likelihood of elevated PTS symptoms and ongoing distress. After September 11, Brown and Goodman (2005) assessed children bereaved as a result of the terrorist attacks on the New York World Trade Center. Youths who coped by watching television or reading, seeking information about the attacks, venting anger, avoiding people, using creative outlets, and doing volunteer work had significantly higher traumatic grief scores than those who did not. Traumatic grief scores correlated with trauma symptom scores. Although volunteer work and information seeking might be considered active coping strategies, seeking information through TV may exacerbate symptoms by providing traumatic images during an event (chapter 10) or by acting as traumatic reminders that may exacerbate reactions following events (Brown & Goodman).

Avoidance Coping

In the assessment of PTSD, avoidance has been described both as a symptom and as a coping method. Kirmayer, Young, & Hayton (1995) summarized the following theoretical precursors to "psychological trauma": Fear is the memory of pain that permits individuals to anticipate and avoid injury. Anxiety is the capacity to imagine pain and not merely to recollect it. Avoidance is one method of coping with this anticipatory anxiety. Foa, Riggs, and Gershuny (1995) proposed that when a trauma victim's avoidant defensive strategies are not sufficient to ward off trauma symptoms, the affective system shuts down (e.g., numbing occurs; Box 5.1b). Avoidance may be mediated by other variables. Street, Gibson, and Holohan (2005) found that women with greater childhood trauma exposures were more likely to respond to domestic violence with guilt and a sense of responsibility for their victimization. Guilt was directly associated with PTSD levels, and guilt was linked to an increase in avoidance coping strategies—self-distraction, alcohol/drug use, giving up, denial, and stoicism or ignoring emotions. Guilt and avoidance coping were associated with increased current levels of PTSD.

Culture and Coping

Each culture promotes specific coping strategies to foster health and development and to deal with stress (Shiang, 2000; chapter 6). Cultures and social groups influence coping efforts such as the expression of emotions (e.g., ventilation or suppression) and help seeking. In a post-9/11 study of New York police officers, Pole, Best, Metzler, and Marmar (2005) found that coping style was an important explanatory variable for the differences in PTSD levels. Officers who endorsed elevated *wishful thinking coping* (belief in miracles, faith, or luck; wishing, daydreaming, or fantasizing that things would be different) or *self-blame coping* (a tendency to blame, criticize, or lecture themselves) had higher levels of symptoms. These coping styles were prevalent among Hispanic police. Pole et al. speculate that the prevalence of *wishful thinking* and *self-blame* coping may be related to the fatalism and religiosity (e.g., Catholic emphasis on personal responsibility, sin, and redemption) often found in the Hispanic culture. Perhaps due to differences in culture, age, or exposure, similar coping proved helpful in a study of youths bereaved by the September 11, 2001 terrorist attacks. In this primarily Caucasian sample, bereaved children who told themselves that their lives would improve and who used prayer to cope reported more positive memories of the deceased (Brown & Goodman, 2005).

Temperament and Coping

The relationship between coping and temperament as well as the repertoire of coping skills is likely to change with age as children develop greater capacities for self-regulation, cognitive thinking (e.g., hypothetical and abstract thinking), and social interaction (Compas, 1998; Rothbart, 2001). Temperamental characteristics are likely to influence the types of coping responses that can be assimilated by an individual. Compas suggests that behaviorally *inhibited* children (chapter 6) may have greater difficulty acquiring engagement coping responses (e.g., information seeking, instrumental problem-solving skills). Conversely, *uninhibited* youths may find it challenging to develop coping responses that involve the regulation of emotions and behavior (e.g., self-distraction, delay).

Trauma, Youths, and Coping

Studies of youths' coping strategies and traumatic reactions have emerged in the last few years (e.g., Brown & Goodman, 2005; La Greca, Silverman, Vernberg, & Prinstein, 1996; Nader, 1992; Stallard et al., 2001). While the war was ongoing, Bosnian refugee youths (ages 8 to 17) reported information seeking (e.g., watching the news) to cope significantly more often than using distraction (e.g., reading, playing), support seeking (e.g., talking to someone), or other methods (e.g., social withdrawal) (Nader). Three, seven, and ten months after Hurricane Andrew, La Greca and colleagues studied children's use of four types of coping strategies: wishful thinking, positive coping, blame/anger, and social withdrawal (La Greca et al.; Vernberg, La Greca, Silverman, & Prinstein, 1996). PTS symptoms increased with general use of coping (especially wishful thinking) at 3 months; with positive coping, social withdrawal, and especially blame and anger at 7 months; and with blame and anger coping strategies at 10 months (La Greca et al.). Similarly, for youths (ages 7–18) assessed 6 weeks (n = 97) and 8 months (n = 36) after their involvement in a road traffic accident (Stallard et al.), younger children and those with PTSD used more strategies than older youths and those without PTSD. Youths with PTSD used more avoidant and emotion-focused coping (e.g., distraction, social withdrawal, emotional regulation, and blaming others).

Although the consensus is that *problem-focused* coping is important in aiding trauma adaptation for children and adults, the coping strategies that are helpful are likely to be specific to the actual traumatic event and will depend upon factors such as subjective appraisal of the event, time since or phase of the trauma, personality, social support, and other resources (Joseph, Williams, & Yule, 1997; Stallard et al., 2001). For example, information gathering becomes especially important *during* war when knowing the proximity of the enemy and the location of resources may be crucial to survival (Bleich, Gelkopf, & Solomon, 2003; Nader, 1992).

Kidcope
Age range: Adolescent unless adapted
Format: Youth completion

Kidcope (Spirito, Stark, & Williams, 1988) permits children to assess which of 10 coping strategies they used in a specific situation. The strategies and items are *distraction* (e.g., try to forget it; do something else to forget it); *social withdrawal* (stay on your own; keep quiet about the problem); *cognitive restructuring* (try to see the good side of things); *self-criticism* (blame yourself for causing the problem); *blaming others* (blame someone else for causing the problem); *problem solving* (try to sort the problem out by thinking of answers or talking to someone about it; try to sort it out by doing something); *emotional regulation* (shout, scream, get angry; try to calm yourself down); *wishful thinking* (wish the problem had never happened; wish you could make things different); *social support* (try to feel better by spending time with others like family—parents, brothers, or sisters—or with friends); and *resignation* (do nothing because the problem could not be solved). Use and perceived effectiveness of each strategy are rated on a four-point scale (from 1 = Not at all to 4 = Almost all of the time). Originally developed for use with adolescents, Kidcope has been adapted for use with younger children (7 to 12; Pretzlik & Hindley, 1993; Vernberg et al., 1996).

TRAUMA-SPECIFIC RISK AND RESILIENCE

A number of risk and protective factors have been identified clinically and statistically for children exposed to traumas (Table 5.4). The list of identified risk and protective factors may change as more variables and youths' trajectories of change across time are included in analyses. Study results have sometimes been mixed. More study is needed to identify and confirm each factor's role in mediating or moderating traumatic reactions for children with different backgrounds, personalities, and experiences.

Generalizing or Limiting Assessment

Ideally, all children exposed to traumas would be screened for their reactions within the first several weeks after safety has been restored. After large-scale mass traumas such as war, the numbers of children affected have prohibited interview of the entire exposed population. Representative sampling, using multiple measures (e.g., symptom, exposure, personality, and history scales) and multiple sources (e.g., child, parent, teacher, and research observer), has permitted subsequent use of appropriately comprehensive exposure and personal history questionnaires alone to identify children at risk. When possible, intervention programs implemented in schools and communities have provided available treatment for all youths.

For the effective use of less than a full battery of tests for each child, it is essential to identify all aspects of risk (personal and general) for traumatic and associated reactions as well as to remain attuned to the signs of late-occurring reactions. Individuals have had adverse reactions to traumatic events even without direct exposure (Nader, Pynoos, Fairbanks, Al-Ajeel, & Al-Asfour, 1993; Winje & Ulvik, 1998). Youths who have not reported PTSD or who have reported few symptoms sometimes have had later emotional, behavioral, and functioning disturbances clearly associated with traumatic exposure (Fletcher, 2003; Greenwald, 2002b; Yule, Bolton, Udwin, Boyle, O'Ryan, & Nurrish, 2000). School psychologists have complained about the disservice of limiting assessments and interventions to youths who fit a short risk factor list. Youths who do not fit these lists have sometimes had difficulties. Some youths with delineated risk factors have fared well. Caution is advised against anything other than a full assessment when such assessment is possible.

Posttrauma Risk Factors

Risk factors found for increased traumatic reactions in youths can be found in Table 5.4. Some risk factors may be event-specific. Following the

TABLE 5.4.
Some Identified Risk Factors for Increased Posttrauma Reactions and Protective Factors

Variables	Risk Factors
Youth characteristics	Sensitivity levels, issues of attachment, temperament, learning difficulties, poor use of coping strategies, birth order, gender, age, competence, behavioral inhibition
Youth's history	Behavior problems, truancy, anxiety, other psychopathology, previous traumatic or loss experiences, childhood illness
Family	Genetics, parent reactions (e.g., distress or trauma, unequal reactions by parents, guilt inducement, avoidance), family issues (e.g., family chaos, conflict, or violence at home; aspects of the parent-child relationship), lack of support, specific cultural issues, socioeconomic status, multiple problems, isolation, prior psychopathology, parent's previous trauma, parent's psychopathology (e.g., depression, grief, anxiety), parental death
Event factors	Magnitude of the stressor, duration, intensity, degree of life threat, disruption to life, losses, injuries, occurrence of betrayal, proximity, the number of traumas experienced
Proximity	Life threat, injury, emotional involvement, intensity of emotional reaction during the event, sense of responsibility, views of horrible images, fear, panic, worry about another, interactions with or relationship to injured or deceased victims
Postevent factors	Specific posttrauma symptoms (e.g., guilt, amnesia, grief, fear, prolonged anxiety, depression), posttrauma life experiences (e.g., additional traumas, subsequent deaths, extreme stress), posttrauma environment, continued threat
Environment	Deficiencies in social support, lack of school support, an unsafe environment

Resilience or Protective Factors

General	Secure early attachments to caregivers, adaptive competence, internal locus of control, good coping skills, developmental competencies
During traumatic events	Successful protective actions, protection from horrible perceptions, perceptions of having helped, freedom from a sense of responsibility for poor outcomes
Following traumatic events	Social support (from school, family, friends), feeling safe

Sources: Biederman et al., 1990; Briere & Elliott, 1997; Brock & Lazarus, 2002; Costello, Keeler, & Angold, 2001; Daviss, Mooney, Racusin, Ford, Fletscher, & McHugo, 2000; De Bellis, Keshaven et al., 1999; de Jong et al., 2001; Fletcher, 2003; Greenwald, 2002b; Haine, Ayers, Sandler, Wolchik, & Weyer, 2003; La Greca, Silverman, Vernberg, & Roberts, 2002a, 2002b; McCleery & Harvey, 2004; Nader, 1999d; Nader, Pynoos, Fairbanks, & Frederick, 1990; Rabalais, Ruggiero, & Scotti, 2002; Rousseau & Drapeau, 1998; Scheeringa & Zeanah, 1995, 2001; Udwin, Boyle, Yule, Bolton, & O'Ryan, 2000.

sinking of the cruise ship *Jupiter* near Greece (n = 400 British children), youths who had poor or no swimming skills reported significantly more PTSD symptoms (Udwin, Boyle, Yule, Bolton, & O'Ryan, 2000). Timing may be a factor in risk. McCleery & Harvey (2004) point out that interventions may be ineffective or even harmful if they are provided before the environment is sufficiently safe. Children may be at greater risk for specific symptoms based on their personal characteristics. Youths are at greater risk of committing more serious violence in adolescence if in early childhood they were aggressive (e.g., hitting, kicking, and verbal insults and threats) and peer-rejected. Greater risk of both violent victimization and perpetration exists for youths who lack the skills and competencies to resolve conflicts or solve problems (Flannery et al., 2003). In a study of adults in four different regions (Algeria, Cambodia, Ethiopia, Gaza) exposed to similar traumas (war, conflict, mass violence), de Jong et al. (2001) found that risk factors varied by culture. Conflict-related trauma after age 12 was the only risk factor shared by subjects from all four regions.

Predicting Increased Response

No single variable or measure is 100% effective in predicting the level of youths' traumatic reactions. Increased physical or emotional/subjective exposure to traumatic experiences has very consistently predicted increased traumatic response. Following a sniper attack on an elementary school ground, higher exposure and grief levels were associated with elevated and persistent traumatic reactions (Nader, Pynoos, Fairbanks, & Frederick, 1990; Pynoos et al., 1987). La Greca et al. (1996) discovered that children's traumatic symptoms were less likely to decrease between 3 and 7 months after a hurricane if they had a combination of higher exposure levels, more subsequent life events, less social support, and ethnic minority status. Udwin et al. (2000) found differences in the risk factors associated with *PTSD* (e.g., viewing blood, being trapped), with *severity* of response (e.g., low school support, amnesia for most or all of the event, strong fear after the event), and with *duration* of traumatic reactions (e.g., low social support, illness in childhood, high depression scores 5 months after the event).

It is likely that combinations of factors determine the results of traumatic experiences. Culture, personality, or circumstances may alter the effects of risk or protective factors such as intelligence or a nurturing parent. Punamaki et al. (2001) tested 86 Palestinian youths during the last, very violent months of the 1993 Intifada and again 3 years later. PTSD was predominantly related to exposure. Exposure to experiences such as witnessing violence, loss of family members, and being wounded increased neurotic symptoms during the violence and predicted PTSD 3 years later. The more traumatic experiences youths had, the more they suffered from PTSD after 3 years. Child characteristics such as creative intelligence and specific attitudes, and family characteristics such as parenting, served as resilience or risk factors. Youths who believed they would respond actively to violence suffered less from PTSD and emotional disorders 3 years later than those who projected a passive response. Children who perceived a discrepancy between their mother's and father's parenting were particularly vulnerable to PTSD. Creativity, good and harmonious parenting, and the perception by the youth that he or she would have chosen an active response to military violence served as resiliency factors against emotional disturbances other than PTSD. The more intelligent children suffered more from emotional disorders (e.g., mood, anxiety, obsessive-compulsive, and behavioral disorders) if they rated their fathers as highly rejecting and hostile and their mothers as loving and caring. Less creative youths suffered fewer emotional disorders if they perceived their mothers to be loving and caring than children without such a perception. Creativity predicted a decrease in neuroticism (Eysenck's Neuroticism Scale, Eysenck, 1967) and an increase in self-esteem as peace approached.

In addition to risk and protective factors, there is some statistical evidence that specific symptoms or symptom complexes may be predictive of a PTSD diagnosis, severity of response, functional impairment, or prolonged response. Replication and additional study are needed. Pynoos et al. (1987) found that the combination of disturbed sleep and difficulties with concentration most differentiated severe trauma reactions from moderate ones. Carrion, Weems, Ray, & Reiss (2002) found that the *intensity* of avoidance, distress in response to cues, difficulty concentrating, and feelings of recurrence each predicted a PTSD diagnosis or a child's functional impairment. The *frequency* of a "restricted range of affect" or "a sense of foreshortened future" was predictive of impairment. Sack, Seely, and Clarke (1997) revealed that avoidance of situational reminders, loss of interest, detachment, and restricted affect had the greatest predictive power. After a tornado collapsed a school wall, killed nine children, and injured numerous others (Nader, 1991), some children who reported few symptoms but endorsed an increased startle response had later difficulties functioning.

Protective Factors

Researchers and clinicians have also identified protective factors for traumatized youths (Table 5.4). Prior to a traumatic event, resolution of a previous traumatic response, healthy development, and good grades may serve as protective factors in children's traumatic reactions. During an event, ignorance of the magnitude of the occurrence; protection from traumatic sights, sounds, and feeling responsible for events and outcomes; and opportunities for successful actions have been linked to reduced reactions (Nader, 1998; Pynoos et al., 1987; Udwin et al., 2000). Assigning culpability for the event and its outcomes to an external source and having a good support system may prevent the escalation of symptoms (Nader; Pynoos et al.; Rabalais, Ruggiero, & Scotti, 2002; Udwin et al.). A good support system included feeling protected, believing that adults were in control during and after the event, and maintaining healthy relationships with parents and peers. Appropriate assessment methods (Nader et al., 1990) or one or more intervention sessions following an event have reduced reactions (Goenjian et al., 1997; Vila, Porche, & Mouren-Simeoni, 1999).

As stated earlier, a sense of safety and trust, esteem and self-efficacy, and power and control may enhance recovery from traumas (Regehr, 2001). Researchers have confirmed that an early foundation of supportive parenting and the resulting competence engendered is associated with later positive adaptation even if the child goes through a period of maladaptation (Yates et al., 2003). This suggests that, for some children, resilience is not extinguished but may go underground for a time (Anthony, 1987, cited in Yates et al.). On the other hand, trauma may undermine these schemas and create risk or vulnerability. In studies of resilience and child maltreatment, few children have met empirical definitions of resilience over time. When small percentages of maltreated youths are rated as resilient, most of them lose such status over time (Bolger & Patterson, 2003). Nevertheless, some maltreated children achieve higher levels of adaptive functioning than others. Better adjusted youths more often have been older at onset and exposed to fewer stresses, shorter duration of maltreatment, and less severe and pervasive maltreatment. Internal locus of control, higher self-esteem, increased self-regulatory skills, and friendships have been associated with more positive outcomes. These traits along with good support systems (chapter 7) and secure attachments (chapter 8) have provided a measure of protection with regard to a number of types of trauma.

CONCLUSIONS

Resilience, risk, and vulnerability factors may serve as mediating or moderating variables in association with traumatic reactions. Major or minor life events that disrupt the mechanisms that maintain the stability of a person's physical, emotional, and cognitive functioning represent a strain on the person's adaptive capabilities. Risk factors typically co-occur with other risk factors and usually include a sequence of stressful events rather than a single event. Cumulative risk has been associated with increased maladaptation over time. Resilience, the ability to function and feel well despite adversity, has been associated with protective and competence factors. Among them are secure attachments, effective parenting, intellect, and coping skills. Risk and vulnerability, in contrast, have been linked to a large number of traits and conditions such as negative emotionality, traumas, and other adverse experiences: premature birth, poverty, an impoverished early environment, parental mental illness, and divorce. Self-schemas such as safety and trust, esteem and self-efficacy, and power and control and other protective factors may enhance recovery from traumatic experiences. Trauma may undermine resilience and the traits associated with it.

Part II

Aspects of Youth and Environment: Their Influence on the Assessment of Trauma

6

The Nature of the Child

A youth's age, gender, personality, and temperament are likely to affect his or her reactions to trauma and to the associated assessment process. Findings regarding the association of traumatic symptoms with age and gender have been mixed (Fletcher, 2003; Udwin, Boyle, Yule, Bolton, & O'Ryan, 2000). The complexity of associations as well as aspects of assessment may contribute to these conflicting results (chapter 3). Determining the relationship between childhood trauma and the child's characteristics is somewhat problematic. Specific fears and types of reactions appear prominently at different ages or phases of development. Pretrauma ratings of personality or temperament are rarely available, whereas alterations in these child qualities have followed traumas (Nader, 2001b; Terr, 1991; Box 1.1e, 6.1). Even when traits and behaviors can be identified after an event, trauma may change aspects of them. For example, youths may become more concrete in focus, more sensitive to changes in the environment, or more difficult behaviorally. Thus, traits found in association with PTSD may be a result of trauma rather than a cause of symptoms. Factors such as culture or life experiences are among the significant predictors of personality characteristics (see McDermott, 1991; Oakland, 2001; chapter 7). Such variables, therefore, must be considered when assessing trauma's affects on personality and vice versa. Prospective studies are needed to distinguish the results of PTSD from pre-existing traits and qualities.

AGE, DEVELOPMENT, AND GENDER

Age and Development

Age and developmental level affect children's appraisals of threat, the meaning assigned to aspects of the event, emotional and cognitive coping,

---

BOX 6.1
Trauma May Shape or Alter Personality

a. *Mathew.* Before the massacre, Mathew was a happy, easygoing, and outgoing boy. He was friendly and made friends easily, enjoyed playing, was curious, and was very active. He had well-adjusted friends. Afterward, he was withdrawn, angry/hostile, aggressive, pessimistic, and unable to feel any positive emotions. In fact, he became adept at not feeling anything. He began to associate with other troubled and aggressive youths and to get into trouble.

b. *Joanie.* In the face of her mother's neglect and her father's sexual molestation, Joanie learned to fend for herself and to protect and care for her brother. She became very competent and grown up in some ways. She prepared cereal for her brother in the morning while her mother slept. She fixed her brother's afternoon snack. Taking control of things became her style (see Box 1.1e).

---

capacities to tolerate their reactions, and abilities to address secondary life changes (Nader, 2001b; Pynoos & Nader, 1993). Maturation also affects a youth's ability and willingness to report symptoms, to understand questions or directions, and to give information that may please or displease an adult. Age may not only influence perception and meaning attributed to aspects of the traumatic experience but may also affect the aspects of the event that assume prominence both initially and later. For example, the importance of a parent to survival (James, 1994) may influence the initial focus of a young child's experience.

Reporting Symptoms

Age and developmental level directly affect a child's ability to report symptoms and experiences. Very young children's preverbal or barely verbal capacities render them unable to report their subjective experiences (Scheeringa & Zeanah, 1995). Studies of young children have underscored the need for collecting information from multiple sources (Scheeringa, Peebles, Cook, & Zeanah, 2001; see chapter 4). Between 18 months and 2 years of age, children begin to use symbolic play and language to represent experience (Piaget, 1952, pp. 335-338) and to demonstrate their perceptual memories (Terr, 1985). Children under age 5 have been assessed using a combination of observation, questions during or directions regarding play, and supplemental information from caretaking adults (Nader, Stuber, & Pynoos, 1991; Scheeringa et al., 2001). Children as young as age 4 are able to report basic emotions—happy, sad, angry, mad, or scared (Gully, 2000).

When relying on self-reports or peer ratings to gather data, researchers must speak the language of their informants (McCrae & John, 1992). In addition to cultural adaptations (chapter 4, 7), instruments have been adapted for specific age groups through rewording of questions, breaking down questions into simpler units for younger children, and use of age-related answering systems. Children under the age of 8 may have difficulty with the concept of time, even when time is narrowed to the preceding month. Research is needed to determine the efficacy of using a culturally appropriate identifying time period (e.g., Chanuka/Christmas/ Kwanza/Ramadan, Halloween, a birthday) near the time of the event or the period in question (e.g., "since school started" = in the last month). Youths under 8 may also have difficulty with the complexities of a five-point scale.

Emotional sophistication or how "street-wise" the child is may also affect age cutoff levels. For example, the CPTS-RI (chapter 11) has been successfully used without adaptation in wording with children ages 5 and older in south-central Los Angeles (Pynoos et al., 1987; Nader et al., 1990), ages 7 and older in rural New York (Nader & Pynoos, 1993), and a translated version with children ages 11 and older in Kuwait (Nader, Pynoos, Fairbanks, Al-Ajeel, & Al-Asfour, 1993). It was used as a Yes-No questionnaire, with minor alterations in wording, for children ages 5 to 7 in rural New York and for children ages 7 to 10 in the Middle East. Depending on sophistication levels (language and emotional), children ages 5, 6, and 7 (or older in some cultures) may need simplification of terms and shortening of questions (Nader, 1993b). Inasmuch as minor changes in wording can change the meaning of a question, it is important to use standard, recommended changes (e.g., as suggested in the instrument's manual).

As described in chapter 4, the order of questions as well as wording and the contributions of the interviewer (e.g., focus, acceptance, tone of questions) may be particularly important for children. The wording of questions has affected an interviewer's success in eliciting accurate symptom reports. For example, it may be impossible for adults or children to avoid reminders in the aftermath of traumatic events. Although children may wish to avoid some reminders of the event, they may have even less control than an adult over the actual ability to avoid. Therefore, asking if a child stays away from reminders rather than if he or she wishes to avoid them may elicit a misleading negative response. Wording issues may explain why some studies have found high levels of intrusive re-experiencing and relatively few avoidance symptoms. Similar wording difficulties exist for "survivor guilt." Asking children, without additional clarification, if they feel bad because someone else was killed or hurt worse than they were may not discriminate between traumatized and nontraumatized children, because most children feel bad that other children were killed or hurt worse than themselves.

Children (especially young children or children from particular cultures) may respond to cues from the interviewer when answering questions. It is essential that the youth sense a willingness to hear any answer and that there is no wrong answer. When there are open-ended questions, or questions asking for a general list of results (e.g., "Has anything really bad ever happened to you?" or "Do you want to stay away from things that remind you of [the event]?"), asking the open-ended question and waiting for an answer *before* giving specific examples (e.g., "Do you stay away from windows [after exposure to the hurricane]?") or asking specific probe questions (e.g., "What things do you want to stay away from?") can be helpful. Young children may recognize that they want to avoid reminders, but may have difficulty thinking of specific reminders.

Development and Symptoms

More study is needed to determine clearly the variations in traumatic reactions at different developmental stages. Study is needed to delineate a traumatic response's mutations over time from specific developmental phases and from specific symptomatic forms. Symptom and exposure criteria altered from the current *DSM-IV* PTSD criteria may be important to the accurate diagnosis of infants and children (Carrion, Weems, Ray, & Reiss, 2002; Scheeringa, Zeanah, Drell, & Larrieu, 1995; Scheeringa et al., 2001). In assessing youths' behavior and reactions, it is essential to be aware of developmentally normal characteristics, maturation, and change (Tables 6.1A,B). For example, by around 8 months, infants become more hesitant in approaching novel or intense objects. Effortful control of impulses develops slowly from age 1 to 4 through the grade school years. Neural areas (e.g., those subserving memory and attention) undergo extensive maturation during adolescence (Putnam, Ellis, & Rothbart, 2001). Some researchers have found it more useful to examine results in relationship to development (e.g., pubertal stage) rather than age (Carrion et al.).

Particular reactions (e.g., fear) manifest differently at different ages (e.g., clinging or crying for infants, internalized for adolescents) (Putnam et al., 2001). For example, for neonates, activity tends to covary with behavioral distress (Rothbart, Chew, & Gartstein, 2001). Tables 6.1A,B lists some of the developmental occurrences that may be relevant to the assessment of trauma and essential to assessing temperamental differences. Responses by age may reflect the changing nature of symptoms over time or may vary depending on the type of trauma. In a study primarily of maltreated children ages 3 to 13 (n = 219) using a parent report measure (Briere et al., 2001), maltreated younger children were rated higher on anger, and maltreated older children were rated higher on depression.

Some behaviors are common at specific phases of development and signal disturbances at other age levels (Nader, 1997a). For example, when measuring dissociation, it is important to recognize that young children are often likely to exhibit forgetfulness, shifts in attention, and a variable sense of identity; that daydreaming may be a common behavior for youths; and that feeling unreal and detached from one's experience may be common for adolescents (Putnam, 1997; Friedrich, Jaworski, Huxsahl, & Bengston, 1997). Similarly, when measuring sexual concerns or behaviors, some thoughts or actions that are common to an adolescent male (e.g., thinking about sex, having sexual feelings in the body, thinking about touching the opposite sex, and having difficulty stopping thinking about

TABLE 6.1A
Some Findings on Age, Temperament, and Development: Infants

Age Emergence or Stability of Behavior	Observable or Reportable Behavior	Predicts, in a Significant Number of Study Subjects
Newborns • Not an ideal period for assessing temperament characteristics • Smiling and laughter not stable from initially but stable from 3 months	• Differences in irritability and orienting • Differences in susceptibility to distress to overstimulation and colic • Differences in activity level, distress to limitations, and duration of orienting	• Not predictive • Stability in activity level, distress to limitations, and duration of orienting at 12 months
Infants, 2–3 months • Emergence of positive emotionality • Emergence of orienting attention	• Differences in smiling, laughter, and rapid approach • Smiling, laughter (also at 6.5 and 10 months) • Distress • Parent report distress to limitations • High parent-reported fear (also at 6.5 and 10 months)	• Approach tendencies in infants and at ages 6–7; age 7 extraversion, susceptibility to anger and frustration, and low attentional and inhibitory control • Age 7 positive anticipation and impulsivity • Empathy, childhood guilt/shame • Anger/frustration at age 7 • Fear at 7 years
Infants, 4–6 months • Behavioral approach can be measured between 4 and 6 months; at 6 months, it is also manifested in latency to reach and grasp objects • Beginnings of appraisal process at 6 months: comparison of one perception to another	• Differences in distress and body movement to stimulation • Motor reactivity coupled with positive affect • Motor reactivity coupled with distress • NYLS "difficult" temperament • Adaptability • Kagan's low reactive	• Later fear/behavioral inhibition; age 7 parent reported frustration & anger • Approach oriented behavior, 14 mo • Behavioral inhibition • Home & school adjustment at ages 4 & 5, behavior problems at age 3 • School adjustment & behavior problems • Age 2: uninhibited (sociable, spontaneous approach to unfamiliar)

TABLE 6.1A (continued)
Some Findings on Age, Temperament, and Development: Infants

Age Emergence or Stability of Behavior	Observable or Reportable Behavior	Predicts, in a Significant Number of Study Subjects
Infants, 6–12 months • Overall distress, stable from 6.5 months	• Differences in approach-withdrawal • In lab frustration (6.5 and 10 months) • Fear (also at 10 and 13.5months)/shyness, sadness	• Stable from 6 to 12 months and to 2 years • Anger/frustration at age 7; plus activity, positive anticipation, impulsivity, aggression, and high intensity pleasure • Shyness, sadness
Infants, 9–12 months • The onset of fear or behavioral inhibition at this age may work in opposition to earlier rapid approach to novel objects; approach tendencies should not be assessed in this period but between 4 and 6 months • May now show distress to potentially threatening objects • Capacity to attribute mental intentions to another person	• Fear and behavioral inhibition	• Fearful inhibition at ages 8 and 18; (when combined with gentle discipline) highly internalized conscience; later tendency to be empathetic and susceptible to guilt reactions

Derived from the following references: Caspi, 1998; Caspi, Henry, McGee, Moffitt, & Silva, 1995; Caspi & Silva, 1995; Derryberry & Rothbart, 2001; Kochanska, 1997; Knox, 2004; Nelson, Martin, Hodge, Havill, & Kamphaus, 1999; Rothbart, 2001; Rothbart, Chew, & Gartstein, 2001.

TABLE 6.1B
Some Findings on Age, Temperament, and Development: Toddlers, Children

Age Emergence or Stability of Behavior	Observable or Reportable Behavior	Predicts, in a Significant Number of Study Subjects
Toddlers, 13–22 months • Emergence of effortful control (e.g., ability to inhibit and correct movement) • Attention persistence from 14 to 20 months; distractibility stable from 18 to 24 months and from 2 to 12 years • Activity level (not stable before 12 months; generally stable from 14 to 20 months and from 2 to 12 years)	• Intentional movement among laboratory toys • In laboratory, fear at 13.5 months	• Age 7 high positive anticipation, impulsivity, motor activation, and low sadness • At 7 years: fear, low intensity (non-risk taking) pleasure; low positive anticipation, low impulsivity, low activity level, low aggression
Toddlers, 2–3 years • Ability to attend or not to stimuli permitting children the ability to delay reward, to suppress reactive tendencies, take in additional information, and plan more efficient coping strategies (e.g., constrain fear by attending to environmental sources of safety) • Ability to inhibit dominant response in favor of subordinate response improves from 27 to 36 months	• Differences in effortful attention • Performance on spatial conflict task • Fearful inhibition • High fear combined with maternal gentle discipline or low fear combined with secure attachment/maternal responsiveness	• Adolescent ability to concentrate • Mother reported higher attentional focusing, higher inhibitory control, and lower impulsivity • Ages 4, 8, and 18 fearful inhibition • Higher conscience at ages 4 and 5

TABLE 6.1B (continued)
Some Findings on Age, Temperament, and Development: Toddlers, Children

Age — Emergence or Stability of Behavior	Observable or Reportable Behavior	Predicts, in a Significant Number of Study Subjects
Children, 5–6 years	• Internalizing patterns	• Decrease in aggression between kindergarten and first grade
Children, 6–7 years	• Surgency	• Aggression is negatively related to guilt/shame
	• Negative affectivity	• Low aggression, anger; high empathy, guilt/shame, help-seeking, and negativity
• Able to replay positive and negative experiences	• Fear (fear-related inhibition is stable across childhood into adolescence)	• Combines with discomfort, anger/frustration, sadness, and low soothability/falling reactivity to form a general negativity; does not predict anger/frustration

Derived from the following references: Caspi, 1998; Caspi, Henry, McGee, Moffitt, & Silva, 1995; Caspi & Silva, 1995; Derryberry & Rothbart, 2001; Kochanska, 1997; Knox, 2004; Nelson, Martin, Hodge, Havill, & Kamphaus, 1999; Rothbart, 2001; Rothbart, Chew, & Gartstein, 2001.

sex) may be a sign of disturbance (e.g., sexual molestation) in an 8-year-old male (Friedrich et al.).

Gender

Findings regarding gender differences among children exposed to traumas have been mixed. Some researchers have found no differences between the sexes, whereas others have discovered higher levels of symptoms among girls (Carrion et al., 2002; Fletcher, 2003; La Greca, Silverman, Vernberg, & Prinstein, 1996; McFarlane, Policansky, & Irwin, 1987; Nader, Pynoos, Fairbanks, & Frederick, 1990; Pfefferbaum et al., 1999; Pynoos et al., 1987; Stallard, Velleman, Langsford, & Baldwin, 2001; Udwin et al., 2000). When differences have emerged, they have been modest and their meaning uncertain (Silverman & La Greca, 2002). A number of factors must be taken into account when evaluating gender differences. For adults, some research has demonstrated a gender bias in reporting the symptoms of PTSD (e.g., females are more likely to report symptoms than males; Bleich, Gelkopf, & Solomon, 2003). Children's histories (e.g., previous trauma, psychiatric conditions), circumstances (e.g., support systems, cultural issues), traits (e.g., temperament), or levels of distress may also be factors in contradictory findings (Ahadi, Rothbart, & Ye, 1993; Fletcher, 2003; Kroll, 2003). For example, although bivariate analysis revealed gender differences for children exposed to Hurricane Mitch, the differences disappeared in a multivariate analysis that included levels of fear, horror, and helplessness during the hurricane (Goenjian et al., 2001).

Cultural differences also must be considered when assessing the differences between genders as well as when considering other variables (e.g., temperament) and traumatic response. For example, in a study of 6- to 7-year-old children in the People's Republic of China (PRC) and the United States (Ahadi et al., 1993), U.S. children showed higher activity levels, lower inhibitory control, and less smiling for boys than for girls. Gender differences in these traits for the PRC children were reversed: Girls had higher activity, lower inhibitory control, higher impulsivity, and high intensity pleasure (i.e., sensation seeking). Higher levels of sensitivity to low levels of stimulation (perceptual sensitivity and low intensity pleasure) were found to be greater for girls in the United States and for boys in the PRC.

The type of trauma may be a factor in each gender's rate of exposure and their responses to trauma. Silverman, Reinherz, and Giaconia (1996) found that females were 3 times more likely to report any type of abuse and 11 times more likely to report sexual abuse than males. In a study of 2000 10 to 16 year olds exposed to one or more of several types of violence (see chapter 10), Boney-McCoy and Finkelhor (1995) found that the most common form of victimization reported by female adolescents was sexual assault; for male adolescents, it was aggravated assault by a nonfamily member. There was some symptom variation between the sexes. For example, sexually assaulted boys reported significant PTSD-related symptomatology (10 items measured), trouble with a teacher, and sadness. Sexual assault for girls and nonfamily member assault for both boys and girls was significantly associated with PTSD-related symptomatology and trouble with a teacher but not with sadness.

PERSONALITY

A child's personality is a collective of the physical, mental, emotional, and social qualities that are reflected in his or her thoughts, feelings, attitudes, beliefs, behaviors, and patterns of reaction (Chaplin, 1975; Gramercy Books, 1989). Personality traits are the individual tendencies to think, feel, and behave in certain consistent ways (Caspi, 1998). Caspi suggests that individual differences within a group are usually greater than those between groups. Behavior is likely determined by multiple traits that influence how individuals organize their behavior to meet developmental and environmental demands and challenges (Caspi). Personality theories emphasize different elements (e.g., biological, emotional, environmental, self-regulation and intentionality, perceptions, consistency) or their complex interdependence (van Lieshout, 2000).

Many personality and temperament characteristics are genetically influenced and are considerably heritable (Caspi, 1998; Rothbart & Bates, 1998; van Lieshout, 2000). In fact, studies of nonhuman species suggest that temperamental systems are evolutionarily conserved. Rothbart (2001) has summarized findings for 12 nonhuman species. Among the species examined, researchers found aspects of extraversion (energy and enthusiasm), neuroticism (negative affectivity, nervousness), openness (originality, open-mindedness), and agreeableness (altruism, affection). Attention openness was found in some animal species. Conscientiousness or effortful control was found among chimpanzees only. Studies of human twins and adoptees have especially substantiated the heritability of extraversion and neuroticism (see Factor Analytic Models, below) (Caspi). Relatives do not resemble each other, however, in direct correspondence to gene dosage. Therefore, genes may interact with one another in different ways.

Issues related to and measures for assessing temperament traits and personality types are presented in the following sections. Among the items discussed are theories (often research-based) that have influenced the measurement and study of temperament and type. Among them are the New York Longitudinal Study (NYLS), the Five Factor Model, Jeffrey Gray's theories, Jungian-based theories, and more (Table 6.2).

TABLE 6.2
Trait Theories

Theory	Trait Category	Definition of Trait Category
New York Longitudinal Study (Chess & Thomas)	Activity Level	• Amount of physical motion
	Rhythmicity	• Regularity of physiologic functions
	Approach/Withdrawal	• Initial responses to new stimuli
	Mood	• Amount of pleasant or unpleasant behavior
	Intensity	• Energy level of responses (positive or negative)
	Threshold of Sensitivity	• Amount of stimulation to evoke responses
	Distractibility	• Degree stimuli interferes with ongoing behaviors
	Attention Span/Persistence	• Length of time particular activities are pursued
	Adaptability	• Ease or difficulty of modifying reactions to stimuli
Five Factor	I. Extraversion or Surgency or Extraversion/Positive Emotionality (E)	• Sociability, dominance, activity, or the extent to which the person actively engages others or avoids social experiences
	II. Agreeableness (A)	• Helpfulness, manageability, honesty, sincerity; continuum from warmth and compassion to antagonism
	III. Conscientiousness or Conscientiousness /Constraint (C)	• Carefulness, faithfulness, diligence, or the extent and strength of impulse control; ability to delay gratification in favor of more distant goals or to modulate impulsive expression
	IV. Emotional Stability or Neuroticism or Negative Emotionality (N)	• Emotional reactivity; self-confidence, anxiety, fearfulness or low emotional stability or the extent to which the person experiences the world as distressing or threatening
	V. Intellect or Openness to Experience (O)	• Openness, interest, intelligence

TABLE 6.2 (continued)
Trait Theories

Theory	Trait Category	Definition of Trait Category
Neurological Systems (Jeffrey Gray)	Behavioral Activation System (BAS)	• Neuroanatomical system that is sensitive to cues of reward and controls behaviors such as exploration and approach responses; includes medial forebrain bundle, lateral hypothalamus, and the neurotransmitters dopamine and norepinephrine
	Behavioral Inhibition System (BIS)	• Neuroanatomical system that is sensitive to cues of punishment and nonreward; includes the orbital frontal cortex, medial septal area, hippocampus, and Ascending Reticular Activating System, and involves the neurotransmitters norepinephrine and serotonin
Jungian Mental Functions (Carl Jung)	Sensation vs. Intuition (S vs. N)	• Focus on concrete vs. abstract realities, facts/details vs. symbolic, theoretical
	Thinking vs. Feeling| (T vs. F)	• Use objective, logical decision making vs. subjective, personal judgment criteria
	Extroverted or Introverted (E vs. I)	• Outward turning (e.g., think out loud; seek outward interests, stimulation) vs. inward turning (e.g., process internally)
(Myers)	Judging vs. Perceiving (J vs. P)	• Wanting things settled (closure) vs. keeping options open (flexibility)

© Nader, 2003.

TEMPERAMENT

Studied in both infants and animals, temperament characteristics are the early dispositions (e.g., affect, attention, arousal) upon which personality is based (Caspi, 1998; Rothbart, 2001). Temperament, often defined as a substrate of personality, refers to a person's characteristic emotional style or disposition or to the individual differences that index a person's style of approach and response to the environment. In addition to its prominence in the psychological health of very young children, temperament has been identified as a factor in children's vulnerability to traumatization (Bagley & Mallick, 2002; Strelau, 1995), their traumatic and stress reactions (Carey & McDevitt, 1995b; Schwarz & Kowalski, 1992; Strelau), behavioral problems (Dodge, Bates, Pettit, & Valente, 1995; Nelson, Martin, Hodge, Havill, & Kamphaus, 1999; Ruchkin, Schwab-Stone, Koposov, Vermeiren, & Steiner, 2002), psychiatric symptoms (Teerikangas, Aronen, Martin, & Huttunen, 1998), and memory for traumatic experiences (Howe, 1997). In humans and primates, temperamental traits may serve as protective or risk factors. In two studies of veterans (Dalton, Aubuchon, Tom, Pederson, & McFarland, 1993; Otis & Louks, 1997), introversion was prominent among PTSD samples. Primate studies reveal, however, that solitary orangutans seem less affected by social isolation than highly social chimpanzees (Maestripieri & Wallen, 2003).

Some developmental research suggests that temperament encompasses an infant's innate patterns of reacting to stimulation (reactivity) and the parallel capacity for emerging self-regulation (Neisworth, Bagnato, Salvia, & Hunt, 1999). Studies of early temperament and adult adjustment have yielded mixed results. The predictive accuracy of early assessments of temperament has varied to some extent by age and gender (Martin, Wisenbaker, Huttenen, & Baker, 1997; Teerikangas et al., 1998). To interpret the role of temperament as a risk or a protective factor, it is essential to assess the cumulative effect of multiple risk factors of infancy and later childhood (Teerikangas et al.).

Theories of Temperament

Theorists define temperament differently (Rothbart, Ahadi, Hershey, & Fisher, 2001). Most measures of temperament in infants and young children have been based on dimensions identified by the NYLS (Table 6.2, 6.3) and by Buss and Plomin (emotionality, activity, sociability) (Rothbart, Ahadi et al., 2001). From the NYLS of infants, Thomas and Chess (1977) elaborated nine major dimensions of temperament and behavioral style for young children in response to their environments (activity level, rhythmicity, approach/withdrawal, mood, intensity, threshold of sensitivity, distractibility, attention span/persistence, and adaptability) (Chess & Thomas, 1991; Thomas & Chess). NYLS also identified three types of infants

TABLE 6.3
Personality Type Theories

Theory	Type	Trait Combination
NYLS	Easy	• Regular, approaching, adaptable, mild, and predominantly positive in mood
	Difficult	• Timid in initial reactions (withdraw in novel situations), low adaptability, high intensity, predominantly negative mood, and low regularity
	Slow to warm	• Slow initial response (withdrawal), low adaptability but tend to adapt with increased exposure, lower energy levels of response (low intensity), low activity, and a more negative mood
Block's Q-Sort	Ego-resilients or resilients	• Well-functioning cognitively, emotionally, and interpersonally
	Vulnerable overcontrollers or overcontrollers	• Few interpersonal skills, shy, inward; low extraversion and emotional stability; average agreeableness, conscientiousness, and openness
	Unsettled undercontrollers or undercontrollers	• Hostile, disagreeable, show little concern for others, extraverted; average stability and openness; low conscientiousness
Kagan	Low reactive infants (possible uninhibited toddler)	• Respond to stimulation with minimal motor activity and distress; may become uninhibited in the second year
	High reactive infants (possible inhibited)	• Display vigorous motor activity combined with distress in response to stimulation (auditory, olfactory, and visual); may become inhibited (initial avoidance, distress, or subdued emotions)

Myers		
	ENTJ	• Intuitive, innovative organizer
	ESTJ	• Fact-minded practical organizer
	INTP	• Inquisitive analyzer
	ISTP	• Practical analyzer
	ESTP	• Realistic adapter in material world
	ESFP	• Realistic adapter in human relationships
	ISTJ	• Manager of facts/details in organizations
	ISFJ	• Manager of facts/details among people
	ISFP	• Loyal helper, sees needs of the moment
	INFP	• Independent helper, sees possibilities
	ESFJ	• Practical harmonizer
	ENFJ	• Imaginative harmonizer
	INFJ	• Innovator of ideas, people-oriented
	INTJ	• Innovator of ideas, logical, decisive
	ENFP	• Enthusiastic planner of change
	ENTP	• Inventive, analytic planner of change
Keirsey-Bates	NT	• Rational: knowledge, competence, expertise, logic, pragmatism, trust logic
	NF	• Idealist: unity, self-actualization, authenticity, trust their intuition
	SJ	• Guardian: responsibility, security, stability, community, trust authority
	SP	• Artisan: aesthetics, performance, variety, stimulation, trust their impulses

representing a percentage of those studied (difficult, easy, and slow to warm; see "Personality Types," below). Factor analytic results have confirmed some of the constructs proposed by Thomas and Chess (Presley & Martin, 1994). Other researchers have included additional concepts such as self-regulation in the study of temperament and personality (Neisworth et al., 1999; Rothbart, 2001). They conclude that a young child's failure to develop a mature ability to delay or to inhibit a dominant action in order to perform a nondominant action is strongly linked to the difficulties in self-regulation that are associated with various problems in thinking and behavioral organization (DeGangi, 1991a, 1991b; Neisworth et al.).

Jeffrey Gray (1972, 1985, 1987, 1991) highlighted two neurological systems that compete to control motor behavior and have been linked to behavior and temperament (Martin & Bridger, 1999; Rothbart & Bates, 1998). The *Behavioral Inhibition System* (BIS) is a neuroanatomical system that is sensitive to cues of punishment and nonreward (Martin & Bridger). Its neural substrates include the orbital frontal cortex, medial septal area, hippocampus, and Ascending Reticular Activating System and involve the neurotransmitters norepinephrine and seratonin (Rothbart & Bates, 1998). BIS sets in motion inhibition or anxiety responses to novelty, high-intensity stimulation, cues of punishment, and evolutionarily prepared fears (Martin & Bridger, 1999; Rothbart & Bates, 1998). The *Behavioral Activation System* (BAS) (similar to Panksepp's 1986 *Expectancy-Foraging System* or Depue & Iacano's 1989 *Behavioral Facilitation System, or BFS*) is a neuroanatomical system (brain: medial forebrain bundle, lateral hypothalamus; neurotransmitters: dopamine and norepinephrine) that is sensitive to cues of reward (Martin & Bridger; Rothbart & Bates). It controls behaviors such as exploration and approach responses when there are cues of reward (Martin & Bridger). According to Depue and Iacano, when reward is blocked or a desired avoidance impossible, the BFS may facilitate aggression toward removing an obstacle or threat (cited in Rothbart & Bates). Gray sees a stronger BAS than BIS in extraverts who are high on approach and active avoidance and a strong BIS in introverts who are high on inhibition and anxiety.

Factor Analytic Models

In the past 2 decades, personality psychologists have debated the applicability of a five factor model (or "the Big Five") to account for measurable individual personality differences in adults (Eysenck, 1967; John, Caspi, Robins, Moffitt, & Stouthamer-Loeber, 1994; McCrae & John, 1992; Zhang, Kohnstamm, Slotboom, Elphick, & Cheung, 2002). As one of the methods that have proven useful in hypothesizing, organizing, and integrating personality findings (Caspi, 1998), the five factor model has influenced the study of adult personality development and has begun to be tested for children and adolescents (John et al.; Zhang et al.). For adults, the five factors identified have been given varying names and descriptions (Caspi; McCrae & John; van Lieshout, 2000) and have included the following (Table 6.2): (1) extraversion or surgency (E; sociability, dominance, activity) or extraversion/positive emotionality (the extent to which the person actively engages others or avoids social experiences); (2) agreeableness (A; helpfulness, manageability, honesty, sincerity; continuum from warmth and compassion to antagonism), (3) conscientiousness (C; carefulness, faithfulness, diligence) or conscientiousness/constraint (the extent and strength of impulse control—ability to delay gratification in favor of more distant goals or to modulate impulsive expression); (4) emotional stability (N; emotional reactivity; self-confidence, anxiety, fearfulness) or neuroticism (low emotional stability) or negative emotionality (the extent to which the world is experienced as distressing or threatening); and (5) intellect or openness to experience (O; openness, interest, intelligence).

Factor analyses seek to reveal simple clusters of variables that are structure-discrete and define a dimension (McCrae & John, 1992). Many important personality traits, however, are blends of two or more of the five dimensions (McCrae & John). Measures of shyness, for example, typically combine elements of N and low E (Briggs, 1988). Traits such as "hostile" and "temperamental" may include attributes of high N or low A (McCrae & John). Moreover, in a factor analysis, a different selection of variables can result in a different set of dimensions within the same factor (McCrae & John; Rothbart & Bates, 1998). Nevertheless, although fine-grain analyses permit more specific examination of particular aspects of temperament than factor analyses, factor analyses explore interrelationships among temperament dimensions and between temperament and other variables (Putnam et al., 2001).

Proponents of the five factor model agree that the five factors do not exhaust the description of personality. Instead, they suggest, it represents the highest hierarchical level of trait description (Zhang et al., 2002). Some researchers and theoreticians have argued that five factors are insufficient to summarize all known individual differences in personality. Although earlier theorists have combined personality into fewer than five dimensions, some researchers have found more than five factors for youths (e.g., John et al., 1994; Tellegen & Waller, 1992).

The number of factors appears to vary by age as well as by traits studied. Using the Child Behavior Questionnaire (CBQ), Rothbart, Ahadi et al. (2001) found three main factors for 4 to 5 and for 6 to 7 years olds, but four factors for 3 year olds. Although the five factor model may reasonably represent personality structure in late adolescence and adulthood, Dutch and American analyses suggest an additional two factors (activity and irritability) are needed to describe children and early adolescents (Caspi, 1998). The two additional factors have been statistically related to outcomes also associated with traumatic response: school performance, juvenile delinquency, and internalizing and externalizing behavior problems.

Temperament in Relationship to Trauma

Adults and children vary in the characteristic vigor or intensity of their emotional reactions (Martin & Bridger, 1999). Some are more sensitive to the rewarding aspects and some more sensitive to the punitive and novel aspects of their environments. Although its role has not been widely studied, a child's style of reacting to stress can make a significant difference both during an experience and to the event's outcome for the child (Carey, 1997). Sensitivity and reactivity contribute to a child's immediate responses to stress or crisis. Adaptability, mood, persistence, and other qualities help to shape the ongoing outcome. In addition to differential intensities and sensitivities associated with child traits, nonsimilar youths evoke different responses from others and selectively attend and react to circumstances (Caspi, 1998; Dalgleish, Taghavi, Neshat-Doost, Moradi, Canterbury, & Yule, 2003; Dodge et al., 1995; chapter 3, 13). Kagan (2001) suggests that researchers must find theoretically fruitful ways to discover the temperaments and characteristics that bias children to develop particular profiles and must determine how social factors maintain or alter the profiles acquired during the childhood years.

Temperamental functioning (including aspects related to posttrauma assessment) is influenced by maturation and experience (Rothbart, 2001). For example, behavioral fear appears at 6 to 7 months of age, attentional self-regulation at 10 to 12 months, and the beginnings of effortful control develop rapidly between the toddler and preschool years. The associations between brain locations and development have begun to be identified (Caspi, 1998; Rothbart; Rothbart & Bates, 1998; chapter 2). Temperament also varies between cultures. For example, Ahadi et al. (1993) found that for Chinese respondents, effortful control correlated negatively with extraversion but did not correlate with negative affectivity. In studies of U.S. adults and children, effortful control correlated negatively with negative affectivity and did not correlate with extraversion (Rothbart, Ahadi et al., 2001). Rothbart and her colleagues suggest that effortful self-regulation may be employed to inhibit culturally discouraged tendencies (negative affect in the United States, extraversion in China).

A number of theoreticians and statisticians have suggested that personality factors play a part in psychopathology including PTSD. Traits may create vulnerabilities to particular kinds of stressors such as failure to achieve impossible goals for the obsessive-compulsive or abandonment for the dependent personality (Otis & Louks, 1997). Boehnlin (2001) suggests that an obsessive personality style may be more vigilant for the cascade of symptoms that lead to panic (or, for Cambodians, to *kyol goeu*; see chapter 7). Although most inhibited children will not be diagnosed as adults with one of the anxiety disorders, Biederman et al. (1990) found increased risk of multiple anxiety, overanxious, and phobic disorders for inhibited children (see Kagan, Snidman, & Arcus, 1995).

Personality may affect a youth's response to and needs in treatment and assessment. Youths whose trust has been damaged, introverts (Myers & Myers, 1995), or youths with slow-to-warm personality styles (Chess & Thomas, 1991) may need additional time to develop trust. Silence or temporary "shutdown" may indicate an introvert's need to reflect on thoughts, feelings, and ideas before sharing them; tendency to share thoughts and feelings in bits and pieces; and proneness to "shut down" if deprived too long of "alone time" (Kurcinka, 1998a, 1998b). Berens (1998) explains that *idealists* (emphasis: intuition and feeling) are especially stressed by betrayal, insincerity, and lack of integrity. *Rationals* (emphasis: intuition and thinking/knowledge) are particularly stressed by powerlessness, incompetence, and lack of knowledge (see also Keirsey & Bates, 1978). Some youths are particularly attuned to injustice, are sensitive to stimuli and the emotions of others, are prone to focus on the future or the past, or have different paces at processing information. Traits affect initial and ongoing response.

Scales and Measures

A number of scales are available to assess the temperamental traits of infants (see Rothbart, Chew et al., 2001) and children. At this time, fewer are available for adolescents. Some of the scales are described here and in Table 6.4.

The Child Behavior Questionnaire (BQ)
Age range: 3–8 years (see Associated Scales for other age groups' scales)
Translation: Spanish
Format: Parent-report (self-report: EATQ and ATQ)
Associated scales: IBQ-R (3–12 months); ECBQ (18–30 months); EATQ (9–16 years); ATQ (17 and older)

CBQ (Rothbart & Gartstein, 2000) is a parent report questionnaire theoretically derived from temperament dimensions (e.g., emotional reactivity, arousability, self-regulation) and their associated subconstructs (Rothbart, Ahadi et al., 2001). Unlike factor-derived scales, which are often heterogenous, CBQ's larger constructs are relatively homogenous. Because temperamental functioning is influenced by maturation, there are Behavioral Questionnaires for Infancy (IBQ-R), Early Childhood (ECBQ), Childhood (CBQ), Early Adolescence (EATQ), and Late Adolescence into Adulthood (ATQ) (see age ranges in "Associated scales," above; Rothbart, Ahadi et al.). Scales and subscales vary accordingly. The CBQ scales include positive anticipation, smiling/laughter (mood), high intensity pleasure (sensation seeking), activity level, impulsivity (speed of response initiation), shyness (behavioral inhibition), discomfort (distress), fear (fear and withdrawal), anger/frustration (related to the strength of expectation of reward and

TABLE 6.4.
Measures of Personality and Temperamental Traits

Measure (Age range)	∝ Internal Consistency	Interrater r	Test-retest r	Assesses/Measures (Scale or Subscale r; distinguishes)	Authors (Available from)
CBQ (age 3–8 + scales for older ages)	.64–.94 s	.69. .28–.79 P-P		Temperament characteristics	Rothbart & Gartstein, 2000 (www.darkwing.uoregon.edu/~maryroth)
Poz (infants to age 5)				Temperament characteristics	Carey & McDevitt, 1978; 1995a (www.preventiveoz.org or The Preventive Ounce, a Nonprofit, Preventive Mental Health Organization, 354 63rd Street, Oakland, CA 94618)
TABSC-R (age 2–7)	.71–.90 P s .86–.95 T s	.34–.66 P-P .25–.35 P-T	.59–.76 s 1 yr. .54–.72 s 2 yr. .53–.61 s 3 yr.	Temperament characteristics (Low r between inhibition and impulsivity)	Martin & Bridger, 1999 (Roy Martin, rpmartin@coe.uga.edu)
TABS (infancy to almost age 6)	.83 Split-half r = .72 no risk C (.68–.86 s) .91 C w/disabilities (.64–.84 s)		.90 2–3 wk.	Dysfunctional behaviors	Bagnato, Neisworth, Salvia, & Hunt, 1999 (www.brookespublishing.com or Brookes Publishing Company, P.O. Box 10624, Baltimore, MD 21285-0624)

RCMAS (age 6–19)	.60–.80 (except m over 15) KR20 = .83–.85 (.78 for black f ages 10–11)	.69 9 mo. .98 3 wk.	Levels and nature of anxiety (RCMAS and State-Trait Anxiety Inventory for Children Trait Scale [Spielberger, 1973])	Reynolds & Richmond, 1978 (WPS, 12031 Wilshire Blvd., Los Angeles, CA, 90025-1251; 310-478-2061 or 800-648-8857; Fax: 310-478-7838)
MMTIC (age 7–14)	Spearman-Brown split-half r = .62–.75 s	Significant with no change for 70% of C	Jungian based traits.	Murphy, 1986; Murphy & Meisgeier, 1987 (www.capt.org or Consulting Psychologists Press, 3803 E. Bayshore Road, Palo Alto, CA 94303)
SSQ (age 8–17)		.67–.80 7 mo.	Jungian based traits. (Distinguishes cultural differences in trait preferences)	Oakland, Glutting, & Horton, 1996 (Harcourt Assessment, Inc., 19500 Bulverde Road, San Antonio, TX 87259-3701; 800-221-8378)

$\propto$ = alpha; C = children; dis = disabilities; f = females; KR20 = Kuder-Richardson formula 20; m = males; mo. = months; P = parent; s= for subscales; T = teacher; wk. =weeks; yr. = year

Sources: Martin & Bridger, 1999; Murphy & Meisgeier, 1987; Neisworth, Bagnato, Salvia, & Hunt, 1999; Reynolds & Richmond, 2000; Rothbart, Ahadi, Hershey, & Fisher, 2001.

aggressive self-regulation), sadness, soothability, inhibitory control, attentional focusing, low intensity pleasure (nonrisk-taking pleasure), and perceptual sensitivity (threshold of sensitivity or external sensitivity). For U.S., Chinese, and Japanese children, factor analysis of CBQ recovered three broad dimensions of temperament: extraversion/surgency, negative affectivity, and effortful control.

The Preventive Ounce (Poz)
Age range: 4–12 months; 1–3 years; 3–5 years
Translations: Spanish
Format: Parent completion

The Preventive Ounce Questionnaires are derivatives of the Carey questionnaires (Carey & McDevitt, 1978, 1995a) and years of research studies with Kaiser Permanente in Oakland, CA. The major differences between these questionnaires and those of Carey and his associates are (1) the scoring for the preschooler questionnaire generates more scales than the toddler measures and flows more from the toddler than from the infant questionnaire; (2) frustration tolerance questions are added; and (3) redundant mood questions are removed. Subdividing the intensity levels for toddlers or preschoolers into positive events, negative events, and new situations improved predictability to specific behavioral problems and helped parents better understand their children's temperaments (Cameron, 2002). All three questionnaires include basic information (e.g., birth order, infant characteristics) and a sheet to list current concerns. The infant questionnaire is 46 items; the toddler, 67 items; and the preschooler, 69 items. Items are rated as true for the child on a six-point scale (1 = Almost never . . . 6 = Almost always). A Web site provides scales, scoring, and profiles.

The Temperament Assessment Battery for Children-Revised (TABC-R)
Age range: 2–7
Scales: Parent and teacher on child temperament
Format: Caretaker or teacher completion

The Temperament Assessment Battery for Children-Revised (Martin & Bridger, 1999) consists of two forms, a 37-item parent form (PF) and 29-item teacher form (TF). It includes theory-based measures of children's temperamental characteristics based on NYLS dimensions of temperament (Chess & Thomas, 1977) and the neuropsychological theory of Jeffrey Gray (Table 6.2). TABC-R was primarily designed to determine temperamental types or groups of children with a common pattern of temperamental characteristics (i.e., impulsive, inhibited, highly emotional, typical, reticent, and uninhibited). Traits assessed include impulsivity, inhibition, negative emotionality, activity level, and lack of task persistence. On the teacher form, an additional passive type is identified. The TABC-R inhibition scale was developed as a measure of BIS functions, and the impulsivity scale, as a measure of BAS functions. The inhibition scale measures withdrawal from new social situations, hesitance in approaching strangers, and cautiousness about engaging in activities in novel situations. The impulsivity scale is designed to measure the child's inability to control intense emotion, gross motor activity, and attention in three related scales: (1) negative emotionality (the tendency to engage in emotional behaviors such as crying, screaming, and temper tantrums resulting primarily from frustration or denial of wants); (2) activity level (gross motor activity and the inability to control gross motor behaviors); and (3) lack of task persistence (the inability of the child to continue to engage in learning new tasks or to maintain attention over relatively long periods of time). Normative data are available (Martin & Bridger). The caretaker or teacher rates the frequency of a context-specific item regarding the child's behavior.

The Temperament and Atypical Behavior Scale (TABS)
Age range: 11–71 months (i.e., almost 1 to almost 6 years)
Format: Parent or professional completion

TABS (Bagnato, Neisworth, Salvia, & Hunt, 1999) is a 55-item measure of dysfunctional behavior for infants and young children (Neisworth et al., 1999). TABS is intended to identify children at risk for, or already, developing atypically with regard to temperament and self-regulation. Learned and developmentally delayed behaviors are excluded. The 15-item TABS screener permits rapid identification of children in need of more thorough assessment. The TABS assessment tool contains a checklist of specific behaviors. One or both parents can record (Yes or No) whether the child in question exhibits a behavior and whether the parents need help with the behavior. Four subtests are *detached* (withdrawn, aloof, self-absorbed, difficult to engage, and disconnected from everyday routines involving adults or other children; commonly associated with autism spectrum disorder); *hypersensitive/active* (overreactive to even slight environmental stimulation, impulsive, highly active, negative, and defiant; commonly associated with attention-deficit/hyperactivity disorder); *underreactive* (unresponsive and requires intense environmental stimulation to elicit a response, limited awareness, low alertness, passivity, and lethargy; commonly associated with a variety of severe neurodevelopmental problems); and *dysregulated* (difficulty controlling or modulating neurophysiological behavior and oral-motor control) (Neisworth et al.).

Trait Anxiety

The Revised Children's Manifest Anxiety Scale (RCMAS)
Age range: 6–19
Format: Child completion with examiner present (individually or in a group setting for children 9 1/2 or older; individually for younger children)

RCMAS ("What I Think and Feel"; Reynolds & Richmond, 1978), a revision of CMAS, is a 37-item, self-report instrument designed to assess the level and nature of anxiety in children and adolescents. It is based on theories of trait anxiety (Taylor, 1951; Spielberger, 1972), which, in contrast to state anxiety, is a more lasting predisposition to experience anxiety in a variety of settings (Reynolds & Richmond, 2000). Statements are answered by circling "Yes" or "No" to indicate whether the item is descriptive of the child's feelings or actions. The scale yields a total anxiety score and four subscale scores: (1) physiological anxiety, (2) worry/oversensitivity, (3) social concerns/concentration, and (4) lie. A high score indicates a high level of anxiety or lie on that subscale (Reynolds & Richmond, 2000). The RCMAS is intended to assist the assessment of anxiety and should be used with other sources of information (e.g., clinicians, teachers, and parents). Normative data are available.

PERSONALITY TYPES

> Because temperament encompasses organized systems of emotional and attentional processes, rather than separate traits, studies of relationships among temperament variables allow a much richer view of development. (Rothbart, 2001, p. 15590)

Classifications of personality that identify categories of individuals based on configurations of traits (e.g., types, factors) may improve communication among researchers, provide a usable structure for assessment or analysis, help to generate hypotheses, and assist the integration of findings (Caspi, 1998). Personality taxonomies (e.g., the Big Five/Seven, Type) are too broad to capture all of the interesting variations in personality and relationships to other variables that may be obtained in examining more specific traits. However, as Caspi has pointed out, it is possible that trait dimensions and person typologies are complementary rather than competing systems. Examining the association between different types of personalities (to follow) and traumatic reactions also may help to prevent the canceling out of effects (Lipschitz, Morgan, & Southwick, 2002; chapter 2). As can be seen in the descriptions that follow, type theories share some of their components (Table 6.3). For example, Gray's BIS, Kagan's inhibited, Chess and Thomas' slow to warm, and Block's over-controller all have aspects of Jung's introversion function.

Types Derived from the Preceding Studies and Theories of Traits

NYLS

The NYLS of temperament dimensions identified three types of infants representing a percentage of those studied (difficult, easy, and slow to warm) (Carey, 1997; Carey & McDevitt, 1995b; Chess & Thomas, 1977, 1991; Kurcinka, 1998a; Rothbart, Chew et al., 2001). The *difficult* (*challenging* or *spirited*) child was characterized by low rhythmicity, high withdrawal, slow adaptation to change, intense reactions, and high frequency of negative mood. *Easy* children were the opposite. *Slow-to-warm* children had low-intensity negative reactions to new stimuli/situations but tended to adapt after repeated exposures. These temperament clusters when found in infancy (but not at age 3) have correlated with home and school adjustment at age 5 (Nelson et al., 1999). The difficult temperament is reportedly vulnerable to stress reactions (W. B. Carey, personal communication, 1999; Carey & McDevitt, 1995b).

Block's Q-Sort Types

Block (1971; cited in Caspi, 1998) used a Q-sort technique (sorting personality attribute cards in order from those least like to those most like an individual) and an inverse factor analysis to identify clusters of individuals with similar profiles. Three of the five personality types Block identified have remained stable across adolescence into adulthood, been replicated for males and females, and found for Finnish, Icelandic, and U.S. youths (as well as among five New Zealand youth types). The three types are *ego-resilients* or *resilients* (well-functioning cognitively, emotionally, and interpersonally; most prevalent); *vulnerable overcontrollers* or *overcontrollers* (few interpersonal skills, shy, inward); and *unsettled undercontrollers* or *undercontrollers* (hostile, disagreeable, show little concern for others). Differences in these types or traits found in very young children have been linked to particular kinds of problems (e.g., internalizing, externalizing) in later childhood and adolescence (Caspi).

Resilients score moderately high on all Big-Five personality factors (Caspi, 1998; van Lieshout, 2000). *Undercontrollers* score high on extraversion, low on conscientiousness, very low on agreeableness, and average on stability and openness. *Overcontrollers* score low on extraversion and emotional stability, and average on agreeableness, openness, and conscientiousness. For infants, Rothbart & Bates (1998) identified two kinds of negative affectivity: (1) fearful distress and anxiety when confronted with novelty and (2) angry distress and irritability when confronted with limitations and frustration. *Overcontrollers* tend to show fearful distress and anxiety (van Lieshout). Undercontrollers tend to show angry distress and irritability. Researchers have found differences among cultures in the tendency toward overcontrolled or undercontrolled problems (Mash & Dozois, 2003). For example, in separate study comparisons with U.S. youths who were rated higher on undercontrolled problems, Jamaican, Thai, and Kenyan youths were rated higher on overcontrolled problems.

Kagan's High and Low Reactive Infants

Kagan (1997) described a modest correlation between temperamental reactivity in infancy and behavior style in toddlers (e.g., inhibited, uninhibited). He also found an association between reactivity and physiological qualities (e.g., high reactive: narrower faces; higher resting heart rate for 4-year-old boys; more allergies; heritability) and psychological dispositions (e.g., inhibited: more social phobias). High reactive infants (about 20% of healthy European American samples) assessed at 4 months displayed vigorous motor activity combined with distress in response to stimulation (auditory, olfactory, and visual) (Kagan et al., 1995). Low reactive infants (about 40% of healthy European American samples) responded to stimulation with minimal motor activity and distress. Low reactives were most likely to become uninhibited in the second year; high reactives, more prone to be inhibited. Inhibited children reacted with initial avoidance, distress, or subdued emotions.

It is common for temperamentally high or low reactive infants to develop a less extreme profile (Kagan et al., 1995). It is less likely for the environment to create a consistently uninhibited style in a high reactive infant or a consistently inhibited profile in a low reactive. Whether children classified in infancy (4 months old) as high reactive or low reactive become inhibited or uninhibited at age 4 is influenced by environment (e.g., parenting). For example, high reactive infants raised by overprotective mothers in a nontraumatic environment have been rated more inhibited as toddlers.

Kagan (1997) suggested that most youths and adults who think about committing a crime are restrained by anticipatory anxiety, shame, or guilt. Accordingly, children with a less excitable amygdala or a less responsive ventromedial surface would not have the typical intensity of the restraining feelings. If they grow up in neighborhoods and homes that deter antisocial or delinquent behavior, they may become leaders. If not, they may become candidates for a violent delinquent career (Kagan). From studies that found that low resting heart rates in children correlated with antisocial and aggressive behavior, Lipschitz et al. (2002) observed that youths with chronically underaroused autonomic nervous systems may be biologically prone to thrill-seeking behavior and less responsive to punishment. Greater skin conductance and higher heart rates in noncriminal adults with histories of delinquency or family histories of criminality may mean that either increased autonomic responsiveness serves as a protective factor against criminal outcomes or there are two biological subtypes of conduct disturbances. Lipschitz et al. suggest that early and severe childhood trauma that alters the stress-sensitive neurobiological systems may be among the factors that explain differences in autonomic reactivity and its relationship to conduct disturbances.

Biederman et al. (1990) found that compared to controls and "not inhibited" (but not uninhibited by Kagan's definition) children, a small sample of inhibited children were more likely to have all evaluated disorders (major depression, attention-deficit, oppositional, overanxious, phobic, separation anxiety, and avoidant disorders) and significantly more often had overanxious disorder. From the Kagan et al. (1995) longitudinal cohort (mean age approximately 8), Biederman et al. found oppositional disorder was significantly lower, phobic disorder significantly higher, and multiple anxiety disorders substantially higher for the inhibited than the uninhibited children.

Jung's Mental Functions

One set of theorists base personality types on Carl Jung's idea that people favor one from each of two kinds of mental functions (Table 6.2): (1) perception: sensation versus intuition (S vs. N; focus on concrete vs. abstract realities) and (2) judgment: thinking versus feeling (T vs. F; use objective vs. subjective judgment criteria). Jung described eight types characterized by the predominance of one of the functions expressed in either an extroverted (E) or introverted (I) way (Berens & Nardi, 1999; Berens, 1985, 1998; Lawrence, 1993; Jung, 1971; Myers & McCaulley, 1985). Myers added an additional dichotomy to Jung's set (J vs. P; judging vs. perceiving—wanting things settled vs. keeping options open), resulting in 16 personality profiles (Myers & McCaulley; Table 6.3). Keirsey and Bates (1978) outlined four main types (sensing-judging, SJ; sensing-perceiving, SP; intuitive-feeling, NF; intuitive-thinking, NT), each including 4 of the 16 personality types. A dominant type is believed to emerge between ages 6 and 14 (Meisgeier & Murphy, 1987). Well-balanced type development includes unequal but adequate (1) development of a judging function/process and perceiving function/process with superior skill in one of the two processes and (2) facility in using both the extraverted and the introverted attitudes, with one predominating (Myers & Myers, 1995; Otis & Louks, 1997). As in left- or right-handedness, people are happier and perform better when they are able to use their preferred personality style (Oakland, Glutting, & Horton, 1996). Moreover, function preferences are associated with differences in information processing, needs, and value judgments as well as with differences in brain wave patterns and hemispheric bias in response to stimuli (Alcock & Murphy, 1998).

Theoreticians suggest that extreme and prolonged stress may result in exaggeration of a function, dominance of a less refined function, or the extension of a function to inappropriate domains (Quenk, 1985; Otis & Louks, 1997). Studies of type and PTSD are few and have generally examined adults. Two studies of veterans (Dalton et al., 1993; Otis & Louks) suggest a strong tendency toward introversion in the PTSD samples. Both studies found more practical analyzer (ISTP) and inquisitive analyzer (INTP) types (Tables 6.2, 6.3) among those with PTSD. Because symptoms of PTSD can change personality characteristics, it is not known whether the traits measured precede or follow from trauma. For example, social isolation may be a result of PTSD and has been associated with the probability of PTSD (Dalton et al.). Lack of social support has been a risk factor for children (Udwin et al., 2000). At least after combat, not all INTPs or ISTPs develop PTSD. Other factors (e.g., family environment), therefore, also play a part in the results (Dalton et al.).

Rather than to label or categorize children, proponents of Jungian type theory strongly encourage that type assessment be used to accurately describe preferences and to (1) identify talent, (2) adjust for possible weaknesses, (3) enhance personal and social development, (4) promote an understanding of others, (5) assess learning styles, (6) promote educational development, (7) explore prevocational interests, and (8) facilitate research and evaluation studies (Oakland et al., 1996).

The Murphy-Meisgeier Type Indicator for Children (MMTIC)
Age range: 7–14
Format: Child completion, group completion

MMTIC (Murphy, 1986; Murphy & Meisgeier, 1987) is a 70-item measure that assesses the same four preference scales as the Myers-Briggs Type Indicator for Adults (Myers & McCaulley, 1985). It is a self-report instrument designed to assess individual type differences in children. It examines a child's report of how he or she best perceives and processes information and prefers to interact socially and behaviorally with others. The manual provides a description of the 16 types and the characteristics of the dichotomies as well as suggestions for how type may be applied in the classroom (Meisgeier & Murphy, 1987).

The Students Style Questionnaire (SSQ)
Age range: 8–17
Format: Child completion, individually or in groups

SSQ (Oakland et al., 1996) includes 69 items to measure individual differences in students' preferences for eight styles as well as temperaments and personal styles (Oakland et al.; Horton & Oakland, 1997). SSQ includes the following styles: extroverted or introverted (i.e., ways students prefer to gain energy and direction; E-I), practical or imaginative (preferred manner of generally orienting their lives; instead of S-N), thinking or feeling (preferred ways of making decisions—based on thinking or on feeling; T-F), and organized or flexible (preferred timing/manner of making decisions—as soon or as late as possible; instead of J-P). SSQ is intended to identify personal preferences that constitute strengths (Oakland et al.).

CONCLUSIONS

In the assessment of traumatic reactions, age and developmental level help to dictate a youth's ability to respond to self-report measures or to instructions (for diagnosis or treatment), the nature of symptoms and reactions, the character and focus of memories, and the normalcy of behaviors. Temperamental differences also affect youths' traumatic reactions, reporting styles, vulnerabilities, and needs in treatment. A number of traits or trait combinations have been associated with vulnerability to traumatic reactions or to outcomes that occur over time that also have been linked to trauma. In order to clearly understand the effects of these variables and their outcomes, detailed information is needed regarding children and adolescents' characteristics (e.g., temperament, worldview, behaviors, level of inhibition) before, during, and after traumatic events and into adulthood.

7

Culture and Family Background

Differences in sociopolitical and historical backgrounds, linguistic expressions, health terminology, the articulation of distress, customs, beliefs, shared experiences, worldviews, and other background factors affect the recounting, expression, and experience of traumatic events and recovery needs (Kirmayer, Young, & Hayton, 1995; Phan & Silove, 1997; Westermeyer, 1987, 1990; Box 7.1). Family variables such as culture, religion, other group membership, parenting style, relationships, and socioeconomic status (SES) influence or define characteristic reactions to extreme stress, access to assistance, and therapeutic needs. For instance, studies of anxiety disorders in varied cultures have revealed differences in the prevalence of types of anxiety, the prominence of specific symptoms, and the nature and pathology levels of particular behaviors and syndromes (e.g., somatic, dissociative, and affective; Kirmayer et al.). A youth's background may affect his or her ability to establish rapport and understand an interviewer as well as the youth's reporting style, willingness to answer questions accurately, and understanding of questions, experiences, and words. To follow are some aspects of a youth's history and background that may affect the nature of traumatic reactions and the assessment process. This chapter primarily focuses on culture after a brief discussion of other family issues.

FAMILY CIRCUMSTANCES

Levels of environmental stimulation and opportunities to develop skills affect a child's physical (e.g., brain, size), emotional (e.g., awareness, understanding), behavioral (e.g., skills, reactions), and cognitive development. The circumstances that occur for adopted children underscore the need to explore a youth's history and background in order to accurately

BOX 7.1
Case Examples

a. *The Hate Crime*. John was a 17-year-old Native American youth who was restrained by large adolescent boys and forced to watch while they beat his friend to death. John attended a school in which there was much prejudice against Native Americans. In an attempt to fit in, he had rejected much of his heritage and adopted mainstream values. The boys who beat his Native American friend to death with a baseball bat had punched John in his mid region and in the face. It is likely that he was spared more deadly injuries because of his football-playing skills. After his friend's death, he was extremely depressed. His injuries only reminded him that he was safe while his friend was dead. He felt guilty and expressed anger at any attempt to help him. John's grandfather, a tribe elder, arranged a sweat lodge in order to cleanse his spirit and provide an avenue for self-examination.

   The elder decided to include two of the "White" football players who were friends of John. A permanent lodge was available for the sweat lodge ceremony, but the elder had the boys build a sweat lodge from flexible tree branches and blankets. One of the football players had a distant Native American relative. Both were sympathetic and unhappy about the prejudice in the school. It was not until the elder began to smudge (ceremonially cleanse) the lodge that John's resistance began to fade. When they invited in the Grandfathers and Grandmothers (sacred Spirits), he felt fully at home. The mental images or visions that John saw during the 3-hour ceremony were meaningful to him. His friends had their own images that seemed to relate both to John and to their personal histories. The sweat lodge experience appeared to change John's attitude. He was able to process his experience with a therapist after that. The two other boys became protective of John and began to advocate for changes in the school after the sweat lodge.

b. *The War*. Abdul was 17 and had tried to help the Kuwaiti resistance during the war. Other adolescents had helped as well. During his assessment interview, Abdul described an image that haunted him. He had seen a 16-year-old girl whom he knew running dazed and exposed through the street. He knew what had happened to her at the hands of the Iraqi soldiers. He knew that her family would kill her because of it. He wanted to change things. "Did not the girls fight with us during the war? Do not they deserve to be honored as well?" he asked. He described the details of the red splotches on her body. He wanted to run to help her but was afraid of being shot. He wanted to go to her family to tell them . . . Always when he dreamed of the war, he dreamed of this girl, helpless and out of his reach.

c. *The Sniper Attack*. Lu was 7 when the sniper fired on her elementary school ground. Several children were killed and others were injured. After the shootings, Lu, her parents, and her friends were afraid for the children to return to the school. They believed that the bad spirit of the sniper and the angry spirits of the dead children could not pass from this world but instead would wander about the schoolyard. Lu and her friends thought that the unsettled spirits might grab them and take them into the next world. The children returned to school after Cambodian and Vietnamese Buddhist monks, a Vietnamese Catholic priest, and Protestant ministers performed a blessing ceremony that included ceremonies for the dead souls.

d. *The International Adoption*. Jennifer was adopted from an orphanage in the former U.S.S.R. In the orphanage, all decisions were made for her. She did what everyone else did, ate when everyone else ate, went to school when everyone else did, and used the restroom on a schedule. No one ever asked her how she felt emotionally, told her how they felt, or reflected her emotions back to her. There was no opportunity to develop decision-making, labeling of her own or others' feelings, awareness of specific likes and dislikes, or other "normal" skills and aspects of self-awareness.

assess and compare their posttrauma behaviors and symptoms (see Box 7.1d, "International Adoptions" below).

Shared and Nonshared Influences

A child's personality, behavior, and postevent symptoms are influenced by genetic and environmental factors. Shared environmental factors (such as divorce or economic status) enhance similarities between family members, whereas nonshared environmental factors (such as favoritism or attending different schools) promote differences between family members (Caspi, 1998). Specific shared environmental influences (e.g., childhood parental loss through death or divorce) have increased the adult risk of symptoms (e.g., depression, anxiety) and traits (e.g., neuroticism, see chapter 6). In addition to differences within a family, youths have differential experiences with peers, with teachers, and in their neighborhoods. When longitudinal studies follow youths into adult life, the primary influence shifts from the family of origin to the family of destination (Caspi, 1998). Nonshared environmental factors account for substantial variation in temperamental traits and may affect coping styles, reactivity, sociability, and other variables associated with posttrauma reaction levels. Subscales that assess the family environment are included in some of the comprehensive scales in chapter 15. The Family Environment Scale (Moos & Moos, 1986) has been used to evaluate global family behaviors without identifying the specific actor (parent or child) for Euro American, Hispanic, and Southeast Asian populations (Rousseau & Drapeau, 1998).

Research indicates that genetic influences on childhood temperament and on adolescent and adult personality are substantial (Caspi, 1998). Genes interact with one another and with the environment. Gene-environment interactions, for example, have been implicated in some studies of aggression and crime (outcomes that also have been linked to trauma). Age may be a factor in genetic influence, however. Research has established a substantial genetic influence on adult criminality but less so for juvenile delinquency (Caspi). The association between genetics and behaviors may be indirect. For example, the link between parental divorce, or the stress it engenders, and child conduct problems may be at least partially a function of parental psychopathology (e.g., antisocial personality disorder) or other factors (e.g., economic, neighborhood).

Socioeconomic Status

Low socioeconomic status is a powerful correlate of multiple risk factors that may combine to thwart positive adaptation. Researchers have found that SES disadvantage has a deleterious effect on youths' cognitive, intellectual, social, and emotional development (Yates, Egeland, & Sroufe, 2003). Poverty has been associated with lower IQ, verbal ability, and achievement test scores; grade retention, special education placement, and school dropout; and psychiatric disorders and behavioral and emotional problems (Costello, Farmer, Angold, Burns, & Erkanli, 1997; Yates et al.). Parenting has served as a primary mediator of the effects of poverty on child development. Poverty, however, may contribute to poor parental emotional well-being, harsh and punitive parenting, insufficient attention to offspring, inadequate time and other resources to provide sensitive care, and less stable caregiving patterns and daily routines. Consequently, poverty may contribute to insecure attachments and the related risk factors (see chapter 5, 8).

Family factors such as SES and location have been associated with levels of traumatic response in adults and children. Inner-city locations, minority status, and low SES, for example, have been linked to increased exposure to stressful life events (Cohen & Kasen, 1999). Differentiating the effects of each of these variables may be difficult because they so frequently co-occur. When cultural groups split along SES lines, SES differences may underlie findings with regard to cultural or ethnic group membership. Similarly, samples of maltreated children often have economic hardships (see Bolger & Patterson, 2003), making it important to rule out these influences from findings.

Youths living in urban communities in the United States frequently are exposed to daily violence (Self-Brown, LeBlanc, & Kelley, 2004). Self-Brown et al. studied 80 adolescent high school students. Daily stress and violence exposure were significantly, moderately, and positively correlated. At higher but not lower levels of daily stress, there was a significant positive correlation between violence exposure and externalizing problems and between violence exposure and internalizing problems. Thus, for adolescents chronically exposed to violence, daily stress increases risk.

Residents of disadvantaged communities struggle with higher unemployment rates, fewer available jobs, access to fewer resources, declines in social organization, and a reduced sense of efficacy among residents (Deardorff, Gonzales, & Sandler, 2003). Recent studies indicate that community poverty predicts poor adjustment for children and adolescents. Adolescent depression, for example, is influenced by family poverty and community violence. Conditions of family and neighborhood poverty and disadvantage, often found in U.S. inner cities, may predispose youths to symptoms and disorders because these conditions expose them to repeated proximal negative life events.

Social Support

Survival as a species is dependent upon the ability to successfully form and maintain relationships (Bowlby, 1969/1982; Perry, 2006). "Of the 250,000 years or so that our species has been on the planet, we spent 245,000 years living in small transgenerational hunter-gatherer bands of 40–50 individuals. The human brain evolved specific capabilities that are . . . adaptations of living in the natural world in transgenerational groups . . . . For each child under the age of six, there were four developmentally more mature persons who could protect, educate, enrich and nurture the developing child . . . ." (Perry, pp. 44–45). Perry suggests that, contrary to our brains' preference, we currently live in a relationally impoverished world. Relational support is important to physical survival and emotional health. Following traumatic events, higher levels of social support have been associated with lower levels of trauma for both children and adults (Boehnlein, 2001; Compas & Epping, 1993; de Silva, 1999; Kaniasty & Norris, 1993; La Greca, Silverman, Vernberg, & Prinstein, 1996; Rabalais, Ruggiero, & Scotti, 2002).

Some researchers have found that social support serves as a protective factor when the type of support provided matches the type of support needed—emotional support, advocacy, providing needed resources (Rabalais et al., 2002). In addition to instrumental and emotional support, Harter, Waters, and Whitesell (1998) have added approval support and validation support (a subtype of approval; people show interest and respect in what the individual thinks, says, and feels). The two types of support have been strongly linked to self-worth.

A few studies have examined the role of social support in relationship to youths' traumatic reactions. Children exposed to Hurricane Andrew reported moderate levels of social support, primarily from parents and close friends and some from classmates, at 3 months after the hurricane (Vernberg, La Greca, Silverman, & Prinstein, 1996). At 7 and 10 months after the hurricane, higher amounts of social support were associated with lower levels of trauma symptoms (La Greca et al., 1996). At 10 months after the hurricane, low support from teachers was especially predictive of symptoms (La Greca et al.). Udwin, Boyle, Yule, Bolton, & O'Ryan (2000) also found that lack of school support was associated with increased symptoms over time. Research is needed to determine the differences in outcome for perceived versus received support, for support that restores resources, and for support that does or does not match the type of support needed (Rabalais et al., 2002). Measures of social support have been included in scales such as MAGIC and CAPA (see chapter 15). The Network of Relationships Inventory (NRI; Fuhrman & Buhrmester, 1985) includes 30 items to assess 10 relationship qualities such as companionship, conflict, instrumental aid, antagonism, intimacy, nurturance, admiration, relative power, and reliable alliance.

CULTURE

Although development essentially proceeds in the same manner across cultures, the events, circumstances, and conditions called history as well as the beliefs and attitudes relevant to assessment vary by culture (McCrae, 2001). Hofstede (1980) defined culture as the collective mental programming that people of a group, a tribe, a geographical region, a national minority, or a nation have in common. Culture encompasses a number of individuals who were conditioned by the same educational and life experiences. In addition to national cultures are the cultures that develop for groups with regional, occupational, academic, religious, and experiential elements in common. A resemblance among symptom clusters in the study of more than one culture does not certify that the same disorder or experience has been validly identified in each of the cultures (Phan & Silove, 1997; see Cultural Adaptation chapter 4). Each culture defines accepted reactions to catastrophic experiences and the tolerated expression of emotions. In many ways, directly and indirectly, trauma is defined by an individual's sociocultural internalized beliefs and attitudes (de Silva, 1999). The meaning of the event to a culture affects the community's reactions to and labeling of an event and the victims. Cultures dictate responses of ostracism, admiration, sorrow, pride, pity, shame, or support. They help to determine reactions to an event by defining its nature. A war, for example, may be called a necessary action, a just and holy war, an unsought invasion, an act of terrorism, or a mercenary intrusion. Cultures label the proponents or recipients of an event as hero, martyr, victim, survivor, tainted/shamed, evil, or mercenary.

The assessment of culture's influence on outcomes is complicated by issues of acculturation (Kirmayer et al., 1995; Triandis, Kashima, Shimada, & Villareal, 1986) and the fact that travel, electronic communication (radio, television, the Internet), and the availability of written materials place many of the world's populations in a "complex connectedness" (Weine, 2001). Members of an original culture and their descendents have varied rates of adaptation and acculturation to the nation in which they are assessed. Blended or original sociocultural beliefs and values interact with personal, familial, social/political, and economic factors in producing and maintaining panic and other trauma symptoms (Boehnlein, 2001; Kirmayer, et al.). Attitudes regarding ethnophysiological response, attentional focus, expectations, and spiritual beliefs may combine variously with individual personality and physiological traits including autonomic arousal.

Cultural issues are important to many aspects of assessment such as translating measures (chapter 4), comparing age and gender groups (chapter 6), assessing temperamental and behavioral change (chapter 6), and conducting clinical and diagnostic interviews. Cultural and religious differences contribute to the meaning attributed to the event; reactions to helping professionals; acknowledgment or silence about injuries and reactions; the response to loss; the need for action, inaction, or reclusion; the methods of restoring safety; the management of anxiety; the support for or suspicion of one another; coping styles; symptoms; and more. Spiritual beliefs may influence or dictate responses to crises. As sources of comfort and as anchors, they may mitigate traumatic reactions, or they may promote a sense of hopelessness and helplessness (Hines, 1998; Tully, 1999).

Culture and Perception

Cultural conditioning may influence research findings by shaping researchers' descriptions and definitions of terms, their limitations on assessment, and interpretations of findings. As a result, defined symptoms, types, and levels as well as the information gathered may not adequately describe traumatic reactions in all cultures. In a classroom exercise to demonstrate the impact of culture, Hofstede (1980) used an ambiguous picture that can be interpreted two ways: "an attractive young woman" or "an ugly old woman." Half of the students view one picture (the young woman), and half view the other picture (the old woman) for 5 seconds before being presented the combined ambiguous picture. When viewing the combined image picture, most of the students could only see the picture they saw initially (i.e., if "conditioned" by seeing the old woman, they tended to see only the old woman; if conditioned by seeing the young woman, they saw only her). Members of each group found it very difficult to explain what they saw to the other group and, sometimes with considerable irritation, complained of the other group's *stupidity.* Thus, only 5 seconds of conditioning can have a strong effect on perception and behavior (Hofstede). For most individuals (including researchers), culture has a lifetime to influence expectations, perceptions, values, and behaviors.

Culture and Other Variables

Pacing in treatment, the appropriate manner for reframing treatment methods or aspects of the traumatic experience as well as worldview, normal behaviors, and the ways that reactions and emotions are expressed may all reflect personal traits, group allegiance, local mores, family experiences, and environmental factors. Caution about sharing aspects of self and experience and a tendency to focus on the positive or the negative in a situation can be a function of culture or personality. Cultural factors may emphasize the importance of specific personality traits. Zhang, Kohnstamm, Slotboom, Elphick, & Cheung (2002) found that Chinese in mainland China, Hong Kong, Taiwan, and the United States possess some common traits that are deeply rooted in the Chinese culture and characterized by Confucian thought, such as self-discipline and moderation. They also found that Chinese parents more often used negative (or critical) terms than did Dutch parents to describe their children. A culture's emphasis on certain traits, such as conscientiousness, and variations in descriptive style are important when assessing parent reports and child self-reports of multicultural groups.

Socially accepted biases may influence clinical and research expectations and interpretations of behavior. In some Native American cultures, for example, renaming a relative after a dead person is a way of honoring the dead (Stamm & Stamm, 1999). In other cultures, it may be considered morbid or an attempt to replace the dead. To counteract the effects of cultural biases, it is important to recognize their intrusions (Laird, 1998).

Birth Cohort

Birth cohort is the term used to describe all of the people born in a particular year. It has been applied more generally to those born in a particular generation. Youths born at different times grow up in different sociocultural environments (Roberts & Helson, 1997; Twenge & Campbell, 2001). Development, social norms, and other variables important to the assessment of trauma and its possible outcomes may vary for different birth cohorts. Growing up in the 1950s or the 1970s in the United States, for example, may have produced very different developmental changes than growing up in the first decade of the 21st century. Levels of exposure to information (e.g., via television, the Internet), skill-building toys, historical events, changing gender roles, and other developments as well as increasing divorce, mobility, crime, and homeland terrorist threat rates have contributed to these differences. Anxiety and depression have escalated with increases in crime rates and social disconnection (Twenge, 2000; Twenge & Campbell). Changes in women's roles parallel changes in gender-linked attitudes and personality traits. Even differences of 3 to 4 years may affect study results (Mullis, Mullis, & Normandin, 1992; Twenge & Campbell).

Twenge (2002) recommends the use of *time lag* and *cross-temporal meta-analyses* to examine birth cohort or time period effects. *Time lag* analysis investigates same-age samples at different points in historical time. *Cross-temporal meta-analysis* correlates mean scores and the year in which data were collected. A significant positive correlation indicates that the trait has increased, and a significant negative correlation, that it has decreased over time. Regression analysis determines the amount of variance explained by birth cohort. Twenge found evidence for change in attitudes, behavior, life choices, and personality across time. Over the 20th century, depression and anxiety rose. Individuals born in the 1940s, for example, were 5 to 10 times more likely to be depressed than those born in the 1910s. Although the increase in depression has been attributed in part to increased social isolation, multiple factors have likely contributed. The close-knit Pennsylvania Amish, whose customs are rooted in the 19th century, experience depression one fifth to one tenth the amount of the general U.S. population. Mean scores on measures of anxiety increased from the 1950s to the 1990s. Average scores on the Children's Manifest Anxiety Scale were higher in normal youths in the 1980s than for child psychiatry patients in the late 1950s. The average youth from the 1980s or 1990s would outscore all but 16% of those from the 1950s. Increasingly across these decades, youths do not agree "most people can be trusted" and do agree that "you cannot be too careful with people." Social disconnection is highly correlated with anxiety. Individualism, self-esteem, and extraversion have increased especially since the 1960s. Female assertiveness increased between 1930 and 1945, decreased from 1946 to 1967, and increased from 1968 to 1993 (Twenge).

National Cultures

National cultures include the common elements within a nation, the national norm (Hofstede, 1980). Hofstede identified four dimensions for defining the values associated with national culture by studying international organizational cultures (i.e., IBM): power distance, individualism versus collectivism, masculinity versus femininity, and uncertainty avoidance (Hodgetts, 1993; Hofstede). According to Hofstede, organizational cultures are a more superficial phenomenon than national cultures, which reside mainly in deeply rooted values (Hodgetts; Hofstede).

The people of a nation become programmed to have particular expectations, beliefs, and behaviors. In nations with high levels of uncertainty avoidance (e.g., Latin and Catholic cultures; Soeters, 1996), citizens are used to greater career stability, more formal rules, belief in absolute truths, the attainment of expertise from others, and intolerance of deviant ideas and behaviors (Hofstede, 1980). Higher levels of aggressiveness and anxiety that, among other things, promote compliance and induce people to work hard also characterize these countries. In most societies (masculine or feminine), the majority of men have masculine values (directed toward ego goals, achievement, careers, and high salaries) (Hofstede, 1980; Lloyd, 1999; Soeters). Feminine societies, such as Scandinavian countries, also value social goals—caring for the poor, weak, and needy and the environment (Soeters). Relationships are more important than money, and quality of life, more important than performance (Hofstede, 1980). In masculine nations, such as Japan, Austria, and Venezuela, men's values differ more from women's, and older people's values differ more from younger people's (Hofstede, 1998; Lloyd).

Subsequent researchers have added cultural dimensions to Hofstede's list. In a Hong Kong assessment, Michael Bond added long-term versus short-term time orientation (long-term future planning versus immediate access to and usage of resources; Arrindell, 2003). In their study of Russian cultures, Naumov & Puffer (2000) included the long-term/short-term dimension in a *paternalism* dimension. High paternalism exists when the protective functions of the family are transferred to the state, lower paternalism when protective functions remain within the family. Cultural coping styles (chapter 5), issues of control, and culture-bound syndromes have been well-discussed and sometimes assessed as additional national qualities (Ahadi, Rothbart, & Ye, 1993; Pole, Best, Metzler, & Marmar, 2005).

More recent studies have contradicted some of Hofstede's 1980 findings. Oyserman, Coon, and Kemmelmeier (2002) found that Japanese and Koreans were often more individualistic and less collectivistic than Americans

(Yoo & Donthu, 2002). Similarly, some 3- to 6-year-old Japanese children's personality traits resembled U.S. rather than Chinese children (Rothbart, Ahadi, Hershey, & Fisher, 2001). Yoo and Donthu suggest two possible explanations for the differences. First, national cultures change over time. Events such as the breakdown of Arab and communist nations, industrialization of underdeveloped countries, international trade and travel, globalization of corporations, and information technology have helped to reshape cultures. Second, 3 decades ago, IBM workers in developed countries represented an average social class, whereas those in underdeveloped countries who had advanced technology, good education, and global mind-sets must have belonged to their nations' elite classes.

Some of the characteristics of national cultures have been discussed in other chapters (4 to 6). Elements of national cultures that are important to the assessment of children, not discussed elsewhere, are provided here.

Independence versus Interdependence

Individuals in different regions of the world define themselves and parent their children in relationship to independence or to connectedness (Markus, Kitayama, & Heiman, 1996; Shiang, 2000; Shiang, Kjellander, Huang, & Bogumill, 1998; Triandis et al., 1986). Independence-oriented regions such as the United States, northern Europe, and Australia stress that the good, moral self is highly individualistic and autonomous, and seeks to conquer new frontiers. Interdependence-oriented nations such as China stress that the good, moral self puts the good of the group before individual needs. Although *Western* societies tend to be individualistic rather than collectivistic, many American subcultures (e.g., African American, Chinese American) include values of interdependence (Boyd-Franklin & Franklin, 1998; Watson, 1998). Pole et al. (2005) suggest that a greater value on interdependence may result in an enhanced need for social support. Hispanic adults with poor familial and social relationships, for example, have had higher and more intense PTSD symptoms.

Culture-Bound Syndromes

Basic patterns and signs of psychopathology (e.g., insomnia, worry, crying spells, weakness, reduced energy, suicidal ideation, hallucinations) exist worldwide (Westermeyer, 1987). Nonpsychotic disorders that include a combination of emotional distress, behavioral abnormality, transient cognitive disturbances, and crises or situational problems have been observed across cultures. Nevertheless, the same situation may evoke widely different emotional expressions. Conceptualizations and word meanings differ from society to society (de Silva, 1999). Multiple deaths, for example, may elicit tears in one culture and laughter in another (Mills, 2001). "Culture-bound syndromes," such as Hispanic *ataques de nervios* and Cambodian *kyol goeu* or "wind illness," provide culturally recognized and sanctioned ways of expressing depression or anxiety (Boehnlein, 2001; de Silva; Laria & Lewis-Fernández, 2001; Lee, Lei, & Sue, 2001; Velez-Ibanez

& Parra, 1999). After overwhelming emotionally distressing events, traditional Hispanic cultures sanction the expression of brief outbursts of intense emotionality and undercontrolled behavior such as intense fear, anger, grief, lashing out, and crying (Laria & Lewis-Fernández; Velez-Ibanez & Parra). Cambodia's *kyol goeu* includes orthostatic panic and associated somatic changes (Boehnlein).

Similar conditions may differ in important ways among cultures or may be correlated with a number of different Western disorders (Kirmayer et al., 1995). The Rwandan African illness, *Agahinda gakabije,* includes sadness, poor relationships, lack of self-care, loss of mental ability, inability to work, isolation, and feeling that life is meaningless. Although it is the Rwandan disorder most similar to depression, it is a more general disorder that includes depression (Bolton, 2001). Some cultures describe psychological problems in a way that emphasizes the unity between mind and body. The Chinese use a diagnosis of neurasthenia for worries, sadness, lethargy, body pains, and problems with others (Shiang, 2000). Some African, Hispanic, and Asian groups attribute physical and psychological disturbances to mystical or spiritual causes (Velez-Ibanez & Parra, 1999). Culture-bound syndrome labels have been used by communities to categorize deviant or socially problematic behaviors, which vary among cultures. Moreover, differences in biomedical, dietary, and environmental conditions, and traumatic exposure rates among cultures and the distress of migration, can influence rates and types of psychopathology (Westermeyer, 1987).

Issues of Self-Control

Cultures prescribe the nature of stress release. In societies that require controlled behaviors, children exhibit more *overcontrolled* problems such as fears, feelings of guilt, somatic concerns, depression, and anxiety (Mash & Dozois, 2003). In a study of Kenyan, Thai, and U.S. children (ages 11 to 15), Kenyan children were rated particularly high on overcontrolled problems (Weisz & Sigman, 1993). U.S. children were rated particularly high on *undercontrolled* problems like arguing, disobedience at home, and cruelty to others. Similarly for children ages 6 to 11, Buddhist-oriented Thai parents reported higher overcontrolled behavior problems, whereas American children were rated higher on undercontrolled behaviors (Weisz & Suwanlert, 1987). Significantly more overcontrolled problems were reported for Jamaican than for American youngsters as well—a finding consistent with Afro-British Jamaican cultural attitudes and practices that foster inhibition and other overcontrolled behaviors and discourage child aggression and other undercontrolled behaviors (Lambert & Weisz, 1989).

Cultural Groups within a Nation

Each country houses a wide range of personalities and a variety of personal and political attitudes. Groupings of characteristics for the purposes of assessment are limited by current conceptualizations (Rothbart & Bates, 1998), and theories of human characteristics (e.g., culture, personality, motivation, psychology) generally reflect national intellectual middle-class cultural backgrounds (Hofstede, 1980). Not every member of a national culture fits a defined cultural profile. Age, nationalization, acculturation, regionalization, peer influence, and personal and family histories contribute to the differences within cultures. Cultural groups develop experientially, regionally in a nation, and among religions. Shared or similar experiences—perhaps especially traumatic ones—may bring a group of people together to create a new subculture. Groups emerge in response to common experiences such as parents' professional training as well as specific traumatic experiences. The inner-city culture of south-central Los Angeles is composed primarily of Latino and African American cultures. Their attitudes and life experiences differ from those of the same cultures living in less populated neighboring counties. New York inner-city subcultures differ from rural cultures in upstate New York, in their majority politics, lifestyles, attitudes, and their expectations of people and life. Similarly, in each religion, different sects, regions, and organizations hold different beliefs. Sects or organized groups of Christians (e.g., Baptist, Catholic, Mormon), Hindus (e.g., worshipers of Dhurga, Ramakrishna, Siva), and Jews (e.g., Orthodox, Conservative, Reform) may vary in their specific beliefs, politics, and practices. Southern Baptists differ from northern Baptists, and attendees at the downtown temple may differ from those of the uptown temple. In some cultures (e.g., African American) or regions (e.g., Texas), church, religion, or spirituality is a focal point of activities and beliefs.

Categorizing individuals as members of an ethnic or cultural group may contribute to errors in findings when the category includes diverse populations. For example, Asian Americans are from 48 ethnic groups. Among them are Cambodian, Chinese, Filipino, Indian, Japanese, Korean, Vietnamese, and Pacific Islanders. Varied experiences (e.g., immigrants, third-generation Americans), select populations of a culture (e.g., college students), disparate backgrounds (e.g., traditional vs. acculturated parents, social class/resource differences), or different circumstances (e.g., low or high levels of social support) may represent significant differences in the subgroups of a population (Lee et al., 2001). Higher depression rates have been found, for example, in Asian American college students (especially foreign-born Chinese, Korean, and Japanese Americans) with traditional rather than "modern" parents and in immigrants with few social supports. Higher anxiety levels in Chinese students may reflect problems such as acculturative stress, minority status difficulties, parental pressures to achieve, and cultural values to maintain interpersonal and social harmony (and thus greater sensitivity to others and the environment). Decreases in anxiety scores at later assessments have been associated with a move to the United States at an earlier age, integration into a new community, ability to obtain employment, and hardy personality traits (Kinzie, Boehnlein, & Sack, 1998; Lee et al.). Recognizing the subgroups within cultures may be important to finding differences among cultures. For example, Pole et al. (2005) summarized findings suggesting that Puerto Ricans may be more vulnerable to PTSD than other Hispanic groups: (1) when subgroups were compared, Puerto Ricans were often the most distressed, (2) studies observing no Hispanic effect have tended not to include Caribbean Hispanics, and (3) studies reporting a Hispanic effect have included Hispanics in locations heavily populated by Caribbean Hispanics.

Age differences may define contrasts within a culture. In the mid-1990s, the Russian culture as a whole appeared to be moderate in individualism, masculinity, and power distance, and fairly high in paternalism and uncertainty avoidance. The younger generation, however, had the highest scores in masculinity and the lowest scores in paternalism (Naumov & Puffer, 2000). Individuals employed in business had higher uncertainty avoidance than those in the university.

Immigrant Groups

Researchers have identified a condition affecting large numbers of migrants and refugees that may persist for years after migration (Kirmayer et al., 1995; Westermeyer, 1990; Westermeyer & Uecker, 1997). It is marked predominantly by depressive symptoms and includes the symptoms of PTSD (Westermeyer, 1990). It also includes mistrust or suspiciousness, mild to moderate anxiety, physiological symptoms, social withdrawal or isolation, and hostility marked by annoyance and irritation, temper outbursts, urges to harm someone or break things, and arguments (Westermeyer, 1987; Westermeyer & Uecker). Even though this syndrome has not been validated for young immigrant children, some of its symptoms have been found in adolescents (Kinzie, Boehnlein et al., 1998). Most migrant groups (refugees and immigrants) have higher rates of psychiatric disorders than nonmigrant groups (Westermeyer, 1990). Most refugees have had high levels of exposure to traumatic experiences. Empirically developed and tested instruments covering the complete range of their experiences and responses are not currently available (Hollifield et al., 2002).

Hollifield et al. (2002) have stated that accurate assessment of health and trauma status in refugee groups has been limited primarily by the lack of use of sound measurement principles and of theory-based construct definitions to guide the design of scales and interviews. Although a few child measures that can be used for local refugee populations have been translated and adapted for use in other countries, the measures focus primarily on posttraumatic reactions and not the full range of symptoms identified for refugees and immigrants (see Hollifield et al.; Kirmayer et al., 1995).

International Adoptees. Between 1988 and 2001, the number of international adoptions nearly doubled from about 19,000 to over 34,000 (Kapstein, 2003). Adoptions in early infancy have become less frequent, and adoptions of older youths with special needs, after adverse life events or with disabilities, have become more frequent (Rutter & O'Connor, 1999). Even when newborns are sought for adoption, placing countries often delay referral until children are 1 or 2 years of age. International adoptees often have been abandoned early in life for economic or social reasons, removed from neglectful or abusing parents, or orphaned in war-torn nations (Johnson, 1998).

For adoptees, separation from the mother has been described as *the primal wound* (Verrier, 1993), *cumulative adoption trauma* (referring to the initial separation and the subsequent realization of loss of family; Lifton, 1994), and *adopted child pathology* or *adoption syndrome* (Hoksbergen, ter Laak, van Dijkum, Rijk, Rijk, & Stoutjesdijk, 2003). International adoption adds to this the loss of a homeland (Hollingsworth, 2003). Rutter (1997) suggests that, although separations may be stressful, noncontinuity in caregiving and the lack of opportunity to form selective attachments is likely to be more damaging for children in institutions (see chapter 8).

Lack of information about the adoptive child's history can be problematic to assessment. For example, the number of placements and positive attachment relationships with a caregiver vary among adoptees and are associated with aspects of development and pathology. Singer, Burkowski, and Walters (1985) found no increase in the risk for impaired security or pattern of attachment with early adoption, but an increased risk with multiple previous placements (Rutter & O'Connor, 1999). Similarly, infants placed with secure-autonomous foster mothers before 12 months were found secure in their attachments, whereas those placed after 12 months with secure-autonomous mothers were insecurely attached (Hesse, 1999). Similar to findings for children adopted from poor-quality Rumanian institutions, Howe (1997) observed relatively common relationship difficulties (including difficulty forming relationships), indiscriminate behavior toward others, and poor developmental outcomes for adopted children with histories of neglect, abuse, or multiple placements (Rutter & O'Connor). Adoptees who remained at length in institutions are unlikely to have had the kinds of caregiving that promote resilience under stress (Fosha, 2003). From research on the qualities of effective caregiving, Fosha has concluded that caregivers' affective competence and reflective capacity help to foster optimal development and secure attachments as well as to reduce vulnerability to psychopathology. Affective competence in the regulation of a caregiver's own and the child's emotions is at the foundation of the child's sense of security. The caregiver assists the child through stressful or distressing situations that are beyond the child's resources to manage. Being able to reflect on one's own and another's emotional experience is another aspect of affective competence (see Fonagy's *reflective self function*, Main's *coherent and cohesive autobiographical narrative*, and Siegel's *autonoetic capacity* cited in Fosha; Knox, 2003, 2004; chapter 8). This ability to self-reflect is evidenced in the caregiver's empathetic response to the child's distress.

International adoptees may have been exposed to traumatic experiences such as physical and emotional neglect, or witnessing or experiencing assault, rape, torture, starvation, natural disasters, and war (Hoksbergen et al., 2003; Johnson, 1998; Williams, in press). Because of their struggles in violent homes (physical, sexual, or emotional abuse), children from institutionalized settings often have PTSD, chronic fear, insecurity, and feelings of abandonment (Federici, 2003; Hoksbergen et al.). Attachment, learning, language, behavioral, developmental, emotional, sensitivity, and attentional disorders are common for international adoptees (Federici; Williams). In addition to the signs and symptoms of trauma and abandonment, international adoptees have been diagnosed with reactive attachment, separation anxiety, generalized anxiety, or anxiety disorders not otherwise specified (Hoksbergen et al.; Williams). Hoksbergen et al. found that, although after an average of 5 years in adoptive homes the PTSD group did not differ from the norm group on physical development, parents rated them as significantly lower on all other developmental aspects (e.g., in language development and interactions with peers).

Researchers have found behavior problems, high pain thresholds, and excessive attention-seeking especially common in adoptees. In a group of 80 Rumanian children adopted in the Netherlands, Hoksbergen et al. (2003) found that adopted boys and girls often scored in the clinical range on the Child Behavior Checklist (CBCL). Externalization and attention-seeking were most prominent (more so for girls than for boys). Adoptees without PTSD scored significantly lower on internalizing symptoms than the clinical norm group and somewhat lower than the general norm group, were no different from the norm group on ratings of social problems, and had negligible differences on cognitive problems and delinquency. When adoptees met criteria for PTSD (29%), however, they scored higher on all CBCL syndromes (except physical complaints) than other adoptees and the normal group.

Institutionalized youths may not have had opportunities to develop some of the characteristics of a normally developing child such as a conscience, comfort in exploring the environment, decision-making skills, and emotional self-awareness (Williams, in press). They may have always lived in a group situation with little or no privacy, known only a very structured environment, owned no personal property (e.g., clothes, toys), never received encouragement, had limited exposure to variations in feelings, and had no experience with noises that are normal in an American home such as stereos, lawn mowers, alarm clocks, pets, washing machines, televisions, or computers. Therefore, they may react to sounds, people, and situations differently than noninstitutionalized children.

Normal brain development requires appropriate environmental input during early life as well as an intact genome; the greater the deficit (in genome or environmental stimuli), the more problems are observed in development (Johnson, 1998). Adoptees may have had limited stimulation and little conversation, and may never have had their emotions labeled for them or had someone ask how they feel (Williams, in press). Consequently, they may not have the words to describe physical or emotional states. Adoptees from an institution or other deprived environment may not have the social or emotional language to describe or the cognitive schemas to know their symptoms (Williams).

Culture and Psychopathology

Cultural differences in pathology often reflect the influence of other associated variables. Comparisons controlling for a number of variables found that African American and Hispanic American samples were identified and referred for pathology at the same rates as other children, but they were much less likely to actually receive specialty mental-health services or psychotropic medications (García Coll & Garrido, 2000; Mash & Dozois, 2003). European American and Native American children have had similar mental-health problems with one exception: Substance abuse rates have been higher for Native American youths (Costello, Farmer, & Angold, 1999; Mash & Dozois). Higher levels of externalizing behaviors found for African American children in some small studies of child psychopathology may be related to SES or other environmental factors. Studies with larger national samples of Euro American, African American, and Hispanic American children have found either no or very small differences related to race or ethnicity when SES, sex, age, and referral status were controlled for (Mash & Dozois).

Cultural Risk and Protective Factors

Ethnic or cultural experiences can influence vulnerabilities or sensitivities. Chronic exposure to discrimination stresses, acculturation stress, and lack of access to services have been associated with increased susceptibility to trauma (Kinzie, Boehnlein et al., 1998; Pole et al., 2005; Rabalais et al., 2002). For Hispanic and African American Vietnam veterans, perceived racism in the military has been associated with higher rates of PTSD and greater sensitivity to the victimization of villagers than was found for other soldiers (Boehnlein & Kinzie, 1997; Pole et al.). Researchers have reported increased vulnerabilities in the offspring of Nazi Holocaust survivors (Danieli, 1998). Clinical and research evidence has demonstrated how unresolved loss or trauma may contribute to these vulnerabilities via subsequent distressed attachment relationships (Hesse, Main, Abrams, & Rifkin, 2003; see chapter 8).

Culture-bound dissociative symptoms and syndromes may explain higher rates of PTSD among adults in some groups. For example, peritraumatic dissociation (the tendency to experience altered states of consciousness during a trauma) has been a robust predictor of PTSD (Pole et al., 2005). Following September 11, Hispanic police officers who reported significantly more peritraumatic dissociation, wishful thinking coping, and self-blame coping had more cumulative PTSD and somatic symptoms than non-Hispanic officers (Pole et al.). Boehnlein (2001) suggests that cultural attitudes may be a trigger for some symptoms such as panic symptoms in Asians (see "Culture-Bound Syndromes," above). A study of Cambodian combat veterans with PTSD revealed significantly higher levels of physiological responses to viewing trauma scenes than found in American combat veterans (Boehnlein, 2001; Kinzie, Denney, Riley, Boehnlein, McFarland, & Leung, 1998).

Qualities such as a supportive community and culturally acceptable outlets for emotional responses may be protective. Value for and levels of social support vary by culture. Pole et al. (2005) suggest that, because of a greater value placed upon collectivism, Hispanics may place greater emphasis on social support than other ethnic groups. As mentioned earlier, studies of traumatized adults have found that Hispanic patients with poor familial and social relationships had higher and more intense PTSD symptoms (Pole et al.).

Culture and Coping

Cultural differences in coping styles or preparation for coping may explain some of the differences in traumatic reactions (see chapter 5). The current consensus is that active or problem-solving coping is associated with better outcomes than passive or avoidance coping (Pole et al., 2005; Stallard, Velleman, Langsford, & Baldwin, 2001). In 2002, Perilla and colleagues found that traditional Hispanic adults strongly endorsed fatalistic beliefs (cited in Pole et al.). They had a tendency to see events as inevitable and unalterable. A belief that little can be done to alter the outcome may result in a propensity toward passive coping with traumatic events.

For children, guilt (self-blame coping) has been associated with increased trauma symptoms and the maintenance of PTSD (Irwin, 1998; Manion, Firestone, Cloutier, Ligezinska, McIntyre, & Ensom, 1998; Paunovic, 1998; Pynoos et al., 1987). Religious beliefs that emphasize personal responsibility or interpret adverse events as punishment for sins or as inevitable, karmic consequences may create vulnerability for guilt or self-blame after traumatic events (Pole et al., 2005; Nader, 2001a).

Religion may also provide methods of coping by providing answers, solace, and methods of dealing with specific symptoms. Following tragedy, "Why [me, him, her, us]?" is a frequently asked question. In Buddhist and Hindu faiths, *karma* provides an answer. Some faiths furnish practices to ward off future suffering or to make amends when there is guilt (Bible/Torah: Leviticus 6; Quaran [Koran] 9:5, 9:11; Nader, 2001a).

Research Findings for Trauma and Culture

Studies of adults have revealed small but significant cultural differences in the prevalence of PTSD (Pole et al., 2005). Even when higher levels of PTSD were associated with minority cultural background, there were no differences in the levels of functional impairment between cultures (Pole et al.). In some studies, somatization has emerged as an important predictor of PTSD symptoms. The expression of distress in somatic terms is well-documented among some cultures (e.g., Hispanic, Southeast Asian) (Kinzie, Boehnlein et al., 1998; Shiang, 2000). Such findings may suggest the need for a culture-specific variant of PTSD that includes somatic features (Pole et al.). The International Classification of Disorders (ICD-10; World Health Organization, 1992) includes somatoform disturbances in the definition and categories of dissociation (Laria & Lewis-Fernández, 2001; Lee et al., 2001).

Children's ethnic, religious, and cultural backgrounds have been relatively understudied in relation to traumatic reactions (La Greca, Silverman, Vernberg, & Roberts, 2002b). A few researchers have found small effects for ethnic groups. Shannon, Lonigan, Finch, & Taylor. (1994) found increased symptoms for African Americans exposed to Hurricane Hugo but not larger numbers meeting *DSM* PTSD criteria. La Greca et al. (1996) confirmed increased symptoms at 3, 7, and 10 months after Hurricane Andrew for Hispanic and African American children. However, comparisons have sometimes been confounded by the presence of other variables such as numbers and levels of traumatic exposures, SES, access to mental-health services, or other risk factors (Costello, Keeler, & Angold, 2001; Fletcher, 2003; La Greca et al., 1996; Silverman & La Greca, 2002). In a post-September 11 study of highly exposed preschool children and their parents, DeVoe, Klein, and Linas (2003) found no significant differences in rates of PTSD for White, Mixed, and Minority children (or adults) with high SES. In addition to economic status and greater ability to obtain and use resources, differences in coping may contribute to findings. Compared to Minority parents of Minority children, the White parents of White children reported the most negative shift in worldview. DeVoe et al. reported that, perhaps because they are used to serving as buffers against racism for their children, Minority parents reported the most positive parenting changes.

Culture and Assessment

Cultural beliefs and attitudes affect a number of issues important to the measurement of childhood trauma such as the way questions are interpreted, views about acceptable emotions and behaviors after a death or disaster, issues of trust, establishment of a time frame, and the admission and expression of emotions (Gerber, Nguyen & Bounkeua, 1999; Nader, Dubrow, & Stamm, 1999). Cultural beliefs influence informal labeling practices as well as diagnostic practices (Mash & Dozois, 2003). Consequently, the form, frequency, and predictive significance of labels, behaviors, and emotional expressions vary across cultures. For example, in Western cultures, shyness and oversensitivity in children have been associated with peer rejection and social maladjustment. In Chinese children in Shanghai, they are associated with leadership, school competence, and academic achievement (Chen, Rubin, & Li, 1995; Mash & Dozois).

Measures of posttrauma reactions reflect cultural values. Cultural biases and values infiltrate the questions asked to assess traumatic reactions, labels attached to behaviors and patterns of interaction, and interpretations of findings. Behaviors, symptoms, and traits must be translated into the ratable experiences, thoughts, or activities that define them. That means, for example, to assess accurately such concepts as withdrawal or social functioning, it is important to recognize that in Western countries, being sociable may include being lively, active, and talkative, whereas in many Asian countries, it may include being deferent, conscientious of others' needs, and family oriented (Ahadi et al., 1993). A label of pathology sometimes refers to how far a particular personality style or characteristic is from the predominant one in a given culture.

Reporting Symptoms

Self-reports of trauma symptoms tend to reflect social norms and desirability (Pole et al., 2005). Cultural values may affect a youth's willingness to share information as well as his or her awareness of desired or expected responses (Yee, Pierce, Ptacek, & Modzelesky, 2003). The concern about what people will say (for Latinas, "el que diran") may affect what is reported (Garcia-Preto, 1998). Park (1996) described three concepts considered positive cultural values that are strongly imbedded in Korean interpersonal behaviors (Park): *che-myon* (responses resulting from overconsciousness and anticipation of other's possible reactions to what is said); *kee-been* (self-conception or self-feeling at being exposed to others); and *noon-chi* (ability to comprehend what one person wants from another and to know how to respond accordingly—achieved by looking for explicit signs as well as implicit messages). Even under anonymous testing conditions, some collectivistic (e.g., Confucian-based) cultures discourage displays of emotion in order to maintain harmony and to avoid exposing personal weakness (Lee et al., 2001). On the other hand, some cultures sanction a greater or more passionate expression of emotions that may contribute to differences in reporting (Pole et al.).

Voicing mental-health problems may shame or stigmatize in some cultures (e.g., Asian, Arabic) (Kinzie, 1993; Shiang, 2000; Yee et al., 2003). For example, a Kuwaiti adolescent explained that if one family member was diagnosed with mental-health problems, the whole family was tarnished. In order to avoid acknowledging psychological problems, the members of a culture in which shame is associated with emotional disturbances may complain instead of physical symptoms (Lee et al., 2001). This allows the elicitation of social support without the stigmatization and shame of a mental problem (Shiang). For these cultures, physical complaints alone may represent a significant traumatic impact.

Cultural biases may affect both adults' and children's reporting styles. Following World War II, Williams suggested a cultural reason that may have contributed to British combat personnel's 3 1/2 times higher levels of postwar psychiatric illness than Asian Indians (de Silva, 1999). Showing anxiety resulted in a great loss of face for Indians. Parent reporting of children's symptoms may include cultural response biases (Ahadi et al., 1993; de Silva; Mash & Dozois, 2003). In a study of Chinese, Japanese, and American children, American mothers rated their children higher on motivational, academic, and intellectual characteristics. However, they rated their low-achieving children as high as Japanese and Chinese mothers rated their high-achieving children (Ahadi et al.).

The Diagnostic Interview

Sanction and rapport are key steps in eliciting relevant information from and providing treatment for intracultural and intercultural groups (Westermeyer, 1987; Yee et al., 2003). There is no substitute for learning within a community and engaging community and religious leaders, community members, and the individual patient to learn and to be guided through a group's or an individual's specific needs in assessment and treatment. In addition to developing appropriate measures for different countries and for immigrant groups when assessing children (and adults), sanction from community leaders, language proficiency, and the recognition of cultural differences in the willingness to report symptoms are also essential, inside and outside of a native country (Stamm & Stamm, 1999; Yee et al.; Nader, 1997c; see also chapter 4). Stamm and Stamm have recounted the need for those who intervene to identify and include elders (not all older people are elders) for support and in planning for interventions in Native American communities. Yee et al. have described the effectiveness of including community leaders in outreach, assessment, and treatment programs within the Asian population of New York (see chapter 4). Lee et al. (2001) suggest that cross-generation and qualitative methods such as open-ended interviews and focus groups as well as quantitative methods of research are needed to determine the complexities of disorders for disparate cultures.

Making an effort to understand traditional methods of intervention as well as those who are sanctioned to perform them is important to assessment and treatment. A number of cultures have traditional healers or dream interpreters (Nader, Dubrow, & Stamm, 1999), whereas in the United States and Western Europe, mental-health professionals serve that role. In some Latino, African, and Native American cultures, dreams are interpreted, disorders are assessed, and interventions are provided by a medicine man or woman or by recognized dream interpreters (Brown, 1989; Dubrow & Nader, 1999). Spiritual counselors may be sought to address traumas or emotional disturbances or disease.

Establishing Trust. The number of weeks, months, or years it takes for a person to reveal the extent of personal traumatic reactions varies by culture (Kinzie, 1993). Those who have experienced racial, economic, legal, or political prejudice in the United States (Westermeyer, 1987) as well as those who have concerns about American values that differ from their own (Meleis, 2003) may not trust someone from a different culture. In addition to gaining basic knowledge of the ways a patient may respond to and in treatment because of cultural and subcultural membership, the clinician may enhance rapport by conducting a skilled interview, demonstrating the commitment to understanding the patient's point of view, and beginning with open-ended nonthreatening questions. In diagnostic interviews with parents and adolescents, questions regarding sleep, appetite, and energy level sometimes serve as nonthreatening early inquiries (Westermeyer). A longer period may be needed to establish trust with a nonnative clinician (Canive, Castillo, & Tuason, 2001; Kinzie).

Interpreting Body Language and Information. Thought patterns (e.g., orientation to time) and behaviors (e.g., body language) commonly assessed or referred to in therapeutic sessions vary across cultures. Cultural differences exist in physical signs of stress or illness (e.g., lower tension levels in Japanese than in Westerners). What is valued in one culture (e.g., shyness) can be the cause of concern in another (Chen et al., 1995; Mash & Dozois, 2003). Behaviors that signify one thing in one culture may signify something very different in another (Westermeyer, 1987). Direct eye contact, for instance, may indicate honesty or openness in one culture and be interpreted as anger or disrespect in another. Silence may be considered a sign of denial or resistance in some clinical settings. In the context of PTSD for Southeast Asian cultures, however, it may represent one of the following: (1) shame, (2) lack of trust, (3) fatalistic acceptance or resignation, or (4) repression or suppression of intimate issues such as "emotional pain" (Ton-That, 1998). Kirmayer et al. (1995) suggest that locating the source of anxiety or distress in the spirit world, the social world, or the individual's existential predicament are all cultural coping strategies. Cultural differences may either mask or be mistaken for disorders (Canive et al., 2001; Kirmayer et al.). For example, repetitious religious rituals are sanctioned and expected in many cultures including Southern Baptist, Buddhist, Catholic, and Hindu groups. Being homebound is normal for a female from Qatar or Saudi Arabia. Belief in supernatural forces, magic, or witchcraft is common among Caribbean African Americans, Asian Indians, and traditional Hispanics. For adults to live with or preadolescents to sleep with parents is common in some Hispanic or Asian cultures. When they are culturally valued, the experiences and behaviors are generally supported by family and community; are preceded and followed by socially appropriate, productive, and coping behaviors (not psychological, behavioral, or social deterioration); do not diminish self-esteem or prestige; do not include pathological signs and symptoms; and are culturally congruent (Westermeyer). Cultural discontinuities as well as apparent contradictions, excessive emotional reactions, or unlikely behaviors indicate the need for clarification. Study and an educated and trained translator from the culture in question can clarify whether behaviors are culturally congruent or idiosyncratic (Westermeyer).

CONCLUSIONS

Shared and nonshared family factors influence posttrauma reactions. Low SES, for example, has been linked to increased exposure to stressful life events and reduced access to services. Some evidence suggests that having the resources to obtain services and to provide other forms of relief may be protective. When cultural memberships split along SES lines, accurately assessing the effects of culture or SES membership may be hindered.

Along with personality and experiential factors, culture may color a youth's perceptions and reactions to trauma as well as reporting style, willingness to answer questions accurately, and understanding of questions, experiences, and words. Religious, national, peer, and other group cultures define acceptable posttrauma behaviors, emotional expressions, and coping styles. Cultural biases may affect the assessment process. The sanction by cultural leaders for assessment and interventions with exposed individuals or communities, understanding what is normal within a group, and understanding cultural hindrances to accurate reporting are essential to valid evaluations.

8

Attachment

Several studies in the 1940s and 1950s suggested that, after prolonged separation from their mothers, very young children proceeded through phases of "protest," "despair," and "detachment" (Marvin & Britner, 1999). Bowlby (1958) decided that it was loss of the specific mother figure that spurred these reactions. Bowlby (1969/1982) posited that genetic selection favored attachment behaviors, which increased mother-child proximity. In turn, proximity increased the likelihood of protection and survival. From an evolutionary perspective, infants that stayed close to their mothers were less likely to be killed by predators (Cassidy, 1999).

Secure attachment relationships facilitate growth and development in a number of ways. In addition to the protection provided by attachment relationships, these early relationships become the prototype for subsequent relationships (King, 2002). Secure attachments provide environments conducive to the proliferation of neuronal connections and the integration of brain systems (Schore, 2001; Stein & Kendall, 2004). In turn, this development assists the capacity to cope with stress.

Insecure attachments have been implicated in vulnerability to a variety of emotional and behavioral problems and disorders including PTSD. Insecure attachments have been suspected or identified in the etiology of most of the non-biologically induced infant psychological disorders defined by the Diagnostic Classification: 0–3 (DC:0–3; National Center for Infants, Toddlers, and Families, 1994). Insecure attachments have been associated with depressive, anxiety, dissociative, somatic, externalizing, internalizing, and overall psychopathology in childhood, adolescence, and young adulthood (Lyons-Ruth, Zeanah, & Benoit, 2003).

Attachment affects symptoms and behaviors. Adults traumatized as children who have insecure attachment styles (e.g., dismissing, fearful, or preoccupied styles) have had higher levels of posttraumatic symptoms (Muller, Sicoli, & Lemieux, 2000). A parent's unresolved trauma or loss has been linked to the occurrence of disturbed parent-infant attachments that, in turn, significantly often are followed by psychopathology (Hesse, Main, Abrams, & Rifkin, 2003). Early and adolescent attachment organization has predicted future behavior with offspring and with marital partners (Allen & Land, 1999). To follow are theories and findings associated with attachment as well as aspects of attachment that are related to trauma and assessment.

Attachment and Neurobiology

Exposure to early life stress has been associated with neurobiological changes that may lead to increased risk of pathology (Schore, 2003). Studies suggest, for example, that toddlers with insecure attachments have higher cortisol levels in response to stressful or novel situations than children with secure attachments (Gunnar, Brodersen, Krueger, & Rigatuso, 1996; Nachmias & Gunnar, 1996). A post-Strange Situation (see below) rise in salivary adrenocortisal has been documented in disorganized infants as well (Hesse et al., 2003). Animal studies suggest that reactive elevated cortisol levels can be inherited by offspring (Suomi, 1995; Suomi & Levine, 1998). Thus, the effects of trauma and of insecure attachments may be inherited by subsequent generations (Danieli, 1998).

THE ATTACHMENT BEHAVIORAL SYSTEM

The *attachment behavioral system's* biological function is the protection of the child from a variety of dangers. "According to Bowlby, the goal of the child is not an object (e.g., the mother), but rather a state—a maintenance of the desired distance from the mother, depending on the circumstances" (Cassidy, 1999, p. 6). The fear system activates the attachment behavioral system. That is, anxiety, fear, threat, fatigue, illness, distress, hunger, and the withdrawal or absence of the attachment figure activate proximity-seeking (Rutter, 1997).

The child is protected by maintaining proximity to the attachment figure and learns about the environment through exploration. Bowlby posited that the *exploratory system* enhanced survival by providing information about the environment such as how to use tools, obtain food, or find shelter (Cassidy, 1999). The exploratory system may reduce the attachment behavioral system. Empirical evidence has demonstrated that when the attachment behavioral system is not activated—when the child is comfortable with the proximity and availability of the attachment figure—exploration or play with others is enhanced (Bowlby, 1969/1982; Cassidy; Rutter, 1997). The manner in which caregivers and children organize protective proximity and contact, and the way that children use their caregivers as a secure base for exploration, is important during later as well as early development (Marvin & Britner, 1999; see "Age and Assessing Attachment," below). For adolescents and adults as well as infants and young children, the attachment system is evidenced in the tendency to maintain proximity to selected individual(s), to use these individuals as a "secure base" for exploring unfamiliar environments, to seek support from them in times of stress or alarm, and to protest against involuntary separations (Ainsworth, 1989; Allen & Land, 1999; Hesse et al., 2003).

The Attachment Bond

The *attachment bond* is only one aspect of the child's relationship to the mother or other attachment figure (Bowlby, 1969/1982; Cassidy, 1999). The *attachment bond* is among the larger class of *affectional bonds. Affectional bonds* are the child's affectional tie to the attachment figure rather than the bond between them. These bonds are persistent, involve a specific person (are not interchangeable), are emotionally significant, include a desire for proximity to or contact with the person (the nature of which varies by age, emotional state, and environmental and other conditions), and result in distress upon involuntary separation from the person (Bowlby, 1979). To define attachment bonds, Bowlby added to the five criteria of affectional bonds that the child seeks security and comfort from the relationship. Parental attempts to seek security from a child are usually a sign of pathology in the parent and a cause of it in the child (Bowlby, 1969/1982; Cassidy; Rutter, 1997). According to Bowlby, many of the most intense emotions—love, sadness, and grief—arise during the formation, maintenance, and disruption of attachment relationships (Cassidy). The strength of an attachment bond does not equate with the strength of attachment behavior (Ainsworth, 1972, Cassidy). A child's fearful clinging, for example, may either reflect insecure attachment or secure use of the mother as a safe haven. Theorists originally thought that the first 2 years of life were the sensitive period for developing attachments. Researchers have found the sensitive period to be broader and that failure of attachment in the critical period is less fixed and irreversible than originally believed (Rutter).

The Attachment Figure

Even though there are hierarchies in selective attachment, most children develop a few selective attachments to people involved in their care. Bowlby (1969/1982) suggested that the caregiver behaviors relevant to attachment are responsiveness to crying and readiness to interact socially. Nevertheless, infants prefer the primary attachment figure for comfort and security, and tolerate major separations from other attachment figures with less distress (Cassidy, 1999). Colin (1996) suggested factors likely to contribute to the attachment hierarchy: (1) amount of time in the figure's care, (2) the quality of care, (3) the adult's emotional investment in the child, and (4) social cues (Cassidy). The patterns of communication found to be most conducive to *secure attachments* involve reciprocal, contingent, collaborative communication (Siegel, 2003). Hesse et al.

(2003) suggest that it is because attachment is based on contingent social interactions that infants can develop attachments to nonrelated individuals who do not participate in their primary care. Infants become attached even to an abusing or insensitive parent (Cassidy; Hesse et al.; Rutter, 1997; Box 8.1a). Animal studies demonstrate that infants attach or imprint to adults who are not the source of their food. In 1935, Lorenz found that geese imprinted on humans. In 1958, Harlow showed that rhesus monkeys chose cloth-covered surrogate mothers that afforded contact comfort over wire-mesh surrogates providing food (cited in Cassidy). As a child gets older, new opportunities for and changes in the nature of attachments occur. For the sake of assessment, differences and similarities (concordance) in the quality of attachments become relevant. Social development is affected by later as well as early relationships.

Although much research suggests that maternal attachments have greater predictive power than paternal for later psychosocial functioning, Cassidy (1999) suggests that differences in attachment to the father compared to the mother may be related to the degree of sensitive responsiveness. Thompson (1999) showed that different caregivers are likely to develop qualitatively different relationships with offspring (sometimes in different contexts and circumstances), and these differences may predict qualitatively different aspects of a child's functioning. Some studies of self-esteem in children have suggested that the same-sex parent has more of an impact on outcomes such as level of self-esteem, whereas other

---

BOX 8.1

Case Examples: Attachment

a. *Lacey.* Both of Lacey's parents were attentive to her and spent time caring for her, playing with her, teaching her, and disciplining her. Her father, however, was violently abusive to her mother for many years before her mother left him. Lacey's mother took her to therapy after the separation. Even though Lacey had witnessed her father's abuse of her mother and expressed some fear toward him, she also talked of him lovingly and with admiration. In her hand-drawn family pictures, her father was elevated above her, and she was elevated above her mother. In supervision, her intern therapist expressed concerns about her admiration for, and perhaps identification with, a violent father.

b. *Mathew.* When Mathew was 3, his parents divorced. Before the massacre, his mother had a few long-term boyfriends and a second husband who, according to Mathew's mother, were around long enough for him to become attached, and then they left. The man she was with when the massacre occurred was abusive to Mathew's mother and was very critical of Mathew's efforts to obey. To protect him, his mother sent Mathew to live with his father for a year. Mathew's father was struggling with his own PTSD because of his military war experiences. He nevertheless provided Mathew with firm discipline, interest, and good care. After Mathew's return to his mother, a neighborhood man he introduced to her became his stepfather. Perhaps to some extent because of his traumatic detachment combined with early abandonments, Mathew seemed unattached to his stepfather. Even though Mathew sometimes became aggressive toward his mother in response to reminders of the massacre, he was close to her before and after the massacre. Their relationship was a positive one. She was his best advocate.

studies have suggested that the mother is more relevant for both boys and girls than the father (Heinonen, Räikönnen, & Keltikangas-Järvinen, 2003). Disorders such as a parent's depression or trauma may interfere with the quality of care and the sensitivity of response. In 1985, Radke-Yarrow, Cummings, Kuczynski, and Chapman found a greater incidence of insecure attachment among 2 to 3 year olds when the parent had a major affective disorder than when he or she had minor or no depression (cited in Atkinson, 1997).

Recent studies have focused on multiple attachment relationships when families include more than one child (Rosen & Burke, 1999). When there is more than one child, mothers' and fathers' interactions with each child will lead to distinct relationships. Each relationship will include its own qualitative organization of attachment behaviors (Rosen & Burke). Researchers have not yet determined the effects of having multiple attachment figures that contribute in contrasting manners to the child's internal working models about relationships, attachment figures, and him- or herself (Cassidy, 1999; Box 8.1b). Do they become integrated into a single model, result in different self-models in different relationships, or contribute to conflict in relationships? More information is needed regarding their effects on a child's functioning and later relationships.

Affective Competence and Self-Awareness

Clinical and statistical research suggest that a caregivers' affective competence promotes the child's healthy development and secure attachments (Fosha, 2003; Knox, 2003a). A parent's affective competence may provide protection against the damaging effects of abuse and other traumas, and it reduces vulnerability to the transgenerational transmission of psychopathology (Fosha; Slade, 1999). Affective competence includes the caregiver's ability to regulate her or his own and the child's emotions, to assist the child through stressful or distressing situations beyond the child's resources, and to help the child make others' behaviors meaningful and predictable (Slade).

The ability to step back and consider one's own cognitive processes as objects of thought or reflection has been called *metacognitive monitoring* or *reflective self function*. Mary Main (1995) observed that an adult's ability to engage in a coherent and cohesive autobiographical narrative that includes *metacognitive monitoring* is evidence of that adult's single, internally consistent working model of attachment (Fosha, 2003; Knox, 2003b, 2004; Slade, 1999). Main suggests that such an adult has access to all aspects of consciousness without contradiction or distortion (Slade). Fonagy and his colleagues concluded that this capacity for metacognitive monitoring or *reflective self function* suggests the ability to perceive and understand one's own and others' behaviors in terms of mental states or psychological experiences (Knox, 2003a; Slade). Knox has identified four key elements of the reflective function: (1) *narrative competence*—recognition of the psychological cause and effect that links events in a meaningful way; the basis for a sense of agency; (2) *intentionality*—the capacity to pursue goals and desires; (3) *appraisal*—the capacity to evaluate the relative importance or significance of information; (4) *individuation*—awareness of one's own and other people's individual subjectivity. She explained that failure to develop a reflective function results in the lack of a capacity to empathize with others and to place personal emotions in a meaningful context (e.g., to be aware of and evaluate the meaning of one's own emotions). The ability to self-reflect is essential to the capacity to learn from one's behaviors and experiences. Defensive avoidance of the reflective function may occur when information or reflection are perceived as a threat. This avoidance may occur after childhood traumatic experiences such as emotional, physical, or sexual abuse. Disturbances associated with trauma and with the defensive avoidance of reflection include borderline personality disorders, bulimia, self-harm, projective identification, and the loss of a sense of self (Knox, 2003a).

ATTACHMENT STYLES

Bowlby (1969/1982, 1973) suggested that early attachment styles become "working models" for significant social ties or interactions throughout life (Main, Kaplan, & Cassidy, 1985; Rutter, 1997). His theories on attachment were furthered by Mary Ainsworth (1973), who provided the empirical means for its study (Cassidy, 1999). Ainsworth and colleagues' observations of children in the laboratory with their parents and with a stranger resulted in the classifications of (1) *secure (B)*, (2) *insecure avoidant (A)*, and (3) *insecure resistant (C)* attachment styles (Ainsworth, Blehar, Waters, & Wall, 1978; Table 8.1). Early and subsequent studies suggest that most infants' attachments are classified secure, approximately a fourth are insecure avoidant, less than 20% are insecure resistant/ambivalent, and some are unclassifiable (Hesse et al., 2003). Main and Solomon identified a fourth classification, *disorganized/disoriented (D)* (Solomon & George, 1999). Rutter noted that the categories of secure, insecure (avoidant insecure or resistant insecure), and disorganized do not describe all children. Despite their severe relationship problems, autistic children do not stand out in their responses to the Strange Situation as traditionally measured. Measures of insecurity do not capture the patterns of indiscriminant proximity-seeking found in institutionally raised children (Rutter).

The four main attachment styles are described in Tables 8.1 and 8.2 and are discussed here. Studies have shown attachment styles to be stable at least to age 6 (Hesse et al., 2003). Individuals with any of the infant attachment styles may fare well or have difficulty (Hesse et al.; Rutter, 1997). Hesse et al. noted, for example, that early, disorganized attachments may contribute to intellectual, introspective, artistic, and other advantages.

It is generally agreed that infant characteristics such as temperament, parental attributes such as responsiveness, cultural issues such as parent-

TABLE 8.1
Attachment Styles (Infancy to Age 6 or 7)

Attachment Style	Brief Descriptions of Child
Secure (B)	*Infancy: Uses the mother as a secure base for exploration. Misses parent during separation. Actively greets parent (with gesture, smile, or vocalization) upon reunion. When upset, signals for or seeks parent, and returns to exploration after comforted. Prefers parent to stranger.* *Early childhood: Uses parent as secure base for exploration. Reunions are smooth, positive, warm, open, confident, relaxed. Positive, reciprocal interaction or conversation; relaxed, intimate, direct expression of feelings or desires. Able to negotiate conflict or disagreement.*
Insecure avoidant (A)	*Infancy: Explores readily. Seeks distance from parent. Responds minimally to separation and with little visible distress to being left alone. Looks away or focuses on toys and actively avoids parent upon reunion. May stiffen or lean away if picked up. Little or no proximity-seeking; no distress or anger. Response to parent seems unemotional.* *Early childhood: Avoids physical or psychological intimacy but does not avoid interaction. Detached, neutral nonchalance. Subtly minimizes and limits opportunities for interaction. Focuses more on play. Is defended—acts to reduce emotional involvement or confrontation.*
Insecure resistant or ambivalent (C)	*Infancy: Fails to engage in exploration. Is visibly distressed upon entering the strange room. Is often fretful or passive. Preoccupied with parent. May alternate seeking contact with angry aggression or tantrums or may appear passive or too upset to seek contact. Does not find comfort in the parent.* *Early childhood: Heightened intimacy and dependency on parent. Strongly protests separation. Reunions characterized by strong proximity-seeking and exaggerated babyish, cute, or coy behavior or by ambivalence and subtle hostility. Is coercive—maximizes psychological involvement with parent, exaggerates conflict and problems, threatens or disarms.*
Disorganized/Disoriented (D)	*Infancy: Exhibits a variety of odd, inexplicable, conflicted, apprehensive, or apparently not goal-directed behaviors in the presence of the parent. Demonstrates a collapse of attention and behavioral strategies. Behaviors may include contradictory, interrupted, incomplete, or stereotypic movement or sequences and may indicate fear, apprehension, confusion, or disorientation.* *Early childhood: Disorganized behaviors disappear and are replaced by role reversals and controlling behaviors. Role reversals have included controlling-punitive behaviors such as harshly ordering about, rejecting, or humiliating the parent or controlling-caregiving such as excessively solicitous behaviors (cheering, reassuring, falsely positive).* *Assigned in combination with A, B, or C.*

References: Ainsworth, 1973; Cassidy & Shaver, 1999; Hesse, 1999; Hesse, Main, Abrams, & Rifkin, 2003; Lyons-Ruth, Zeanah, & Benoit, 2003; Solomon & George, 1999.

ing norms, family factors such as SES and functioning, and environmental factors such as exposure to stress interact in complex ways to affect relationship quality, interactive behaviors, and even the assessment process (Hesse, 1999; Rosen & Rothbaum, 1993). Rothbaum, Rosen, Ujiie, and Uchida (2002) described how family structure and cultural norms contribute to attachment patterns. Studies cited provided evidence that relationships between females with *preoccupied/ambivalent* attachment styles and males with *dismissive/avoidant* styles are common and quite stable in the United States, although unhappy. Emotional distance between spouses often results in the preoccupied parent's overinvolvement with offspring and in children who comfort, distract, or defend parents (especially mothers) during conflicts. Children's illness, emotional difficulties, or problem behaviors may serve as distractions. Although the families with an "overinvolved" mother who turns her focus to her children and distant fathers who turn their energy to their jobs is considered maladaptive in the West, they are considered normal, are less conflictual, and fare better in Japan.

A strong association has been found between specific attachment styles in caregivers and attachment patterns in infants (Hesse, 1999; Hesse et al., 2003). A strong relationship has emerged, for example, between behavior that is extremely rejecting or abusive and insecure attachments (Rosen & Rothbaum, 1993). Table 8.2 includes the caregiver styles that are associated with each infant attachment pattern.

Secure Attachments

An attachment is considered secure if the security and comfort sought from the attachment figure are achieved (Bowlby, 1969/1982). Secure attachments originate when an infant develops confidence (has a mental representation) that his or her help-seeking signals will receive prompt and appropriate adult response (Cassidy, 1999; James, 1994). Sensitive and responsive caregiving is conducive to secure attachments (Hesse et al., 2003). The psychobiologically attuned caregiver synchronizes to the infant's rhythmic structure (Schore, 2003; Siegel, 1999). The caregiver behaves in sync with the infant's affect, communications, gestures, and play, and modifies his or her behavior to fit the infant's rhythms, capacity for stimuli, length of ability to remain engaged, and nature (Schore; Stein & Kendall, 2004). The child and caregiver re-create similar inner psychophysiological states. Schore explains that, when the "good-enough" primary caregiver induces a stress response in her infant through a misattunement, she rapidly reinvokes a reattunement. This reattunement permits a shift from negative affective states to a state of positive affect. Through these experiences, infants learn to regulate their emotions (Stein & Kendall). Through emotional reciprocity (the sharing of emotional states), the infant learns to shift emotional states. Through communicat-

TABLE 8.2
Attachment Styles for Older Adolescents and Adults

Attachment Style	Brief Descriptions
Secure autonomous (B or F)	*Adolescent: Recognition that other relationships may meet attachment needs better than parents can may lead to greater openness, flexibility, and objectivity in re-evaluating relationships. Likely expect minimal disruption to relationship for a minor transgression; concerned with trust-building after a severe breach to restore the relationship. Autonomy and relatedness in disagreements and other interactions with parents. Tendency to turn to parents when very distressed. A smoother process of balancing autonomy and attachment needs. Tendency to engage in productive, problem-solving discussions (even if heated or intense) that balance autonomy with preserving the parent-child relationship. Coherence in discussing attachment-related experiences and affect.* *Adult: Coherent, clear discourse. Descriptions of attachment experiences/relationships (favorable or unfavorable) seem objective and internally consistent. Values the attachment relationship.* *As Caregivers: Secure/autonomous adults most often have infants with secure attachments. Most likely to be empathetic as parents. The only parents found to mirror infant negative expressions.*
Insecure dismissing (A or D)	*Adolescent: Recognition that other relationships may meet attachment needs better than parents can may lead to derogatingly dismissive attitudes toward "deficient" parent(s). Disengagement, dysfunctional anger, or hostility. Show the least autonomy and relatedness in interactions with parents. Avoidance of problem-solving and of renegotiation of relationships; lower levels of confidence in the relationship. Recounts of caregiver's parenting range from glowing but vague to detailed, negative descriptions, both of which steer away from in-depth consideration of negative feelings.* *Adult: Not coherent. Dismissing of attachment-related experiences and relationships. Denial of memories of childhood. Idealizing or normalizing of parents with unsupported or contradicted generalized representations of history. Excessively brief in information provided.* *As Caregivers: Most often associated with insecure/avoidant infant offspring. Appear to be the least interested and responsive to infants and older offspring. Use of pressuring techniques with adolescents that tend to undermine autonomy.*
Insecure preoccupied (C or E)	*Adolescent: Recognition that other relationships may meet attachment needs better than parents can may lead to angry preoccupation with the "deficient" parent(s). Use of passive thought processes reflecting mental entanglement between self and caregiver. Recounts of caregiver's parenting range from glowing but vague to detailed, negative descriptions.* *Adult: Not coherent. Preoccupied with or by past attachment experiences/relationships. Appears angry, passive, or fearful. Often long, grammatically entangled sentences, or vague language.* *As Caregivers: Most often associated with insecure resistant/ ambivalent infant offspring. Inappropriately responsive to offspring. Overengagement with adolescent offspring.*

TABLE 8.2 (continued)
Attachment Styles for Older Adolescents and Adults

Attachment Style	Brief Descriptions
Unresolved disorganized (D or U)	*Adult: Striking lapse in metacognitive monitoring of reasoning or discourses during discussions of loss or trauma. Incompatible ideas. State or time-space shifts. Recurring catastrophic fantasies not based on experience. Attempts to control others by becoming punitive or overly solicitous—especially when stressed or fearful of or for the person. May exhibit confusion, eulogistic speech, strange movement, or prolonged silence.* *As Caregivers: Most often linked to disorganized infant attachments.*
Hostile-helpless disorganized	*Adult: The individual unconsciously identifies with either an aggressive or helpless-fearful caregiver; has held and holds globally negative representations of caregivers; may hold contradictory attitudes toward caregivers (both devaluation and identification); exhibits pervasive indicators of hostile and/or fearful states of mind; may see self as bad or unworthy; affective numbing may be demonstrated by laughter at painful anecdotes; evidence of affectively intense, unstable relaltionships, such as ruptures in contact with family members in adulthood.* *As Caregivers: Linked to infant disorganization at 18 months of age.*

References: Ainsworth, 1989; Allen & Land, 1999; Cassidy & Shaver, 1999; Hesse, 1999; Hesse, Main, Abrams, & Rifkin, 2003; Lyons-Ruth, Yellin, Melnick, & Atwood, 2003; Solomon & George, 1999.

ing with responsive adults, infants begin to develop a strong sense of self (Stein & Kendall).

Secure attachments can instill in a child the expectation that adults can be turned to for nurturance, support, guidance and need fulfillment as well as instilling representations of self-worth and competence (Yates, Egeland, & Sroufe, 2003). Secure attachments are adaptive, and they foster the gradual and appropriate self-reliance that leads to mastery and autonomy (James, 1994; Luthar, 2003). Attachment security has correlated positively with enthusiasm, compliance, and persistence in toddlers (Atkinson, 1997). Compared to children insecurely attached as infants, securely attached children have been found to be more ego-resilient, happier, more popular with peers, and more competent (Weinfield, Sroufe, Egeland, & Carlson, 1999; Yates et al.). They have had better quality peer relationships, later first intercourse, and a tendency to require emotional commitment for intimacy. Infant attachment behaviors have predicted autonomy and relatedness with parents in adolescence, but they have not predicted attachment classification in adolescence. Autonomy-seeking behaviors in adolescence and an underlying positive relationship with parents have tended to be highly correlated (Allen & Land, 1999). Differentiation of self and others permits a view of self as separate from caregivers and a move away from a script-oriented view of self in relationships. Formal operational thinking allows analysis and comparison of relationships. With the capacity to evaluate the nature of relationships, increased ability to take another person's perspective, and a reduced need to monitor the availability of parents for attachment needs, adolescents attain a level of cognitive and emotional freedom (Allen & Land). For adults and youths, a close, confiding relationship is protective against stress (Rutter, 1997).

Insecure Attachments

When the quality of caregiving is inconsistent or sporadic or if care is regularly insensitive, infants develop insecure attachments (Ainsworth, 1973; Bowlby, 1969/1982, 1973; Thompson, 1991). Among the types of insecure attachments are *avoidant* and *ambivalent/resistant* attachments. Rejecting or disinterested caregiving has predicted *insecure-avoidant* attachments (Hesse et al., 2003). *Avoidant* infants have learned that the attachment figure may reject their advances. As a result, they suppress need and distance themselves from the caregiver. They communicate directly with the caregiver only when feeling well; when distressed, they mask negative emotion and self-soothe (Knox, 2003b). Inconsistent or preoccupied caregiving has predicted insecure *resistant/ambivalent* attachments (Hesse et al.). *Ambivalent/resistant* children fear the attachment figure will either fail to respond or will intrude in a way they cannot control. They cling and try to control the caregiver's response (Knox).

The temperamental dimension of negative emotionality is associated with insecure attachment (Rutter, 1997). In adolescence, insecure attachments are more often characterized by increased hostility, poorer social skills with peers, more romantic but less qualitative relationships, and ongoing problems with parents (Allen & Land, 1999). Attachment insecurity has been associated with depression, distress, dissociative states, anxiety disorders, suicidality, and personality disorders (Alexander, Anderson, Brand, Schaeffer, Grelling, & Kretz, 1998; Blizard, 2001; Fergusson, Woodward, & Horwood, 2000; West, Adam, Spreng, & Rose, 2001), with relationship problems during childhood and adult life (Styron & Janoff-Bulman, 1997), with internalizing symptoms in boys (Atkinson, 1997), and with behavior problems (Scheeringa & Zeanah, 2001; Thompson, 1991). Adolescent psychiatric disturbance has predicted insecure attachments in young adults (Allen & Land).

Adolescents' *insecure-dismissing* attachments (A) have been linked to externalizing problems such as aggression or delinquency, conduct disorder, and substance abuse (Allen & Land, 1999). Maternal control does not serve as a buffer against deviance for this attachment style. Insecure-dismissing adolescents may develop symptoms that serve to distract themselves and others from stress-related cues. Kobak and Cole (1994) found that college-age youth with eating disorders disproportionately used insecure-dismissing strategies (cited in Allen & Land). The attention given to the eating disorders provided distraction from their emotional distress. Preoccupied insecure adolescents (C) have been predicted by overpersonalized arguments with fathers 10 years earlier as well as by a lack of avoidance or withdrawal from arguments and unproductive overengagement with parents that undermines autonomy. Use of preoccupied attachment patterns in adolescence has been linked to depression and other internalizing problems. When unresolved, these problems may include suicidality. Research has produced mixed findings regarding the direct or indirect association of preoccupation with externalizing behaviors. Preoccupied adolescents have had symptoms or problem behaviors that maintain focus on distress-related cues and keep the attachment system highly activated.

Disorganized/Disoriented Attachments

In experimental settings in which toddlers are deliberately given conflicting signals, they exhibit disorganized behavior (Hesse et al., 2003). Each infant has an optimal level of stimulation (Stein & Kendall, 2004). When underaroused, infants usually seek additional stimulation. Attuned caregivers will match and exaggerate the infant's behavior. If the child looks away because of overstimulation, the sensitive mother responds accordingly. If the caregiver continues to excite rather than disengage, the infant will eventually disorganize. Fear of the parent is believed to lead to disorganized/disoriented (D) attachments. The infant's normal biological safe haven becomes simultaneously the source of alarm. The parent's behavior may drive the infant away from and toward the parent at the same time, producing an unsolvable experience. Assessment of D attachments frequently are made in combination with one of the other main attachment classifications (A, B, or C). The disorganized/disoriented attachments characteristic of abused and neglected youths predict later chronic disturbances of affect regulation, stress management, hostile-aggressive behavior, risk of PTSD, and a predisposition to relational aggression (Lyons-Ruth & Jacobvitz, 1999; Schore, 2003). D attachments in combination with traumatic experiences have been linked to dissociative disorders (Liotti, 2004). Liotti posits that youths' increased vulnerability to trauma when their parents have been traumatized may be mediated by attachment disorganization. He explains, for example, for children of Nazi Holocaust survivors who develop disorders (see Danieli, 1998), their parents' unresolved traumatic memories may have interfered with parental behavior and induced disorganized attachments.

Main and Hesse reported a link between parental death in childhood and infant disorganization in the next generation (Hesse et al., 2003; Lyons-Ruth, Yellin, Melnick, & Atwood, 2003). Hesse, Main, and their colleagues explained that both maltreating caregivers and nonmaltreating parents with a history of trauma or loss may behave in ways that result in disorganization. Maltreating parents do so with directly frightening behaviors. Nonmaltreating parents with a history of unresolved trauma or loss may create a state of alarm or even terror in infants with frightening behaviors such as sudden shifts in expressions or haunting tones of voice that are frightening and confusing to the child. The parent may exhibit frightened, absorbed or dissociative, and unexplained or anomalous forms of frightening or threatening but not physically abusive behavior. Some unresolved parents may also display sexualized, timid/deferential or protective, and brief periods of disorganized or disoriented behaviors likely occurring during dissociative states. In interviews, these parents' slippages in language and reasoning may occur especially during discussion of a loss or traumatic experience (Hesse et al.; Siegel, 2003). These behaviors may be most likely to appear in stressful situations. In contrast, frightened and alarming parental behaviors related to an identifiable external source are unlikely to produce disorganization and are usually followed by comfort, contact, or "repair" (Hesse et al.; Lyons-Ruth & Jacobvitz, 1999).

Although a number of studies have confirmed the link between parental losses or severely distressing events to infant offspring's disorganized attachments (Liotti, 2004), research has also shown that some infants classified as disorganized do not have parents classified as "unresolved" on the Adult Attachment Interview (AAI) (see "Attachment Measures," below), suggesting that there may be multiple pathways to disorganization (Lyons-Ruth, Yellin et al., 2003). Lyons-Ruth, Yellin et al. studied a small group of parents (n = 45) to determine whether the severity of trauma or loss experienced before age 16 is related to parental unresolved states of mind and parental hostile-helpless states of mind. Whereas the 1985–1998 Main and Goldwyn coding system classifies mothers as unresolved when they show lapses of monitoring of reason or discourse in response to material related to trauma or loss, the coding system for hostile-helpless states of mind examines discourse patterns throughout the AAI interview regardless of relevance to loss or trauma. Neither the severity of childhood abuse nor the experience of parental death in childhood was related to AAI unresolved states of mind. Studies have also found a differential effect of trauma versus loss on parent-infant interactions. Lyons-Ruth and colleagues found that parental death or separation/divorce, lack of structure and supervision, and number of family moves as well as sexual abuse in a mother's childhood correlated with reduced involvement with infant offspring at 12 to 18 months. On the other hand, family conflict, severe punishment, lack of warmth, and parental mental-health problems as well as witnessed violence and childhood physical abuse were related to hostile-intrusive behavior toward infants. An unresolved state of mind and the experience of childhood parental death contributed independently and additively to the prediction of infant disorganization at 12 months. At 18 months, the severity of trauma had no direct relation to infant disorganization but was associated with hostile-helpless states of mind, which in turn predicted infant disorganization. Parental loss and unresolved states did not add to the prediction of disorganization at 18 months, suggesting that maternal trauma may become more important to attachment when infants make the transition to toddlerhood.

A single infant may exhibit disorganized attachment behavior toward an unresolved caregiver, organized-avoidant attachment toward a separate "dismissing" caregiver, and organized secure attachment behaviors toward a third attachment figure (Liotti, 2004). This suggests that the attachment relationship reflects aspects of caregiver behaviors and the individual relationship rather than something inherent in the child. Although some studies support the belief in a minimal influence on attachment disorganization by child-intrinsic factors such as temperament or neurobiology (Lyons-Ruth & Jacobvitz, 1999; Liotti), one study has revealed the influence of a genetic factor. Lakatos, Toth, Nemoda, Ney, Sasvari, & Gervai (2000) found a gene allele of the DRD4 gene, related to defective dopaminergic brain functions and reduced efficiency of attentional systems, that may contribute to attachment disorganization (Liotti). Less than 40% of infants carrying the allele develop a disorganized attachment. Liotti hypothesizes that gene-environment interactions contribute to many, but not all, cases of infant attachment disorganization.

Siegel (2003) suggests that parental behavior that produces mental disorganization in the child may create current functional impairment and, if repeated, a tendency toward future disintegration. D attachments in infancy have been associated with aspects of psychopathology from middle childhood to late adolescence, with unusual levels of aggression, and with dissociative-like behaviors in elementary and high school (Hesse et al., 2003). D infant attachments predict role inversion with the parent by age 6 as well as response inhibition, dysfluent discourse, and narratives with catastrophic fantasies. In a 1987 study of 6 year olds classified D in infancy, Kaplan found fear, resistance, silence, disorganization, and disorientation when the children were presented with pictured separations from a parent (cited in Hesse et al.). Kaplan suggested that these behaviors in the children may have been related to continued confused and fearful behaviors in the parents regarding an important loss.

Cannot Classify

A small percentage of adults and children do not fit any of the attachment classifications (Hesse, 1999; Hesse et al., 2003). Adults with high idealization scores (usually associated with dismissing insecure attachment styles) who later discuss parents in an angry preoccupied manner (associated with insecure preoccupied attachment styles) have been classified as *cannot classify*. Parents of unclassifiable children also have exhibited frightened and frightening behaviors within play sessions.

TRAUMA AND ATTACHMENT

Faulty attachments may precede, occur during, or follow traumas. Insecure attachments have resulted in vulnerabilities to traumas or traumatic reactions. Shared traumatic experiences may create traumatic attachments. Children's traumas caused by caregivers or caregivers' unresolved traumas may produce insecure or disorganized attachments in infants or children. Research evidence suggests that significant major life events can disrupt the continuity of attachments and attachment patterns and strategies (Allen & Land, 1999; Box 8.1b).

Attachment styles may affect a youth's interactions with and expectations of a treating clinician, peers, and authority figures. Relationships are encoded in memory and help to shape the brain circuitry that enable memories, relationships, and self-regulatory processes (Siegel, 2003). Research evidence suggests that parental attachment styles affect children's memory capacity and responses to stressful or novel situations (Howe, 1997). For example, children whose parents had an avoidant or anxious/ambivalent attachment style made more errors than other children did in recalling stressful medical procedures (Goodman & Quas, 1996).

Traumatic Attachment

In addition to the normal attachment bonds between infants/children and parents are the bonds that occur during the perception that one's life is in another's hands (e.g., with a physician or another patient during life-threatening illness) or when individuals go through intense experiences together. Thus, attachments may occur under traumatic circumstances. Children may develop increased attachments to those with whom they endure a traumatic experience or with perpetrators of traumatic experiences (Nader & Mello, 2002; Nader & Pynoos, 1993). *Hostage syndrome* denotes the increase of attachment to perpetrators during traumatic events (Ochberg & Soskis, 1982). The child victim perceives outside help as unavailable; a dominant person alternates terroristic and nurturing behaviors, thus strengthening the bonds; responses such as dissociation, numbing, or self-blame, among others, lead to a confusion of pain and love; the victim's need for attachment overcomes fears (James, 1994). Such trauma bonding is based on terror, the sense that one's life is in danger, and the assailant is in total control. Relief over survival may be experienced as gratitude toward the perpetrator.

Trauma's Impact on Attachment Style

Childhood traumas may disrupt youths' attachments and alter their interactional styles (Lyons-Ruth & Jacobvitz, 1999; Roche, Runtz, & Hunter,

1999). Changes in interactional styles with peers, caretakers, and other adults sometimes follow, for example, posttrauma increases in irritability, impulsiveness, aggressive reactivity, fears, or reactivity to reminders. Because of their natures, ongoing traumas such as child abuse or prolonged hostage situations make or change attachments or attachment patterns (Herman, 1992b; Ochberg & Soskis, 1982). Single-incident traumatic events can result in impaired functioning, feeling overwhelmed, prolonged separation, fear, anxiety, and misinterpretation of behaviors. Any of these occurrences can lead to patterns of child or parent behavior that seriously interfere with the attachment relationship. Following catastrophic events, a parent might not be able to recognize or respond adequately to the child's needs; the child might not be able to adequately express needs or respond to the adult (Field, Seligman, Scafidi, & Schanberg, 1996; James, 1994; Scheeringa & Zeanah, 2001). The parent's own trauma or response to the young child's trauma has sometimes resulted in inadequate, withdrawn, overprotective, smothering, endangering, or constrictive caretaking (James; Scheeringa & Zeanah). Disorganized/disoriented infant attachments are linked to a variety of subsequent pathology. Among other results, Schore (2003) proposes that a trauma-generated disorganized/disoriented insecure attachment may result in an inability to generate a coherent strategy for coping with relational stress.

ASSESSING ATTACHMENT

Research has been inconsistent and has shown only a modest relationship between parental caregiving and the quality of attachment relationships (Hesse, 1999; Rosen & Rothbaum, 1993). A number of factors may contribute to these disparate findings (Atkinson, 1997, Cassidy, 1999). Study samples with extremely negative forms of parenting are likely to produce stronger associations between parental behavior and attachment categories (Allen & Land, 1999; Rosen & Rothbaum). After a certain period of time, an infant or child's behaviors may change because of habituation to or expectations of parental responsiveness. Studies have shown that maternal sensitivity at 1 month is a better predictor of attachment security patterns at age 18 than when parental sensitivity was measured at 8 or 24 months (Hesse). Maternal sensitivity at 12 years showed no relationship to adolescent status.

The location of the observations (home or laboratory), the duration and number of assessment periods, the degree to which children's responses contribute to ratings of parent's quality of assistance, the focus of interpretation, and the level of distress produced during the assessment session may all affect findings (Rosen & Rothbaum, 1993). Allen & Land (1999) explain, for example, that continuities between infant Strange Situation behavior and adolescent attachment patterns primarily reflect continuities in the parenting received instead of reflecting stable internal working models (see "Attachment Styles," above). Attachment styles may predict later outcomes because they represent stable, ongoing aspects of parenting.

Of course, age differences have important implications for accurate assessment (see "Age and Assessing Attachment," below). Solomon and George (1999) believe that the greatest uncertainty in assessing attachment patterns is for preschool-age children. Allen and Land (1999) have suggested that adolescents' efforts to establish autonomy make assessing their attachment organization difficult. Adolescents, regardless of attachment style, exhibit an intensity in their efforts to overcome dependence on parents. An adolescent may therefore avoid a parent when stressed. In addition, adolescents have exhibited a greater reticence than adults in participating in attachment interviews.

Allen and Land (1999) have proposed that attachment organization primarily may reflect strategies for handling intense affect. Strange Situation behavior, then, could be interpreted in terms of affect regulation. Then, similar to adolescent dismissing behaviors, infant avoidance (A) of a parent on reunion may reflect attempts to minimize affect on reunion. Like preoccupied adolescents, ambivalent or resistant (C) infant attachment patterns may indicate an overwhelmed, arousal-enhancing coping style.

It is important, when assessing attachment relationships, to distinguish between attachment and other behaviors. For example, in addition to attachment figure, the caregiver may serve as playmate, disciplinarian, or teacher. Playful interactions between caregiver and child such as peek-a-boo and reading are not attachment behaviors. Moreover, even when an attachment component exists in a relationship, an attachment bond cannot be presumed from it (Bowlby, 1969/1982; Cassidy, 1999). If separated from its mother, a distressed 1 year old will direct attachment behaviors to a stranger. Similarly, a child may regularly direct attachment behavior to a close friend and feel comfort in the friend's presence. Close spacing of assessments has produced lower stability in findings, presumably due to sensitization of infants to the procedure (Solomon & George, 1999).

Age and Assessing Attachment

Age is an important factor in measuring the quality of attachment. Defining the differences in attachment behavior at different ages poses a problem to assessment. Infants may cry, vocalize, or reach out in order to elicit the mother's proximity (Cassidy, 1999). Toddlers may run, walk, crawl, leap, or even roll toward the caregiver. Older children are cognitively able to maintain relationships with an absent person (Rutter, 1997). With the child's increasing age, the timing and quality of distance interactions including conversation, the quality of parent-child negotiations related to separations and reunions, and the child's symbolic representations become important to assessment (Solomon & George, 1999).

Assessments of infant attachments have focused primarily upon prox-imity-seeking and exploration as well as the quality of caregiving. Rosen and Burke (1999) found an association between parental caregiving and attachment for 18 to 24 month olds but not for 4 to 5 year olds. Solomon and George (1999) suggest that attachment security and insecurity are based primarily on those instances in which the attachment security system is activated. Attachment behavior is best elicited and observed, therefore, in situations that are stressful, fear-inducing, or threatening. Sickness, calamity, danger, and disaster naturally engage the adult attachment sys-tem (Bowlby, 1969/1982). In such cases, it is normal to seek the proximity of another known and trusted individual. Any type of suffering activates the attachment system in adults and youths (Liotti, 2004).

The interactions that define an attachment style differ across time (see Tables 8.1, 8.2). Specific behaviors or classifications may be more prevalent at particular ages or in different cultures. Research evidence suggests, for example, that the number of disorganized/disoriented infants increases between 12 and 18 months of age (Solomon & George, 1999). During ado-lescence, attachment behaviors are gradually transferred to peers. Like early attachment behaviors, emerging romantic attachments are biologi-cally rooted in the survival of the species (Allen & Land, 1999). Perhaps awkwardly at first, adolescents transfer parental functions to peers—they "obey" their directives and desire to please them. Allen and Land suggest that autonomy-seeking can be seen as a part of the exploratory system. A central function of the adolescent's attachment relationship may be to provide an emotional safe haven or secure base that permits exploration of a wide range of emotional states. From a survival standpoint, develop-ing the capacity for self-regulation of emotions may enhance the ability to form and sustain relationships and to nurture offspring.

Attachment Measures

Ainsworth provided rating scales of parent-child interaction and a 21-to 24-minute laboratory procedure (the Strange Situation) that includes a series of everyday stressors to measure the quality of attachment (Atkin-son, 1997; Rosen & Burke, 1999; Solomon & George, 1999). Brief separa-tions and reunions do not have the same meaning for all children (Rutter, 1997). For example, responses to the absence of a main caretaker is likely to differ for Japanese infants who are rarely separated from their moth-ers versus institutionalized children who are used to multiple caretak-ers. In addition to the Strange Situation procedure, other methods have been devised to assess attachment across age groups including other videotape observation ratings of parent-child interactions in prescribed activities at home or in the laboratory, Q-sort parental ratings of children (see below), narrative techniques, picture response procedures, doll play methods, and, for older youths and adults, self-report measures (Solomon & George). Adult evaluations have been used to predict infant or adult attachment patterns. As measured by the Adult Attachment Interview, the coherence of parents' autobiographical narratives when telling of their lives from their earliest experiences with their own parents has predicted infant attachment (Hesse et al., 2003; Siegel, 2003). The Inventory of Parent and Peer Attachment (Armsden & Greenberg, 1987; for youths as young as 12) and measures of romantic attachments have been used to study adolescent attachments (Allen & Land, 1999). As of 1999, AAI was the only measure that demonstrated an empirical connection to attachment as assessed in infancy.

Methods have been adapted for older children by lengthening the time of separation, changing the instructions, or changing the gender of the stranger or investigator (Solomon & George, 1999). The validity and reliability of methods is still under assessment. Results have been best when researchers have been well-trained.

Strange Situation

The *Strange Situation* (Ainsworth et al., 1978) is a laboratory procedure designed to assess the balance between exploratory and attachment behavior (Solomon & George, 1999). The Strange Situation procedure usually includes an introduction to the new room and a series of seven 3-minute episodes. The episodes are designed to activate the attachment behavioral system and to produce mild but increasing levels of stress (Rosen & Burke, 1999). The child is first introduced to the new room in the company of a parent and then to an unfamiliar adult. The stranger is the same gender as the parent in studies including both mothers and fathers. After introduction to the room, the series presents the following 3-minute episodes (Rosen & Burke; Solomon & George): (1) the infant settles in and explores. The parent assists only if necessary; (2) the strange adult is introduced and, in the final minute, plays with the child; (3) the parent leaves the infant with the stranger; (4) the parent returns, and the stranger leaves quietly; (5) the parent leaves the child alone in the room; (6) the adult stranger enters and interacts with the infant as necessary; and (7) the parent returns, and the stranger leaves quietly. Videotapes of these episodes capture the child's exploration of the environment, the child's reactions to separation and reunion, and the child's use of the parent as a secure base or to gain comfort. Coding results in discrete categories rather than continuous dimensions (Rutter, 1997). Schneider-Rosen, Braunwald, Carlson, and Cicchetti (1985) and Rosen and Burke used a modified scoring procedure to classify 24-month-old infants and their proximity-seeking, contact maintenance, avoidance, resistance, search, and distance interaction. Solomon and George have described three systems of classification criteria that use the Strange Situation procedure to evaluate preschool children. Main and Cassidy developed a system to classify 2.5 to 6 year olds. Crittendon's Preschool Assessment of Attachment and Cassidy and Marvin's system have been used with 2.5 to 4.5 year olds. Both methods identify communicative and defensive goals underlying attachment patterns (see Solomon & George for a summary of the these and other methods).

Attachment Q-Sort

The Attachment Q-sort (AQS; Waters, 1987) was developed to evaluate the secure-base behaviors—the use of parents for comfort and exploration—in 1 to 5 year olds (Rosen & Burke, 1999). Parents/raters familiarize themselves with the 90 behavioral statements and then observe the child for a prescribed period (a few weeks) while thinking about how well each item describes the child. An experimenter then directs the parent/rater to sort the 90 Q-sort cards into nine piles of 10 cards as indicated in the instructions. Q-sort distributions are then correlated with a criterion Q-sort developed from experts' descriptions of the optimally secure child (Rosen & Burke). AQS procedures are based on longer in-home observations and interviews with mothers (Rutter, 1997). Although Q-sort classifications have correlated moderately with assessments of attachment security using the Strange Situation (Rosen & Burke), the observations extend beyond the stress situations used to measure attachment in the Strange Situation procedures (Rutter).

Picture Response Procedures

Kaplan (1987) developed a classification system for children's responses to pictures using the picture response protocol of Hansburg's (1972) Separation Anxiety Test (cited in Solomon & George, 1999). Scenes ranged from mild to stressful (from a parent's bedtime "Goodnight" to watching a parent leave). Attachment groups are differentiated based on children's emotional openness and ability to imagine constructive solutions to the idea of feeling endangered by separation. Children are classified as *resourceful* (B; discuss coping in constructive ways), *inactive* (A; indicate feelings of vulnerability or distress but no method to cope), *ambivalent* (C, give contradictory responses), or *fearful* (D, respond with inexplicable fear, lack of constructive strategies for coping, or disorganized or disoriented thought processes).

Adult Attachment Inventory

AAI (George, Kaplan, & Main, 1984, 1996) has been used with older adolescents and adults. It is a semistructured, hour-long protocol that assesses the degree of coherence, clarity, and organization when discussing situations that are highly affectively charged (Allen & Land, 1999; Hesse, 1999). Its 18 questions elicit descriptions of the family and of childhood relationships with parents, the relationship with the mother and with the father (five adjectives for each parent and related memories for each adjective), behaviors and responses when distressed/hurt/ill, salient separations, possible experiences of rejection, parental threats, abuse, impact of early experiences on current personality, setbacks to development, other close adults, loss of a parent or other loved one, changes in relationships with parents, and the current relationship with parents. If interviewees are parents, they are asked about relationships with their offspring. Verbatim transcribed interviews are assessed by trained raters (Hesse, 1999).

Coding Systems. The AAI interview is scored to indicate the degree to which each parent was described as loving, neglecting, rejecting, involving, and pressuring the infant to achieve (Lyons-Ruth, Yellin et al., 2003). A second set of scales is used to assess the participant's state of mind and discourse style, including coherence of thought, idealization, insistence on lack of recall, derogation, fear of loss of the child, metacognitive monitoring, passivity of speech, involved anger, lack of resolution of loss or trauma, and the coherence of the total transcript. Based on scale scores, an adult is assigned to one of four major attachment classifications: secure, insecure/dismissing, insecure/preoccupied, and unresolved with respect to loss or trauma (Main & Goldwyn, 1998). A fifth category, currently designated *cannot classify*, is characterized by shifting from one strategy to another over the course of the interview (e.g. dismissing to preoccupied) or displaying low coherence on the interview as a whole without an elevated score on any of the indicators of an insecure state of mind (Hesse, 1999). Newly developed classification codes for a hostile-helpless category (Yellin, Atwood, Melnick, & Lyons-Ruth, 2003) were derived empirically to operationalize the states of mind that might present on the AAI secondary to chronic relational trauma, including sexual, physical, or emotional abuse. Hostile-helplessness codes include (1) *global devaluation of a caregiver* (each globally negative past representation of caregivers that continued to be active in the present); (2) *identification with a hostile caregiver* (each negative evaluation of a caregiver in which the participant also identified with or appeared to value or accept similarities between the negatively evaluated attachment figure and the self without noting the tension between these two views and expressed without involved anger); (3) *recurrent references to fearful affect* (each reference to participant's own experiences of fearful affect states); (4) *sense of self as bad* (uncritically related anecdotes that depicted participants themselves as guilty, responsible, deserving of disrespectful treatment, or undeserving of positive attention; perhaps indexing an ongoing need to preserve a positive view of caregivers by continuing to blame oneself); (5) *laughter at pain* (whenever laughter followed anecdotes about psychological or physical distress); and (6) *ruptured attachments* (each reference to no longer having contact with one or more nuclear family members through a deliberate decision to terminate contact).

CONCLUSIONS

Infant-caregiver attachments are rooted in biological survival needs. Infants may have different attachment styles with different caregivers. Attachment behaviors vary with age. Insecure attachments have been linked to traumas in more than one way. Insecure attachments have been implicated in vulnerability to a variety of emotional and behavioral problems and disorders including PTSD. Shared traumatic experiences may create attachments among survivors or between perpetrators and victims. Traumas may disrupt attachments and relationship styles. Caregivers' own unresolved traumas or losses may produce disorganized/disoriented attachments.

Disorganized/disoriented attachments are characteristic of abused and neglected youths. Multiple pathways may lead to the parental behaviors and states that induce attachment disorganization in infants including a parent's own unresolved traumas and losses. Disorganized/disoriented attachments predict later chronic disturbances of affect regulation, stress management, hostile-aggressive behavior, risk of PTSD, and a predisposition to relational aggression and, in combination with traumatic experiences, have been linked to dissociative disorders.

Part III

Methods and Measures for Assessing Trauma in Youths

9

Interviewing Children and Adolescents Following Traumatic Events

Individual interviews are used to question and observe youths for diagnostic purposes, to assess symptoms and functioning, and to make decisions about the treatment or care of youths (Waterman, Blades, & Spencer, 2004). For thousands of children yearly, individual interviews are used to determine the nature of a youth's experience for forensic purposes. Assessment and diagnostic interviews may have a therapeutic as well as an evaluative purpose. The goal of a forensic interview, however, is to discover the truth without influencing the information gathered. Because an interviewer's or clinician's questions and interventions may influence a child's recall of a traumatic experience(s), cognizance of whether the child's testimony will be needed is important when conducting an interview.

The success of a diagnostic or assessment interview with a youth depends on several factors. The interviewer must be able to establish rapport with the child, gain his or her trust, and demonstrate an interest in the youth and his or her emotional state. Establishing trust and good rapport is essential to truthful and timely completion of a scale regardless of the format used to obtain information (Reich & Todd, 2002b; Reynolds & Kamphaus, 1998). The rater must also be able to attune to nonverbal cues and to contradictions in the child's verbal report.

With traumatized youths, ensuring a child's physical safety and well-being must precede any attempts to assess formally his or her traumatic reactions (McCleery & Harvey, 2004). Initially after a traumatic event, it is important to restore safety, attend to physical injuries and needs, prevent additional traumatization, and provide support (Nader, 1999d). A youth

215

may not feel safe, even after he or she has been made safe—protected from harm, taken to a safe location, given any needed medical care, placed in the care of protecting and nurturing caregivers, and/or provided needed information. Restoring the youth's sense of safety may require, for example, time spent in the protective presence of adults, alterations in day- and night-time routines (e.g., sitting with them until they go to sleep), age-appropriate and accurate information, and the ongoing experience of safety.

Interviewing a child is quite different from interviewing an adult, requiring special skills (Wandersman, 1998). Play, toys, or drawings may assist the very young child and older youths who are not comfortable verbalizing personal information, uncomfortable feelings, and traumas that they may want to forget. This chapter presents some of the issues important to interviewing traumatized youths. It includes a discussion of general principles for interviewing youths, children's memories and what influences memory, and important aspects of forensic interviews including appropriate methods of questioning children. A thorough under-standing of childhood trauma, mental-health issues, and developmental issues as well as skilled and experiential training can provide some of the safeguards needed in the assessment process with distressed youths. This chapter is not intended to replace skilled training or supervised practice.

Special Methods

Specialized methods are often required in interviewing victims of trauma. A thorough understanding of the meaning and nature of specific posttrauma symptomatic reactions as well as of appropriate interview questions is a necessary but not sufficient prerequisite to successful and harmless assessment. Understanding the respondent's state of mind and issues of closure are essential (Nader, 1997c; Ochberg, 2002). During the war, health professionals in the former Yugoslavian Republics reported a variety of harmful effects after survivors of rape were interviewed by journalists, mental-health professionals, and other personnel. These results included suicides and suicide attempts, severe depressions, and acute psychotic episodes (Swiss & Giller, 1993). Similarly, studies of adults suggest that one to three psychological debriefings may worsen outcomes for some participants (Mayou, Ehlers, & Hobbs, 2000; Raphael & Wilson, 2001; Ruzek & Watson, 2001). Consequently, Ruzek and Watson recom-mended that, if debriefings are employed, only experienced, well-trained practitioners conduct them.

Training that includes cultural issues is important not only to increase accuracy but also to prevent harm. In Kuwait following the Gulf Crisis, adolescent girls were unwilling to admit a rape experience unless assured of confidentiality and separate record keeping (Nader, 1997a). Views and reactions to trauma and mental-health intervention vary across cultures. Understanding the beliefs and practices of the person being interviewed is crucial to ensuring the collection of complete and accurate information and for the protection of those affected by the event (Box 9.1).

GENERAL PRINCIPLES FOR INTERVIEWING YOUTHS

Whether conducting assessments using trauma and other scales in a large group or conducting individual assessments in a private office, specific principles apply. The interviewer's competence, credibility, and demeanor are important to the success of assessment. The youth's safety with, trust for, and rapport with the interviewer are also essential. Although the impact of interviewer/clinician characteristics is not yet fully clear, these characteristics may become important following traumas (Nader, 2001b). After violent or other human-induced traumas, for example, the gender and other characteristics of the perpetrator may

---

BOX 9.1
Case Examples: Youth Interviews

a. *Noura.* When she was 16, Noura was raped by an enemy soldier. She told no one. After a year, she worked up the courage to tell her family that she had been raped during the war. The next day, her brother killed her. A Kuwaiti clergyman explained that Arab females are considered tainted if raped.

b. *Lilly.* Lilly was a 3 year old who, at the age of 2, was in the back seat during a car accident. Her previously violently traumatized mother was driving when they were struck by another car. Although there were no visible injuries, her mother was extremely upset by the accident and began to tremble and cry. Lilly froze and looked dazed for several minutes following the accident. Subsequently she ate poorly, cried more, was anxiously attached to her mother, and cried out in her sleep. In the interview room, her play included normal doll play and re-enacting play with cars. Lilly moved two cars in their respective lanes in opposite directions toward each other. When the two cars became close to one another, she would freeze and remain frozen in place. By the second session, Lilly was comfortable with the clinician. She seemed to feel obligated to include her mother in her play, often as an afterthought. Her mother was then excused from the room, but stayed nearby in case she was needed.

c. *Marie* (Nader, 2001b). While her mother washed their clothes, 8-year old Marie sat reading on a bench against the front glass wall of the Laundromat. A car drove through the glass, propelling Marie head-first into the corner of a washing machine. Marie only remembered her confusion as she went flying and her mother's shocked and frightened face as her mother held Marie's head in her arms. Marie's doctor said that she would never regain memory of hitting the washing machine because of her head injury. In the course of therapy, Marie was prompted to begin before the car hit her and to recall, out loud, in slow detail, each aspect of her experience. At first, she seemed to rush past the segment in which she hit the washing machine. After backing up and slowing down the mental image, she was able to regain memory of the moments preceding, during, and after the impact. This memory recovery provided relief from an ongoing sense of confusion and separateness from her witnessing family members.

d. *Jenny.* Jenny was 16 when she was abducted with her family by a substance-abusing man who was paying his drug debt by acting as an assassin. He mistook Jenny's innocent family for his assigned hit. The family was held hostage for 3 days. Each day, the man murdered one of the family members. Jenny was rescued while the man was preparing to kill her. Every time the police detectives tried to interview her, she began to tremble and sob uncontrollably and could not speak. A few months of therapy and the opportunity to retell her experience in a safe environment with a trusted therapist enabled her to testify and to begin to grieve.

affect how the child responds to an interviewer (D'Urso, Esquilin, Fiore, Haldapoulus, & Heiman, 1995). From beginning to end, the interviewer must be able to create a safe environment, maintain rapport, adapt to the needs of the youth being interviewed, and provide appropriate closure and reorientation to the present.

Creating a Safe Environment

During a traumatic event, the youth's safety or feelings of safety have been threatened. The youth may have been exposed to threat perpetrated by an adult whom the youth should have been able to trust as well as to horrible and/or frightening sensory experiences. The youth's reactions may be additionally complicated by previous stressful experiences or disturbed trust (chapters 5, 7). Very distressed youths may need breaks during an extended interview or if extremely upset by an interview question (Reich & Todd, 2002b). A skilled interviewer must learn when to press forward and when to pause. Too little faith in the child's ability to provide information despite discomfort or the interviewer's insensitivity to the level of the child's distress can be problematic for the youth and for the assessment.

Any reluctance to hear aspects of the child's experience and any perceived judgment (positive or negative; approval or disapproval) of responses or experiences is likely to undermine the accuracy of reporting and may even disrupt the youth's memory (Nader, 1997c; Reich & Todd, 2002b; Santtila, Korkmana, & Sandnabba, 2004). If the child feels that the interviewer is upset by or negatively judging the information given, the youth may withhold information, exaggerate, or tone down answers. The youth may overreport the positive. Spoken or unspoken admiration or approval of qualities, achievements (such as grades), or behaviors may result in attempts to please the interviewer or to gain his or her approval (Reich & Todd). Reich and Todd suggest a moderate conversational or "storytelling" tone and avoidance of a singsong cadence. Both a balanced sense of empathy and a balance between genuine interest and neutrality are important. Conveying warmth and friendliness are usually beneficial.

When the traumatic event has affected a large group of youths, community or school interventions may be a part of an initial or ongoing assessment and intervention process. Immediately following a catastrophic event after safety is restored, classroom or other group venues may be used to provide support, factual information, normalization of responses (i.e., all responses are okay), and availability of helping professionals (Nader, 1993b). Depending upon youths' stress levels and needs for comfort and safety, initial discussions may be brief and supportive. In the first 2 to 3 weeks following a major catastrophic event, much effort may be necessary to restore a safe environment and attend to physical needs. During that time, there may be some false highs and false lows in children's reports of their reactions (Nader).

The Interview Setting

A primary goal is to maintain the best interests of the youth by creating a supportive environment while maximizing the information disclosed (D'Urso et al., 1995). The nature of the event or the time and circumstances that lead to a request for assessment may, at least in part, dictate the setting in which the youth is interviewed. Caregivers may seek assistance from a clinician who sees the youth in a private office. Following mass traumas, classrooms full of children or adolescents have been interviewed individually or asked to complete a questionnaire or scale simultaneously (Nader, 1997b; Nader & Muni, 2002; Pynoos & Nader, 1988; Shaw, 1997; Williams, 1994). School is a familiar, often comfortable setting for assessing traumatized children (Carlson, 1997; Nader, 1997c). It is important that a youth feel that he or she is answering in private. Youths tend to answer in a socially accepted fashion especially when aware of their peers' presence in the interview (chapter 4). The feeling of privacy can be created even in a classroom full of youths. For elementary school children, a private corner with the child facing and well-engaged with the assessor can permit the presence of others to fade from awareness.

In order to develop a sense of privacy and safety, with increasing age of youths, it may take more time and attention to the setting. Adolescents may be more concerned about appearances, especially in the presence of peers, and may need greater privacy in order to feel comfortable sharing accurate information. Hodgman and Jack (1992) recommend having unlined paper and pencil and an inviting hand-sized object available for adolescents to handle when difficult matters are discussed in an interview.

The Presence of Others

Poole and Lamb (1998) have concluded that the presence of other persons in an assessment interview is best avoided (Poole & Lindsay, 2001). There is no evidence that the presence of "support persons" is beneficial. They can interfere with an interview by interrupting, answering for the child, or prompting the child (Santtila et al., 2004). The presence of an attached (personally related to the child) adult may contaminate the interview; the presence of a detached person (e.g. a social worker or other professional) can be helpful (Santtila et al.; see also Pelligrini, 2001).

With very young children (preschoolers), the caregiver's presence may be necessary, at least initially, for the comfort of the child (Box 9.1b). The parent's presence, however, can become a hindrance to diagnosis and treatment. In a small study of young children (mean age 6), Santtila et al. (2004) found that a known person's presence in the interview was associated with an increase in the number of suggestive utterances by interviewers and a coinciding decrease in the number of descriptions by the child. Some diagnostic interviews with small children have included indirectly observing or videotaping the child while simultaneously discussing the traumatic experience with one of the parents (Scheeringa, Peebles, Cook, & Zeanah, 2001). Santtila et al. posit that this procedure could seriously contaminate the child's subsequent memory or narration. Because young children, especially, find it difficult to consider that a mother is capable of telling a lie, they might only believe and repeat what has already been stated by a parent.

Introductions

Preparation by a parent or teacher can assist in the development of trust and rapport. Trusted adults may impart in advance the purpose of the interview and the expertise and qualifications of the interviewer(s). The initial contact with a youth acknowledges that the interview is prompted by an actual event in the child's life (Nader, 1993b). Assessors may introduce themselves by saying, "I am (We are) the kind of (doctors/individuals) who talk with children who have gone through something like [what happened to the youth or at the youth's school]. I am (We are) here to find out how you are doing since [the event] was over." D'Urso et al. (1995) recommend the following to help put the youth at ease: "I talk with a lot of children. I want to know what they think and feel so I can help them if they have any worries or problems" (p. 9).

Establishing Rapport

Establishing rapport has also been described as establishing an alliance or engaging the interviewee/patient/client (Lehmann & Coady, 2001). Good rapport between the interviewer and the interviewee is crucial to motivate the interviewee to fill out the questionnaire or answer the interview questions truthfully, completely, and in a timely fashion (Reynolds & Kamphaus, 1998). In any assessment interview with children, the level of trust and ease with which the youth can communicate personal information is paramount to a successful interview or measure completion (Reich & Todd, 2002b). The interviewer's comfortable competence and unspoken authority can be beneficial. Adolescents particularly may be disturbed by any *defensive* authoritativeness (Hodgman & Jack, 1992). One method of establishing rapport (as well as assisting assessment and treatment) is to have the child draw a picture and tell a story about it. The interviewer's genuine interest in a youth, his or her experience, and his or her picture and story have assisted in establishing a comfortable relationship (Nader, 1993b).

Beginning an interview with neutral questions or with age- and culturally appropriate biographic questions can facilitate engagement, permit time to establish trust, and allow youths to demonstrate and feel competence and comfort in answering questions (Gilgun, 1998; Hodgman & Jack, 1992; Nader, 1997a). Such questions also permit the interviewer to become familiar with the youth's level of functioning and manner of speaking/wording (Faller, 1998b). Although it is important to avoid stilted professional terminology, using youthful jargon may be experienced by youths as patronizing and manipulative (Hodgman & Jack). The evaluator's pace must honor the youth's own rhythm and pacing as well as the need to increase or decrease pressure to enhance self-revelation. Nonverbal as well as verbal communications are important to a youth's comfort. Children are often glad to be able to tell someone about their traumatic experiences, when the interviewer is perceived to be willing to hear everything nonjudgmentally.

Issues of Trust

In order to trust the interviewer, a youth must feel safe in his or her presence. This includes feeling respected personally, individually, culturally, and in general as well as feeling that the interviewer is trustworthy, genuinely interested, and willing to hear anything. In order to be respectful, eye contact, for example, should be appropriate to the child's (or parent's) practiced cultural and personal patterns. When interviewing adolescents, some are more comfortable with direct eye contact, others feel awkward when looked at directly (Hodgman & Jack, 1992). Gilgun (1998) recommends that, with sexually abused youths, the interviewer refrain from either staring or avoiding the eyes.

After exposure to a single horrific experience, most children will readily rely upon an adult for protection and safety. Youths whose trust has been injured by specific or repeated traumatization, especially at the hands of adults, are likely to have more difficulty developing trust. The interviewer's actual trustworthiness and genuine interest in the youth are important. For some youths, more than one session will be needed to establish that the interviewer is trustworthy. In face-to-face interviews, a child's lack of initial trust is informative and signals the need for additional information.

Talking about the trauma may be particularly difficult for children who have been sexually abused (Lubit, Hartwell, van Gorp, & Eth, 2002). Such youths may need more time to establish rapport and more than one session to answer all of the relevant questions (D'Urso et al., 1995; Lubit et al.). Children are not always aware of the source of their anxiety (D'Urso et al.). Trust is enhanced with abused or chronically traumatized youths when the interviewer protects the child from additional coercion while enabling discussion of the abuse in a safe, secure atmosphere (Gilgun, 1998). The interviewer's patience, empathy, and respect as well as calm, quietly compassionate listening (rather than emotional reactions) are important. Gilgun points out that communicating, verbally or nonverbally, that sexual abuse is horrible and forever damaging can interfere with recovery. A better message is sent by the interviewer's belief that, although sexual abuse is a painful and difficult experience, help is possible. Ideally, discussions of sexual abuse occur in the context of a relationship. Gilgun suggests that interest in all aspects of a child's life—happy and sad memories, favorite things to do, friends, what's not fair in life, things they would someday like to do—can help to build a relationship. Doing things (e.g., walks, games) with children, even briefly, can aid trust. Children love gentle, kind attention from adults (Gilgun).

Age and Rapport

Although no set of actions are *correct* for all young children under all circumstances, and traumas may require specific adaptations in methods, House (2002) has described some basic and general methods to assist in building rapport with youths of different ages. In a private clinic or office, rapport begins with a greeting in the waiting area. After introductions to accompanying adults, the adults typically introduce the young child to the clinician. A quick separation from parents establishes a precedent for private conversation, permits observation of the child's reaction to separation, and establishes the clinician's role as the one who structures the contacts. The professional's confidence, leadership, planning, and organization can help to put adults at ease. If a young child resists separation, the clinician negotiates for one parent to accompany him briefly.

With young children, standard rapport building includes commenting on the youth's clothes, possessions, plans following the appointment, and objects in the office that seem to intrigue him or her (House, 2002). Responding with words and actions to the child's facial expressions and emotional reactions, taking him or her seriously, noticing how he or she feels, and trying to accommodate his or her situation can help to build security and trust. Questions can determine the child's concept of numbers, time, or other concepts. A young child may be able, for example, to count to 10 without understanding the quantity of 10 (10 days, 10 experiences; Faller, 1998b). Thus the interviewer learns about the youth's memory for details, verbal skills, thought organization, and expression of affect.

With school-age children, House recommends discussing their favorite activities (2002). This discussion helps to build a database about the child and to establish a pattern of communication. The evaluator can elicit the youth's description of self and his or her environment and may explore fantasies such as "If you had three wishes . . ." or "If you could change one thing about yourself . . .". The clinician can then move on to less comfortable topics. Issues of family loyalty and secrets may become important. When confidentiality is part of the agreement (it may not be in legal cases), House recommends reiterating the rules of the therapeutic relationship. Sensitivity to the child's conflict over sharing complaints or secrets is important. Reframing sharing information as a positive action for the long-term benefit of the family may help to reduce the youth's conflict.

With adolescents, tolerance of differences in motives, honesty, and respect for those in weaker positions is essential to rapport (House, 2002).

Tolerance has limitations for most people. Recognizing and accepting, for example, that not everyone wants to make good grades or do their share of the chores may be difficult for some. Adolescents often question or feel ambivalent toward *normal* assumptions, and they may resist the imposition of values from adults. Rapport requires accepting adolescents' ambivalence, assisting discovery of what they think, and helping articulation of a *common cause* between the youth and adult family members. House points out that adolescents are "often exquisitely sensitive to mendacity. They hear the reverberation of the half-truth, the slight evasion, the less than total candor in our voices; see the shift of our eyes; feel the changes in our body language" (p. 17). Adults often avoid certain topics and withhold some information for good reasons. Unless the lie is congruent with what the adolescent would like to believe (e.g., that he or she can come up with car payments), an un- or half-truth will confirm the expectation that adults lie. Hodgman and Jack (1992) suggest that the interviewer's *abnormal candor* marks the interviewer as different from usual adults whom adolescents may expect to dissimulate, to rely on appearances, or to assert authority to hide their own discomforts. House indicates that this "demanding commitment to honesty" (p. 17) may require careful inspection of words and actions with the adolescent and his or her family. Such candor sets the stage for honesty and directness. For youths of every age, it is important to avoid lying in order to elicit information or to protect the youth from the truth (D'Urso et al., 1995). Age-appropriate, accurate information can prevent later confusion.

Explaining the Procedure

Youths can be prepared for the nature of the interview/questionnaire, allowed a chance to ask questions about the interview/question process, and advised of the confidential nature of the interviews. In an individual interview, the youth is advised of the conditions of danger to self or others for which confidentiality will be breached (Vitulano & Tebes, 1991). Reich and Todd (2002b) underscore the importance of being certain that youths know that they do not have to answer any question, but that it is very helpful to the study (or assessment) for them to answer. Establishing the importance of truthful answers may include statements such as, "It's important that you tell me the truth, that you tell me about things the way they really happened," or "We need to know the truth about how you are doing" (Kay 2002; Nader, 1993b; Santtila et al., 2004). Assessments of multiple youths in a classroom often include an introduction of the interviewers, a brief description of the event (e.g., "As you know, last week a sniper shot at children on the playground, and one student was killed."), and that different youths react differently to such an event (e.g., "Some children are very upset after something like this happens, and some children feel okay. When we talk to you [when you fill out this form], we just need to know the truth about how you are doing") (Nader).

In order to enhance the possibility that adult respondents will answer completely and truthfully, Kessler, Mroczek, and Belli (1999) use techniques that may be applicable to adolescents and children ages 8 and older as well as to caregivers and teachers. Among their suggestions are research goals that include altruistic purposes and clarifying instructions that are worded to motivate. Altruistic purposes may include that (1) the answers assist the interviewers to help those exposed to the current event, (2) what is learned will help others who are exposed to these experiences in the future, and (3) the information gathered will influence policies that affect us all. Instructions, such as those that describe that the questions will be hard work, may elicit indirect commitment to serious and complete reporting. The request for an explicit commitment can also be used. Kessler et al. give the following example used for adults:

> This interview asks about your physical and emotional well-being and about areas of your life that could affect your physical and emotional well-being. It is important for us to get accurate information. In order to do this, you will need to think carefully before answering the following questions. Are you willing to do this? (p. 263)

Studies have shown that commitment questions improve the accuracy of recall. Structured feedback questions have been used, as well, to encourage thoughtful response. A difficult question may be prefaced with, for example, "The next question may be difficult, so take your time before you answer." Similarly, after a response, an interviewer can point out that the person answered quickly and ask if there is anything else (even something small). Research has found that the use of all three methods—motivating instructions, structured feedback questions, and a commitment question—increases the level of memory search and accuracy more than any one component alone (Miller & Cannell, 1977; Vinokur, Oksenberg, & Cannell, 1979; Kessler et al., 1999).

Recognizing the Needs of Youths

Each child is a unique individual who has had a very personal experience of a traumatic event. In addition to understanding childhood trauma, personality, and developmental issues, it is important to identify specific needs, tendencies, and behaviors related to culture, background, and personality (chapters 6, 7). The ability to modify the setting (location, toys, materials) permits flexibility in meeting the youth's individual needs (Linder, 2000). Depending on the type of interview and specific child or group, the interviewer may need to adapt in any of the following ways: (1) choose a scale/measure appropriate for the age and culture of the youth;

(2) use culturally appropriate toys and trauma-specific replicas for dem-onstration; (3) alter the level or type of language used, (4) gather informa-tion from different sources—include parents or peers as much or as little as is reasonable and beneficial for the success of the assessment; and (5) adapt to the youth's emotional state and level of functioning (Linder; Sant-tila et al., 2004).

Each person exposed directly or indirectly to a traumatic event will have his or her own timing for response and recovery (Nader, 1999d; Nader & Pynoos, 1993). Individual children, adolescents, and adults will be ready at varying times to speak, grieve, express anger, or move out of regression (Nader). Each youth will develop a particular posttrauma rhythm that includes personal reactions to the traumatic experience, the need to regress to differing degrees over time, the ability to process the event, the need for time-out from the memories and emotions related to the event, the ability to receive support, the ways aspects of his or her reactions interact and effect his or her life, and other trauma-related and personal issues. Interviewers and clinicians must adapt their actions and responses to meet the individual's reactions, timing, and processing of the event (Nader).

Younger children may present a challenge because of their shorter atten-tion spans and their lack of verbal sophistication (Reich & Todd, 2002b). After traumatic exposure, youths of all ages may regress, become more concrete and less imaginative, or function at more primitive levels (Nader, 1999d). In addition to age-level language and expectations, it is important to recognize functioning emotional and developmental age (which may change from contact to contact) following the event (Nader; Witkin, 2005). Because thinking may be more concrete, it is important that instructions be stated simply and with willingness to repeat. Faller (1998b) provides the rough guideline that the shorter the child's communications are, the shorter the interviewer's questions should be.

The Child's Language and Thinking

Younger children may have difficulties with temporal order, time, and number (D'Urso et al., 1995; Lubit, Hartwell, van Gorp, & Eth, 2002). Fail-ure to recognize the child's language skills and thinking processes may result in the child's confusion (D'Urso et al.). The examiner may make erroneous assumptions without taking into account the child's literal and concrete understanding and personal language. D'Urso et al. tell of an evaluator who asked a child if the abuser tickled his "pee pee." The child responded *"No"* initially, but later acknowledged being touched on his "pee pee" during the tickle game. The child explained he is not ticklish (therefore, the man did not *tickle* his penis). Not until about age 3-1/2 does a child understand and respond reliably to questions such as "Where," "Who," "What," or "How." Children may use idiosyncratic words, words from other languages, or correct terminology for body parts. Children may incorrectly use words. A child who had been fondled said that she was afraid of being "raped" by the assailant. She understood the word "rape" to mean "murder" (D'Urso et al.).

Closure

Skillful assessment and treatment sessions provide a sense of resolution, closure, and reorientation at the end of the session (Nader & Mello, 2001). Closure usually includes feeling heard by someone who understands what the youth went through; it is essential after speaking to a child about his or her traumatic experience. Achieving the proper closure at the end of each session prevents leaving the child with renewed anxiety and an unnecessary avoidance of the diagnostic or therapeutic situation (Nader, 1994; Pynoos & Eth, 1986). An inner-city school psychologist reported having read numerous articles on trauma/grief-focused therapy, but when she and her colleagues tried the techniques, students felt worse instead of better afterwards (Nader, 1997c). Reviewing an experience with a traumatized individual must be done skillfully and only when the goals of a session can be achieved. Training is advised. When done well, the interview can assist the processing of traumatic thoughts and emotions, help provide a new view of aspects of the experience, or contribute to repairing the self-concept (Nader, 1997c; Ochberg, 2002). At the end of an evaluation, the interviewer may need to assist the youth to resolve distress, problematic perspectives, or other issues that may have arisen during the interview (Lubit et al., 2002).

During an interview, it may become important to comfort a child and/ or to help her or him to remember or discover her or his own working coping mechanisms. Different methodologies have disparate views about the appropriateness of physical comfort. The decision about the method of comfort is also influenced by the nature of the youth's traumatic experience. Inappropriate touch may have been a part of the trauma. In some therapeutic methods, harmless, nurturing touch is a part of the intervention (see James, 1994). Nonverbal and verbal methods also have been used successfully to comfort youths. If a child has drawn or described a horrible scene, for example, after a personal interview, measure completion, or discussion, she or he may need to draw a repaired image of an injured person or site or to draw a happy memory of a person or location (Galente & Foa, 1986; Nader & Pynoos, 1991). This introduction of something that did not actually happen may be inadvisable for a forensic interview.

At the beginning of an individual assessment or treatment interview, the trauma survivor must be oriented to the trauma. Introducing oneself as a trauma therapist, at the first session, is the beginning of this process. In a well-conducted assessment interview, a youth may become so focused upon the trauma that she or he loses awareness of the external environment (Nader, 1997c). Children who have been traumatized repeatedly or who become easily entranced with some aspect of a personal experience may need reorientation to the present and to an aspect of his or her existence that promotes coping. In some diagnostic interviews, if it is appropriate, an interviewer may focus on something positive or neutral at the beginning of the interview or on the way into the interview room. The interviewer may then return to this early focus at the end of the session. The clinician may notice the beautiful day/view/picture, ask about activities, or engage in a conversation about other nonrelated topics before addressing the trauma and after closure. For these children, reorientation to the present may prevent mishap after the session.

CHILDREN'S MEMORIES

Under normal circumstances, memory may be affected by age, stress, biological factors, and the nature of an experience. Distinctive, unique, and personally consequential experiences are best remembered; distinctive items are the easiest to learn and hardest to forget (Howe, 1997). Studies of children's memories have been conducted in stressful situations, but, for obvious and ethical reasons, traumatically stressful conditions are not created in order to study memory. Scientists who study the brain and neurobiology posit that moderate stress enhances memory but extreme or prolonged stress interferes with memory (Sapolsky, 1998). In contrast, a wealth of evidence suggests that traumatic experiences produce detailed, "etched-in," and long-lasting memories (Terr, 1991; Koss, Figueredo, Bell, Tharan, & Tromp, 1996; Nader, 1997c; Pynoos & Eth, 1985). In fact, studies confirm that emotional arousal and elevated stress hormones such as plasma cortisol enhance declarative memory (McCleery & Harvey, 2004). Memories for highly emotional episodes contain information not found in other recall narratives including a focus on beliefs that have been violated due to the nature of the event (Howe; Stein, Wade, & Liwag, 1996).

Age and Memory

Even young children accurately recall, over considerable time, participatory and nonparticipatory (e.g., witnessing), single incident or ongoing traumatic experiences (Howe, 1997; Lewis, 1995; Nader, 2001b; Nigro & Wolpow, 2004). A number of memory studies have demonstrated that young children outperform adults for some aspects of recall (Lubit et al., 2002). Research has confirmed that young children are capable of remembering accurately even their complex personal experiences (Gilstrap, 2004). In a study of initial and 6-month recall of preschoolers (30, 36, and 48 months old), Howe, Courage, & Peterson (1995) found that memory increased with age. Whether or not they had initial intrusive thoughts, these preschool children demonstrated an ability to recall considerable information about their traumatic experiences. In a study of children 18 months to 5 years of age who had undergone emergency-room treatments, Howe discovered little decline in memory of the central aspects of events even though decline in memory of peripheral issues was substantial. Notwithstanding a tendency to "dissociate" during an experience, the memory of the experience as well as the dissociated object (e.g., a spot on the ceiling) may be well-preserved. Children younger than age 6 have more difficulty distinguishing fact from fantasy and may confound what they did with what they thought of doing. They are, however, able to distinguish their thoughts from other people's actions (Lewis).

Although children can accurately recall and retain memories of an event, faulty pre- and postevent information can result in distortions in recall (Gilstrap, 2004; Siegel, 1996). For nontraumatic events, children ages 3 and 4 are more suggestible than 5 and 6 year olds (Siegel). By age 4, children usually resist attempts to suggest a history of abuse. Children may have difficulty challenging parents' perceptions of events, however, and, if repeatedly told something did not occur, will come to doubt their own perceptions.

Repetition and Recall

Research supports the beneficial effects on recall of repeating accurate information (Melnyk & Bruck, 2004). Repeated neutral interviews can consolidate memory for an event and thus protect against forgetting, prevent normally occurring errors of commission, promote reminiscence (the reporting of previously unmentioned details in later recall), and increase the likelihood of hypermnesia (increase in the amount of new information recalled over increasing retention intervals that exceeds the amount of information forgotten) (see "Types of Questions," below). Some studies of young children did not confirm repetition's ability to increase memory. Moreover, some evidence suggests that the benefits may only occur when the neutral interview is conducted within a period of about 1 week after the event.

Misinformation poses the greatest risk to accurate recall when it is further in time from the event and closer in time to the memory test (Melnyk & Bruck, 2004). In a 1-week memory test, Warren and Lane (1995) found that interviewing with or without misinformation shortly after presentation of a video did not negatively affect the accuracy of 9 year olds' reports. Two studies of preschoolers over several weeks or years found that reports of false events and misinformation effects decreased substantially over time (Ceci, Huffman, Smith, & Loftus, 1994; Huffman, Crossman, & Ceci, 1997; Poole & Lindsay, 2001). Poole and Lindsay reported that children gave fewer false details in response to open-ended prompts as well as to Yes/No questions. In a test of recall 40 days after a magician event, Melnyk and Bruck found that, overall, children produced more accurate than inaccurate utterances in their free recall of the event. When the effects of timing were minimized, repeated exposure to misinformation did not increase children's suggestibility nor did repetition of true information increase facilitation of memory. In a second experiment, with leading or suggestive accurate information, Melnyk and Bruck found that memory was facilitated only for those children who received a very early suggestive interview (within 4 weeks of the event). Misinformation effects, on the other hand, were only heightened when children underwent both "very early" and "very late" (2 days before testing) suggestive interviews. Findings suggest that timing of interviews/testing is a key ingredient in the influence of intervening interviews.

Trauma and Repetition

Most trauma interventions include retelling or verbal review (sometimes repeatedly) of the traumatic experience or parts of it (Nader, 2001b; Pynoos, Nader, & March, 1991). Repeatedly recounting a traumatic memory decreases associated anxiety, thus allowing its reorganization (Foa & Rothbaum, 1998; March, Amaya-Jackson, Foa, & Treadwell, 1999). Trauma is often a fragmented emotionally and cognitively disorganized experience (Silva et al., 2003). For some cognitive behavioral methods, treatment progress is reflected in an increasingly coherent narrative of the trauma that can be more readily integrated into the victim's existing mental schemas (March et al.; Silva et al.).

McKenna, Foster, and Page (2004) have used the terms *cognitive interviewing, verbal probing* (nondirective questions to clarify reactions), and *think-aloud* (speaking aloud about experiences) to describe techniques used to study children's (ages 8 to 16) recall of physical activities. Cognitive interviewing has four stages: (1) context reinstatement (e.g., "What was on your mind when the day began? What did you have planned for that day?"); (2) reporting all details (e.g., "Start right before the event happened and take me through it step by step." Nader, 2001b); (3) changing the order of reporting events (e.g., "Tell me again what happened, but this time start from the time when . . . ."); and (4) changing the perspective of viewing the event (e.g., "If your friend/mother/brother/other were describing what happened, what would she/he say?") (McKenna et al.; see also Nader, 2001b; Pynoos & Nader, 1989). McKenna et al. found that all of these methods refined children's recall of experiences. Landmarks and important events were especially helpful elements around which the children could develop their accounts of their experiences (McKenna et al.; Nader, 1993b). Procedures that focused on context as well as frequent prompts and identifying what others were doing assisted recall. Within a framework of play therapy, trauma/grief-focused therapy (Nader, 2001b, 2002d; Nader & Mello, 2001; Pynoos & Eth, 1986; Pynoos & Nader, 1993) elicits a child's free and directed recall of a traumatic experience in a similar manner (Box 9.1c).

Encoding Memories

More than one kind of memory is encoded in the brain (Byrnes, 2001; Siegel, 2003). *Implicit memories* include behavioral or procedural memories (such as riding a bike or walking down the stairs) and emotional memories (such as fear associated with an injurious or threatening experience) (Sapolsky, 1998; Siegel). Implicit memories are mediated by nonhippocampal brain circuits and do not require conscious attention for encoding (Siegel; see chapter 2). The effects of their recall occur within conscious awareness but are only experienced in the "here and now." In contrast, *explicit memory* requires conscious focal attention for encoding. Explicit memories include semantic (factual) and episodic (autobiographical) memories. They activate the medial temporal lobe, including the hippocampus. Maturation of the prefrontal cortex during the preschool years may explain the emergence and ongoing development of self-awareness and autobiographical memory. Orbitofrontal development may help to explain the mind's ability to see the self in the past, present, and possible future (Siegel).

An individual's state of mind during the encoding of information or events may determine or contribute to the information's accessibility to later retrieval (Siegel, 1996). For example, when sad, it can be easier to recall events experienced when one was sad in the past. *State of mind* can include combinations of dominant emotional tone, perceptual biases, behavioral response patterns, and increased accessibility of particular memories. Activation profiles may include clusters of emotional tones, associated sensations, memories, and mental models. For dissociatively disordered patients, shifts in state of mind can be accompanied by varying degrees of memory barriers (Siegel).

Forgotten Memories. The debate continues about whether memories are ever lost or instead just become more difficult to access (Sapolsky, 1998). Studies of small samples of adults suggest that individuals with higher scores on measures of creative imagination or dissociation are more likely to recover false or previously unavailable true events when asked to form a mental image of an event (ISTSS, 1998). Physicians have sometimes told children that they would never regain specific memories of injuries, especially head injuries. These "lost memories" have been regained in the process of step-by-step (slow-motion) review and re-review of children's experiences using neutral prompts (e.g., "What happened next?"; Nader & Mello, 2001). Creating a safe, therapeutic environment is conducive to remembering (McCann & Pearlman, 1990; Parson, 1999). In this manner, a 12-year-old girl regained memories of being hit by a flying table during a tornado (see also Box 9.1c).

Trauma and Memory

Distortions of time and space have been observed in children following traumas (Terr, 1983a; Pynoos & Nader, 1989). Some researchers have found that children try to fill in gaps in their memories by confabulating; however, if given prompts or cues, children remember quite well (Lewis, 1995; Johnson & Foley, 1984; Pynoos & Nader). Pynoos and Nader found that children incorporated wishful thinking into their unassisted retelling of their experiences after a mass traumatic event. They were able to report their experiences accurately when assisted to begin at a specific point and proceed through the details of the event. With abuse cases, some evidence indicates that the probability of remembering can increase with the number of abuse incidents (Goleman 1992; Howe, 1997). Repeated exposure to similar events, however, may produce memories that blend into a single script-like representation. Individual incidents may lose their uniqueness, details may become blurred (Lindsay & Read, 1995; Howe).

FORENSIC INTERVIEWS

When conducting initial interviews with youths, it is important to be cognizant of the possibility of litigation for damages or the need for eye-witness testimony. Forensic cases require familiarity with the rules of evidence, legal requirements of mental-health professionals, and aspects of the law that might affect normal guidelines such as limitations on confidentiality and acceptable methods of questioning (see chapter 16). Future civil litigation may be initiated when a technology-related or human-made event occurs (Saylor & Deroma, 2002). Suits have been filed after builder negligence led to structural collapse in natural disasters. Such suits require knowledge of local civil law. Initial youth interviews for forensic purposes are usually unstructured interviews. They are often conducted by police officers or protective agency personnel. As the case of Jenny suggests, some youths are unable to testify regarding their experiences as witnesses or victims of crimes without some intervention (Box 9.1d).

Functioning Age

As stated earlier, traumatized youths may not be functioning at age-appropriate levels. As an indicator of developmental level, chronological age is accurate less than half the time in the general population, and even less frequently for children in the foster system (Witkin, 2005). Witkin explains, "Equating age with developmental level often leads to both errors of inclusion and exclusion" (p. 8). For courtroom purposes, lawyers can estimate receptive language and verbal abstract thinking in approximately 20 minutes with the use of two tests. The Peabody Picture

Vocabulary Test-III estimates receptive language (Dunn & Dunn, 1997). The Similarities Subtest on the Wechsler instruments estimates verbal abstract reasoning level (Wechsler, 2002, 2003, 2004).

Using Piaget's findings, Witkin (2005) suggests that children with language and abstract reasoning skills under the age of 4 rarely make reliable witnesses. They can be easily misled and misunderstood. Their statements are often inconsistent over retellings. Children with language and reasoning skills between ages 4 and 7 are reasonably consistent over time. They can answer concrete questions about a wide range of topics but are usually unable to draw inferences. They can often orient successfully to time. Children with the skills of 8 to 12 year olds can answer questions that require inferences or have multiple parts. They can work with more abstract concepts. These children usually can present their points of view effectively in court when questioning is developmentally sensitive. Youths with developmental skills over the age of 12 are typically capable of the cognitive tasks required of them in the courtroom.

Competence to Testify

In the legal arena, a child's competence to testify is demonstrated by his or her ability to tell the difference between the truth and a lie (McCarron, Ridgway, & Williams, 2004). In order to assess a child's understanding of the concepts of truth and lies, he or she is asked to (1) define the two concepts, (2) explain the difference between truth and lies, or (3) identify example statements or stories of truth and lies. Concepts such as truthfulness are abstract and can be difficult for children. *The Truth or Lie Story* is a method that has been successfully used (McCarron et al.). By age 4, most children have an understanding of what a lie is. They usually find it easier to identify examples of lies rather than truths. D'Urso et al. (1995) have used questions such as, "If I said that you are a boy, would that be the truth or a lie?"

The Truth or Lie Story

The Truth or Lie Story (McCarron et al., 2004) has been used with children as young as age 3 to establish their ability to distinguish between the truth and a lie. A story is told about a child, John or Mary, who tells a lie to his or her mother about breaking a window, or an adolescent, Tony, tells a lie to his mother about smoking. Three questions meet the requirements for establishing competency: correct identification of whether a truth or a lie has been told, identification of the correct response the youth in the story should have given, and some understanding of the importance of telling the truth (why the child in the story might respond in the way he or she did).

Accuracy and Interviewing

The accuracy of children's eyewitness testimony may be influenced by (1) factors under the control of forensic investigators, such as the way questions are phrased, and (2) factors that cannot be controlled by investigators, such as the age of the child or the nature of the event (Poole & Lindsay, 2001). Children ages 3 to 8 participated in science demonstrations, and then listened to their parents read a story that described events experienced and not experienced in the demonstration. Poole and Lindsay found that, in response to open-ended prompts, many children of each age group described fictitious events. In response to direct questions, especially for the younger children, accuracy markedly declined. After the children were reminded of the story, told that some things described in the story might not actually have happened, the older children retracted many of their false reports, but the younger children did not. Poole and Lindsay recommend that judgments about the accuracy of children's testimony must include awareness of possible previous exposure to misinformation. For forensic evaluations, it is important to be cognizant of what the youth or the caregiver may have learned from previous interviews and assessment measures about the right answers to questions (D'Urso et al., 1995; Lubit et al., 2002).

Researchers agree that the accuracy of children's testimony can be affected by a number of factors related to interviewing (Santtila et al., 2004; The Forensic Echo, 2002). Option-posing and suggestive utterances, for example, elicit less reliable information from a child witness. Moreover, there appear to be changes in the interview dynamics related to the phase of an interview. Focused questions, in contrast to open-ended questions, should be used as late as possible in an interview. Some investigators urge interviewers to use open-ended prompts or questions throughout their interviews. Using open-ended questions to elicit intensity levels (see chapter 4; e.g., "How much did it hurt?" or "How difficult was it?"), however, may result in relatively undifferentiated answers from youths (McKenna et al., 2004). Youths use words like *really* or *a lot* to describe varying levels of intensity.

Children may incorporate elements that have been introduced by interviewers (when questioning) into their memories of events and, then, report these elements in later interviews (Santtila et al., 2004). As mentioned above, youths might learn to answer in a manner perceived to please the interviewer (Reich & Todd, 2002b; Santtila et al.). As long as interviews are conducted in an appropriate manner, repeated interviewing does not seem to have a negative influence on children's eyewitness testimony. Repeated interviews that include misleading questions result in significant increases in erroneous responses (Santtila et al.).

For therapeutic purposes, clinical interviews may include fantasized action or directed drawings. Taping a youth's free recall before these inclusions may be important for legal purposes. With the parent's and youth's permission, the initial interview may be audio- or videotaped. Lubit et al. (2002) point out that transcripts and audiotapes lack visual conversational cues. Consequently, they may give the wrong impression of what happened in the interview. When it does not inhibit the youth, videotaping is superior.

Assisted Recall with Props: Anatomically Correct Dolls, Toys, and Replicas

Studies have shown that, although young children (ages 3 to 4) usually provide highly accurate information in their free recall of an event, their recall is often sparse (Nigro & Wolpow, 2004; Poole & Lindsay, 2001). The use of physical props such as toys or other replicas related to the experience has consistently increased the volume of information provided by young children. Nigro and Wolpow explain that props may serve as both memory-retrieval cues and aids to communication of complex or emotionally difficult information. In the case of childhood trauma, toys and replicas may be provided for the purpose of demonstrating the traumatic experience or its episodic segments.

By age 4, children are able to relate a scale model to its real counterpart. Research suggests, however, that young children may have trouble negotiating the boundary between play and reality. In a study by Harris, Brown, Marriott, Whittall, and Harmer (1991) in which children were asked to imagine a bunny or a monster inside a box, children were able to say that the creatures were only imaginary. Nevertheless, children later claimed uncertainty that the creatures would not be in the box, and a fourth of the 4 year olds were afraid for the experimenter to leave the room (Nigro & Wolpow, 2004). Some researchers have concluded that children will behave as if the creatures are real only while they remain in pretence mode and not after it is terminated. Additionally, they may tell fictitious tales if they think that adults are playing with them.

Nigro and Wolpow (2004) confirmed that the manner in which toys are presented and used in interviews with young children is critical. They interviewed 4-year-old children 1 to 2 days after they participated in a staged event (preparing for a camping trip). Five groups of children were studied: (1) those who played with toy replicas of items from the event prior to an interview with toy props; (2) those who matched toy replicas to real items from the event prior to the interview with toy props; (3) those who colored before an interview with toy props; (4) those who colored before an interview with the real items; and (5) those who colored before an interview with no props, only verbal cues. When the children played with toy props prior to the interview, their verbal accuracy was lowest during the interview. Children who saw toys for the first time during the interview behaviorally enacted the highest amount of correct information about the event. Nigro and Wolpow concluded that, when the use of toys signals to 4-year-old children that a pretence mode is acceptable, it affects their recall of an event.

Anatomically Correct Dolls

Some studies show that accuracy does not suffer from the use of anatomically correct dolls (Goodman, Quas, Batterman-Faunce, Riddlesberger, & Kuhn, 1997; Nigro & Wolpow, 2004). In other studies, accuracy has diminished with specific use of toy props (see above). Santtila et al. (2004) state that, although findings have been mixed, overall, interviews involving the use of anatomically correct dolls have not differed significantly from the ones where dolls were not used. The number of new details reported by the child has been similar with and without the dolls. When dolls were actively used in an interview, however, on average interviewers' questions were generally longer with increased suggestive utterances, and children's answers generally shorter and less detailed, and included more unclear utterances (answers that make no sense in context).

Child Abuse Interviews: Props and Questions

Some states and agencies provide guidelines for interviews and evaluations of abused youths. The American Professional Society on the Abuse of Children (Myers, Berliner, Briere, Hendrix, Reid, & Jenny, 1990), for example, provides guidelines for the psychosocial evaluation of suspected abuse in children (D'Urso et al., 1995). Faller (1998a, 1998b) contributes a checklist for determining the likelihood of sexual abuse as well as other interview methods appropriate for forensic purposes. She uses, for example, a multidisciplinary team, age-appropriate questions that follow the guidelines presented below, and abuse-specific drawings as a method of investigation.

Recognizing the importance of avoiding leading and coercive questions, Faller (1998a, 1998b) has provided examples of the types of questions that may be used to discover abuse: (1) people-focused, (2) circumstances-focused, and (3) body parts-focused. *People-focused* questions include those about who lives in the youth's house, his or her favorite family member, what is liked about and activities with the favorite person, and things not liked about the person ("Is there something you don't like about . . . ?"). *Circumstance-focused* questions may be about what happens when [the suspected abuser] visits or baby-sits ("What happens when Uncle Bud comes to visit?"). *Body parts-focused* questions may include the use of anatomically correct dolls or pictures. The interviewer may start at the top and ask, "Where is her hair?" ". . . eyes?" "What color are her eyes?" "How many eyes does she have?" Then work down to the child's names for the nipples ("What is this?"), navel, genitalia, and anus. Anatomical drawings, rather than dolls, may be used to corroborate a disclosure. Faller uses anatomically correct male and female pictures appropriate for the youth's age and culture. The child can show where he or she was hurt. The interviewer can write the questions asked and the youth's answers on the picture so that they can be used as a part of court proceedings.

In contrast to the generic drawing methods described in chapter 12, which may not elicit much sexual content, Faller (1998b) has described abuse-specific drawings to permit the youth to show and tell about his or her experience. These directed artworks include drawings of the offender ("Draw a picture of Uncle Bud") and of the abuse itself. Drawings of the offender are followed by questions such as "Tell me about Uncle Bud." "What makes him happy?" What makes him sad?" ". . . scared?" ". . . angry?" Drawing pictures of the abuse may be difficult for the child and is not requested until after a number of other drawings have been completed.

Types of Questions

The types of questions used to assess trauma are discussed in chapter 4. In diagnostic interviews that may precede court hearings, the nature of questions about the youth's experience becomes particularly important. Child abuse cases have been lost or incorrectly filed because a clinician's questions were leading or suggestive. Studies have shown that particular types of questions are more likely than others to elicit inaccurate information, especially from younger children. Such questions include (1) those that introduce information, (2) those that introduce a preference, (3) repeated questions, and (4) requests for imagination or speculation (Gilstrap, 2004). *Forced-choice* or *option posing* questions provide a set of responses from which to choose the correct answer (e.g., "Was it red or blue?"; Gilstrap; Santtila et al., 2004). They imply that the correct answer is one of the options. Santtila and colleagues suggest that *option posing* questions that (1) focus the youth's attention on incident-related issues not mentioned by the youth or (2) require a choice between alternate answers (e.g., "Yes" or "No") usually elicit less reliable responses (Santtila et al.; Waterman et al., 2004). Whether specific or nonspecific, *suggestive utterances* prompt for specific answers and may influence the youth to answer inaccurately. Suggestive statements may include assumptions of details not mentioned such as, "Were you inside or outside of the school when he hit you?" when the youth did not say the person hit him, or when the man was wearing a green jumpsuit, saying, "The man's jumpsuit was blue, wasn't it?" *Nonspecific suggestive utterances* point the child in a particular direction (Santtila et al.). They may make assumptions not obvious by the youth's demonstration of what happened or attributions not mentioned by the youth (e.g., ". . . the horrible thing that happened . . ."). In addition to demeanor and tone, an interviewer can indicate a preference by question structure (e.g., "He was doing ___, wasn't he?" or "I think he was ___.") (Gilstrap). When a question that includes misinformation is repeated across multiple interviews, children are more likely to acquiesce to the suggestion and to provide additional details.

After reading a story to young children, Lampinen and Smith (1995) showed them a video of a person talking about and including misinformation about the story (Waterman et al., 2004). When the person providing the misinformation was an adult, the children subsequently incorporated the inaccurate information into their reports about the story. However, when the person was a child or an adult who was introduced as a "silly" adult, children did not incorporate the incorrect information. Waterman et al. suggest that this study highlights the importance of the social demands of an interview to children's accuracy. It also demonstrates the ability of a credible adult to introduce inaccuracy (Gilstrap, 2004; Waterman et al.).

Neutral questions either contain no information or only the information provided by the child (Gilstrap, 2004). For court purposes, appropriate questions about a child's personal experience include open-ended questions, facilitating questions, and clarifications (Santtila et al., 2004). Research findings indicate that the most accurate testimony about youths' personal experiences is obtained by using free-recall questions, followed, if needed, by open-ended questions including *wh- questions* (e.g., what, when, where, who) or prompts to elicit additional information (Waterman et al., 2004). In studies of children ages 3, 5, and 7, similar accuracy and very little intrusion of inaccurate information has been demonstrated in children's free recall of medical examinations. Open-ended questions, statements, and imperatives may be used to elicit the youth's free recall of the event(s) (Santtila et al.). They include, for example, "Can you tell me what happened?" or "Where were you right before [the event] happened?" and, after the youth's response, "Can you tell me what happened after that?" Facilitating questions and statements include nonsuggestive utterances that encourage the youth to continue his or her response. These might include brief indicators that the interviewer is listening (e.g., "OK." or "Mmhuh."), nonjudging reflective or echoing statements (e.g., Child: "He took my panties off." Interviewer: "He took off your panties?"), and accurate verbalizations of what the child has demonstrated with toys (e.g., "You ran and got under the table?"). Questions asking what the child said or meant are used for clarification (e.g., "What did you say?" or "Can you help me to understand what you mean by that?" or "How do you mean he was bad?" or "Did it happen this Christmas or another Christmas?").

The Freedom to Say, "I Don't Know."

When youths feel that they are expected to know the answers, this perceived expectation may influence answers or omissions. It is important that youths feel free to say that they did not understand. The interviewer might say, for example, "If you don't understand any of my questions, just tell me and I will try to say it another way" (Faller, 1998b). It is also important that youths feel free to say, "I don't know." The interviewer might say, for example, "I'd like to ask you some questions about what happened [during the event]. If you don't know the answer to a question, that's OK, and you can tell me that you don't know" (Waterman et al., 2004).

Evidence suggests that children are more likely to say, "I don't know" to misleading questions when they do know the answer if (1) preinterview instructions or attitudes suggest that they are expected to know all of the answers, or (2) they are rated to have high self-esteem (Howie & Dowd, 1996; Waterman et al., 2004). A "don't know" response, when the child in fact does know that the questioner is wrong, does not acquiesce to the misleading question with its false information, but it is not a correct response. "Don't know" is an accurate response when the answer was not provided. Following a story and a staged event, Waterman, Blades, & Spencer, (2001) and Waterman et al. (2004) found children much more likely to admit correctly that they did not know the answer in response to a wh- question than to a Yes/No question. In the forensic context, a youth is questioned about an actual experience. Following an actual, nonstressful event (an adult discussed pets and food using color photographs), the interviewer was present during the presentation for half of the children and not for the other half (Waterman et al., 2004). Children (ages 6 to 8) were generally accurate about answerable questions whether they were wh- or Yes/No questions. They gave more correct "don't know" responses to unanswerable questions when the interviewer had been absent from the staged event. Waterman et al. offer this possible explanation: when an already knowledgeable interviewer questions children, the context created is similar to a "test" situation. During classroom tests, if the child does not know an answer, guessing may result in the right answer or in praise for trying. When the interviewer does not have knowledge of the event, questions may appear more like genuine requests for information and engender less pressure to provide a response.

CONCLUSIONS

Evaluators may conduct interviews with traumatized youths for assessment, diagnostic, and forensic purposes. The goals of assessment/ diagnostic interviews may include therapeutic endeavors as well as evaluation. Such interviews may include reworking traumatic memories. The goal of a forensic interview is to discover the truth without influencing the information gathered. The success of a diagnostic or assessment interview with a youth depends on several factors. Among these factors are the youth's sense of safety, rapport, and trust and the evaluator's genuine interest in and respect for the youth and his or her emotional state. An evaluator must be aware of the youth's culture, background, personality, and personal needs. For the safety of the youth, closure is essential when traumatic memories are elicited.

Because the questions, statements, and interventions of the interviewer or clinician can influence a youth's accuracy of recall, it is important to be cognizant of whether the child's testimony will be needed when conducting a diagnostic interview. Free recall and open-ended questions as well as the interviewer's nonjudgmental demeanor are likely to elicit the most reliable responses.

10

The Nature of the Event
Assessing Exposure Levels and Complicated Reactions

Whether they are single incidents or repeating episodes, traumatic events vary immensely. Each event includes multiple impressions that may register or imprint with intensity on an individual's mind (Nader, 1997c; Terr, 1991). In addition to children's profound emotional (e.g., horror, helplessness, agitation), physiological (e.g., pounding heart, neurochemical changes), or numbing experiences (e.g., dissociation, amnesia, being stunned), the intense impressions engendered by traumatic events may include strong desires to act (e.g., to fight, flee, hide, rescue, or find), imagined actions or fantasies (e.g., to intervene, be elsewhere), role identifications (e.g., victim, rescuer, perpetrator, runner, witness, peacemaker), sensory impressions (e.g., physical sensations, images, sounds, smells), attempts to understand (e.g., feelings or actions of others; "Why me?"), self-rejection (e.g., disdain for the helpless or ineffectual self), senses of injustice (e.g., bad things happen to good people, bad people have success), senses of betrayal (e.g., after the unwelcome actions of known others, harmful behaviors from those who acted like they had goodwill toward the youth), and changes of focus (e.g., prominence of ineffectual self or of negative events over positive) (Nader; Nader & Mello, 2001). Event-related traumatic memory representations, interlinked with each other and with aspects of the child and his or her history, become a part of traumatic response and recovery (Nader).

Some aspects of a youth's history, circumstances, and personality may increase the likelihood of exposure to traumatic events. Some psychological disorders such as conduct disturbances (Greenwald, 2002a, 2002b) or manic-type bipolar disorders (Cohen & Mannarino, 2004) may increase the likelihood of traumatic exposure as well. Major stressful events may lead to smaller or other negative events that affect mental health (Haine, Ayers, Sandler, Wolchik, & Weyer, 2003). Traumatic events may result in economic changes, the emotional absence of a caregiver(s), and changes in multiple life domains. In addition to or as a part of the symptoms of post-traumatic stress disorder (PTSD), event-specific traumatic impressions may affect the youth's quality of life, patterns of thought and behavior, and responses to treatment (Nader, 2001b).

In order to assess traumatized youths' reactions and recovery, it is essential to understand the nature and details of the event and of the child's personal exposure to them. Knowing the details of a traumatic event will assist the assessor in understanding the nature and depth of the youth's reactions, in identifying traumatic reminders, and in predicting how the event may later integrate into the child's life or translate into complex patterns of behavior and response across life. This chapter describes aspects of a traumatic event that are important to assessment and issues related to the *Diagnostic and Statistical Manual* (*DSM-IV*; APA, 1994) PTSD Criterion A. Instruments used to assess exposure to stressful life events and to assess degree of exposure are also presented here.

Mass Media

Jerome Kroll wrote:

> The violence and genocide and the uprooting and resettlement of whole populations throughout the world in the 20th and 21st centuries increasingly shown as they happen by the news media; the high-profile domestic exposure of childhood abuse in its various forms; the awareness of the psychological effects of the Vietnam War on all exposed to it have made posttraumatic stress disorder (PTSD) a familiar concept. . . . The benefits are ... recognition that the effects of trauma do not disappear just because broken bones are mended, that children are deeply affected by exposure to violence, that collections of peoples and their cultures are irrevocably altered by exposure to violence and subsequent uprooting . . . (Kroll, 2003, p. 667)

Mass traumatic events (e.g., school shootings, terrorist attacks, and conditions of war) affect entire countries or large populations of a country either directly or via mass media. Bleich, Gelkopf, & Solomon (2003) found no significant differences between those who were actually injured in a terrorist attack and those who were not directly exposed. The researchers suggest that this could be because the respondents understated their reactions (see chapter 4 regarding telephone interviews) or because a major national trauma is not limited to those who experience it directly (see also Silver, Holman, McIntosh, Poulin, & Gil-Rivas, 2002 regarding

September 11). Exposure to traumas via television has been associated with increased traumatic reactions in exposed children (Nader, Pynoos, Fairbanks, Al-Ajeel, & Al-Asfour, 1993; Pfefferbaum et al., 1999; Brown & Goodman, 2005) and with symptomatic reactions in those not directly exposed (Schuster et al., 2001). In a national survey following the September 11 terrorist attacks, parents who reported that their children were stressed were likely to restrict their children's TV watching (Schuster et al.). Among youths whose parents did not restrict TV watching, the number of youths' stress symptoms (parent-reported) was associated with the number of hours of postattack TV watching. Although *DSM-IV* does not exclude television exposure as a form of witnessing, North & Pfefferbaum (2002) suggest that the symptoms and reactions of those in settings outside of directly affected areas should be recognized as psychological sequelae distinct from PTSD.

Viewing television following or during the ongoing threat of violence or disaster has been used as a coping or preparative mechanism by adults and youths (e.g., Bleich et al., 2003; Nader, 1997a). In 2003, during the Iraq War, television and radio communication was cut off in Iraq. No access to the news meant not knowing how near the threat was, from what direction it might come, if loved ones were threatened, if the war was over, or if needed resources (e.g., food and water) were available. In April of 2002, following 19 months of terrorism, Israeli and Arab-Israeli adults reported via telephone interview that their most prevalent methods of coping were gathering information (about friends and family, watching/listening to TV and radio news reports) and seeking/finding and giving social support (Bleich et al.; see chapter 5).

THE NATURE OF THE EVENT

A hundred children in the same room during a single traumatic incident will have, in addition to their common experiences, individual memories and reactions colored by aspects of their personal event experiences, personal attributes, and previous life experiences. Even traumatic events of the same genre (e.g., fires, hurricanes, shootings, wars) vary widely in their content, unfolding, phase (e.g., ongoing conflict, end of war), duration, intensity, frequency (e.g., single assault or molestation, multiple assaults or molestations over time), visibility, material destructiveness, injuriousness, relationships, interactions (e.g., with perpetrator, friends, or family), perpetrator characteristics, and personal meaning to the victim (Boney-McCoy & Finkelhor, 1995; Nader, 1997c). Bolger and Patterson (2003) found that the types, timing, and duration of maltreatment helped to account for differences in adjustment. Either neglect or sexual abuse (and especially both) were associated with higher levels of internalizing problems and lower levels of perceived control. Youths abused over a longer period of time had more problems with peers, externalizing problems, and lower self-esteem. Early onset heightened problems and was likely to result in lower self-esteem, more behavior problems, and an external locus of control. The pathways to particular symptoms may differ. For example, trauma may lead to aggression, which in turn may lead to peer rejection (chapter 3). In contrast, youths with a stronger internal locus of control may be less likely to accept aversive situations passively and more likely to make efforts to meet challenges, and have better outcomes (Bolger & Patterson). For children ages 3 to 13 (n = 219), Briere et al. (2001) found differences on caregiver-rated TSCYC scale (chapter 13) scores for different types of abuse experiences—sexual abuse, physical abuse, or witnessing domestic violence. All three groups were associated positively with posttraumatic stress total and intrusion score ratings. Sexually abused children and children who witnessed domestic violence linked to higher PTS-avoidance ratings. Physically abused children and domestic violence witnesses had higher PTS-arousal ratings. Sexually abused youths had increased sexual concerns ratings, whereas witnessing domestic violence was negatively associated with sexual concerns. Physical abuse was linked to dissociation.

Intensity and Duration of Events

The intensity and duration of events may affect youths' traumatic reactions. For child abuse, studies often have shown that the degree of trauma increases with greater violence and greater emotional closeness to the abuser (Clinton & Jenkins-Monroe, 1994). For adults, a number of symptoms have been identified that occur most frequently if trauma has been chronic and occurs early in life (Herman, 1992a; van der Kolk, Roth, Pelkovitz, & Mandel, 1992; Terr, 1991). Among the symptoms that are not included in the *DSM-IV* PTSD diagnostic criteria are affect dysregulation, somatization, loss of beliefs, dissociative symptoms, self-destructive behaviors, loss of faith in authority or adults, and unrelenting hopelessness (chapter 1). In addition, "victim coping" in response to persistent posttraumatic distress in childhood can lead to impairment in the body's stress response systems, the physiology of the brain, and the ability to process social information and deal with interpersonal conflict (Ford, 2002; chapters 1, 3). A number of the additional symptoms are addressed in the extended questions, for example, on the CAPS-CA, CITES-R, CPTS-RI, TSCC, and WBTH (chapter 11).

Number of Stressors

In a U.S. National Comorbidity Survey, Kessler, Davis, & Kendler (1997) found that individual adversities, even those that do not occur in clusters, significantly predict onset of adult disorders. Nijenhuis, van der Hart, & Steele, (2002) found that adult psychiatric patients who reported more than five types of traumatization during their lives had higher levels of PTSD and dissociative symptoms than those who reported fewer than five traumas, only emotional abuse and neglect, or no traumatization. The number of negative life events has correlated positively with depression and conduct problems for youths (Haine et al., 2003). Fergusson and Horwood (2003) studied the effects of adverse factors (stress) on resilience and risk in New Zealand youths between ages 0 and 21 (n = 991). Adverse factors included (1) family economic: low SES, standard of living, and parent education; (2) parental relationship: single-parent, changes of parent, parental violence; (3) child abuse: excessive punishment or abuse or sexual assault; and (4) parental adjustment: parental alcoholism, criminality, or drug use. They found that youths exposed to six or more adverse factors had 2.4 times more externalizing and 1.8 times more internalizing disorders than youths with low adversity. With increases in childhood adversity, youths had corresponding, significant increases in externalizing problems such as property crimes, violent crimes, substance abuse, and conduct/antisocial disorders as well as in internalizing problems such as anxiety, depression, and suicidal ideation or attempts.

Single versus Chronic Traumas

Differences between single incident and ongoing traumas are in need of additional investigation (Fletcher, 2003; Herman, 1992a; Nader, 1997c; Terr, 1991; van der Kolk et al., 1992). Traumatic events that are ongoing or chronic (e.g., abuse, domestic violence, war, chronic illness, repeated surgeries, inner-city violence) lead both to similar and to different outcomes than do nonabuse events of short duration (e.g., a single hurricane, fire, transportation accident, shooting) (Famularo, Kinscherff, & Fenton, 1990; Fletcher; Green, 1985; Kiser, Heston, Millsap, & Pruitt, 1991; Nader; Terr). Terr observed that Type II ongoing or chronic traumas are characterized by prolonged and sickening anticipation, and Type I nonabusive events of short duration, by extreme fear and intense surprise. Events that are equal in type, however, are not always equal in intensity, impact, or meaning to the child. Clearly, determining an accurate profile for children exposed to ongoing versus single-incident experiences is complicated by differences in phase of response, phase of development, the nature of the traumatic event, a youth's relationship to the perpetrator, a youth's personality, and other variables.

Some indicators suggest that the long-term consequences of ongoing traumas emphasize re-experiencing and avoidance. When children exposed to single incidents of violence were compared to children exposed to ongoing, painful treatments for catastrophic illness (including bone-marrow transplantation, BMT), the most striking differences were the predominance of avoidance symptoms and the reduced number of arousal symptoms in the BMT patients (Nader & Stuber, 1992). Similarly, Realmuto and his colleagues (1992) found a greater frequency of re-experiencing and avoidance symptoms and a lower frequency of arousal symptoms in adolescents who had been exposed between 1975 and 1979 to the wartime atrocities of the Pol Pot regime in Cambodia. They suggest the possibility that massive trauma exposure in childhood might result in chronic re-experiencing, avoidance, and vulnerability to arousal. Over time, recent reminders, biochemical factors, or current stress may trigger intermittent hyperarousal episodes. Subsequent studies of children exposed to chronic or abusive stressors have demonstrated more symptoms of avoidance or numbing, more frequent distress in response to reminders, more symptoms of arousal, and more negative affect than for children exposed to single traumatic incidents (Fletcher, 2003).

Researchers and clinicians continue to compare different kinds of traumatic experiences in order to delineate event-specific reactions. In addition to their appearance following ongoing traumas, the symptoms of complicated trauma have been observed after single, dual, or multiple unrelated traumas, or a single trauma combined with a loss, or with consequent homelessness, handicap, or disfigurement, for example (Nader, 1997c; Terr, 1991; van der Kolk et al., 2005). Some of the reactions associated with repeated or intense traumas, such as unremitting sadness, may be more likely following single traumas if a friend or relative has died, if a previous interaction with a deceased person is now unresolvable, or if a death has been witnessed whether or not the deceased was previously known. For example, a child who witnessed an unknown woman shoot herself experienced ongoing sadness. Other reactions, such as self-anesthesia or dissociative symptoms, may be more common when there is danger or injury to personal physical integrity. For example, a child who was hit in the face by a table, an adolescent who was raped, and a child who was in an explosion with her classmates had periods of dissociation and subsequent amnesia for portions of their experiences. Aggression toward the self, including self-mutilation, has occurred following a single traumatic experience when the child has had a prior unrelated single-incident trauma or a prior loss. More information is needed to discover if self-aggression may occur for specific children following a single severe trauma. For example, specific symptoms or disorders have been linked to personality traits or vulnerabilities (Dalton, Aubuchon, Tom, Pederson, & McFarland, 1993; Otis & Louks, 1997). No matter what differences may be found in the symptoms associated with the duration or type of trauma, individual youths' reactions to personal traumas are subjective and are a consequence of multiple aspects of the youth and his or her background. Consequently, scales such as the Dimensions of Stressful Events (DOSE), History of Victimization Form (HVF), and Exposure Questionnaire (EQ), described in this chapter, focus on the youth's subjective response to the trauma rather than on the type of event.

Type of Event or Experience

Some efforts have been made to examine the differences between specific types of traumatic events and experiences (Boney-McCoy and Finkelhor, 1995; de Silva, 1999; La Greca, Silverman, Vernberg, & Roberts, 2002a). Comparisons of separate studies of the same type of event are complicated by differences in methodology. In addition, as Briere and Elliott (1997) point out, the aversive quality of some traumatic events may result in avoidance strategies. This avoidance may result in emotional or cognitive denial, dissociation, memory distortion, suppression, self-distraction, or self-medication, which interfere with accurate psychological evaluation.

After controlling for the effects of location, age, social class, race, and quality of parent-child relationship, Boney-McCoy and Finkelhor (1995) compared 2,000 children (ages 10 to 16) who reported (1) aggravated assault by a family member (physical assault involving either the use of a weapon or injury of the victim), (2) simple assault by a nonfamily member (without a weapon or injury), (3) physical assault by a parent, (4) physical assault by a nonparent family member (usually a sibling), (5) attempted or completed kidnapping, and (6) sexual assault, and for boys, violent assault to the genitals (e.g., kick or punch to the genitals during a fight or argument). They assessed 10 symptoms of PTSD, sadness in the last month, and trouble with a teacher in the past year for the children reporting these traumas. In their association with the psychological measures, all other forms of victimization were equivalent to sexual assault except simple assault and nonparental family assault, which were associated with distinctly fewer symptoms. Studies of a more comprehensive list of reactions over time are needed.

Although the studies represent different samples of youths, a group of studies using the same instrument have determined different mean trauma scores for different groups: children diagnosed with PTSD (group mean = 323.55; n = 11; Kohr, 1995); a clinical sample (mean = 139.55; Kohr); hurricane-exposed youths (group mean = 103.89 for mixed exposures—with and without life-threat or witnessing of injury; n = 122; Goldwater, 1993); and children of divorced parents (group mean = 87.27; Berna, 1993). Zahn (1994) compared 30 sexually abused children (SA; mean = 274.5) to an equivalent number of children from Berna's regular education group (mean = 86.58) and a subsample of emotionally disturbed children (mean = 117.13; Rea, 1994) and found significantly greater symptoms for the SA group than the other two groups.

Studies about the persistence of symptoms after the cessation of danger and violence have been inconsistent (Punamaki, Quota, & El-Sarraj, 2001). Punamaki and colleagues have pointed out that violent traumatic events such as kidnappings (Terr, 1983a, 1991), incarceration in concentration camps (Kinzie, Sack, Angell, Manson, & Rath, 1986), and school shootings (Nader, Pynoos, Fairbanks, & Frederick, 1990) have shown prolonged (years) symptoms, in contrast to studies of natural disasters, which were followed by a considerable decrease in traumatic symptoms (La Greca, Silverman, Vernberg, & Prinstein, 1996; Swenson, Saylor, Powell, Stokes, Foster, & Belter, 1996). On the other hand, children's symptoms were reduced after the Gulf War for Israeli children following cessation of SCUD missile attacks (Schwarzwald, Weisenberg, Waysman, Solomon, & Klingman, 1993) and for Iraqi children 2 years after the bombing of their shelter (Dyregrov & Raundalen, 1993). Following the sinking of the cruise ship *Jupiter* near Greece (Udwin, Boyle, Yule, Bolton, & O'Ryan, 2000), the length and intensity of youths' symptoms was associated with specific reactions and risk factors. These findings suggest that a number of variables, in addition to the nature of the event, can influence persistence of symptoms. These might include the perception of whether or not the threat persists, whether or not support systems are in place, or the nature of previous and subsequent experiences.

Kessler et al. (1997) adjusted for overlap among 26 childhood adversities: traumas, parental psychopathology, and permanent or prolonged parental loss. They found that parental psychopathology (especially maternal) and interpersonal traumas (especially rape and kidnap) had comparable substantive import in adult psychopathology. Kessler et al. concluded that some of the variation in effects of different adversities is related to differential clustering of adversities rather than to unique effects of particular adversities.

Events with Deaths

The death of a significant individual during a traumatic event has been associated with increased PTSD symptoms in children (Nader et al., 1990; Pfefferbaum et al., 1999; Pynoos et al., 1987). In addition, traumatic events that include deaths have been associated with a more complex set of reactions than normal bereavement (Burnett, Middleton, Raphael, Dunne, Moylan, & Martinek, 1994; Eth & Pynoos, 1985b; Gray, Prigerson, & Litz, 2004; Nader, 1997b; Stamm, 1999). A new diagnosis, traumatic grief or complicated grief, has been proposed for the upcoming *DSM-V* for people whose grief has been complicated by trauma or the nature of the lost relationship (Jacobs, 1999; Prigerson et al., 1996; Stamm).

Complicated grief reactions are distinguished from "normal" or uncomplicated grief reactions primarily by "the presence of unremitting and incapacitating distress that interferes markedly with functioning" (Gray et al., 2004). Some theoreticians and researchers suggest that complicated grief may occur not only in response to deaths that occur during traumatic events but also in response to any death that is personally devastating (Jacobs, 1999). Cohen, Mannarino, Greenberg, Padlo, and Shipley (2002) have described two distinct theoretical pathways proposed for adult traumatic or complicated grief. One is based on attachment theory, and the other is based on the traumatic nature of some deaths. Prigerson et al. (1996) have attempted to integrate the two concepts (Cohen et al.). This conception of complicated grief for adults is not based on the event but on the relationship between the deceased and the bereaved and the bereaved's dependency on the relationship (Cohen et al.). The proposed diagnostic criteria for complicated grief in adults includes significant separation distress (Criterion A), as evidenced by the frequent occurrence of at least three of the following symptoms: intrusive preoccupation or thoughts of the deceased, yearning for the deceased, searching for the deceased, or excessive loneliness. The person experiences significant symptoms of traumatic distress for longer than 6 months as evidenced by the frequent occurrence of at least six of the following: intrusive recollections about the deceased, avoidance, assuming the symptoms or harmful behaviors of the deceased, futility about the future, numbness or detachment, being stunned or dazed, disbelief about the death, emptiness, feeling unfulfilled without the deceased, feeling that part of the self has died, shattered worldview (e.g., lost or fragmented sense of trust, security, or control), or bitterness (Gray et al.; Silverman et al., 2000). In 2005, Prigereson and Maciejewski called for studies of the following guidelines for a possible DSM V diagnosis of complicated grief: (1) Criterion A requires chronic and disruptive yearning, pining, or longing for the deceased; (2) at least four symptoms from Criteria B—trouble accepting the death, inability to trust others, excessive bitterness, difficulty moving on, numbness/detachment, feeling life is empty or meaningless, feeling the future is bleak or holds no meaning, agitation) and (3) Criteria C—marked and persistent dysfunction in social, occupational, and other important domains (see also Prigerson & Vanderwerker, 2005). For adults, complicated grief has been associated with long-term physical and mental-health impairments (Prigerson et al., 1997), with lower social functioning scores, worse mental-health scores, and lower energy levels than normal bereavement (Silverman et al.), and with increased suicidal ideation (Prigerson et al., 1999).

In contrast to adult complicated grief, children's traumatic grief has been observed when, as a result of trauma symptoms, youths are unable to complete the tasks of uncomplicated bereavement (Cohen et al., 2002; Nader, 1997b; Webb, 2002a). Children whose loved ones have died in traumatic events may experience normal bereavement (Cohen et al.). On the other hand, in addition to experiencing the trauma, witnessing the death, or discovering the body, learning about the traumatic nature of the death may be sufficiently traumatic for the occurrence of traumatic grief (Cohen et al.; Nader, 1997b). After traumatic events with deaths, children who have learned that such an event was occurring in a loved one's possible location, heard about and imagined the traumatic event, or seen media images related to the event have also experienced trauma or traumatic grief (Nader, 1997b; Nader et al., 1993; Pfefferbaum et al., 1999). Cohen et al. have summarized the findings related to diagnostic criteria for childhood traumatic grief. These findings include that (1) the circumstances of the death were objectively or subjectively perceived to be traumatic; (2) significant PTSD symptoms resulted; (3) reminders of the loss or of the consequent change in circumstances segue into intrusive traumatic reminders, thoughts, or imagery; (4) attempts to cope with the triggered traumatic reactions follow (e.g., avoidant or numbing strategies may follow); and (5) PTSD symptoms and efforts to contend with them may impinge on the child's ability to complete the tasks of uncomplicated bereavement (Cohen et al.; Nader, 1997b). Thus, adult complicated grief is related to the loss of a security-enhancing relationship, whereas childhood traumatic grief is associated with the intrusion of traumatic thoughts or imagery and the related coping strategies (Cohen et al.). A study of adolescents (n = 87) has confirmed this difference. Layne, Pynoos et al. (2001) found that symptoms pertaining to the loss of a security-increasing relationship (excessive loneliness, purposelessness, yearning for the deceased, feeling a part of oneself has died, feeling that life is meaningless, shattered worldview) were not characteristic of adolescents with traumatic grief. Following September 11, 2001, Brown and Goodman (2005) confirmed, for youths (ages 8 to 18), a distinct construct for normal versus traumatic grief. They found that complicated grief included yearning for the deceased. More studies are needed to examine childhood traumatic grief.

Actions or Failure to Act During an Event

In addition to the traumatic injuries that result from being victimized, a youth's thoughts, actions, or failure to act during a traumatic event can cause deep emotional pain (Nader & Mello, 2001; Box 10.1a, 10.1b). Empathy may moderate the emotional impact of hurting another person. Experiences, such as intense helplessness, that deflate the self-image can be desolating. Behaviors or omissions that lead to guilt such as failing to rescue or assist another or doing something to injure or kill another person (even an enemy) can be personally devastating and can increase trauma symptoms. Nader et al. (1993) found that youths who had injured someone else during the 1991 Gulf War had more trauma symptoms than traumatized youths who had not injured anyone. Both younger and older children sometimes overestimate what they should or could have done during a catastrophic event (see also Herman, 1997; Box 2.1c, 10.1c).

Aspects of Timing: Event and Phase of Response

The phase of the trauma, intervention, or response is an additional factor influencing reactions and measurement. Although children may need and want to speak about their experiences following traumatic events, they may need family contact, some restoration of order, reestablishment of a sense of safety, and/or time for initial recovery before they

---

BOX 10.1
Case Examples: Factors Influencing Personal Traumatic Reactions

a. Ahmed. When he was 16, Ahmed had survived the ongoing horrors of war for more than a year without physical injury. Throughout most of his therapy session, Ahmed appeared to feel ashamed. He sat slumped, looked down at his hands, and mumbled softly while he described his experiences. An Iraqi soldier who patrolled their neighborhood during the occupation forced neighborhood residents to watch while he tortured or killed someone. Ahmed heard how the soldier had sawed off someone's leg while he screamed, had gutted a cat, and had made boys walk naked in front of their mothers before he shot them. One night, Ahmed was playing chess with an "older man" (aged 40). The Iraqi soldier came in, accused the older man of working with the resistance, and began to beat him mercilessly. Ahmed stood frozen behind the television set, unable to speak. When he started to move toward the man to help him, the soldier warned him that if he moved, he would be shot. Ahmed stood motionless and silent while the soldier beat the man to death. Ahmed was unable to move for several seemingly long minutes after the soldier left. He did not know why the soldier had spared him. He wished he had died. He could not bear to be alive because he had let the soldier beat the man to death and had done nothing.

b. Mathew. A number of factors contributed to Mathew's self-contempt following the massacre, including his helplessness and failure to fight back or help his friend. Mathew took a Barbie doll, cut her hair and colored it to look like his hair, dressed her in boys' clothes that looked like his, and wrote a symbol on the arm of her jacket that was exactly like the one on his jacket. Mathew began to beat the doll, break her arms, slam her against the table, and hang her.

c. Shawn. During an earthquake, Shawn ran toward the school cafeteria exit door because debris was flying toward him and the wall near his table was spewing concrete blocks. He looked back briefly before exiting the room and saw a girl lying motionless on a table near the collapsing wall. He later agonized over not having gone back to help the girl. Learning that she was already dead did not relieve his feelings that he should have gone back to help her.

d. Ivo. After Ivo was finally rescued from wartime incarceration, his family fled to a town in his country that was no longer in the midst of the war. When asked if he had been injured during the war, this adolescent Bosnian boy answered, "No." Knowing that Ivo had been captured and imprisoned for weeks by enemy soldiers who tended to torture their victims, the interviewer pursued the issue. Ivo admitted that he had been beaten daily during his imprisonment. He explained that it was much worse for his defiant friend, who had been permanently crippled by beatings. At this stage, the boy was more worried about his father, who was still imprisoned, and about the greater harm to his friends and others who had not yet returned. From his current perspective, he could only consider his own injuries in comparison to the injuries of others.

---

can give detailed answers regarding their reactions. Rumors are common and fear is contagious in the aftermath of a traumatic event (Pynoos & Nader, 1988). Arousal symptoms may be common to the traumatized and untraumatized. Within the first 2 days to 2 weeks following a catastrophic incident, some initial symptoms (e.g., bad dreams, fears) may disappear for those who are not traumatized. Moreover, the initial numbing and denial may decrease for children who are traumatized. Assessment may be more accurate after order and safety are restored and rumors are dispelled. There is also a need for assessment over time. Some symptoms may appear immediately (e.g., sleep disturbance), whereas others have a delayed onset (e.g., behavior problems) (Frederick, 1985; Schwarz & Kowalski, 1992). Not all of those who develop PTSD do so within the first 6 months of the event (Fletcher, 2003; Yule, Bolton, Udwin, Boyle, O'Ryan, & Nurrish, 2000). Yule and his colleagues found that 10% of the children with PTSD following the sinking of the *Jupiter* did not develop PTSD for 7 months to 5 years later. PTSD was persistent rather than transitory with delayed onset. For some, with the passage of time, the process of PTSD subsides and other mental-health symptoms (e.g., depression) become more prominent (Kroll, 2003) or reactions translate into patterns of behavior or vulnerabilities.

For ongoing traumas, the phase of the event itself is important to recognize. For example, in 1991, after the Gulf War was over, children in Kuwait seemed to be in a different phase of their reactions than refugee children in Croatia in 1992, where that war continued (Nader, 1997a). Kuwaiti children became focused upon the extent of the physical and psychological damage that occurred, upon rebuilding, and upon issues of accountability. In contrast, Croatian children were still focused upon surviving the war and its horrors; they found watching the news and staying informed a useful coping mechanism. As the war was ongoing, numbing appeared to be prevalent. Symptoms appeared to be warded off or ignored, because there might be more to endure.

When an event is perceived to be over rather than ongoing, there will likely be a reassessment of the experience and its results (Nader, 1997c). Children suffering from ongoing traumas such as abuse or inner-city violence with no end in sight, like the children exposed to ongoing war, may of necessity ward off symptoms or disavow their importance until "the war is over" (Box 10.1d). From both a clinical and a research standpoint, the event phase and the length of exposure will affect assessment of trauma symptoms and reported levels of severity of response over time.

TRAUMAGENIC EVENTS: *DSM-IV* CRITERION A

There is continued debate over which events cause traumatic reactions in children and over the nature of childhood traumatic response. Some of the issues are presented here. Children and adolescents may have symptoms described under the *DSM* criteria of PTSD (e.g., repetitive unwanted thoughts, physiological or emotional distress in response to reminders, irritability or outbursts of anger) in response to troubling events such as embarrassment, hurt feelings, or a romantic break-up. One way that *DSM-IV* distinguishes between the symptoms that occur in the normal course of life events and those associated with traumatic events that engender

PTSD is in Criterion A. *DSM-IV* Criterion A defines the event as one in which there was (A1) "actual or threatened death or serious injury, or a threat to the physical integrity of self or others" and (A2) "the person's response involved intense fear, helplessness, or horror . . . [or] disorganized or agitated behavior" (APA, 1994, pp. 427–428).

What constitutes a catastrophic stressor for children remains a controversial issue (see "Symptom Ratings" in chapter 4). Some professionals argue to abolish *DSM* Criterion A requirements, whereas others argue that the diagnosis be restricted to those who have experienced extreme, life-threatening events (Scheeringa & Zeanah, 1995). Some have suggested that re-experiencing phenomena should be sufficient to warrant the diagnosis whether or not the experience involved life threat (Drell, Siegel, & Gaensbauer, 1993). Some have suggested that, if the child meets symptom requirements of *DSM-IV* PTSD Criteria B through D, the diagnosis should be given (Hyman & Snook, 2002). Still others have suggested that, because children and adolescents who experience other life stressors and mental-health problems are likely to respond affirmatively to questions about re-experiencing symptoms (Wolfe & Birt, 2002b), the severity of the child's reaction during the experience should define it as traumatic. Costello, Angold, March, & Fairbank (1998) have defined two types of events to examine in relation to trauma symptoms: the "extreme stressor" or "high magnitude" event as defined by *DSM-IV* PTSD Criterion A, and the "low magnitude" event (e.g., stressful events covered by most life event scales used in research on depression and anxiety). Similarly, theoreticians who have proposed a diagnosis of traumatic or complicated grief for the more complex grief reactions experienced after traumatic deaths suggest that the diagnosis may be applicable to any death that is personally devastating (Jacobs, 1999; Nader, 2002c).

The current stressor criterion becomes particularly problematic for infants and preschool children (Scheeringa & Zeanah, 1995). Experiences that are not traumatic for older children or adults can be traumatic for very young children (Drell et al., 1993; Scheeringa, Peebles, Cook, & Zeanah, 2001; Scheeringa & Zeanah). Scheeringa and colleagues (Scheeringa et al., 2001; Scheeringa, Zeanah, Myers, & Putnam, 2005) have recommended removing the *DSM IV* requirement for an "experience of intense fear, helplessness or horror" from Criterion A and altering algorithms for a PTSD diagnosis by reducing the number of symptoms required in other criteria.

Fear, Helplessness, and Horror

Studies have confirmed the association of PTSD with fear, helplessness, and horror for many but not all adults exposed to traumatic events (Brewin, Andrews, & Rose, 2000). Brewin et al. have suggested that individuals who do not experience intense fear, helplessness, or horror during a trauma may have subsequent PTSD associated with other noxious emotions such as shame or anger or with other psychological or biological factors. In addition to fear, helplessness, and horror, anger with others and shame are also strong predictors of PTSD (Andrews, Brewin, Rose, & Kirk, 2000). In an undergraduate population, Roemer, Orsillo, Borkovec, and Litz (1998) correlated retrospective reports of fear, helplessness, and horror with current PTSD symptoms. They found that only helplessness was significantly related to level of symptoms (Brewin et al.). In a nonrepresentative sample of adults (n = 138) who rated their fear, helplessness, and horror approximately 3 weeks after being assaulted, Brewin et al. found that fear, helplessness, horror, shame, and anger at others were all associated with PTSD 6 months after the event. Fear and helplessness were equally common and were more common than horror. The few respondents with PTSD who had not experienced fear, helplessness, or horror during the event had experienced high levels of shame or anger with others. Shame and anger with others have effects on later PTSD, independent from those of intense peritraumatic fear, helplessness, or horror.

EXPOSURE QUESTIONNAIRES

The degree and frequency of exposure to stressful or traumatic events may affect a child's reaction to the specific event under assessment. Stress assessments do not always distinguish between chronic and episodic traumatic or stressful events or determine the qualitative differences in aspects of stress experiences (Deardorff, Gonzales, & Sandler, 2003). With some overlap, a few scales are presented below that measure primarily (1) stressful events across a child's lifetime or (2) the degree or intensity of exposure to traumatic events or a specific event. Both life events and exposure levels have been associated with the degree, course, and nature of traumatic reactions (Daviss, Mooney, Racusin, Ford, Fleischer, and McHugo, 2000; Daviss, Rascusin, Fleischer, Ford and McHugo, 2000; Nader et al., 1990; Pynoos et al., 1987; Udwin et al., 2000).

Some studies suggest that degree of exposure (e.g., life threat, fear, or subjective involvement) rather than life events are more strongly and significantly associated with PTSD scores (Fletcher, 1996b; Pynoos et al., 1987; Udwin et al., 2000). La Greca et al. (1996) found that children who reported more major life events during the recovery period 3 to 7 months after a traumatic event reported more PTSD symptomatology. Complex or repeated traumas, however, may result in symptoms beyond those defined in the criteria of PTSD or acute stress disorder (ASD; Carlson & Briere, 2002; APA, 1994; Herman, 1992a, 1992b; Terr, 1991; chapter 1).

Studies have demonstrated a strong association between minor daily stressors and youths' psychological functioning even after controlling for major life stressors (Self-Brown, LeBlanc, & Kelley, 2004). Daily stressors may serve as mediating or moderating variables in the outcomes of major life stressors. A number of assessment tools have been used to evaluate the general range of stressful life events (e.g., relocating, divorce, broken bone; Coddington, 1972; Huete, 2001). The measures presented here were developed to assess traumatic events (see Table 10.1).

Stressful Life Events

Several studies have demonstrated that as the frequency of major life stressors increase, youths' psychological functioning declines (Self-Brown et al., 2004). Some scales assess the incidence of specific stressors (e.g., Screen for Adolescent Violence Exposure; Hastings & Kelley, 1997). The following measures primarily assess the frequency of exposures to stressful life events.

The Child and Adolescent Psychiatric Assessment (CAPA) Life Events Scale

Age range: 9–17
Parent interview: Included
Format: Semistructured child interview
Relevant subscales: Family Structure; PTSD; other disorders
Training: Required

The CAPA Life Events Scale is a subscale of the Child and Adolescent Psychiatric Assessment (v. 4.2; Angold, Cox, Prendergast, Rutter, & Simonoff, 2000). The Life Events section uses the same general structure as the rest of CAPA (see chapter 15). It combines both respondent- and interviewer-based methods of assessment. The CAPA life events module contains questions about two types of events: the "extreme stressor" or "high magnitude" event as defined by *DSM-IV* PTSD Criterion A, and the "low magnitude" events, stressful events covered by most life event scales used in research on depression and anxiety. High magnitude life events are assessed for the child's whole life; low magnitude events for the past 3 months (Costello et al., 1998). Screening questions establish from parent and child interviews whether the child has the three core symptoms of PTSD: reexperiencing, hypervigilance, and avoidance. Hypervigilance and avoidance are asked only if the child experiences painful recall (i.e., reexperiencing). The full PTSD assessment is administered only if all three core symptoms are present and are linked causally to the event (Costello et al.).

The History of Victimization Form (HVF)

Age range: 8–16
Format: Compiled from clinical and protective agency records and inter-
    views with guardians and social workers
Associated scales: CITES-R, CPEQ

TABLE 10.1
Exposure Measures

Measure (Age Range)	∝ Internal Consistency	Interrater r	Test-Retest r	Assesses/Measures (Scale or Subscale r; Distinguishes)	Author (Available from)
CAPA Life Events (age 8–16)			2 wk. high magnitude ICC =.83 P, .72 C; low magnitude events ICC = .58 P, .62 C	High (traumas) and low (stressors) magnitude life events (distinguishes trauma outcomes)	Angold, Cox, Prendergast, Rutter, & Simonoff, 2000 (Center for Developmental Epidemiology, Department of Psychiatry and Behavioral Sciences, Duke University Medical Center, Box 3454, Durham, NC 27710-3454)
HVF (age 9–17)				Abuse, neglect, and family violence events (distinguishes trauma outcomes)	Wolfe, Gentile, & Bourdeau, 1987 (Vicky Veitch Wolfe, Ph.D., Child & Adolescent Centre, 346 South Street, London Health Sciences Centre, London, Ontario, Canada N6A 4G5; wolfev@lhsc.on.ca)
LITE (age 8 and older)				Traumatic or loss events and intensity of response (distinguishes trauma outcomes)	Greenwald, 1999 (Sidran Institute; sidran@sidran.org; www.sidran.org; 200 E. Joppa Road, Suite 207, Towson, MD 21286, phone: 410-825-8888, fax: 410-337-0747)
TTTc (age 12–17)				Stressful and traumatic life events and intensity of response (distinguishes trauma outcomes)	Fletcher, 1992b (Kenneth Fletcher, Ph.D., Psychiatry Department, University of Massachusetts Medical Center, 55 Lake Avenue North, Worcester, MA 01655; Kenneth.Fletcher@umassmed.edu)

TESI-C (age 8–17)	k =.73 –1.00	k = .50–.70 2–4 mo. C	Traumatic life events and intensity of response (child report) (distinguishes trauma outcomes)	Ford et al., 2005 (Dr. Julian Ford, Ford@Psychiatry.uchc.edu)
TESI-PRR (age 0–18)		k = .50–.70 2–4 mo. P	Traumatic life events and intensity of response (parent report) (distinguishes trauma outcomes)	Ghosh Ippen et al., 2002 (Chandra Ghosh Ippen, Chandra@itsa.ucsf.edu)
YAUTC (age 13 and older)			Stressful and traumatic life events and intensity of response; includes sexual abuse items (distinguishes trauma outcomes)	Fletcher, 1992c (Kenneth Fletcher, Ph.D., Psychiatry Department, University of Massachusetts Medical Center, 55 Lake Avenue North, Worcester, MA 01655; Kenneth. Fletcher@umassmed.edu)
CPEQ (age 8–16)	.81–.89 s		Traumatic life events and intensity of response; includes sexual abuse items (distinguishes trauma outcomes)	Wolfe, Gentile, & Bourdeau, 1987 (Vicky Veitch Wolfe, Ph.D., Child & Adolescent Centre, 346 South Street, London Health Sciences Centre, London, Ontario, Canada N6A 4G5; wolfev@lhsc.on.ca)

TABLE 10.1 (continued)
Exposure Measures

Measure (Age Range)	∝ Internal Consistency	Interrater r	Test-Retest r	Assesses/Measures (Scale or Subscale r; Distinguishes)	Author (Available from)
DOSE (age 0–17)	.63–.70			Intensity of subjective reactions to traumatic life events (WBTH; CPTSD interview; CRTES; TSCC; CBCL; Parent Report, CRS; predicted trauma symptoms)	Fletcher, 1992a (Kenneth Fletcher, Ph.D., Psychiatry Department, University of Massachusetts Medical Center, 55 Lake Avenue North, Worcester, MA 01655; Kenneth. Fletcher@umassmed.edu)
EQ (age 7–17)				Traumatic life events and intensity of response (distinguishes trauma symptoms/outcomes)	Nader, 2002b (measures@twosuns.org; fax: 512 219-0486)
CGA-C[CGA-P] (age 8–17)				Complicated grief reactions (assesses proposed complicated grief disorder; short and long scales) (new scale)	Short: Prigerson, Nader, & Maciejewski, 2005; Long: Nader, Prigerson, & Maciejewski, 2005 (measures@twosuns.org; fax: 512 219-0486)

PPTIM (age 8–17)		Bereavement and other cumulative losses (people, pets, places, things) (new scale)	Nader & Prigerson, 2005 (Dr. Kathleen Nader, measures@twosuns.org; fax: 512 219-0486)
ICG-C (age 8–18)		Complicated grief reactions (assesses complicated grief symptoms)	Dyregrov, Yule, Smith, Perrin, Gjestad, & Prigerson, 2001 (Dr. William Yule, w.yule@iop.kcl.ac.uk)
EGI (age 8 and older)	.93; .70 — .90 s	Complicated grief reactions (distinguishes trauma outcomes)	Layne, Savjak, Saltzman, & Pynoos, 2001 (Dr. Christopher Layne, 284 TLRB, Brigham Young University, Provo, UT 84602; christopher_layne@byu.edu; fax 801 422-0163)

C = child; k = kappa; KR = Kuder-Richardson; P = parent; r = correlation; s = subscales; wk. = weeks

Sources: Fletcher, Cox, Skidmore, Janssens, & Render, 1997; Ford & Rogers, 1997; Greenwald & Rubin, 1999; Layne, Pynoos et al., 2001; Nader, & Fairbanks, 1994; Nader, Pynoos, Fairbanks, Al-Ajeel, & Al-Asfour, 1993; Wolfe & Birt, 2002a.

The History of Victimization Form (Wolfe, Gentile, & Bourdeau, 1987) was developed to provide detailed information regarding sexual abuse, physical abuse, neglect, emotional maltreatment, and exposure to family violence. Information is gathered regarding timing, duration, and cessation of abuse. Six sexual abuse scale scores are derived: severity of abuse, use of coercion/force, number of perpetrators, relationship to perpetrators, duration of abuse, and frequency of abuse. Exposure to physical abuse, neglect, emotional maltreatment, and family violence items are recorded on a Yes/No format.

The Lifetime Incidence of Traumatic Events (LITE)
Age range: 8 and older
Translations: German, Persian, Spanish, Swedish
Format: Child and parent completion forms
Associated scales: CROPS, PROPS

LITE (Greenwald, 1999) permits a Yes or No response to 16 potentially traumatic or loss events (e.g., been in a car accident; someone in the family died), indication of the number of exposures to each, age during exposure, and three-point scales (None, Some, Lots) for how much the event upset the child "then" and bothers the child "now." It is not considered by its author to be an objectively scorable instrument, but when a trauma/ loss exposure score was needed, based on clinical judgment, a researcher has rated each participant's exposure severity on a scale of 1 to 4, with a higher number representing an estimate of greater exposure (Greenwald & Rubin, 1999). LITE has also been scored by tallying the number of events endorsed (Greenwald, Satin, Azubuike, Borgen, & Rubin, 2001). Parent and student forms are available.

The Teen Tough Times Checklist (TTTC)
Age range: 12–17
Translations: Spanish
Format: Child completion
Associated Scales: Parent Report of Child's Stress Reaction, DOSE, YAUTC, WBTH, World View Survey, Child and Parent PTSD Iinterviews

The Teen Tough Times checklist (Fletcher, 1992b) is similar to the Young Adult Upsetting Times Checklist (YAUTC; see below). It is a 70-item checklist (e.g., "Kids made you do something horrible or did something horrible to you") that does not include the sexual abuse items on the Young Adult checklist (see YAUTC, below, and WBTH, chapter 11).

The Traumatic Events Screening Inventory for Children (TESI-C)
Age range: 8–17
Format: A structured child interview and a child self-report measure

The Traumatic Events Screening Inventory for Children (Ford et al., 2002; Ford et al., 2005) is a 19-item survey designed to elicit children's exposures to or witnessing of severe accidents, severe illness or injury of self or someone close, death of someone close, prolonged separation from someone depended on, natural disaster, family or community conflict or violence, kidnap, threat or violence to self, television or actual exposure to war or terrorism, incarceration of family, animal attacks, someone's suicide or self-harm, sexual molestation, neglect, and emotional abuse. The questions are arranged hierarchically (gradually increasing the intimacy of the experiences; sexual trauma is toward the end of the interview) to help the child tolerate the possible stress of disclosing traumatic experiences. Probes determine the presence or absence of (1) the child's and the interviewer's assessment of the degree of threat of death or injury (*DSM* Criterion A1) and (2) the child's endorsement of fear, helplessness or confusion, and disgust or horror (A2). If A1 and A2 items are endorsed, the interviewer inquires about age at occurrence, what happened, who was in the event, if anyone was hurt, and the need for medical attention. The TESI-Self Report Revised, for youths ages 10 to 16, asks about the same types of events and about witnessing drug usage. It (1) elicits the youth's age at the first, last, and worst experience under each category, (2) asks if the youth felt really bad, upset, scared, sad, or mixed up by the worst experience, and (3) inquires about the type of experience, injury, or death. The interview is designed for use only by qualified mental-health professionals or advanced trainees supervised by a qualified mental-health professional.

Traumatic Events Screening Inventory-Parent Report Revised C (TESI-PRR)
Age range: 0–18
Translations: Spanish
Format: Semistructured parent interview or parent completion

The Traumatic Events Screening Inventory-Parent Report Revised C (Ghosh Ippen et al., 2002) is a screening instrument for a child's exposure to traumatic events based on TESI-C and includes simplified language and additional items relevant to young children ("Has your child ever been in a serious natural disaster where someone could have been [or actually was] severely injured or died [like a tornado, hurricane, fire, or earthquake]?"). Administering the questionnaire as an interview whenever possible is recommended. TESI-PRR is part of a two-stage screening plan. Stage I involves screening the parent regarding the child in multiple settings (e.g., court, home, school) using a brief version of TESI-PRR (the basic questions with no follow-up questions). Stage II involves following up positive screens (i.e., parent indicates yes to an event) with codeable clinical interviews or questionnaires specific to the item that screens positive.

The Young Adult Upsetting Times Checklist (YAUTC)
Age range: 13 and older
Translations: Spanish
Format: Child completion
Associated scales: Parent Report of Child's Stress Reaction, DOSE, TTTc,
     WBTH, WVS, Child and Parent PTSD interviews

The Young Adult Upsetting Times Checklist (Fletcher, 1992c) is
based on a Life Events and Coping Inventory (LECI; Dise-Lewis, 1988)
designed for children. Minor items (e.g., "You felt angry or upset," "You
felt rushed or pressured") have been excluded. Traumatizing events,
such as abuse and exposure to violence and disasters, have been added.
The checklist includes stressful ("You moved to a new home") and traumatic events ("Someone you know was caught in a disaster like a fire,
flood, earthquake, or tornado"). Each of 75 experiences is rated for their
occurrence (in the "last year" and "before the last year") and the intensity of the worst experiential occurrence (on a four-point Likert scale:
1 = Not upsetting; 2 = Somewhat upsetting; 3 = Very upsetting; or 4 =
Extremely upsetting). There is a page to describe the worst experience
and why it happened. To use the checklist for younger adolescents, it is
appropriate to assess their ability to understand and to omit questions
referring to after the age of 18.

Exposure Levels

The following scales primarily assess the degree or intensity of exposure (e.g., degree of life threat, level of emotional response during the
event) to one or more specific traumatic event(s) (see Table 10.1).

The Children's Peritraumatic Experiences Questionnaire (CPEQ)
Age range: 8–16
Format: Child completion
Associated scales: CITES-R, HVF

The Children's Peritraumatic Experiences Questionnaire (Wolfe & Birt,
1993) is a 33-item scale (originally 78) developed to assess children's emotional reactions (e.g., feelings of helplessness, fear, terror, sadness, and
anger) during their sexual abuse experiences (or their most negative life
experience for nonabused participants). Based upon a principal components analysis, the five scales are extreme reactions, fear/anxiety, negative
affect, dissociation, and guilt (Wolfe & Birt, 2002a). The extreme reactions
(e.g., feared being killed or dying, felt like killing offender or self, felt like
fainting) and the fear/anxiety (e.g., shaky, frightened, worried) scales
closely parallel *DSM-IV* PTSD Criterion A2 ("intense fear, helplessness, or
horror"). Items are rated on a three-point scale (None, Some, and A lot).

The Dimensions of Stressful Events (DOSE)
Age range: 0–17
Format: Rater completion with information from parent and child
Associated scales: Parent Report of Child's Stress Reaction, TTTc, YAUTC,
    WBTH, WVS, Child & Parent PTSD interviews

The DOSE (Fletcher, 1992a) scale was developed to assess the degree to which an event is traumatizing. It measures exposure and resulting variables (e.g., number of traumas, relationship to perpetrator and to deceased victims, sense of stigmatization, and moral and religious conflicts). Twenty-five items (e.g., "Did the child suffer any lasting losses [other than death of friends or relatives] due to the stressful event[s]?") address frequency and degree of exposure to single-incident events. Items include, for example, proximity, view of blood, unexpectedness, duration, and more. Twenty-four items (e.g., "Was the child ever threatened with harm if the abuse was revealed?" "Was anyone physically injured due to the event[s]?") assess frequency and degree of exposure to child abuse experiences. A scoring key accompanies the scale.

The Exposure Questionnaire (EQ)
Age range: 7–17
Translations: Croatian, Kuwaiti Arabic
Associated scales: CPTS-RI, CPTSR-PI

The EQ (Nader, 1993a, 1999b, 2002b) assesses exposure levels (e.g., life threat, injury, subjective response, emotional proximity) and other variables (e.g., relationship to deceased and injured, worry about another, property damage, helping efforts) that affect the child's subjective experience during and after a traumatic event. A page for the general description of the child's experience and two questionnaires are included (postwar questions and postdisaster or postviolence questions). Items are rated either "Yes" or "No" or on a five-point scale (0 to 4) appropriate to the question. For emotional reactions that have been statistically associated with increased traumatic symptoms (e.g., fear, panic, horror, helplessness, guilt), the questionnaire first inquires about frequency, then about the intensity of the reactions.

MEASURES OF COMPLICATED REACTIONS TO TRAUMA

Researchers and clinicians have identified more complicated reactions to trauma and to traumatic deaths. Complicated trauma reactions include symptoms in addition to PTSD most commonly associated with multiple or ongoing traumas (see "Intensity and Duration of Events," above; Table 1.4). A symptom complex distinct from uncomplicated bereavement, childhood traumatic grief (see "Events with Deaths," above), may occur when the death is perceived by the child to be traumatic. Like *DSM-IV* PTSD, childhood complicated trauma or grief reactions appear to be different from the adult syndromes in a number of ways. Moreover, evidence suggests that treatments for simple PTSD may not be applicable to more complex posttrauma reactions (Ford, Courtois, Steele, van der Hart, & Nijenhuis, 2005; van der Kolk, Roth, Pelcovitz, Sunday, & Spinazzola, 2005). Accurate diagnosis of complex PTSD or developmental disorder (van der Kolk & Courtois, 2005) is important. Measures of complicated trauma and complicated grief have been developed and tested for adults. New child measures are in progress. Several instruments that measure trauma in youths include some or many of the symptoms of complicated trauma (e.g., revised CPTS-RI and Additional Questions). New instruments have been developed to measure childhood traumatic grief (see Table 10.1).

Complicated Trauma

The Structured Interview for Disorders of Extreme Stress-Not Otherwise Specified (SIDES) (Pelcovitz, van der Kolk, Roth, Mandel, Kaplan, & Resick, 1997) measures the symptoms of complex trauma in adults. It has been used with adolescents. SIDES is intended for administration after a *DSM* PTSD scale (e.g., the CAPS). SIDES has demonstrated good psychometric properties (van der Kolk & Pelcovitz, 1999). An additional scale for children is under construction (see CPTS-RI and AQ, chapter 11).

Traumatic Grief

Inventories of childhood traumatic grief are undergoing revision and testing. The authors of these measures consider them to be "under construction." Additional studies are needed to assist the process of their development as well as to aid our understanding of this syndrome in children. The inventories presented here are similar in their content but differ in their wording (see Table 10.1).

The Complicated Grief Assessment for Children and Adolescents (CGA-C)
Age range: 8–17
Associated scales: Exposure (PPTIM), short form, long form, parent forms

The Complicated Grief Assessment for Children and Adolescents is a new instrument that includes a short form (Prigerson, Nader, & Maciejewski, 2005) and long form (Nader, Prigerson, & Maciejewski, 2005) as well as parent-, self-, and interview-report forms. Its precursor is the Inventory of Complicated Grief (ICG; Prigerson et al., 1995), an adult measure with good psychometric properties (Prigerson et al., 1999). The scales include symptoms of childhood bereavement and traumatic grief described in the literature over the last 20 years. The People, Places, and Things I Miss (PPTIM; Nader & Prigerson, 2005) is an exposure questionnaire that permits a comprehensive description of a youth's bereavement and other cumulative losses. Youths list and describe their relationships to the valued people who have died, moved, or otherwise left their lives; the pets and valued items that have been lost; and the living places and resources that may have been lost or destroyed. The instruction sheet for PPTIM includes a practice page. The CGA-C short form is a questionnaire designed to address the symptoms and behaviors associated with the complicated grief diagnosis proposed for *DSM-V*. The CGA-C long form is a questionnaire designed to address the feelings, symptoms, and behaviors associated with bereavement and complicated grief. The first half of the questionnaire examines symptoms related to the person who died. The second half of the questionnaire examines general symptoms and functioning. The time frame is the last month. Parent forms are also available. The measures are currently undergoing psychometric testing.

The Inventory of Complicated Grief for Children (ICG-C)
Age range: 8–18
Format: Child completion

ICG-C (Dyregrov, Yule, Smith, Perrin, Gjestad, & Prigerson, 2001) is a 23-item self-report measure. Its precursor is the Inventory of Complicated Grief (formerly the Inventory of Traumatic Grief; Prigerson et al., 1995). The current version is 23 items and uses a five-point rating scale from "Almost never" (1, less than once a month) to "Always" (5, several times a day). Use and psychometric testing of the scale is in progress.

The UCLA/BYU Extended Grief Inventory (EGI)
Age range: 8 and older
Translations: Bosnian
Format: Child completion

EGI (Layne, Savjak, Saltzman, & Pynoos, 2001) is a 28-item self-report measure that assesses the frequency of adaptive and potentially maladaptive grief reactions during the past 30 days. The inventory is a revised version of the UCLA Grief Screening Inventory (Nader, 1993b; Nader et al., 1990; Pynoos et al., 1987). EGI contains three factor-analytically derived subscales: positive connection (e.g., "I enjoy good memories of him/her"; "I feel that, even though the person is gone, he/she is still an important part of my life"), existentially complicated grief reactions (e.g., "Life for me doesn't have much purpose since his/her death"; "I don't see myself having a good life without him/her"), and traumatic intrusion and avoidance (e.g., "I don't *talk* about the person who died because it is too painful to think about him/her"; "Unpleasant thoughts about *how* the person died get in the way of enjoying good memories of him/her") (Layne, Savjak et al., 2001). The inventory uses a five-point frequency scale ranging from "Never" (0) to "Almost always" (4). The new version is under construction. Consequently, scoring and interpretation guidelines are still being developed. A (no-fee) user agreement contract must be signed in order to use the instrument for research or clinical purposes.

CONCLUSIONS

Traumatic events vary in their intensity, duration, and nature. Knowing the details of a traumatic event will assist the assessor in understanding the nature and depth of the youth's reactions, identifying traumatic reminders, and predicting how the event may later interplay in the child's life or translate into complex patterns of behavior and response across life. Debate continues over which events cause traumatic disorders in children. The controversy has resulted in (1) proposed alterations in *DSM-IV* Criterion A that take into account age and developmental issues and (2) interviews that separate Criterion A events from other stressful events. Similarly, proponents of a new diagnosis of traumatic or complicated grief for the more complex grief reactions experienced after traumatic deaths recommend its applicability to any personally devastating death.

With some overlap, scales are available that measure primarily (1) stressful events across a child's lifetime or (2) the degree or intensity of exposure to traumatic events or a specific event. Some of the measures include issues related to nonabuse and some to child abuse traumas. Others have versions that can be used with or without sexual abuse components. The degree and frequency of exposure to stressful or traumatic life events may affect a child's reactions to the specific trauma under assessment. The kinds of experiences that are emotionally overwhelming vary by age group and individual child. Differences have been observed in the intensity of reactions in response to specific stressful events and to degrees and types of traumatic exposures. Both life events and exposure levels have been associated with the degree, course, and nature of traumatic reactions.

11

Self-Reports of Trauma Symptoms
School-Age Children and Adolescents

Descriptions of posttraumatic stress disorder (PTSD), acute stress disorder (ASD), and complex trauma symptoms are presented in chapter 1. Self-report measures to assess them are presented here. A number of self-report measures have been updated for the assessment of childhood trauma. Self-report measures permit the reporting of internalized reactions and tendencies that cannot be measured by observation (Putnam, Ellis, & Rothbart, 2001). As discussed in chapter 4, youths generally report more symptoms for themselves than adults report for them. Adults are often better at reporting some of the observable, undesirable behaviors, such as conduct disturbances, for children until they reach adolescence and can better hide such behaviors.

Measures of childhood trauma symptoms may differ in their format, focus, age range, length, and comprehensiveness. Some of them require an identified trauma; others do not. Based on clinical and statistical findings for children and adolescents exposed to traumatic events, many of the measures include symptoms in addition to those specified in the *Diagnostic and Statistical Manual of Mental Disorders* (*DSM-IV*) Criteria B through F. Shorter scales may be quicker and easier to administer, whereas scales and interviews with probe or additional questions for each item permit endorsement of symptoms missed due to wording issues or state of mind. The longer measures allow exploration of the accuracy of initial responses and/or explore additional trauma-related symptoms. The measures and interviews presented in this chapter permit the assessment of a trauma level, *DSM-IV* (and sometimes *DSM-III*) PTSD symptoms/diagnosis, or *DSM* and additional symptoms. Scales used primarily for assessing abused and molested children, those used primarily for single incidents of trauma, and separate measures of functional impairment are described.

The controversy over applying adult *DSM* PTSD criteria to children is also discussed in this chapter.

The Importance of Youth Self-Reports

In the last half of the 20th century, researchers demonstrated the effectiveness of interviewing children directly regarding their traumatic experiences and responses (McFarlane, Policansky, & Irwin, 1987; Nader, Pynoos, Fairbanks, & Frederick, 1990; Pynoos et al., 1987; Terr, 1979; Yule, Bolton, Udwin, Boyle, O'Ryan, & Nurrish, 2000). Interviews with children continue to reveal the need to reword, arrange, and effectively present questions in order to best assess children and to make the assessment process easier for them. Moreover, we are still learning about children's responses to trauma and the elements before, during, and after traumatic exposure that contribute to reactions. As a consequence, many of the instruments undergo periodic revisions and/or updates. Several of the instruments represented below were undergoing revision or psychometric testing during the writing of this book.

The importance of interviewing children regarding their psychological reactions has been well-established (Terr, 1979; Reich & Earls, 1987; Nader & Pynoos, 1989; Praver, Policansky, & Irwin, 2000; Weissman et al., 1987). Following the Three Mile Island nuclear accident, children reported stronger and more symptomatic responses for themselves than parents reported for them (Handford et al., 1986). Kinzie, Sack, Angell, Manson, and Rath (1986) found that Cambodian children exposed to concentration-camp-like experiences were more anxious about schoolwork and more worried about friends, and complained of symptoms of depression at a higher rate than reported by their parents or guardians. In an acute-phase study of children exposed to a sniper attack (Pynoos et al., 1987), children reported more and different symptoms than parents reported for them (Nader & Pynoos). Parents reported more objective symptoms (e.g., rudeness, anxiety/arousal, bullying, argumentativeness, irritability, and regression); children reported more subjective symptoms (e.g., intrusive thoughts and images, avoidance of feelings, sense of estrangement, impaired concentration, and sleep disturbance).

Interviewing children directly may be most effective (1) after physical needs are met and a sense of safety is restored (Nader, 1999d; Scheeringa & Zeanah, 1995) and (2) when the interviewer is appropriately knowledgeable and deemed caring and trustworthy by the children. Children may be traumatized by their experiences, yet may not report the full range of PTSD symptoms. In addition to timing and method, avoidance of traumatic emotions and reminders may affect the accuracy of assessment. For example, sexually abused children who denied the abuse have reported significantly fewer symptoms than nonabused children (Elliot & Briere, 1994a). Traumatized children who underreport may exhibit specific indicators of traumatic response. There is some evidence, for example, that the suppression of reexperiencing phenomena in children with direct exposure to traumatic events may result in increased arousal symptoms (e.g., difficulties with impulse control, somatic complaints, startle response; Carrion, Weems, Ray, & Reiss, 2002; Nader & Fairbanks, 1994). Additionally, over time, children may minimize their symptoms, thinking that other children are no longer symptomatic, or that they should not be symptomatic after months have passed. Symptoms or their links to a trauma may become less overt. For example, earlier symptoms or traumatic impressions may later translate into vulnerabilities or cognitive and behavior patterns.

Problems Common to Self-Report Measures

Self-report instruments, in general, have several significant problems (Kagan, 2001). Among them are a number of semantic constraints on assessments of self. After affirming a trait or symptom on a questionnaire, a youth may be biased to respond affirmatively to all questions semantically related to that statement to maintain consistency. Relevant items may be missing if a human trait does not have a popular semantic name or if the trait or symptom has not yet been defined by current theoretical constructs. Whether or not some symptoms or patterns of behavior have been well-defined, they may be difficult to ask about or to describe. Some behaviors vary depending on context and may be omitted if the youth does not have a particular context in mind when answering or if the measure does not include some contexts. When answers to questionnaires are influenced by a comparison of past with present, accuracy depends on how well the past is retrieved. Individuals may use the information that is most accessible to construct judgments "on the spot" about their moods and behaviors. Answers may represent a sense of meaning, but not the referential meaning when it is the latter that determines whether the item is true or false (Kagan).

In an effort to create reliable and valid measures, researchers statistically, accurately eliminate questions/items from scales and interviews. This process has occurred, however, before all subgroups, patterns of response across time, and the importance of particular rare symptoms have been established. There are likely to be variations in the ways that specific groups of children (large or rare subgroups) react to traumas initially and over time. Gantt and Tabone (1998) found, for example, that some art indicators are rare, only drawn by members of the patient population (not the nonpatient group), and indicative of cognitive disorders or young age (chapter 12). One assessment measure often used to assess abused youths elicits ratings of emotions (sad, angry, scared, fine, or happy) during the first phase of the test (Gully, 2000). Psychometric evaluation found a Cronbach's α of only .42 for angry. Although angry was omitted from the study analysis, angry was not then omitted from the test. Obviously, anger must be one possible selection among emotions and can be clinically important.

Cautions

Issues important to assessment such as personality, wording, and culture have been described in earlier chapters. It is worth reiterating that these issues may dramatically affect study outcomes. Pre-existing personality traits and those associated with other disorders sometimes overlap with trauma symptoms. Introversion and negative emotionality (chapter 6), for example, correspond to some aspects of traumatic response and may predate traumatic exposure.

Wording must take into account natural tendencies, such as propensities to respond in a socially accepted manner, as well as culture, age, and structural issues. Asking a youth if he or she has always been that way (preliminary version of the Clinician-Administered PTSD Scale for Children and Adolescents, or CAPS-CA) instead of whether he or she has always or how long he or she has had bad dreams, for example, may elicit a defensive rather than an accurate response. For four distinct cultural groups, McInerney, Lillemyr, & Sobstad (2004) found a method effect related to how positive and negative question components were ordered (see chapter 4). McInerney et al. caution the researcher to "look at the emic composition of scales and not to assume that broad-based analyses will be replicable amongst subgroups" (p. 5).

Well-established scales with demonstrated good to excellent reliability and validity may elicit different outcomes from culturally or socially distinct subgroups of youths. McInerney and colleagues (2004) demonstrated this problem for two well-established self-rated competence scales. In their study of two mainstream individualist cultures (one Australian and one Norwegian) and two indigenous collectivist cultures (one in each nation), the Norwegian SAAMI, a collectivist culture, were significantly lower than three other groups on the *Perceived Competence Scale for Children* social scale (Harter, 1982) and were significantly higher than the three other groups on the *General Achievement Goal Orientation Scale* social scale (McInerney, Yeung, & McInerney, 2001). Although the researchers found a few broadly universal items on Harter's competence and social scales, they concluded that some well-proven instruments may be unsatisfactory in some multicultural and socioculturally diverse settings.

APPLICABILITY OF *DSM-IV* CRITERIA

Most childhood trauma assessment scales are based on *DSM* PTSD symptoms, with or without additional symptoms. Cantwell and Rutter (1994) have pointed out that the modification over time of the *Diagnostic and Statistical Manual* (from *DSM-III* to *DSM-III-R* and *DSM-IV*) testifies to the need for a flexible and evolving evaluation system that accommodates new empirical findings (Caspi, 1998). The debate over the nature of childhood traumatic response includes concerns over the applicability of *DSM-IV* symptom criteria. Some of the issues are presented here.

DSM Criteria B, C, and D

Researchers continue to debate the nature of childhood traumatic response (Fletcher, 2003). There is some evidence that three symptoms of denial or avoidance (Criterion C) may be too restrictive or difficult to assess for children (Green, 1993; Schwarz & Kowalski, 1991). A number of studies have found children with subsyndromal but clinically significant PTSD (Carrion et al., 2002; Daviss, Mooney, Racusin, Ford, Fleischer, McHugo, 2000; Vila, Porsche, & Mouren-Simeoni, 1999). Some researchers suggest that youths may alternate long periods of re-experiencing with long periods of avoidance and numbing (Lubit, Hartwell, van Gorp, & Eth, 2002; Realmuto, Masten, Carole, Hubbard, Groteluschen, & Chun, 1992; Schwarz & Kowalski, 1991). In addition, the question arises regarding whether *DSM-IV* PTSD criteria take into account the changing nature of symptoms over time or the complexity of reactions to intense, ongoing, or multiple traumas.

Some researchers have suggested that the *DSM-IV* criteria symptom lists are too limited (Armsworth & Holaday, 1993; Fletcher, 2003), that Criteria C and D lists should be adjusted for children in the same manner that A and B have been adjusted (Carrion et al., 2002), or that childhood PTSD should be studied as a continuous rather than a dichotomous variable (Fletcher; Kirmayer, Young, & Hayton, 1995; Putnam, 1998). Sack, Seeley, & Clarke (1997) found four PTSD factors instead of three for Cambodian refugee youths. They suggest that numbing and effortful avoidance comprise separate criteria (see also Foa, Riggs, & Gershuny, 1995). A number of adult studies demonstrate that the correlates of numbing and avoidance differ, and effective treatment methods vary when one or the other predominates (Asmundson, Stapleton, & Taylor, 2004). Still others have suggested a greater focus on the effects of trauma that lead to referral for clinical services such as a youth's functioning among others (e.g., peers, school, family; Angold, Costello, Farmer, Burns, & Erkanli, 1999; La Greca, Silverman, Vernberg, & Roberts, 2002b). Carrion et al. found that children with below established *DSM-IV* criteria thresholds did not differ significantly from children meeting all three criteria (B, C, and D) thresholds with regard to assessed impairment and distress (e.g., Criterion F symptoms, CBCL internalizing symptoms, and comorbidity). Perry, Pollard, Blakely, Baker, and Vigilante (1995) suggest that, especially for deliberately inflicted traumas, *DSM-IV* does not have adequate descriptive categories for the majority of trauma-related neuropsychiatric syndromes observed in children. In a study of maltreated children (n = 120; Perry, 1995), only

70% of severely traumatized children with dramatic symptoms of physiological hyperarousal met diagnostic criteria for PTSD. There are also children whose symptoms or impairment do not appear until months or years later, and there is evidence that individual symptoms, such as exaggerated startle response, may predict PTSD or functional impairment but not both (Carrion et al., 2002). To be effective, assessments of distress and impairment must encompass multiple manifestations of impairment and fluctuations in the appearance and evolvement of symptoms. Asmundson et al. recommend empirically supported subtypes of PTSD.

Another aspect of the controversy over *DSM-IV* Criteria B through D is related to the overlap in symptoms or the manner in which they become interlinked. For example, sleep difficulties must be distinguished from trauma-relevant nightmares, hypervigilance, and intrusive thoughts not present before the trauma occurred (Kimerling, Prins, Westrup, & Lee, 2004). Some questionnaires (e.g., Children's Reaction to Traumatic Events Scale, or CRTES; Children's Impact of Traumatic Events Scale-Revised, or CITES-R) include an item regarding whether thoughts and images of the trauma keep the youth from going to sleep. Wolfe and Birt (2002a) found, in a factor analysis of CITES-R results, that the item (thoughts interfering with sleep) loaded with re-experiencing rather than hyperarousal symptoms. Although this might engender some discussion about types of sleep disturbance, it demonstrates the link between some arousal and reexperiencing symptoms. Moreover, although increased heart rate and perspiration may be indications of arousal, *DSM-IV* Criterion B includes them among the reexperiencing symptoms (B5, physiological reactivity to reminders). The diagnosis of childhood PTSD using *DSM-IV* needs additional study and discussion.

TRAUMA QUESTIONNAIRES

To some extent, the differences among trauma questionnaires are influenced by the scale or interview's format, the age range, the authors' theoretical beliefs, research findings, and the desire to be brief or thorough. The length of each interview or time for scale completion is affected by the length of the questionnaire, the degree of a child's symptomatic presentation, and the rater or interviewee's interactional or contemplative style (Egger & Angold, 2004). Youths differ, for example, in the amount of time and the nature of their thinking about each question. Different interviewers may engage in varying amounts of processing and probing for the truth and meaning of a youth's response. Below are trauma measures for school-age children and adolescents and trauma measures that include questions on sexual abuse (see Table 11.1). Because children frequently present with symptoms in addition to PTSD and ASD and because treatments for "simple" PTSD can be ineffective for more complex (and comorbid) traumatic reactions (Ford et al., 2005), the scales presented here are those that include symptoms in addition to the *DSM-IV* disorders.

Scales that measure only *DSM-IV* PTSD (e.g., CRTES-R; Jones, Fletcher, & Ribbe, 2002) can be found elsewhere (Nader, 2004). Trauma and comorbidity measures for preschoolers are included in chapter 13.

Trauma Symptoms—School-Age Children and Adolescents

To follow are measures for school-age children and adolescents that include symptoms in addition to those described in *DSM-IV* PTSD and ASD criteria.

The Child Report of Post-Traumatic Symptoms (CROPS)
Age range: 5–17
Translations: Bosnian, Dutch, German, Italian, Persian, Spanish
Associated scales: PROPS, LITE
Format: Child completion; structured phone interview

The Child Report of Post-Traumatic Symptoms (CROPS 1.1xr; Greenwald, 1996a, 1997; modified from the Trauma Reaction Indicators Child Questionnaire) is a 26-item scale (e.g., "I daydream"; "I worry that bad things will happen") and includes symptoms in addition to those defined by *DSM-IV* PTSD criteria. The CROPS was developed based on a meta-analysis of the child trauma literature (Fletcher, 1996a) and on the diagnosis of PTSD in *DSM-IV*. It can be used with or without an identified trauma. The child is asked to rate the validity of symptom-endorsing statements, over the preceding week, on a 0- to 2-point scale (None, Some, Lots) (Greenwald & Rubin, 1999; Wiedemann & Greenwald, 2000). Scores are continuous rather than subdivided into diagnostic algorithms.

The Clinician-Administered PTSD Scale for Children and Adolescents (CAPS-CA)
Ages: 8–17
Translations: German
Format: Semistructured child interview

The Clinician-Administered PTSD Scale for Children and Adolescents (Nader, Kriegler, Blake, & Pynoos, 1994; Nader, Kriegler, Blake, Pynoos, Newman, & Weathers, 1996; Nader, Newman, Weathers, Kaloupek, Kriegler, & Blake, 2004) is an instrument developed to measure *DSM-IV* PTSD symptoms and associated symptoms in children and adolescents. This clinician-administered scale provides a method to evaluate the frequency, intensity, and reporting validity of individual symptoms toward a current or lifetime diagnosis of PTSD. It also assesses social, developmental, and scholastic functioning. The CAPS-CA includes standardized prompt questions and supplementary probe questions. Two five-point rating scales accompany each item: one assessing the frequency

TABLE 11.1
Child Trauma Self-Report Scales and Assessments of Functioning

Instrument[1] (Age Range)	Number of Items for PTSD B-D+ Other Symptoms	Interraterr	Cronbach's alpha (α) for Total Scale	Test-Retest	Scoring	Assesses/Measures (Scale or Subscale r; Distinguishes)	Current Authors (Available from)
CAPS-CA (8–17)	17+ probes +E-F	k = .80 –.97	α = .89		PTSD	*DSM-IV PTSD* Associated symptoms *(Child PTSD Checklist; CPTS-RI; distinguishes trauma and recovery)*	Nader, Newman, Weathers, Kaloupek, Kriegler, & Blake, 2004 (www.ncptsd.va.gov/ncmain/ assessment/assessment/assessmet_ request_form.html or from Western Psychological Services, 12031 Wilshire Blvd., Los Angeles, CA, 90025-1251; 310-478-2061 or 800-648-8857; fax: 310-478-7838)
CITES-2 (8–16)	78		α = .89–.91		PTSD+	*DSM-IV PTSD* Associated symptoms Sexual abuse symptoms *(distinguishes trauma from nontrauma groups)*	Wolfe & Gentile, 1991 (Vicky Veitch Wolfe, Ph.D., Child & Adolescent Centre, 346 South Street, London Health Sciences Centre, London, Ontario, Canada N6A 4G5 or wolfev@lhsc.on.ca)
CPTS-RI + AQ (7–17)	20 11 + probes	r = .94 –.97	α = .83–.89 K = .88		PTS level PTSD+	Trauma level, DSM-IV PTSD, associated symptoms (DSM-IV PTSD; CAPS-CA, WBTH, UCLA PTSD scale; distinguishes trauma by exposure)	Frederick, Pynoos, & Nader, 1992, Nader, 1995, 1999a (measures@twosuns.org; fax 512-219-0486)

Measure (age)	Number of items	Reliability		Validity	Assesses	Source
CROPS (5–17)	26	α = .91	r = .70 –.80	PTSD+	*DSM-IV PTSD Associated symptoms (TSCC, A-DES, neuroticism; distinguishes trauma by exposure)*	Greenwald, 1997 (Sidran Institute; sidran@sidran.org; www.sidran.org; phone: 410-825-8888, fax: 410-337-0747, 1-888-825-8249)
CRTES-R (6–18)	23	r = .91	α = .73–.85	PTSD	*DSM-IV PTSD and sexual anxiety (distinguishes trauma by level of distress)*	Jones, Fletcher, & Ribbe, 2002 (Russell T. Jones, Ph.D., Department of Psychology, 4102 Derring Hall, Virginia Tech University, Blacksburg, VA 24060)
CTRI (2–4, 5–7, *8–12, *13–17 Parent) *Currently available	(Multiple optional scales)	(New)		PTSD+	*DSM-IV PTSD, ASD, sexual concerns, complex trauma, PT cognitive bias, additional symptoms, developmental disruption*	Nader & Fletcher, in press (measures@twosuns.org; fax 512-219-0486 or Kenneth.Fletcher@umassmed.edu)
TSCC (8–16)	10 PTS 54 total	α = .86–96		Trauma score+	Trauma score Anxiety, depression, anger, dissociation, sexual concerns (Child Depression Inventory; MMPI scale 8; CBCL; CDC)	Briere, 2005 (Available from Psychological Assessment Resources Inc., 1-800-331-TEST)

TABLE 11.1 (continued)
Child Trauma Self-Report Scales and Assessments of Functioning

Instrument[1] (Age Range)	Number of Items for PTSD B-D+ Other Symptoms	Interrater r	Cronbach's alpha (α) for Total Scale	Test-Retest	Scoring	Assesses/Measures (Scale or Subscale r; Distinguishes)	Current Authors (Available from)
WBTH (8–19)	56		α = .92 K-R =.91		PTSD+	*DSM IV PTSD, Associated symptoms* (CPTS-RI; distinguishes traumatized youths from comparison youths)	Fletcher, 1991b (Kenneth Fletcher, Ph.D., Department of Psychiatry, University of Massachusetts Medical Center, 55 Lake Avenue North, Worcester, MA 01655; Kenneth.Fletcher@ umassmed.edu)
CGAS (4–16)		ICC = .65				Functional impairment (CIS; distinguishes functional impairment related to psychopathology)	Shaffer, Gould, Bird, & Fisher, 1983 (published in Bird, 1999)
CIS (9–17)		ICC = .63		ICC = .89 P ICC = .63 C		Functional impairment (CGAS; distinguishes functional impairment related to psychopathology)	Bird et al., 1993 (www.jaacap.com)

[1] Statistics may be for an earlier version, are for the total scale or the PTS scale, and refer to the English version. C = child; ICC = intraclass correlation; K = kappa; K-R = Kuder-Richardson; P = parent; PT = post traumatic; r = correlation.

Sources: Aaya-Jackson, McCarthy, Newman, & Cherney, 1995; Bird, 1999; Bird et al., 1993, 1996; Briere, 1996, 2001, 2005a, 2005b; Chaffin & Shultz, 2001; Crouch, Smith, Ezzell, & Saunders, 1999; Daviss et al., 2000; Erwin, Newman, McMackin, Morrissey, & Kaloupek, 2000; Fletcher, 1996b, 2003; Greenwald & Rubin, 1999; La Greca, Silverman, Vernberg, & Prinstein, 1996; Lanktree, Briere, & Hernandez, 1991; Lonigan, Shannon, Finch, Daugherty & Taylor, 1991; Nader, 1998; Nader, Pynoos, Fairbanks, & Frederick, 1990; Punamaki, Quota, & El-Sarraj, 2001; Pynoos et al., 1987; Schwarz & Kowalski, 1992; Vernberg, La Greca, Silverman, & Prinstein, 1996; Weidemann & Greenwald, 2000; Wolfe & Birt, 2002a, 2002b.

and the other the intensity of each symptom assessed. The scale provides a practice section to introduce the child or adolescent to the interview format and to establish relevant time frames. It provides optional picture (icon) response scales to correspond to frequency and intensity ratings (Nader, Blake, & Kriegler, 1994; Newman et al., 1997). An updated manual is available (Newman et al.).

The Child Posttraumatic Stress Reaction Index and Additional Questions (CPTS-RI&AQ)
Age range: 7–17
Translations: Canadian French, Croatian, Kuwaiti Arabic, Norwegian, Vietnamese
Associated scales: CPTS-RI-parent, EQ, CPTSR-PI
Format: Semistructured child interview

The Child Posttraumatic Stress Reaction Index (Frederick, Pynoos, & Nader, 1992) is a 20-item scale, and the Additional Questions (AQ; Nader, 1999a) include 11 main questions (and 48 probe or clarification questions). CPTS-RI items include some of the *DSM-IV* PTSD symptoms from each of three main subscales and two associated features (guilt, regression). AQ includes other *DSM-IV* items. A five-point Likert frequency rating scale ranges from "None" (0) to "Most of the time" (4). For the 20-item index, the scoring system establishes a level of PTSD. Comparisons of CPTS-RI scores with clinical assessments for severity levels of PTSD have resulted in the following guidelines: A total score of 12 to 24 indicates a mild level of PTS reaction; 25 to 39, a moderate level; 40 to 59, a severe level; > 60, a very severe reaction. An associated training manual provides detailed instructions (Nader, 1993b, 1999c). Although CPTS-RI will remain available to provide a trauma level that correlates well with *DSM-IV* PTSD, it is the precursor to two other scales: UCLA PTSD Reaction Index for *DSM-IV* (Pynoos, Rodriguez, Steinberg, Stuber, & Frederick, 1998; Rodriguez, 2001) and the comprehensive scales currently being completed by Nader and Fletcher. The Nader and Fletcher scales will include *DSM* ASD and PTSD, complex trauma, and additional scales (e.g., associated symptoms and information processing items) (see Table 11.1).

When Bad Things Happen (WBTH)
Age range: 8–19
Translations: Armenian, Hebrew, Spanish
Format: Child completion
Associated scales: Parent Report of Child's Stress Reaction, DOSE, TTTc, YAUTC, WVS, Child and Parent PTSD interviews

The When Bad Things Happen scale (WBTH, R4; Fletcher, 1991b) assesses *DSM-IV* PTSD, *DSM-III-R* PTSD, and associated symptoms. More than one question per symptom permits the endorsement of symptoms missed due to wording or the child's state of mind. Four questions assess *DSM* Criterion A, and 56 questions (2 to 6 questions per criterion item) assess *DSM* re-experiencing, numbing/avoidance, and arousal. Associated symptoms are examined in two to five questions for each category: anxiety, depression, omens and future prediction, survivor guilt, guilt/self-blame, fantasy/denial, self-destructive behavior, possible dissociation, aggressive/antisocial behavior, risk taking, and changed eating habits. Items are scored on a three-point scale (Lots, Some, Never; or the reverse). A rating scale with a coding key accompanies the scale, assisting computation of the *DSM-III* or *-IV* diagnosis or a continuous score. A computer-scoring program and a tape to assist younger children in completing the instrument are available.

Trauma and Child Abuse

The measures presented here have been used to assess trauma symptoms in abused as well as other children. CITES-2 defines a traumatic event to which the child is instructed to endorse related symptoms. The Trauma Symptom Checklist for Children (TSCC) does not link responses to a specific, defined traumatic event, and thus is particularly useful when the trauma has not been identified (e.g., trauma history unknown or questionable) (Wolfe & Birt, 2002b).

The Children's Impact of Traumatic Events Scale (CITES–2)
Age range: 8–16
Format: Semistructured child interview; child completion is possible
Associated scales: HVF, CPEQ

CITES (Wolfe, Wolfe, Gentile, & Larose, 1986; CITES-R, Wolfe & Gentile, 1991) is a self-report measure for sexually abused children's PTSD symptoms, attributions, and perceptions of social reactions. CITES-2 (Wolfe & Gentile, 2003) includes the CITES-R, the CPEQ (chapter 10), and additional items for the clinician's possible use. It has the original 54 items, 24 items based on *DSM-IV* PTSD diagnostic criteria or identified factors, and some new experimental items. Its 11 subscales have four dimensions: *PTSD* (intrusive thoughts, avoidance, hyperarousal, and sexual anxiety); *social reactions* (negative reactions from others and social support); *abuse attributions* (self-blame/guilt, empowerment, distrust, and dangerous world); and *eroticism* (Wolfe, Gentile, Michienzi, Sas, & Wolfe, 1991). PTSD questions are patterned after the HIES (Horowitz, Wilner, & Alvarez, 1979) and *DSM-IV* hyperarousal and additional avoidance items. The sexual anxiety scale is comprised of items from a Finkelhor and Browne (1985) model of traumagenic factors including helplessness, betrayal, stigmatization, and traumatic sexualization. Items on the abuse attributions scale were patterned after revised learned helplessness theory (Abramson, Seligman,

& Teasdale, 1978; Peterson & Seligman, 1983) including internal versus external, stable versus unstable, and global versus specific items. Although its intention is to measure the impact of childhood sexual abuse, CITES-2 permits the examination of trauma factors, social reactions, and other subjective responses common to traumatized children in general (e.g., loss of friends, being made fun of by others, loss of faith in adults, distrust). It includes symptoms common to more complicated forms of PTSD. As intended, many of the additional symptom questions are worded specifically for sexual abuse (Wolfe & Birt, 2002a). CITES-2 is to be scored as a continuous measure; however, it can also be used to examine *DSM-IV* PTSD symptom criteria and diagnostic status. Although it is worded for children with good reading skills, it is recommended for use in a semistructured interview. Items are rated on a three-point scale from 0 to 2 (Not true, Somewhat true, or Very true). A scoring CD is available.

The Trauma Symptom Checklist for Children (TSCC)
Age range: 8–16
Translations: Cambodian
Format: Child completion
Associated scales: Detailed Assessment of Post-traumatic Stress (DAPS; for 17 or 18 year olds and older; Briere, 2001)

The Trauma Symptom Checklist for Children (Briere, 1989, 1996, 2005a, 2005b) is intended for use in the evaluation of children who have experienced traumatic events such as childhood physical and sexual abuse, victimization by peers (e.g., physical or sexual assault), major losses, the witnessing of violence to others, and natural disasters. It is a 54-item scale with six clinical subscales: anger (ANG; 9 items), anxiety (ANX; 9), depression (DEP: 9), dissociation (DIS; 10; two subscales), posttraumatic stress (PTS; 10) and sexual concerns (SC; 10; two subscales). Some symptoms overlap subscales (e.g., Item 11: PTS and dissociation; Items 24 and 25: PTSD and anxiety). Subscales are not intended to provide a diagnosis of specific disorders (e.g., PTSD or dissociative disorder). The TSCC has two validity scales, one that taps a tendency to deny any symptomatology (underresponse, UND), and one that indexes a tendency to overrespond to symptom items (hyperresponse, HYP). An alternate version, the 44-item TSCC-A, is identical to the full version with two exceptions: It contains no sexual items, and it has seven critical items (Briere, 1996). The scale is rated on a four-point Likert frequency format ranging from "Never" (0) to "Almost all of the time" (3). Scores are cumulative for each subscale. Extensive normative data are available.

FUNCTIONAL IMPAIRMENT

Distress or impairment in social, occupational, school, or other important areas of functioning is a part of the *DSM-IV* PTSD diagnosis (Criterion F; APA, 1994). Functional impairment suggests the need for intervention whether or not *DSM* PTSD diagnostic criteria are met. In early life, it can undermine the normal progression of important developmental skills such as social and intellectual skills, self-control, self-integration, and self-worth. Trauma's power to undermine a youth's ability to function adequately is influenced by many factors, including the nature of the child and the event as well as age at occurrence, length and degree of exposure, support received afterward, and comorbidity (Albano, Chorpita, & Barlow, 2003; Nader, 2001b; van der Kolk, 2003; Webb, 2004).

Age

The specific behaviors and skills that connote competence and normal functioning change dramatically from infancy to toddler age to school age. Normalcy covers a range of skills and behavior at each age. Young children are likely to have difficulty identifying their own competence levels. In addition to the reading skills and understanding required to respond to questionnaire items, children between the ages of 4 and 7 may have trouble distinguishing between reality and wished-for traits and behaviors, between the ideal self-image and the real self (Harter & Pike, 1984). Pictorial scales (e.g., Harter's Self-Perception Scales; Harter, 1982; Harter & Pike) have sometimes been used for children between the ages of 4 and 7 to sustain a child's interest, understanding, and attention.

Measures of Functioning

Youths or their parents may find it difficult to accurately attribute impairments to one disorder when there are comorbid disorders (Bird, 1999; Bird, Cohen, Narrow, Dulcan, & Hoven, 1994). Most informants will be able to report changes in the ability to function that occurred after a traumatic experience. Some of the measures presented above and in chapters 13 and 15 include assessments of functional impairment. Some scales and interviews provide self- or parent-report *functioning* subscales (e.g., CAPS-CA; DISC-IV) or request endorsement of a symptom as present only when it is clinically significant and indicates impairment (e.g., CAPA; Bird). The following are additional methods of assessing problematic functioning. One is for clinician completion.

The Children's Global Assessment Scale (CGAS)
Age range: 4–16
Format: Clinician completion
Associated scales: Nonclinician scale

CGAS (Shaffer, Gould, Bird, & Fisher, 1983; published in Bird, 1999; Shaffer, Gould, Brasic et al., 1983), an adaptation of the Global Assessment Scale for adults (Endicott, Spitzer, Fleiss, & Cohen, 1976), reflects a subject's lowest level of functioning during a specified time period. Scores are assigned based on a broader evaluation in which the rater must have gathered clinical information about the child's past history, behavior at school and at home, symptomatology, and social relations (Bird). A rater is expected to synthesize his or her knowledge about a youth's psychological and social functioning, and to assign a numerical score of psychological impairment that can lie at any point within a 10-point range for each of 10 defined spectrums, from needs constant supervision to superior functioning. Scores range from 1 (for the most impaired youths) to 100 (for youths at the healthiest level of adaptive functioning) (Bird). Although Shaffer, Gould, Brasic, et al. (1983) recommended a cutoff score of 70 to distinguish clinically significant cases from nonclinical cases, data from a Puerto Rico field study established any score below 61 as clinically significant (Bird; Bird, Yager, Staghezza, Gould, Canino, & Rubio-Stipec, 1990).

The Columbia Impairment Scale (CIS)
Age range: 9–17 (younger for parent scale)
Format: Child and parent completion forms

The Columbia Impairment Scale (Bird et al., 1993) is a 13-item scale devised to assess four major areas of functioning: *interpersonal relations* (items 2, 3, 7, 9, 10); broad areas of *psychopathology* (items 1, 4, 8, 13); *functioning at school or work* (items 5, 12); and use of *leisure time* (items 6, 11). Items are scored on a Likert scale ranging from 0 ("No problem") to 4 ("A very bad problem"). A card is available for the respondent to point to or give the score for each item (Bird, 1999). The Brief Impairment Scale (BIS; Bird et al., 2005) is a 23-item parent-report measure that assesses *interpersonal relationships* (with parents, siblings, peers, teachers and other adults), *school/work* (responsibility, attendance, performance), and *self-fulfillment* (hobbies, sports, self-care, enjoyment). BIS uses a "past-year" reference. Ratings range from 0 (No problem) to 3 (A serious problem).

CONCLUSIONS

Youths are an important source of information about their posttraumatic reactions. School-age children and adolescents generally report more symptoms for themselves than others report for them. Researchers continue to explore and question the differences in childhood (versus adult) traumatic response. Debate persists over the applicability to children of *DSM-IV* Criteria B through D symptoms and algorithms. Moreover, children have frequently exhibited symptoms in addition to those listed in the *DSM-IV* criteria. Youth subgroups, patterns of response across time, and the importance of particular rare symptoms must be established before measures of trauma and diagnostic criteria can be accurately formulated.

Many scales and interviews are available for the assessment of childhood trauma. The measures of childhood trauma symptoms may differ in their content, format, focus, age range, length, and comprehensiveness. Shorter scales may be quicker and easier to administer, whereas scales and interviews with probe or additional questions for each item permit endorsement of symptoms missed due to wording issues or state of mind. The longer measures allow exploration of the accuracy of initial responses and/or of symptoms in addition to *DSM* PTSD symptoms. The time it takes for scale or interview completion is affected by the degree of symptomatic response and presentation, the rater or interviewee's interactional or contemplative style, as well as the length of the questionnaire. Based on clinical and statistical findings for children and adolescents exposed to traumatic events, many of the measures include additional symptoms to those specified by *DSM-IV* criteria. The impact of traumatic events on a child's ability to function (*DSM-IV* Criterion F) has been measured clinically, through the additional questions on trauma scales and interviews, and by scales that specifically measure functional impairment. Recognition of children's symptoms and their manifestation over time continues to evolve.

12

The Use of Projective Tests in the Evaluation of Trauma

Projective tests are based on the assumption that people *project* their feelings, thoughts, and needs into their drawings, sentence completions, and descriptions of nonspecific art or specific scenes (Wandersman, 1998). Gordon (2002) suggests that if a person draws, writes about, or interprets ambiguous pictures with an unusually high degree of a particular emotion (e.g., aggression), it is likely that the person has a lot of the emotion (e.g., aggressive feelings). That a person has such emotions is, however, not equivalent to acting on such emotions or fantasies, nor does it necessarily indicate that the person has engaged in related past actions, for example, of aggression. Youths especially may have difficulty verbalizing their thoughts and feelings about issues that provoke anxiety or discomfort (Wandersman). Projective techniques like drawings, storytelling, play, and sentence completion provide indirect methods of communicating how they see themselves and their world. When youths are guarded about discussing their families and themselves, these methods may be particularly useful. Projective tests have sometimes identified symptomatic youths missed by traditional measures.

Evaluators emphasize the need for caution when interpreting projective tests (Wandersman, 1998). When a child tells a story about killing a parent, for example, he or she may be expressing anger without an actual intention of doing harm. During and after traumatic experiences or illness, individuals may regress (Gantt, 2004a; Nader, 1997c; Peterson & Hardin, 1997). Their thinking may become concrete and/or disordered. Regression or disordered cognition may be reflected in play, drawings, and stories and must be taken into account when assessing youths against age-related norms. No test, including nonprojective tests, is foolproof in determining trauma.

Projective tests provide a method for generating hypotheses to be explored. They are subjective measures: Examiners make qualitative interpretations about the meaning of an individual's responses (Wandersman, 1998). Observers may disagree about the meaning of the same reactions or elements of art. Consequently, some researchers have devised quantitative methods of assessing projective measures. This chapter describes a number of projective methods that have been used to assess trauma in youths. Among them are drawings, interpretations of pictures or inkblots, and, briefly, sentence completion and storytelling. As is true for other methods of assessment, the proper training and supervision, and learning standardized methods of practice and interpretation, are essential.

The Utility of Projective Tests

When children have difficulty expressing feelings such as distress or their strong emotions have been sequestered from conscious awareness, projective measures permit the indirect expression of these emotions (Briere & Elliott, 1997; Lubit, Hartwell, van Gorp, & Eth, 2002; Pynoos & Eth, 1986; Terr 1994). Projective measures may reveal unexpressed, additional information about children or adolescents' reactions to their traumatic experiences. Such tests can assist the evaluation of a youth's fears and coping styles as well as the traumatic themes that continue to influence the child's sense of self and relationships (Drake, Bush, & van Gorp 2001; Lubit et al.). In addition, projective tests permit the opportunity to avoid the constraints of objective testing, wherein the youth must respond to a specific test item in a prescribed manner (Briere & Elliott).

Cautions in the Use of Projective Tests

Cohen and Kasen (1999) have noted that the validity of projective tests for measuring affective problems "has long been in doubt" (p. 304). Because they are subjective measures, there is the possibility of faulty interpretations about the meaning of an individual's responses (Wandersman, 1998). It may be difficult to determine the validity of an interpretation; therefore, it is important to describe what led to the interpretation. Idiosyncratic methods and interpretations can undermine validity, result in misdiagnoses, and lead to other faulty conclusions (Cohen & Kasen; Wandersman; see chapter 16). Errors of diagnosis may result if the interpreter is not well-versed in the possible overlap of symptoms among diagnostic categories.

A common practice in projective tests is to develop diagnostic decisions or concerns based on responses outside of those established as normal.

For projective tests, like for *DSM* categories, it is possible that indicators of deviance from the norm may be shared among multiple diagnostic categories (Holaday, 2000; White, Wallace, & Huffman, 2004). The same projective indicators, for example, might be found for adolescents with depression, attention-deficit/hyperactivity disorder, or PTSD. The potential overlap between personality-disordered, psychotic, and posttraumatic Rorschach presentations requires the clinician to be familiar with all three diagnostic scenarios (Briere & Elliott, 1997). Nonpsychotic PTSD sufferers may present with signs of thought disorder and/or impaired reality testing on the Rorschach or drawing tasks (Briere & Elliott; Holaday; Holaday, Armsworth, Swank, & Vincent, 1992; Holaday & Whittenberg, 1994).

Variables such as verbal language skills, SES, culture, and tester bias are relevant to assessment and performance (Cohen & Kasen, 1999). Youths with poor language skills or cultural differences in attitudes may respond to pictures and blots differently than other youths. The Thematic Apperception Test (TAT) for Urban Hispanic Children has remedied, at least in part, the cultural problem for Hispanic youths. There are, however, cultural differences in problem disclosure and normative responses. Even when making quantitative determinations, assessments can be somewhat subjective. In art therapy, artistic skill may be a confounding variable (Gantt, 2004a; White et al., 2004). Youths with impaired fine motor skills may have difficulties completing a drawing task (Peterson & Hardin, 1997).

Art therapists suggest parallels between Freud's dream interpretation or Jung's archetypes and the use and interpretation of projective tests or drawings (Gantt, 2004a; Malchiodi, 1998). Although dreams or artwork may be trying to tell you something, it is important to remember that the dream or picture is drawing on personal symbolism to do so. Symbols vary among cultures, groups, eras, and persons. Symbols may change in response to environments, life phases, and past or recent experiences (see Box 12.1). Gantt emphasizes: "Context is the key to understanding how the symbol functions" (p. 22). Specific symbols may have certain meaning in one context but not another.

The Effects of an Era: Cohort Differences

Cohort and school cultures are important to consider when comparing youths to norms. In 1984, following a sniper attack, children directly exposed to the shooting were more likely to include blood in their drawings (Nader & Pynoos, 1991). Study is needed to determine whether drawing or seeing blood in blots or pictures is normal 20 years later for youths who are more often exposed to the sight of blood through the media. In the 1980s, researchers provided some evidence that Western children's art does not reflect nudity in the home, sexual education, or access to sexually explicitly materials (Peterson & Hardin, 1997). Cable and some regular television programs include sexually explicit scenes that some children have seen despite their parents' best efforts to prevent it. More recent stud-

---

BOX 12.1
Case Example: The Nature of Symbols

Marilyn. Marilyn took a psychology course at the local university during the summer after
her junior year. When she studied Freud, including his dream interpretations, Marilyn
dreamed about floating logs and her flying. When she studied Gestalt methods and its
related dream theory, she dreamed that she was multiple characters (representing parts of
herself) within her dream. Later she read a book about Native American symbolism and
the symbols were incorporated into her dreams. A friend of hers was reading a book
about dream symbols that presented different and additional meanings for dream symbols
and for persons and items that appeared in dreams. Her friend's interpretation of
Marilyn's dream left her feeling very confused. She did not feel the sense of
understanding or relief that she usually felt after examining her dreams.

---

ies are needed to determine if children's exposure to media depictions
(cable and other television) affects their art, interpretations, or behavior. A
3-year-old girl told her mother that she wanted to kiss like they do on television after seeing *ER*, a show about emergency room doctors. When her
daughter's attempts at passionate kissing persisted, the mother became
concerned about her daughter trying to passionately kiss someone outside
of the family.

ART AND DRAWING TECHNIQUES

Directed drawing techniques have been used extensively in order to
establish rapport with youths, to permit youths to demonstrate their experiences, and as a part of treatment methods (Faller, 1998b; Nader, 1993b;
Nader & Pynoos, 1991). For more than half a century, art therapists have
attempted to standardize quantitative and qualitative methods of interpreting drawings for diagnostic purposes (Gantt & Tabone, 1998; Peterson
& Hardin, 1997). Frequently used drawing techniques and the methods
used to assess them are described in this section. Youths' art is different
from adults' art in that children often disregard proportion and perspective (Peterson and Hardin). Their art may be less graphic and different in
composition. Like adults, distressed youths may include happy elements
in their drawings.

Art as an Assessment Tool

In addition to their therapeutic use, art methods have been employed to
provide insights into a person's emotional status (White et al., 2004). Art
techniques have been used as a diagnostic tool to assess symptoms, provide specific profiles, and examine coping styles of trauma victims and
their siblings (Nader & Pynoos, 1991; Peterson & Hardin, 1997; Wallace et
al., 2004). Aspects of drawings have been associated with emotional dis-

orders such as bipolar disorder, depression, anxiety, and schizophrenia as well as with level of self-esteem, suicidal ideation, and sexual abuse. One difficulty in assessing problems such as suicidal thinking or sexual abuse in art is the variation in degree, type, and nature of these problems (Gantt, 2004a). Suicidal ideation may include, for example, transient thoughts about suicide, intermittent but recurrent desires to kill oneself, chronic and persistent suicidal thoughts, or plans of the method and time to carry out suicide. Sexual abuse ranges from fondling to sadistic torture. Findings regarding the use of these methods to identify certain outcomes have been mixed (White et al.).

Among the benefits of using art in assessments of youths are the following: (1) Art provides a method of establishing rapport; (2) it enables an uncensored view into a youth's thoughts and feelings; (3) it is a nonverbal method for children with age, cognitive, or cultural limitations in their language skills; and (4) it is a nonthreatening means of assessment that children are most likely to engage in even if they are unwilling or uncomfortable verbalizing feelings and emotions (Wallace et al., 2004). Drawings provide a way to engage a child in discussions or in an elaboration of their ideas or feelings (Wandersman, 1998). Projective drawings have proven to be an excellent means of revealing youths' traumatic reactions in a less threatening way (Wallace et al.; White et al., 2004). Wandersman reminds us that drawings may represent wishes, fantasies, or imitations rather than reflect reality. Drawings may, nevertheless, provide a window into the youth that more direct questioning does not.

Age

Normal characteristics of drawings by age have been provided and discussed by DiLeo (1983), Gantt and Tabone (1998), and Peterson and Hardin (1997). Art elements may indicate different things at different ages. Perseveration (repeated graphic activity), for example, may be found normally in the art of young children and in art of the elderly. It also can be an indicator of frontal lobe disorders such as autism, learning disabilities, ADHD, pervasive developmental disorder, Alzheimer's, or dementia.

Assessing developmental level and drawing is complicated by the possibility of regression following trauma or other disorders. Normally, very young children draw in scribbles or masses of lines and shapes (Gantt & Tabone, 1998). In the drawings of 4 to 6 year olds, the person's arms may extend from the neck or head, and objects may be geometric shapes (Gantt & Tabone; Peterson & Hardin, 1997). Children may mix front and side views in depictions of persons (Gantt & Tabone). Latency-age youths may line up everything on a baseline. Adolescents' drawings are usually more realistic and include overlapping of objects (e.g., a hand overlapping a tree branch). Gantt and Tabone found that adolescents sometimes become creative or add humorous touches when asked to make a second drawing, while complaining that they already did that. In artistically creative works of art, a concept can be abstracted. The concept behind a schizophrenic person's art, in contrast, leaves the viewer unable to make sense of it.

Culture

Gantt (1998) recommends image-based research continue to be conducted in the art therapy field. Although symbolism or symbolic meaning is important, it is the primary realm of anthropologists and art historians. Youths may incorporate personal, familial, peer group, and other cultural symbolism into their drawings and other projections (Nader, 1997a, 1997c). The same criteria are not applicable to all cultures. Children from some African cultures frequently omit eyes from their drawings (Peterson & Hardin, 1997). Some cultures routinely include accurate genitalia in depictions. Other cultures draw only primitive (stick) figures but may sculpt more accurate figures. Gantt points out that current fads appear in drawings, such as angels and Teenage Mutant Ninjas, during particular eras or in a particular time in American youth cultures.

Color

Although art therapists and evaluators have proposed qualitative meanings for specific colors in drawings, theorists disagree about their meanings. Peterson and Hardin (1997) have stated that the subject of color has not been researched and is likely to differ for different societal groups and cultures. Nevertheless, some researchers have found an association between specific patient populations and the amount of color used or the appropriateness of colors used for real objects such as an apple or a tree (Gantt & Tabone, 1998). Shading has often been referred to as an indicator of anxiety (DiLeo, 1983; Gantt, 2004a). However, as Gantt points out, there are many forms of shading. In one 1971 study, 92% of normal children used shading (Gantt).

Patient Populations

A growing body of research has examined the association of specific experiences and disorders with art content in requested drawings (see "Drawing Techniques," below). Gantt and Tabone (1998) provide a table listing observations for major depression, bipolar disorder, schizophrenia, and cognitive disorders. They found that people drawn completely in dark blue or completely in yellow were rare and only drawn by members of the patient population and not the nonpatient group. More than one observer has noted hollow figures and fragmented composition in a schizophrenic person's drawings. Art researchers have found either fewer or darker colors and constricted use of space in depressed patients' drawings.

Research has demonstrated that certain characteristics in drawings distinguish abused from nonabused youths (Clinton & Jenkins-Monroe, 1994). Across the studies, however, there are few common trends, and even for the same types of drawings, findings are disparate. Earlier studies lacked interrater reliability and standardized, objective evaluation methods. Items that appear in specific cases, such as a phallic tree drawn by a sexually abused youth, do not appear in the art of all such youths (Gantt, 1998). A number of researchers have stated that projective tests such as drawings can be helpful in evaluating incest victims but are not sufficient alone for diagnostic purposes (Peterson & Hardin, 1997). Peterson and Hardin suggest that the presence of sexual or abuse indicators in drawings should alert the clinician to possible molestation. Such items may serve to raise a *clinical flag* for additional investigation (Gantt).

Ethics and Art

Hammond and Gantt (1998) have pointed out a number of ethical considerations in the clinical use of art. Of course, a mental-health professional should not practice beyond what he or she was trained to do. This does not mean that a clinician cannot reasonably discuss a patient's work of art the way he or she would discuss a dream or an experience. Artwork is a form of communication and includes spontaneous unconscious imagery as well as depiction, creativity, and fantasy. It can sometimes trigger unexpected emotional reactions. Some clinicians point out that premature translation of nonconscious materials into verbal terms has inherent risks.

A reasonable assumption of confidentiality and respect for privacy are encompassed in a therapeutic relationship (Hammond & Gantt, 1998). Exceptions in confidentiality, mandates to disclose, possible presentations to a treatment team, and possible academic use of art can be presented to youths or parents in initial discussions and written outlines of confidentiality (see chapter 16). Among other issues that may warrant delineation are ownership of the art, its inclusion in the record in original or replicated form, and any possible display of the artwork. Hammond and Gantt believe that including all of a person's art in his or her record can compromise his or her privacy. Agencies vary in their requirements about what is included in a person's record. Art may be represented as a summary, description, the actual art, or replicated art. Evaluations for a court case may necessitate presentation of the actual document (Faller, 1998a, 1998b).

Pattern Matching

Therapists who use art as an assessment method with a particular population come to recognize pictures that are typically drawn by members of that population. They recognize the pattern associated with the disorder simply by looking at the picture, without a list of guidelines. A number of researchers have found this to be true with more than one population (Gantt & Tabone, 1998; White et al., 2004; Zalsman et al., 2000). Zalsman et al. discovered that the evaluator's overall impression of the picture was the best predictor of suicidal behavior scores. Although scores for the Formal Elements of Art Therapy Scale (FEATS; see "Standardized Assessment Methods for Drawings" below) have been validated in the diagnosis of severe depression, for the renal transplant patients studied by Wallace et al. (2004), the FEATS method did not appear to be a sensitive means to identify depression. Wallace et al. offer that art therapy using nonquantitative analysis may be more effective at detecting depression with this population. Their art therapist interviewers reported that focusing on specific features of drawings missed drawings that, when viewed as a whole, suggested the youth's depression or traumatization. Talking with the youth when he or she is drawing also may be more sensitive than a quantitative approach. They recommend the administration of art-based assessment in conjunction with self-reporting assessments and patient interviews.

Drawing Techniques

Formally scored drawings include the Human Figure Drawing (HFD), Draw a Person (DAP), House-Tree-Person (HTP), Draw a Person Picking an Apple from a Tree (PPAT), and Kinetic Family Drawing (KFD) (Peterson & Hardin, 1997; Wallace et al., 2004; Wandersman, 1998). As discussed in the section to follow ("Standardized Assessment Methods for Drawings"), assessments rely on symbolic, descriptive, and positioning aspects of items included or excluded from the drawings (White et al., 2004). The methods are easily administered. They require motor performance skills and visual motor control (Zalsman et al., 2000). Supplies and instructions vary slightly among groups and methods (Peterson & Hardin, 1997; White et al.).

Draw a Person or Human Figure Drawing

The DAP or HFD task has the youth draw a picture of a person. It is generally believed to produce a youth's self-representation (Peterson, Hardin, & Nitsch, 1995). It may include the idealized, actual, or feared self (Gantt & Tabone, 1998). The drawing is evaluated for developmental level, self-concept, and indications of anxiety or other emotional content (Wandersman, 1998). Evaluators also use it to assess group values, personality, intellect, self in relationship to others, attitudes, schizophrenia, suicidal ideation, or the likelihood of victimization (Peterson & Hardin, 1997; White et al., 2004).

Kinetic Family Drawing

In KFD, a youth is asked to draw a picture of his or her family doing something together (Peterson & Hardin, 1997; Wandersman, 1998). KFD is analyzed for styles, actions, and symbols (Peterson & Hardin). It is believed to depict the youth's perception of interpersonal relationships and support among family members (Peterson et al., 1995; Box 8.1a). The drawing may indicate, for example, the youth's perceptions regarding who is a part of the family as well as power, closeness, and distance. Most young children draw family members facing forward, standing in a line. Older children can use profiles or full faces and can depict movement.

Draw a Person Picking an Apple from a Tree

PPAT requires an integrative approach—combining three items (person, tree, and apple) to solve a problem (White et al., 2004). Sequential thinking and logical integration of several elements is necessary. Youths with impaired thinking may have difficulty organizing their thoughts to draw such a picture. PPAT has been used to assess the *DSM* Axis I disorders of major depression, schizophrenia, bipolar disorder (manic phase), and the organic mental disorders. It has been applied to a number of youth populations including traumatized and suicidal youths.

House-Tree-Person

The HTP task asks the youth either to draw a house, a tree, and a person on one page or to draw each on separate pages. HTP was designed to elicit information regarding the youth's perception of and interaction with his or her environment (Peterson & Hardin, 1997). It suggests how the youth sees him- or herself in the world (Niolon, 2003). HTP has also been used to examine the youth's intelligence, sensitivity, maturity, and personality integration. HTP's originator, John Buck, developed quantitative scoring for intelligence and qualitative methods of appraising personality characteristics.

Practical Matters

Art assessment techniques vary to some extent in their setup, questions, and note-taking. These matters are discussed briefly here and are detailed in manuals for the different assessment methods.

Preparation and Setting

The supplies used for the individual techniques are defined in a method's manual. The standard FEATS method for PPAT includes providing each youth with white card stock (12- by 18-inch), Mr. Sketch Scented Markers, and unlimited time to complete the drawing (Gantt & Tabone, 1998; White et al., 2004). Peterson and Hardin (1997), on the other hand, provide 8 1/2- by 11-inch white paper and no. 2 pencils, and permit the use of colored pencils for HFD and KFD. They say that markers do not allow the detail needed for interpretation. The issues of rapport and trust discussed in chapter 9 apply for these interviews as well. Peterson and Hardin recommend a semiprivate location in which the youth is unlikely to copy or imitate others and unlikely to feel scrutinized. The area should be free of other drawings. The youth should not be watched by family, friends, or others while drawing. A board can be provided for a hospital patient to use as a hard surface for drawing.

Prompts

Prompts and directions that precede a drawing must be administered in the prescribed manner in order for the data elicited to be legitimately compared to other studies and normative data. The acceptable prompts used with an assessment method are defined in the method's manual. Peterson and Hardin (1997) recommend specific prompts when using their method. An individual may ask questions after being asked to draw a picture. If the youth asks who to draw, the clinician or researcher may say, "Whoever you want." If the youth says, "I can't draw," Peterson and Hardin suggest saying, "Don't worry about making it perfect, I'm not judging your drawing skills" (p. 34). If she or he asks if she or he should draw a girl or boy, they suggest saying, "Whatever you want to draw." In contrast, when a youth asks what gender the figure should be after being asked to draw a picture of a person picking an apple from a tree, Gantt and Tabone (1998) simply repeat the instructions with emphasis on the word *person*.

Each method provides recommended probes to elicit information about a picture once it has been drawn. Research suggests that children are unlikely to be able to describe their drawings after a week has passed (Peterson & Hardin, 1997). Peterson and Hardin recommend a number of prompts or questions to gain information about the picture just after it has been completed: "Tell me about your drawing." "Tell me more about your drawing." "What is this?" "What time is it in the picture?" or "What does the person need the most?" A material item such as a computer game or skateboard is a typical answer for the last question. For KFD, an interviewer might ask, "What is the person doing?" Gantt (2004b) recommends questions like, "If you were in the picture, where would you be?" "What would happen . . .?" and "What would you be doing?" to elicit more about the artist (p. 3). If the case is a forensic one, special care must be taken in the wording of questions (see chapters 9, 16).

Notes

Making notes about what the child is doing during the drawing process can be useful to assessments. Evaluators recommend writing down behaviors rather than interpretations of behaviors (Peterson & Hardin, 1997; Wandersman, 1998). Notes may include, for example, any relevant data about how rapidly the youth drew and his or her facial expressions, posture, movements, or breathing. Gantt and Tabone (1998) have observed that, in the height of their manic episodes, patients dash off several pictures instead of the single picture requested, giving little energy to each picture. Paying attention only to the content of these pictures misses this detail.

Number of Drawings

Many evaluators recommend that a series of drawings be used (Gantt, 2004a; Gordon, 2002). A single picture provides a circumscribed view of an individual's art-making and individuality (Gantt & Tabone, 2003). A single drawing may reflect, for example, current concerns, last night's movie, or recent events. Early drawings may include more censoring than subsequent ones. Peterson et al. (1995) found that older sexually abused youths disclosed subtle clues to abuse in their initial drawings and more explicit signs in later artwork. Drawings have been used serially to observe changes over time such as progress before and after treatments (Gantt & Tabone).

Standardized Assessment Methods for Drawings

Efforts have been made to develop a quantifiable assessment method of using a youth's artwork to determine or assist the determination of pathology. Among the currently used methods (Table 12.1) are FEATS (Gantt & Tabone, 1998), Draw a Person: Screening Procedure for Emotional Disturbance (DAP:SPED; Naglieri, McNeish, & Bardos, 1991), Diagnostic Drawing Series (DDS; Cohen, 1986/1994), and Hardin/Peterson methods (Peterson & Hardin, 1997). Qualitative and quantitative methods have been used. Qualitative methods consider how well the drawing was composed—structure, symmetry, size, shape, slant, shading, placement, omissions, and pencil pressure (Peterson et al., 1995). The scales described here rate similar and different content items.

The Diagnostic Drawing Series

DDS is a three-picture art interview (Cohen & Mills, 2000). Materials used include a 12-color pack of square, soft chalk pastels (Alphacolor or Faber Castell) and 18- by 24-inch, 70 lb. white drawing paper with a slight tooth, or texture. Administration takes 20 to 50 minutes (most individuals require 20 minutes to draw). Instructions and clearly defined and illustrated criteria that highlight the structure, rather than the content, of the drawings can be found in the *DDS Rating Guide* (Cohen, 1986/1994). Individuals, ages 13 and older, are instructed to draw a series of three pictures: (1) an unstructured task, or free picture ("Make a picture using these materials"); (2) a structured task, or tree picture ("Draw a picture of a tree"); and (3) a semistructured task, or feeling picture ("Make a picture of how you're feeling, using lines, shapes, and colors"). Pictures are rated using the *DDS Rating Guide* for the presence of 23 criteria: color type, blending, idiosyncratic color, line/shape mix, integration, abstraction, representation, image, enclosure, groundline, people, animals, inanimate objects, abstract symbols, word inclusion, landscape/water, line quality/pressure, line length, movement, space usage, tree, tilt, and unusual placement. The free picture is believed to reveal the artist's defense system. DDS has been

TABLE 12.1
Projective Methods

Measure[1]	∝ Internal Consistency	Inter-rater r	Test-retest r	Assesses (Scale or Subscale r; distinguishes)	Author (Available from)
DDS		95.7%		Free drawing, tree drawing, and picture drawing (distinguished between 4 diagnostic groups with 77% accuracy)	Cohen & Mills, 2000 (The DDS Project at P.O. Box 9853, Alexandria, VA, 22304 or email Barry Cohen at <b4rtime@cox.net>)
FEATS	.45-.47	.73-.93		PPAT drawing (distinguished ADHD, low self-esteem in adolescents, and depression and anxiety in pediatric transplant patients; traumatized youths missed by separate measures; groups with impaired thinking; Coopersmith SEI)	Gantt & Tabone, 1998 (www.traumatherapy.us; Intensive Trauma Therapy; 314 Scott Avenue, Morgantown, WV; 304-291-2912)
Hardin/Peterson				Drawings: HFD & KFD (distinguished sexually abused from nonabused youths)	Peterson & Haradin, 1997 (www.tlcinstitute.org; http://fammedn.med.unr.edu/peterson/index.html)
TAT		.89-.95		Stories about picture cards (distinguished dissociative patients from control group)	Morgan & Murray, 1935 (Harvard University Press; 79 Garden Street, Cambridge, MA 02138; www.hup.harvard.edu)
Roberts-2		.92	Median .75	Stories about pictures (distinguished normal from clinical groups)	Roberts, 2005 (Western Psychological Services, 12031 Wilshire Blvd., Los Angeles, CA, 90025-1251; 310-478-2061 or 800-648-8857; FAX: 310-478-7838
Rorschach				Stories about inkblots (distinguished traumatized or abused youths from nontraumatized group)	Rorschach, 1921 (www.rorschach.com)

© Nader, 2006

[1] Statistics may be for an earlier version. C = child= P = parent; r = correlation;

Sources: Clinton and Jenkins-Monroe, 1994; Frey, 2002; Gantt & Tabone, 2003; Holaday, 2000; Mills, Cohen, & Meneses (1993); Peterson et al., 1995; Pica et al., 2001; Wallace et al., 2004; White et al., 2004, Roberts & Gruber, 2005.

administered individually and in groups with psychiatric and medical populations. The method has been used with children determined to have major depressive disorder, adjustment disorder, or conduct disorder and youths who have been sexually abused or exposed to domestic violence. It has been used with adults who have PTSD, dissociative disorders, schizophrenia, depression, bipolar disorder, and borderline personality disorder, among other disorders. Translations include Japanese, Spanish, German, Dutch, and French. Introductory and advanced training sessions last from 6 to 12 hours and are provided by DDS originator Barry M. Cohen and his associates.

The Formal Elements of Art Therapy Scale

FEATS (Gantt & Tabone, 1998) utilizes 14 scales that focus on specific features of a PPAT drawing. Configurations of scale items have been variously associated with specific Axis I psychological problems (Wallace et al., 2004). The 14 scales are *prominence of color* (amount of color used), *color fit* (appropriateness of objects' colors), *implied energy* (amount of energy used to make the drawing), *space* (amount of space used), *integration* (degree items are balanced into a cohesive whole), *logic* (extent that the picture is a logical or an intentionally humorous depiction of a PPAT), *realism* (degree that items are recognizable as real items), *problem-solving* (whether and how the person gets the apple from the tree), *developmental level* (age level at which pictures are drawn), *details of object and environment* (details pictured in addition to the tree, person, and apple), *line quality* (consistence and normalcy), *person* (dimension and wholeness of the person), *rotation* (amount of tilt), and *perseveration* (repetition of a graphic element or motor act of drawing) (Gantt & Tabone, 1998; White et al., 2004). The scale focuses on art content rather than symbolism (White et al.). The FEATS manual (Gantt & Tabone, 1998) provides illustrations and methods for collecting two types of data (Gantt, 1998). Global formal variables include, for example, implied energy, prominence of color, and use of space. Content variables include categories such as what the person is doing in the picture (standing, jumping, sitting) and the specific colors used for the person and the tree. Gantt and Tabone (2003) consider the drawings to be "a barometer of psychological state" (p. 426). The signs of trauma include weapons, negative themes, black and red predominance, hostile ways of getting the apple out of the tree such as cutting it down. Some of these themes may be included in youths' drawings because they are copying from movie or other characters. FEATS uses a Likert rating system (0–5). Higher scores do not necessarily indicate higher or better levels of the quality measured (Gantt & Tabone, 1998). FEATS normative values are available for adults (Gantt) and for youths based on evaluations of the art from 322 students in suburban Virginia schools (Wallace et al., 2004). Although *rotation* and *perseveration* are rare even in patients' drawings, the scales are retained because their items have been found in drawings of very young children and patients with dementia.

Hardin/Peterson Forms

Peterson and Hardin (1997) have provided methods of assessing HFD and KFD. Their HFD method is purely quantitative. Their KFD method is both quantitative and qualitative, although the qualitative ratings are not included in the scoring. Scores provide clues to the presence or absence rather than a diagnosis of physical, sexual, or emotional abuse. After the drawing is completed, the evaluator questions the youth and rates the picture. Notes are made about the youth during the drawing process as well as regarding the picture and the youth's description of it. A history of the youth may assist in determining whether or not the picture represents reality. Peterson and Hardin provide a discussion of age-level differences in drawing skills.

Hardin/Peterson Screening Inventory for the Child HFD. The Hardin/Peterson HFD scoring sheet rates 28 items weighted from most serious to least serious. Items 8 to 15 are 2 points if present; 16 to 20 are .5 (one half) point if present. Items include (1) explicit genitalia, (2) concealment of genitalia, (3) omission of genital area, (4) omission of central part of figure, (5) encapsulation, (6) fruit trees added, (7) opposite sex drawn, (8) tiny figure, (9) poor integration of body parts or a monster figure, (10) hands cut off, (11) omission of arms and legs, (12) belly button, (13) jagged teeth, (14) big hands, (15) transparency, (16) slanting figure, (17) genitals emphasized, (18) legs tightly together, (19) waist cut off, (20) extensions or long limbs, (21) rainbows, (22) butterflies, (23) hearts, (24) flying birds, (25) rain or clouds, (26) shading of face, (27) unicorns, and (28) X's for eyes. The first seven items are considered the "serious seven" and have a 3-point value if they are present. Peterson and Hardin (1997) provide guidelines for rating each item present or absent. A total score of 0 to 2 is normal, 3 to 5 points is considered undetermined, and a score of 6 or more is considered suspicious. Scores of 3 or more require an additional interview.

Hardin/Peterson Screening Inventory for the KFD. On the Hardin/Peterson KFD form, the evaluator first makes qualitative ratings. The evaluator is asked to recognize an overall impression of the drawing including an impression of its mood, order versus chaos, and whether anything is strange or peculiar. In addition, the interviewer notices each figure's size, shape, and distortion level. The assessor's developing hypothesis is based on these items and the youth's history and presentation in the interview. The authors recommend a follow-up interview if a drawing shows excessive chaos. The quantitative section of the inventory provides weighted scores for 24 items under three main categories: styles, treatment of figures, and actions with negative aspects. A score of 0 to 2 is normal, 3 to 5 is undetermined, and 6 or more is suspicious and should be referred. Peterson and Hardin point out that youths who show no problems in the scales of the three quantitative sections but show problems in the three qualitative sections may have vision, perceptual, or motor difficulties such as muscular dystrophy, mild head injury, poor eyesight, attention deficit, or cerebral palsy. Problems in the qualitative section may also indicate situational distress.

YOUTHS' DESCRIPTIONS OF PICTURES AND INKBLOTS

Projective tests such as the Thematic Apperception Test and Rorschach have been widely used to assess patterns of thought, observational capacity, attitudes, and emotional responses (Frey, 2002). They may be especially useful when the youth or adults are guarded about talking (Wandersman, 1998). Such tests vary in their primary focus: TAT or the Children's Apperception Test (CAT) focuses on general needs and perceptions, the Roberts Apperception Test (Roberts, 1994; now Roberts-2) focuses on family relationships, and the Projective Storytelling Test focuses on abuse and neglect. These tests present a picture, ask the person to tell a story about it, and then assess the responses for coping style, feelings, needs, and themes. Rorschach uses inkblots in a similar manner. Researchers have sometimes developed methods specific to trauma symptoms or have found exceptions in the use of predominant methods of assessment. CAT is considered to be obsolete. Although TAT has been used with children as young as age 4 (Nova, 2005), Rorschach and TAT were not intended for use with young children. The Roberts Apperception Test (Roberts, 1994) has undergone revision and is presented in the "Sentence Completion and Storytelling" section.

The Thematic Apperception Test (TAT)

TAT is a set of 31 black-and-white cards depicting individuals and groups in "classic" human, social, and interpersonal situations (Frey, 2002; Murray, 1943/1971). An individual's stories are believed to include conscious and unconscious defenses, drives, impulses, wishes, motives, fantasies, conflicts, interpersonal attitudes, and perceptions (Pica, Beere, Lovinger, & Dush, 2001). Critics have pointed out its lack of a universal scoring system, concerns about adequate validity and reliability, limited emotional range of the pictures, and problems with its ethnic and cultural generalizability (Frey; Pica et al.). In studies with trained or experienced raters administering TAT, however, validity has been acceptable (Pica et al.). Subjects are usually shown 10 of the cards at each of two sittings (Frey). Responses to TAT (Murray, 1943/1971) vary by age, culture, and SES (Byrd & Witherspoon, 1954). In general, young children's stories are briefer than older children's stories. Young children's responses to the cards frequently lack plots, cause-and-effect relationships, and spontaneity.

The Rorschach

The Rorschach consists of relatively unstructured inkblot (stimulus) cards (Leavitt, 2000). The person being tested looks at each card and describes what he or she sees. Responses may reflect an integration of complex memory traces from previous experiences in response to or triggered by the stimulus figure. Normative tables (Exner, 1993) suggest that what one person sees, others also generally see. For some, however, responses are colored by their personal internal world and are outside of the normal range of reactions (Leavitt). For both adults and children, a number of studies have demonstrated a significant relationship between sexual abuse and sex-trauma content in Rorschach responses. Like other tests, the Rorschach test signs do not establish an absolute certainty that sexual abuse actually occurred. Failure to show the signs does not mean the absence of sexual abuse. Nevertheless, Rorschach findings may alert the clinician to the possibility of trauma when none has been reported (Holaday, 2000).

Leavitt (2000) explains that the Rorschach responses that researchers have identified as signs of trauma, such as the *sex-abuse signs,* do not comprise accurate images of the Rorschach stimulus field. Studies have shown that the vast majority of nonabused patients do not see the *sex-abuse signs* in the Rorschach stimuli. Signs of trauma in Rorschach responses may demonstrate a preoccupation with victimization rather than actual experience.

Studies of Traumatized Youths

Abused and severely burned youths have been studied using the Rorschach. Across studies, evidence has led Holaday (2000) to recommend changing the label for Exner's Schizophrenic Index scale (see "PTSD and ODD," below). Comparisons of traumatized youths to Exner's (1993) normative scales have demonstrated differences. Compared to the Exner Comprehensive System normative data for children and adolescents, Holaday, Armsworth, Swank, and Vincent (1992) found differences for traumatized youths in the following variables: space, texture, weighted sum color (WsumC), coping (D Score), passive movement, perceptual accuracy (X+%), and the egocentricity index (EgoC, 3r+2/R). They did not find significant differences in active movement or morbid or aggressive responses.

Sexually Abused Youths. Clinton and Jenkins-Monroe (1994) studied the Rorschach responses of 94 sexually abused youths ages 6–9, 10–12, and 13–16. Of the 18 Rorschach variables studied, 17 were significantly different from Exner's normal group for the abused youths. For all three age groups, scores suggested (1) restriction and inhibition of emotional expression (higher achromatic color, C', (2) depression (higher suicide constellation, S-CON, demonstrates high levels of false positives and negatives for child suicidality), (3) avoidance of emotional situations (lower affective ratio, Afr), (4) lack of emotional involvement, guardedness, and defensiveness about revealing personal information (high lambdas), (5) impairment in relationships (one of the following: human content, H; human movement with unconventionality and perceptual distortion, M-; texture, T; and aggressive movement, Ag), and (6) reduced perceptual processing (lower on perceptual processing, X+%). For older youths, high levels of diffuse shading (Y) and low D scores signify feeling overwhelmed, helpless, and unable to cope. The two older groups had lower-than-normal animal movement (FM), suggesting intrusive thoughts related to unmet needs. The two older groups demonstrated poor self-worth (significantly lower egocentricity and personal responses, PER). Adolescents' scores indicated a tendency to neglect aspects of the environment when processing information (lower on cognitive organization, Zd). Not surprisingly, adolescents demonstrated distorted perceptions or rejection of adult authority (low on popular responses).

Burned Youths and Lambda Group. In a study of 98 severely burned youths (ages 6 to 21), Holaday and Whittenberg (1994) found that patients' Rorschach responses included positive clinical indices demonstrating learned helplessness, depressive feelings, and inner struggles to master the trauma: 49% Coping Deficit Index, 26% Depression Index, and 23% Schizophrenic Index. Youths' responses also indicated poor perceptual accuracy (X+%), disturbed interpersonal relationships (T), low self-esteem (3r+2/R), and increased anxiety (m). Compared to the normative sample, 91% of the burn victims had very poor perceptual accuracy (X+%); 70% had negative self-images (EGOCEN); 86% had problems with interpersonal relatedness (T); 49% felt helpless, believed they no longer had power to control what happened to them, and likely experienced social crises (CDI); and 26% were depressed (DEPI). The authors observed the importance of examining two groups of traumatized youths: (1) constricted (numb), regressed, and overcontrolled, and (2) acting out (aroused), undercontrolled, and emotionally flooded youths (see chapter 6). According to Exner (1993), the Rorschach response style of people with *high lambdas* is to ignore, reject, or avoid stimulus complexity (Holaday & Whittenberg). Those with *low lambdas* exhibit conflicts, emotions, unfulfilled needs, and overinvolvement with surrounding stimuli. Holaday and Whittenberg found that the *high lambda* group had fewer color responses (WsumC) and fewer human movement responses (M), which yielded an Experience Actual score (EA) signifying reduced accessibility of psychological resources. They were constricted, regressed, less involved with people and their environments, and more guarded. They had fewer responses indicating active movement, aggression (AG), and diffuse shading (Y). The *low lambda* group, in contrast, had more achromatic color responses (C') and inanimate movement responses (m). They appeared more depressed, uncomfortable, and anxious. Both groups had low perceptual accuracy (X+%) scores (more than 3 standard deviations, or SDs, below the normative mean), egocentricity scores (2 SDs below the mean), and texture scores (1 SD below the mean).

Burned and Otherwise Traumatized Youths. Holaday, Warren-Miller, and Whittenberg (1994) examined 10 Rorschach content variables for severely burned youths, two groups of traumatized youths, and the predictions of experienced and inexperienced individuals working with severely burned youths (86 severely burned youths; Holaday & Whittenberg, 1994; and 75 nonburned traumatized youths). Contrary to adult prediction, both groups of traumatized youths reported the same number of explosion (54%) and fewer fire contents (54%) than the normative group. Except for an increased sexual content in the traumatized group, the two traumatized groups gave similar Rorschach responses. The two patient groups reported significantly different responses from the normative group in two categories: human and animal contents. Youths normally identify high numbers of animals in blots. Fewer H responses were recorded for 48% of burned and 40% of the nonburned traumatized group. Although this is interpreted to imply conflicts in self-image, identity, or interpersonal relationships, the number of A contents was normal for a younger age group. It may indicate regression. Inexperienced burn-unit workers' expectations/predictions of content were 60 to 90% inaccurate for the youths' Rorschach contents. Experienced workers were 43% accurate (Holaday et al., 1994). Rorschach experts in the Exner Comprehensive Method with no experience in work with burn victims gave only 27% correct predictions. Their predictions were based on the adult literature for PTSD.

PTSD and Oppositional Defiant Disorder (ODD). Holaday (2000) found that, for traumatized youths, 12 items differed from the Exner Rorschach normative tables. Holaday studied youths referred by school districts for testing because of academic, behavioral, and interpersonal difficulties. She found differences in Rorschach scores between children and adolescents with PTSD and those with oppositional defiant disorder (n = 35 for each group). Both groups were significantly different from normative values on the same 12 variables: the Schizophrenic Index (SCZI), Depressive Index (DEPI), Coping Deficit Index (CDI; helplessness), Perceptual Accuracy (X+%; criterion test for the Schizophrenic Index), Egocentricity Index (EgoC), Affective Ratio (Afr), T (Texture), Experience Actual (EA), Passive Movement (P), Weighted sum color (WsumC), Raw Sum Scores (RawSumSS; a criterion test for the Schizophrenic Index), and Weighted Sum Scores (WgtSumSS; a criterion test for the Schizophrenic Index). Both groups scored higher than the normative tables on EB styles (introversive, extratensive, or ambient). More than half of each group was ambient: They had inconsistent behavioral patterns or approach styles that could lead to inefficiency and uncertainty in problem-solving and to intra- or interpersonal problems. A large percentage of both groups scored positive on CDI. Not all of the individuals with PTSD, but a significantly greater percentage than the ODD group, scored 4 or higher on SCZI. Although other means were not significant, there was a trend toward higher scores for the PTSD group on DEPI, morbid content (MOR), and T scores.

Holaday's (2000) findings contradict Exner's (1993) statement that only people with schizophrenia have problems of both disordered thinking and inaccurate perception. Although the children in the PTSD group had positive scores on SCZI, they did not exhibit schizophrenic behaviors, such as delusions, disorganized speech, hallucinations, or disorganized or catatonic behaviors, for a period of at least 6 months, described in the *DSM–IV* for a diagnosis of schizophrenia. According to Holaday, when trauma interrupts a youth's "naive belief that the world has predictable rules, the people in it are trustworthy and fair, and punishment and pain are consequences of bad behavior," traumatized youths also display the problems revealed by Rorschach SCZI (p. 143). For young trauma victims, "life becomes irrational, illogical, and confusing" (p. 143). Although Exner's SCZI 1991 revision data revealed false positive rates of 0 to 11%, and false negative rates between 12 and 22%, these data apparently did not include protocols from children (Exner). Two studies since 1991 (Franklin & Cornell, 1997; Murray, 1992) have assessed adolescents (Holaday). Murray found high false positives in youths with severe learning disabilities and attention-deficit/hyperactivity disorders. Franklin and Cornell found falsely elevated SCZI for intellectually gifted adolescent girls. Holaday recommends renaming SCZI as the Perception and Thinking Index (PATI) to reflect its actual function (revealing perceptual accuracy and disordered thinking) rather than viewing it as a diagnostic category.

SENTENCE COMPLETION AND STORYTELLING

Sentence completion tests, briefly described here, are another form of projective measure (Lubit et al., 2002). The tests consist of 40 to 50 sentence stems. The youth is encouraged to complete the sentence stem with his or her true feelings. Interpretations of manual-based scoring systems are often qualitative. Among the well-known sentence completion tests are the Rotter Incomplete Sentence Blank (Rotter & Rafferty, 1950) and the Sentence Completion Series (Brown & Unger, 1992; Lubit et al.). Incomplete sentences have been used to assess feelings, perceptions, and needs. Cautions that apply to interpretation of other projective methods apply also to sentence completion tasks. Storytelling techniques have been used to assess such issues as information processing attitudes and biases (chapter 14). The highly recommended Roberts-2 (formerly the Roberts Apperception Test) has undergone revision and psychometric testing. It is presented here.

Roberts-2

Roberts-2 (Roberts, 2005) provides 16 pictures depicting social situations with peers or family members (Roberts & Gruber, 2005). The pictures are provided in sequence. The child is asked to tell a story about each picture that includes a beginning, middle, and end and a reference to feelings. Social cognitive competence in comparison to peers is assessed. Scales include *Theme Overview Scales* (popular pull—provides a popular response; complete meaning—provides requested aspects and a resolution); *Available Resources Scales* (includes support for self, support for or from others, reliance on others, and limit-setting); *Problem Identification (PID) Scales* (PID 1—simple recognition of the problem; PID2—description; PID3—clarification; PID4—definition; PID5—explanation); *Resolution Scales* (RES1—simple closure or easy outcome; RES2—easy and realistically positive outcome; RES3—constructive resolution; RES4—constructive resolution of feelings and situation; RES5—elaborated process with possible insight); *Emotion Scales* (anxiety, aggression, depression, or rejection); *Outcome Scales* (unresolved, nonadaptive, maladaptive, unrealistic); *Unusual* or *Atypical (ATYP) Responses* (unusual—refusal, no score, antisocial; ATYP1—illogical; ATYP2—misidentification of theme; ATYP3—misidentification of person; ATYP4—violence or excessive aggression; ATYP5—abuse; ATYP6—imaginary content such as monsters or ghosts; ATYP7—death of a main character; ATYP8—sexual content; ATYP9—other unusual content). Detailed scoring and examples are provided in the manual (Roberts & Gruber).

CONCLUSIONS

Projective techniques like drawings, storytelling, play, and sentence completion provide indirect methods of communication for youths who are guarded about discussing their families and themselves. These methods have served as excellent techniques for establishing rapport and opening personal discussions with traumatized youths. Recognition of personality types, possible regression, and cognitive disturbances are important when assessing traumatized youths using these and other methods of assessment. Symbolism is often unique to an individual, group, or culture.

Caution is advised in interpreting or drawing conclusions from projective measures. Indicators of abuse, aggression, or other pathology or experience have been found among normal individuals without pathology or traumatic experiences. The signs do not appear in the projections of all who have such pathology or experiences. Nevertheless, with the use of projective techniques, researchers have found symptoms such as dissociation and cognitive disturbances and have identified Axis I disorders such as depression, mania, and schizophrenia. Projective tests and methods have delineated signs of trauma that signify the need for additional investigation or intervention. Importantly, these methods have sometimes identified symptomatic youths missed by traditional measures.

13

Adult Reports
Parent, Teacher, and Clinician Assessments of Trauma

Information is needed from multiple informants to most accurately assess trauma and other psychopathology in youths (Achenbach & Rescorla, 2001; Ferdinand et al., 2003). Although children are able to report symptoms that permit a diagnosis of PTSD and associated difficulties, studies have shown that youths, parents, teachers, and clinicians make unique contributions to the prediction and the diagnosis of signs of maladjustment and psychopathology (Ferdinand et al.). For different observers, variations occur in the kinds of situations observed, what children are willing to reveal or display, the occurrence of low-frequency behaviors, and the youth's reaction to observers (Martin, Wisenbaker, Huttenen, & Baker, 1997).

Some biases and access issues become apparent in adult reports of children's behaviors and symptoms. Biases may be related to issues such as gender and personal perspectives. For example, in 1976, college students rated an infant's emotional reactions to various intense and novel stimuli (e.g., a jack-in-the-box). Condry and Condry (1976) found that students who believed the infant to be male more often labeled the reaction anger; students who assumed the infant was female more often labeled the reaction fear (cited in Martin et al., 1997). The continuity over time of adult raters' reports may be affected by constancy in the adult's characteristics and expectations as well as in the child's characteristics and behaviors (Caspi, Henry, McGee, Moffitt, & Silva, 1995). Parents generally observe children in a greater variety of situations than do teachers or clinical observers (Putnam, Ellis, & Rothbart, 2001). In factor analyses of children's temperaments, different factors have emerged for parents than for teachers (Presley & Martin, 1994).

Parents

Parents observe children in a wide range of situations that are logistically or ethically impossible to recreate in a laboratory (Putnam et al., 2001). Parents have provided information regarding changes in children's behaviors at home and with peers (Reich & Earls, 1987; Nader & Pynoos, 1989). For most psychiatric disorders, children generally report more symptoms for themselves than either parents or teachers report for them (McDermott & Palmer, 2002). Some studies have found that children report more symptoms of all disorders for themselves (Weissman et al., 1987), whereas others have suggested variations by disorder. For example, research demonstrates that parents often report more conduct disorders or objective behavioral symptoms than youths report for themselves (Herjanic & Reich, 1982; Kisiel & Lyons, 2001). In a study of high-risk youths, Lau, Garland, Yeh, McCabe, Wood, Hough (2004) found this pattern only for Caucasian parents. Minority parents reported fewer problems for their children than youths reported for themselves. Youth reports indicated no differences between ethnic groups for internalizing or externalizing symptoms. Using measures of both dissociation and other symptoms/ behaviors, Kisiel and Lyons found that scores on dissociation measures (A-DES youth report and CDC caregiver report) were primarily associated with the outcomes reported by the same informant. That is, child-reported dissociation was associated with child-reported symptoms, and parent-reported dissociation with parent-reported symptoms. This may be because youths are better able to describe their internal experiences and adults are better able to describe their external behaviors.

Loeber, Green, Lahey, and Stouthamer-Loeber (1991) found that parents' and teachers' reports of children's disruptive behaviors were significantly better predictors of future problems than were children's reports. It has been suggested that as children grow older, they are better able to conceal their activities from their parents, and adolescents are therefore better reporters of their own conduct disturbances (Edelbrock, Costello, Dulcan, Conover, & Kalas, 1986; Reich & Earls, 1987). Parents and children may identify or define behaviors differently. Although correlations were generally low between parent's and children's and between children's and teacher's reports, Reynolds and Kamphaus (1998) found that parent's ratings of children on a depression subscale were more closely related to children's reported symptoms on a child self-reported clinical maladjustment composite subscale.

Parents' own traumatic reactions may affect reporting. Distressed parents may minimize their children's reactions or may consciously or unconsciously require the child to hide or suppress symptoms. In contrast, parents who have attended parent groups or training sessions have been observed to be better reporters of their children's reactions. This educational process has sometimes been assisted by a thorough parent interview (Nader, 1984, 1995; see "CPTSR-PI," below). One year after a tornado, parents who had attended parent meetings every 2 months with a trauma consultant were better reporters than their children of the children's ongoing traumatic reactions (symptoms were confirmed with the clinicians and teachers working with the children).

Clinical descriptive and statistical studies of children's postdisaster symptoms have suggested that parents may underreport children's exposure levels as well as an event's impact on their children (Daviss, Rascusin, Fleischer, Mooney, Ford, & McHugo, 2000; Richters & Martinez, 1993). Parents' needs to contend with anxiety through suppression or attempts to deny the event's impact, lack of awareness of less overt symptoms or of exposure levels, and children's protecting them from some of their reactions may all contribute to underreporting (Bloch, Silber, & Perry, 1956; Kupersmidt, Shahinfar, & Voegler-Lee, 2002; McDermott & Palmer, 2002). Sternberg et al. (1993) suggest that some parents may prefer not to recognize signs of damage wrought by children's traumatic experiences, whereas some children may be biased defensively. They found fathers, in contrast to mothers, least likely to report problem behaviors in their children. In contrast, there is some evidence that a small percentage of parents may perceive more or more intense symptoms than are present in their traumatized children (Scheeringa, Peebles, Cook, & Zeanah, 2001; see "Trained Raters," below).

Agreement. Agreement between a parent and other informants has generally been low (Ferdinand et al., 2003). Long-standing evidence suggests that mothers tend to score their children higher than fathers on behavioral assessment scales (Achenbach & Rescorla, 2001; Briere et al., 2001; Friedrich, 1997b). Concordance between parents' reports is higher for disruptive behaviors (e.g., aggression, hyperactivity, conduct problems) than for children's internalizing behaviors (e.g., somatization, anxiety) (Achenbach & Rescorla; Reynolds &Kamphaus, 1998). Reynolds and Kamphaus found stronger agreement between mothers' and fathers' ratings for children and adolescents than for preschool-age groups. Ferdinand et al. found higher agreement between clinicians' and teachers' assessments of 8- to 16-year-old youths' externalizing symptoms than between clinicians' and parents' assessments. They speculate that this pattern of agreement may occur because clinicians and teachers see many more children than parents do. Agreement may also reflect differences in public versus home behaviors.

Teachers

Reich and Earls (1987) found the reports of teachers to be particularly helpful in making behavioral diagnoses for a variety of disorders. Teachers are also of assistance in reporting visible symptoms of depression and anxiety, and marked changes in school performance or academic style (Nelson, Martin, Hodge, Havill, & Kamphaus, 1999; Reich & Earls). McFarlane, Policansky, and Irwin (1987) found that anxiety and behavioral disturbance, observed at school but not observed by parents at 2 and 8 months following a destructive fire, were associated with post-traumatic phenomena at 26 months.

Because of constraints in the school environment (Presley & Martin, 1994), the classroom may not be the best place to observe emotional intensity. Children feel freer to express emotions at home than in a public environment (Nelson et al., 1999). Children may find it possible to suppress symptoms in the classroom and focus on schoolwork. They may become quieter or more inhibited at school, a behavioral change that is sometimes appreciated. On the other hand, teachers are excellent raters of task-oriented behavior (motoric/attentional self-regulation) (Nelson et al.; Presley & Martin). Teachers who are traumatized, or who feel guilty, may underreport children's symptoms (Pynoos & Nader, 1988) or conversely become supersensitized to children's symptoms (Nader & Pynoos, 1993). Following a tornado, teachers reported fewer PTSD and reduced self-esteem symptoms for children than children reported for themselves.

Agreement. Agreement between parents' and teachers' reports of youths' behaviors has generally been low to moderate (Martin & Bridger, 1999; Reynolds & Kamphaus, 1998, p. 180). Agreement has been stronger at the child and adolescent levels than at the preschool level (Achenbach, McConaughy, & Howell, 1987; Reynolds & Kamphaus). Parents and teachers have agreed most closely in their ratings of behaviors that are easiest to observe: disruptive behavior problems (e.g., hyperactivity and conduct problems), attention problems, and adaptive skills. Parents and teachers agree least on internalizing problems.

Trained Raters

In addition to training's importance to issues of safety and accuracy, training raters to appropriately use specific instruments helps to ensure consistency among raters in definitions of symptoms, traits, and ratings. Evidence suggests that trained raters sometimes observe behaviors in children that contradict caregivers' reports (Scheeringa et al., 2001). In a small study of children younger than 48 months, raters were better able than parents to recognize reactivity to reminders and a restricted range of affect in children. In this study, a small percentage of caregivers of traumatized children, but not those of nontraumatized children, had a tendency to overendorse some symptoms (i.e., numbing/avoidance and hyperarousal symptoms) (Scheeringa et al.). Rater observations of children and thorough follow-up questions regarding onset, frequency, duration, and intensity of symptoms have helped to establish whether or not a behavior reported by a parent legitimately met symptom endorsement (Scheeringa et al.).

CAREGIVERS' REPORTS OF TRAUMA SYMPTOMS

Many trauma and behavioral assessment measures have correspond-ing parent or teacher measures. The following scales and interviews can be used to obtain information from parents (or teachers) independently of or in addition to child report measures. Most of them include items in addition to *DSM-IV* criteria symptoms (Table 13.1).

Scales for Children and Adolescents

To follow are the scales and interviews that elicit caregiver reports of trauma symptoms in school-age children and adolescents. Scales and interviews regarding younger children are in the next section.

The Child Posttraumatic Stress Reaction Parent Inventory (CPTSR-PI)
Age range: 5–17
Format: Semistructured parent interview

The Child Posttraumatic Stress Reaction Parent Inventory (Nader, 1984, 1995; R4 in progress) elicits, from the parent, clinical and research infor-mation on a child's reactions to a traumatic experience. The interview includes trauma and additional symptoms in five sections: I. *Pretrauma Descriptors:* family background information; descriptions and ratings of the child's behaviors and personality before and after the event (e.g., moods, confidence, social behaviors); II. *Prior Experiences:* descriptions of the child's and the family's previous traumatic events; III. *The Traumatic Event:* the parent's report of the child's and of personal descriptions of the relevant traumatic event; parental reactions that may have had an impact on the child; descriptions of the child's initial response to the event (may be omitted by researcher); IV. *Post-trauma Reactions:* the child's ongoing response to the event (divided into *DSM-IV* criteria); and V. *Associated Symptoms* (Nader). The time frame is in the last month. The manual provides a list of the questions that correspond to each *DSM-IV* criteria symptom (A through F) and a list of those that correspond to each of the CPTS-RI questions (chapter 11).

The Parent Report of Posttraumatic Symptoms (PROPS)
Age range: School age and adolescent
Translations: Bosnian, Dutch, German, Italian, Persian, Spanish
Format: Parent completion or structured phone interview

The Parent Report of Posttraumatic Symptoms (1.2xr; Greenwald, 1997; modified from Greenwald, 1996b) is a 32-item scale (e.g., difficulty concen-trating; clings to adults) updated to reflect the *DSM-IV* PTSD diagnosis and symptoms in addition to those described in *DSM-IV* PTSD criteria.

TABLE 13.1 (continued)
Adult Report Measures of Trauma and Related Symptoms

Measure (Age Range)	∝ Internal Consistency	Interrater r	Test-Retest r	Assesses/Measures (Scale r; Other Validity)	Author (Available from)
CPTSR-PI (5–17)		94–97%		Parent interview regarding C's previous traits and behaviors, initial reactions to the trauma, and posttrauma symptoms (ERev; distinguished traumatized from nontraumatized children; serves as aid to treatment)	Nader, 1984/1995 (measures@twosuns.org; fax: 512-219-0486)
PROPS (5–17)	.87–.93	.93	.79	Parent report of DSM-IV PTSD and associated symptoms (ERev; CROPS; neuroticism, loneliness, mastery scales)	Greenwald, 1997 (Sidran Institute; sidran@sidran.org; www.sidran.org; phone: 410-825-8888, fax: 410-337-0747, 1-888-825-8249)
PRCRS (5–17)				Parent report of DSM-IV PTSD and associated symptoms	Fletcher, 1991a (Kenneth Fletcher, Ph.D. Kenneth.Fletcher@umassmed.edu)
PSIOR (0–4)		86–93% K = .74 or higher K = .67–1.0 s		Parent report of young children's symptoms for DSM-IV and alternative rating (distinguishes nontrauma from trauma group with more PTSD, symptoms, comorbidity, and decreased heart period)	Scheeringa & Zeanah, 2005 (Dr. Scheeringa, Department of Psychiatry and Neurology, 1440 Canal Street, TB52, New Orleans, LA 70112; mscheer@tulane.edu)
PAPA (2–5)			ICC = .56–.89	Parent report of DSM-IV, ICD-10, DC:0-3, and RDC-PA symptoms and disorders	Egger, Ascher, & Angold, 2002 (Duke University; 919-687-4686) Center for Developmental Epidemiology

Measure (age)	Reliability		Validity	Source
TSCYC (3–12)	.81–.93 s reg .78–.81 s clin		Parent report posttraumatic stress, sexual concerns, anxiety, depression, dissociation, and anger/aggression (distinguishes sexual abuse, physical abuse, and witnessing of domestic violence groups)	Department of Psychiatry and Behavioral Sciences Duke University Medical CenterBox 3454 Durham, North Carolina 27710-3454 Briere, 2005a (Psychological Assessment Resources Inc., 1-800-331-TEST; Psychological Assessment Resources, Inc.16204 North Florida Avenue Lutz, Florida 33549)
Interact/Bliss	K = .8 2–.83 s		Observation of styles of communication (effective vs. disruptive) (distinguishes aggressive from nonaggressive youths)	Dumas, Blechman, & Prinz, 1994
POKIT (2–4)			Observation of play and child's ability to learn and interact with others (distinguishes autistic children)	Mogford-Bevan, 2000 (www.eggheadpublications.co.uk/pokit.html)
POS (preschool)	K = .87–.94		Observation of types of play (distinguishes inhibited groups; inhibited had frontal brain asymmetry at 9 or 14 mo.)	Rubin, 1989 (Dr. Kenneth Rubin, University of Maryland, 301-405-7735)
PPBS (preschool)	.61–.89 s	.39–.66	Teacher or parent observations of play (T reticence r T internalizing; P shyness r P emotionality; shyness r -solitary activity; +activity; social play r sociability; rough play r externalizing, activity, -attention)	Coplan & Rubin, 1998

TABLE 13.1 (continued)
Adult Report Measures of Trauma and Related Symptoms

Measure (Age Range)	∝ Internal Consistency	Interrater r	Test-Retest r	Assesses/Measures (Scale r; Other Validity)	Author (Available from)
SRPB (school age)				Observation of recess and playground play (males' rough and tumble play r aggression and dominance scores)	Pellegrini, 1995 (www.sunypress.edu)
TPOS (3–9)		.85		Observation of normal and traumatic play (earlier version distinguished bone-marrow transplant patients from controls)	Nader, Fletcher, & Stuber, 2005 (measures@twosuns.org)
POSA (2–5)		ICC = .78K = .79–.93		Play observation of anxiety (scores r P and T but not C reports of children's anxiety; r with mother's absence; assessed reductions in anxiety)	Glennon & Weisz, 1978
SBI	.72–.86 s	ICC= .27–.79 s	ICC = .77–.84	Observation of children's social communication styles (normative data available for violence exposed youths)	Gully, 2003d (www.peakascent.com)

- = negative correlation; C = child; clin = clinical sample; ERev = expert review; ICC = intraclass correlation; K= kappa; mo. = months; P = parent; s =sub-scales; r = correlation; reg = regular sample; T = teacher

Sources: Briere, 2005a; Briere et al., 2001; Coplan, 2000; Coplan & Rubin, 1998; H. L. Egger, personal communication, 2003; Egger, Erkanli, Keeler, Potts, Walter, Angold, 2006; Fox, Henderson, Rubin, Calkins, & Schmidt, 2001; Greenwald & Rubin, 1999; Gully, 2001; Mori & Armendariz, 2001; Nader & Pynoos, 1989; Nader, Stuber, & Pynoos, 1991; Pellegrini, 2001, 2003; Scheeringa, Peebles, Cook, & Zeanah, 2001; Zeanah, Myers, & Putnam, 2003; Scheeringa, Zeanah, Myers, & Putnam, 2004; Stuber, Nader, Yasuda, Pynoos, & Cohen, 1991.

CROPS and PROPS are not parallel questionnaires but have some overlap of content and can be used individually or in combination. The parent is asked to rate the prevalence of symptoms over the past week, on a 0- to 2-point scale (None, Some, Lots). The scale can be scored as a continuous measure; a tentative "clinical" cutoff of 16 has been used (Greenwald & Rubin, 1999).

The Parent Report of the Child's Reaction to Stress (PRCRS)
Age range: School and adolescent (some preschool)
Translations: Spanish
Format: Parent completion
Associated scales: WBTH, DOSE, TTTc, YAUTC, WVS, Child and Parent
    PTSD interviews

The Parent Report of the Child's Reaction to Stress (Fletcher, 1991a) includes a description of the event, four items assessing *DSM* Criterion A, and one to six questions for each *DSM* Criteria B through D item. The PRCRS includes questions that examine the associated symptoms included on the WBTH scale: anxiety, depression, superstitious beliefs ("omens and future prediction" on the WBTH), survivor guilt, guilt/self-blame, fantasy/denial, self-destructive behavior, possible dissociation, aggressive/antisocial behavior, risk taking, and changed eating habits. Items do not correspond exactly to items on the WBTH.

Caregiver Reports of Children Under 6

Whether or not diagnostic systems are appropriate for preschoolers is under continued debate (Egger, Ascher, & Angold, 1999). It is agreed that there are important differences in the manifestations and assessments of disorders in the very young. Proposed criteria for diagnosing in preschool children is under preliminary investigation (Egger, Ascher, & Angold, 2002; Scheeringa et al., 2001). Interviews are likely to undergo fine-tuning and additional revision as more is learned about the nature of disorders in preschool children.

As a preventive effort, preschool measures must include early manifestations of disorders as well as symptoms found in diagnostic schema (Egger & Angold, 2004). Specialists have pointed out that clinical disturbances in infants and young children are not simply behavioral problems but are relationship disturbances (Egger & Angold; Zeanah, 2000) and may hinder development. The Diagnostic Classification: 0-3 (DC:0-3; National Center for Infants, Toddlers, and Families, 1994) provides a diagnostic scheme for conceptualizing and classifying mental-health and developmental disorders in infancy and early childhood. It posits a transactional model rather than a psychopathological model to describe behavior differences in early development. DC:0-3 highlights the relationships among the infant's temperament, neurophysiological differences, and self-regulatory behavior and between the infant and those in his or her environment (Neisworth, Bagnato, Salvia, & Hunt, 1999).

Psychological disorders may be different in very young children than in older children and adults for a number of reasons (Scheeringa et al., 2001). Among the reasons are very young children's rapid developmental changes, cognitive immaturity, and limited ability to communicate symptoms, and the importance of the infant-caregiver relationship as a context for development and psychopathology (Mogford-Bevan, 2000; Zeanah, Boris, Scheeringa, 1997). Evidence to date has indicated that highly symptomatic children under the age of 6 often fail to meet the diagnostic threshold of *DSM-IV* PTSD (Scheeringa, Zeanah, Myers, & Putnam, 2005). Scheeringa et al. (2001) demonstrated that alternative rather than *DSM-IV* criteria showed superior criterion validity for assessing trauma in preschool children: (1) The nine cases with the most total alternative criteria symptoms were the ones that received the alternative diagnosis, whereas three of the five cases with the most total *DSM-IV* symptoms did not receive a *DSM-IV* diagnosis; (2) six very symptomatic cases barely missed achieving a *DSM-IV* PTSD diagnosis, suggesting that the *DSM-IV* algorithm was not sufficiently sensitive; and (3) cases diagnosed using the alternative criteria showed significantly more signs and symptoms than the cases not diagnosed by the alternative criteria. In contrast, the mean number of signs and symptoms recorded for the 3 cases diagnosed using *DSM-IV* criteria was not significantly different from the number recorded for the 12 cases not diagnosed by the *DSM-IV* criteria. Alternative criteria as well as alternative algorithms (i.e., fewer required symptoms under individual *DSM-IV* criterion) for the diagnosis of PTSD in infants and young children are still under investigation (Scheeringa, Zeanah, Myers, & Putnam, 2003). In prelude to a final conclusion about numbers and patterns of symptoms, there are new measures and interviews that assess the very young (Table 13.1).

The PTSD Semistructured Interview and Observational Record (PSIOR) for Infants and Young Children
Age range: 0–48 months (or up to 6 years)
Format: Semistructured interview with caregiver; child observation

PSIOR (V1.2; Scheeringa & Zeanah, 1994, 2001; V1.4, Scheeringa & Zeanah, 2005) is a parent-report interview regarding traumatized children under the age of 6. Version 1.4 consists of one page that elicits the dates and other details of the young child's traumatic exposures and an interview containing the following 30 items: *DSM-IV* Criterion A: 2 items; reexperiencing: 6 items; dissociation: 1 item; numbing/avoidance: 7; hyperarousal symptoms: 5; associated symptoms: 4; disability and distress questions: 5. PSIOR contains *DSM-IV* PTSD criteria items and other developmentally sensitive trauma items for children less than 48 months old (Scheeringa

& Zeanah, 1995). All items were distilled from ratings of actual cases of severely traumatized infants. Item descriptions are focused on observable behaviors rather than subjective experiences (Scheeringa, Zeanah, Drell, & Larrieu, 1995; Scheeringa et al., 2001). The interviewer reads a stem question about each symptom. If the answer is positive, specific examples, onset, frequency, and duration are explored until it is clear whether the symptom is present. Currently, observation of the child during the caregiver interview provides supplemental information (Scheeringa et al., 2003). The interview permits a diagnosis either by the *DSM-IV* algorithm or by proposed alternative algorithms, provided at the end of the scale.

The Preschool Age Psychiatric Assessment (PAPA)
Age range: 2–5
Translations: Spanish in process
Format: Structured interview with parent/guardian

PAPA (Egger et al., 1999, 2002; see CAPA) is an interviewer-based structured parent or guardian interview that collects symptom and impairment information. PAPA includes developmentally relevant symptoms from *DSM-IV, ICD-10, DC:0-3*, and the Research Diagnostic Criteria-Preschool Age (*RDC-PA*). The authors recommend that a full assessment of a preschooler include direct assessment of the child (e.g., developmental/intellectual level), information from or interviews with others involved with the child's care (e.g., teacher or daycare provider), and other measures (e.g., assessment of parental psychopathology) as well as a structured interview such as PAPA. The parent interview includes subsections for gathering background and symptom information as follows: introduction (information and consent forms; a brief checklist on the child's symptoms and their results), brief development assessment, family structure and function, childcare, play and peer relationships, depression, conduct problems, attention-deficit/hyperactivity disorder, regulation/habits, eating and food, elimination, somatization, sleep, separation anxiety, anxious affect, worries, rituals and repetitions, reactive attachment, life events, PTSD A events (stressor occurring in the last 3 months such as birth of a sibling, change of daycare), PTSD B events (lifetime major traumatic events such as death of a parent, being physically abused), incapacity, socioeconomic status, ending the interview, and debriefing questionnaire (interviewer's feedback on the interview format and questions) (Egger & Angold, 2004; Egger et al., 2002). PAPA is comprised of (1) a glossary that contains detailed definitions of symptoms and (2) an interview schedule, which is a series of questions guiding the interviewer in determining whether symptoms, as defined in the glossary, are present. Rather than asking one fixed question, the interviewer asks mandatory probe questions but can continue to refine his or her understanding of the symptom until he or she is confident that the symptom is or is not present. If the symptom is present, its severity is assessed across the following dimensions: the intensity of the symptom itself; the frequency of the symptom; the duration of the symptom; the relationship context of the behavior; the onset date of the symptom; and psychosocial impairment related to the presence of the symptom. The primary reference period for symptoms (except for lifetime major traumatic events) is the 3 months prior to the interview date. For each stressor or traumatic event, PAPA assesses symptoms and behaviors (e.g., regression in language, sleep difficulties, increased crying) that started or intensified after the event. If the parent reports these changes in the child's behavior since the event, the interviewer completes a comprehensive assessment for the symptoms of posttraumatic stress disorder. Psychiatric diagnoses are generated by computerized algorithm after the interview. A computerized and a clinical version of PAPA and an online training program are in process.

The Trauma Symptom Checklist for Young Children (TSCYC)
Age range: 3–12
Format: Parent completion
Associated scales: TSCC, DAPS

The Trauma Symptom Checklist for Young Children (Briere, 2005a) is a 90-item caretaker-report measure developed to assess trauma-related symptoms in children ages 3 to 12. Clinical scales include the following: posttraumatic stress-total (PTS-TOT), PTS-Intrusion, PTS-Avoidance, PTS-Arousal; Sexual Concerns; Anxiety; Depression; Dissociation; and Anger/Aggression. TSCYC asks about observable behaviors such as looking sad, throwing things at other children, and pretending to have sex. Two validity scales determine atypical responses (overreporting = sum of least reported items such as hearing voices or forgetting one's own name) and response level (underreporting = denial of thoughts, feelings, or behaviors usually reported to a degree by caregivers for children such as arguing or telling a lie) (Briere; Briere et al., 2001). Respondents are asked how many hours in a specific location, such as home, the caregiver spends with the child when the child is awake. Caregivers rate each item on a four-point scale (1 = Not at all to 4 = Very often) for how often the symptom has occurred in the previous month. A *DSM-IV* PTSD diagnosis is possible from the parent scale. Normative data are available for gender and age groups (3–4, 5–9, and 10–12 years) (Briere). Normative data are based on a sample of 750 electronically surveyed caregivers randomly selected from a national marketing research company list. Scale wording approximates a 6.8-grade reading level.

CLINICIAN/RATER ASSESSMENTS

In addition to measures that elicit caretaker, teacher, or youth reports, clinician and other rater report methods assist the assessment of interaction styles, specific traumatic and other symptoms, functioning, and clinical status and progress. Among them are the observational techniques, individualized assessment procedures, and measures of specified goal attainment presented here (see also "Functional Impairment," in chapter 11).

Observation

To assess youths' behaviors, symptoms, and skills, clinicians have observed them in clinical settings, at home, at school, or in other institutional settings. Kagan (2001) suggests that if researchers video recorded children's behaviors for 24 hours over a 6-month period in different contexts before analyzing their personalities or reactions, it is likely that different or additional personality and symptom categories or dimensions would emerge. Kagan believes that doing so might also increase agreement between parent and clinician reports. Observation techniques may be less often used because of the time and cost requirements associated with them: staff and video equipment.

Observation has been used to assess a youth's attachment or interactional styles with peers or parents (Ainsworth, Blehar, Waters, & Wall, 1978; Hesse, Main, Abrams, & Rifkin, 2003; Mori & Armendariz, 2001; Roberts, 2001) and to measure competence levels (Pellegrini, 2001). Such methods have assessed family interactional patterns as well (Harvey, 2000). Observation has been employed extensively in studies of temperament. As described in chapter 6, Kagan, Reznick, and Snidman (1988) used observational methods to study temperamentally inhibited and uninhibited children. Observational methods have evaluated disordered behaviors such as ADHD, antisocial behaviors, impulsivity, anxiety, traumatic re-experiencing, and impaired functioning (Mori & Armendariz; Roberts; Nader & Pynoos, 1991; Terr, 1981a).

Informal and Formal Observations

Clinical observations range from informal to formal. Informal observations during an interview or test session may include inspections of the person's tone of voice, style, patterns of behavior, posture, and intensity (Wandersman, 1998). The interviewer might notice, for example, the youth's ability to maintain attention, startle reactions, whether a parent kept shifting the focus to their own problems instead of the child's, the nature of the parents' reactions to each other in conjoint parent interviews, or the parent's stiffness in response to the youth (Gordon, 2002; Wandersman). Structured observations may be conducted in different settings or situations—in the waiting room, at home, at school, in the playroom, and in social settings (Wandersman). For very young children, observations during play may be structured around a specific task, such as playing or drawing with the parent. Behavioral observations permit a view of actual interactions, reactions, and responses to different parents or situations and of the quality of attachment relationships (Wandersman; chapter 8). Testing or observation situations may not reflect a person's usual behavior, however. *Observer effects* must be considered when observation is used (Kay, 2002). The observer's presence may impact the youth's behavior or may indirectly influence the youth because of changes in the teacher or parent's behavior when the observer is in the classroom or home.

Behavior Sampling

To sample child behaviors, researchers generally record a youth's dominant behaviors or play in a sampling segment. Coded behaviors are usually selected from a predefined "mutually exclusive and exhaustive taxonomy" (e.g., a prespecified classification list; Coplan, 2000, p. 571.) Behavior sampling techniques have included group or individual methods. In *event sampling* coding schemes, the event rather than a period of time is the unit of analysis (Coplan). The assessor observes a child or scans a group during the event until a specific behavior commences. The behavior is then coded until it runs its course. This method is useful for sampling low-frequency behaviors such as solitary play on the playground. In *time sampling*, an individual or each child is observed for a series of short-term segments (e.g., 10-, 15-, or 30-second segments). Time sampling can be carried out for a specified number of segments across a prescribed number of days or once per week/month during a school year or treatment course.

Setting and Context

A number of factors influence the usefulness and accuracy of observational methods. *Analogue* observational assessments are those conducted in experimental settings using simulated circumstances to elicit behaviors of interest in children (Mori & Armendariz, 2001). Contrived settings may inhibit a child's exhibition of competence until trust for the assessor or clinician and familiarity with surroundings has been accomplished (Pellegrini, 2001). Pellegrini recommends two observation sessions in each context chosen for assessment: home, school classroom, playground, or clinician's office. The question arises regarding whether behaviors in experimental settings will generalize to normal situations (Mori & Armendariz). In field settings, children exhibit behaviors and competences of their choosing rather than those selected by the researcher.

Observation of young children can be a particularly fruitful method of gathering information about the child's competence, interactional style, mental imagery, and traumatic preoccupations. A child's performance in an assessment situation varies considerably with variations in test conditions such as the assessor/clinician's race and gender, assessment format, and familiarity with any toys or props that might be used (Pellegrini, 2001). When toys are employed, for example, if too few toys are available, children's play tends to follow themes suggested by the toys or props.

Young children demonstrate highest levels of competence when stereo-typically gender-appropriate toys are available to them. Evidence suggests that children exhibit higher levels of cognitive, linguistic, and social skills when assessed in play with a friend than with an acquaintance.

In order to observe youths' behaviors, researchers have used direct observation in person, from a second source, through a one-way mirror, or from video recordings. Forms exist for teachers, peers, parents, and trained observers to record their observations of a youth (Coplan, 2000). As discussed in chapter 9, the presence of known adults can inhibit or contaminate children's exhibition of fantasy and its associated language (Pellegrini, 2001). The level of concern about remaining unobtrusive and the purpose of the interview dictate the method used.

Play Observations

Mental representations that include imagery and mental language allow an individual to cognitively take apart and recombine the world. Events and objects can be held in mind, mentally disassembled, analyzed, and recombined/synthesized to create new ideas and new responses to the world (Barkley, 2003). This process permits creativity and problem-solving. Barkley likens children's play to this mental process. Play contributes to children's development into mentally healthy and socially competent individuals (Pellegrini, 2001). It is also a method through which a child represents and, sometimes, works through troubling mental representations. In their play, children may dramatically rework their traumatic moments and experiences (Nader & Pynoos, 1991; Webb, 2002a).

Children's play interests are somewhat manipulated by the media (e.g., TV, movies, commercials), toy manufacturing industry, video games, video recordings, and books or comics (Marsh, 2000). These interests include, for example, the dramatic appeal of the superhero figure that can perform beyond the normal limitations set by life and adults. Solnit (1987) points out that children take their play very seriously, expending large amounts of emotion during play. In addition to this quality, traumatic play can take on an almost driven quality (Nader & Pynoos, 1991; Terr, 1981a). As long as a child progresses to the next step in a needed progression in play, he or she appears to enjoy the play. Resolution is not always possible without therapeutic assistance (chapter 1; Box 13.1).

Forms of Play. Play can be social or solitary, goal-directed or seemingly purposeless, and symbolic or physical. Researchers have described *functional* play: manipulation of an object to determine its properties and what it does, *construction play:* goal-directed play behaviors such as building something, and *symbolic* or *dramatic* play: one thing may represent something else, reality is suspended (Coplan & Rubin, 1998; Pellegrini, 2001; Rubin, 1989). Pellegrini suggests that normal play is governed by the question, "What can *I* do with it?" (p. 866). In contrast, functional or exploration is guided by "What can *it* do?" With novel toys, youths are likely to explore them before they play with them. The social dimensions of play—solitary, parallel, and group—are summarized in the description of the Play Observation Scale (POS) to follow (Coplan, 2000). Pellegrini adds to these forms of play *interactive play:* two youths engaging in reciprocal interaction.

Pellegrini and Smith (1998) have described different forms of physical play. *Rhythmic* play predominates in infancy and includes gross motor movements such as body rocking, arm waving, and foot kicking without an apparent goal. *Exercise* play increases from toddlerhood to its peak during preschool years and then declines in the elementary school years. It includes physically vigorous gross motor locomotion such as chasing a ball, running, jumping, climbing, lifting, fleeing, and pushing and pulling. For 9 to 10 year olds, it may become running, walking fast, games, sports, and cycling. *Rough and Tumble* (R&T) behavior combines (1) "soft" or open-hand hitting, pushing, or teasing; (2) positive affect: smiling or laughing; and (3) staying together after the *rough* act. *Aggressive* behavior combines (1) hard, closed-hand hitting or kicking; (2) negative affect: frowning or crying; and (3) separation after the *aggressive* act. R&T play peaks in middle childhood and includes playful tumbling, hitting, grappling, wrestling, and kicking, and sometimes chasing. Research demon-

---

BOX 13.1
Traumatic Play

a. *A Sniper Attack.* Following the sniper attack, a 10-year-old boy attempted to engage his peers in shooting games. He was agitated when his friends would not allow him always to be the successful good guy. Another 10-year-old boy enacted, in his play, the successful rescue by police and firemen of several schools endangered by snipers, fires, and earthquakes. He fully enjoyed his play and seemed relieved afterward. Rashida played over and over the segment of her experience when she heard the gunshots, traced the bullets path, and ran for safety, leaving her friend behind her. She always stopped play and became very upset after the segment when she started to run (before her friend was shot).

b. *Mathew.* In his treatment sessions more than 2 years after the massacre, Mathew (see Box 1.1a, 10.1b) began each session by protesting that he did not need treatment. He then readily engaged in directed demonstrations of his experience with toy replicas or spontaneously engaged in play. A few examples of his spontaneous play are provided here: He arranged the clinician as a silent witness to the side of a somewhat wooded and rocky section of the grounds while he became a sniper hiding behind rocks and shooting at shooters before they could do any harm. He used toy soldiers with weapons and spray disinfectant to kill an army of ants just outside the treatment room. He spoke to the ants to let them know that they would be killed so that they could do no harm. He built a Lego fortress with a large wall and mote and defended it against knights with spears. Two days after Mathew discussed how helpless he felt during the siege at the hands of the shooter, in a hospital group session peers teased him about his short bleached hair and called him a girl. He went to the floor like he sometimes did when feeling helpless (as though again on the floor under the restaurant table). On that day in his treatment session, Mathew made a female doll look like him and attacked and tore her/him apart (Box 10.1b). After completion of this play a half hour later, when the treating clinician summarized what he had done ("You've taken a girl doll, dressed her, and made her look exactly like you ..."), he blurted, "I am not a girl!" Then he discussed his feelings of helplessness and anger at himself during the shootings and when teased by his peers.

strates that aggression and R&T are separate systems. Before adolescence, R&T does not correlate with nor tend to escalate to aggression for most youths. In many mammalian species, R&T and aggression appear to be linked to different neural and endocrine controls.

The Purpose of Play. Although many researchers believe that play permits the practice of skills necessary to later adult functioning, research has demonstrated its immediate developmental purpose as well. Piaget (1962) and other researchers have suggested that play, in general, is associated with a sense of mastery and well-being in children that, in turn, has implications for functioning and resilience (Pellegrini & Smith, 1998; chapter 5). The purpose of symbolic play has been distinguished from that of physically active play.

Symbolic play is characterized by the suspension of reality, the representation of one thing by another, and/or the symbolic enactment of real or imaginary experiences. Play does not demand censoring, orderliness, or the inhibiting influence of reality (see Freud, 1965; Nader & Pynoos, 1991; Solnit, 1987). It need not be consequential or unchangeable. In their play, children do not simply repeat actions but are able to manipulate objects and outcomes. Pellegrini (2001) describes what he calls Fein's (1979) "catharsis-like" theory: The motivation for children's play is the desire to attain the unattainable. It includes a tension between this motivation to fulfill wishes and the desire to impose social rules. In addition and as opposed to wish fulfillment, symbolic play may combine external reality with the child's personal internal reality (Nader & Pynoos; Winnicot, 1971). In this way, youths reenact, in their play and behaviors, aspects of their traumatic and other experiences. In therapeutic interventions, play can be directed or permitted to facilitate the youths' facing emotional moments with the associated affect (Nader & Mello, 2001). The youth may reenter the traumatic moment or fantasy in order to release, reprocess, and redefine aspects of his or her experience (Boik & Goodwin, 2000; Levy, 1938; Nader & Mello; Nader & Pynoos; Pynoos & Eth, 1986).

Pellegrini and Smith (1998) have summarized research evidence that suggests active play's developmental purpose. *Rhythmic* play is linked to neuromuscular development. Specific rhythmic movements appear to increase just prior to achievement of voluntary control of the associated system and specific motor pattern. This play may proliferate, eliminate, or modify neural growth or synapse formations (chapter 2). *Exercise* play appears to assist the development of physical strength, endurance, and economy of movement. Although frequent play tends to maximize cognitive performance, it appears that any break, not necessarily play, serves this purpose. Research evidence shows that vigorous play correlates with preschool children's abilities to decode emotional expressions (happy, sad, scared, angry, neutral), and elementary school children's R&T is linked to the ability to decode play signals (e.g., signals that "this is play"). Pellegrini (2003) demonstrated that R&T practices are used to establish dominance in adolescence. Through R&T, youths can often evaluate the strength of others or establish the dominance of their own strength. Males tend to engage in exercise and R&T play more than girls (Pellegrini & Smith). In most mammalian species and cultures, males engage in more R&T. Evidence suggests that the gender differences for R&T may be related to hormonal influences—increased androgens—and socialization practices. In contrast to boys, girls primarily use verbal rather than physical means to gain/keep resources. In contrast to adolescents, preadolescents' R&T does not correlate with peer nomination revealed dominance status. For adolescents, the stronger boy may escalate the intensity of behaviors such as fighting if the weaker boy does not yield or show distress.

Traumatic Play. Regardless of the mechanisms involved, traumatized youths may appear to be compelled to enact their traumatic experiences in their play or activities (see chapter 1). Traumatic play is a form of re-experiencing and may represent an attempt to reprocess aspects of the experience. Many traumatized youths seem unable to rework their experiences through their play, however, without assistance. Following a kidnapping during which schoolchildren were buried alive in their school bus, Terr (1981a) observed that traumatic play differed from normal play. In contrast to usual play, children's traumatic play failed to provide relief, aggravated rather than soothed the condition, and ended unsatisfactorily. Nader and Pynoos (1991) found that children's traumatic play either provoked anxiety or provided relief for a child. The differences in the play's effects may be related to the degree (1) of perceived control over outcomes, (2) a satisfactory ending is achieved, (3) the youth feels free to express prohibited affects, or (4) a cognitive reworking is assisted. Youths exposed to a sniper attack and to a massacre provide examples (Box 13.1a, 13.1b).

Methods of Analysis. Many qualities can be assessed when observing children's play: the function of play, the roles enacted, affect, goals, interactions, agreement or disagreement with playmates, replication of home life or life events, resolution, and more. Several protocols exist for observing children at play (Mori & Armendariz, 2001; Nader & Stuber, 1993; Pellegrini, 2001; Roberts, 2001; Scheeringa et al., 2001). Although they no longer use all of them, Scheeringa and colleagues have used the following observation contexts for very young children exposed to traumas: (1) during the caregiver interview, (2) in free play with the caregiver, (3) in examiner-child free play, (4) in examiner-guided trauma re-enactment play, and (4) during an interview regarding the parent's PTSD symptoms (Scheeringa et al.). A few play observation methods are listed here and in Table 13.1.

The Play Observation Kit (POKIT)

The Play Observation Kit (Mogford-Bevan, 2000) was developed for use with 2 to 4 year olds who have evidenced developmental delays and deviations. POKIT employs a standard set of toys, five observational checklists, and a qualitative summary to obtain specific, objective, and concrete descriptions of children's play. The qualitative summary of the child's ability to learn and interact with others includes initial play level, manipulation and hand-eye coordination, quality of play and exploration, variation and flexibility in play, persistence, learning and problem solving, attention, communication, and picture and storybook handling sections. Collected findings are entered into a developmental status summary. POKIT has diagnosed cases of autism later confirmed by child psychiatry specialists.

The Preschool Play Behavior Scale (PPBS)

The Preschool Play Behavior Scale (Coplan & Rubin, 1998; Coplan, 2000) is an 18-item teacher-rated scale that assesses free-play behaviors in preschool children. It is based on the Play Observation Scale (described next) and uses a five-point Likert rating scale. Its completion by teachers is recommended after several school weeks and the opportunity to get to know children. PPBS subscales include *reticent behavior* (onlooker/spectator, aimless wandering, watching or listening without trying to join in, and alone and unoccupied, possibly staring into space), *solitary-passive behavior* (playing alone examining toy/object; playing alone building or creating with toys), *solitary-active behavior* (engaging in solitary pretend or "make-believe" play), *social play* (talking to others during play, engaging in make-believe play with others, joining group play); and *rough-play* (engaging in "rough and tumble" with others, playing at mock or playful fighting with others).

The Play Observation Scale (POS)

The Play Observation Scale (Rubin, 1989) is a play behavior taxonomy that was originally designed for use with early and middle childhood (Coplan, 2000). The behaviors observed include *unoccupied* (absence of focus or intent; wandering aimlessly; staring blankly) *onlooking* (watching others' activities without attempting to enter them); *solitary play* (playing alone, independently, and with different toys at least 3 feet from others); *parallel play* (engaging in own activities within 3 feet of others with awareness of other children); *peer conversation*; and *group play* (playing directly with other children). Play may be *functional* (simply for physical enjoyment), *exploratory* (examination of an object to learn its properties), *constructive* (manipulating objects to construct or create something), or *dramatic* (pretense; taking on roles). The quality of play, as described earlier, is functional, constructive, exploratory, dramatic, or games with rules. Quality and type of play form a matrix for observation. Researchers have observed youths for multiple 10-second intervals, 90 intervals in each of two free-play sessions (Fox, Henderson, Rubin, Calkins, & Schmidt, 2001; Henderson, Marshall, Fox, & Rubin, 2004).

The School Recess and Playground Behavior (SRPB)

The School Recess and Playground Behavior scheme (Pellegrini, 1995) is a method of assessing playground behavior of primary schoolchildren.

The behaviors observed include the following: passive/noninteractive, passive/interactive, adult directed, adult organized, aggressive, rough and tumble play, vigorous behavior, games, object play, and role play. Pellegrini (2001) found that kindergartners' playground behavior better predicted first-grade achievement than did their test scores. Higher levels of time in adult-directed behavior was a negative indicator of social competence. Cooperative play with peers and object play were each positively correlated with first-grade achievement.

The Traumatic Play Observation Scale (TPOS)

The Traumatic Play Observation Scale (Nader, Fletcher, & Stuber, 2005) provides taxonomy of normal and traumatic play behaviors for a variety of traumas. TPOS includes a solitary play rating scale and a social play rating scale to assess the presence and nature of traumatic play. The 3- to 5-year-old Child Trauma Checklist (Nader & Stuber, 1993) is a precursor to the TPOS. The current measure permits the observational assessment of traumatic play versus normal play. Because a child's specific types of play are of interest following traumatic events, the TPOS expands the list of types of play to include exploratory, doctor/hospital, monster/evil person, family, superhero, being a baby, baby doll, eating play food, good child/bad child, guns/weapons, games, dress up, being left, transformer, cowboys/Indians, building things/construction, specific trauma play (e.g., tornado, earthquake, shooting, assault/beating, hitting, molestation/rape, calling for help, and other forms of trauma-enacting play), normal-role play, trauma-role play, or other forms of play. The associated toys are made available. Children are video recorded in 15 minutes of free play and then, If desired, for 15 minutes during and after questions about the traumatic event. Each 15- or 30-second increment of play is recorded for its predominant play mode. The child's affect and demeanor during the play is also recorded—fascinated, smiling, laughing, serious, sad, angry, relaxed, engrossed, intense/driven, perseverative, agitated, fatigued.

Classroom Observations

Classroom observations have been used with children of all ages. Kay (2002) points out the importance of observing qualitative as well as quantitative differences. Children sometimes are able to "hold it together" in the classroom so that difficulties are not obvious. Although the youth may continue to complete schoolwork, problems with concentration, intrusive thoughts, or other symptoms may alter aspects of performance. A youth who functioned at a normal or rapid pace before the trauma may become slow and his or her efforts laborious in doing schoolwork or other tasks. Qualitative differences such as a greater struggle to function may exacerbate symptoms, such as fatigue, frustration, and impulsive reactivity, and may cause additional and ongoing life hindrance in a competitive environment.

A youth's reactivity has become an important issue as a result of or a precursor to trauma. Reactivity has multiple components (Sutton, 2002). Among them are onset, peak amplitude, and recovery or decay. Discovering these aspects of a youth's reactivity is difficult without observational methods.

The Student Observation System (SOS). The Student Observation System (Reynolds & Kamphaus, 1998) is a companion method for the *Behavior Assessment System for Children (BASC, chapter 15)*. Clinicians or raters directly observe youths' classroom behavior. Momentary time sampling includes systematic coding during 3-second intervals after 30 seconds of observation, for 15 minutes. SOS assesses maladaptive and adaptive behaviors ranging from repetitive motor movements to positive peer interactions.

Laboratory or Office Observations

Laboratory or office observations have been used to study a variety of behaviors and disorders (Ainsworth et al., 1978; Mori & Armendariz, 2001; Roberts, 2001). Methods include naturalistic or simulated situations. Naturalistic and simulated findings are not always in accord (Mori & Armendariz). This issue requires consideration when designing studies. Among the scales with demonstrated reliability and validity are the Preschool Observation Scale of Anxiety, a 30-item measure of situation anxiety (Glennon & Weisz, 1978), and the INTERACT/BLISS, a coding system that permits assignment into communication typologies (effective or disruptive; Dumas, Blechman, & Prinz, 1994) (Mori & Armendariz).

Sexual Abuse. For possible sexual abuse cases, Wandersman (1998) has described play interviews that may be especially useful for very young children who have difficulty verbalizing or drawing. Puppets, dolls, or animals and a dollhouse or sandtray are made available so that a child may be asked to use fantasy to communicate about difficult issues. A situation may be set up in a dollhouse, for example, with the child waking up at night crying. The child may then be asked to play out what happened and what will happen next. A child might be asked to set up and describe a world in a sandtray. The child may use a doll family to show what he or she does when scared. Even if the play does not reflect what happens, it can be used to assess the child's feelings and wishes.

Social Behavior. The Social Behavior Inventory (SBI; Gully, 2003d) is a 30-item checklist of interpersonal behavior for use with youths, ages 3 to 17 (Gully, 2003e). Gully (2003d) urges caution in interpreting results for very young children who have a limited capacity to demonstrate some of the behaviors measured. A youth can be rated in approximately 4 minutes by parents, or by other raters who have spent 1 to 2 hours with the youth. The SBI includes five scales: *aversive-miscommunication* (nervous movement, complaints, put-downs, false beliefs, threats, blaming, paranoia, manipulation, does not listen, is not truthful), *aversive-insensitive* (raises voice when angry, does not give compliments, states negative feelings, does not accept responsibility, is not sensitive, does not compromise, threatens, is blaming, is demanding), *aversive-argumentative* (nervous movement, begins conversations, makes requests, complains, interrupts, blames, demands, disagrees, manipulates), *prosocial-genuine* (gives compliments, makes requests, expresses beliefs, requests feedback, states positive feelings, states negative feelings, accepts responsibility, is sensitive, compromises, laughs, demonstrates leadership, is open about feelings), and *prosocial-direct* (eye contact, clarity and volume, begins conversations, makes requests, expresses beliefs, laughs, demonstrates leadership, listens). An additional *total social competence* scale is derived by subtracting items that load uniquely on the aversive scales from those that load uniquely on the prosocial scales (Gully, 2001). Parents or clinicians rate each of the 30 items as either "Not or rarely true" (= 0), "Somewhat or sometimes true" (= 1), or "Very or often true" (= 2) (Gully, 2003d). Data is available for 318 parent reports of normal youths (nonclinical sample) and for 594 clinician reports of youths who were part of a child abuse treatment program (clinical sample). Comparative data and scale correlations are available for the clinical and nonclinical samples and for the five violence risk groups of the clinical sample: sexual abuse, physical abuse, exposure to family violence, sexual aggression, and physically assaultive behavior.

Individualized Clinical Assessments

When clinical assessments are tailored to the individual youth, they can include his or her personal traumatic experience(s) and reactions. Such evaluations can compare a youth to his or her personal previous or current levels of functioning instead of to a defined or average level. An individualized trauma or progress assessment might include, for example, documentation and progress toward resolution of the following (discussed in more detail in the other chapters of this book): (1) specific traumatic episodes including worst and troubling moments; (2) symptoms that impair functioning and quality of life; (3) trauma-related roles and trauma-induced script-like behavioral patterns; (4) problematic information processing; (5) traumatic grief; (6) guilt or self-blame; (7) shame; (8) injured self-systems (e.g., self-esteem, self-control/regulation, locus of control, systems of belief, self-confidence); (9) relationship disruptions and interactional difficulties (e.g., trust, support, changes in relationships); (10) undesirable personality changes (e.g., increased negativity, supersensitivity to sounds and other stimuli, irritability); (11) loss of acquired or normal developmental skills; (12) externalizing behaviors (e.g., increased aggressive reactivity, impulsiveness, oppositional behaviors); (13) internalizing symptoms (e.g., depression, anxiety); (14) reactivity to reminders; (15) suicidal ideation or self-harm; and (16) personal meaning of the traumatic experience (e.g., its link to past experiences).

Goal Attainment Scaling (GAS)

Goal Attainment Scaling (Hogue, 1994; Kiresuk, Smith, & Cardillo, 1994) has been used as a method of individualized assessment. Rather than rating patients on a fixed set of psychiatric symptoms, GAS requires the development of outcome scales specifically tailored to the individual or group whose progress is to be measured. It creates a list for examination of those characteristics, behaviors, or symptoms that intervention is intended to change, alleviate, or prevent. A clinician may create five-point *level of attainment* scales and additional scales with specific indicators of each level of success for an identified goal (Kiresuk et al.).

CONCLUSIONS

Multiple sources of information are best used in assessing youths' reactions to traumatic events. Clinicians, parents, or teachers report some symptoms more effectively than children do. Adults are generally better at reporting children's observable externalized problem behaviors than their internalized symptoms. Measures designed for parent and teacher completion or interview add to the assessment process and are available for use in combination with PTSD inventories (chapter 11) as well as with measures of child behaviors (chapter 15). Parents' or teachers' own traumatic reactions may affect the accuracy of their reports.

New measures for children under the age of 5 have been designed taking into account the specific differences in preschool and older children's reactions and needs. Alternative PTSD algorithms and symptoms as well as measures of psychopathology have been proposed for use with very young children. These measures are currently being statistically tested.

In addition to the standardized parent-, teacher-, and child-reported assessments described in the other chapters of this book, specific clinician or trained rater assessments of youths include observational and individualized methods. Protocols for youth observations have been used in a variety of settings and contexts. Among settings are the classroom, playground, clinical office, experimental setting, and home. Youths have been observed alone, in interactions with peers or parents, and with other adults. They have been observed at play, during schoolwork, in simulated circumstances, and amid a normal routine. These additional clinician methods can add to the richness of information gathered about an individual child and serve to assess progress during treatment.

Part IV
Assessing Additional Trauma Symptoms

14

The Integration of Information Following Traumas
Information Processing and Dissociation

Information processing includes a number of cognitive functions: (1) *receptive:* the acquisition, classification, processing, and integration of information, (2) *memory* and *learning:* the storing and recall of information, (3) *thinking:* the organization and reorganization of information, and (4) *expressive:* the communication and enactment of information (Werry, 1991). Problematic information processing may be related to attention, memory, interpretation, response search, response selection, or failure of integration (Crick & Dodge, 1994; Mash & Dozois, 2003). Such processing has been implicated in a number of childhood disorders and problems (Mash & Barkley, 2003; Mash & Dozois). Theorists suggest that knowledge acquired throughout life is represented in memory in the form of *schemas:* abstract, generic knowledge structures (Siegel, 1996). Within an information processing framework, PTSD is characterized by dysfunctional schemas; for example, the world is conceived as indiscriminately dangerous, and the self as incompetent to cope with stress (March, Amaya-Jackson, Foa, & Treadwell, 1999). Siegel (2003) points out, "Impairment in representational integration in general, including the bilateral integration of information processing between right and left hemispheres in particular, may be a core deficit in unresolved trauma" (p. 15). Some aspects of information processing were discussed in earlier chapters. Information processing, dissociation, and their relationships to trauma and assessment are discussed here.

Memory Networks

An individual's information processing system includes networks of memory associations referred to variously as schemata, scripts, or working models of relationships (Bowlby, 1969/1982; Crick & Dodge, 1994; Shapiro & Maxfield, 2003). When they are natural and normal, these networks permit adaptive movement through life (Shapiro & Maxfield). Schemata directly affect cognition, emotion, and body sensation. Within or outside of awareness and with or without effort, cognitive processes, including memory, attention, and other aspects of information processing, accompany emotions (Heller, Schmidtke, Nitschke, Koven, & Miller, 2002). Emotions can affect information processing, and information processing can affect emotions (Crick & Dodge). Cognitions, emotions, and neurochemical reactions combine across time and contexts and result in specific associations that engender states of mind and body as well as enactments or inaction. Shapiro and Maxfield explain that new situations may elicit memory networks of previous experiences that affect current perceptions, reactions, and behaviors. This replay is significant to re-enactment, transference, and other posttrauma reactions.

Integration, Differentiation, and Compartmentalization

Integration has been addressed in more than one manner (Siegel, 2003). It is the process by which the parts or traits of an individual's personality or brain circuitry work together as a whole. *Integration* is the process of coordinating neurological impulses, encoded information, and memories into a whole (Chaplin, 1975). Brains are genetically programmed to *differentiate* their circuits. *Integration* is achieved during normal development but can be impaired by trauma. Suboptimal or traumatizing experiences can injure the brain's ability to balance the integration-differentiation process.

Compartmentalization refers to the separation of areas of awareness and memory or the failure of integration of knowledge and experience. Everyone periodically experiences context- or state-dependent compartmentalization of recall information (Putnam, 1997). Sad memories, for example, may be easiest to recall when in a sad state (Siegel, 1996). Dissociative compartmentalization permits an individual to store and recall emotionally laden information separately from other information (Putnam; see "Dissociation," below). Compartmentalization also permits an individual to hold different views of self.

Showers (2002) studied integration versus compartmentalization of negative and positive attributions to self and others. Under normal circumstances, individuals may display relatively stable differences in the structure of beliefs about self and, yet, may change to fit a situation. From an information processing perspective, the self-concept is seen as "an enormous repertoire of self-relevant information, including both episodic and semantic knowledge . . . organized into categories . . . that help to activate subsets of self-knowledge . . ." (Showers, pp. 272-273). Subsets may include, for example, the core self and the working self. Showers suggests that individuals evaluate their multiple selves through a process of either *compartmentalization* or *integration*. In *compartmentalization* evaluation of self-states, positive and negative attributes are segregated into separate self-attribute categories. Compartmentalized Harry has a scholar-self with all positive attributes (e.g., curious, disciplined, creative, motivated) and a test-taking self with all negative attributes (e.g., worrying, tense, distracted, insecure). *Integration* evaluation of self-roles includes positive and negative characteristics in each self-state category. For integrated Sally, humanities-self includes such characteristics as creative, insecure, motivated, and moody, whereas her science-self is disciplined, worrying, analytic, and tense. *Compartmentalization* minimizes access to negative self-beliefs and either permits the individual to ignore them or creates vulnerability to overwhelm by important negative self-states.

Although negative self-attributions are linked to positive associations in the *integration* method, its advantage is that it minimizes the impact of inevitable negative self-beliefs. Showers found for college students that greater compartmentalization was associated with less negative mood, demonstrating its use as an effective coping mechanism during stressful life events. During relationship stress, it was associated with greater likelihood of staying in the relationship. Individuals who remained integrative under stress had low vulnerability to depression and experienced only minor stress. Some evidence suggests that well-adjusted individuals (in conditions of nontraumatic stress) can shift from a compartmentalized self-structure to an integrative style when negative attributes are prominent.

Group Membership

Among variables associated with information processing findings are temperament and brain hemispheric tendencies. Research has begun to support the hypothesis that the left frontal lobe is relatively more specialized for approach functions, and the right frontal lobe for withdrawal (see Gray's BIS and BAS, chapter 6). Accordingly, hemispheric laterality may be an important variable for understanding and assessing individual differences in processing negative affective stimuli, including threat stimuli. Individual differences in perceptual asymmetry (PA) have been associated with diagnostic subtypes. For a small sample of adults, Otto, McNally, Pollack, Chen, and Rosenbaum (1994) failed to find the explicit memory bias for threat words in panic disorder patients found in earlier tests after arousal induction. Otto et al. used a dichotic listening procedure to assess brain hemispheric processing biases as evidenced by PA: a more than 20 decibel sound identification acuity difference between the left and right ears. There were no PA differences between the patient and control groups. All three groups had greater recall for panic-threat, general-threat, and positive words than for neutral words. PA scores alone and in combination with group membership significantly predicted explicit memory bias for threat words. A greater right-ear advantage was implicated in a greater bias toward threat stimuli for the patient groups. Higher PA scores were associated with greater memory bias for threat in patients than control subjects. Low PA scores, in contrast, demonstrated the opposite effect: Memory bias scores for threat were less in anxiety patients than for control subjects. The study suggests a lower right-ear advantage is associated with cognitive avoidance. Blaustein (2000) found, for 36 adolescents with a history of maltreatment, that high-avoidance youths demonstrated an increased bias toward threatening information compared with low-avoidance youths.

Trauma and Information Processing

Individuals with PTSD appear to sample and categorize experience in ways that are qualitatively significantly different from nontraumatized people (van der Kolk, 2003). Developmentally, youths' social information processing changes as they acquire additional cognitive skills, experience, a broader social database, and greater competence such as improved attentional abilities and increased mental organizational skills (Crick & Dodge, 1994). Exposure to catastrophic events is likely to change youths' thinking to varying degrees. Variations may be attributed to age, child traits and temperaments, history and background, or aspects of the traumatic experience. Young children, for example, may lose a sense of protection from and faith in adults as well as the framework for resilience (competence, trust, control; Yates, Egeland, & Sroufe, 2003). Adolescents' sense of self and autonomy may be undermined.

Empirical evidence demonstrates that traumatic experiences may result in information processing biases (Crick & Dodge, 1996; de Castro, Slot, Bosch, Koops, & Veerman, 2003; Dodge, Bates, Pettit, & Valente, 1995; Schippell, Vasey, Cravens-Brown, & Bretveld, 2003). Aggressive abused youths exhibit attributional biases: They perceive, interpret, and make decisions about social interactions that increase the likelihood of their aggressive acts (Crick & Dodge; de Castro et al.; Dodge et al.; Schippell et al.; chapter 3). Whether because of posttrauma neurobiological reactivity, victim consciousness, changed information processing, or other traumatic sequelae or personality factors, a youth may develop a sense of entitlement or a keen attentional awareness of injustice that influences his or her character and behaviors. He or she may, in fact, see injustice when none exists. Research has demonstrated that cognitions and symptoms can be bidirectional.

Information Processing and Depression versus Anxiety

Some theoreticians have suggested that depression is based on perceived past losses and failures, whereas anxiety is based on fear of future losses and failures (Malcarne & Hansdottir, 2001). Their associated patterns of attention, perception, and information processing may be temporary or persistent. They may have a major impact on the youth's functioning, style, and quality of life. Chorpita and Barlow (1998) posit that early experiences with uncontrollable or unpredictable stimuli generate perceptions of low control and lead to increased activity in the Behavioral Inhibition System (chapters 5, 6) and to risk of anxiety and depression (cited in Malcarne & Hansdottir). With cumulative low control experiences, cognitive schemas may become rigid and resistant to evidence of control. These schemas may result in biased processing of later input.

Posttrauma or other depressive patterns of thinking may include underevaluation of self, helplessness, a sense of futility, and negative expectations of the future. Depressed individuals may evaluate themselves negatively, underestimate their competence, set unrealistic and perfectionistic goals for themselves, believe that efforts to achieve goals are futile, or feel hopeless or pessimistic about the future (Hammen & Rudolph, 2003). Evidence suggests that negative views of self and the world mediate the association between negative affect and later underestimation of competence. Depressed individuals are more likely to attend to and recall unpleasant rather than pleasant information. They are likely to make more negative judgments about real and hypothetical life events. Depressive symptoms have been linked to biased information processing regarding interpersonal interactions, such as negative interpersonal expectations and perceptions, and maladaptive relationship-oriented beliefs (Rosenbloom & Williams, 2002).

Studies have demonstrated that anxious children engage in both depressive and anxious self-talk. Anxious youths engage in more off-task thoughts, negative self-statements, and negative cognitive errors (e.g., more negative evaluations) (Malcarne & Hansdottir, 2001). Anxiety has been associated strongly with attentional biases to threatening stimuli (Heller et al., 2002; see "Attentional Biases," below).

INFORMATION PROCESSING BIASES

Among information processing biases are attentional biases, self-attributional biases (self-representations), other-attributional biases (expectations of others or of relationships), and biased expectations of events and outcomes. An attributional style is an individual's general tendency to form similar causal explanations across events (Yee, Pierce, Ptacek, & Modzelesky, 2003). Trauma frequently leads to mild to severe alterations in attention and processing. Unhealed trauma associations implicitly set the groundwork for future perceptions (Shapiro & Maxfield, 2003). Trauma-engendered alterations in cognitive processing may be a part of posttrauma symptoms such as anxiety, aggression, depression, and dissociation.

Attentional Biases

Attentional selectivity is a process by which some information is selected for processing and other information ignored (Bijttebier, Vasey, & Braet, 2003). Individual differences in susceptibility to negative emotion and to selective attention have been associated with brain hemispheric differences (Otto et al., 1994). Negative affect and depression have been linked to relatively greater right hemisphere activation, particularly in the right frontal lobe.

Laboratory Studies of Attention

Laboratory studies of anxiety disorders and attentional biases have found that anxious patients selectively process disorder-specific or trauma-specific threat words (Freeman & Beck, 2000; McNally, Kaspi, Riemann, & Zeitlin, 1990). In a Stroop paradigm, delays in color-naming of words occur when the meaning of the word automatically attracts the subject's attention despite efforts to attend to the word's color. McNally et al. used variously colored neutral, positive, trauma, and OCD (e.g., filth, feces, germs) words to study veterans with and without PTSD. PTSD patients, but not controls, exhibited Stroop interference for war-trauma words but not for OCD, positive, or neutral words. In a study of 53 girls ages 11 to 17 (20 sexually abused [SA] with PTSD, 13 SA without PTSD, and 20 controls), Freeman and Beck discovered that overall color-naming was significantly slower for the PTSD group than controls. All participants in this study showed cognitive interference for sexual-trauma-related words.

Youths who experience traumatic events may become selective in their attention to negative events (Dodge, Bates, & Pettit, 1990). Although some methodology problems exist in the measurement of information processing in youths (Vasey, Dalgleish, & Silverman, 2003), attentional biases in favor of threat-related information have been found in youths who are subclinically anxious or diagnosed with generalized anxiety disorder (GAD), PTSD, or simple phobias, and whose parents have PTSD (Dalgleish, Taghavi, Neshat-Doost, Moradi, Canterbury, & Yule, 2003). Clinicians have also repeatedly observed increased attention to negative events for youths and sometimes communities after traumatic events. The modified Stroop task has elicited inconsistent findings in young samples (Dalgleish et al.). For small samples of youths with PTSD (n = 24), GAD (n = 24), major depressive disorder (MDD; n = 19), and controls (n = 26), Dalgleish et al. showed no significant differences in profiles of anxious and depressed youths' performances on a modified Stroop paradigm. Using a dot-probe task, however, they found the GAD (but not the PTSD or MDD) group had an attentional bias toward threat material; the PTSD group had an attentional bias away from depressogenic material. Anxious youths with both GAD and PTSD rated negative events as more likely to happen to others than to themselves, whereas depressed youths did not.

Attributional Biases: Self and Others

Mental representations are based on interconnected, developing representations that emerge successively and interactively with age (Thompson, 1999). *Internal Working Models* (IWMs; Bowlby, 1969/1982; chapter 8) are continuously revised and updated throughout development. Aspects of IWM may have different timetables and differing critical periods. Cognitive schemas regarding the self (self-representations) and the world directly affect the way an individual acts and interacts in the world. They influence or may result from a youth's responses to traumatic events. Trust or distrust, high or low self-esteem, and internal or external locus of control, among other represented models, have their individual and interrelated sets of cognitive thought processes. Early and traumatic experiences as well as temperamental characteristics may set up anticipatory attitudes that affect interactions and relationships (Caspi, 1998). Youths with attributional biases may search a situation for fewer cues before making an attributional decision and find evidence for their biases through selective attention or biased interpretation. When biases lead to aversive nonverbal, verbal, or behavioral expressions, they are likely to elicit reactions that reinforce them such as increased actual hostility and rejection from peers following aggression (Crick, 1995).

Biases about self include perceptions of image, worth, control, and competence. Biases about others include expectations of their characteristics and behaviors. Many of these biases have been discussed in chapters 3 and 5. Biases may result in positive or negative self-talk, tendencies toward inhibition or action, and variations in self-control. These IWM, internal constructs, or internal role representations translate into attitudes, expectations, interpretations, response selections, and behaviors. Faulty views of self may precipitate problematic or pathological behaviors such as a dissociative or aggressive style or disorder (Dodge et al., 1995; Silberg, 2004).

Role Attributions: Self and Others. In diagnostic interviews following a sniper attack on an elementary school ground in the early 1980s, I mentioned to my colleague that youths appeared to be identifying primarily with victim, perpetrator, or rescuer roles. Subsequently, in ongoing treatment of multiple traumatized youths, it became clear that a number of *trauma-related roles* or *trauma-engendered scripts* influence a traumatized youth's behavior and thinking about self and others. These role attributions often require processing or resolution (see chapter 1). Whether viewed as schema, scripts, IWMs, identifications, internalizations, defenses, intense impressions, conversions, reenactments, a process of new integration of information and perceptions, or other occurrences, this phenomenon is relevant to a youth's attention, behavior, and perceptions of the world as well as his or her treatment and recovery. It may be important in the future to assess these schemas in determining the effects of trauma and the outcomes of treatment.

Some attentional and attitudinal biases appear to represent rather stable changes in aspects of information processing. For example, the *victim coping* that may be persistently characteristic of violently traumatized youths denotes the defensive attitudes, sense of numbing and emptiness, spaced out/disorientation or *brain fog*, expectation of danger and betrayal, and unspoken belief that distrust and defiance are essential for self-protection or for coping with unmanageable emotions (Ford, 2002; chapter 3). In other instances, youths may shift in and out of *trauma-related roles* or *trauma-engendered scripts* and their accompanying biases (Box 13.1b, 14.1a).

A number of clinician/researchers have observed posttrauma IWMs, *trauma-related roles,* or *trauma-induced scripts* that influence attention, perception, and response selection. As discussed in chapter 1, these IWMs or trauma-related roles may result in reenactment or other trauma symptoms and behaviors. Although researchers have described specific groups of roles as they apply to particular traumatized youth populations, any number of trauma-specific roles may be possible. In addition to the roles of perpetrator, rescuer, victim, or witness, trauma-related roles may reflect aspects of a youth's individual experience. Among them are mobilized witness, helpless child, bad child, perpetrator's assistant, voice of reason, soother/calmer, aggravator, tainted one, or searcher. Boxes 1.1e, 13.1b, and 14.1a and 14.1b demonstrate roles engendered by a single incident trauma. Roles related to abuse or disorganized attachments follow.

Expectations of Protection. Thomas (2005) proposes that, because their caregivers did not protect them at crucial moments, abused children do not internalize adequate constructs of protection from self or others. Consequently, they lack a template for developing self-defense behaviors. Children who are well-protected form mental models of a safe child, a strong protector, and a self-controlled or curbed aggressor. In contrast, abused children encode representations of an unsafe child, an inadequate protector, and an out-of-control and dangerous aggressor. Consequently, abused individuals tend to see others as dangerous aggressors, even when the people simply intend to make a request, express disagreement, or strike a negotiating stance (Box 1.1e). When abuse survivors do not feel strong enough to counter these perceived acts of aggression effectively,

BOX 14.1

Case Examples: The Integration and Expression of Information

a. *Mathew*. Before his trauma-focused treatment, Mathew (Box 1.1a) frequently dressed like the shooter, instigated physical fights, and exhibited aggressive behaviors that frightened his mother and teachers. In early treatment sessions, Mathew moved in and out of roles such a victim, attacker, witness, and rescuer, sometimes within a single session or a single role over several sessions. As his treatment progressed, he no longer acted out the role of aggressor with school peers, his mother, or teachers. His desire to fight continued, however. He moved through other roles and returned to processing aspects of the violent perpetrator through a period of obsession with stories, movies, and histories of bloody murderers. He processed aspects of one trauma-related role and then seemed primarily driven, cognitively and behaviorally, by another role. During a hiatus from treatment, he fully embraced the rescuer role and fought as protector. The nonconscious or implicit memories that appeared to be a force during this phase were related to his intense peritraumatic desire to have saved the friend who died in the massacre. Many of his intense trauma-related desires and impressions have since translated into socially normal behaviors (see Box 17.1).

b. *Jalal*. After a sniper attack, one elementary school boy searched frantically for his sister, who disappeared when everyone ran for cover. Throughout his life, he repeated aspects of the frantic search and the role of the frantic searcher in his relationships, recreation, and career.

c. *Forgotten Segments of Experience*. Lila was held hostage with her classmates when she was 10 years old. After one of the hostage-takers accidently set off the bomb, Lila could not recall the period of time between the bomb explosion and finding safety outside of the smoke-filled room. An 8 year old who was hit by a car and propelled into a washing machine did not recall the time between flying toward the washer and seeing the panicked look on her mother's face, until she slowly reviewed her experience with a therapist (Box 9.1c). Joanie did not recall performing fellatio on her father up to age 12 until, as an adult, she described a recent dream to her therapist (Box 1.1e).

d. *Randa*. Randa was held hostage with her classmates by a woman who dictated a suicide note and then shot herself in front of them. Eleven-year-old Randa seemed to become confused and "spacey" when asked about her distressing symptoms. Her teacher reported that she responded with the same confusion/spaceyness when her schoolwork was difficult.

they feel violated. When challengers hold a role with greater real or perceived power, an abused youth is likely to respond with acquiescence, helplessness, and/or feeling violated along with harsh and critical self-talk. Unable to defend themselves from both external and internal attack, survivors may feel overwhelmed and dissociate. In severe cases, depersonalization, amnesia, or identity-switching may occur (Thomas).

Attributions of Personal Badness. Loewenstein (2004) describes the emergence in abused children of a sometimes wordless and all-encompassing belief in personal *badness* that becomes an "agonizingly ego-syntonic postulate of the survivor's assumptive world, excruciatingly and repetitively reenacted" (p. 258). An abuser's negative attributions and blame directed to the child may reinforce or contribute to the belief in the child's *badness* (Herman, 1992c, 1997; Loewenstein). Beliefs and their repeated reenactment may instigate a self-fulfilling prophecy (Loewenstein). When victimization repeats itself, the child may feel that somehow, something about him or her makes the bad things happen. Belief in the good parent and the bad self suggests that change is possible. If the child becomes good, all will be better. Otherwise, the child must contend with truths such as that the parent treated him or her like an object for personal gratification alone and did not care what happened to the child. The child dissociates and internalizes the parent's badness (p. 259).

The Drama Triangle: Attributions of Self and Caregiver. Liotti (2004) describes the basic structure of fairy tales and tragic plays as they apply to issues of trauma and attachment. For the child with a disorganized attachment, the three basic positions of the *drama triangle* (persecutor, rescuer, and victim) become representations of the self and the attachment figure. The self is victim of a persecutor. The caregiver who both frightens and comforts is both persecutor and rescuer. Liotti explains that the IWM of disorganized attachment also includes a representation of a powerful, evil self (persecutor) or powerful comforter/rescuer self and a fragile or devitalized attachment figure (victim). Also possible is the representation of both self and attachment figure as the helpless victims of a separate and mysterious, invisible source of danger. Research has provided some support that, when they reach school age, youths with early disorganized attachments behaviorally exhibit either caregiving (rescuer) or punitive (persecutor) attitudes toward their caregivers (Hesse, Main, Abrams, & Rifkin, 2003; Liotti; Lyons-Ruth & Jacobvitz, 1999).

Disorganized attachments increase vulnerability to dissociative reactions. The multiple representations of self and caregiver in which each of them shift among the three incompatible roles of persecutor, rescuer, and victim metaphorically describe the contradictory preverbal emotional schemata that arise in disorganized attachments (Liotti, 2004). The contradictory roles may be experienced simultaneously or in rapid sequence. The associated implicit memory structures are too complex and contradictory to be later synthesized or integrated in a unitary, cohesive structure of explicit, semantic memory and thus interfere with integration and are intrinsically dissociative.

Measures of Information Processing

Information processing is nonlinear: Individuals engage in multiple information processing activities simultaneously (Crick & Dodge, 1994). Although occurring simultaneously, steps are used sequentially in the study of information processing. For example, social information processing study steps include "(1) encoding of external and internal cues, (2) interpretation and mental representation of those cues, (3) clarification or selection of a goal, (4) response access or construction, (5) response decision, and (6) behavioral enactment" (Crick & Dodge, p. 76). Studies of information processing have enlisted a number of assessment methods. Memory and cognition assessments have been applied to traumatized youths and to some of the symptoms associated with trauma, such as aggression (chapter 3). For example, lack of memory specificity (see "Autobiographical Memory Test (AMT)," below) has been associated with a history of trauma and with a diagnosis of major depression in adults (de Decker, Hermans, Raes, & Eelen, 2003). Evaluations such as audio- or videotaped vignettes, written stories, pictures, cue words, observational methods, cue card or computer memory tasks such as dot-probe or Stroop memory tasks (e.g., color-naming of words), and imagination tasks are used to assess information processing. Methods of assessing social information processing include, for example, presenting youths with one or more hypothetical social situations followed by questions designed to elicit their various processing patterns. Such presentations may include reading vignettes about social situations (with or without illustrations), showing youths a videotape of same-age peers acting out a situation (Crick et al., 1998), engaging youths in an actual provocation situation (arranged by the experimenters), using a self-report inventory (e. g., Harter, 1982), or showing youths pictures of individuals interacting (Roberts, 2005, chapter 12). A few information processing methods are described here (Table 14.1).

The Autobiographical Memory Test (AMT)

AMT (Williams & Broadbent, 1986) includes a total of 10 (alternating negative and positive) emotional cue words presented by the experimenter (de Decker et al., 2003). In response to each of the words—happy, sad, safe, angry, interested, clumsy, successful, emotionally hurt, surprised, and lonely—participants are asked to generate a specific memory. Participants are allowed 30 seconds per response. If the response is not a memory, the individual is prompted by a question such as, "Can you think of a specific time—a particular episode?" until the 30 seconds is concluded.

The Expectations Test (ET)

ET (Gully, 2003a) requires youths, ages 4 to 16, to report their expectations of (1) how children in 16 ambiguous photographs feel, (2) what will happen to the child in the picture, and (3) whether they have control over the outcome (Gully, 2000, 2003b). For each picture, first the youth is asked whether the child is feeling scared, sad, angry, fine, or happy. After answering, he or she is asked what he or she thinks is going to happen to the child. Expected experiences are classified as (1) negative—*sexual abuse* (e.g., privates touched, raped, molested), *physical harm* (e.g., spanked, injured, killed), *separation* (e.g., divorced, lost a parent, kidnapped, put in a foster home), *other negative* (e.g., given a time-out, yelled at, becomes ill), or *distress* (e.g., feeling sad, lonely, crying); (2) neutral (e.g., watching television, eating, going to bed); (3) positive—*contact* (e.g., being hugged, kissed) or *other positive* (e.g., feeling happy, being saved, playing); or (4) unknown

TABLE 14.1
Measures of Information Processing and Dissociation

Measure (Age Range)	∝ Internal Consistency	Interrater r	Test-Retest r	Assesses/Measures (Scale or Subscale r; Distinguishes)	Author (Available from)
AMT		87–93%		Autobiographical memory (memory deficits r trauma experiences but not with depression, state and trait anxiety, hopelessness or worry)	Williams & Broadbent, 1986 (see de Decker, Hermans, Raes, & Eelen, 2003)
ET	.42 (angry) – .83 (sexual abuse) s	K = .66–1.0 s		Expectations related to picture cards (TSCC; distinguishes nondistressed—no distress history, from distressed youths—psychiatric inpatients, outpatients, sexually abused, sexually aggressive, and court cases related to custody or abuse)	Gully, 2003a (PEAK Ascent, 4079 Diana Way, Salt Lake City, UT 84124; peakascent@comcast.net; www.peakascent.com)
A-DES (11–17)	.92 Split-half: .94		.77	Adolescent dissociative symptoms (distinguishes abused from nonabused youths and dissociative disordered from nonpsychotic diagnostic groups; higher scores for risk-taking, self-destructive, and lower competence youths)	Armstrong, Putnam, & Carlson, 1993 (Sidran Press, 1-888-825-8249; www.sidran.org)
CDC (5–12)	.86—.95 Split-half: .79–.94		.61–.73 1yr. 57–.92 s	Children's dissociative symptoms (P-report) (distinguishes nonabused from abused and psychiatric inpatient and sexually abused from physically abused; CI-report distinguishes some types of dissociative disorders)	Putnam & Peterson, 1994 (Frank Putnam, M.D.; Frank.Putnam@chmcc.org)
DFP				Children's dissociative symptoms (CI-report) (identifies 93% of a dissociative target group)	Silberg, 1996 (Sidran Institute, sidran@sidran.org)

CI = clinician; K = kappa; P = parent; r = correlations; s = subscales; yr = year
Sources: Armstrong, Putnam, Carlson, Libero, & Smith, 1997; de Decker, Hermans, Raes, & Eelen, 2003; Gully, 2000, 2003b, 2003c; Kisiel & Lyons, 2001; Putnam, Helmers, & Trickett, 1993; Putnam & Peterson, 1994; Silberg, 1996; Smith & Carlson, 1996.

(says, "I don't know"). After all 16 pictures are completed sequentially, for each picture rated negative or positive, the youth is reminded of what she or he expected and then asked if the child can stop the expected experience from happening or can make something else happen. Administration instructions, norms for 300 control youths, and the correlated associations for each of the possible feelings (scared, sad, angry, fine, happy) and expectations selected are provided in the manual (Gully, 2003b).

DISSOCIATION

Research has demonstrated that environmental factors, particularly stressful childhood experiences, contribute to the development of dissociation (Becker-Blease, Deater-Deckard, Eley, Freyd, Stevenson, & Plomin, 2004; Liotti, 2004; Pasquini, Liotti, Mazzotti, Fassone, & Picardi, 2002). Although dissociative symptoms occur without identifiable traumatic precursors, severe dissociative disorders such as dissociative identity disorder (DID) in children and adolescents have generally been attributed to severe stressors such as chronic physical and sexual abuse or, in some cases, to repeated surgical procedures or imitation of family dissociative disorders (Silberg, 1998b, 2004). Silberg (1998a) has observed a number of cases of DID in children without a history of trauma or related disorders. In these cases, youths experienced a series of events viewed as intolerable or threatening. The youths learned a pattern of avoidance to cope with the perceived stresses and binds characteristic of the situations. Mersky (1992) has suggested that multiple personality disorder (MPD, now DID) is a socially created artifact (cited in Silberg, 1998a). Nevertheless, Mersky has observed that children use imaginary friends and additional identities to deal with severe emotional conflict or to protect themselves from intolerable experiences. The prevalence of dissociative symptoms varies by culture and by age (Pole, Best, Metzler, & Marmar, 2005). Its many and changing definitions affect its assessment. The concern that interviewing and treatment techniques may compel dissociative behaviors or reports of dissociation from eager-to-please youths underscores the need for nonsuggestive and nonreinforcing questioning and intervention (Silberg, 1998a).

Functioning. Thomas (2005) suggests that even mild, fleeting dissociative episodes may signal vulnerability and an immediate need for protection. More intense dissociative episodes may portend intense feelings or perceptions of vulnerability or overwhelm. Dissociative behaviors that may have served effectively as a problem-solving strategy to psychologically "switch off" from traumatic experiences in childhood can become debilitating and may seriously impede healthy adult functioning (Sutton, 2004). Even mild dissociation can be disabling for trauma survivors. When they are dissociating, even basic protective actions are impossible. They are unable, for example, to leave a situation to buy time or to provide constructive reasons for refusal (Thomas). Thomas has observed that survivors typically, passively or superficially, acquiesce to challenge often through incongruent agreement signaled by a mixture of acquiescence and resistance messages. These behaviors may elicit a *challenger's* withdrawal or taking advantage. Frequent dissociation interferes with development "because it separates a child mentally from the contexts in which development occurs" (Haugaard, 2004; p. 149). Youths fail to learn and integrate academic and social skills. Their behaviors elicit criticism or rejection from others that may in turn trigger dissociation. High levels of dissociation are associated with increased aggression towards others and self-destructive behaviors (Putnam, Helmers, & Trickett, 1993).

Age and Dissociation

Data suggest that children are more dissociative than adults. Putnam (1997) and colleagues found, on average, dissociation is highest for 5 to 6 year olds; it declines with age through the seventh decade of life. Other researchers place the normal dissociative peak in late childhood or early adolescence followed by steady decline (Haugaard, 2004). In a study of twins and adoptive children for whom trauma history was not assessed, Becker-Blease et al. (2004) found that nonpathological dissociative symptoms were moderately stable from middle childhood through middle adolescence. Ogawa, Sroufe, Weinfield, Carlson, and Egeland (1997) observe that young children may normally exhibit dissociation in response to trauma because they tend to resolve conflict through fantasy play. With age, dissociative behaviors become less and less normative and are more likely to indicate a pathway to pathology. Research has shown that scores are moderately higher for late adolescents than for nonclinical adults and that individuals with PTSD often have clinically significant scores (Waller, Putnam, & Carlson, 1996).

Culture and Dissociation

Culture is an important factor in the assessment of dissociative symptoms. Dissociative behaviors that are normal in some cultures may be considered pathological in others (Kirmayer, Young, & Hayton, 1995; Westermeyer, 1987, 1990). Hindu and New Age meditative practitioners, for example, may seek states of altered awareness such as viewing life as though witnessing it from outside of oneself. Dissociative states serve as an indicator of evolvement in some cultures or religions. Hindu, New Age, and some Christian sects consider dissociated meditative experiences and visions as an indication of spirituality. On the other hand, expected cultural practices may mask relevant symptoms (Kirmayer et al.; see chapter 7 and "Dissociation as a Coping Mechanism," below).

Conceptual Focus

The manner in which clinicians and researchers define and view dissociation shapes the content of assessment measures and treatments. More than one and combined methods of treatment have assisted dissociative patients. Silberg's 2004 article highlights the role of family and environment in perpetuating dissociative disorders. In 2004, Loewenstein described "dissociation of the parent's badness" as the *ultimate dissociation* "most central to the treatment of dissociative psychopathologies" (p. 259). These foci, extracted from well-defined and successfully used methods, demonstrate how different emphases may affect treatment and assessment procedures and needs.

Predisposition to Dissociation

Silberg (1998a) points out that severe trauma is not a necessary or a sufficient condition to engender severe dissociative reactions (see also Waller et al., 1996). Researchers have attempted to delineate factors that comprise a predisposition to dissociation. Early theoreticians postulated that traumatized individuals used an innate hypnotic capability to self-hypnotize in order to cope with repeated traumas (Putnam, 1997). Although a substantial percentage of patients with dissociative disorders have an above-average hypnotic capacity, the correlations between measures of hypnotizability and those of dissociation have been low. Studies have demonstrated that absorption appears to be normally distributed throughout the population and accounts for most of the correlation between hypnosis and absorption scales (Putnam). Herman (1992c, 1997) reminds us that the capacity for induced trance or dissociative states is normally high in young children. Youths who have been regularly severely punished or abused may develop the ability to a fine art. They may learn to hide memories in complex amnesias, ignore pain, or induce hallucinations. These sometimes-deliberate behaviors may become automatic and involuntary. They may form separate personality fragments, each with its segmented memories, psychological functions, and personal names.

Silberg (1998a, 2004) summarized researchers' findings regarding the components of being dissociative-prone: (1) fantasy proneness, (2) well-developed imaginative ability, (3) a capacity for empathic perceptiveness, and (4) the capacity for trance induction. Empathic perceptiveness, the well-developed prowess or personality characteristic of readily intuiting the thoughts and affects of others (Kurcinka, 1998a; Silberg, 1998a), may be an asset under normal circumstances. Within a pathological family environment in which parents do not tolerate a youth's affective responses of sadness, anger, and disappointment, empathic perceptiveness may engender "the basic confusion about the nature of self and emotions which underlies dissociative disorders" (Silberg, 1998a, p. 6). Silberg adds to the list of dissociative-prone traits: symbolic and mimicry abilities and deficits in achieving flexible coping and adaptive skills (see also Putnam, 1997). Normal self-organizing skills permit the fluid and flexible movement between affective states without reliance on activation of separate identities (alters).

Defining Dissociation

The term *dissociation* has been used to describe a variety of phenomena. The term's changing definition(s) continue to be discussed by professionals treating trauma-related dissociative symptoms (Carlson, 2002; Ogawa et al., 1997). The diversity of theoretical stances or symptom definitions has implications for assessment and treatment.

Presentation

The many and varied presentations of dissociative symptoms and disorders may complicate attempts at definition, assessment, and prognosis. Dissociation has been defined as a normal characteristic of the psychobiology of human consciousness, an aspect of the hypnotic process, a response to overwhelming or traumatic circumstances (chapter 2), an intrapsychic defense, and a psychopathological disturbance that is a central feature of *DSM-IV* dissociative disorders and a criterion symptom for other *DSM-IV* disorder groups such as PTSD, ASD, or somatoform disorder (E. Carlson, personal communication, August 2002; Lowenstein, 2002). Symptoms may be pathological or nonpathological. They may refer to daily occurrences, an occurrence during trauma, or a style of functioning. Dissociative symptoms such as absorption and mild depersonalization occur in nonclinical contexts (Carlson, 1997). Dissociation may occur during overwhelming and intolerable episodes of trauma; portions of a traumatic experience may remain dissociated from consciousness and compartmentalized in memory (Carlson; Herman, 1992c, 1997; Sutton, 2004). Psychologists have referred to parallel streams of consciousness or divided attention as dissociation. Herman uses George Orwell's term, *doublethink,* to refer to the capacity to hold two contradictory beliefs simultaneously through dissociative alterations in consciousness. Individuals who have undergone prolonged war, captivity, or abuse may use this process (1) to live simultaneously in the trauma while moving through current circumstances or (2) to have hope and meaning despite ongoing danger of violence and a sense of helplessness. Carlson points out that dissociative symptoms are among PTSD reexperiencing (e.g., flashbacks) and numbing/avoidance (e.g., gaps in awareness) symptoms. Shifting between multiple self-states is normal (Silberg, 2004). Dissociation may become a style of adaptation. In one of its extremes, aspects of self separate into individual personalities (DID).

Continuum or Separate Typology?.

Psychopathological dissociation has been examined as a set of symptoms on a continuum from extreme to innocuous or as a completely separate construct that is inherently pathological (Ogawa et al., 1997). Scales that measure dissociation may change as dissociation becomes more clearly defined. The *continuum* versus *typology* debate is that either (1) pathological dissociators are fundamentally different from normal individuals or (2) a dissociative continuum exists that ranges from normal absorptions to fugue states (Putnam, 1997). Scales that emerged in the 1980s were based on the continuum theory: Dissociation occurred on a continuum ranging from minor normative dissociations (e.g., daydreaming) to psychiatric conditions (e.g., DID; Putnam et al., 1993). The fragmentations of consciousness and reductions of ordinary awareness characteristic of dissociation may occur as momentary confusion, blank spells, or memory lapses; as more unusual states such as trance or shock; or as extreme states such as fugues or personality alters (Thomas, 2005).

For adults, Waller et al. (1996) confirmed Janet's 19th century theory that individuals without mental illness rarely experience pathological dissociative symptoms. They concluded that there are two types of dissociation rather than a continuum of dissociative experiences from normal to pathological: (1) Nonpathological dissociative experiences represent a dissociative trait, and (2) pathological dissociative experiences represent a separate taxon or typology. Nonpathological dissociative symptoms such as absorption measure a dimensional construct. Pathological dissociation such as derealization/depersonalization, identity confusion, and amnesia, instead, tap a typological construct. The pathological dissociative class (taxon or typology) is identified using a brief questionnaire, the Dissociative Experiences Scale-Taxon (DES-T). Individuals not a part of the pathological dissociative class received moderate scores on the DES (but not on the DES-T) because of elevated scores on the nonpathological dissociative dimension (Waller et al.). Ogawa et al. (1997) found support for this separate pathological taxon for youths. Despite these findings, Putnam (1997) points out that each theory accounts for some of the variance in findings.

Some theorists divide dissociation into *negative* and *positive*, *psychoform* and *somatoform* symptoms (Nijenhuis, van der Hart, & Steele, 2002). Among *psychoform* dissociative symptoms are (1) *negative* or unintegrated dissociative systems of ideas and functions (Janet's "mental stigmata"): amnesia, depersonalization, and derealization, and (2) *positive* or retrieved systems without integration (Janet's "mental accidents"): reexperiencing memories or flashbacks, such as thoughts, images, and feelings or hearing voices (Laria & Lewis-Fernández, 2001; Nijenhuis et al.). *Somatoform* dissociative symptoms include motor inhibitions (e.g., paralysis, inability to feel parts of the body) and anesthesia of one or more sensory modalities (e.g., visual tunneling and haziness, deafness) and include pain, sexual sensations, flight, freeze, submissive states, and fight. Nijenhuis et al. have observed that many measures of dissociative symptoms do not include all of the symptoms.

Nonpathological Dissociation

In a workshop aimed at self-improvement, the speaker assigned attendees, as homework for the week, to meditatively recall each day of their lives beginning in infancy. At the end of the week, no one claimed to have been able to do so. Most individuals forget portions of their lives. Momentary confusions, divided attention, absorption, blank spells, state shifts, daydreams, fantasies, somatoform symptoms, mild depersonalization, and memory lapses are within normal experience. Individuals of all ages may compartmentalize aspects of memory and fail to integrate some emotions, experiences, or aspects of events. These minor to major dissociations may occur more easily when fatigued, distressed, overwhelmed, or threatened. Ogawa et al. (1997) suggest that, when trauma is so threatening that it overwhelms normal defenses, even the healthy self must resort to dissociation. In contrast to the *vulnerable self* (a child with weak defenses and a poorly integrated sense of self), the healthy self is able eventually to integrate disturbing experiences. Dissociations are of clinical and research focus when they impede functioning, thwart living, hamper relationships, follow experiences of interest (e.g., faulty attachments or traumas), or increase symptoms and reactions.

Dissociation as a Coping Mechanism

Dissociation has been identified as a coping mechanism in the face of overwhelming stress, trauma, or severe injury. In the early 20th century, Jung described dissociation as a normal part of the psyche's defenses against the potentially damaging effects of trauma (Kalsched, 1996). During a traumatic experience, the psyche may withdraw from the scene or experience of injury (Box 5.1b). When withdrawal is not possible, a part of the self must withdraw. Dissociation permits the mind or body to split off or compartmentalize pain, traumatic memories, or other disquieting thoughts from normal consciousness (Sutton, 2004). Kalsched states that dissociation can allow life to go on by dividing up the unbearable experience and distributing it to different mind and body compartments, especially those that are unconscious. Thus, generally unified elements of consciousness—imagery, affect, sensation, and cognitive awareness—are not allowed to integrate. A full and coherent narrative history becomes impossible because the memory has holes in it or because mental imagery, for example, is split off from affect.

Dissociation has been used to cope during horrible experiences such as rape, molestation, or torture. It is believed that certain imprisoned Tibetan monks' meditative training assisted their coping with torture by the Chinese (Laria & Lewis-Fernández, 2001). Dissociation is one method by which children separate abuse experiences from conscious awareness (Becker-Blease et al., 2004; Herman, 1997). Children have amnesias for difficult-to-bear segments of a traumatic event that are recoverable in a safe clinical setting (Box 14.1c). Dissociation's usefulness as a coping method also has been demonstrated by the clinical application of anxiety management techniques with a dissociative component: progressive muscle relaxation with visualizations and meditation techniques (Cohen, Berliner, & Mannarino, 2000; Meadows & Foa, 1998).

From Coping to Habit

Dissociation is a common response to disruption and stress in early childhood but, when persistent, is indicative of pathology in adolescence (Ogawa et al., 1997). Loewenstein (2004) points out that, although treatment is often based on the idea that dissociative conditions result as an "originally adaptive, protective intrapsychic process" that permits psychological survival and growth despite overwhelming circumstances, research on "peritraumatic dissociation" suggests its role in a poorer clinical outcome after trauma (p. 256). Peritraumatic dissociation—dissociation that occurs during or immediately after a traumatic experience—is one of the most robust predictors of PTSD (Pole et al., 2005). Dissociation may become a style of coping with stress (Box 14.1d). Sutton (2004) explains that, when used repeatedly as a problem-solving strategy in childhood, dissociation can develop into a conditioned response to any stressful situation. Regarding pathological dissociation, Silberg (2004) states, "Dissociative symptoms are complex adaptations that evolve into learned habits that are then reinforced in environments in which parent-child interaction patterns continue to promote and reinforce maladaptive functioning" (p. 487).

Pathological Dissociation

Pathological dissociation has been conceptualized as a disturbance in the integrative functions of identity, memory, and consciousness (APA, 1994; Putnam et al., 1993). In young children, the brain regions that include major integrative functions and the sense of self are immature (Nijenhuis et al., 2002; Putnam, 1997). The integrative functions and other brain functions can be hampered (and possibly injured) by the neurochemicals released during severe threat (De Bellis, Baum et al., 1999; De Bellis, Keshavan et al., 1999; Nijenhuis et al.; chapter 2).

Failure of Integration

Theoreticians suggest that dissociative patients are unable to manage inevitable conflicts that arise between self-states or roles (Ogawa et al., 1997; Silberg, 2004). Ogawa et al. explain the effects of failure of integration:

> When salient experience must be unnoticed, disallowed, unacknowledged, or forgotten, the result is incoherence in the self structure. Interconnections among experiences cannot be made, and the resulting gaps in personal history compromise both the complexity and the integrity of the self. Important meanings are lost (pp. 871-872).

Dissociative patients may have received conflicting messages, for example, that communicate simultaneously that the child is loved and that the child is a usable object (Silberg, 2004). Dissociative youths do not develop cohesive organization across shifts in emotional states nor easily process strong emotions and painful experiences. Dissociative symptoms are "manifestations of these integrative failures so that consciousness is erratic (trance states), relevant information is discarded (forgetfulness), and conflicting, unprocessed emotions dictate behavior (fluctuations in identity or behavior)" (p. 488). Dissociative processes interfere with the development of a coherent and developmentally appropriate sense of self (Haugaard, 2004).

Haugaard (2004) points out that most youths forget things but can recall them when prompted to do so. This has been proven true for traumatic experiences as well (Pynoos & Nader, 1989). Haugaard notes that for dissociative youths, it is as though the memories were never encoded. The lack of memory for experiences that others recall can be very confusing for the dissociative child and may be at the basis of depression or acting-out behaviors. Repeated confrontations can lead to a sense of helplessness and hopelessness.

Dissociative Disorders

Pathological forms of dissociation include *DSM-IV* DID, dissociative (D) fugue, D amnesia, D disorders not otherwise specified (DDNOS), and depersonalization disorder (DD) (APA, 1994; Carlson, 1997; Herman, 1992c, 1997; Sutton, 2004; Table 14.2). Dissociative symptoms such as amnesias are commonly found in adults with PTSD, ASD, and dissociative disorders. Dissociative *amnesia* denotes the inability to recall important information (beyond ordinary forgetfulness) regarding aspects of traumatic or highly stressful experience. Dissociative *fugue* combines amnesia, sudden travel, and identity confusion or the assumption of a new identity. Such fugues and total amnesias following traumas are considered to be rare (Carlson). *Depersonalization* disorder is characterized by severe distortions in perceptions of body and self. *Depersonalization* symptoms may occur after a single or prolonged trauma (Carlson; Herman). Adults have described feeling removed from their bodies or watching from a distance or have described "going through the motions" of rescue efforts or other posttrauma behaviors without feeling like they were actively directing their own behavior.

TABLE 14.2
Adult Dissociative Disorders

Disorder	Symptoms	Descriptors/Observable Behaviors
Dissociative amnesia	Persistent loss of memory of significant personal information, typically of a traumatic or stressful nature, not explained by normal absent-mindedness	Inability to recall information
Dissociative fugue	An abrupt, nonscheduled journey away from one's home or usual place of work, accompanied by a loss of memory of one's past, confusion over one's identity, or assuming a new identity	Identity confusion or lack of an identifiable past
Dissociative identity disorder	Most extreme form of dissociation; characterized by two or more separate identities or personality states that recurrently take control of the individual's behavior, accompanied by loss of memory of significant personal information not explained by normal absent-mindedness	Identity shifts; loss of segments of time
Depersonalization disorder	An unrelenting or frequent feeling of disconnection or detachment from oneself (mind-body split), during which reality testing remains intact	"Looking down on, inside, standing beside, or outside myself"; "blank spells"; floaty; foggy, dazed out, phased out, or zoned out; trance-like feeling
Derealization	A sense that the external world feels strange or unreal sometimes accompanies depersonalization	Feeling two-dimensional, strange, unreal; perceiving an uncanny alteration in the size and shape of objects
Dissociative disorder not otherwise specified	Disorder in which dissociative symptoms predominate but does not meet criteria for any specific dissociative disorder	Staring into space with inability to arouse

Sources: APA, 1994; Carlson, 1997; Herman, 1992c, 1997; Putnam, 1997; Sutton, 2004.

Adult dissociative symptoms have not always applied as readily to children and adolescents (Carlson, 1997). *DSM-IV* adult diagnostic categories do not clearly fit childhood manifestations of dissociation (Silberg, 2004; see Table 14.2). Children's dissociative symptoms may include trance-like states, forgetfulness for past or current behavior, fluctuating behavior including rapid regressions, rage reactions, vivid imaginary friends, divided identities, and depersonalization and derealization symptoms. Dissociative amnesias may be difficult to detect in very young children (Carlson). The dissociative fugues described for adults are unlikely for youths who are too young to travel. Children's dissociative disorders may be misdiagnosed as ADHD, mood disorders, or conduct disorders (Haugaard, 2004).

Dissociation and Self-Injury

Dissociative processes, particularly dissociative amnesia, depersonalization, and derealization, have been associated with self-injury such as cutting or burning self-mutilations (Herman, 1992c, 1997; Sutton, 2004). Many self-injurers describe feeling emotionally numb, detached from physical and mental processes, detached from themselves, or "dead inside." They may feel little or no pain during self-injury. Some self-injurers report feeling more alive, more grounded, or more real following self-inflicted injury (Sutton). An unbearable agitation and a compulsion to attack one's body may accompany derealization, depersonalization, and anesthesia (Herman). Self-injury may induce dissociation or diminish it (Sutton; see Table 1.3).

Environment and Dissociation

Parents and children repeatedly alter or influence each other's states of consciousness (Putnam, 1997; chapters 2, 8). Researchers have found an association between dissociative tendencies and environments that lack restorative experiences (Kluft, 1996), such as available parenting and emotional support from extended family, other adults, or peers (Becker-Blease et al., 2004; Ogawa et al., 1997).

Attachment

Loewenstein (2004) points out that, for the sake of survival, a child must form an attachment even if a caregiver is murderously abusive. A caregiver's abuse of an infant or his or her own previous trauma or loss around the time of an infant's birth has been linked to an infant's disorganized attachment (Hesse et al., 2003; Liotti, 2004; Pasquini et al., 2002). Ogawa et al. (1997) found a relationship between both infants' disorganized and anxious/avoidant attachment styles and dissociation. Anxious/avoidant infants were more likely than anxious/ambivalent or securely attached infants to have high dissociation in elementary school and dur-

TABLE 14.3
Alerting Signs for Possible Childhood Dissociative Disorders

Category of Behavior	Indicators of Possible Dissociative Disorders (If beyond Normal Frequency and Intensity)
Out of touch (lack of awareness of environment)	Trance-like states; spacing out; dazed; daydreaming; prolonged staring; intense absorption in books, TV shows, or movies; out of touch from schoolwork or activities; sleep-walking
Memory lapses/amnesias (inability to recall even when prompted)	Forgetfulness for past or current behavior, segments of time, where items appeared from, or how he or she got to a location; denies behaviors observed by others and may be adamant or perplexed by their disbelief of the denial; unexplained changes in a youth's environment such as items' arrangement, appearance, and disappearance; failure to remember developed skills
Fluctuations in behavior (dramatic changes in skills, style, and preferences)	Rapid age regressions; dramatic variability in school performance; inability to complete a task that was easy before; dramatic changes in preferences for food, clothes, activities, projects, etc.; inconsistencies in language, voice quality, accent, handwriting, and demeanor; significant changes in attitude toward people and situations; dramatic differences in responses to questions or pictures (such as psychological tests)
Parts of self (separate identities)	Vivid imaginary friends well into school years; divided identities; hearing voices inside his or her head that are engaged in arguments; blames a separate identity for undesirable behaviors or emotional outbursts
Impulsive or self-destructive	Sudden rage reactions; unprovoked aggression; risk-taking; suicideality; self-mutilation
Depersonalization/derealization	Complaints of a sense of unreality of self/environment; out-of-body experiences or watching self as if watching someone else; feeling split into observed and observer; internal dialogue between voices without external alters
Other symptoms	Sleep disturbance; constantly on edge and checking dates/times
Peer reactions	Child does not know why several relationships end suddenly or people are angry with him or her; the child is periodically called by other names, often by people that he or she does not recall meeting; peers think he or she is strange; peers may ignore or reject the child in response to fluctuations in and unusual behaviors

Sources: Carlson, 1997; Haugaard, 2004; Putnam, 1997; Silberg, 1998a, 1998b, 2004.

ing adolescence. Infants who exhibited disorganized attachment styles more often had high dissociation scores in adolescence and young adulthood. As Susman-Stillman, Kalkose, Egeland, & Waldman (1996) point out, youths with avoidant attachment styles have learned to cope with rejection by defensively excluding feelings and information that activate the attachment system (cited in Ogawa et al.). These youths may, however, have more mature defense mechanisms by young adulthood. Longitudinal studies have linked persistent dissociation to disorganized attachments (Weinfield, Sroufe, Egeland, & Carlson, 1999).

Adults given a classification of *unresolved trauma* (chapter 8) evidence dissociation in either a level of mental absorption that hampers attention to the external environment or in a sudden lack of continuity in discourse, thought, or behavior (Hesse et al., 2003; Liotti, 2004). The adult may suddenly discontinue speech and stare into a void for seconds or for minutes, nonresponsive to queries or attempts to arouse. A previously traumatized adult might suddenly utter fragmented, incoherent comments about intrusive trauma-related mental images. In the most extreme variety of dissociation, an alternate ego state may appear. This pattern of dissociation may be transgenerational. During the Strange Situation interview (chapter 8), infants rated *disorganized* also demonstrate dissociative-like behaviors (Liotti). For 30 seconds or longer in the middle of approaching the parent, these infants may suddenly become immobile with a blank look and be unresponsive to the parent's call. Infants may exhibit contradictory movement patterns, as if pursuing two incompatible goals. Infants may engage in an aggressive gesture with an unusual facial expression in the middle of a display of affection. They may interrupt pleasant interactions with the parent and suddenly assume a dazed or trancelike expression, strike at the parent's face or eyes, and then resume affectionate behavior. Ogawa et al. (1997) found that elevated dissociative symptoms at age 19 were best predicted by disorganized attachment between 12 and 18 months and mother's psychological unavailability between 0 and 24 months.

Environmental Reinforcement

Dissociative disorders are created and sustained within an interpersonal context (Silberg, 1998a). Recognizing the interpersonal nature of symptoms and their preservation may be essential to the assessment and recovery process, especially for youths (Loewenstein, 2004; Silberg, 2004). Families may engage in complex reinforcing patterns (Silberg, 1998a). Particular behavioral states may be demanded in response to specific family stimuli. For dissociative youths, the patterns of response have become ingrained and persistent. Silberg (1998a) points out that clinicians may also reinforce dissociative patterns by oversubscribing to the belief in a child's *alters* (alternate personalities) or by too rigidly following an adult treatment model. Silberg (1998a) provides guidelines to help avoid these reinforcing behaviors.

Dissociation and Its Associations

Dissociation has been highly correlated with somatic symptoms in those suffering from PTSD or who have histories of sexual abuse or multiple hospitalizations (Laria & Lewis-Fernández, 2001). Studies of twins and adoptive children have permitted investigation of the relative contribution to nonpathological dissociative symptoms of genetic, shared environmental, and nonshared environmental factors. Findings among studies have been mixed (Becker-Blease et al., 2004). A number of variables are linked to the severity of dissociation.

Circumstances. Among the factors found in association with the severity of dissociation following traumatic events are the age at onset, chronicity, and severity of traumatization as well as disorganized and avoidant patterns of attachment (Nijenhuis et al., 2002; Ogawa et al., 1997). The number of *violent* perpetrators has been implicated in the development of dissociative symptoms (Trickett, Noll, Reiffman, & Putnam, 2001; Lyons-Ruth, Zeanah, & Benoit, 2003). Traumatic experiences during infancy and childhood have proven to be strong risk factors for dissociative disorders (DDs; Pasquini et al., 2002). For a group composed primarily of adults (52 with DDs; 146 controls), Pasquini et al. found that individuals with a history of infant or childhood trauma were more than 7 times as likely to develop one of the DDs than others. Individuals whose parent had experienced a severe life event within 2 years of their birth were 2 times as likely to develop one of the DDs.

Mixed findings regarding the effects of early onset of trauma on dissociation may reflect the confounding of early onset and chronicity (Ogawa et al., 1997). Most studies show that sexual abuse, especially severe sexual abuse, has the predominant effect on dissociation (Kisiel and Lyons, 2001). Kisiel and Lyons found, however, that *severity* of sexual abuse for a group of 106 youths (ages 10 to 18) with histories of various types of severe abuse (physical, sexual, neglect, or combined) was not associated with dissociation or psychopathology. The group studied reported only nonpathological dissociation. Higher levels of dissociation were reported for sexual than for physical abuse. Dissociation appeared to mediate problematic outcomes for sexual abuse such as self-mutilation, sexual aggression, and suicidality. Dissociation was associated with higher levels of symptoms, increased risk-taking behaviors, and lower levels of competent functioning.

Age Links. Ogawa et al. (1997) followed 126 low-income youths from infancy to young adulthood (age 19). Lower infant IQ and sexual abuse predicted higher dissociation when youths were toddlers. If the mother was abused as a child or single at the child's birth, the youth was more likely to have dissociative symptoms in elementary school. Infant and concurrent physical abuse predicted higher dissociative symptoms in elementary school. Elevated dissociation in adolescence was predicted by disorganized or avoidant infant attachment style, witnessing interpersonal violence in infancy, and concurrent physical abuse. Infant's attention span, parent's unavailability in the child's infancy, and infant disorganized attachment style were associated with dissociative symptoms in young adulthood. Correlations between self measures and dissociation for the group with later-onset abuse (in elementary school or adolescence) lent some support for the hypothesis that a stronger sense of self in the face of trauma served as a protective factor for later dissociation.

Dissociation Scales

The Child Dissociation Checklist (CDC), the Adolescent Dissociative Experiences Scale (A-DES), and the Dissociative Features Profile (DFP) are presented here. These scales are, respectively, a caregiver-report measure, a youth-report measure, and a clinician-evaluation measure. As Kisiel and Lyons (2001) have pointed out, the measures may reflect separate constructs. Different informants may be better able to observe different aspects of youths' reactions. Ogawa et al. (1997) observe that it is difficult for an outside source to assess experiences such as derealization and depersonalization. Although some studies have shown a correlation between the two measures (Friedrich, Gerber et al., 2001), Kisiel and Lyons found that the A-DES and the CDC were not highly correlated with one another. Although there were some cross-informant relationships, the two measures were primarily associated with outcomes reported by the same informant.

The Adolescent Dissociative Experiences Scale (ADES)
Age range: 11–17
Translations: Numerous
Format: Semistructured interview or adolescent completion

A-DES (v. 1.0; Armstrong, Putnam, & Carlson, 1993) is a 30-item self-report measure designed to assess four areas of youths' dissociation: dissociative amnesia, passive influence, depersonalization and derealization, and absorption and imaginative involvement (Armstrong, Putnam, Carlson, Libero, & Smith, 1997). It uses a 10-point rating scale (Never to Always). Initial studies suggest a mean item score for the 30 items of 4.8 for dissociative adolescents with a standard deviation of 1.1. The authors suggest a mean item score above 3.7 warrants additional evaluation for dissociative disorders.

The Child Dissociative Checklist (CDC)
Age range: 5–12
Translations: Numerous
Format: Caretaker or other observer completion

CDC (V3.0-2/1990; Putnam et al., 1993; Putnam & Peterson, 1994) is a 20-item adult-report instrument that adds 4 items to version V2.0 (Putnam, 1985). The CDC measures the following: (1) dissociative amnesias; (2) rapid shifts in the following: demeanor, access to information, knowledge, abilities, and age appropriateness of behavior; (3) spontaneous trance states; (4) hallucinations; (5) alterations in identity; and (6) aggressive and sexual behavior (Putnam et al., 1993). A CDC score of 12 or higher is highly suggestive of significant dissociative psychopathology (Putnam & Peterson; Putnam et al., 1993; Putnam, Helmers, Horowitz, & Trickett, 1995). Observable behaviors are rated using a three-point scale (2 = Very true, 1 = Somewhat or sometimes true, and 0 = Not true) that best describes the child's behavior on a given item over the past 12 months (Putnam et al., 1993; Putnam & Peterson). Scores range from 0 to 40. Mean scores reported for sexually abused girls were established at 6 ±6.4 and, for comparison girls, 2.3 ± 2.7 (Putnam et al., 1993; for ages 7 to 13, Malinosky-Rummel & Hoier, 1991). Higher scores were found in a psychiatric inpatient population (ages 4 to 12; Wherry, Jolly, Feldman, Adam, & Manjanatha, 1994). Scores vary somewhat by dissociative disorder (Putnam & Peterson).

The Dissociative Features Profile (DFP)
Age range: 5–17
Format: Clinician completion

DFP (Silberg, 1996) has been used clinically to help identify specific dissociative pathology in children and adolescents. DFP is used in combination with at least two other measures (e.g., projective and IQ tests). It is not recommended for use as a sole diagnostic instrument for dissociative disorders. It consists of two parts (Part I: Behaviors and Part II: Markers). The behaviors section notes the patient's unusual behaviors or presentations (e.g., amnesia, staring, anger, odd movements, fluctuations, fearfulness, dividedness, physical complaints) during the testing. The markers section describes actual test responses (e.g., multiplicity, dissociative coping, torture, transformation, mutilation, religiosity). Predictive validity improves when both parts of the measure are used, but Part II (markers) may be used alone. A one-page reference guide elaborates procedures for scoring of weighted items. The dissociative disorder cutoff score is 15. The scales' use in clinical assessment is described by its author (see Silberg, 1998b).

CONCLUSIONS

Changes in attention, attributions, memory, interpretation, and response search and selection may follow traumatic experiences. Posttrauma impairments in information processing and the integration of representations may lead to faulty relationships, aggression, depression, anxiety, dissociation, or other symptoms. Trauma-related role assumptions and attributions may be a part of disrupted information processing. Youths may feel compelled to enact problematic expectations, attitudes, and behaviors when processing these roles that are observed, desired, or experienced during a traumatic event. Temperamental traits and brain hemispheric tendencies affect the assessment of biased attention.

Many measures of dissociation do not include all types of dissociation. Evidence suggests that nonpathological and pathological dissociation constitute separate typologies rather than a continuum of dissociative experiences. Dissociation used as a coping mechanism may become pathological when it becomes habitual and severe. Trauma and disorganized and avoidant attachments have been linked to the severity of dissociation. Dissociation is associated with increased symptoms such as self-mutilation, sexual and other aggression, suicidality, increased risk-taking, and lower levels of competent functioning.

15

Assessing Comorbidity and Additional Symptoms

Psychopathology can be broadly defined as "impairment in the individual's established, or expected, roles at a given developmental period . . . typically accompanied by reports of emotional distress" (Ingram & Price, 2001, p. 6). A specific disorder may be reached through a variety of different conditions and processes (epifinality); the same vulnerability processes may lead to no or different types of disorders for different individuals (multifinality). PTSD captures only limited aspects of posttraumatic psychopathology (van der Kolk & Courtois, 2005). Youths may respond to their traumatic experiences with disorders, symptoms, and/or patterns of thought and behavior other than those described in the *DSM* diagnostic criteria of PTSD (Nader, 2001b). Accurate diagnosis is important to successful interventions. Research suggests that treatments for simple PTSD may not be applicable to PTSD with comorbid disorders (Ford, Courtois, Steele, van der Hart, & Nijenhuis, 2005; van der Kolk, Roth, Pelcovitz, Sunday, & Spinazzola, 2005). Some of the instruments designed for youths that measure behaviors, symptoms, disorders, and attitudes associated with traumatic response are described in this chapter. The scales and interviews are listed by category: comorbidity, attitudes toward life, and child behaviors.

Childhood Adversities and Adult Comorbidity

Most studies focus on one disorder without taking into account the frequent comorbidity of disorders and the effects of disorder combinations on the nature of response and recovery (Kessler, 2000). Studies have demonstrated substantial comorbidity among adult psychiatric disorders (de Graaf, Bijl, ten Have, Beekman, & Vollebergh, 2004). PTSD presents with high rates of comorbidity (Kessler, 2000). When studies control for lifetime comorbidities, the effects of a variety of adversities, whether or not they meet PTSD Criterion A, are distinguished more by similarities than differences. Retrospective studies have consistently found that adults with psychiatric disorders significantly more often than others report exposure to childhood adversities (Kessler, Davis, & Kendler, 1997). Such adversities often occur in clusters. Kessler et al. found that the effects of particular adverse events are not confined to any one class of disorders. Comorbidity between mood and anxiety disorders is particularly common; mood disorders most often arise after anxiety disorders (de Graaf et al.). Neuroticism (chapter 6), childhood trauma, and parental (especially maternal) psychiatric history have been more strongly associated with comorbidity than with solitary disorders (de Graaf et al.; Kessler et al.). De Graaf et al. found that difficulties functioning were more strongly associated with comorbid than with single disorders. Women were more likely than men to develop anxiety or mood disorders and less likely to develop substance abuse disorders.

Course and Severity. Comorbidity can have a substantial impact on the course and severity of PTSD (Kimerling, Prins, Westrup, & Lee, 2004). In addition to explicitly trauma-related disorders, the many other symptoms and disorders associated with an adult's history of trauma include dissociative, depression, substance abuse (SUD), anxiety, personality (PD), psychotic, and medical disorders (Gold, 2004; Kimerling et al.). For women (in order of frequency), major depression, simple or social phobias, and SUD have been identified as the most common comorbid disorders (Kimerling et al.). For men, SUD, major depression, and conduct disorders are most common. Sexual dysfunction is frequent for both genders whether or not the trauma was sexual in nature.

Directionality. The relationship between other disorders and PTSD may be bidirectional (Carlson, 1997). Disorders may occur because trauma places individuals at increased risk of psychological disorders; psychological disorders may render individuals at increased risk of traumatization after exposure to extreme experiences. For example, depression is both a possible result of PTSD and a risk factor for the development of PTSD (Kimerling et al., 2004). Major life events including exposure to trauma are important in the etiology of depression and may, in part, explain gender differences in the development of PTSD. In the general population, depressive disorders are more common among women, and substance abuse disorders are more common among men.

Medical Disorders. Stress has been associated with increased medical disease (Kimerling et al., 2004; Schnurr & Jankowski, 1999). For adults, PTSD has been linked to increased cardiovascular, pain, gastrointestinal, and reproductive disorders as well as increased risk of sexually transmitted disease, cancer, and chronic lung disease. Women with histories of childhood traumas are at increased risk of gynecological disorders

(Kimerling et al.). Although more study is needed to determine any pre-existing toxic exposures (or trauma-related exposures), habits, or vulnerabilities and propensities that may contribute to these ailments, the diseases' prevalence among PTSD groups suggests its important role in vulnerability to these conditions (see chapter 2). PTSD is also associated with a poorer course for diseases.

Age, Traits, and Comorbid Disorders

Although findings are often mixed, specific symptoms and disorders tend to increase or decrease in likelihood with age, ethnicity, temperament, or family circumstances (Malcarne & Hansdottir, 2001). Age-related changes result from changes in brain chemistry or cognitive processes. Behaviors that are normal at one age can be pathological at another. Personality disorders, which have been associated with childhood traumas as well as specific emotional and environmental characteristics (Krug, 1996), provide an example. The narcissistic tendencies, antisocial behaviors, and immature sense of self that are characteristic of PD are normal behaviors for adolescents. Research findings suggest that measures of PD in adolescents may not be tapping the same constructs as adult measures (Geiger & Crick, 2001). Separation anxiety disorder and symptoms decrease with increasing age. Panic disorder and agoraphobia are rare before the onset of puberty. Several studies have found that social phobias or combined social phobias and overanxious disorder are more common among African Americans than Caucasians. School refusal, in contrast, was more common among Caucasians than African Americans. Studies of youths have demonstrated an association between Gray's Behavioral Inhibition System (BIS) prominence or Kagan's inhibited type (chapter 6; Kagan, Snidman, & Arcus, 1995; Martin & Bridger, 1999; Rothbart & Bates, 1998) and later anxiety disorders (Biederman et al., 1993; Caspi, Henry, McGee, Moffitt, & Silva, 1995; Caspi, Moffitt, Newman, & Silva, 1996; Malcarne & Hansdottir). Evidence supports a genetic role for some anxiety disorders such as phobic disorders, but not for others such as PTSD (Malcarne & Hansdottir).

TRAUMA, COMORBIDITY, AND CHILDREN

Comorbidity is a term used to describe the occurrence, more often than expected by chance, of a second condition with the first or studied condition (Silberstein, 2001; Table 15.1). When symptoms of the two disorders overlap, diagnosis may be confounded. Alternate and comorbid diagnoses among traumatized children have recently become the subject of more in-depth focus. Among the disorders found in association with PTSD are attention-deficit disorder (ADD), attention-deficit/hyperactivity disorder

(ADHD), conduct disorder (CD), oppositional defiant disorder (ODD), depressive disorders (e.g., major or not otherwise specified), phobias (e.g., social or specific), and anxiety disorders (e.g., separation, panic) (Carrion, Weems, Ray, & Reiss, 2002; Cicchetti, 2003b; Ford, 2002; Greenwald, 2002b; Udwin, Boyle, Yule, Bolton, & O'Ryan, 2000; Weinstein, Staffelbach, & Biaggio, 2000). In addition to the comorbid disorders found in traumatized children are disorders diagnosed in adulthood (e.g., antisocial personality disorder, borderline personality disorder, generalized anxiety disorder, and multiple personality or dissociative identity disorder) that have correlations with childhood traumatic experiences (Krug, 1996). For both youths and adults, substance abuse, dissociative, and eating disorders have been associated with childhood traumas (Pasquini, Liotti, Mazzotti, Fassone, & Picardi, 2002).

Some disorders, such as depression and anxiety, are commonly comorbid for youths and adults in both clinic and nonclinic samples (Malcarne & Hansdottir, 2001). As noted above, PTSD often precedes the development of depressive disorders. In a study of youths exposed to a hurricane (La Greca, Silverman, Vernberg, & Prinstein, 1996), predisaster anxiety levels predicted PTSD 3 and 7 months after the disaster. This suggests that other anxiety disorders may predispose youths to developing PTSD (Cohen & Mannarino, 2004). Some disorders may appear to be comorbid, but may have different courses. Kinzie, Boehnlein, & Sack (1998) found depression and PTSD in Cambodian refugee youths. In a 6-year follow-up study, although their depression greatly decreased over time, PTSD remitted only slightly. In addition to their PTSD symptoms, for 72% of them, ongoing distress included continued worry about family left in

TABLE 15.1
Mechanisms that May Explain Comorbidity

Mechanism	Explanation
Coincidence or artifact	It may be coincidental that the two disorders occur in proximity to each other. Individuals who visit a physician's office or clinic tend to have more than one disorder. The disorders may not be considered comorbid.
Causation	One disorder may cause the other. The contribution of one disorder to the other may be unidirectional or bidirectional.
Environmental or genetic	The two conditions may share environmental or genetic etiologies.
Predisposition	Independent factors such as personality, environmental, or genetic risk factors may predispose an individual to a state resulting in both conditions.

Based on information from Silberstein, 2001.

Cambodia, and for close to a third of them, family conflict over doing things the Cambodian versus the American way persisted.

Overlapping Symptoms

A number of overlapping symptoms among disorders may make differential diagnosis difficult (Table 15.2 and 15.3). For *DSM* disorders, a PTSD diagnosis, if possible, supercedes other diagnoses when symptoms are directly related to PTSD Criterion A experiences (APA, 1994). PTSD may present with symptoms similar to other disorders, or the two disorders may coexist. Depressive and anxiety disorder symptoms overlap considerably (APA, 1994; Cohen & Mannarino, 2004; Ingram & Price, 2001; Kimerling et al., 2004). Like PTSD, obsessive-compulsive disorders include hypervigilance and intrusive thoughts (Cohen & Mannarino). Dissociative symptoms such as disorganized behavior, flat affect, and social withdrawal may have a similar presentation to psychotic disorders. Under certain conditions, severely traumatized youths may be particularly likely to display transient psychotic symptoms. Severely traumatized abused or incarcerated and tortured youths, for example, may display psychotic symptoms when frightened by being restrained in an inpatient psychiatric unit (Cohen & Mannarino). Table 15.2 relates the overlap in possible symptoms of trauma and other disorder categories. Sleep disturbance, difficulties concentrating, and diminished interest in activities are symptoms shared by PTSD and depression (Kimerling et al.). Health disorders may also influence symptoms or have overlapping symptoms such as confusion, agitation, poor concentration, periods of dissociation, depression, or anxiety.

Scales and Differential Diagnosis

Although many standardized psychological tests have now added trauma subscales, most were not developed at a time when psychological trauma was well-recognized. Such measures often underidentify or distort trauma effects (Briere & Elliott, 1997). Briere and Elliott note that older instruments (or faulty interpretations of them) may, for example, (1) confuse intrusive or reliving PTSD symptoms with hallucinations, obsessions, primary process, or faked responses; (2) misidentify dissociative avoidance as chaotic internal states, fragmented thinking, or signs of schizophrenia; and (3) misinterpret hypervigilance or generalized distrust as evidence of paranoia or other delusional processes. Nonschizophrenic PTSD patients with or without dissociation may rate high on signs of schizophrenia because life may become irrational, illogical, and confusing following traumas (Holaday, 2000; chapter 12). When they involve chaotic internal states, interpersonal difficulties, and tension-reduction or other affect-avoidance behaviors and activities, the effects of childhood trauma have been mislabeled as personality disorders. Scales presented

TABLE 15.2
Risk Factors and Overlap of Comorbid Disorders with PTSD

Disorder	Risk Factors*	Possible Overlap with PTSD Symptoms
Anxiety disorders	Slow to habituate in infancy; fearful/inhibited temperament; diminished sense of control over events or situations; neurochemical and affect dysregulation; insecure resistant attachment; social withdrawal and avoidance; genetic predisposition	Anxiety; avoidance; diminished sense of control over events or situations; neurochemical and affect dysregulation; social withdrawal and avoidance
Attention disorders	Information processing deficits; variability in negative mood and in arousal; problems in maintaining attention; attention allocated to fewer stimuli; distractibility; impulsivity; difficulty processing emotional cues; difficulty planning; poor social competence; poor problem-solving; irregular metabolism of monamines; lower dopamine; underarousal of reticular activation system	Attention deficits; hypervigilance; impulsiveness; variability in negative mood and arousal; difficulty planning; difficulty processing cues and information; lack of social competence
Conduct disorders	Lack of empathy; poor self-control/impulsivity; hostile attributions to others/the world; aggressive/hostile attribution bias; low self-esteem; increased anger or depression; emotional intensity and lability; avoidant insecure attachments and relationships; lack of social competence/social failure; poor problem-solving skills; social rejection; neurological or genetic predisposition; noradrenergic and serotonergic deficits; history of family mental illness or substance abuse, ADHD; parental psychopathology; socioeconomic disadvantage; affiliation with deviant peers	Dysregulation of affect; neurochemical responses; emotional intensity and lability; impulsivity; attributional biases; lack of social competence; increased anger or depression; low self-esteem; emotional intensity and lability; affiliation with deviant peers
Mood disorders	Shy temperament; learned helplessness; negative or otherwise dysfunctional attributional biases toward self and others; anxious insecure attachments; withdrawal; genetic predisposition; HPA axis dysfunction	Social estrangement or avoidance; lack of interest in activities; learned helplessness; attributional biases; withdrawal; HPA axis dysfunction
Personality disorders	Poor emotion regulation skills; negative home environment (e.g., abuse, violence, disorganization); avoidant insecure attachment; negative emotionality; attention problems; lack of empathy; perfectionism combined with maladaptive evaluation tendencies; relational aggression; faulty information processing; poor interpersonal competence; reduced emotional responsiveness	Emotional dysregulation; restricted range of affect; attention problems; faulty information processing; aggression; poor interpersonal competence; reduced or overreactive emotional responsiveness; negative emotions

*Any of the risk factors may occur in combination with specific other risk or environmental factors to increase the likelihood of pathology.
Sources: Cassidy & Shaver, 1999; Ford, 2002; Geiger & Crick, 2001; Greenwald, 2002b; Ingram & Price, 2001; Price & Lento, 2001; Weinfield, Sroufe, Egeland, & Carlson, 1999.

TABLE 15.3
Symptoms in Common: PTSD and Comorbid Disorders*

Disorder	Symptoms Associated with the Disorder that May Occur In Traumatized Youth
Attention-deficit disorder (ADD) or ADHD	Memory and learning difficulties; problems in maintaining attention; distractibility; impulsivity; difficulties processing information; variability in mood and arousal; difficulty processing emotional cues; difficulty planning; poor time sense; poor social competence; poor problem-solving; appears not to listen when spoken to; may not follow through on tasks or may not finish schoolwork or other tasks; loses things; forgetful; fidgety; difficulty engaging in activities; low frustration tolerance; temper outbursts; demoralization; dysphoria; poor self-esteem; rejection by peers; poor self-control; underperforming relative to ability
Borderline personality disorder (BPD)	Suspiciousness or transient, stress-related paranoid ideation; hostile attribution bias; dissociative symptoms; unstable self-image, lacking or negative sense of self; impulsivity; marked reactivity of mood; intense, unstable, and inappropriate emotional expression; increased sensitivity to stressful events or misinterpretation of events; outbursts of anger; paralyzing anxiety; excessive dependency; heightened emotionality about relationships; fears of abandonment
Conduct disorder (CD)	Aggression; hostile/aggressive attributions to others; PTSD; social detachment, emotional numbing, and hypervigilance; may appear to be callously indifferent to the rights of others; anger; depression; insecure relationships and attachments; low self-esteem; low frustration tolerance; irritability; temper outbursts; recklessness; early-onset sexual behavior; initiates fights or bullies others; may be truant from school; destruction of property; use of alcohol or drugs
Major depression (MD)	Depressed mood; faulty appraisal of self and others; low self-esteem; withdrawal; increased sensitivity to stressful events; irritability; sleep disturbance; excessive crying; sadness; sense of emptiness, worthlessness, and/or hopelessness; fatigue or low energy; suicidal ideation; poor appetite or overeating; difficulty concentrating or making decisions; decreased interest or pleasure in activities; may also be anxious, agitated, or listless; excessive guilt feelings
Oppositional defiant disorder (ODD)	Oppositional behaviors; negative, hostile behaviors (e.g., arguing with authority figures, frequently losing temper, defiance); low self-esteem; mood lability; low frustration tolerance; oppositional defiance to engage in specific activities may represent traumatic avoidance; PTSD hypervigilance may give rise to the resentful suspiciousness common to ODD; irritable, touchy, or easily annoyed by others; angry and resentful; high reactivity; difficulty being soothed; substance abuse; low self-esteem; low frustration tolerance

*In some cases, differences exist in the normal prevalence of behaviors by age and type of trauma.
Sources: APA, 1994; Barkley, 2003; Ford, 2002; Geiger & Crick, 2001; Hammen & Rudolph, 2003; Holaday, 2000; Price & Lento, 2001.

here provide information useful to an overall clinical picture that may not be provided by PTSD scales. The scales have been well-tested and may include PTSD scales.

Validity Scales. Lie or validity scales in measures of trauma may or may not be useful in assessing trauma in youths. Gordon (2002) points out that lie scales on psychological tests are often about defenses in general, and not about the specific credibility of reporting or testimony. Briere and Elliott (1997) note that individuals who have experienced interpersonal victimization tend to have more deviant scores on validity scales, thereby decreasing their usefulness. Rather than motivate to overendorse symptoms, chronic posttraumatic difficulties or comorbid affective symptoms may result in elevated validity or lie scale scores for those with severe traumas.

The Child and Adolescent Psychiatric Assessment (CAPA)
Age range: 9–17
Parent interview: PAPA (ages 6–17)
Format: Semistructured with structured questions and ratings
Relevant subscales: Family Structure; Life Events; PTSD; other disorders
Training: Required

CAPA (v. 4.2; Angold, Cox, Prendergast, Rutter, & Simonoff, 2000) combines both respondent- and interviewer-based methods of assessment. It is based on *DSM-III, DSM-IV, ICD-9*, and *ICD-10* glossaries as well as a variety of additional symptoms of psychopathological interest (e.g., among PTSD symptoms: emotional responses, somatic responses, intervention fantasies). The interviewer's conversational style in an introductory section is designed to establish rapport, elicit an overall picture of any problems, and gain a picture of the child's life (e.g., home and family life, school life, peer groups, and spare-time activities). Items that children do not report accurately (e.g., attention-deficit/hyperactivity disorders, delusions, hallucinations, and thought disorders) have been omitted from the child interview. Items that are involved in more than one diagnosis, such as sleep disturbance, are represented in only one place. Symptoms are rated for intensity, frequency, and duration on scales from two up to five points (e.g., 0 = Absent; 2 = Present to a specified degree; 3 = More pervasively or intensely present as defined) (Angold et al., 2000; Angold, Prendergast, Cox, Harrington, Simonoff, & Rutter, 1995). The reference period is 3 months unless *DSM* criteria require otherwise. A symptom is counted whether reported by parent or child (Costello, Angold, March, & Fairbank, 1998). After a symptom has been thoroughly investigated (e.g., context, aggravating and ameliorating factors, and consequences of the symptom; observation of the child in the interview), all the information obtained is used to match the subject's symptom description (i.e., behavior, emotion, or thought) to detailed glossary definitions and levels of severity. Questions are asked verbatim. The interviewer continues appropriate questioning until all the necessary information for making a rating has been obtained. There are three levels of questions. "Screening questions" serve as entry points to certain sections of the interview. If the screening question is convincingly negative, there is no need for additional questioning regarding the specific symptom. If, however, the subject changes his or her mind or provides contradictory information, the interviewer returns to the appropriate sections (Angold et al., 1995).

With regard to an event established as traumatic by three screening symptoms, the PTSD section of CAPA first asks about acute emotional (e.g., surprise, helplessness, derealization, feeling out of control) and somatic (e.g., dizziness, dry mouth, rapid breathing, trembling) responses and about fantasies of intervention, rescue, or revenge (Angold et al., 2000; Costello et al., 1998). It then explores, in much more detail, symptoms of the three main *DSM* symptom criteria (B, C, and D; APA, 1994), coping responses (e.g., normal, obsessional, compulsive), and additional symptoms (e.g., guilt, religious beliefs, risk-taking behaviors). Date of onset is reported for each symptom (*DSM* Criterion D). To be coded as present, distress (*DSM Criterion F*) is a necessary consequence of most symptoms. Assessment of impairment (Criterion F) in the ability to function normally with adults (i.e., parents, teachers, others), siblings, or peers is also included (Angold et al.; Costello et al.).

The Missouri Assessment of Genetics Interview for Children (MAGIC)
Age range: 7–12, 13–18
Translations: English, Spanish, Indian Kannada
Relevant subscales: Home Environment; Sibling Relations; Peer Relations; Psychosocial Stressors; Perinatal and Early Life; PTSD; other disorders
Format: Semistructured interview
Training: Required

MAGIC is a new version of the Diagnostic Interview for Children and Adolescents (DICA; Reich, Herjanic, Welner, & Gandhy, 1982; Herjanic & Reich, 1982; Reich, 2000; Reich & Kaplan, 1994). MAGIC includes both *DSM-III-R* and *DSM-IV* disorders. Each version of MAGIC includes age-specific language and examples: child (ages 7 to 12); adolescent (13 to 17); young adult (18 to 25); adult (26+); parent (parents reports on their children ages 7 to 17). A number of rating scales are used. For example, length of time (e.g., in days, weeks, or months), frequency (e.g., number of times), and intensity of disruption scales (e.g., 1 = Not at all, 2 = Not too much, 3 = Somewhat, 4 = Quite a bit) are used. Web-based computer programs are available (Reich & Todd, 2002b). The MAGIC manual describes the assessment-relevant issues and meanings of items. MAGIC includes an initial question and specified probe questions. When the answer is determined to be "No" to some questions, others may be omitted as specified. Simple probes are used, and a written explanation must be given for a response when the word "Specify" appears after the question. For other questions, lines are available for recording (under "Record") but are not mandatory. Interviewers must be highly trained so that they will be able to clarify questions and assess symptoms accurately (Reich & Todd). MAGIC is fully computerized.

ADDITIONAL SYMPTOMS

Traumatized children often present with other symptoms in addition to those included in *DSM-IV* and *ICD-10* PTSD diagnoses (Fletcher, 2003; Saigh, Yasik, Sack, & Koplewicz, 1999; Terr, 1991). Among the additional symptoms endorsed more than a third of the time by traumatized children are dissociative responses, guilt, generalized anxiety or fears, and low self-esteem (Fletcher). Other symptoms include a changed outlook toward life, depression, separation anxiety, regressive behaviors, self-destructive behaviors, risk-taking, aggressive or antisocial behaviors, changed morality, changed attachment behaviors, panic attacks, eating problems, warped time perspective, and sleepwalking (Fletcher; Garbarino, 1999; Glodich, 1999; Nader, 2001b; Terr). Many of these symptoms are discussed in the other chapters of this book. Measures of youths' attitudes toward life, behavioral and emotional problems (and sometimes self-perceptions), and sexualized behaviors are presented here. Although they are discussed in chapters 1 and 3 in relationship to trauma and to aggression, shame and guilt, and a scale to measure them, are also offered in this section.

Attitudes Toward Life

Measures of life satisfaction and worldview may be used to assess current views and possible changes in a youth's sense of subjective well-being (Huebner, Funk, & Gilman, 2000). Life satisfaction is an individual's personal judgment of his or her quality of life and is an important component of subjective well-being (Huebner, Suldo, Valois, Drane, & Zullig, 2004). Evidence suggests that neither high nor low levels of life satisfaction are necessarily synonymous with clinical syndromes (Huebner et al., 2000). A youth's family and life circumstances may significantly affect life satisfaction (e.g., the conflicting demands of modern versus traditional cultural values; Park, 1996). Some individuals report overall life satisfaction despite experiences with associated intense negative emotions or behaviors, and some individuals report low overall life satisfaction without these experiences (see "Temperament," chapter 6).

Studies of traumatized adults have confirmed a marked decrease in life satisfaction after severe multiple traumas (Anke & Fugl-Meyer, 2003). Anke and Fugl-Meyer described an orientation toward life (*sense of coherence*, SOC) that assists in coping with stress. SOC includes a pervasive and enduring dynamic sense of confidence that (1) internal and external stimuli will be structured, predictable, and explicable; (2) resources are available to meet the demands of these stimuli; and (3) the demands or challenges of the stimuli are worthy of engagement and investment. Years after multiple traumatic injuries, subjects experienced a pronounced decrease in satisfaction with life as a whole as well as in the life domains of work, leisure, sex, contacts with friends, and self-care. A strong SOC and a qualitatively adequate social network served as buffers against the negative influence of disabilities.

Data suggest that adolescent reports of life satisfaction are somewhat consistent in nature, rather than primarily based on momentary influences (e.g., current mood; Huebner et al., 2000). Suldo and Huebner (2004) found support for a relationship among adolescents' life satisfaction, adverse life events, and externalizing behaviors. In contrast to youths who reported dissatisfaction with their lives, adolescents with positive life satisfaction scores were less likely to develop externalizing behavior problems after adverse life events. Life satisfaction, then, may operate as a protective factor that buffers the effects of adverse life events in adolescence. Studies of pre- and posttrauma levels of life satisfaction are needed.

An individual's worldview (including core assumptions and expectations) is largely determined by his or her culture (including religious culture; de Silva, 1999) and experience (Terr, 1979). Studies of posttrauma changes in worldview have suggested that a pessimistic attitude is more likely to occur for more extreme chronic or abusive stressors (Fletcher, 2003). In a small laboratory study, children's estimates of future negative events, however, did not distinguish those with PTSD from comparison groups (Dalgleish, Taghavi, Neshat-Doost, Moradi, Canterbury, & Yule, 2003).

The Students' Life Satisfaction Scale (SLSS) and Multidimensional SLSS (MSLSS)
Age range: 8–18
Format: Child completion (monitored)

SLSS (Huebner, 1991b) is a 7-item self-report scale that assesses children's overall life satisfaction (e.g., "I have a good life"). It differs from the 40-item Multidimensional SLSS (Huebner, 1994b), which assesses satisfaction within five specific domains (i.e., family, friends, school, self, and living environment; Huebner, 2001; Huebner, Gilman, & Laughlin, 1999). Items are scored on a four-point Likert scale (1 = Never; 2 = Sometimes; 3 = Often; 4 = Almost always) or a six-point Likert scale (1 = Strongly disagree; 2 = Moderately disagree; 3 = Mildly disagree; 4 = Mildly agree; 5 = Moderately agree; and 6 = Strongly agree). Negatively keyed items are reverse scored. Hence, higher scores indicate higher levels of life satisfaction. Normative data are available (Huebner, 2001). A five-item Brief MSLSS (BMSLSS) is also available (Huebner et al., 2004; items presented in the text). The BMSLSS, completed by 5,545 students from schools in a southeastern state (Huebner et al., 2004), asks one question for each of the five domains of satisfaction.

The World View Survey (WVS)
Age range: 12 and older
Format: Child completion

WVS (Fletcher, 1997) measures posttrauma beliefs. The survey is comprised of nine subscales (Fletcher & Skidmore, 1997). Five of the subscales (the trauma reactive beliefs scale) appear to be associated with exposure to traumatic stress: anxious uncertainty (AU), inadequacy (I), dangerous world (DW), self-abnegation (SA), and lack of control (LC). The other four subscales (the negative beliefs scales) do not appear to be associated with exposure to traumatic stress: poor ego-strength (PES; low resilience), negative social relations or poor attachment (PA), lack of personal empowerment (LPE), and negative outlook (NO). Each belief is rated on a four-point Likert scale (1 = Strongly agree, 2 = Mostly agree, 3 = Mostly disagree, and 4 = Strongly disagree). Higher scores indicate disagreement with a belief. Thirty-six items are scored in reverse order.

Child Behaviors and Problems

Measures that assess child behavioral and emotional symptoms and adaptive behaviors are often used in the study of trauma and other disorders. Some frequently used measures to assess children's behavior problems are included here after a discussion of frequently assessed problems. Many instruments now include trauma subscales.

Internalizing and Externalizing Problems

Measures of youths' behaviors often assess internalizing and externalizing problems. *Internalizing* problems include those experienced within the child such as withdrawal, somatic complaints, depression, suicidal ideation, and anxiety symptoms. *Externalizing* behaviors include external, observable behaviors such as attention problems, aggression, delinquency, and antisocial behaviors. Maltreatment during childhood has been associated with increased risk for both internalizing and externalizing problems (Bolger & Patterson, 2003). Bolger and Patterson found that an internal locus of control, however, served as a protective factor against internalizing problems. Assessing attachment style is also important to the analysis of internalizing and externalizing symptoms (chapter 8). Lyons-Ruth, Easterbrooks, and Cibelli (1997) found that both early avoidant and disorganized attachments predicted comorbid internalizing and externalizing symptoms. Early organized avoidant attachments predicted purely internalizing symptoms.

Personality and other factors influence the effects of life experience on symptoms. Such factors may induce differences, for example, in thresholds of reactivity to the environment, coping, and other behaviors and choices that affect outcomes. For 991 New Zealand youths (ages 0 to 21), Fergusson and Horwood (2003) found that youths exposed to six or more adverse factors had 2.4 times more externalizing and 1.8 times more internalizing disorders than youths with low adversity (see chapter 10). Being male reduced the risk of developing internalizing problems, whereas being female reduced the risk of developing externalizing problems. For externalizing problems, low novelty seeking, avoidance of delinquent peer associations, and high self-esteem mitigated the effects of exposure to adversity. For internalizing problems, high parental attachment, low novelty seeking, and low neuroticism mitigated the effects of adversity.

Determining whether a youth has purely internalizing, purely externalizing, or mixed problems is important to assessment. For example, Jackson, Frick, and Dravage-Bush (2000) found that, when *internal, external*, and *unknown* control domains were assessed as dependent variables for youths with externalizing and mixed behavior problems, the externalizing behavior group demonstrated a higher *unknown* locus of control. Externalizing children consistently endorsed unknown locus of control for school situations, physical activities, and everyday situations, but not for social situations. Jackson et al. theorize that acting-out behavior may result or be maintained by a perception that the controller of events in the environment is unknown and possibly unpredictable. Failure to identify context, to separate youths into mixed or solely externalizing groups, and to list *unknown* under types of locus of control may explain why some studies have found both an external and an internal locus of control for externalizing youths.

The Achenbach System of Empirically Based Assessment (ASEBA)
Age range: 6–18
Translations: 65 additional languages
Format: Parent, youth, or teacher completion or interviewer completion

ASEBA provides scales for individuals ages 1.5 to 90+. For school-age children, ASEBA consists of parallel forms for the parent, youth, and teacher, respectively: the child behavior checklist for ages 6 to 18 (CBCL/6-18; formerly CBCL/4–18), youth self-report (YSR), and teacher's report form (TRF) (ASEBA, 2002; Achenbach, 1966, 1991; Achenbach & Rescorla, 2001). The current version includes revised empirically based scales, new *DSM*-oriented scales, and new national norms. The CBCL/6–18 has 118 items that describe specific behavioral and emotional problems, plus two open-ended items for reporting additional problems. Parents rate the child for how true each item is now or within the past 6 months (teachers rate each item for the last 2 months on the TRF) using the following three-point scale: 0 = Not true (as far as you know); 1 = Somewhat or sometimes true; 2 = Very true or often true. Normative data are provided for *total competence* and its three subscales (activities, social, and school). *Total problems* consists of eight syndromes (aggressive behavior; anxious/ depressed; attention problems; rule-breaking behavior; social problems; somatic complaints; thought problems; and withdrawn/depressed) that subdivide into internalizing and externalizing. The total problems score includes some problems that are not in any syndrome or *DSM*-oriented scale. Six *DSM* scales are also included (affective problems; anxiety problems; somatic problems; attention-deficit/hyperactivity problems; oppositional defiant problems; and conduct problems). In addition, ASEBA forms elicit descriptive data and open-ended reports of the "best things" and "greatest concerns" about the youth (ASEBA; Achenbach & Rescorla). The CBCL/6–18 is normed for youths ages 6 to 18; YSR is normed for ages 11 to 18; the current TRF is normed for ages 6 to 18 (okay for first graders age 5; Achenbach & Rescorla). Software is available for scoring and analysis.

The Behavior Assessment System for Children (BASC)
Age range: Preschool (2 1/2–5), child (6–11), and adolescent (12–18)
Translations: Spanish, Dutch
Format: Youth, parent, or teacher completion or interview
Requirements: Supervised test experience

BASC is a multimethod, multidimensional approach to evaluating children's behavior and self-perceptions (Reynolds & Kamphaus, 1992, 1998). BASC has five components, which may be used individually or in any combination: (1) *Self report of personality* (SRP-C, ages 8 to 11; SRP-A, ages 12 to 18) elicits "True" or "False" response to items regarding thoughts, emotions, and self-perceptions: clinical maladjustment, school maladjustment, other problems, personal adjustment, and composite scores. An audiotape is available for children with limited ability to read English. (2) *Teacher rating scale* (TRS) elicits school observers' descriptions of the child's observable school behaviors: externalizing problems, internalizing problems, school problems, other problems, adaptive skills, and composite. (3) *Parent rating scale* (PRS) permits caretakers' descriptions of the child's observable behaviors in the community or home. It is the same as the TRS without school problems, learning problems, and study skills. (4) A *structured developmental history* (SDH) is an extensive history and background questionnaire. (5) The *student observation system* (SOS) is used for time-sampling—30 second observation intervals for 15 minutes with 3 seconds for recording—directly observed classroom behavior. BASC measures positive (adaptive) dimensions of behavior as well as personality and behavioral problems and emotional disturbances. The BASC scales include validity checks (the tendency to be excessively negative, positive, or implausible) that allow the clinician to assess the accuracy and consistency of informants. For PRS and TRS, items are rated on a four-point scale (0 = Never, 1 = Sometimes, 2 = Often, 3 = Almost always).

Normative data based on large, representative samples is differentiated by age, gender, clinical or general status, and informant. Computer software is available for scoring and analysis (Reynolds & Kamphaus, 1998).

The Personality Inventory for Youth (PIY)
Age range: 9–18
Format: Child completion
Associated scales: PI for Children (PIC-2)

PIY (Lachar & Gruber, 1995a, 2001) is a multidimensional, 270 item, self-report measure that is a companion measure to the caretaker-report Personality Inventory for Children-Revised (PIC-R; Lachar, 1982). The first 80 items constitute the short form of the scale. PIY consists of two main scales: *clinical scales* and *response validity scales*. Nine main clinical scales contain 24 subscales: *cognitive impairment* (poor achievement and memory; inadequate abilities; learning problems); *impulsivity and distractibility* (brashness; distractibility and overactivity; impulsivity); *delinquency* (antisocial behavior; dyscontrol; noncompliance); *family dysfunction* (parent-child conflict; parent maladjustment, marital discord); *reality distortion* (feelings of alienation; hallucinations and delusions); *somatic concern* (psychosomatic syndrome; muscular tension and anxiety; preoccupation with disease); *psychological discomfort* (fear and worry; depression; sleep disturbance); *social withdrawal* (social introversion; isolation); and *social skill deficits* (limited peer status; conflict with peers). An audiocassette is available for individuals with less than a low- to mid-third-grade reading level. Hand- and computer-scoring services are available (Lachar & Gruber, 1995a).

Sexualized Behaviors

When sexualized behaviors include sexual interest, self-stimulation, sexually intrusive behavior, gender-based behavior, and personal boundary permeability, children's sexualized behaviors vary by age, gender, problem behaviors, life stress, family sexuality, and personality (Friedrich, 1993a; Friedrich, Fisher et al., 2001; Hoyle, Fejfar, & Miller, 2000). Friedrich et al. (1992) found that these behaviors usually decrease with age for 2 to 12 year olds, particularly for girls. Sexually abused boys, however, tend toward broader and more aggressive sexual behaviors when they are older (Friedrich, 1995). Data indicate that psychiatric outpatients and inpatients without a history of sexual abuse exhibit significantly more sexual behaviors than a nonpsychiatric sample but fewer behaviors than sexually abused children (Friedrich et al., 2001). Similarly for children with ADHD, parents reported problems of masturbation and problems with interpersonal boundaries; however, as a group, ADHD children exhibited less sexual interest and less sexual aggression than sexually abused children (Friedrich, 1995).

The Children's Sexual Behavior Inventory 3 (CSBI-3)
Age range: 2–12
Translations: French, Spanish, German, and Swedish
Format: Parent completion

CSBI-3 (Friedrich, 1990, 1993a, 1997a, 1997b) is a 38-item measure that permits parents or primary caregivers to rate sexual behavior in children ages 2 to 12 (Friedrich, 1993a, 1993b, 1995, 1997b; Friedrich, Fisher et al., 2001). The CSBI-3 assesses a wide variety of sexual behaviors related to sexual interest, self-stimulation, sexually intrusive behavior with other children and adults, gender-based behavior, and personal boundary permeability. It includes validity and attitudinal items (Friedrich et al., 1992; Friedrich, 1995). Three clinical scales of the CSBI are normed by age group (Friedrich, 1997b; Friedrich, Grambsch, Broughton, Kuiper, & Beilke, 1991): *CSBI total* (sum score of all 38 CSBI items); *developmentally related sexual behaviors* (distinguishes sexual behaviors more common at specific ages); and *sexual abuse-specific items* (includes sexual behaviors often related to sexual abuse). Friedrich (1997b) reminds us that sexual abuse cannot be predicted on the basis of a test score alone. CSBI-3 uses a four-point frequency rating scale indicating occurrence for the past 6 months: 0 = Never, 1 = Less than once per month, 2 = One to three times per month, and 3 = At least once per week. Total score is determined by summing all of the items less the validity items.

Shame and Guilt

Although often used interchangeably, studies have demonstrated that shame and guilt are distinct affective experiences (Tangney, 1990). Earlier measures of the two concepts have often failed to distinguish between them. Most individuals have the capacity to and do experience shame and guilt at some point in daily living. Moderate levels of shame and guilt may have an adaptive function. Siegel (1999) explains that shame occurs when the infant's aroused sympathetic nervous system urges him or her to action but the caregiver's protective "No!" activates the parasympathetic system to put on the brakes. Schore (1996) notes that, when shame-inducing interactions are coupled with sustained caregiver anger and/or lack of repair of the disconnection between caregiver and child, then shame leads to humiliation. The inability to experience either shame or guilt has been, at least theoretically, linked to sociopathic and antisocial tendencies (Tangney). Experiences that engender shame can be paralyzing in their intensity (Leeming & Boyle, 2004). Kaufman (1989) suggested that repeated shame experiences, especially in childhood, may become internalized as a part of a shame-based identity (cited in Leeming & Boyle). Exaggerated guilt and shame have been implicated in depression, social withdrawal, low self-esteem, obsessive reactions, and prolonged PTSD.

Although some research evidence suggests that individuals either are shame-prone or are guilt-prone (Tangney, 1990), Tangney, Wagner, Fletcher, and Gramzow (1992) found a correlation between guilt- and shame-proneness in studies of college students. Shame and guilt do share features in common and can occur in tandem: both include dysphoric affects that have some form of internal attribution. Each can arise from a specific behavior or transgression (Tangney, Miller, Flicker, & Barlow, 1996). Tangney et al. (1996) found that both shame and guilt can be fairly intense and long-lasting emotions that are related to serious situations. Both are self-conscious emotions and may include intense feelings of responsibility, regret, and desire to make amends. Shame and guilt can be associated with a sense of failure or transgression as well as disgust, contempt, fear, anger, and sadness. Tangney (1996) suggests that the two affects become intertwined when guilt is maladaptive. Maladaptive guilt is characterized by chronic self-blame, obsessive rumination, and a linking of the focus on "the horrible thing that I have done" and "the horrible person that I am." Intense, unrelenting posttraumatic and other forms of maladaptive guilt thus may be guilt fused with shame.

As outlined here, shame and guilt also have important differences. The failure to distinguish between them may result in contradictory findings. For example, findings have been mixed regarding guilt's relationship to aggression. Shame- or guilt-proneness may be important to assess in determining their relationship to trauma.

Shame

With shame, the object of concern is the entire self (Tangney et al., 1992). With or without actual public exposure, shame arises from negative self-evaluation of the entire self rather than of specific behaviors (Tangney, 1990). Tangney et al. (1996) state, "In shame, the self is both agent and object of observation and disapproval, as shortcomings of the defective self are exposed before an internalized observing 'other'" (p. 1257). Shame is significantly related to self-perception and is often accompanied by a sense of exposure, shrinking, smallness, worthlessness, and powerlessness. The expression of a sense of shame includes words like *unworthy, inferior, inadequate, bad, immoral,* or *unprincipled* (Tangney, Niedenthal, Covert, & Barlow, 1998). Shame is tied to perceived deficiencies in the *core self* and with wanting to undo aspects of self (Tangney et al., 1996). In an assessment of self-reported discrepancies in the three domains of self, Tangney et al. (1998) found that discrepancies among any of the perceived actual, ideal, and obligated-to-be selves were associated with shame.

Tangney et al. (1992) found that the tendency to experience shame across a variety of situations correlates strongly with the tendency to externalize cause or blame. Shame can motivate anger, "a kind of hostile, humiliated fury" (Tangney et al., p. 670). Lewis (1971) observed that, because shame includes the idea of a rejecting, disapproving other, hostility can instigate a rage reaction and be redirected in retaliation (cited in Tangney et al.). Extreme shame has been noted as a component of extreme aggression such as terrorism or murder (Gilligan, 2003; Scheff, 1997; Volkan, 2001; chapter 3).

Peri- and posttraumatic shame and humiliation usually include feelings of intense degradation. Herman (1992c, 1997) describes posttraumatic shame as a response to helplessness, violation, and indignity suffered in the eyes of another: "The survivor's shame and guilt may be exacerbated by the harsh judgment of others, but is not fully assuaged by simple pronouncements absolving her from responsibility, because simple pronouncements, even favorable ones, represent a refusal to engage with the survivor in the lacerating moral complexities of the extreme situation" (p. 69). Shame has been associated with increased and prolonged trauma symptoms. Feiring, Taska, and Lewis (1998) studied abused youths (82 children, 60 adolescents) within 8 weeks of discovery of abuse. Shame and self-blaming attributional style were associated with depression, low self-esteem, and other traumatic event sequelae even after controlling for age, gender, and abuse characteristics. One year later (80 children, 57 adolescents), shame was among the important predictors of symptom level (Feiring, Taska, & Chen, 2002). For 103 Australian university students, proneness to shame and proneness to guilt contributed significantly to the prediction of dissociative tendencies (Irwin, 1998). Women, sexually victimized either in childhood or in adulthood, who had increased self-blame demonstrated poorer recovery (Ullman, 1997).

Guilt

The object of concern, with guilt, is a specific action or inaction (Tangney et al., 1992). Guilt focuses on past behavior that is inconsistent with internalized moral or other standards (Tangney, 1990); it often includes a nagging preoccupation with a specific transgression (Tangney et al., 1996). Tangney et al. (1998) found that guilt was unrelated to discrepancies between the actual self and self-guides—what the individual or others think is the person's ideal self or the self that the person should feel responsible to be or is obligated to be. Guilt is more often focused on wanting to undo an aspect of behavior (Tangney et al., 1996).

Although both may be experienced as very real, Danieli (1984) and Lifton (1993) make a distinction between *real/active* guilt and *imagined/passive* guilt (Nader, 2001a). Following traumatic experiences, an individual may experience *real guilt* for acts of commission or omission that result in the physical or emotional endangerment or harm of others. *Imagined guilt* (e.g., survivor guilt, guilt with an element of wishful thinking about one's ability to act) includes guilt that occurs in the absence of having acted harmfully. Following traumas, youths' guilt may be maladaptive. Both types of guilt can include self-condemnation and can result in self-punishing acts such as the action or elicitation of rejection, disdain, and/or self-harm.

For adults and children, guilt has been associated with increased trauma symptoms (Kinzie, Sack, Angell, Manson, & Rath, 1986; Lacey, 1972; Nader, Pynoos, Fairbanks, & Frederick, 1990; Pynoos et al., 1987). For 63 women exposed to domestic violence, Street, Gibson, and Holohan (2005) found that women with greater childhood trauma exposures were more likely to respond to domestic violence with guilt and a sense of responsibility for their victimization. Trauma-related guilt was directly and indirectly linked to current levels of PTSD. Guilt was also linked to an increase in avoidance coping (chapter 5). Such coping strategies were also associated with elevated current levels of PTSD. One month and again 1 year after a sniper attack on an elementary school playground, guilt was associated with increased trauma symptoms (Nader et al.; Pynoos et al.). Children reported guilt for being unable to provide aid, being safe when others were harmed, or believing their actions endangered others. Youths with none to mild PTSD reactions almost never reported guilt. Twenty-five percent of youths with severe reactions reported guilt. Both guilt and degree of acquaintance with the deceased victim were associated with increased mean reaction index scores in all exposure groups. Street et al. point out the reciprocal relationship between many variables and trauma outcomes. In their study, guilt increased avoidant coping. Avoidant coping may prevent cognitive and emotional processing of traumatic reactions including guilt. Individuals with more severe levels of PTSD may use avoidant coping strategies because of the pain of traumatic thoughts and emotions (chapter 5).

Assessment of Guilt- and Shame-Proneness

A number of problems exist in the assessment of proneness to shame or guilt (Tangney, 1996). Measures may fail to distinguish between the two distinct concepts. Scales may confound proneness to guilt (an affective disposition) with moral standards or other sets of beliefs and attitudes that guide behavior. Likewise, shame (an affective state) must be distinguished from self-concept, a generally stable trait usually independent of a specific situation. Scales that assess shame- or guilt-proneness may be comprised of a list of adjectives for a subject to select as self-descriptions (Harder & Lewis, 1987) or may be scenarios followed by the selection of responses related to guilt or shame (Tangney, Wagner, Burggraf, Gramzow, & Fletcher, 1990; Tangney, Wagner, Gavlas, & Gramzow, 1991).

Adjective lists do not permit reference to specific situations that might distinguish shame or guilt (Tangney). Scenarios may make moral judgments difficult to distinguish from guilt-proneness. As is true with many aspects of assessing traumatized youths, shame- or guilt-proneness assessed prior to the traumas is rarely available. Most of the scales that assess shame- or guilt-proneness were developed for adults. A brief description of the Tangney scales for youths is provided here. These measures assess guilt- and shame-proneness and do not assess state-guilt or -shame nor do they assess maladaptive or traumatic guilt or posttraumatic shame.

The Test of Self-Conscious Affect (TOSCA)

Tangney and colleagues have devised measures of shame- or guilt-proneness for adults, children ages 8 to 12 (Tangney et al., 1990), and adolescents (Tangney et al., 1991). Stegge and Ferguson (1990) have developed a version of TOSCA for young children, ages 5 to 12. The scales consist of 10 negatively and 5 positively valenced scenarios that represent shame, guilt, externalization, and detachment/unconcern rated on a five-point scale. Measure scenarios include a small subset of possible transgressions or failures experienced by respondents in an age group (Tangney, 1996). Scenarios are familiar, everyday types of situations that do not include more serious or traumatic situations.

CONCLUSIONS

Disorders other than or in addition to PTSD may occur after youths' traumatic experiences. Comorbidity can have a substantial impact on the course and severity of PTSD. Anxiety, depression, substance abuse, and medical disorders are commonly associated with adult PTSD. For youths, ADD, ADHD, CD, ODD, depressive disorders, phobias, and anxiety disorders have been found in association with PTSD. Some disorders are more likely at specific ages. Differential diagnosis is sometimes difficult because of the overlap in symptoms among disorders. Specific symptoms in addition to PTSD symptoms also occur in children following traumatic events. Some of them have been endorsed often by youths (e.g., dissociative responses, guilt, generalized anxiety or fears, and low self-esteem). Measures of disorders and of child behaviors have been used frequently to assess the problem behaviors of traumatized youths. Following traumas, youths have endorsed increased internalizing and externalizing behaviors. Sexualized behaviors may serve as indicators of sexual abuse. Comorbid disorders and symptoms such as shame or guilt may increase and prolong traumatic response and require treatment adaptations.

Part V
Pulling It All Together

16

Writing Reports Regarding Traumatized Youths

Following actual or alleged traumatic events, a treating mental-health professional or agency, physician, forensic source, school, or insurance or other compensating agency may request a formal report. Reports for forensic and nonforensic purposes should provide accurate, relevant, and ethical information. With or without the submission of a report, evaluation of youths requires informed consent from the parent or both parent and youth. Up-to-date knowledge is essential regarding laws related to investigations, reports, the limitations of confidentiality, and other relevant issues that vary by state, country, and the purpose of the report. Practitioners must also remain cognizant of age and developmental, cultural, and personal factors throughout the assessment and writing process.

Preparatory efforts such as identifying appropriate sources of information are essential to an accurate and reliable report. When determining the sources of information to be gathered, one method of protecting a youth is to decide whether the information is necessary to the report and if its collection would cause unnecessary distress. For example, would interviewing peers help or hinder? Trauma issues and concerns about the accuracy of information reported may vary depending on the context. Parents may underreport a youth's symptoms in a clinical or school setting and may exaggerate symptoms in a forensic setting (Lubit, Hartwell, van Gorp, & Eth, 2002). In sexual abuse cases, it is fairly common for an abused child to recant allegations (D'Urso, Esquilin, Fiore, Haldapoulus, & Heiman, 1995). In a custody case, a child may be coached to make allegations. This chapter addresses issues important to psychological and forensic report writing related to actual or alleged traumatic events.

PRELIMINARY ISSUES OF REPORT WRITING

> . . . a high quality psychological evaluation offers a compact and efficient way to provide a multidimensional picture of a person's psychological capacities and needs. A good psychological evaluation is focused on providing data from a range of situations and responses to answer a specific referral question. (Wandersman, 1998, p. 8)

Trauma and other report writing requires attention to the report's focus, possible personal biases, and laws that apply in the report writer's jurisdiction. Effectively documenting in-depth information requires the capacity to view a topic from multiple perspectives (Vassallo, 2002).

Focus and Attitude

Report preparation serves to document, in an integrated manner, the most significant findings and conclusions related to the referral question (Donders, 2001a). The professional who writes a report must address the specific issues required by the agency, court, or individual requesting the report. A comprehensive report is likely to require assessments of the youth and interviews with other informants such as family, teachers, investigating agents, and peers. Assessing the child before gathering other information may help to prevent bias in the evaluation process. The child, on the other hand, may have been interviewed by researchers, police investigators, or others as well as by the clinician prior to the request for a report (see chapter 9).

The style used in report writing varies across disciplines and purposes. Buzzard (1972) states that, in scientific report writing, style "is in some ways a question of good manners" (p. 202). The aim is to provide the clearest and simplest presentation of facts and arguments appropriate for the readers for whom the report is written and to make it as easy for the reader as possible. Such a presentation requires taking the time to give the readers all that they need to know in order to have a critical understanding of the text. Consideration also must be given to the report's impact on the lives of those involved. This consideration necessitates careful thought about what must be included and what need not be included in the report, given its purpose.

Preparation

An understanding of childhood development, psychopathology including traumatization, and current findings regarding the possible initial, delayed, complex, and long-term consequences of youths' traumatic exposure is essential to accurate posttrauma report writing. The timing of certain preparatory efforts may be influenced by the desire to assist youths and to prevent bias. Assessments for traumatization, for example, may follow briefing regarding a traumatic event such as a shooting or tornado at a school but may precede knowledge of the youth's exposure and personal history. Forensic evaluators disagree about how much preliminary information an evaluator should have prior to conducting an evaluation (D'Urso et al., 1995). Many feel that preparation prior to the actual interview is vital and may help to ensure a more positive experience for the youth. Others prefer that the evaluator begin without prior knowledge.

Prior to assessment, the report-writing professional will need up-to-date information about relevant laws such as psycho-legal issues and rules of evidence, informed consent, and releases of information from other informants (e.g., schools, physicians) and to the agent requesting or in need of a report (Gordon, 2002; Wilson & Moran, 2004). Court cases may require specific kinds of preparation such as review of the formal charges or allegations and police summaries. Prior to the assessment, the clinician will need an understanding of the youth's culture and background. The youth's qualities and background may influence the nature and methods of assessment as well as the findings.

Sources of Information

Valid and reliable scales and interviews that elicit youths' self- and adult-reports of youths' symptoms and behaviors have been described in the chapters of this book. In addition to verbal reports or scale-completions, informal or formal observations will likely add to the accuracy of the evaluation (Wandersman, 1998; chapter 13). An examining physician may provide reports of a youth's injuries and medical care. Police reports and eyewitnesses hold information about the nature of the event and the youth's experience (Wilson & Moran, 2004). Caregivers, teachers, school records, and sometimes peers can provide needed data about the youth's history and functioning. Caregivers may be able to provide additional sources of information. When the caregiver or the youth is under investigation, individuals aware of the person or the event such as the police, paramedics, neighbors, or eyewitnesses may suggest other sources.

Biases

It is difficult or impossible to remain completely free of bias in making evaluations. Bias need not, however, result in ignoring information that contradicts or confirms a result or opinion. The professional may have to evaluate his or her own reactions to the individual being assessed. In the case of a crime or injury to a child, personal feelings about the perpetrator or the victim may be automatic. As Allnutt and Chaplow (2000) point out, "Psychiatric findings are largely subjective and the psychiatrist's opinion is vulnerable to influence of social and cultural variables" (p. 986). The professional must be aware of his or her limitations and biases and must be able to make an objective evaluation of a youth and his or her condition. Otherwise, it is ethically reasonable to disqualify him- or herself from the process.

Knowing the purpose of the report introduces possible bias. Awareness, for example, that a court, attorney, investigating agency, or other is assessing (1) child abuse, (2) a youth's committed aggression, (3) the financial responsibility for the youth's emotional and physical injuries, or (4) other specific questions is likely to elicit, in the evaluator, a set of beliefs and reactions. One mental-health professional never accepted requests from lawyers defending youths who committed violence. Although traumatization may be an important factor in a youth's commission of a crime, the professional believed that using traumatization as a defense gives permission for traumatized youths to engage in criminal acts. He explained, "There are just too many traumatized youths out there for it to be reasonable to justify violence with traumatization. Most traumatized youths do not assault others, so traumatization is an insufficient reason for the commission of violence anyway." Another professional took many cases in which traumatized individuals committed crimes. He worked with veterans before becoming an expert witness. He was well aware of the strength of a compulsion to self-protect and the nature of adults' flashback experiences that could lead to harm of others by an otherwise good person. Clinicians are aware of the need to examine personal attitudes toward perpetrators, victims, and specific traumatic situations as well as aspects of *compassion fatigue* associated with ongoing trauma work (Figley, 2002). An evaluator's own or loved one's previous traumatic experience can color reactions to a current situation as well.

Related to child abuse and other criminal evaluations, police officers and mental-health professionals have sometimes been accused of forming an opinion and then attempting to prove it to the exclusion of other possibilities. Investigators fearing for the safety of children may ignore certain aspects of the situation, whereas investigators attuned to the difficulties of raising children may minimize others. Bias may also affect assessments following natural or other human-precipitated traumas. An anonymous principle investigator tells the story of assessing a large group of community youths following a mass traumatic event. All interviewers were blind to exposure and other relevant factors regarding youths assessed. An entire dataset was thrown out because a compassionate assessor rated almost every child he interviewed to be severely traumatized. Other blind interviewers found variations in reactions among the children that later analysis revealed to be associated with specific event and child factors. A reinterviewed subsample of the children from the excluded dataset confirmed this variation in reactions in relation to child and event factors.

Personal assumptions can occur in the language of the assessor with or without his or her awareness. During early practice assessment interviews in a culture in which having many children is valued, a trainee asked, "Of course, you will have children when you grow up?" instead of "Will you have children when you grow up?" She was surprised and amused at herself when the trainer told her how she had worded the question.

Ease of Reading

A single report may have a varied audience. Professionals who write for the courts, for business organizations, and for clinical reasons recommend the use of logic, clarity, brevity, simplicity, and humanity (Allnutt & Chaplow, 2000; Vassallo, 2002). Clarity is assisted, for example, by avoiding use of technical jargon, double negatives, hedging statements, and ambiguity. If technical terms must be included, they can be explained in parentheses or in a glossary of terms at the end of the report (Allnutt & Chaplow). Brevity and simplicity can be enhanced by using short words, short paragraphs, and sentences that do not exceed 20 to 25 words as well as by avoiding multisyllabic words, making verbs nouns, and unnecessary or meaningless sentence introductions. Simplicity also can be facilitated by writing in a pattern familiar to the audience. Allnutt and Chaplow suggest avoiding superfluity, repetition, apologies, vagueness, adjectives, adverbs, words that end in "tion," pejorative language, and generalities. The report may be read aloud to a jury, team, or committee and should be easy to read aloud. Buzzard (1972) says that repetition in a report is usually the result of bad ordering. The order in which the contents of the report are presented can clarify the subject for the writer as much as for the reader. If the outline of the report is presented in the introduction, presenting the rest of the report in the same order makes reading easier.

In books and manuscripts, using alternate words with the same meaning may be desirable. In report writing, however, it can be confusing (Buzzard, 1972). Similarly, using the same word to mean two different things can be perplexing to the reader. Buzzard recommends using one word to represent a single concept consistently throughout the report. Subsequently, the reader does not have to stop and try to determine if the writer is intending something different. A report may, for example, refer to caregivers when consistently identifying the mother, the father, the grandmother, or Mrs. X. "Mrs. X, the babysitter," would be clearer.

When possible, writing a rough draft and setting it aside for later rewording is desirable (Buzzard, 1972). An objective colleague's review, questions, and feedback can be a valuable part of the process. The requesting agent may also provide feedback prior to the final report. In this way, the requesting agent may indicate whether or not the report has addressed all of the issues that need addressing (Wandersman, 1998). Donders (2001b) found that neuropsychologists who work with pediatric populations were more likely to permit caregivers to review the report before its finalization than neuropsychologists who work with other populations. The advisability of doing so, again, depends upon the circumstances and the nature of the report. Sharing it with the parent can allow the parent to participate in or feel more a part of the final intervention plan.

THE ELEMENTS OF A NONFORENSIC REPORT

No single format will meet the reporting needs of all clinicians and circumstances (Donders, 2001a). The providing and requesting agency, those who might have access to the report, available information, and specific issues under scrutiny, as well as the evaluator's discipline, influence a report's content and structure. In a report on a traumatized youth, some of the sections described below are combined, reordered, or otherwise changed depending on these variables. Although some may be written in letter form, reports are often divided into sections. Generally, reports include an introduction, relevant history, current presentation, findings related to the question or purpose of the report, and a conclusion or opinion. Some reports include a section that lists the sources of information for the report and include a summary of findings that precedes an opinion (Allnutt & Chaplow, 2000). Table 16.1 is a general worksheet for organizing the contents of a report. In the following pages, excerpts from a school report and treating agency illustrate report sections.

Purpose or Reason for Referral

Reports often begin with a statement of the purpose, focus, and scope of the report. The *purpose* section includes what the document sets out to do, what questions it addresses, and what or who instigated the assessment (Donders, 2001a; Vassallo, 2002). It may include the problems the youth is having (Kay, 2002). When a youth's ability to function normally at school has been impaired by his traumatic injuries and reactions, for example, the purpose of the psychoeducational report may be to determine (1) the best method of schooling and (2) whether special treatment is necessary for the youth given the problems he or she is having.

Methods: Sources of Information, Measures Used

The methods section may include a list of the sources of information, authorization and consent for the assessment and report, documents reviewed, assessment procedures, and evaluation measures used (Donders, 2001a; Vassallo, 2002; Wilson & Moran, 2004). Medical, legal, school, and other documents may be reviewed as a part of the assessment. Injury and treatment reports, educational and psychological test data, and school records, for example, help to compare the youth's past and present functioning. Assessments may include tests of cognitive and social func-

TABLE 16.1
Worksheet for Trauma Report

Contents	Report Notes
Requesting agent (style, preferences . . .	
Purpose/questions Address the following: 1. 2. 3. 4. 5.	
Methods: Sources of information, measures, interviews	
Youth's presentation	
Findings/results	
Conclusions, recommendations, or opinions	
Limitations or contradictions	
Addendum or attachments	

tioning as well. Some measures of academic functioning do not reveal difficulties that occur under certain conditions and do not reveal specific problems such as nonverbal, right hemispheric learning problems (Kay, 2002). Kay recommends use of the Wechsler Individual Achievement Test (2nd edition) for the latter. As Gordon (2002) points out, each assessment measure and methodology has its advantages and disadvantages. Each result should be a part of a working hypothesis to be confirmed by the use of other methodologies.

Sources of Information

Measures: Child Posttraumatic Stress Reaction Index; Exposure Questionnaire; Child Posttraumatic Stress Reaction Parent Inventory; Missouri Assessment of Genetics Interview for Children

Interviews: Youth, parent, joint mother-son, teacher, neighbor, peer, psychiatrist

Records reviewed: Medical, psychiatric, school, police reports

Observations: Classroom, in hospital

Examiner Qualifications

The examiner's credentials, agency, and contact information may appear in the letterhead, signature, or a separate section. Separate presentation may be required in a forensic report. When writing reports regarding traumatized youths, the evaluator's opinions must be grounded in knowledge of the field, peer-reviewed scientific research, the multiple levels of trauma and its multiple impacts on youths, related developmental issues, and the influence of background and other factors that may impact the symptomatology of a youth (Wilson & Moran, 2004). The evaluator must be able to competently use diagnostic testing measures and methods.

Current Presentation, Identifying Data, or Behavioral Observation

The youth's (and sometimes family's) current presentation may be included among the findings or as a separate section. This section may include identifying data and mental status information.

Tony is an attractive 8-year-old boy who attends the 3rd grade at . . . Tony insisted upon his mother's presence in the interview. Tony's appearance was clean and age appropriate. He appeared nervous and expressed anxiety about what would be decided by his interview. He did not want to go back to school. His affect was congruent with his mood. He denied hallucinations and was oriented to time, place, and person. His stream of thought was normal except . . . During most of the interview, Tony was easily distracted by sounds or movement. He jumped under the table and covered his neck when there was a loud banging noise outside that made the windows rattle . . .

Mathew is currently an inpatient at . . . Mathew is a 15-year-old boy who appears physically somewhat younger than his age. He has inked "Dead Kennedy's Society" and skull and crossbones on his jacket sleeve. By his own design, his short hair is bleached blond with darker roots. Mathew disavowed the need for hospitalization or for treatment. He explained that his teacher had grabbed his arm so he punched him . . . Mathew was oriented to time and place . . .

History and Background

History and background information may include any information about the youth's history and background and about the event that is needed to understand fully the situation under assessment (Vassallo, 2002). Depending on its purpose and audience, history and background may include a description of the precipitating event, the youth's emotional and physical exposure to it, his or her prior history, relevant demographics, and background information (Donders, 2001a). Agencies have differing policies about including cultural information in reports. If the report's purpose is to determine damages to be awarded the youth and his or her family because of the traumatic experience, the history and background section may include the youth's psychological history and previous functioning in order to determine how much of his or her condition is related to the event.

When the earthquake of 5.6 magnitude resulted in the collapse of the school gymnasium during third period gym class, Tony was in the gym. He sustained multiple injuries . . . leg was broken in three places . . . Sixteen of his classmates and Tony's teacher also were injured. Five of his peers were killed. Tony was hospitalized for three weeks, and required a period of recuperation after he returned home . . .

Before the gym collapsed, Tony, a well-behaved 8-year-old boy, was well liked by his peers and adults. From kindergarten to 3rd grade, teachers described him as intelligent, conscientious, active, and imaginative. His grade point average was 3.4. He was reading at a 7th grade level. Tony's mother described him as well behaved although occasionally playfully mischievous . . .

Mathew lives with his mother and stepfather. Mathew's parents were divorced and his father moved out of state when he was 7. He has had little contact with his father since then. His mother had a series of relationships before her current marriage. She explains that the men stayed long enough for Mathew to become attached and then left. Mathew has a close and comfortable relationship with his mother. Mathew states that he likes his stepfather okay. He does not appear to have formed an attachment to him ....

On [date], Mathew went with John, his best friend, and his best friend's parents to [location] to visit [amusement park]. They were having lunch in a small restaurant when a man entered and shot "an old man" sitting across from Mathew and then started walking around shooting others . . . [see Box 1.1].

Prior to the shootings, Mathew was a happy, well-behaved, easygoing, well-liked boy who enjoyed life.

The Findings

Findings include the results of assessments, interviews, and observations. This section presents findings but does not make conclusions (Buzzard, 1972). Subsections may cover (1) interviews with, observations of, and self-reports by the youth; (2) caregiver reports; (3) teacher reports; (4) medical and psychological reports from other sources; (5) school information from records and school personnel; and, possibly, (6) peer reports. If appropriate, this or an earlier section may include a mental status exam and a description of the assessed individual's appearance, demeanor, and presentation. Whether or not to include previous medical history or current medical information will depend on the needs of the report and the laws of the land. Some states, for example, ban the disclosure of HIV-positive status (Donders, 2001a).

> *Homeschooling.* When his physician approved school attendance, Tony refused to return to school. Homeschooling was attempted in May. According to the teacher, Tony was anxious, exhibited poor concentration, and frequently displayed angry outbursts. He would not let his mother leave the room. When other youths came to visit him, he became extremely upset if they hovered around him or were noisy. On several occasions, he covered his ears and screamed in response to loud noises or his friends' chatter.

The discussion of findings should be sufficiently logical and thorough that when readers approach the closing section, they would make the same conclusions and recommendations as the report writer (Vassallo, 2002). Quotations from the youth or others, vignettes of the youth's behaviors, and tables or figures may help to paint a picture of the youth's condition and functioning. The following excerpts from *interview* findings demonstrate Tony's symptoms, his anxious attachment, and its impact on his mother.

> . . . Tony's mother complained, "Tony will not let me out of his sight. He holds onto my clothes . . . I can't get anything done. I have no privacy. I feel guilty because I am irritable and exhausted . . ." According to his mother and two neighbors (one of Tony's friends and his mother), Tony has been constantly frightened and irritable. He startles easily. He jumps in response to any rattling or rumbling sound and sometimes startles when the clock ticks . . .

> . . . More than two years after the traumatic event, even though some of his original symptoms (e.g., startle reactions and physiological reactions to reminders) are no longer apparent, Mathew scored 75 (*very severe*) on the Childhood Posttraumatic Stress Reaction Index. He continues to have intrusive thoughts and dreams about his experience, engages in repeated re-enactments of aspects of his experience [see Box 1.1], avoids reminders or lashes out in response to their imposition, . . . Mathew is unable to concentrate at school. He is quick to aggression in response to traumatic reminders, expects aggression from others, and seeks opportunities to fight . . . Mathew continues to exhibit and report a complicated form of PTSD as well as unresolved complicated grief for his dead friend. Although prior to the massacre, Mathew exhibited intelligence, conscience, adequate coping skills, good self-control, and quality peer attachments, his symptoms have undermined these aspects of his personality, skills, and personal resources. His relationships are among aggressive and other troubled peers. Mainstream peers avoid him. He demonstrates hostile attribution biases and is quick to aggression . . .

Opinion or Conclusions

The *conclusions, recommendations,* or *opinions* should arise from the findings (Buzzard, 1972). Whether or not this includes a diagnosis or a description depends, again, on the purpose of the report. In order to have the reader agree with the conclusions, the report must address every issue that may concern the reader (Vassallo, 2002). Conclusions may be presented in narrative form or as an itemized list (Donders, 2001b). The purpose of the report may suggest the need for a prognosis section or information about appropriate interventions. Diagnoses may or may not be necessary. For neuropsychiatric reports, Donders found that private practitioners were more likely to provide diagnostic information than clinicians employed in medical or rehabilitative settings, perhaps because they routinely provide them for reimbursement agencies.

Recommendations:

1. Continued homeschooling for two more weeks while Tony, his mother, and his classmates and teacher are prepared for his reentry into the classroom.
2. With his mother's permission, meeting of his therapist with his classroom to help them to understand his symptoms and needs (e.g., that they avoid noisily hovering around him, warn him of their approach . . .).
3. His mother's presence in his classroom and her gradual removal—from next to him, to the back of the room, to outside the door, to the school library. . . .

. . . Mathew is currently unable to function acceptably in a normal classroom environment. His hyperreactivity, poor impulse control, and outbursts pose a threat to his teachers and peers. If he does not lash out, he self-medicates or sleeps in response to unavoidable stress . . .

Mathew would benefit from special schooling and ongoing, specialized trauma treatment. . . . Prognosis is guarded. Early resilience factors, his willingness to engage in treatment, and a strong support system are advantages. Comprehensive intervention is advisable.

Limitations

A section or subsection on the limitations of the evaluation is appropriate in some cases but not in others. *Limitations* are factors that may prevent the report from being current, thorough, or conclusive (Vassallo, 2002). This section provides a format for review of any inconsistencies or information contradictory to the findings. It may identify the possible influence of unavailable data, time limitations, the state of current knowledge, or the need for additional observation. If not specifically requested, including such a section in a report for schools or insurance agencies may only create confusion. For court purposes, however, this section may permit a jury or judge to evaluate more accurately the report provider's findings in relationship to the case.

Additional Aspects of the Report

Additional or optional elements may enhance the reader's understanding. A cover page or letter may include the report title, date, and name of both provider and recipient and may include an abstract of the report (Vassallo, 2002). A table of contents and a glossary of terms may facilitate the ease of reading (Allnutt & Chaplow, 2000; Vassallo). The report's audience may benefit from a description of the possible results, course, and long-term effects of trauma that may be relevant to the case. Illustrations such as figures or tables may demonstrate a point such as the infrequency of a behavior or symptom among the normal population for this age group, if such information is available. These materials can be provided throughout the text or in an addendum. If the conclusions or opinions of the report are in narrative form, a point-by-point list may be used to summarize the findings, conclusions, or recommendations.

ADDITIONAL ISSUES FOR FORENSIC REPORTS

Traumatic experiences may result in civil or criminal litigation, custody cases, and juvenile court proceedings. Civil cases may follow the perception or actuality that someone is responsible for the damages or injuries (physical or psychological) that occurred during the event. Criminal cases may follow human-perpetrated events such as violence or fires. The juvenile justice system may become involved in determining child abuse, neglect, or molestation as well as in placement of children. Family courts may oversee custody cases in which traumatization has been alleged. Any of these forensic circumstances may require report writing.

Courts demonstrate continued uncertainty about the exact nature of what the behavioral sciences can contribute, for example, to sorting out allegations of child sexual abuse (The Forensic Echo, 1998, 2002). The standard for reports has moved from opinion-based findings to scientific-based expert testimony (The Forensic Echo; Wilson & Moran, 2004). A report may have a major impact on multiple lives because of its content and consequences. If conclusions provided in reports and testimony cannot be defended when challenged during cross-examination, they are likely to be discredited or impeached by a skillful opposing attorney. Rawdon (1994) recommends trying to read the report with the jury's eyes or hear the testimony from the jury's ears.

Forensic reports may necessitate attention to specific details such as documentation of results and maintenance of records (Donders, 2001b). When compiling a forensic report, the steps to be taken often include instruction regarding the requirements of the report, evaluation, information-gathering, formulating an opinion, and drafting the report (Allnutt & Chaplow, 2000). The report then includes a statement of purpose and sources of information, relevant history and background, the nature of assessments and findings, and an opinion.

It is important to remember that the court process may be trying for traumatized youths. The American Bar Association has guidelines for the fair treatment of child witnesses (Wilsey, 2004). Among its recommendations are the following: (1) the use of a multidisciplinary team; (2) awareness of the impact of a continuance on the well-being of the youth; (3) accommodating court protocols to meet the needs of the child; (4) the court's discretion in the use of leading questions with children; (5) avoidance of intimidating or confusing the child witness; (6) as long as the defendant's right to cross-examine is not impaired, permitting the child to testify from a location other than that normally reserved for witnesses, via closed-circuit television, or through a one-way mirror; (7) allowing the noninfluencing presence and accessibility of a supportive person for the child witness at all times during his or her testimony; (8) excluding unnecessary individuals from the courtroom at the request of the child witness or his or her representative; and (9) the use of videotaped depositions.

The Expert Witness

For the field of trauma, the expert witness serves as "an impartial neutral witness with specialized experience and expertise in the area of trauma and PTSD" (Wilson & Moran, 2004, p. 617). State and federal laws may determine who can provide reports or expert testimony as well as what is required for an acceptable report. A state may require, for example, that an expert witness who writes a report be currently engaged in a clinical practice or respected training position. Reports may specify board certification, relevant publications, professional memberships, knowledge of assessment techniques, knowledge of treatment modalities, knowledge of scientific literature, and experience (Kay, 2002; Wilson & Moran). During most of the 20th century, expert testimony was based on the Frye Rule (Wilson & Moran). An expert's opinion had to be based on data, information, and conclusions that were generally accepted among the majority of colleagues in a specialty (The Forensic Echo, 1998, 2002; Wilson & Moran). In 1993, the *general acceptance* rule was replaced by the Daubert standard (Supreme Court case: Daubert v. Merrell Dow Pharmaceuticals Inc.), which emphasized whether a technique/theory could be scientifically tested, has been peer reviewed and published in scientific journals, and has known and potential rates of error, as well as the general acceptance of the theory (Wilson & Moran).

In addition to the need for scientifically tested information about trauma in children, the expert will need to use multiple sources and methods of information (Wilson & Moran, 2004). Interviews conducted by different examiners can be useful. Although a single evaluator is acceptable, a number of professionals suggest the use of a team, especially for sexual abuse cases (D'Urso et al., 1995; Faller, 1998b). Ethical practices include that professionals maintain high standards of competence and provide only services for which they are qualified by training and experience. As discussed earlier, maintaining objectivity is also important (D'Urso et al.).

The Evaluator's Role

When writing reports for the court, the forensic or nonforensic professional may find him- or herself in ethical conflict in relationship to role and ethical/moral obligations (Allnutt & Chaplow, 2000; D'Urso et al., 1995). When the professional is both therapist and evaluator, the therapeutic alliance may be disrupted. Under normal circumstances, a primary goal is to act in the best interest of children and adults without doing harm. When the clinician has a therapeutic relationship with family members in a custody or abuse case, the duty to protect children overrides benefi-cence or avoidance of providing evidence that may damage or distress others. Allnutt and Chaplow recommend clarifying roles, any limitations to confidentiality, and boundaries at the beginning of an evaluation that is conducted to enable a forensic report. Decisions must be made about what is relevant to the case and what might cause unnecessary damage to those under review and any third parties that may be injured by the report. In all cases, it is essential that the report writer be aware of the possible impact of the report.

Appelbaum (1990, 1997) describes the forensic psychiatrist as primarily an evaluator rather than a therapist (cited in Allnutt & Chaplow, 2000). He delineates the principles of forensic psychiatry as "subjective truth tell-ing," "objective truth telling," and "respect for the person." Although a final opinion involves subjective truth telling, the expert should have gen-uine belief in his or her testimony and must acknowledge the limitations of the testimony and of current scientific knowledge. Allnutt and Chap-low point out that the forensic report should be written for the purpose of assisting the court, judge, or jury to make an appropriate determination (see also Wandersman, 1998). They recommend that the evaluator resist giving opinions on the ultimate issue or legal determination even when justice system members encourage them to do so.

Readiness for Testimony

Self-examination and discussions with attorneys, other team members, and/or court personnel can assist readiness to testify. Examination of per-sonal history (especially previous testimony), biases, and weak areas can help readiness. Preparation with anticipated hypothetical questions that may be posed by attorneys from both sides can prevent awkward answers (Schultz, 1989). Materials may be taken to court that support findings such as charts or prepared notes on the qualities and validation of measures used. It is important to be able to *state aloud* the limitations of findings, measures used, and personal expertise. The evaluator/expert witness may be asked questions about his or her qualifications, or any *skeletons* in his or her own closet, and for a copy of a personal vita or resume. Aware-ness of the court setup and legal audience can be invaluable. Knowing the demographics of jury members (e.g., location, educational level) as well as judge's style or special expectations, for example, can help to shape the presentation (Schultz).

For a forensic report, the evaluator may want to review legal text such as the court's specific request and the legal issues pertaining to it, formal charges made against a defendant, medical reports or a police summary of facts, police video interviews and transcripts, relevant statements and affidavit material, psychological and psychiatric reports, and clinical notes (Allnutt & Chaplow, 2000). Evaluations for compensation may require atten-tion to the impact of the stressor event on mental state and emotional and behavioral functioning. Causality may be the focus of such an assessment.

An understanding of the child's previous psychiatric and developmental history is essential to assessing the impact of a traumatic experience.

Consent

States and countries may have codes of ethics regarding consent. In Australia and New Zealand, the Psychiatrists Code of Ethics requires an informed consent in which the assessed individual is advised of the purpose of the report, the nature of the assessment, and the potential risks and benefits of undertaking the assessment. Allnutt and Chaplow (2000) recommend, in addition, advising the individual of the following: for whom the report is being written, for what agency the professional is working, the consequences of making incriminating statements, and any possibility that the information may be made available to a wider public. Unlike confidential clinical reports, forensic reports may be distributed to parties in a lawsuit or other legal proceeding. Opposing legal counsel, the judge, juries, insurance companies, and opposing expert witnesses may receive copies (Wilson & Moran, 2004). Aspects of the report may be read aloud in court. Youths and families affected by traumatic events will have to contend with court proceedings, hear repeated discussions of aspects of the traumatic event, be presented with traumatic images and other reminders, be required to share personal information, and endure other experiences that may be particularly trying to someone who is traumatized (Box 16.1a).

The Rules of Evidence

The rules of evidence control the information that may be introduced in court (Feller, Davidson, Hardin, & Horowitz, 1992). The standard of proof in criminal cases is *beyond a reasonable doubt* and in civil cases is *a preponderance of the evidence.* A number of resources are available online regarding laws and procedures related to reports and testimony in specific states (e.g., search for laws on court testimony; www.findlaw.com). Based on the reliability and prejudicial or nonprejudicial nature of information, evidentiary rules delineate what the judge is allowed to consider and what must be excluded from consideration. The admissibility of investigations, note-taking, and preserved and other evidence are governed by these rules. Feller et al. have described the types of admissible evidence. *Direct evidence* is based on personal knowledge or observation (usually eyewitness testimony). *Real or demonstrative evidence* generally includes objects such as documents, photographs, or x-rays. Before real or demonstrative evidence may be presented to the court, a foundation must be laid that establishes its relevance and authenticity. *Circumstantial evidence* is indirect evidence from which particular inferences can be drawn. In child abuse

---

BOX 16.1

Case Examples: Forensic Cases

a. *Mark.* When he was 16, Mark and his family returned from an outing to find their front door ajar. Mark's father went into the house while the rest of the family waited in the car. They heard gunfire, and then saw a robber run out of the house. Mark chased and tackled the robber just before the police arrived and arrested the man. His two siblings ran into the house and saw their dead father. The experience of successfully apprehending the robber/murderer had served as a protective factor for Mark. He was less symptomatic than his siblings. In court when the deputy district attorney showed him the picture, Mark saw his father's bloody body for the first time. His symptoms increased following his testimony.

b. *Bianca.* When she was 16, Bianca gave police a detailed description of her father fondling her breasts and requested protection. The police investigator was somewhat concerned about inconsistencies in her report. Nevertheless, because of this bright adolescent girl's insistence, she was placed in an upper middle-class foster home similar to her own home. Her father denied the allegations to Child Protective Services investigators, but plead *no contest* in court and permitted his daughter's placement. Bianca discovered that she had no more freedom in placement than she had at home. She grew tired of living away from home. She admitted that she made up the story of abuse because she was angry at her father for not letting her go out.

---

cases, this may include a neighbor who heard a child screaming and an adult shouting, a teacher's observation of the parent's frequent smell of alcohol and slurred speech, or an expert's testimony that a child's injuries are inconsistent with the parents' explanations for them.

Evidence must be *material* (i.e., have a logical connection to any of the issues to be proven) and *relevant* (i.e., it increases the likelihood that a particular fact occurred) (Feller et al., 1992). The *hearsay rule* requires that relevant but unreliable evidence will be excluded. States or localities may differ in the nature of their exceptions to the hearsay rules. Exceptions— out-of-court admissions, excited utterances, regularly and systematically kept records, statements made to a physician for diagnosis or treatment, and information with circumstantial guarantees of trustworthiness—may vary related to the type of case (criminal or civil) and special statutory exceptions. Some states have defined special exceptions for child abuse cases. For example, a 4-year-old child's but not an adult's utterances several hours after a rape may be admissible as excited utterances.

The Purpose of the Report

The purpose of the forensic evaluation is to address the legal question. Upon receipt of the request for a report, the forensic psychiatrist, psychologist, social worker, or other professional must initially clarify the question and information sought as well as the roles, responsibilities, and expectations of the evaluator and the requestor (Allnutt & Chaplow, 2000). Formal legal instruction may be advisable. Evaluation often consists of understanding the past and present behavior and mental/emotional state of the individual to be assessed. The information sought may be case- and circumstance-specific. The requesting agent can specify, for example, how much background information should be collected before the report is written or whether, instead, the report is to be written from the per- spective of a blind expert or observer. For trauma evaluations, the blind observer may be *blind to* the individual's level of exposure, past history, or other specific information until after the initial evaluation. Prosecut- ing or defending attorneys may want testimony from one expert with- out knowledge of the defendant or complainant and one who has directly interviewed either the defendant or complainant.

Measures and Methods

The results obtained from test measures are only as good as the mea- sures used (Kay, 2002). Forensic reports usually enlist a combination of methods and measures (Wilson & Moran, 2004). Methods used must have demonstrated validity and reliability for the population assessed and must be used in the prescribed and validated fashion. Multiple types of assessment permit comparison of data and a fuller picture of the youth and his or her situation. Maltreatment experts recommend that evalua- tions with youths be therapeutic in nature, take place over several ses- sions, and include multiple types of assessment in multiple settings (Lubit et al., 2002; D'Urso et al., 1995; Wandersman, 1998). In addition to individual interviews and measures, assessment may include conjoint interviews with family members in order to evaluate issues such as attach- ment, the quality of interaction, and other aspects of the parent-child relationships (Wandersman). According to Wandersman, in addition to a supportive and respectful process, evaluations that address difficult issues such as traumas should avoid making the child feel rushed, pressured, or misused (see chapter 9). Children need to be heard and taken seriously. Several sessions may be required in order to establish trust, to enhance the youth's opening up, and to increase the depth of the assessment.

Youth and parent assessments may include intelligence tests, per- sonality measures, adaptive behavior tests and observations, academic achievement tests, and diagnostic assessments including trauma mea- sures (Wandersman, 1998). These tests can provide a profile of cognitive strengths and weaknesses, self-confidence, developmental problems, and special needs such as attention, memory, or impulse control problems. Such tests can also elucidate the youth's style in handling challenges, frus- tration, and distractions and the parents' intellectual skills for responsible parenting (Gordon, 2002; Wandersman). Although a battery of normed tests can provide useful general information about developmental level, educational needs, motivation, and behavior, they may or may not be of use for the professional's purposes. Such tests can be expensive to administer (Wandersman).

Interpreting Test Results

To adequately and accurately interpret assessment tools, it is essential to recognize youths' developmental and emotional functioning levels and to be aware of the influence of current circumstances including the effects of the court proceedings. No diagnostic interview, test, or observational method can determine whether or not someone engaged in a past act (Gordon, 2002). From psychological tests, the examiner can hypothesize about whether such behavior is typical or not typical of a particular personality.

The Opinion

Even though other parts of the report focus on information from the past, an opinion is written in the present tense (Allnutt & Chaplow, 2000). The opinion section of the report is likely to be of most interest to the court. It should be based on the findings from interviews, observations, supplementary reports, and other information gathered. The credibility given to the report and to the opinion is apt to depend on the strength of its reasoning. Allnutt and Chaplow recommend logically structuring the opinion by providing the basis for each level of inference. This structure should include establishing the evidence for or against psychopathology, outlining the nature of the psychopathology, explaining the impact of the psychopathology on the person's behavior and functioning, and explaining how the behavior and psychopathology apply to the legal issue. They emphasize an awareness of the limits of inferring causality and suggest that the professional address any inconsistencies and contradictions to the findings.

Allnutt and Chaplow (2000) explain that, in court cases, experts are invited to provide psychiatric information that then can be utilized to determine the applicability of a legal concept. They recommend caution when crossing professional boundaries. When assessing a defendant, legal report writing primarily requires the approach of a phenomenologist, not a diagnostician. Diagnostic classification systems are provided to improve interrater reliability and to facilitate standard individual assessment as well as research about the diagnostic category. Diagnoses were not created for use in the courtroom. Forensic consultants often recommend providing a thorough description of the individual's symptoms and behaviors instead of a diagnosis (Allnutt & Chaplow; D'Urso et al., 1995; Gordon, 2002; Lubit et al., 2002). A diagnosis becomes of greater importance in the sentencing or dispositional phase of court proceedings because it informs of prognosis and treatment (Allnutt & Chaplow).

Specific Types of Reports

Information specific to domestic violence and abuse cases is presented briefly here.

Domestic Violence

Most studies of domestic violence have relied on a single source of information (the mother), have failed to include important other variables such as abuse of children, and have studied only children housed in shelters for battered women (Edleson, 1999). Although more study is needed, court reports must take into account current findings and guidelines for child witnesses to violence who may also have been abused. Witnessing domestic violence is among the experiences linked to PTSD symptoms and to multiple documented problems (Edleson). Among the youths' *psychological and emotional problems* are hostility, aggression, anxiety, social withdrawal, and depression. Problems with *cognitive functioning* may include lower verbal and quantitative skills as well as attitudes that support the use of violence. *Longer-term difficulties* such as depression, trauma-related symptoms among men, and trauma-related symptoms plus low self-esteem among women have also been found. Physical abuse, younger age, more recent witnessing of violence, the mother's increased distress, and the lack of perceived family support for the child have been associated with increased symptoms. Adolescents exposed to both community and domestic violence have coped better if they live in more stable and socially connected households.

Research confirms that approximately half of the men who battered their wives also abused their children (Saunders, 1998). Battered women were half as likely as men to abuse their children and were much *less* likely to direct anger toward their children when they are not in a violent relationship. Physical abuse, harassment, and stalking frequently continue after separation and divorce. Women are at increased risk of homicide during separation, custody hearings, or visitation exchanges of children. Rarely, men kill children in retaliation after being left. Over half of male batterers are repeat offenders.

States have begun to adopt the *Model Code of the Family Violence Project* of the National Council of Juvenile and Family Court Judges (NCFCJ, 1995; Saunders, 1998). These statutes include the presumption that it is detrimental to and not *in the best interest of the child* to be placed in the sole custody of or in joint legal or joint physical custody with a perpetrator of family violence. Some states' statutes now address additional concerns including (1) the prevention of child abduction by the perpetrator through supervised visitation; (2) a defense against child abduction charges if battered women flee with their children; (3) battered women's exemption from mandated mediation; (4) protection of battered women from charges of "child abandonment" if they flee for their safety, (5) permission to check on the criminal charges against a divorce partner; and (6) increased ease for battered women to relocate far from their abusers. Not all courts consider spousal abuse when they assess each parent's willingness to co-parent when making custody decisions. Consequently, battered women may be labeled "uncooperative."

Child Abuse Reports

Courts are reluctant to blindly accept children's testimony about sexual abuse partly because false testimony has helped to convict innocent people (Foote, 2002; Box 16.1b). On the other hand, children sometimes recant their allegations when actual abuse has occurred. No foolproof indicators of past sexual abuse exist (Kamphuis, Kugeares, & Finn, 2000). Symptoms of PTSD can arise from experiences other than sexual molestation, and the behavioral profile of an abused child is also exhibited by nonabused children (Crump, 2002; La Greca, Silverman, Vernberg, & Prinstein, 1996; Nader, Pynoos, Fairbanks, & Frederick, 1990; Udwin, Boyle, Yule, Bolton, & O'Ryan, 2002). From the perspective of the accused, individuals whose tests suggest that they are very disturbed may never hurt anyone, whereas some essentially normal individuals may do some very bad things (Gordon, 2002). All allegations must be taken seriously.

Reports on child neglect and abuse require an astute, objective, and thorough understanding of the youth's familial, social, and systemic environments and their relationship to the presenting symptoms (Allnutt & Chaplow, 2000). Bathing routines, sleeping arrangements, views of nudity, and discussions of sexuality may vary considerably among households and cultures (D'Urso et al., 1995). In some cultures, genital stimulation is used to soothe infants. An evaluator may need to examine the degree to which practices are embedded in the family's culture, and their receptivity to education about the laws and mores in this country.

Among the indicators that a child has been sexually abused are the youth's own statements of abuse; sexualized play and behaviors; sexual interests that are not age-appropriate; atypical responses to sexual stimuli; sexualized responses to projective tests; trauma symptoms; intense anxiety; changes in emotional and performance behaviors; and disruption of key regulatory processes such as appetite, sleep, mood, aggression, and impulsivity; and the content of dreams and nightmares (Burgess, 2002; Gilgun, 1998). Physical findings include sexually transmitted infections, visible injuries to the genitalia or anal regions, and the use of a colposcope to detect pelvic or genital injury not seen in a visual examination (Burgess; Faller, 1998b; Gilgun). Behavioral indicators must be interpreted with cognizance of the context in which the behaviors occur, the youth's age, other relevant circumstances, the relationship of the child to the accused abuser, and the physical and mental health of the child (Burgess). The examiner must distinguish from those arising from sexual abuse, for example, behaviors that follow something a 3 year old walked in on or wanted to imitate after seeing it on television.

Crump (2002) explains that, rather than providing a conclusion—that a child was abused because she or he exhibits symptoms of abuse— accepted expert testimony has assisted the jury in evaluating whether behavior is indicative of a falsehood. The admissibility of psychological testimony is largely dependent upon how the offer of guidance is made, for what purpose, and in what jurisdiction. Collateral information such as medical, behavioral, and psychological reports and observations regarding the child and the environment can help to substantiate the clinical facts. In addition, reports may address the likelihood that an event(s) can be linked (as the proximate cause) to any particular symptoms (Lubit et al., 2002). Multiple interviews may be necessary in order to establish rapport and trust with the child. Multiple interviews may confuse the child (D'Urso et al., 1995). Depending on the youth's needs, evaluators recommend between two and no more than six assessment interviews for sexual abuse cases.

CONCLUSIONS

A treating mental-health professional or agency, physicians, forensic sources, schools, or insurance or other compensating agencies may request a report regarding a youth exposed to a traumatic event. Reports for forensic and nonforensic purposes must provide accurate, relevant, and ethical information and be guided by consideration for all whom the report may affect, professional ethics, and laws related to evaluations/investigations and report writing. The professional is responsible for obtaining up-to-date information about relevant laws and practices, examining personal biases, and clarifying the goals and purposes of the report. The content of reports varies in response to the needs of the requesting agency, available information, and the evaluator's training. Youths' and adults' lives may be affected dramatically by the content and recommendations in a report. In forensic cases, the result may be a change in custody or placement of a child, incarceration, or failure to protect a youth. Training, experience, and good investigative skills can help to prevent faulty conclusions regarding youths actually or allegedly exposed to traumas.

17

An Afterword
Some Conclusions About Assessing Trauma in Youths

For most of us who assess and treat children and adolescents, the goal is to prevent their harm or psychopathology and to help remedy psychological or developmental disruption and difficulties or disorders. The purpose of developing measures and methods of assessment is to assist these goals. The child or adolescent is the most important element of the assessment or diagnosis and treatment process. The individual is assessment's reason for being. Because assessing youths requires time, energy, and other resources, we all want the fastest and most efficient ways to accomplish assessments. Quick methods of sampling such as via telephone and the Internet present obvious concerns even when assessing adolescents. Studies have demonstrated that youths report more symptoms in face-to-face interviews than over the phone or completing forms in groups (Jones & Ribbe, 1991; Todd, Joyner, Heath, Neuman, & Reich, 2003). Evidence suggests the therapeutic value of appropriately conducted face-to-face assessments as well (Nader, Pynoos, Fairbanks, & Frederick, 1990). I believe that part of our roles as assessors is to discover methods and practices that are most helpful to youths as well as revealing of their needs and difficulties. Many of the challenges to achieving accurate assessments are related to the lack of relevant information about youths prior to their traumatic experiences. Routine assessments beginning in early life used only for youths' benefit would be ideal. This would require effective ongoing protections of confidentiality.

This book describes commonly studied and recently contemplated posttrauma reactions in youths, variables important to their assessment, and subgroups or subtypes that may explain the frequently mixed findings in

401

the assessment of youths exposed to traumatic experiences.[1] Especially for children, PTSD captures only limited aspects of posttraumatic psychopathology (Briere & Spinazzola, 2005; Fletcher, 2003; Nader, 2001b; Terr, 1991; van der Kolk & Courtois, 2005; Scheeringa & Zeanah, 2001). Children exposed to ongoing and to single traumas may have the symptoms of complex PTSD and may experience considerable developmental disruption as a result of their experiences (Herman, 1992c; Ford, Courtois, Steele, van der Hart, & Nijenhuis, 2005c; van der Kolk & Courtois). Dramatically altered attitudes and patterns of interaction may derail relationships, successful actions, and opportunities. With his kind permission, the story of "Mathew"[2] has been told in some detail in order to illustrate these and many of the other points made in this book. His trauma assessment and treatment began when the field was just developing measures to assess youths' traumatic reactions. This chapter presents a comparison of Mathew's life 2 years after the trauma and now (Table 17.1). It provides a summary of important points related to assessing trauma.

The Story of Mathew

Mathew provides an excellent example of the ability of youths to recover from the depths of despair and a seemingly destroyed life (Box 1.1). A few minutes is a very long and stressful time to be hiding under a table wondering if you and people you care about will be the next persons killed. Mathew waited for well over an hour, during which people he loved were killed and many others were killed or mutilated, sometimes in front of him. He could not escape seeing still others after the shooting stopped. His every movement to discover what was happening during the siege resulted in the repeated shooting of his best friend's father. Mathew managed only a brief escape when he passed out for a short time. His intense desires to understand what was happening and to fight back or otherwise intervene were impossible to act upon during the experience. He desperately tried to awaken his dead friend. His best friend's mother was clearly dead. He had to walk out through a pool of blood. He endured the images of mutilation and others' screams of pain all the way to the hospital.

By the time his mother finally found someone with experience in treating traumatized youths, he was using alcohol and hard drugs to anesthetize himself, behaving aggressively, and endangering himself repeatedly. For a time, only his mother and his new therapist believed he could recover. Both could see his dynamic spirit and the beautiful heart that were hidden under the noise and commotion of traumatic response. It was

---

[1] Since the completion of this book, a few additional articles have been found or made available (See Reference section).

[2] His name has been changed, of course, to protect his privacy. I trust that those who read about him will also respect his privacy.

TABLE 17.1
Case of Mathew

Symptom	2 Years After the Massacre (Age 15)	Currently
Intrusive thoughts	Quickly put it out of his mind when thoughts intruded. In treatment session, he repeatedly engaged in play that replicated aspects of his experience.	Thinks of it about once every two months when there is a show about it on TV or if asked (e.g., when giving his medical history). The same memories replay at those times—being told that the man was coming down the isles shooting people, being told to move to safety, the initial gunshot, trying to get his dead friend to respond, the SWAT team kicking his friend's dad, a beeping machine, the injured people in the ambulance
Distressing dreams	Dreams and nightmares about the massacre every night	Rarely dreams of it. No nightmares after seeing TV shows about massacre.
Reliving, reenactment, or repetitive behaviors	Smelled gunpowder a lot of the time; jumped and became fearful if heard a popping sound. Repeated reenactments of aspects of his experience. Often engaged in aggressive reenactments after reminders of the event.	None. Goes hunting and is okay with gun sounds. Is aware if gun sounds occur otherwise. No longer compelled to react to reminders with replays. Still likes to fight but only does so in martial arts competitions.
Recurrent Distress w/reminders	Emotional with reminders. Yearly, in the month it occurred became squirmy and unfocused without realizing it. Able to move quickly into emotionless mode; would "shut down" or go to sleep.	For a while, was emotional when saw a TV show about it, but is not so much anymore.
Somatic Complaints w/reminders	Fast heartbeat, sweats, became really fatigued and went to sleep	Fast heartbeat if watches a show about the massacre. Otherwise, none.
Avoidance of thoughts, talk, and feelings	Wanted to avoid thoughts, feelings, and conversations. Learned to "just not feel." Went to sleep or took drugs to avoid being overwhelmed by feelings and thoughts. Did not want to talk about it.	No longer needs to shut down. Does not offer information about the massacre because prefers not to be fussed over. Can talk about it comfortably. Talks things out now rather than hiding his feelings. If feels he is starting to shut down, he catches himself and does not. Because he has overcome his own resentments, he readily talks about the massacre to help others overcome their resentments.

TABLE 17.1 (continued)
Case of Mathew

Symptom	2 Years After the Massacre (Age 15)	Currently
Avoidances of activities, people and places	Avoided all restaurants like where it happened or any similar restaurant. Got drunk when went through the town where it occurred. Avoided some really really scary people but "hung out" with violent people.	Will eat takeout from those places but will not eat inside. Eats in other restaurants. Does not want to go to where it occurred but now will go sober to other locations beyond it that they visited on their trip before the massacre. Is always sober now.
Diminished interest in activities	Liked action figures. Did not lose interest in activities. Changed peer group and main activities. Engaged in less wholesome activity.	Engages in many activities and has many friends. Loves snow and water sports, fishing, and hunting. Enjoys activities with his family. Learned martial arts and enjoys competition…
Amnesias	Forgot large segments of his experience.	Recalled the experience in his treatment and has no missing segments now.
Detachment or loss of engagement	Was very detached.	He has close relationships. Still, in large social gatherings that include some who are close to him, he feels apart and may lock up. Comes out of it when his wife makes him aware of it. Is very social otherwise.
Restricted range of affect	Unable to feel positive emotions like happiness. Did not smile for years. Was guarded with others. Drinking and drugs permitted him to feel invincible.	Experiences the whole range of emotions. Is happy and loves his family. Enjoys friends. Felt an amazing depth of love with the birth of his child.
Sense of foreshortened future/pessimistic outlook	Was sure that he would not live to be 21 and was okay with that. Did not expect to marry or have a family.	Expects a long life despite physical consequences of drug usage. Has a loving family and expects it to grow.
Sleep disturbance	Sleep disturbed by nightmares. Fell asleep under stress during the day. Sleep was his escape. Slept as much as he could.	Sleeps well. No longer needs to sleep when reminded of the event. No nightmares.
Irritability or outbursts of anger	Sought fights. Reacted aggressively in response to reminders. Had hostile attributional biases. Wanted to make the first attack rather than be attacked. Extreme reactivity.	Does not fight now: "It's not me." Only fights in competitions. Is tempted to fight when he meets someone who is really aggressive and might hurt others like the guy who thought the Texas tower murders were cool. Loses his temper on occasion at dysfunctional employees but calms and apologizes for snapping at them.

Poor concentration	Unable to concentrate. Tried special classes, then dropped out of school.	Is a successful businessman who supervises a division of individuals. He takes on new challenges and stays with them until he conquers them.
Hypervigilance, excessive fear, or frozen watchfulness	Hypervigilant. Expected danger. Sought fights. Wanted to be the attacker and not the attacked. Carried a gun for protection.	Vigilance has replaced hypervigilance. Is not really fearful now. He is very aware of those around him when he is in areas he knows unsavory characters frequent. Still faces the door when eats in a restaurant.
Exaggerated startle response	Had an exaggerated startle response that was its worst during his stay in the hospital after the massacre.	None now.
Complex Trauma	*************************************	*************************************
Impaired functioning: academic, social, other	Unable to do schoolwork or function normally socially. "I would say that I was unable to function at all." Unable to have a sustained relationship or hold a job.	Has a good marriage and lovely family, a good job, and teaches others to live successfully. Speaks at AA meetings. Counsels others. Supervises others at work. Is skilled and successful.
Numbing, detachment, or absence of emotional responsiveness	Used sleep or drugs to numb when stressed or reminded of the massacre. Could "just not feel" and could shut people out. Could put himself in a state of mind where he "did not care about anyone or anything."	Is completely sober. Okay to talk and think about the massacre. Cares for others. Is a good support person and counselor to friends and AA members.
Derealization or Depersonalization	None reported	None.
Dysregulation of affect and impulses	Could shut off his conscience. Felt the need to fight. Could be angry or mean without guilt. Excessive risk taking—endangered self repeatedly. Broke the law. Was among dangerous people who could kill him. Engaged in other self-destructive behaviors—drugs, alcohol, smoking, and general "disregard for body or self." Was suicidal—endangered self, thought of overdosing but took a little drugs and felt better. Overengaged in sex.	Can no longer behave that way toward people. Is law abiding and sober. Is cautious and protective of his family if in unsafe locations.

TABLE 17.1 (continued)
Case of Mathew

Symptom	2 Years After the Massacre (Age 15)	Currently
Alterations in attention and consciousness	None reported.	None.
Alterations in self-perception	Some survivor guilt that his friend died and he did not. Sometimes wondered why he did not get up and fight or attack the shooter or do something. Did not want anyone to know what he had gone through; feared being judged. Felt like none could understand what he went through. Felt ineffective as a person. Felt permanently damaged.	Feels good about himself.
Distorted perception of the perpetrator	Experienced rage toward the shooter, and was preoccupied with wanting to kill the shooter. Watched and read about mass murderers to try to understand.	Has forgiven him. Still watches shows about the massacre and other mass killings. No longer feels intense emotions, has nightmares, or needs to sleep afterward.
Alterations in relationships with others	Felt he could not trust anyone. Put self in dangerous situations and was revictimized. Victimized others—behaved aggressively.	Has good relationships. Is respectful of others. Is a support person for others. Takes good care of himself.
Somatization	Physical problems were related to drug usage and wounds.	Covered his wounds and needle marks with tattoos.
Alterations in systems of meaning	"There is no God or He would not have allowed this to happen. If there is a God, I don't want to know him." Felt hopelessness and despair.	Is deeply spiritual and a strong participant in his church. Has hope.
Trauma Complexity Continuum	********	********
Altered self-capacities	Was totally different after the massacre. Had been a "good and happy kid." His self-esteem and confidence "disappeared." He became aggressive toward his mother after the massacre but maintained a close relationship with her.	Is now a happy and good man. Has had to relearn confidence. His confidence is good most of the time. Still sometimes doubts himself but thinks it out. Feels his mother is still overprotective and wants her to trust his adult competence.

Cognitive disturbances	Used to attribute hostile intent to others and think them untrustworthy. Was pessimistic and expected danger. Felt helpless and hopeless. Feared getting close to others because feared loss or rejection.	No longer expects others' hostility or untrustworthiness. Sometimes his first thought is pessimistic but he reevaluates. Does not stay in a pessimistic mode. Like before the massacre, is a social person.
Mood disturbances	Very depressed, angry, and aggressive after the massacre.	No longer.
Overdeveloped avoidance reactions	Engaged in substance abuse. Poked at the sites of his wounds. Scarred himself. Had a ritual with needles—drew blood into syringe and then injected drugs. This gave him pleasure. Suicidal thoughts related to feeling there was no future, feeling hopeless and depressed.	No substance abuse. Does not mutilate or hurt himself. It does not please him to have needles inserted when blood is drawn. Covered arm scars with tattoos. Is happy to be alive. Wants to really live life.

Symptom list is based on DSM-IV PTSD criteria symptoms (Table 1.1), Complex Trauma and Complexity Continuum Symptoms (Table 1.4). This is a comparison of Mathew 2 years after the massacre and now. Some comments are in his own words. His family also provided current information.

primarily his personal competence, strength, and goodness that pulled him through this living nightmare both alive and without having killed anyone as a consequence of intense and rapid reactivity. His ability to use his traumatic enactments and his support systems well were important to his recovery. His mother was a tireless advocate for him, and he counted on her support. Although as an adolescent, he prematurely left treatment, he had a good experience with trauma therapy and was able to return to treatment when he was later ready to seek assistance. In the meantime, he and his mother were prepared for the issues he needed to resolve, and she, more often than he, recognized them as they appeared. His life is still colored by his experience, but the real "Mathew" is back. Others describe him as an admired and valued man, husband, father, boss, and friend (Table 17.1). He says that he has a good marriage and a good job, loves being a father, teaches others to live successfully, and enjoys life most of the time.

Apples and Oranges and Invisible Friends

All too frequently in the study of childhood trauma, the review that precedes a study indicates that there are *mixed findings* regarding the issue(s) under study. In addition to differences in study methodology, samples, and sample sizes, these differences in findings are likely related to attempts to compare nonequivalents, because there are invisible or unrecognized subgroups and variables that have not been considered among some or all of the studies, or because different trajectories or specific variables cancel otherwise discernable effects. We are still discovering the ways that youths distribute into groups related to specific posttrauma outcomes. Sometimes we assume trauma is the cause when it is only one of the factors that contribute to results. Variables can be complexly interrelated. Reviews such as comparisons of interventions may ignore important differences such as the fact that goals and target symptoms of specific methods differ from those of other methods. Some treatments focus on visible symptoms, whereas others primarily focus on issues related to right and other invisible brain processing.

A Summary of Important Points for Assessing Trauma in Youths

The following list of principles is not hierarchical but includes important issues related to assessing youths.

1. *Youths' traumatic reactions and their styles of reporting their reactions differ from those of adults.* Based on intuition, observation, and research evidence, children have been studied in a variety of age groups: infancy (0 to 1 or 2), toddlerhood (2 or 3 to 4 or 5), early childhood (5 or 6 to 8 or 9), later childhood (9 or 10 to 12), early adolescence (13 to 15 or 16), and late adolescence (16 or 17 and older). Although trauma researchers often condense youths into three age groups, there are clearly differences among age groups that necessitate adaptations in methods and measures of assessment. These differences affect youths' immediate reactions and needs as well as the ongoing or long-term effects of trauma. Therefore, assessing youths using a single set of criteria and algorithms based primarily on adult reactions to trauma is inadvisable.

2. *Multiple factors contribute to youths' traumatic reactions and to the amount and manner in which traumas disrupt development.* Aspects of a child's life combine and transact in complex manners. Multiple pre- and posttrauma factors, in addition to age, contribute to youths' traumatic reactions. Among these variables are the nature of the child, the experience, the youths' personal and family history and circumstances, and other environmental factors such as support systems and resources (Nader, 2001b; Webb, 2004; Williams, in press). A youth's resilience, personality, competencies (e.g., IQ, self-control), and skills (e.g., coping, problem-solving) mediate and moderate his or her traumatic reactions. Aspects of personal history such as previous experiences influence the prominence and meaning of segments or impressions from the event (Pynoos & Nader, 1993). Parents' cultures, economic status, mental health, emotional availability, and parenting and attachment styles may create vulnerabilities or resilience factors for youths. The nature of the event, including its content, unfolding, phase, duration, intensity, frequency, visibility, material destructiveness, injuriousness, relationships, interactions, perpetrator characteristics, and personal meaning to the victim (Boney-McCoy & Finkelhor, 1995; Nader, 1997c), influences the nature of symptoms, traumatic impressions, comorbidity, and more. Environmental factors such as peer and school support, neighborhood safety, and resources may diminish or worsen reactions. These factors singly or in combination affect symptoms, the nature of the developmental disruption created by trauma, and other issues that affect assessment and treatment.

3. *Multiple methods, sources, and measures are needed for the accurate and comprehensive assessment of youths.* Youths behave and report differently in different settings, amid different individuals, and at different times. Although there is overlap, teachers observe a particular set of traits and behaviors, parents another set, clinicians another, and peers still another. Specific behaviors, symptoms, and traits are best discovered

by observation. No single source or method of assessment provides a full picture of youths before or after their traumatic experiences.

4. *The shaping of measures has often preceded the identification of important variables, variable combinations, subgroups or subtypes, and rare but important indicators of posttrauma difficulties.* It is important to develop measures that meet reasonable standards. It is essential to honor the individual youth and his or her personal needs. As a result of psychometric testing, we eliminate questions from measures before discovering which symptoms, although rare, are important indicators of particular pathology, before discovering all subgroups and subtypes, and before assessing whether differences in timing or trajectories cancel effects.

5. *The flexibility to honor a youth's individual needs is an important issue in the treatment and assessment of trauma in children and adolescents.* Developing assessment measures and methods is often about uniformity and consistency. Working effectively with children, including diagnosing/assessing and developing treatment plans for them that may be assessed, is often about flexibility and individuality. Consistency in questions and methods is important to the accuracy of assessments and comparisons. We recognize the need to change these questions and methods to adapt to cultural and other group differences. Hofstede (1980) has pointed out that the differences within a culture can be greater than those between cultures. We have only in the last decade or so begun to apply the need for adaptation of methods, measures, and disorder descriptions to very young children (Scheeringa, Zeanah, Drell, & Larrieu, 1995). Trauma assessments for youths with cognitive impairments are just beginning to emerge. Needed adaptations for a youth or their lack affect research and the interpretation of findings. The point is to elicit an accurate evaluation of each individual youth. Standardized measures and methods can be used in combination with adjustments for youths' needs. Part of what needs discovery is the factors that influence the accurate and beneficial (or at least harmless) elicitation of information from youths with different personal characteristics.

6. *The Rhythm and Needs of the Youth.* The success of assessments and interventions depends in part on the ability to adapt to the needs and the rhythm of the youth (Nader, 1994). Successful adaptation can facilitate rapport and the youths' willingness or ability to share personal information. It can enhance the therapeutic nature of questioning.

7. *In addition to expertise in using particular methods, other researcher or therapist qualities are important to assessment and treatment.* Among the qualities repeatedly found to benefit treatment outcomes are therapist warmth and empathy (Loneck, Banks, Way, & Bonaparte, 2002; Marshall et al., 2002). Genuine interest and respect have also been in these lists of important qualities. The story of Mathew

suggests that the parent's and clinician's belief that the youth's healthy individuality can be restored may be a matter for study. The study of attachment has demonstrated the importance of valuing and attuning to a child's rhythms and needs (Kalsched, 1996; Knox, 2003a; Schore, 2003; Siegel, 2003; Wilson, 2004). Youths usually respond to positive attention from adults. Feeling respected and valued is especially important to youths, their comfort levels, and their self-views.

8. *Evidence-Based Methods.* Most clinicians use a variety of methods in order to meet the needs of an individual seeking assistance. A friend who lived some distance from me once asked for a referral for her traumatized daughter. I called known colleagues in her area and found three well-respected clinicians who might be able to assist her. After describing their treatment/study protocols, the two most highly recommended therapists each made a point to let me know that they would introduce other methods to meet the needs of the patient. Study results for evidence-based methods are not always results of only the methods described in treatment protocols. Moreover, differences in methods, treatment goals, the alterations in symptoms over time, and the still incomplete knowledge of youths and their ongoing reactions to traumas makes comparison of the effectiveness of methods difficult.

Methods must be defined in order to be assessed. Some treatments are easier to define than others, however. A recent computer study of attitudes toward making play therapy a manualized treatment method instigated a series of e-mail conversations among a large group of clinicians about the problems with making strict guidelines for a treatment that should be tailored to a youth's needs. A number of clinicians/researchers have demonstrated the importance and effectiveness of having a repertoire of therapeutic methods and approaches to assist traumatized youths and their families (Cohen & ACAAP, 1998; Gil, 2006; Lehmann & Coady, 2001; Nader, 2001b). Gil demonstrates this fact well. She points out that rigid therapy agendas can overwhelm the individual seeking help. They may undermine clinician and treatment.

9. *We are in a perpetual state of discovery with regard to trauma in youths.* A prime directive of the field of health and mental health is to do no harm. Equally important is to be of preventive and reparative assistance. Assessing youths to gain knowledge can be fulfilling and important. The point of psychological research is *to discover* in order to better prevent or treat the problems and symptoms that impair life.

A great deal has been learned, in the last 35 years, regarding youths' traumatic reactions. There is much yet to learn. For example, we have much more to learn about how clinician characteristics, youth characteristics, and aspects of specific traumatic experiences combine in ways that affect the success of interventions. Methods and measures have changed repeatedly in response to a growing body of research, and they will continue to evolve as we fill in the gaps in our knowledge.

REFERENCES

Gil, E. (2006). *Helping abused and traumatized children: Integrating directive and nondirective approaches.* New York: Gilford Press.

Loneck, B., Banks, S., Way, B., & Bonaparte, E. (2002). An empirical model of therapeutic process for psychiatric emergency room clients with dual disorders. *Social Work Research, 26*(3), 132–143.

Marshall, W. L., Serran, G., Moulden, H., Mulloy, R., Fernandez, Y. M., Mann, R., & Thornton, D. (2002). Therapist features in sexual offender treatment: Their reliable identification and influence on behaviour change. *Clinical Psychology and Psychotherapy, 9*, 395–405.

Glossary

antagonist — Compound that prevents a neurotransmitter's action by either competing for its receptor or modifying the receptor or its environment. (An *irreversible antagonist* is able to directly activate a receptor.)

attachment — Bonds that develop between infants and their caregivers that are rooted in biological survival needs.

attentional biases — Selective attention; the tendency to attend to specific stimuli, behaviors, and verbalizations more than others. A fearful person, for example, may attend more to signs of possible threat than to other stimuli.

attributional biases — Perceptual or information processing biases; tendencies to see in or attribute to others specific attitudes, beliefs, or motives. People with hostile attributional biases, for example, tend to assume or perceive hostile intent from others even when it is not present.

comorbidity — The occurrence, more often than expected by chance, of a second condition or additional conditions with the first or studied condition.

culture — National groups and religious, regional, or experiential subgroups that develop a common history, expectations, beliefs, values, and behaviors.

dendrite — The branching portion of a neuron that receives neurotransmitters.

diathesis — The predisposition toward a particular state or condition.

dissociation — Disengaging from stimuli in the external world and attending to an "internal" world; fragmentations of consciousness and reductions of ordinary awareness that may occur as momentary confusion, blank spells, daydreams, or memory lapses, as more unusual states such as trance or shock, or as extreme states such as fugues or personality alters.

dominance — A hierarchy of control or leadership in affiliative relationships.

encoding — The transformation of signals, stimuli, or perceptions into signals or memories.

endorphins — Peptides that act as internally produced painkillers and have a structure similar to codeine and heroin.

externalizing — Emotions, behaviors, or symptoms that are expressed externally such as conduct disturbances.

glial cells — Cells that provide firmness and structure to the brain and form the myelin sheath.

information processing — Cognitive information processing includes a number of cognitive functions: (1) acquisition, classification, processing, and integration of information, (2) storing and recall of information, (3) organization and reorganization of information, and (4) communication and enactment of information. Problematic information processing may be related to attention, memory, interpretation, response search, response selection, or failure of integration.

integration — The process of coordinating neurological impulses, encoded information, and memories into a whole; when the parts or traits of an individual's personality work together as a whole.

internalizing — Symptoms or emotions expressed internally such as feelings of depression or anxiety.

latency age — Ages 7 through 10.

locus of control — A person's belief that control over external events, behaviors, or emotions is internal (within the person: internal locus of control) or external (outside of the person: external locus of control).

mediate — To be a link or an intervening variable between two processes or events. For example, if trauma affects self-esteem and self-esteem affects competence, self-esteem is a mediating or intervening variable between trauma and competence.

moderator — Any variable that affects (reduces or increases) another variable.

myelin sheath — The fatty acid coating that surrounds the axons of long neurons, provides scaffolding for neuron migration, and takes up and removes some of the neurotransmitters released during synaptic transmission; the layer that speeds up axonal firing.

neuron — A nerve cell that plays a role in information processing.

resilience — Protective and competence factors that increase the ability to function and feel well despite adversity.

schema — A cognitive framework or knowledge structure consisting of a number of inputs, ideas, or memories.

self-esteem — Evaluative judgments about oneself; high self-esteem indicates positive self-regard; low self-esteem indicates poor self-regard.

sensitivity — The percentage of youth identified as having a diagnosis by a scale or measure who actually have the diagnosis; the number of true positives identified by the measure.

specificity — The percentage of youth who do not have a diagnosis that are accurately identified by a measure as not having the diagnosis; the number of true negatives identified by the measure.

stimulus — A internal or external signal that activates a brain receptor or an organism.

stress-moderation — The presence of the moderator reduces or increases the relations between negative events and mental health problems, and acts as a stress-buffer or stress-exacerbator.

stress-mediation — Negative events that influence the mediator, which in turn impacts mental health; the mediator is a plausible mechanism through which stress may affect mental health.

synapses — The junction between nerve cells.

References

Aber, J. L., Brown, J. L., & Jones, S. M. (2003). Developmental trajectories toward violence in middle childhood: Course, demographic differences, and response to school-based intervention. *Developmental Psychology, 39*(2), 324–348.

Abramson, L. Y., Seligman, M. E., & Teasdale, J. D. (1978). Learned helplessness in humans: Critique and reformulation. *Journal of Abnormal Psychology, 87*, 49–74.

Achenbach, T. M. (1966). The classification of children's psychiatric symptoms: A factor analytic study. *Psychological Monographs, 80*(7), 1–37.

Achenbach, T. M. (1991). *Manual for the Child Behavior Checklist/4–18*. Burlington: University of Vermont, Department of Psychiatry.

Achenbach, T. M., McConaughy, S. H., & Howell, C. T. (1987). Child/adolescent behavioral and emotional problems: Implications of cross-informant correlations for situational specificity. *Psychological Bulletin, 101*(2), 213–232.

Achenbach, T. M., & Rescorla, L. A. (2001). *Manual for the ASEBA school-age forms & profiles*. Burlington: University of Vermont, Research Center for Children, Youth, & Families.

Ahadi, S. A., Rothbart, M. K., & Ye, R. (1993). Children's temperament in the U.S. and China: Similarities and differences. *European Journal of Personality, 7*, 359–377.

Ainsworth, M. D. (1972). Attachment and dependency: A comparison. In J. L. Gewirtz (Ed.), *Attachment and Dependency* (pp. 97–137). Washington, DC: V. H. Winston.

Ainsworth, M. D. (1973). The development of infant-mother attachment. In B. M. Caldwell & H. N. Ricciuti (Eds.), *Review of child development research* (Vol. 3, pp. 1–94). Chicago: University of Chicago Press.

Ainsworth, M. D., (1989). Attachments beyond infancy. *American Psychologist, 44*, 709–716.

Ainsworth, M. D., Blehar, M. C., Waters, E., & Wall, S. (1978). *Patterns of attachment: A psychological study of the strange situation*. Hillsdale, NJ: Erlbaum.

Albano, A. M., Chorpita, B. F., & Barlow, D. H. (2003). Childhood anxiety disorders. In E. J. Mash & R. A. Barkley (Eds.), *Child psychopathology* (1st ed., pp. 279–329). New York: Guilford Press.

Alcock, M., & Murphy, E. (1998, March). Type development: From unconscious perfection through conscious imperfection to conscious completion. Paper presented at Counter attack: Rising to the challenges of education. The Role of Psychological Type Conference, Orlando, FL.

Alexander, P. C., Anderson, C. L., Brand, B., Schaeffer, C. M., Grelling, B. Z., & Kretz, L. (1998). Adult attachment and long-term effects in survivors of incest. *Child Abuse and Neglect, 22*(1), 45–61.

Allen, J. P., & Land, D. (1999). Attachment in adolescence. In J. Cassidy & P. R. Shaver (Eds.), *Handbook of attachment: Theory, research, and clinical applications* (pp. 319–335). New York: Guilford Press.

Allen, J. S., Bruss, J., & Damasio, H. (2004). The structure of the human brain. *American Scientist, 92*(3), 246–253.

Allnutt, S. H., & Chaplow, D. (2000). General principles of forensic report writing. *Australian and New Zealand Journal of Psychiatry, 34*, 980–987.

Altman, N. (2002). *Endorphins Q & A.* Retrieved May 25, 2005, from http://www. healing springs.com/ENDORPHINS.htm

Alvarez, A. (1997). Adjusting to genocide: Techniques of neutralization and the Holocaust. *Social Science History, 21*, 139–178.

Amaya-Jackson, L., McCarthy, G., Newman, E., & Cherney, M. (1995). *Child PTSD checklist.* Unpublished manuscript, Department of Psychiatry, Duke University, Durham, NC.

American Psychiatric Association. (1994). *Diagnostic and statistical manual of mental disorders* (4th ed.). Washington, DC: Author.

American Psychiatric Association. (2001). *Diagnostic and statistical manual of mental disorders, DSM-IV-Text Revision* (4th ed.). Washington, DC: Author.

Anderson, K. E., Lytton, H., & Romney, D. M. (1986). Mothers' interactions with normal and conduct-disordered boys: Who affects whom? *Developmental Psychology, 22*, 604–609.

Andreou, E. (2004). Bully/victim problems and their association with Machiavellianism and self-efficacy in Greek primary school children. *British Journal of Educational Psychology, 74*, 297–309.

Andrews, B., Brewin, C. R., Rose, S., & Kirk, M. (2000). Predicting PTSD symptoms in victims of violent crime: The role of shame, anger, and childhood abuse. *Journal of Abnormal Psychology, 109*, 69–73.

Angold, A., Costello, E., Farmer, E., Burns, B., & Erkanli, A. (1999). Impaired but undiagnosed. *Journal of the American Academy of Child & Adolescent Psychiatry, 38*(2), 129–137.

Angold, A., Cox, A., Prendergast, M., Rutter, M., & Simonoff, E. (2000). *Child and Adolescent Psychiatric Assessment.* Unpublished manuscript. ©Angold et al., 1987, 1990, 1992, 1996, 1999.

Angold, A., Prendergast, M., Cox, A., Harrington, R., Simonoff, E., & Rutter, M. (1995). The Child and Adolescent Psychiatric Assessment. *Psychological Medicine, 25*, 739–753.

Anke, A. G. W., & Fugl-Meyer, A. R. (2003). Life satisfaction several years after severe multiple trauma—A retrospective investigation. *Clinical Rehabilitation, 17*, 431–442.

Anthony, E. J. (1987). Risk, vulnerability, and resilience: An overview. In E. J. Anthony & B. J. Cohler (Eds.), *The invulnerable child* (pp. 3–48). New York: Guilford Press.

Appelbaum, P. S. (1990). The parable of the forensic psychiatrist: Ethics and the problem of doing harm. *International Journal of Law and Psychiatry, 13*, 249–259.

Appelbaum, P. S. (1997). A theory of ethics for forensic psychiatry. *Journal of the American Academy of Psychiatry and the Law, 25*, 233–247.

Armsden, G. C., & Greenberg, M. T. (1987). The Inventory of Parent and Peer Attachment: Individual Differences and Their Relationship to Psychological Well-being in Adolescence. *Journal of Youth and Adolescence, 16,* 427–454.

Armstrong, J. G., Putnam, F. W., & Carlson, E. B. (1993). *Adolescent Dissociative Experiences Scale.* Self-report measure.

Armstrong, J. G., Putnam, F. W., Carlson, E. B., Libero, D. Z., & Smith, S. T. (1997). Development and validation of a measure of adolescent dissociation: The Adolescent Dissociative Experiences Scale. *Journal of Nervous Mental Disorders, 185,* 491–497.

Armsworth, M. W., & Holaday, M. (1993). The effects of psychological trauma on children and adolescents. *Journal of Counseling and Development, 72,* 49–56.

Arrindell, W. A. (2003). Cultures' consequences: Comparing values, behaviors, institutions, and organizations across nations. *Behaviour Research & Therapy, 41*(7), 861–862.

ASEBA. (2002). Child Behavior Checklist for ages 6–18. Retrieved September 11, 2002, from www.aseba.org/products/cbcl6–18.html

Asmundson, G. J. G., Stapleton, J. A., & Taylor, S. (2004). Are avoidance and numbing distinct PTSD symptom clusters? *Journal of Traumatic Stress, 17*(6), 467–475.

Atkinson, L. (1997). Attachment and psychopathology: From laboratory to clinic. In L. Atkinson & K. Zucker (Eds.), *Attachment and psychopathology* (pp. 3–16). New York: Guilford Press.

Ayalon, O. (1983). Coping with terrorism: The Israeli case. In D. Meichenbaum & M. Jaremko (Eds.), *Stress reduction and prevention* (pp. 293–339). New York: Plenum Press.

Ayres, A. J. (1978). Learning disabilities and the vestibular system. *Journal of Learning Disabilities, 78*(11), 18–29.

Bagley, C., & Mallick, K. (2002). Prediction of sexual, emotional, and physical maltreatment and mental health outcomes in a longitudinal cohort of 290 adolescent women. *Child Maltreatment, 5*(3), 218–226.

Bagnato, S. J., Neisworth, J. T., Salvia, J., & Hunt, F. M. (1999). *Temperament and Atypical Behavior Scale (TABS).* Baltimore: Brookes.

Barber, B. K., Olsen, J. E., & Shagle, S. C. (1994). Associations between parental psychological and behavioral control and youth internalized and externalized behaviors. *Child Development, 65,* 1120–1136.

Barkley, R. A. (2003). Attention deficit/hyperactivity disorder. In E. J. Mash & R. A. Barkley (Eds.), *Child psychopathology* (1st ed., pp. 75–143). New York: Guilford Press.

Bar-On, D. (1999). Israeli society between the culture of death and the culture of life. In K. Nader, N. Dubrow, & B. Stamm (Eds.), *Honoring differences: Cultural issues in the treatment of trauma and stress* (pp. 211–233). Philadelphia: Taylor & Francis.

Barry, C. T., Frick, P. J., & Killain, A. L. (2003). The relation of narcissism and self-esteem to conduct problems in children: A preliminary investigation. *Journal of Clinical Child and Adolescent Psychology, 32*(1), 139–152.

Bartko, J. J. (1976). On various intraclass correlation reliability coefficients. *Psychological Bulletin, 83,* 762–765.

Bartko, J. J., & Carpenter, W. T. (1976). On the methods and theory of reliability. *Journal of Nervous and Mental Disease, 163,* 307–317.

Baumrind, D. (1989). Rearing competent children. In W. Damon (Ed.), *Child development today and tomorrow* (pp. 349–368). San Francisco: Jossey-Bass.

Becker-Blease, K. A., Deater-Deckard, K., Eley, T., Freyd, J. J., Stevenson, J., & Plomin, R. (2004). A genetic analysis of individual differences in dissociative behaviors in childhood and adolescence. *Journal of Child Psychology and Psychiatry, 45*(3), 522–532.

Bellah, R. N., Madsen, R., Sullivan, W. M., Swidler, A., & Tipton, S. M. (1985). *Habits of the heart.* New York: Harper & Row.

Berens, L. V. (1985). A comparison of Jungian function theory and Keirseyan temperament theory in the use of the Myers-Briggs Type Indicator. *Dissertation Abstracts International, 46*(6-B), 2108.

Berens, L. V. (1998). *Understanding yourself and others: An introduction to temperament.* Huntington Beach, CA: Telos Publications.

Berens, L. V., & Nardi, D. (1999). *The sixteen personality types: Descriptions for self discovery.* Huntington Beach, CA: Telos Publications.

Berna, J. M. (1993). *The worst experiences of adolescents from divorced and separated parents and the stress responses to those experiences.* Doctoral dissertation, College of Education, Temple University Graduate Board, Philadelphia.

Biederman, J., Rosenbaum, J., Bolduc-Murphy, E. A., Faraone, S., Chaloff, J., Hirshfield, D., & Kagan, J. (1993). A three-year follow-up of children with and without behavioral inhibition. *Journal of the American Academy of Child and Adolescent Psychiatry, 32,* 814–821.

Biederman, J., Rosenbaum, J., Hirshfield, D., Faraone, S., Bolduc, E., Gersten, N., Kagan, J., Snidman, N., & Reznick, J. (1990). Psychiatric correlates of behavioral inhibition in young children with and without psychiatric disorders. *Archives of General Psychiatry, 47,* 21–26.

Bijttebier, P., Vasey, M. W., & Braet, C. (2003). Special section: Information-processing factors in child and adolescent psychopathology. *Journal of Clinical Child and Adolescent Psychology, 32*(1), 2–9.

Bird, H. R. (1999). The assessment of functional impairment. In D. Shaffer, C. Lucas, & J. Richters (Eds.), *Diagnostic assessment in child and adolescent psychopathology* (pp. 209–229). New York: Guilford Press.

Bird, H. R., Andrews, H., Schwab-Stone, M., Goodman, S., Dulcan, M., Richters, J., Rubio-Stipec, M., Moore, R., Chiang, P., Hoven, C., Canino, G., Fisher, P., & Gould, M. (1996). Global measures of impairment for epidemiologic and clinical use with children and adolescents. *International Journal of Methods in Psychiatric Research, 6*(4), 295–307.

Bird, H. R., Canino, G. J., Davies, M., Ramirez, R., Chavez, L., Duarte, C., & Shen, S. (2005). The Brief Impairment Scale (BIS): A multidimensional scale of functional impairment for children and adolescents. *Journal of the American Academy of Child and Adolescent Psychiatry, 44*(7), 699–707.

Bird, H. R., Canino, G., Rubio-Stipec, M., & Ribera, J. (1987). Further measures of the psychometric properties of the Children's Global Assessment Scale. *Archives of General Psychiatry, 44,* 821–824.

Bird, H. R., Cohen, P., Narrow, W., Dulcan, M., & Hoven, C. (1994). Global impairment and impairment attributed to specific disorders: A comparison of available measures. In N. Alessi & S. Porter (Eds.), *Scientific proceedings: 41st annual meeting of the American Academy of Child and Adolescent Psychiatry, New York* (p. 12). Washington, DC: American Academy of Child and Adolescent Psychiatry.

Bird, H. R., & Gould, M. (1995). The use of diagnostic instruments and global measures of functioning in child psychiatry epidemiological studies. In F. C. Verhulst & H. M. Koot (Eds.), *The epidemiology of child and adolescent psychopathology* (pp. 86–103). New York: Oxford University Press.

Bird, H. R., Shaffer, D., Fisher, P., Gould, M., Staghezza, B., Chen, J., & Hoven, C. (1993). The Columbia Impairment Scale: Pilot findings on a measure of global impairment for children and adolescents. *International Journal of Methods in Psychiatric Research, 3*(3), 167–176.

Bird, H. R., Yager, T., Staghezza, B., Gould, M., Canino, G., & Rubio-Stipec, M. (1990). Impairment in the epidemiological measurement of childhood psychopathology in the community. *Journal of the American Academy of Child and Adolescent Psychiatry, 29*(5), 796–803.

Birleson, P. (1981). The validity of depressive disorder in childhood and the development of a self-rating scale: A research report. *Journal of Child Psychology and Psychiatry, 22*, 73–88.

Blair, R. J., Jones, L., Clark, F., & Smith, M. (1997). The psychopathic individual: A lack of responsiveness to distress cues? *Psychophysiology, 34*, 192–198.

Blaustein, M. E. (2000). Individual differences in posttraumatic stress symptomatology following childhood sexual abuse. Doctoral dissertation, Duke University, 2000. *Dissertation Abstracts International, 60*(10-B), 5219.

Bleich, A., Gelkopf, M., & Solomon, Z. (2003). Exposure to terrorism, stress-related mental health symptoms, and coping behaviors among a nationally represented sample in Israel. *Journal of the American Medical Association, 290*(5), 612–620.

Blizard, R. A. (2001). Masochistic and sadistic ego states: Dissociative solutions to the dilemma of attachment to an abusive caretaker. *Journal of Trauma and Dissociation, 2*(4), 37–58.

Bloch, D., Silber, E., & Perry, S. (1956). Some factors in the emotional reaction of children to disaster. *American Journal of Psychiatry, 113*, 416–422.

Block, J. (1971). *Lives through time.* Berkeley, CA: Bancroft Books.

Boehnlein, J. K. (2001). Cultural interpretations of physiological processes in post-traumatic stress disorder and panic disorder. *Transcultural Psychiatry, 38*(4), 461–467.

Boehnlein, J. K., & Kinzie, J. D. (1997). Cultural perspectives on posttraumatic stress disorder. In T. W. Miller (Ed.), *Clinical disorders and stressful life events* (pp. 19–43). Madison, CT: International Universities Press.

Boik, B. L., & Goodwin, E. A. (2000). *Sandplay therapy: A step-by-step manual for psychotherapists of diverse orientations.* New York: W. W. Norton.

Bolger, K. E., & Patterson, C. J. (2003). Sequelae of child maltreatment: Vulnerability and resilience. In S. S. Luthar (Ed.), *Resilience and vulnerability: Adaptation in the context of childhood adversities* (pp. 156–181). New York: Cambridge University Press.

Bolton, B. (2003). Test review: Coopersmith Self-Esteem Inventory. *Rehabilitation Counseling Bulletin, 47*(1), 58–60.

Bolton, P. (2001). Cross-cultural validity and reliability testing of a standard psychiatric assessment instrument without a gold standard. *The Journal of Nervous and Mental Disease, 189*(4), 238–242.

Boney-McCoy, S., & Finkelhor, D. (1995). Psychosocial sequelae of violent victimization in a national youth sample. *Journal of Consulting and Clinical Psychology, 63*, 726–736.

Bonner, B., Walker, G., & Berliner, L. (1996). *Behavioral interventions for children with sexual behavior problems.* Unpublished manuscript, University of Oklahoma Health Sciences Center, Oklahoma City.

Bowlby, J. (1958). The nature of the child's tie to his mother. *The International Journal of Psycho-analysis, 39*(5), 350–373.

Bowlby, J. (1969/1982). *Attachment and loss. Volume 1: Attachment.* New York: Basic Books.

Bowlby, J. (1973). *Attachment and loss. Volume 2: Separation.* New York: Basic Books.

Bowlby, J. (1979). *The making and breaking of affectional bonds.* London: Tavistock.

Bowlby, J. (1980). *Attachment and loss. Volume 3: Loss.* New York: Basic Books.

Bowlby, J. (1988). *A secure base: Parent-child attachment and healthy human development.* New York: Basic Books.

Boyd-Franklin, N., & Franklin, A. J. (1998). African American couples in therapy. In M. McGoldrick (Ed.), *Re-visioning family therapy* (pp. 268–281). New York: Guilford Press.

Bremner, J. D. (1999). Does stress damage the brain? *Biological Psychiatry, 45*(7), 797–805.

Bremner, J. D. (2003). The effects of stress on the brain. *Psychiatric Times, 20*(7), 18–22.

Breslau, N. (1987). Inquiring about the bizarre: False positives in Diagnostic Interview Schedule for Children (DISC) ascertainment of obsessions, compulsions, and psychotic symptoms. *Journal of the American Academy of Child & Adolescent Psychiatry, 26*(5), 639–644.

Brewin, C. R., Andrews, B., & Rose, S. (2000). Fear, helplessness, and horror in posttraumatic stress disorder: Investigating DSM IV Criterion A2 in victims of violent crime. *Journal of Traumatic Stress, 13*, 499–509.

Briere, J. (1989). Trauma Symptom Checklist for Children (TSCC), a copyrighted instrument.

Briere, J. (1996). *Trauma Symptom Checklist for Children (TSCC) professional manual.* Odessa, FL: Psychological Assessment Resources.

Briere, J. (2001). *Detailed Assessment of Posttraumatic Stress (DAPS) professional manual.* Odessa, FL: Psychological Assessment Resources.

Briere, J. (2005a). *Trauma Symptom Checklist for Young Children* (TSCYC). Odessa, FL: Psychological Assessment Resources.

Briere, J. (2005b). *Trauma Symptom Checklist for Young Children.* Description of the TSCYC. Retrieved August 8, 2005, from http://www.johnbriere.com/tscyc.htm//top

Briere, J., & Elliott, D. M. (1997). Psychological assessment of interpersonal victimization effects in adults and children. *Psychotherapy: Theory, Research, Practice, Training, 34*(4), 353–364.

Briere, J., Johnson, K., Bissada, A., Damon, L., Crouch, J., Gil, E., Hanson, R., & Ernst, V. (2001). The Trauma Symptom Checklist for Young Children (TSCYC): Reliability and association with abuse exposure in a multi-site study. *Child Abuse & Neglect, 25*, 1001–1014.

Briere, J. & Spinazzola, J. (2005). Phenomenology and psychological assessment of complex posttraumatic states. *Journal of Traumatic Stress, 18*(5), 401–412.

Briggs, S. R. (1988). Shyness: Introversion or neuroticism? *Journal of Research in Personality, 22*, 290–307.

Brock, S. (2002). Identifying individuals at risk for psychological trauma. In S. Brock & P. Lazarus (Eds.), *Best practices in crisis prevention and intervention in the schools* (pp. 367–383). Bethesda, MD: National Association of School Psychologists.

Brock, S., & Lazarus, P. (Eds.). (2002). *Best practices in crisis prevention and intervention in the schools*. Bethesda, MD: National Association of School Psychologists.

Brown, E. J., & Goodman, R. F. (2005). Childhood traumatic grief: An exploration of the construct in children bereaved on September 11. *Journal of Clinical Child & Adolescent Psychology, 34*(2), 248–259.

Brown, J. E. (Ed.). (1989). *The sacred pipe: Black Elk's account of the seven rites of the Oglala Sioux*. Norman: University of Oklahoma Press.

Brown, L., & Unger, A. (1992). *Sentence Completion Series (SCS)*. Odessa, FL: Psychological Assessment Resources.

Buchanan, A. (1998). Intergenerational child maltreatment. In Y. Danieli (Ed.), *International handbook of multigenerational legacies of trauma* (pp. 535–552). New York: Plenum Press.

Bulman, R. J., & Brickman, P. (1982). Expectations and what people learn from failure. In N. T. Feather (Ed.), *Expectancy, actions: Expectancy-value models in psychology* (pp. 207–237). Hillsdale, NJ: Erlbaum.

Burgess A. (1975). Family reaction to homicide. *American Journal of Orthopsychiatry, 45*(3), 391–398.

Burgess, A. (2002). Abused: Can you tell? Testimony on sex abuse victims challenged. *The Forensic Echo, 2*(7), 1–9. Retrieved March 8, 2005, from http://echo.forensicpanel.com/1998/ 6/1/abusedcan.html

Burke, J., Borus, J., Burns, B., Millstein, K., & Beasley, M. (1982). Changes in children's behavior after a natural disaster. *American Journal of Psychiatry, 139*(8), 1010–1014.

Burnett, P., Middleton, W., Raphael, B., Dunne, M., Moylan, A., & Martinek, N. (1994). Concepts of normal bereavement. *Journal of Traumatic Stress, 7*, 123–134.

Burton, D. L. (1996). Cognitive factors in sexually aggressive children. Doctoral dissertation, University of Washington, 1996. *Dissertation Abstracts International, 57*(5-A), 2208.

Buss, A. H., & Plomin, R. (1984). *Temperament: Early developing personality traits*. Hillsdale, NJ: Erlbaum.

Buss, A. H., & Warren, W. L. (2000). *Aggression Questionnaire (AQ): Manual*. Los Angeles: Western Psychological Services.

Buss, D. M., Block, J. H., & Block, J. (1980). Preschool activity level: Personality correlates and developmental implications. *Child Development, 51*, 401–408.

Buzzard, R. B. (1972). Notes on report writing. *Occupational Psychology, 46*(4), 201–207.

Byrd, E., & Witherspoon, R. L. (1954). Responses of preschool children to the Children's Apperception Test. *Child Development, 25*(1), 35–44.

Byrnes, J. P. (2001). *Minds, brains, and learning*. New York: Guilford Press.

Cameron, J. (2002). *Letter of explanation*. Letter accompanying the Preventive Ounce Questionnaires.

Canino, G., & Bravo, M. (1999). The translation and adaptation of diagnostic instruments for cross-cultural use. In D. Shaffer, C. Lucas, & J. Richters (Eds.), *Diagnostic assessment in child and adolescent psychopathology* (pp. 285–298). New York: Guilford Press.

Canive, J. M., Castillo, D. T., & Tuason, V. B. (2001). The Hispanic veteran. In W. Tseng & J. Streltzer (Ed.), *Culture and psychotherapy: A guide to clinical practice* (pp. 157–172). Washington, DC: American Psychiatric Association Press.

Cantwell, D. P., & Rutter, M. (1994). Classification: Conceptual issues and substantive findings. In M. Rutter, E. Taylor, & L. Hersov (Eds.), *Child and adolescent psychiatry* (3rd ed., pp. 3–22). Oxford, England: Blackwell.

Carey, W. B. (1997). *Understanding your child's temperament.* New York: MacMillan.

Carey, W. B., & McDevitt, S. C. (1978). Revision of the Infant Temperament Questionnaire. *The American Academy of Pediatrics, 61*(5), pp. 735–739.

Carey, W. B., & McDevitt, S. C. (1995a). *Carey Temperament Scale.* London: The Psychological Corporation.

Carey, W. B., & McDevitt, S. C. (1995b). *Coping with children's temperament.* New York: Basic Books.

Carey-Trefzer, C. (1949). The results of a clinical study of war-damaged children who attended the Child Guidance Clinic, the hospital for sick children, Great Ormond Street, London. *The Journal of Mental Science, 95,* 535–559.

Carlson, E. (1997). *Trauma assessments: A clinician's guide.* New York: Guilford Press.

Carlson, E., & Briere, J. (2002). Complex psychological trauma: Its correlates and effects. An ISTSS Web site letter regarding the 18th annual meeting. Retrieved November 8, 2002, from http://www.istss. org/meetings/index.htm

Carrion, V. G., Weems, C. F., Ray, R. D., & Reiss, A. L. (2002). Toward an empirical definition of pediatric PTSD: The phenomenology of PTSD symptoms in youth. *Journal of the American Academy of Child and Adolescent Psychiatry, 41*(2), 166–173.

Caspi, A. (1998). Personality development across the life course. In W. Damon & N. Eisenberg (Eds.), *Handbook of child psychology (5th ed., Vol. 3). Social, emotional, and personality development* (pp. 311–388). New York: Wiley & Sons.

Caspi, A., Begg, D., Dickson, N., Harrington, H., Langley, J., Moffitt, T. E, & Silva, P. A. (1997). Personality differences predict health-risk behaviors in young adulthood: Evidence from a longitudinal study. *Journal of Personality and Social Psychology, 73,* 1052–1063.

Caspi, A., Henry, B., McGee, R. O., Moffitt, T. E., & Silva, P.A. (1995). Temperamental origins of child and adolescent behavior problems: From age three to age fifteen. *Child Development, 66,* 55–68.

Caspi, A., Moffitt, T. E., Newman, D. L., & Silva, P. A. (1996). Behavioral observations at age 3 predict adult psychiatric disorders: Longitudinal evidence from a birth cohort. *Archives of General Psychiatry, 53,* 1033–1039.

Caspi, A., & Roberts, B. W. (2001). Personality development across the life course: The argument for change and continuity. *Psychological Inquiry, 12*(2), 49–66.

Caspi, A., & Silva, P. A. (1995). Temperamental qualities at age three predict personality traits in young adulthood: Longitudinal evidence from a birth cohort. *Child Development, 66,* 486–498.

Cassidy, J. (1999). The nature of the child's ties. In J. Cassidy & P. R. Shaver (Eds.), *Handbook of attachment: Theory, research, and clinical applications* (pp. 3–20). New York: Guilford Press.

Cassidy, J., & Shaver, P. R. (Eds.). (1999). *Handbook of attachment: Theory, research, and clinical applications.* New York: Guilford Press.

Ceci, S. J., Huffman, M. L. C., Smith, E., & Loftus, E. F. (1994). Repeatedly thinking about a non-event: Source misattributions among preschoolers. *Consciousness and Cognition, 3*(3-4), 388–407.

Center, Y., & Ward, J. (1986). A note on the use of two self-esteem inventories with Australian schoolchildren. *Australian Psychologist, 21,* 473–476.

Chaffin, M., & Shultz, S. (2001). Psychometric evaluation of the Children's Impact of Traumatic Events Scale-Revised. *Child Abuse and Neglect, 25,* 401–411.

Chamberlain, P., & Moore, K. (2002). Chaos and trauma in the lives of adolescent females with antisocial behavior and delinquency. In R. Greenwald (Ed.), *Trauma and juvenile delinquency: Theory, research, and interventions* (pp. 79–108). New York: Haworth Press.

Chaplin, J. P. (1975). *Dictionary of psychology.* New York: Dell Publishing.

Chapman, P. L., & Mullis, A. K. (2002). Readdressing gender bias in the Coopersmith Self-Esteem Inventory-Short Form. *The Journal of Genetic Psychology, 163*(4), 403–409.

Chen, X., Rubin, K. H., & Li, Z. Y. (1995). Social functioning and adjustment in Chinese children: A longitudinal study. *Developmental Psychology, 31,* 531–539.

Chess, S., & Thomas, A. (1977). Temperamental individuality from childhood to adolescence. *Journal of the American Academy of Child Psychiatry, 16*(2), 218–226.

Chess, S., & Thomas, A. (1991). Temperament. In M. Lewis (Ed.), *Child and adolescent psychiatry: A comprehensive textbook* (pp. 145–159). Baltimore: Williams & Wilkins.

Chorpita, B. F., & Barlow, D. H. (1998). The development of anxiety: The role of control in the early environment. *Psychological Bulletin, 124*(1), 3–19.

Cicchetti, D. V. (2003a). Foreword. In S. S. Luthar (Ed.), *Resilience and vulnerability: Adaptation in the context of childhood adversities* (pp. xix–xxxi). New York: Cambridge University Press.

Cicchetti, D. V. (2003b). Neuroendocrine functioning in maltreated children. In D. Cicchetti & E. Walker (Eds.), *Neurodevelopmental mechanisms in psychopathology* (pp. 345–365). Cambridge, UK: Cambridge University Press.

Cicchetti, D. V., & Sparrow, S. A. (1981). Developing criteria for establishing interrater reliability of specific items: Applications to assessment of adaptive behavior. *American Journal of Mental Deficiency, 86*(2), 127–137.

Clinton, G. T., & Jenkins-Monroe, V. (1994). Rorschach responses of sexually abused children: An exploratory study. *Journal of Child Sexual Abuse, 3*(1), 67–83.

Coddington, R. (1972). The significance of life events as etiologic in the diseases of children: II. A study of the normal population. *Journal of Psychosomatic Research, 16,* 205–213.

Cohen, B. M. (Ed.). (1986/1994). *The Diagnostic Drawing Series Rating Guide.* Available from Barry M. Cohen, P.O. Box 9853, Alexandria, VA 22304.

Cohen, B. M., & Mills, A. (2000). *Report on the Diagnostic Drawing Series.* Available from The DDS Project, P.O. Box 9853, Alexandria, VA 22304.

Cohen, J. (1960). A coefficient of agreement for nominal scales. *Educational Psychology Measurement, 20,* 37–46.

Cohen, J. (1992). A power primer. *Psychological Bulletin, 112,* 155–159.

Cohen, J. & the AACAP Work Group on Quality Issues. (1998). Practice parameters for the assessment and treatment of children and adolescents with posttraumatic stress disorder. *Journal of the American Academy of Child and Adolescent Psychiatry Supplement, 37*(10), 4S–26S.

Cohen, J. A., Berliner, L., & Mannarino, A. P. (2000). Treating traumatized children: A research review and synthesis. *Trauma, Violence, and Abuse: A Review Journal, 1*(1), 29–46.

Cohen, J. A., & Mannarino, A. P. (1998). Factors that mediate treatment outcome of sexually abused preschool children: Six- and 12-month follow-up. *Journal of the American Academy of Child & Adolescent Psychiatry, 37*(1), 44–51.

Cohen, J. A., & Mannarino, A. P. (2004). Posttraumatic stress disorder. In T. H. Ollendick & J. S. March (Eds.), *Phobic and anxiety disorders in children and adolescents: A clinician's guide to effective psychosocial and pharmacological interventions* (pp. 405–432). New York: Oxford University Press.

Cohen, J. A., Mannarino, A. P., Greenberg, T., Padlo, S., & Shipley, C. (2002). Childhood traumatic grief: Concepts and controversies. *Trauma, Violence & Abuse, 3*(4), 307–327.

Cohen, P., & Kasen, S. (1999). The context of assessment: Culture, race, and socioeconomic status as influences on assessment of children. In D. Shaffer, C. Lucas, & J. Richters (Eds.), *Diagnostic assessment in child and adolescent psychopathology* (pp. 299–318). New York: Guilford Press.

Colin, V. L. (1996). *Human attachment.* New York: McGraw-Hill.

Columbia Encyclopedia (2005). Neurotransmitter. Retrieved February 17, 2005 from http:www.encyclopedia.com/printable.asp?url=/ssi/nl/neurotr.html (see also *hormone* and *catecholamine* and their links at the same website).

Compas, B. E. (1998). An agenda for coping research and theory: Basic and applied developmental issues. *International Journal of Behavioral Development, 22*(2), 231–237.

Compas, B. E., & Epping, J. E. (1993). Stress and coping, in children and families: Implications for children coping with disaster. In C. F. Saylor (Ed.), *Children and disasters* (pp. 11–28). New York: Plenum Press.

Condry, J., & Condry, S. (1976). Sex differences: A study of the eye of the beholder. *Child Development, 47,* 812–819.

Connell, J. P. (1985). A new multidimensional measure of children's perceptions of control. *Child Development, 56,* 1018–1041.

Coopersmith, S. (1967). *Self-Esteem Inventory (SEI).* A research instrument. See Coopersmith, 1989.

Coopersmith, S. (1989). *Coopersmith Self-Esteem Inventories.* Palo Alto, CA: Consulting Psychologists Press.

Coplan, R. J. (2000). Assessing nonsocial play in early childhood: Conceptual and methodological approaches. In K. Gitlin-Weiner, A. Sandgrund, & C. Schaefer (Eds.), *Play diagnosis and assessment* (2nd ed., pp. 563–598). New York: Wiley and Sons.

Coplan, R. J., & Rubin, K. H. (1998). Social play. In D. P. Fromberg & D. Bergen (Eds.), *Play from birth to twelve: Contexts, perspectives, and meanings* (pp. 368–377). New York: Garland.

Costello, A. J., Edelbrock, C., Kalas, R., Kessler, M., & Klaric, S. (1982). *The National Institute of Mental Health Diagnostic Interview Schedule for Children (DISC).* Rockville, MD: National Institute of Mental Health.

Costello, E. J., Angold, A., March, J., & Fairbank, J. (1998). Life events and posttraumatic stress: The development of a new measure for children and adolescents. *Psychological Medicine, 28,* 1275–1288.

Costello, E. J., Farmer, E. M. Z., & Angold, A. (1999). Same place, different children: White and American Indian children in the Appalachian mountains. In P. Cohen & C. Slomkowski (Eds.), *Historical and geographical influences on psychopathology* (pp. 279–298). Mahwah, NJ: Lawrence Erlbaum Associates.

Costello, E. J., Farmer, E. M. Z., Angold, A., Burns, B. J., & Erkanli, A. (1997). Psychiatric disorders among American Indian and White youth in Appalachia: The Great Smoky Mountains Study. *American Journal of Public Health, 87*(5), 827–832.

Costello, E. J., Keeler, G. P., & Angold, A. (2001). Poverty, race/ethnicity, and psychiatric disorder: A study of rural children. *American Journal of Public Health, 91*(9), 1494–1498.

Cowen, E. L., Work, W. C., Wyman, P. A., Parker, G. R., Wannon, M., & Gribble, P. (1992). Test comparisons among stress-affected, stress-resilient, and non-classified fourth- through sixth-grade urban children. *Journal of Community Psychology, 20,* 200–214.

Crick, N. R. (1995). Relational aggression: The role of intent attributions, feelings of distress, and provocation type. *Development and Psychopathology, 7,* 313–322.

Crick, N. R., & Dodge, K. A. (1994). A review and reformulation of social information-processing mechanisms in children's social adjustment. *Psychological Bulletin, 115*(1), 74–101.

Crick, N. R., & Dodge, K. A. (1996). Social information-processing mechanisms in reactive and proactive aggression. *Child Development, 67*(3), 993–1002.

Crick, N. R., Nelson, D. A., Morales, J. R., Cullerton-Sen, C., Casas, J. F., & Hickman, S. E. (2001). Relational victimization in childhood and adolescence: I hurt you through the grapevine. In J. Juvonen & S. Graham (Eds.), *Peer harassment in school: The plight of the vulnerable and victimized* (pp. 196–214). New York: Guilford Press.

Crick, N. R., & Werner, N. E. (1998). Response decision processes in relational and overt aggression. *Child Development, 69*(6), 1630–1639.

Crick, N. R., Werner, N. E., Casas, J. F., O'Brien, K. M., Nelson, D. A., Grotpeter, J. K., & Markon, K. (1998). Childhood aggression and gender: A new look at an old problem. In D. Bernstein et al. (Eds.), *Gender and motivation. Nebraska symposium on motivation* (Vol. 45, pp. 75–141). Lincoln: University of Nebraska Press.

Cronbach, L. J. (1951). Coefficient alpha and the internal structure of tests. *Psychometrika, 16,* 297–335.

Cronbach, L. J. (1988). Internal consistency of tests: Analyses old and new. *Psychometrika, 53*(1), 63–70.

Crouch, J. L., Smith, D. W., Ezzell, C. E., & Saunders, B. E. (1999). Measuring reactions to sexual trauma among children: Comparing the Children's Impact of Traumatic Events Scale and the Trauma Symptom Checklist for Children. *Child Maltreatment, 4,* 255–263.

Crump, S. (2002). *Abused: Can you tell? Testimony on sex abuse victims challenged.* [An interview] *The Forensic Echo, 2*(7), 1–9. Retrieved March 8, 2005, from http://echo.forensicpanel. com/1998/6/1/abusedcan.html

Csikszentmihalyi, M. (1990). *Flow: The psychology of optimal experience.* New York: HarperCollins.

Csikszentmihalyi, M. (1997a). Finding flow. *Psychology Today, 30*(4), 46–48, 70–71.

Csikszentmihalyi, M. (1997b). Happiness and creativity: Going with the flow. *Futurist, 31*(5), 8–12.

Dahl, R. E., Dorn, L., & Ryan, N. D. (1999). Sleep and neuroendocrine measures. In D. Shaffer, C. Lucas, & J. Richters (Eds.), *Diagnostic assessment in child and adolescent psychopathology* (pp. 321–334). New York: Guilford Press.

Dalgleish, T., Taghavi, R., Neshat-Doost, H., Moradi, A., Canterbury, R., & Yule, W. (2003). Patterns of processing bias for emotional information across clinical disorders: A comparison of attention, memory, and prospective cognition in children and adolescents with depression, generalized anxiety, and post-traumatic stress disorder. *Journal of Clinical Child and Adolescent Psychology, 32*(1), 10–21.

Dalton, J., Aubuchon, I., Tom, A., Pederson, S., & McFarland, R. (1993). MBTI profiles of Vietnam veterans with Post-Traumatic Stress Disorder. *Journal of Psychological Type, 26,* 3–8.

Damasio, A. R. (2002). Remembering when. *Scientific American, 287*(3), 66–73.

Danieli, Y. (1984). Psychotherapist's participation in the conspiracy of silence about the Holocaust. *Psychoanalytic Psychology, 1*(1), 23–42.

Danieli, Y. (1998). *International handbook of multigenerational legacies of trauma.* New York: Plenum Press.

Davidson, M. (2004). *Molecular expressions photo gallery: The endorphin collection.* Retrieved May 25, 2005, from http://micro.magnet.fsu.edu/micro/gallery/endorphin/endorphins.html

Davies, D. (1991). Intervention with male toddlers who have witnessed parental violence. *Families in Society: The Journal of Contemporary Human Services, 72*(9), 515–524.

Daviss, W. B., Mooney, D., Racusin, R., Ford, J. D., Fleischer, A., & McHugo, G. J. (2000). Predicting posttraumatic stress after hospitalization for pediatric injury. *Journal of American Academy of Child and Adolescent Psychiatry, 59*(5), 576–583.

Daviss, W. B., Racusin, R., Fleischer, A., Mooney, D., Ford, J. D., & McHugo, G. (2000). Acute stress disorder symptomatology during hospitalization for pediatric injury. *Journal of the American Academy of Child and Adolescent Psychiatry, 39,* 569–575.

Dawes, R. (1988). *Rational choice in an uncertain world.* New York: Harcourt Brace Jovanovich.

Dawson, G., Frey, K., Panagiotides, H., Osterling, J., & Hessel, D. (1997). Infants of depressed mothers exhibit atypical frontal brain activity: A replication of previous findings. *Journal of Child Psychology and Psychiatry, 38,* 179–186.

Deardorff, J., Gonzales, N. A., & Sandler, I. N. (2003). Control beliefs as a mediator of the relation between stress and depressive symptoms among inner-city adolescents. *Journal of Abnormal Child Psychology, 31*(2), 205–217.

De Bellis, M., Baum, A., Birmaher, B., Keshavan, M., Eccard, C., Boring, A., Jenkins, F., & Ryan, N. (1999). Developmental traumatology part I: Biological stress systems. *Biological Psychiatry, 45,* 1259–1270.

De Bellis, M., Keshavan, M., Clark, D., Casey, B., Giedd, H., Boring, A., Frustaci, K., & Ryan, N. (1999). Developmental traumatology part II: Brain development. *Biological Psychiatry, 45,* 1271–1284.

de Castro, B. O., Slot, N. W., Bosch, J. D., Koops, W., & Veerman, J. W. (2003). Negative feelings exacerbate hostile attributions of intent in highly aggressive boys. *Journal of Clinical Child and Adolescent Psychology, 32*(1), 56–65.

de Decker, A., Hermans, D., Raes, F., & Eelen, P. (2003). Autobiographical memory specificity and trauma in inpatient adolescents. *Journal of Clinical Child and Adolescent Psychology, 32*(1), 22–31.

DeGangi, G. A. (1991a). Assessment of sensory, emotional, and attentional problems in regulatory disordered infants: Part 1. *Infants and Young Children, 3*(3), 1–8.

DeGangi, G. A. (1991b). Treatment of sensory, emotional and attentional problems in regulatory disordered infants: Part 2. *Infants and Young Children, 3*(3), 9–19.

de Graaf, R., Bijl, R. V., ten Have, M., Beekman, A. T. F., & Vollebergh, W. A. M. (2004). Rapid onset of comorbidity of common mental disorders: Findings from the Netherlands Mental Health Survey and Incidence Study (NEMESIS). *Actica Psychiatrica Scandinavia, 109*, 55–63.

de Jong, J. T., Komproe, I. H., Ommeren, M. V., Masri, M. E., Araya, M., Khaled, N., van de Put, W., & Somasundaram, D. (2001). Lifetime events and PTSD in 4 postconflict settings. *Journal of American Medical Association, 286*(5), 555–562.

Depue, R.A. & Iacano, W.G. (1989). Neurobehavioral aspects of affective disorders. In M. R. Rosenzweig & L. Y. Porter (Eds.), *Annual review of psychology* (Vol. 40, pp. 457–492). Palo Alto, CA: Annual Reviews.

Derogatis, L. R., & Melisaratos, N. (1983). The Brief Symptom Inventory: An introductory report. *Psychological Medicine, 13*(3), 595–605.

Derryberry, D., & Rothbart, M. K. (2001). Early temperament and emotional development. In A. F. Kalverboer & A. Gramsbergen (Eds.), *Handbook of brain behavior in human development* (pp. 967–988). London: Kluwer Academic Publishers.

de Silva, P. (1999). Cultural aspects of post-traumatic stress disorder. In W. Yule (Ed.), *Post-traumatic stress disorders: Concepts and therapy* (pp. 116–138). Chichester, England: Wiley and Sons.

DeVoe, E. R., Klein, T. P., & Linas, S. (2003, December). *Helping young children and their parents and caregivers: Lessons from Ground Zero.* Workshop presented at the Zero to Three: 18th National Training Institute, New Orleans.

DiLeo, J. H. (1983). *Interpreting children's drawings.* New York: Brunner/Mazel.

Dise-Lewis, J. E. (1988). The life events and coping inventory: An assessment of stress in children. *Psychosomatic Medicine, 50*, 484–499.

Dodge, K. A. (1986). A social information processing model of social competence in children. In M. Perlmutter (Ed.), *The Minnesota Symposium on Child Psychology* (Vol. 18, pp. 77–125). Hillsdale, NJ: Erlbaum.

Dodge, K. A., Bates, J. E., & Pettit, G. S. (1990). Mechanisms in the cycle of violence. *Science, 250*, 1678–1683.

Dodge, K. A., Bates, J. E., Pettit, G. S., & Valente, E. (1995). Social information-processing patterns partially mediate the effect of early physical abuse on later conduct problems. *Journal of Abnormal Psychology, 104*(4), 632–643.

Dodge, K.A. & Coie, J. D. (1987). Social information-processing factors in reactive and proactive aggression in children peer groups. *Journal of Personality and Social Psychology, 53*, 389–409.

Dodge, K.A., Coie, J.D., Pettit, G.S. & Price, J.M. (1990). Peer status and aggression in boys' groups: Developmental and contextual analyses. *Child Development, 61*, 1289–1309.

Donders, J. (2001a). A survey of report writing by neuropsychologists, I: General characteristics and content. *Clinical Neuropsychologist, 15*(2), 137–149.

Donders, J. (2001b). A survey of report writing by neuropsychologists, II: Test data, report format, and document length. *Clinical Neuropsychologist, 15*(2), 150–161.

Drake E., Bush S., & van Gorp, W. (2001). Evaluation and assessment of PTSD in children and adolescents. In S. Eth (Ed.), *PTSD in children and adolescents* (pp. 1–31). Washington, DC: American Psychiatric Publishing.

Drell, M. J., Siegel, C. H., & Gaensbauer, T. (1993). Post-traumatic stress disorder. In C. H. Zeanah, Jr. (Ed.), *Handbook of infant mental health* (pp. 291–304). New York: Guilford Press.

Dubrow, N., & Nader, K. (1999). Consultations amidst trauma and loss: Recognizing and honoring differences. In K. Nader, N. Dubrow, & B. Stamm (Eds.), *Honoring differences: Cultural issues in the treatment of trauma and loss* (pp. 1–19). Philadelphia: Taylor & Francis.

Dumas, J. E., Blechman, E. A., & Prinz, R. J. (1994). Aggressive children and effective communication. *Aggressive Behavior, 20*, 347–358.

Dunn, L., & Dunn, L. (1981). *The Peabody Picture Vocabulary Test-III*. Circle Pines, MN: American Guidance Service.

Dunn, L., & Dunn, L. (1997). *The Peabody Picture Vocabulary Test* (3rd ed.). Circle Pines, MN: American Guidance Service.

D'Urso, A., Esquilin, S., Fiore, M., Haldapoulus, M., & Heiman, M. (1995). *Mental health evaluations of child sexual abuse*. Retrieved March 8, 2005, from http://www.state.nj.us/humanservices/NJTaskForce/mhsae.html

Dyregrov, A., & Raundalen, M. (1993, June). *The impact of the Gulf War on the children of Iraq*. Paper presented at the International Society for Traumatic Stress Studies World Conference, Trauma and Tragedy, Amsterdam.

Dyregrov, A., Yule, W., Smith, P., Perrin, S., Gjestad, R., & Prigerson, P. (2001). *Inventory of Complicated Grief for Children*. Copyrighted inventory, under construction.

Earls, F., Reich, W., & Jung, K. G. (1988). Psychopathology in children of alcoholic and antisocial parents. *Alcohol Clinical and Experimental Research, 12*, 481–487.

Edelbrock, C., Costello, A., Dulcan, M. K., Conover, N. C., & Kalas, R. (1986). Parent-child agreement on child psychiatric symptoms assessed via structured interview. *Journal of Child Psychology and Psychiatry, 27*, 181–190.

Edleson, J. L. (1999). *Problems associated with children's witnessing of domestic violence*. Violence against Women online resources. Retrieved March 8, 2005, from http://www.vaw.umn.edu/documents/vawnet/witness/witness.html

Egger, H. L., & Angold, A. (2004). The Preschool Age Psychiatric Assessment. In R. DelCarmen-Wiggins & A. Carter (Eds.), *A handbook of infant, toddler, and preschool mental assessment* (pp. 223–246). New York: Oxford University Press.

Egger, H. L., Ascher, B. H., & Angold, A. (1999). *The Preschool Age Psychiatric Assessment: Version 1.1*. Unpublished interview schedule. Center for Developmental Epidemiology, Department of Psychiatry and Behavioral Sciences, Duke University Medical Center, Durham, NC.

Egger, H. L., Ascher, B. H., & Angold, A. (2002). *The Preschool Age Psychiatric Assessment: Version 1.3*. Unpublished interview schedule. Center for Developmental Epidemiology, Department of Psychiatry and Behavioral Sciences, Duke University Medical Center, Durham, NC.

Egger, H., Erkanli, A., Keeler, G., Potts, E., Walter, B. K. & Angold, A. (2006). Test-Retest Reliability of the Preschool Age Psychiatric Assessment (PAPA). *Journal of the American Academy of Child & Adolescent Psychiatry. 45*(5), 538–549.

Elander, J., & Rutter, M. (1996). Use and development of the Rutter Parents' and Teachers' Scales. *International Journal of Methods in Psychiatric Research, 6*, 63–78.

Elliott, D., & Briere, J. (1994a). Forensic sexual abuse evaluations of older children: Disclosures and symptomatology. *Behavioral Sciences and the Law, 12*, 261–277.

Elliott, D. & Briere, J. (1994b). *The Trauma Symptoms Checklist for Children: Validation data from a child abuse evaluation center.* Unpublished manuscript, UCLA School of Medicine, Los Angeles.

Endicott, J., Spitzer, R., Fleiss, J., & Cohen, J. (1976). The Global Assessment Scale: A procedure for measuring overall severity of psychiatric disturbance. *Archives of General Psychiatry, 31*(2), 766–771.

Erwin, B. A., Newman, E., McMackin, R. A., Morrissey, C., & Kaloupek, D. G. (2000). Malevolent environmental factors, traumatic life events, and PTSD among criminally involved adolescents. *Criminal Justice and Behavior, 27*, 196–215.

Eth, S., & Pynoos, R. (1985a). Developmental perspectives on psychic trauma in children. In C. Figley (Ed.), *Trauma and its wake, Vol. I: The study and treatment of post-traumatic stress disorder* (pp. 36–52). New York: Bruner/Mazel.

Eth, S., & Pynoos, R. (1985b). Interaction of trauma and grief in childhood. In S. Eth & R. Pynoos (Eds.), *Post-traumatic stress disorder in children* (pp. 171–186). Washington, DC: American Psychiatric Press.

Exner, J. E., Jr. (1993). *The Rorschach: A comprehensive system: Vol. 1. Basic foundations* (3rd ed.). New York: Wiley.

Eysenck, H. J. (1967). *The biological basis of personality.* Springfield, IL: Charles C. Thomas.

Fagan, J., & McMahon, P. P. (1984). Incipient multiple personality in children: Four cases. *Journal of Nervous and Mental Disease, 172*, 26–36.

Faller, K. C. (1998a). *Video manual: Interviewing for child sexual abuse: A forensic guide.* New York: Guilford Press.

Faller, K. C. (1998b). *Videotape: Interviewing for child sexual abuse: A forensic guide.* New York: Guilford Press.

Famularo, R., Kinscherff, R., & Fenton, T. (1990). Symptom differences in acute and chronic presentation of childhood post-traumatic stress disorder. *Child Abuse and Neglect, 14*, 439–444.

Fang, L., & Chen, T. (2004). Community outreach and education to deal with cultural resistance to mental health services. In N. B. Webb (Ed.), *Mass trauma, stress, and loss: Helping children and families cope* (pp. 234–255). New York: Guilford Press.

Federici, R. (2003). *Help for the hopeless child: A guide for families* (2nd ed.). Alexandra, VA: Author.

Fein, G. (1979). Echoes from the nursery: Piaget, Vygotsky, and the relationship between language and play. In E. Winner & H. Gardner (Eds.), *Fact, fiction, and fantasy* (pp. 1–14). San Francisco: Jossey-Bass.

Feiring, C., Taska, L. S., & Chen, K. (2002). Trying to understand why horrible things happen: Attribution, shame, and symptom development following sexual abuse. *Child Maltreatment, 7*(1), 26–41.

Feiring, C., Taska, L. S., & Lewis, M. (1998). The role of shame and attributional style in children's and adolescents' adaptation to sexual abuse. *Child Maltreatment, 3*(2), 129–142.

Feller, J. N., with Davidson, H. A., Hardin, M., Horowitz, R. M. (1992). *Working with the courts in child protection*. McLean, VA: U.S. Department of Health and Human Services Administration for Children and Families, Administration on Children, Youth and Families National Center on Child Abuse and Neglect (this manual was developed and produced by The Circle, Inc., McLean, VA, under Contract No. HHS-105–88–1702).

Fenichel, O. (1945). *The psychoanalytic theory of neurosis*. New York: W. W. Norton.

Ferdinand, R., Hoogerheide, K., van der Ende, J., Visser, J. H., Koot, H. M., Kasius, M. C., & Verhulst, F. C. (2003). The role of the clinician: Three-year predictive value of parents', teachers', and clinicians' judgment of childhood psychopathology. *Journal of Child Psychology & Psychiatry & Allied Disciplines, 44*(6), 867–876.

Fergusson, D. M., & Horwood, L. J. (2003). Resilience to childhood adversity: Results of a 21-year study. In S. S. Luthar (Ed.), *Resilience and vulnerability: Adaptation in the context of childhood adversities* (pp. 130–155). New York: Cambridge University Press.

Fergusson, D. M., Woodward, L. J., & Horwood, L J. (2000). Risk factors and life processed associated with the onset of suicidal behaviour during adolescence and early adulthood, *Psychological Medicine, 30,*(1), 23–39.

Field, T., Seligman, S., Scafidi, F., & Schanberg, S. (1996). Alleviating posttraumatic stress in children following Hurricane Andrew. *Journal of Applied Developmental Psychology, 17*, 37–50.

Fields, R. M. (1979). Child terror victims and adult terrorists. *Journal of Psychohistory, 7*(1), 3–16.

Figley, C. (2002). *Treating compassion fatigue*. New York: Routledge.

Finkelhor, D., & Browne, A. (1985). The traumatic impact of child sexual abuse: A conceptualization. *American Journal of Orthopsychiatry, 55*, 536–541.

Flannery, D. J., Vazsonyi, A. T., Liau, A. K., Guo, S., Powell, K. E., Atha, H., & Dennis, W. V. (2003). Initial behavior outcomes for the Peace Builders Universal School-Based Violence Prevention Program. *Developmental Psychology, 39*(2), 292–308.

Fleiss, J. L. (1981). *Statistical methods for rates and proportions*. New York: John Wiley & Sons.

Fletcher, K. (1991a). *Parent Report of the Child's Reaction to Stress*. Copyrighted scale.

Fletcher, K. (1991b). *When Bad Things Happen Scale*. Copyrighted screening instrument for PTSD.

Fletcher, K. (1992a) Dimensions of Stressful Events (DOSE). Exposure questionnaire. Available from Kenneth.Fletcher@umassmed.edu.

Fletcher, K. (1992b) The Teen Tough Times Checklist. Exposure questionnaire. Available from Kenneth.Fletcher@umassmed.edu.

Fletcher, K. (1992c) Young Adult Upsetting Times Checklist (YAUTC). Exposure questionnaire. Available from Kenneth.Fletcher@umassmed.edu.

Fletcher, K. (1997). World View Survey. A copyrighted scale.

Fletcher, K. E. (1996a). Childhood posttraumatic stress disorder. In E. J. Mash & R. A. Barkley (Eds.), *Child psychopathology* (1st ed., pp. 242–275). New York: Guilford Press.

Fletcher, K. E. (1996b, November). *Measuring school-aged children's PTSD: Preliminary psychometrics of four new measures.* Paper presented at the Twelfth Annual Meeting of the International Society for Traumatic Stress Studies, San Francisco.

Fletcher, K. E. (2003). Childhood posttraumatic stress disorder. In E. J. Mash & R. A. Barkley (Eds.), *Child psychopathology* (2nd ed., pp. 330–371). New York: Guilford Press.

Fletcher, K. E., & Skidmore, G. L. (1997, November). *The World View Survey: Assessing trauma's impact on beliefs.* Paper presented at the Thirteenth Annual Meeting of the International Society for Traumatic Stress Studies, Montreal.

Fletcher, K.E. Cox, W.D., Skidmore, G.L., Janssens, D. & Render, T. (November 1997). Multimethod assessment of traumatization and PTSD among adolescent psychiatric inpatients. A paper presented at the Thirteenth Annual Meeting of the International Society for Traumatic Stress Studies, Montreal, Quebec, Canada.

Foa, E. B., Riggs, D. S., & Gershuny, B. S. (1995). Arousal, numbing, and intrusion: Symptom structure of PTSD following assault. *The American Journal of Psychiatry, 152*(1), 116–120.

Foa, E. B., & Rothbaum, B. O. (1998). *Treating the trauma of rape: Cognitive-behavioral therapy for PTSD.* New York: Guilford Press.

Fonagy, P., Target, M., Steele, M., Steele, H., Leigh, T., Levinson, A., & Kennedy, R. (1997). Morality, disruptive behavior, borderline personality disorder, crime, and their relationships to security of attachment. In L. Atkinson & K. Zucker (Eds.), *Attachment and psychopathology* (pp. 223–274). New York: Guilford Press.

Foote, W. (2002). *Abused: Can you tell? Testimony on sex abuse victims challenged.* [An interview] *The Forensic Echo, 2*(7), 1–9. Retrieved March 8, 2005, from http://echo.forensicpanel. com/1998/6/1/abusedcan.html

Ford, J. D. (2002). Traumatic victimization in childhood and persistent problems with oppositional-defiance. *Journal of Aggression, Maltreatment and Trauma, 6*(1), 25–58.

Ford, J.D., Courtois, C.A., Steele, K., van der Hart, O. & Nijenhuis, E.R.S. (2005). Treatment of complex posttraumatic self-dysregulation. *Journal of Traumatic Stress, 18*(5), 437–447.

Ford, J., Ghosh Ippen, C., Wolpaw, J., Racusin, R., Rogers, K., Ellis, C., Schiffman, J., Ribbe, D., Cone, P., Lukovitz, M., & Edwards, J. (2005). Traumatic Events Screening Inventory for Children (TESI-C) Version 8.5. Dartmouth, VT: National Center for PTSD and Dartmouth Child Psychiatry Research Group.

Ford, J. D., Racusin, R., Ellis, C. G., Daviss, W. B., Reiser, J., Fleischer, A., & Thomas, J. (2000). Child maltreatment, other trauma exposure, and posttraumatic symptomatology among children with oppositional defiant and attention deficit hyperactivity disorders. *Child Maltreatment, 5*(3), 205–217.

Ford, J. D., Racusin, R., Rogers, K., Ellis, C., Schiffman, J., Ribbe, D., Cone, P., Lukovitz, M., & Edwards, J. (2002). Traumatic Events Screening Inventory for Children (TESI-C) Version 8.4. Dartmouth, VT: National Center for PTSD and Dartmouth Child Psychiatry Research Group.

Ford, J. D., & Rogers, K. (1997, November). *Empirically-based assessment of trauma and PTSD with children and adolescents.* Paper presented at the Annual Convention of the International Society for Traumatic Stress Studies, Montreal.

Forensic Echo, The. (1998/2002). *Abused: Can you tell? Testimony on sex abuse victims challenged, 2*(7), 1–9. Retrieved March 8, 2005, from http://echo.forensicpanel. com/1998/ 6/1/abusedcan.html

Fosha, D. (2003). Dyadic regulation and experiential work with emotion and relatedness in trauma and disorganized attachment. In M. Solomon & D. J. Siegel (Eds.), *Healing trauma* (pp. 228–281). New York: W. W. Norton.

Foulkes, D. (1990). Dreaming and consciousness. *European Journal of Cognitive Psychology, 2*(1), 39–55.

Foulkes, D., Hollifield, M., Sullivan, B., Bradley, L., & Terry, R. (1990). REM dreaming and cognitive skills at ages 5–8: A cross-sectional study. *International Journal of Behavioral Development, 13*(4), 447–465.

Fox, N. A., Henderson, H. A., Rubin, K. H., Calkins, S. D., & Schmidt, L. A. (2001). Continuity and discontinuity of behavioral inhibition and exuberance: Psychophysiological and behavioral influences across the first four years of life. *Child Development, 72*(1), 1–21.

Franklin, K. W., & Cornell, D. G. (1997). Rorschach interpretation with high-ability adolescent females: Psychopathology or creative thinking? *Journal of Personality Assessment, 68*, 184–196.

Frederick, C. (1985). Selected foci in the spectrum of posttraumatic stress disorders. In J. Laube & S. A. Murphy (Eds.), *Perspectives on disaster recovery* (pp. 110–130). East Norwalk, CT: Appleton-Century-Crofts.

Frederick, C., Pynoos, R. S., & Nader, K.O. (1992). Childhood Post-Traumatic Stress Reaction Index (CPTS-RI). Copyrighted semi-structured interview.

Freeberg, A. L., & Stein, C. H. (1996). Felt obligations towards parents in Mexican-American and Anglo-American young adults. *Journal of Social & Personal Relationships, 13*(3), 457–471.

Freeman, J. B., & Beck, J. G. (2000). Cognitive interference for trauma cues in sexually abused adolescent girls with posttraumatic stress disorder. *Journal of Clinical Child Psychology, 29*(2), 245–256.

Freud, A. (1965). *Normality and pathology in childhood.* New York: International Universities Press.

Freud, A., & Burlingham, D. (1943). *War and children.* New York: Medical War Books.

Frey, R. J. (2002). *Thematic apperception test.* Retrieved May 10, 2005, from http://www.healthatoz.com/healthatoz/Atoz/ency/thematic_apperception_test. jsp

Friedrich, W. (1990). Children's Sexual Behavior Inventory. Adult report measure.

Friedrich, W. (1993a). Sexual behavior in sexually abused children. *Violence Update, 3*(5), 6–11.

Friedrich, W. (1993b). Sexual victimization and sexual behavior in children: A review of recent literature. *Child Abuse and Neglect, 17*, 59–66.

Friedrich, W. (1995). Evaluation and treatment: The clinical use of the Child Sexual Behavior Inventory: Commonly asked questions. *American Professional Society on the Abuse of Children (APSAC) Advisor, 8*(1), 1, 17–20.

Friedrich, W. (1997a). *Child Sexual Behavior Inventory (CSBI-3).* Odessa, FL: Psychological Assessment Resources.

Friedrich, W. (1997b). *Child Sexual Behavior Inventory professional manual.* Odessa, FL: Psychological Assessment Resources.

Friedrich, W., Fisher, J. L., Dittner, C. A., Acton, R., Berliner, L., Butler, J., Damon, L., Davies, W. H., Gray, A., & Wright, J. (2001). Child Sexual Behavior Inventory: Normative, psychiatric, and sexual abuse comparisons. *Child Maltreatment, 6*(1), 37–49.

Friedrich, W., Gerber, P. N., Koplin, B., Davis, M., Giese, J., Mykelbust, C., & Franckowiak, D. (2001). Multimodal assessment of dissociation in adolescents: Inpatients and juvenile sex offenders. *Sexual Abuse: A Journal of Research and Treatment, 13*(3), 167–177.

Friedrich, W., Grambsch, P., Broughton, D., Kuiper, J., & Beilke, R.L. (1991). Normative sexual behavior in children. *Pediatrics, 88*(3), 456–462.

Friedrich, W., Grambsch, P., Damon, L., Hewitt, S. K., Koverola, C., Lang, R. A., Wolfe, V., & Broughton, D. (1992). Child Sexual Behavior Inventory: Normative and clinical comparisons. *Psychological Assessment, 4*(3), 303–311.

Friedrich, W., Jaworski, T. M., Huxsahl, J. E., & Bengston, B. S. (1997). Dissociative and sexual behaviors in children and adolescents with sexual abuse and psychiatric histories. *Journal of Interpersonal Violence, 12*(2), 155–171.

Furhman, W., & Buhrmester, D. (1985). Children's perceptions of the personal relationships in their social networks. *Developmental Psychology, 21*, 1016–1024.

Galente, R., & Foa, D. (1986). An epidemiological study of psychic trauma and treatment effectiveness for children after a natural disaster. *Journal of the American Academy of Child Psychiatry, 128*, 445–450.

Gantt, L. (1998). Research. *American Journal of Art Therapy, 37*(2), 57–65.

Gantt, L. (2004a). The case for formal art therapy assessment. *Art Therapy: Journal of the American Art Therapy Association, 21*(1), 18–29.

Gantt, L. (2004b). *Suicidal indicators in art* [Brochure]. Trauma Recovery Institute, 314 Scott Avenue, Morgantown, WV 26508, ph. 304–291–2912.

Gantt, L., & Tabone, C. (1998). *The Formal Elements Art Therapy Scale: The rating manual*. Morgantown, WV: Gargoyle Press.

Gantt, L., & Tabone, C. (2003). The Formal Elements Art Therapy Scale and Draw a Person Picking an Apple from a Tree. In C. A. Malchiodi (Ed.), *Handbook of art therapy* (pp. 420–427). New York: Guilford Press.

Garbarino, J. (1999). *Lost boys: Why our sons turn violent and how we can save them.* New York: The Free Press.

Garbarino, J. (2002). Foreword: Pathways from childhood trauma to adolescent violence and delinquency. *Journal of Aggression, Maltreatment and Trauma, 6*(1), xxv–xxxi.

Garber, J., & Flynn, C. (2001) Vulnerability to depression in childhood and adolescence. In R. E. Ingram & J. M. Price (Eds.), *Vulnerability to psychopathology: Risk across the lifespan* (pp. 175–225). New York: Guilford Press.

García Coll, C., & Garrido, M. (2000). Minorities in the United States: Sociocultural context for mental health and developmental psychopathology. In A. J. Sameroff, M. Lewis, & S. M. Miller (Eds.), *Handbook of developmental psychopathology* (2nd ed., pp. 177–195). New York: Kluwer Academic/Plenum.

Garcia-Preto, N. (1998). Latinas in the United States. In M. McGoldrick (Ed.), *Revisioning Family Therapy* (pp. 330–344). New York: Guilford Press.

Geiger, T. C., & Crick, N. R. (2001). A developmental psychopathology perspective on vulnerability to personality disorders. In R. E. Ingram & J. M. Price (Eds.), *Vulnerability to psychopathology: Risk across the lifespan* (pp. 57–102). New York: Guilford Press.

George, C., Kaplan, N., & Main, M. (1984). *Adult Attachment Interview Protocol.* Unpublished manuscript. University of California, Berkeley.

George, C., Kaplan, N., & Main, M. (1996). *Adult Attachment Interview Protocol* (3rd ed.). Unpublished manuscript. University of California, Berkeley.

Gerber, L., Nguyen, Q., & Bounkeua, P. K. (1999). Working with Southeast Asia people who have migrated to the United States. In K. Nader, N. Dubrow, & B. Stamm (Eds.), *Honoring differences: Cultural issues in the treatment of trauma and loss* (pp. 98–118). Philadelphia: Taylor & Francis.

Ghosh Ippen, C., Ford, J., Racusin, R., Acker, M., Bosquet, M., Rogers, K., Ellis, C., Schiffman, J., Ribbe, D., Cone, P., Lukovitz, M., & Edwards, J. (2002). *Traumatic Events Screening Inventory–Parent Report Revised C.* Dartmouth, VT: National Center for PTSD Dartmouth Child Trauma Research Group.

Gilbert, P., Cheung, M. S.-P., Grandfield, T., Campey, F., & Irons, C. (2003). Recall of threat and submissiveness in childhood: Development of a new scale and its relationship with depression, social comparison and shame. *Clinical Psychology and Psychotherapy, 10*, 108–115.

Gilgun, J. F. (1998). *Signs of child sexual abuse.* Retrieved March 8, 2005, from http://ssw.che.umn.edu/img/assets/5661/SW_5706_Handout.pdf

Gilligan, J. (2003). Shame, guilt, and violence. *Social Research, 70*(4), 1149–1180.

Gilman, R., Huebner, E. S., & Laughlin, J. E. (2000). A first study of the Multidimensional Students' Life Satisfaction Scale with adolescents. *Social Indicators Research, 52*(2), 135–160.

Gilstrap, L. L. (2004). A missing link in suggestibility research: What is known about the behavior of field interviewers in unstructured interviews with young children? *Journal of Experimental Psychology, 10*(1), 13–24.

Gislason, I.L. & Call, J. (1982). Dog Bite in Infancy. Trauma and Personality Development. *Journal of the American Academy of Child Psychiatry, 21*(2), 203–207.

Glennon, B., & Weisz, J. R. (1978). An observational approach to the assessment of anxiety in young children. *Journal of Consulting and Clinical Psychology, 46*, 1246–1257.

Glodich, A. M. (1999). *Psychoeducational groups for adolescents exposed to violence and abuse: Assessing the effectiveness of increasing knowledge of trauma to avert reenactment and risk-taking behaviors.* Unpublished doctoral dissertation, Smith College School for Social Work, Northampton, MA.

Goenjian, A. K., Karayan, I., Pynoos, R. S., Minassian, D., Najarian, L. M., Steinberg, A. M., & Fairbanks, L. A. (1997). Outcome of psychotherapy among early adolescents after trauma. *American Journal of Psychiatry, 154*, 536–542.

Goenjian, A. K., Molina, L., Steinberg, A. M., Fairbanks, L. A., Alvarez, M. L., Goenjian, H. A., & Pynoos, R. S. (2001). Posttraumatic stress and depressive reactions among Nicaraguan adolescents after Hurricane Mitch. *The American Journal of Psychiatry, 158*(5), 788–794.

Gold, S. N. (2004). Trauma resolution & integration program. *Psychotherapy: Theory, Research, Practice, Training, 41*(4), 363–373.

Goldwater, A. (1993). *Attributional styles of child victims of natural disasters.* Doctoral dissertation, College of Education, Temple University, Philadelphia.

Goleman, D. (1992, July 21). Childhood trauma: Memory or invention? *New York Times* (Vol. 141, issue 49034), p. C1.

Gonzales, N. A., Tein, J., Sandler, I. N., & Friedman, R. J. (2001). On the limits of coping: Interactions between stress and coping for inner-city adolescents. *Journal of Adolescent Research, 16*, 372–395.

Gonzalez, N. J., & Isaacs, L. (2005). Book I. Manuscript submitted for publication.

Goodman, G. S., & Quas, J. (1996). Trauma and memory: Individual differences in children's recounting of a stressful experience. In N. Stein, P. A. Ornstein, B. Tversky, & C. J. Brainerd (Eds.), *Memory for everyday and emotional events* (pp. 267–294). Hillsdale, NJ: Erlbaum.

Goodman, G. S., Quas, J. A., Batterman-Faunce, J. M., Riddlesberger, M. M., & Kuhn, J. (1997). Children's reactions to and memory for a stressful event: Influences of age, anatomical dolls, knowledge, and parental attachment. *Applied Developmental Science, 1*(2), 54–75.

Gordon, R. (2002). *Child custody evaluations: Psychologist or detective?* Retrieved March 8, 2005, from http://www.mmpi-info.com/custody.html

Gramercy Books. (1989). *Webster's encyclopedic unabridged dictionary of the English language.* New York: Author.

Gray, J. (1972). The psychophysiological nature of introversion-extraversion: A modification of Eysenck's theory. In V. D. Nebylisyn & J. A. Gray (Eds.), *Biological bases of individual behavior* (pp. 182–206). New York: Academic Press.

Gray, J. (1985). Issues in the neuropsychology of anxiety. In A. H. Tuma & J. D. Maser (Eds.), *Anxiety and the anxiety disorders* (pp.5– 25). Hillsdale, NJ: Erlbaum.

Gray, J. (1987). *The psychology of fear and stress.* New York: Cambridge University Press.

Gray, J. (1991). The neuropsychology of temperament. In J. Strelau & A. Angleitner (Eds.), *Explorations in temperament: International perspectives on theory and measurement* (pp. 105–128). New York: Plenum Press.

Gray, M., Prigerson, H., & Litz, B. T. (2004). Conceptual and definitional issues in traumatic grief. In B. Litz (Ed.), *Early intervention for trauma and traumatic loss in children and adults: Evidence-based directions* (pp. 65–84). New York: Guilford Press.

Green, A. (1983). Dimensions of psychological trauma in abused children. *Journal of the American Academy of Child Psychiatry, 22*, 231–237.

Green, A. H. (1985). Children traumatized by physical abuse. In S. Eth & R. Pynoos (Eds.), *Post-traumatic stress disorder in children* (pp. 133–154). Washington, DC: American Psychiatric Press.

Green, B. L. (1993). Disasters and posttraumatic stress disorder. In J. R. T. Davidson & E. B. Foa (Eds.), *Posttraumatic stress disorder: DSM-IV and beyond* (pp. 75–97). Washington, DC: American Psychiatric Association.

Greenberg, M. T. (1999). Attachment and psychopathology in childhood. In J. Cassidy & P. Shaver (Eds.), *Handbook of attachment* (pp. 469–496). New York: Guilford Press.

Greenberg, M. T., DeKlyen, M., Speltz, M. L., & Endriga, M. C. (1997). The role of attachment processes in externalizing psychopathology in young children. In L. Atkinson & K. Zucker (Eds.), *Attachment and psychopathology* (pp. 196–222). New York: Guilford Press.

Greenwald, R. (1996a). The information gap in the EMDR controversy. *Professional Psychology: Research and Practice, 27*(1), 67–72.

Greenwald, R. (1996b). *Parent Reports of Post-traumatic Symptoms.* Copyrighted instrument.

Greenwald, R. (1997). *Child and Parent Reports of Post-traumatic Symptoms* (CROPS & PROPS). Copyrighted instruments.

Greenwald,R. (1999). *The Lifetime Incidence of Traumatic Events (LITE) Scale.* Baltimore, MD: Sidran.

Greenwald, R. (2002a). The role of trauma in conduct disorder. In R. Greenwald (Ed.), *Trauma and juvenile delinquency: Theory, research, and interventions* (pp. 5–23). New York: Haworth Press.

Greenwald, R. (Ed.). (2002b). *Trauma and juvenile delinquency: Theory, research, and interventions.* New York: Haworth Press.

Greenwald, R., & Rubin, A. (1999). Brief assessment of children's post-traumatic symptoms: Development and preliminary validation of parent and child scales. *Research on Social Work Practice, 9,* 61–75.

Greenwald, R., Satin, M. S., Azubuike, A. A. A., Borgen, R., & Rubin, A. (2001, December). *Trauma-informed multi-component treatment for juvenile delinquents: Preliminary findings.* Poster session presented at the annual meeting of the International Society for Traumatic Stress Studies, New Orleans.

Grigorenko, E. L. (2002). In search of the genetic engram of personality. In D. Cervone & W. Mischel (Eds.), *Advances in personality science* (pp. 29–82). New York: Guilford Press.

Grinder, J., & Bandler, R. (1976). *The structure of magic: II.* Oxford, England: Science & Behavior.

Grob, A., Little, T. D., & Wanner, B. (1999). Control judgments across the lifespan. *International Journal of Behavioral Development, 23,* 833–854.

Gully, K. (2000). Initial development of the Expectations Test for Children: A tool to investigate social information processing. *Journal of Clinical Psychology, 56*(12), 1551–1563.

Gully, K. (2001). The Social Behavior Inventory for Children in a child abuse treatment program: Development of a tool to measure interpersonal behavior. *Child Maltreatment, 6*(3), 260–270.

Gully, K. (2003a). *Expectations Test.* Salt Lake City, UT: Peak Ascent.

Gully, K. (2003b). *Expectations Test professional manual.* Salt Lake City, UT: Peak Ascent.

Gully, K. (2003c). Expectations Test: Trauma scales for sexual abuse, physical abuse, exposure to family violence and posttraumatic stress. *Child Maltreatment, 8*(3), 218–229.

Gully, K. (2003d). *Social Behavior Inventory.* Salt Lake City, UT: Peak Ascent.

Gully, K. (2003e). *Social Behavior Inventory professional manual.* Salt Lake City, UT: Peak Ascent.

Gunnar, M. R., Brodersen, L., Krueger, K., & Rigatuso, J. (1996). Dampening of adrenocortical responses during infancy: Normative changes and individual differences. *Child Development, 67,* 877–889.

Haine, R. A., Ayers, T. S., Sandler, I. N., Wolchik, S. A., & Weyer, J. L. (2003). Locus of control and self-esteem as stress-moderators or stress-mediators in parentally bereaved children. *Death studies, 27*(7), 619–640.

Hamlin, V., Jonker, B., & Scahill, L. (2004). Acute stress disorder symptoms in gunshot-injured youth. *Journal of Child & Adolescent Psychiatric Nursing, 17*(4), 161–172.

Hammen, C., & Rudolph, K. D. (2003). Childhood mood disorders. In E. J. Mash & R. A. Barkley (Eds.), *Child psychopathology* (2nd ed., pp. 233–278). New York: Guilford Press.

Hammond, L. C., & Gantt, L. (1998). Using art in counseling: Ethical considerations. *Journal of Counseling & Development, 76,* 271–276.

Handford, H. A., Mayes, S., Mattison, R., Humphrey, F., Bagnato, S., Bixler, E., & Kales, J. (1986). Child and parent reaction to the Three Mile Island nuclear accident. *Journal of the American Academy of Child and Adolescent Psychiatry, 25,* 346–356.

Hansburg, H. G. (1972). *Adolescent separation anxiety: Vol. 1. A method for the study of adolescent separation problems.* Springfield, IL: Charles C. Thomas.

Harder, D. W., & Lewis, S. J. (1987). The assessment of shame and guilt. In J. N. Butcher & C. D. Spielberger (Eds.), *Advances in personality assessment* (Vol. 6, pp. 89–114). Hillsdale, NJ: Lawrence Erlbaum Associates.

Hardin, R. (2001). Conceptions and explanations of trust: In K. S. Cook (Ed.), *Trust in society* (pp. 3–39). New York: Russell Sage.

Harlow, H. F. (1958). The nature of love. *American Psychologist, 13,* 673.

Harris, P. L., Brown, E., Marriott, C., Whittall, S., & Harmer, S. (1991). Monsters, ghosts and witches: Testing the limits of the fantasy-reality distinction in young children. *British Journal of Developmental Psychology, 9,* 105–123.

Hart, J., Gunnar, M., & Cicchetti, D. (1995). Salivary cortisol in maltreated children: Evidence of relations between neuroendocrine activity and social competence. *Development and Psychopathology, 7,* 11–26.

Harter, S. (1982). The Perceived Competence Scale. *Child Development, 53*(1), 87–97.

Harter, S. (1985). *The Self-Perception Profile for Children.* Unpublished manual. Denver: University of Denver.

Harter, S. (1988). *The Self-Perception Profile for Adolescents.* Unpublished manual. Denver: University of Denver.

Harter, S. (1999). *The construction of the self.* New York: Guilford Press.

Harter, S., & Pike, R. (1984). The pictorial scale of perceived competence and social acceptance for young children. *Child Development, 55*(6), 1969–1982.

Harter, S., Waters, P., & Whitesell, N. R. (1998). Relational self-worth: Differences in perceived worth as a person across interpersonal contexts among adolescents. *Child Development, 69*(3), 756–766.

Harvey, S. (2000). Dynamic play approaches in the observation of family relationships. In K. Gitlin-Weiner, A. Sandgrund, & C. Schaefer (Eds.), *Play diagnosis and assessment* (2nd ed., pp. 457–473). New York: Wiley and Sons.

Hastings, T., & Kelley, M. L. (1997). Development and validation of the Screen for Adolescent Violence Exposure (SAVE). *Journal of Abnormal Child Psychology, 25,* 5112–520.

Hattie, J. (1992). *Self-concept.* Hillsdale, NJ: Erlbaum.

Haugaard, J. J. (2004). Recognizing and treating uncommon behavioral and emotional disorders in children and adolescents who have been severely maltreated: Dissociative disorders. *Child Maltreatment, 9*(2), 146–153.

Hawley, P. H., & Little, T. D. (2002). Evolutionary and developmental perspectives, on the agentic self. In D. Cervone & W. Mischel (Eds.), *Advances in personality science* (pp. 177–195). New York: Guilford Press.

Heinonen, K., Räikönnen, K., & Keltikangas-Järvinen, L. (2003). Maternal perceptions and adolescent self-esteem: A six-year longitudinal study. *Adolescence, 38*(152), 669–687.

Heller, W., Schmidtke, J. I., Nitschke, J. B., Koven, N. S., & Miller, G. A. (2002). States, traits, and symptoms: Investigating the neural correlates of emotion, personality, and psychopathology. In D. Cervone & W. Mischel (Eds.), *Advances in personality science* (pp. 106–126). New York: Guilford Press.

Henderson, H. A., Marshall, P. J., Fox, N. A., & Rubin, K. H. (2004). Psychophysiological and behavioral evidence for varying forms and functions of nonsocial behavior in preschoolers. *Child Development, 75*(1), 251–263.

Herjanic, B., & Reich, W. (1982). Development of a structured psychiatric interview for children: Agreement between child and parent on individual symptoms. *Journal of Abnormal Child Psychology, 10*(3), 307–324.

Herman, J. L. (1992a). Complex PTSD: A syndrome in survivors of prolonged and repeated trauma. *Journal of Traumatic Stress, 5*(3), 377–391.

Herman, J. L. (1992b). A new diagnosis. In J. L. Herman, *Trauma and recovery* (pp. 115–127). New York: Basic Books.

Herman, J. L. (1992c, 1997). *Trauma and recovery.* New York: Basic Books.

Hesse, E. (1999). The adult attachment interview: Historical land current perspectives. In J. Cassidy & P. R. Shaver (Eds.), *Handbook of attachment: Theory, research, and clinical applications* (pp. 395–433). New York: Guilford Press.

Hesse, E., Main, M., Abrams, K. Y., & Rifkin, A. (2003). Unresolved states regarding loss or abuse can have "second-generation" effects: Disorganization, role inversion, and frightening ideation in the offspring of traumatized, nonmaltreating parents. In M. Solomon & D. J. Siegel (Eds.), *Healing trauma* (pp. 57–106). New York: W. W. Norton.

Higgins, D. J., & McCabe, M. R. (1996, August). Parent perceptions of children's experiences of maltreatment. Paper presented at the Biannual Conference of the International Society for the Prevention of Child Abuse and Neglect, Dublin, Republic of Ireland.

Hines, P. M. (1998). Climbing up the rough side of the mountain: Hope, culture, and therapy. In M. McGoldrick (Ed.), *Re-visioning family therapy* (pp. 78–89). New York: Guilford Press.

Hodgetts, R. (1993). A conversation with Geert Hofstede. *Organizational Dynamics, 21,* 53–61.

Hodgman, C. H., & Jack, M. S. (1992). Interviewing. In E. McAnarney, R. Kreipe, D. Orr, & G. D. Comerci (Eds.), *The textbook of adolescent medicine* (pp. 180–185). Philadelphia: W. B. Saunders.

Hofstede, G. (1980). *Culture's consequences: International differences in work-related values.* Beverly Hills, CA: Sage Publications.

Hofstede, G. (Ed.). (1998). *Masculinity and femininity: The taboo dimension of national cultures.* Thousand Oaks, CA: Sage Publications.

Hogue, T. E. (1994). Goal attainment scaling: A measure of clinical impact and risk assessment. *Issues of Criminological and Legal Psychology, 21,* 96–102.

Hoksbergen, R. A. C., ter Laak, J., van Dijkum, C., Rijk, S., Rijk, K., & Stoutjesdijk, F. (2003). Posttraumatic stress disorder in adopted children from Romania. *American Journal of Orthopsychiatry, 73*(3), 255–265.

Holaday, M. (2000). Rorschach protocols from children and adolescents diagnosed with posttraumatic stress disorder. *Journal of Personality Assessment, 75*(1), 143–157.

Holaday, M., Armsworth, M. W., Swank, P. R., & Vincent, K. R. (1992). Rorschach responding in traumatized children and adolescents. *Journal of Traumatic Stress, 5*(1), 119–129.

Holaday, M., Warren-Miller, G., & Whittenberg, T. (1994). Biased expectations of burned or traumatized children and adolescents as revealed through predictions of Rorschach responding. *Counseling Psychology Quarterly, 7*(2), 207–219.

Holaday, M., & Whittenberg, T. (1994). Rorschach responding in children and adolescents who have been severely burned. *Journal of Personality Assessment, 62*(2), 269–279.

Hollifield, M., Warner, T. D., Lian, N., Krakow, B., Jenkins, J. H., Kesler, J., Stevenson, J., & Westermeyer, J. (2002). Measuring trauma and health status in refugees. *Journal of American Medical Association, 288*(5), 611–621.

Hollingsworth, L. D. (2003). International adoption among families in the United States: Considerations of social justice. *Social Work, 48*(2), 209–217.

Horowitz, M., Wilner, N., & Alvarez, W. (1979). Impact of Events Scale: A measure of subjective stress. *Psychosomatic Medicine, 41*, 209–218.

Horton, C. B., & Oakland, T. (1997). Temperament-based learning styles as moderators of academic achievement. *Adolescence, 32*(125), 131–142.

Hough, R. L., Vega, W., Valle, R., Kolody, B., del Castillo, R. G., & Tarke, H. (1989). Mental health consequences of the San Ysidro McDonald's massacre: A community study. *Journal of Traumatic Stress, 3*, 71–92.

House, A. E. (2002). *The first session with children and adolescents: Conducting a comprehensive mental health evaluation*. New York: Guilford Press.

Howe, M. L. (1997). Children's memory for traumatic experiences. *Learning and Individual Differences, 9*, 153–174.

Howe, M. L., Courage, M. L., & Peterson, C. (1995). Intrusions in preschoolers' recall of traumatic childhood events. *Psychonomic Bulletin and Review, 2*(1), 130–134.

Howie, P. M., & Dowd, H. J. (1996). Self-esteem and the perceived obligation to respond: Effects on children's testimony. *Legal and Criminological Psychology, 1*, 197–209.

Hoyle, R., Fejfar, M., & Miller, J. (2000). Personality and sexual risk taking: A quantitative review. *Journal of Personality, 68*(6), 1203–1231.

Huebner, E. S. (1991a). Correlates of life satisfaction in children. *School Psychology Quarterly, 6*, 103–111.

Huebner, E. S. (1991b). Initial development of the Students' Life Satisfaction Scale. *School Psychology International, 12*, 231–240.

Huebner, E. S. (1994a). Conjoint analyses of the Students' Life Satisfaction Scale and Piers-Harris Self-Concept Scale. *Psychology in the Schools, 31*, 273–277.

Huebner, E. S. (1994b). Preliminary development and validation of a Multidimensional Life Satisfaction Scale for Children. *Psychological Assessment, 6*, 149–158.

Huebner, E. S. (2001). *Multidimensional Students' Life Satisfaction Scale: Introduction and Rationale*. Columbia, SC: Author.

Huebner, E. S., & Aldeman, G. L. (1993). Convergent and Discriminant Validation of a Children's Life Satisfaction Scale: Its relationship to self- and teacher-reported psychological problems and school functioning. *Social Indicators Research, 30*, 71–82.

Huebner, E. S., Funk, B. A., III; & Gilman, R. (2000). Cross-sectional and longitudinal psychosocial correlates of adolescent life satisfaction reports. *Canadian Journal of School Psychology, 16*(1), 53–64.

Huebner, E. S., Gilman, R., & Laughlin, J. (1999). The multidimensionality of children's well being reports: Discriminant validity of life satisfaction and self-esteem. *Social Indicators Research, 46*, 1–22.

Huebner, E. S., Laughlin, J. E., Ash C., & Gilman, R. (1998). Further validation of the Multidimensional Students' Life Satisfaction Scale. *Journal of Psychological Assessment, 16*, 118–134.

Huebner, E. S., Suldo, S. M., & Valois, R. F. (2003, March). Psychometric properties of two brief measures of children's life satisfaction: The Students' Life Satisfaction Scale (SLSS) and the Brief Multidimensional Students Life Satisfaction Scale (BMSLSS). Paper prepared for the Indicators of Positive Development Conference, Washington, D.C.

Huebner, E. S., Suldo, S., Valois, R. F., Drane, J. W., & Zullig, K. (2004). Brief Multidimensional Students' Life Satisfaction Scale: Sex, race, and grade effects for a high school sample. *Psychological Reports, 94*(1), pp. 351–356.

Huesmann, L. R., Moise-Titus, J., Podolski, C.-L., & Eron, L. D. (2003). Longitudinal relations between children's exposure to TV violence and their aggressive and violent behavior in young adulthood: 1977–1992. *Developmental Psychology, 39*(2), 201–221.

Huete, J. M. (2001). The relationship of daily stress and health in adolescence: Development of the Daily Stress Inventory for Adolescence (DSI-A). Doctoral dissertation, Louisiana State University. *Dissertation Abstracts International, 61*, 6708.

Huffman, M. L., Crossman, A., & Ceci, S. (1997). Are false memories permanent? An investigation of the long-term effects of source misattributions. *Consciousness & Cognition, 6*, 482–490.

Hyman, I., & Snook, P. (2002). *My Worst Experience Scale manual.* Los Angeles: Western Psychological Services.

Ingram, R. E., & Price, J. M. (2001). The role of vulnerability in understanding psychopathology. In R. E. Ingram & J. M. Price (Eds.), *Vulnerability to psychopathology: Risk across the lifespan* (pp. 3–19). New York: Guilford Press.

Irwin, H. J. (1998). Affective predictors of dissociation II: Shame and guilt. *Journal of Clinical Psychology, 54*(2), 237–245.

ISTSS. (1998). *Childhood trauma remembered: A report on the current scientific knowledge base and its applications.* Chicago: Author.

Jackson, Y., Frick, P., & Dravage-Bush, J. (2000). Perceptions of control in children with externalizing and mixed behavior disorders. *Child Psychiatry and Human Development, 31*(1), 43–58.

Jacobs, S. (1999). *Traumatic grief: Diagnosis, treatment, and prevention.* Philadelphia: Brunner/Mazel.

James, B. (1994). *Handbook for treatment of attachment-trauma problems in children.* Lexington, MA: Lexington Books.

Jersild, A. T. (1952). *In search of self.* New York: Teachers College Bureau of Publications.

John, O. P., Caspi, A., Robins, R. W., Moffitt, T. E., & Stouthamer-Loeber, M. (1994). The "Little Five": Exploring the five-factor model of personality in adolescent boys. *Child Development, 65*, 160–178.

Johnson, D. E. (1998). The family physician and international adoption. *American Family Physician, 58*(9), 1958–1963.

Johnson, K. (2006). Posttraumatic stress in children and adolescents. Retrieved 5/8/07 from http://www.brynmawr.edu/psychology/cdpp/johnson.shtml.

Johnson, M. K., & Foley, M. A. (1984), Differentiating fact from fantasy: The reliability of children's memory. *Journal of Social Issues, 40*, 33–50.

Jones, R. T., Fletcher, K., & Ribbe D. R. (2002) *Child's Reaction to Traumatic Events Scale-Revised* (CRTES-R). Self report traumatic stress measure.

Jones, R. T., & Ollendick, T. H. (2002). Residential fires. In A. M. La Greca, W. K. Silverman, E. M. Vernberg, & M. C. Roberts (Eds.), *Helping children cope with disasters and terrorism* (pp. 175–199). Washington, DC: APA Press.

Jones, R. T., & Ribbe, D. P. (1991). Child, adolescent and adult victims of residential fire. *Behavior Modification, 15*(4), 560–580.

Jones, R. T., Ribbe, D. P., & Cunningham, P. B. (1994). Psychosocial correlates of fire disaster among children and adolescents. *Journal of Traumatic Stress, 7*(1), 117–122.

Joseph, S., Williams, R., & Yule, W. (1997). *Understanding post-traumatic stress: A psychosocial perspective on PTSD and treatment*. Chichester, England: Wiley.

Jung, C. G. (1971). *Psychological types: The collected works of C. G. Jung* (Vol. 6). Princeton, NJ: Princeton University Press.

Kagan, J. (1997). Temperament and the reactions to unfamiliarity. *Child Development, 68*(1), 139–143.

Kagan, J. (2001). Commentaries on "Personality development across the life course: The argument for change and continuity" and "Issues in the study of personality development: The need for new constructs." *Psychological Inquiry, 12*(2), 84–103.

Kagan, J., Reznick, J. S., & Snidman, N. (1988). Biological bases of childhood shyness. *Science, 240*(4849), 167–71.

Kagan, J., Snidman, N., & Arcus, D. (1995). The role of temperament in social development. *Annals of the New York Academy of Sciences, 771*, 485–490.

Kalsched, D. (1996). *The inner world of trauma: Archetypal defenses of the personal spirit*. London: Brunner-Routledge.

Kamphuis, J. H., Kugeares, S. L., & Finn, S. E. (2000). Rorschach correlates of sexual abuse: Trauma content and aggression indexes. *Journal of Personality Assessment, 75*(2), 212–224.

Kaniasty, K., & Norris, F. (1993). A test of the support deterioration model in the context of natural disaster. *Journal of Personality and Social Psychology, 64*, 395–408.

Kaplan, N. (1987). *Individual differences in six-year-olds' thoughts about separation: Predicted from attachment to mother at age one*. Doctoral dissertation, Psychology Department, University of California, Berkeley.

Kapstein, E. B. (2003). The baby trade. *Foreign Affairs, 82*(6), 115–125.

Kardiner, A. (1941). The traumatic neuroses of war. *Psychosomatic Medicine Monographs, 1 (2 & 3, Serial No. 258)*. Washington, DC: National Research Council.

Karno, M., Burnam, A., Escobar, J. I., Hough, R. L., & Eaton, W. W. (1983). Development of the Spanish-language version of the National Institute of Mental Health Diagnostic Interview Schedule. *Archives of General Psychiatry, 40*, 1183–1188.

Kassam-Adams, N., & Winston, F. K. (2004). Predicting child PTSD: The relationship between acute stress disorder and PTSD in injured children. *Journal of the American Academy of Child & Adolescent Psychiatry, 43*(4), 403–411.

Katz-Plotkin, S. (1991). Sexual victimization and its impact on children's sexual behavior and behavioral functioning. Doctoral dissertation, Boston College. *Dissertation Abstracts International, 52*(2-A), 475.

Kaufman, G. (1989). *The psychology of shame: Theory and treatment of shame-based syndromes.* New York: Springer.

Kay, M. (2002). *Preparation of a psycho-educational evaluation report.* Retrieved March 8, 2005, from http://www.harborhouselaw.com/article/kay.report.htm

Keirsey, D., & Bates, M. (1978). *Please understand me.* Del Mar, CA: Prometheus Nemesis.

Kessler, R.C. (2000). Posttraumatic Stress Disorder: The burden to the Individual and to society. *Journal of Clinical Psychiatry, 61*(5), 4–14.

Kessler, R. C., Davis, C. G., & Kendler, K. S. (1997). Childhood adversity and adult psychiatric disorder in the U.S. National Comorbidity Survey. *Psychological Medicine, 27,* 1101–1119.

Kessler, R. C., Mroczek, D. K., & Belli, R. F. (1999). Retrospective adult assessment of childhood psychopathology. In D. Shaffer, C. Lucas, & J. Richters (Eds.), *Diagnostic assessment in child and adolescent psychopathology* (pp. 256–284). New York: Guilford Press.

Kimerling, R., Prins, A., Westrup, D., & Lee, T. (2004). Gender issues in the assessment of PTSD. In J. P. Wilson & T. M. Keane (Eds.), *Assessing psychological trauma and PTSD* (2nd ed., pp. 565–599). New York: Guilford Press.

King, V. (2002). Parental divorce and interpersonal trust in adult offspring. *Journal of Marriage & the Family, 64*(3), 642–656.

Kinzie, J. D. (1993). Posttraumatic effects and their treatment among Southeast Asian refugees. In J. Wilson & B. Raphael (Eds.), *The International Handbook of Traumatic Stress Syndromes* (pp. 311–319). New York: Plenum Press.

Kinzie, J. D., Boehnlein, J., & Sack, W. H. (1998). The effects of massive trauma on Cambodian parents and children. In Y. Danieli (Ed.), *International handbook of multigenerational legacies of trauma* (pp. 211–221). New York: Plenum Press.

Kinzie, J. D., Denney, D., Riley, C., Boehnlein, J. K., McFarland, B., & Leung, P. (1998). A cross-cultural study of reactivation of posttraumatic stress disorder symptoms: American and Cambodian psychophysiological response to viewing traumatic video scenes. *Journal of Nervous and Mental Disease, 186,* 670–676.

Kinzie, J. D., Sack, W. H., Angell, R. H., Manson, S., & Rath, B. (1986). The psychiatric effects of massive trauma on Cambodian children: I. The children. *Journal of the American Academy of Child Psychiatry, 25*(3), 370–376.

Kiresuk, T. J., Smith, A., & Cardillo, J. E. (Eds.). (1994). *Goal attainment scaling: Applications, theory, and measurement.* Hillsdale, NJ: Erlbaum Associates.

Kirmayer, L. J., Young, A., & Hayton, B. C. (1995). The cultural context of anxiety disorders. *The Psychiatric Clinics of North America, 18*(3), 503–521.

Kiser, L. J., Heston, J., Millsap, P. A., & Pruitt, D. B. (1991). Physical and sexual abuse in childhood: Relationship with post-traumatic stress disorder. *Journal of the American Academy of Child and Adolescent Psychiatry, 30,* 776–783.

Kisiel, C. L., & Lyons, J. S. (2001). Dissociation as a mediator of psychopathology among sexually abused children and adolescents. *American Journal of Psychiatry, 158,* 1034–1039.

Klain, E. (1998). Intergenerational aspects of the conflict of the former Yugoslavia. In Y. Danieli (Ed.), *An international handbook of multigenerational legacies of trauma* (pp. 279–296). New York: Plenum Press.

Klein, H. (1974). Child victims of the Holocaust. *Journal of Clinical Child Psychology, 3*(2), 44–47.

Kluft, R. P. (1984). Multiple personality in childhood. *Psychiatric Clinics of North America, 7*(1), 121–134.

Kluft, R. P. (1985). Childhood multiple personality disorder: Predictors, clinical findings and treatment results. In R. P. Kluft (Ed.), *Childhood antecedents of multiple personality* (pp. 167–196). Washington, DC: American Psychiatric Press.

Kluft, R. P. (1996). Dissociative identity disorder. In L. K. Michelson & W. J. Ray (Eds.), *Handbook of dissociation: Theoretical, empirical and clinical perspectives* (pp. 337–366). New York: Plenum Press.

Knox, J. (2003b). Trauma and defenses: Their roots in relationship, an overview. *Journal of Analytical Psychology, 48,* 511–530.

Knox, J. (2003a). Reflective function, the mind as an internal object. A presentation based on a chapter in J. Knox (2003b). Archetype, attachment, analysis: Jungian psychology and the emergent mind. NY: Brunner-Routledge.

Kobak, R. R., & Cole, C. (1994). Attachment and metamonitoring: Implications for adolescent autonomy and psychopathology. In D. Cicchetti (Ed.), *Rochester Symposium on Development and Psychopathology: Vol. 5. Disorders of the self,* (pp. 267–297). Rochester, NY: University of Rochester Press.

Kochanska, G. (1997). Multiple pathways to conscience for children with different temperaments: From toddlerhood to age 5. *Developmental Psychology, 33,* 228–240.

Kochanska, G., & Clark, L. (1997). Implications of mother's personality for their parenting and their young children's developmental outcomes. *Journal of Personality, 65*(2), 387–420.

Kohly, M. (1994). *Reported child abuse and neglect victims during the flood months of 1993.* Jefferson City, MO: Missouri Department of Social Services, Division of Family Services, Research and Development Unit.

Kohr, M. (1995). *Validation of the My Worst Experience Survey.* Unpublished doctoral dissertation, Temple University, Philadelphia.

Koss, M. P., Figueredo, A. J., Bell, I., Tharan, M., & Tromp, S. (1996). Traumatic memory characteristics: A cross-validated mediational model of response to rape among employed women. *Journal of Abnormal Psychology, 105*(3), 421–432.

Kovacs, M., & Beck, A. T. (1977). An empirical clinical approach toward a definition of childhood depression. In J. G. Schulterbrandt & A. Raskin (Eds.), *Depression in childhood: Diagnosis, treatment and conceptual models* (pp. 43–57). New York: Raven Press.

Krakow, B., Hollifield, M., Johnston, L., Koss, M., Schrader, R., Warner, T. D., Tandberg, D., Lauriello, J., McBride, L., Cutchen, L., Cheng, D., Emmons, S., Germain, A., Melendrez, D., Sandoval, D., & Prince, H. (2001). Imagery rehearsal therapy for chronic nightmares in sexual assault survivors with posttraumatic stress disorder [on-line]. *JAMA, 286*(5). Retrieved 9/2/02 from http://jama.ama-assn.org/issues/v286n5/abs/joc10245.html

Krakow, B., Sandoval, D., Schrader, R., Keuhne, B., McBride, L., Yau, C. L., & Tandberg, D. (2001). Treatment of chronic nightmares in adjudicated adolescent girls in a residential facility. *Journal of Adolescent Health, 29*(2), 94–100.

Kroll, J. (2003). Posttraumatic symptoms and the complexity of responses to trauma. *JAMA, 290*(5), 667–670.

Krug, R. (1996). Psychological effects of manmade disasters. *Oklahoma Dental Association, 86*(4), 40–44.

Kuder, G. F., & Richardson, M. W. (1937). The theory of the estimation of test reliability. *Psychometrika, 2,* 151–160.

Kunzmann, U., Little, T. D., & Smith, J. (2000). Is age-related stability of subjective well-being a paradox? Cross-sectional and longitudinal evidence from the Berlin Aging Study. *Psychology and Aging, 15*(3), 511–526.

Kupersmidt, J. B., Shahinfar, A., & Voegler-Lee, M. E. (2002). Children's exposure to community violence. In A. M. La Greca, W. K. Silverman, E. M. Vernberg, & M. C. Roberts (Eds.), *Helping children cope with disasters and terrorism* (pp. 381–397). Washington, DC: APA Press.

Kurcinka, M. S. (1998a). *Raising your spirited child* (2nd ed.). New York: Harper Perennial.

Kurcinka, M. S. (1998b). *Raising your spirited child workbook.* New York: Harper Perennial.

Lacey, G. N. (1972). Observations on Aberfan. *Journal of Psychosomatic Research, 16,* 257–260.

Lachar, D. (1982). *Personality Inventory for Children (PIC) revised format manual supplement.* Los Angeles: Western Psychological Services.

Lachar, D., & Gruber, C. P. (1995a). *Personality Inventory for Youth (PIY) manual: Administration and interpretation guide.* Los Angeles: Western Psychological Services.

Lachar, D., & Gruber, C. P. (1995b). *Personality Inventory for Youth (PIY) manual: Technical guide.* Los Angeles: Western Psychological Services.

Lachar, D., & Gruber, C. P. (2001). *Personality Inventory for Children, second edition (PIC-2) manual: Standard form and behavioral summary.* Los Angeles: Western Psychological Services.

La Greca, A. M., & Prinstein, M. J. (2002). Hurricanes and earthquakes. In A. M. La Greca, W. K. Silverman, E. M. Vernberg, & M. C. Roberts (Eds.), *Helping children cope with disasters and terrorism* (pp. 107–138). Washington, DC: APA Press.

La Greca, A. M., Silverman, W. K., Vernberg, E. M., & Prinstein, M. J. (1996). Symptoms of posttraumatic stress in children after Hurricane Andrew: A prospective study. *Journal of Consulting and Clinical Psychology, 64*(4), 712–723.

La Greca, A. M., Silverman, W. K., Vernberg, E. M., & Roberts, M. C. (Eds.). (2002a). *Helping children cope with disasters and terrorism.* Washington, DC: APA Press.

La Greca, A. M., Silverman, W. K., Vernberg, E. M., & Roberts, M. C. (2002b). Introduction. In A. M. La Greca, W. K. Silverman, E. M. Vernberg, & M. C. Roberts (Eds.), *Helping children cope with disasters and terrorism* (pp. 3–33). Washington, DC: APA Press.

Lahey, B., Locher, R., Quay, H. C., Applegate, B., Shaffer, D., Waldman, L., Hart, E. L., McBurnett, K., Frick, P. J., Jensen, P. S., Dulcan, M. K., Canino, G., & Bird, H. R. (1998). Validity of DSM-IV subtypes of conduct disorder based on age of onset. *Journal of the American Academy of Child and Adolescent Psychiatry, 34,* 435–442.

Laird, J. (1998). Theorizing culture: Narrative ideas and practice principles. In M. McGoldrick (Ed.), *Re-visioning family therapy* (pp. 20–36). New York: Guilford Press.

Laird, R. D., Jordan, K. Y., Dodge, K. A., Pettit, G. S., & Bates, J. E. (2001). Peer rejection in childhood, involvement with antisocial peers in early adolescence, and the development of externalizing behavior problems. *Development and Psychopathology, 13*, 337–354.

Laird, R. D., Pettit, G. S., Dodge, K. A., & Bates, J. E. (2003). Change in parents' monitoring knowledge: Links with parenting, relationship quality, adolescent beliefs, and antisocial behavior. *Social Development, 12*(3), 401–419.

Lakatos, K., Toth, I., Nemoda, Z., Ney, K., Sasvari, M., & Gervai, J. (2000). Dopamine D4 receptor gene polymorphism as associated with attachment disorganization in infants. *Molecular Psychiatry, 5*, 633–637.

Lambert, M. C., & Weisz, J. R. (1989). Over- and under-controlled clinic referral problems in Jamaican clinic-referred children: Teacher reports for ages 6–17. *Journal of Abnormal Child Psychology, 17*, 553–562.

Lampinen, J. M., & Smith, V. L. (1995). The incredible (and sometimes incredulous) child witness: Child eyewitnesses' sensitivity to source credibility cues. *Journal of Applied Psychology, 80*, 621–627.

Lanclos, N. F. (2001). Parenting practices as a moderator of exposure to community violence. Doctoral dissertation, Louisiana State University and Agricultural & Mechanical College, 2002. *Dissertation Abstracts International, 63*(2-B), 1035.

Lanktree, C. B., Briere, J., & Hernandez, P. (1991, August). Further data on the Trauma Symptom Checklist for Children (TSC-C): Reliability, validity, and sensitivity to treatment. Presented at the annual meeting of the American Psychological Association, San Francisco.

Laria, A. J., & Lewis-Fernández, R. (2001). The professional fragmentation of experience in the study of dissociation, somatization, and culture. *Journal of Trauma & Dissociation, 2*(3), 17–47.

Lau, A. S., Garland, A. F., Yeh, M., McCabe, K. M., Wood, P. A., & Hough, R. L. (2004). Race/ethnicity and inter-informant agreement in assessing adolescent psychopathology. *Journal of Emotional and Behavioral Disorders, 12*(3), 145–156.

Lawrence, G. (1993). *People types & tiger stripes* (3rd ed.). Gainesville, FL: Center for Applications of Psychological Type.

Layne, C. M., Pynoos, R. S., Saltzman, W. S., Arslanagic, B., Black, M., Savjak, N., Popivic, T., Durakovic, E., Music, M., Jampara, N., Djapo, N., & Houston, R. (2001). Trauma/grief-focused group psychotherapy: School based post-war intervention with traumatized Bosnian adolescents. *Group Dynamics: Theory, Research, and Practice, 5*(4), 277–290.

Layne, C. M., Savjak, N., Saltzman, W. R., & Pynoos, R. S. (2001). *UCLA/BYU Grief Screening Inventory*. Unpublished instrument. Provo, UT: Brigham Young University.

Lazarus, R. S., & Folkman, S. (1984). *Stress, appraisal, and coping*. New York: Springer.

Leavitt, F. (2000). Surviving roots of trauma: Prevalence of silent signs of sex abuse in patients who recover memories of childhood sex abuse as adults. *Journal of Personality Assessment, 74*(2), 311–323.

LeDoux, J. E. (1996). *The emotional brain: The mysterious underpinnings of emotional life*. New York: Simon & Schuster.

Lee, J., Lei, A., & Sue, S. (2001). The current state of mental health research on Asian Americans. *Journal of Human Behavior in the Social Environment, 3*(3/4), 159–178.

Lee, M., Cohen, S., Stuber, M., & Nader, K. (1994). Parent-child interactions with pediatric bone marrow transplant patients. *Journal of Psychosocial Oncology, 12*(4), 43–60.

Leeming, D., & Boyle, M. (2004). Shame as a social phenomenon: A critical analysis of the concept of dispositional shame. *Psychology and Psychotherapy: Theory, Research and Practice, 77,* 375–396.

Lehmann, P., & Coady, N. F. (Eds.). (2001). *Theoretical perspectives for direct social work practice: A generalist-eclectic approach.* New York: Springer.

Levy, D. M. (1938). Release therapy in young children. *Psychiatry, 1,* 387–390.

Levy, D. M. (1945). Psychic trauma of operations in children. *American Journal of Diseases of Children, 69,* 7–25.

Lewis, H. B. (1971). *Shame and guilt in neurosis.* New York: International Universities Press.

Lewis, M. (1995). Embarrassment: The emotion of self-exposure and evaluation. In J. P. Tangney & K. W. Fischer (Eds.), *Self-conscious emotions: The psychology of shame, guilt, embarrassment, and pride* (pp. 198–218). New York: Guilford Press.

Lichtenberg, J. W., & Moffitt, W., III (1994). The effect of predicate matching on perceived understanding and factual recall. *Journal of Counseling & Development, 72*(5), 544–548.

Lifton, B. J. (1994). *Journey of the adopted self. A quest for wholeness.* New York: Basic Books.

Lifton, R. J. (1993). From Hiroshima to the Nazi doctors: The evolution of psychoformative approaches to understanding traumatic stress syndromes. In J. P. Wilson & B. Raphael (Eds.), *International handbook of traumatic stress syndromes* (pp. 11–23). New York: Plenum Press.

Linder, T. (2000). Transdisciplinary play-based assessment. In K. Gitlin-Weiner, A. Sandgrund, & C. Schaefer (Eds.), *Play, diagnosis, and assessment* (pp.139–164). New York: John Wiley & Sons.

Lindley, P., & Walker, S. N. (1993). Theoretical and methodological differentiation of moderation and mediation. *Nursing Research, 42*(5), 276–279.

Lindsay, D. S., & Read, J. D. (1995). "Memory Work" and recovered memories of childhood sexual abuse: Scientific evidence and public, professional, and personal issues. *Psychology, Public Policy, and Law, 1*(4), 846–908.

Liotti, G. (1992). Disorganized/disoriented attachment in the etiology of the dissociative disorders. *Dissociation, 5,* 196–204.

Liotti, G. (2004). Trauma, dissociation, and disorganized attachment: Three strands of a single braid. *Psychotherapy: Theory, Research, Practice, Training, 41*(4), 472–486.

Lipschitz, D. S., Morgan, C. A., & Southwick, S. M. (2002). Neurobiological disturbances in youth with childhood trauma and in youth with conduct disorder. *Journal of Aggression, Maltreatment and Trauma, 6*(1), 149–174.

Lira, E. (2001). Violence, fear, and impunity: Reflections on subjective and political obstacles for peace. *Peace and Conflict: Journal of Peace Psychology, 7*(2), 109–118.

Lloyd, B. (1999). Tough love/tough theory [Review of the book *Masculinity and femininity: The taboo*]. *Psychology, Evolution and Gender, 1*(3), 321–327.

Loeber, R., Green, S. M., Lahey, B. B., & Stouthamer-Loeber, M. (1991). Differences and similarities between children, mothers, and teachers as informants on disruptive behavior disorders. *Journal of Abnormal Child Psychology, 19,* 75–95.

Loewenstein, R. J. (2004). Commentary on "Cherchez la Femme, Cherchez la Femme: A Paradoxical Response to Trauma" Dissociation of the "Bad" Parent, Preservation of the "Good" Parent. *Psychiatry, 67*(3), 256–260.

Lonigan, C. J., Shannon, M. P., Finch, A. J., Jr., Daugherty, T. K., & Taylor, C. M. (1991). Children's reactions to a natural disaster: Symptom severity and degree of exposure. *Advances in Behavioral Therapy, 13,* 135–154.

Lorenz, K. E. (1935). De Kumpan in der Umvelt des Vogels. In C. H. Schiller (Ed.), *Instinctive behavior* (pp 137–215; 289–413.). New York: International Universities Press.

Lowenstein, R. (2002, November). The phenomenology of dissociation and its treatment implications for complex trauma. Plenary presentation for the International Society for Traumatic Stress Studies, Baltimore.

Lubit, R., Hartwell, N., van Gorp, W. G., & Eth, S. (2002). *Forensic evaluation of trauma syndromes in children.* Retrieved March 8, 2005, from http://www.traumahelp.org/forensic.htm

Luthar, S. S. (Ed.). (2003). *Resilience and vulnerability: Adaptation in the context of childhood adversities.* New York: Cambridge University Press.

Lyons-Ruth, K., Easterbrooks, M. A., & Cibelli, C. D. (1997). Infant attachment strategies, infant mental lag, and maternal depressive symptoms: Predictors of internalizing and externalizing problems at age 7. *Developmental Psychology, 33*(4), 681–692.

Lyons-Ruth, K., & Jacobvitz, D. (1999). Attachment disorganization: Unresolved loss, relational violence and lapses in behavioral and attentional strategies. In J. Cassidy & P. Shaver (Eds.), *Handbook of attachment* (pp. 469–496). New York: Guilford Press.

Lyons-Ruth, K., Yellin, C., Melnick, S., & Atwood, G. (2003). Childhood experiences of trauma and loss have different relations to maternal unresolved and hostile-helpless states of mind on the AAI. *Attachment & Human Development, 5*(4), 330–352.

Lyons-Ruth, K., Zeanah, C. H., & Benoit, D. (2003). Disorder and risk for disorder during infancy and toddlerhood. In E. J. Mash & R. A. Barkley (Eds.), *Child psychopathology* (2nd ed., pp. 589–631). New York: Guilford Press.

Maestripieri, D., & Wallen, K. (2003). Nonhuman primate models of developmental psychopathology. In D. Cicchetti & E. Walker (Eds.), *Neurodevelopmental mechanisms in psychopathology* (pp. 187–214). Cambridge, UK: Cambridge University Press.

Magnus, K. B., Cowen, E. L., Wyman, P. E., Fagen, D. B., & Work, W. C. (1999). Correlates of resilient outcomes among highly stressed African-American and White urban children. *Journal of Community Psychology, 27*(4), 473–488.

Main, M. (1995). Recent studies in attachment: Overview with selected implications for clinical work. In S. Goldberg, R. Muir & J. Kerr (Eds.), *Attachment theory: Social, developmental and clinical perspectives* (pp. 407–472). Hillsdale, NJ: Analytic Press.

Main, M., & Goldwyn, R. (1998). *Adult attachment classification system.* Unpublished manuscript, University of California, Berkeley.

Main, M., Kaplan, N., & Cassidy, J. (1985). Security in infancy, childhood, and adulthood: A move to the level of representation. *Monographs of the Society for Research in Child Development, 50*(1/2), 66–104.

Malcarne, V. L., & Hansdottir, I. (2001). Vulnerability to anxiety disorders in childhood and adolescence. In R. E. Ingram & J. M. Price (Eds.), *Vulnerability to psychopathology: Risk across the lifespan* (pp. 271–303). New York: Guilford Press.

Malchiodi, C. A. (1998). *The art therapy sourcebook.* Los Angeles: Lowell House.

Malinosky-Rummel, R. R., & Hoier, T. S. (1991). Validating measures of dissociation in sexually abused and nonabused children. *Behavioral Assessment, 13,* 341–357.

Manion, I. G., Firestone, P., Cloutier, P., Ligezinska, M., McIntyre, J., & Ensom, R. (1998). Child extrafamilial sexual abuse: Predicting parent and child functioning. *Child Abuse and Neglect, 22*(12), 1285–1304.

Mannarino, A. R., Cohen, J. A., & Berman, S. R. (1994). The Children's Attributions and Perceptions Scale: A new measure of sexual abuse-related factors. *Journal of Clinical Child Psychology, 23,* 204–211.

Mansel, J., & Hurrelmann, K. (1991). Alltagsstreß bei Jugendlichen. Eine Untersuchung über Lebensrisiken und psychosoziale Befindlichkeiten im Statusübergang. Weinheim, Deutschland: Juventa.

Manson, S. M., Ackerson, L. M., Dick, R. W., Baron, A. E., & Fleming, C. M. (1990). Depressive symptoms among American Indian adolescents: Psychometric characteristics of the Center for Epidemiologic Studies Depression Scale (CES-D). *Psychological Assessment, 2*(3), 231–237.

March, J., Amaya-Jackson, L., Foa, E., & Treadwell, K. (1999). Trauma focused coping treatment of pediatric post-traumatic stress disorder after single-incident trauma. Version 1.0. Unpublished protocol.

March, J., Amaya-Jackson, L., Murray, M., & Schulte, A. (1998). Cognitive-behavioral psychotherapy for children and adolescents with post-traumatic stress disorder following a single incident stressor. *Journal of American Academy of Child and Adolescent Psychiatry, 37*(6), 585–593.

Markus, H. R., Kitayama, S., & Heiman, R. J. (1996). Culture and basic psychological principles. In E. T. Higgins & A. W. Kruglanski (Eds.), *Social psychology: Handbook of basic principals* (pp. 857–913). New York: Guilford Press.

Marsh, J. (2000). But I want to fly, too! Girls and superhero play in the infant classroom. *Gender & Education, 12*(2), 209–220.

Martin, P. (2003). Taking control of your life: A brief journey and guide. *International Journal of Reality Therapy, 23,* 41–46.

Martin, R. P., & Bridger, R. C. (1999). *Temperament Assessment Battery for Children-Revised, manual.* Copyrighted manual and measure.

Martin, R. P., Wisenbaker, J., Huttenen, M. O., & Baker, J. (1997). Gender difference in infant temperament. *Infant Behavior and Development, 20,* 339–347.

Marvin, R. S., & Britner, P. A. (1999). Normative development: The ontogeny of attachment. In J. Cassidy & P. R. Shaver (Eds.), *Handbook of attachment: Theory, research, and clinical applications* (pp. 44–67). New York: Guilford Press.

Mash, E. J., & Barkley, R.A. (Eds.). (2003). *Child psychopathology* (2nd ed). New York: Guilford Press.

Mash, E. J., & Dozois, D. (2003). Child psychopathology: A developmental systems perspective. In E. J. Mash & R. A. Barkley (Eds.), *Child psychopathology* (2nd ed., pp. 3–71). New York: Guilford Press.

Masten, A. S., & Powell, J. L. (2003). A resilience framework for research, policy and practice. In S. S. Luthar (Ed.), *Resilience and vulnerability: Adaptation in the context of childhood adversities* (pp. 1–25). New York: Cambridge University Press.

Mayou, R. A., Ehlers, A., & Hobbs, M. (2000). Psychological debriefing for road traffic accident victims: Three-year follow-up of a randomized controlled trial. *British Journal of Psychiatry, 176*, 589–593.

McBurnett, K., King, J., & Scarpa, A. (2003). The hypothalamic-pituitary-adrenal system (HPA) and the development of aggressive, antisocial, and substance abuse disorders. In D. Cicchetti & E. Walker (Eds.), *Neurodevelopmental mechanisms in psychopathology* (pp. 324–344). Cambridge, UK: Cambridge University Press.

McCann, I. L., & Pearlman, L. A. (1990). *Psychological trauma and the adult survivor: Theory, therapy, and transformation*. Philadelphia: Brunner/Mazel.

McCarron, A. L., Ridgway, S., & Williams, A. (2004). The Truth or Lie Story: Developing a tool for assessing child witnesses' ability to differentiate between truth and lies. *Child Abuse Review, 13*, 42–50.

McCleery, J. M., & Harvey, A. G. (2004). Integration of psychological and biological approaches to trauma memory: Implications for pharmacological prevention of PTSD. *Journal of Traumatic Stress, 17*(6), 485–496.

McCrae, R. R. (2001). Traits through time. *Psychological Inquiry, 12*(2), 84–86.

McCrae, R. R., & John, O. P. (1992). An introduction to the Five-Factor model and its applications. *Journal of Personality, 60*, 175–215.

McDermott, B. M., & Palmer, L. J. (2002). Wilderness area and wildfire disasters: Insights from a child and adolescent screening program. In A. M. La Greca, W. K. Silverman, E. M. Vernberg, & M. C. Roberts (Eds.), *Helping children cope with disasters and terrorism* (pp. 139–156). Washington, DC: APA Press.

McDermott, J. F. (1991). The effects of ethnicity on child and adolescent development. In M. Lewis (Ed.), *Child and adolescent psychiatry: A comprehensive textbook* (pp. 145–159). Baltimore: Williams & Wilkins.

McFarlane, A. C., Policansky, S. K., & Irwin, C. (1987). A longitudinal study of the psychological morbidity in children due to natural disaster. *Psychological Medicine, 17*, 727–738.

McInerney, D. M., Lillemyr, O. F., & Sobstad, F. (2004, July). Self-concept in cultural context: Harter's Perceived Competence Scale for Children [R]. *Proceedings of Self-concept, Motivation and Identity: Where do we go from here?* Third International Biennial SELF Research Conference, Berlin, Germany.

McInerney, D. M., Yeung, S. Y., & McInerney, V. (2001). Cross-cultural validation of the Inventory of School Motivation (ISM). *Journal of Applied Measurement, 2*, 134–152.

McKenna, J., Foster, L. J., & Page, A. (2004). Exploring recall of physical activity in young people using qualitative interviewing. *Pediatric Exercise Science, 16*(1), 5–14.

McNally, R. J., Kaspi, S. P., Riemann, B. C., & Zeitlin, S. B. (1990). Selective processing of threat cues in posttraumatic stress disorder. *Journal of Abnormal Psychology, 99*, 398–402.

Meadows, E. A., & Foa, E. B. (1998). Intrusion, arousal and avoidance: Sexual trauma survivors. In V. M. Follette, J. I. Ruzek, & F. R. Abueg (Eds.), *Cognitive-behavioral therapies for trauma* (pp. 100–123). New York: Guilford Press.

Meiser-Stedman, R., Yule, W., Smith, P., Glucksman, E., & Dalgleish, T. (2005). Acute stress disorder and posttraumatic stress disorder in children and adolescents involved in assaults or motor vehicle accidents. *American Journal of Psychiatry, 162*(7), 1381–1383.

Meisgeier, C., & Murphy, E. (1987). *Murphy-Meisgeier Type Indicator for Children manual.* Palo Alto, CA: Consulting Psychologists Press.

Meleis, A. I. (2003). Guest editorial: Reflections on September 11, 2001. *Health Care for Women International, 24,* 1–4.

Melnyk, L., & Bruck, M. (2004). Timing moderates the effects of repeated suggestive interviewing on children's eyewitness memory. *Applied Cognitive Psychology, 18,* 613–631.

Mercier, M. H., & Despert, J. L. (1943). Psychological effects of the war on French children. *Psychosomatic Medicine, 5,* 266–272.

Mersky, H. (1992). Manufacture of personalities. *British Journal of Psychiatry, 160,* 327–340.

Mezulis, A. H., Abramson, L. Y., Hyde, J. S. & Hankin, B. (2004). Is there a universal positivity bias in attributions?: A meta-analytic review of individual, developmental, and cultural differences in the self-serving attributional bias. *Psychological Bulletin, 130*(5), 711–747.

Miller, P. V., & Cannell, C. F. (1977). Communicating measurement objectives in the survey interview. In D. M. Hirsch, P. V. Miller, & F. G. Kline (Eds.), *Strategies for communication research* (Vol. 6, pp. 127–151). Beverly Hills, CA: Sage.

Mills, S. (2001). The idea of different folk psychologies. *International Journal of Philosophical Studies, 9*(4), 501–519.

Mitchell, C. E. (1990). Development or restoration of trust in interpersonal relationships during adolescence and beyond. *Adolescence, 25,* 847–854.

Mlot, C. (1998) Probing the biology of emotion. *Science, 280*(5366), 1005–1007.

Mogford-Bevan, K. (2000). The Play Observation Kit (POKIT): An observational assessment technique for young children. In K. Gitlin-Weiner, A. Sandgrund, & C. Schaefer (Eds.), *Play diagnosis and assessment* (2nd ed., pp. 262–299). New York: Wiley and Sons.

Moller-Thau, D., & Fletcher, K. E. (1996). *Diagnosing child PTSD with two self report measures: The Childhood PTSD Reaction Index and the When Bad Things Happen Scale.* Unpublished manuscript.

Moos, H. R., & Moos, S. B. (1986). *Family Environment Scale manual* (2nd ed.). Palo Alto, CA: Consulting Psychologists Press.

Moran, P. B., & Eckenrode, J. (1992). Protective personality characteristics among adolescent victims of maltreatment. *Child Abuse and Neglect, 16,* 743–754.

Mori, L. T., & Armendariz, G. M. (2001). Analogue assessment of child behavior problems. *Psychological Assessment, 13*(1), 36–45.

Muller, R., Sicoli, L., & Lemieux, K. E. (2000). Relationship between attachment style and posttraumatic stress symptomatology among adults who report the experience of childhood abuse. *Journal of Traumatic Stress, 13*(2), 321–332.

Mullis, A.K., Mullis, R.L. & Normandin, D. (1992). Cross-sectional and longitudinal comparisons of adolescent self-esteem. *Adoleslcence, 27,* 51–61.

Murphy, E., & Meisgeier, C. (1987). *Murphy-Meisgeier Type Indicator for Children.* Palo Alto, CA: Consulting Psychologists Press.

Murphy, E. A. (1986). Estimates of reliability and validity for the Murphy-Meis-geier Type Indicator for Children. Doctoral dissertation, University of Houston, 1986. *Dissertation Abstracts International, 47*(6-A), 2091.

Murray, H. A. (1943/1971). *Thematic Apperception Test: Manual.* Cambridge, MA: Harvard University Press.

Murray, J. F. (1992). Toward a synthetic approach to the Rorschach: The case of a psychotic child. *Journal of Personality Assessment, 58,* 494–505.

Myers, I. B., & McCaulley, M. (1985). *Manual: A guide to the development and use of the Myers-Briggs Type Indicator.* Palo Alto, CA: Consulting Psychologists Press.

Myers, I. B., & Myers, P. B. (1980/1995). *Gifts differing.* Palo Alto, CA: Davies Black.

Myers, J. E. B., Berliner, L., Briere, J., Hendrix, C. T., Reid, T., & Jenny, C. (Eds.). (1990). *The APSAC handbook on child maltreatment.* Thousand Oaks, CA: Sage Publications.

Nachmias, M., & Gunnar, M. (1996). Behavioral inhibition and stress reactivity: The moderating role of attachment security. *Child Development, 67*(2), 508–522.

Nader, K. (1984/1995). *Childhood Post-traumatic Stress Reaction, Parent Inventory* (CPTSR-PI) (3rd ed.). Copyrighted instrument. Semi-structured interview about children, for parents of children with traumatic exposure. R4 in progress.

Nader, K. (1991). *Posttraumatic stress assessment following a tornado at a school.* Unpublished report to a school district, February 28.

Nader, K. (1992). *CPTS-RI assessment of Bosnian refugee youth in Croatia.* Unpublished data analysis.

Nader, K. (1993a). *Exposure Questionnaire (EQ).* A measure of children's physical and subjective exposure to traumatic experiences. Available from measures@twosuns.org.

Nader, K. (1993b). *Instruction manual, Childhood PTSD Reaction Index, Revised, English version.* Copyrighted manual.

Nader, K. (1994). Countertransference in treating trauma and victimization in childhood. In J. Wilson & J. Lindy (Eds.), *Countertransference in the treatment of post-traumatic stress disorder* (pp. 179–205). New York: Guilford Press.

Nader, K. (1995). *Additional Questions (AQ):* A supplemental questionnaire for the CPTS-RI. Austin, TX: Two Suns.

Nader, K. (1995). Childhood Trauma: a manual and questionnaires. Austin, TX: Two Suns.

Nader, K. (1996). Children's traumatic dreams. In D. Barrett (Ed.), *Trauma and dreams* (pp. 9–24). Cambridge, MA: Harvard University Press.

Nader, K. (1997a). Assessing traumatic experiences in children. In J. Wilson & T. Keane (Eds.), *Assessing psychological trauma & PTSD* (pp. 291–348). New York: Guilford Press.

Nader, K. (1997b). Childhood traumatic loss: The interaction of trauma and grief. In C. R. Figley, B. E. Bride, & N. Mazza (Eds.), *Death and trauma: The traumatology of grieving* (pp. 17–41). London: Taylor & Francis.

Nader, K. (1997c). Treating traumatic grief in systems. In C. R. Figley, B. E. Bride, & N. Mazza (Eds.), *Death and trauma: The traumatology of surviving* (pp. 159–192). London: Taylor & Francis.

Nader, K. (1998). Violence: Effects of a parent's previous trauma on currently traumatized children. In Y. Danieli (Ed.), *An international handbook of multigenerational legacies of trauma* (pp. 571–583). New York: Plenum Press.

Nader, K. (1999a). *Additional Questions.* Copyrighted supplemental semistructured interview.

Nader, K. (1999b). *Exposure Questionnaire (EQ)*. A measure of children's physical and subjective exposure to traumatic experiences. Available from measures@twosuns.org.

Nader, K. (1999c). *Instruction manual, Childhood PTSD Reaction Index, Revised, English version*. Copyrighted manual.

Nader, K. (1999d). *Psychological first aid for trauma, grief and traumatic grief* (3rd ed.). Austin, TX: Two Suns.

Nader, K. (2001b). Treatment methods for childhood trauma. In J. P. Wilson, M. Friedman, & J. Lindy (Eds.), *Treating psychological trauma and PTSD* (pp. 278–334). New York: Guilford Press.

Nader, K. (2001a). *Guilt following traumatic events*, ©Nader & Gift from Within, 2001 [on-line]. Available: http://www.sourcemaine.com/gift/html

Nader, K. (2002a). *Behavioral Style Scale (child, parent and teacher)*. Copyrighted scale.

Nader, K. (2002b). *Exposure Questionnaire (EQ)*. A measure of children's physical and subjective exposure to traumatic experiences. Available from measures@twosuns.org.

Nader, K. (2002c). Simple formulas best applied to simple grief [Review of the book *A student dies, a school mourns*]. *Contemporary Psychology APA Review of Books, 47*(4), 464–466.

Nader, K. (2002d). Treating children after violence in schools and communities. In N. B. Webb (Ed.), *Helping bereaved children* (2nd ed., pp. 214–244). New York: Guilford Press.

Nader, K., Blake, D. D., & Kriegler, J. A. (1994). *Instruction manual: Clinician Administered PTSD Scale, Child and Adolescent Version (CAPS-C)*. White River Junction, VT: National Center for PTSD.

Nader, K., Dubrow, N., & Stamm, B. (Eds.). (1999). *Honoring differences: Cultural issues in the treatment of trauma and loss*. Philadelphia: Taylor & Francis.

Nader, K., & Fairbanks, L. (1994). The suppression of re-experiencing: Impulse control and somatic symptoms in children following traumatic exposure. *Anxiety, Stress and Coping: An International Journal, 7*, 229–239.

Nader, K. & Fletcher, K. (in press). *The Child Trauma Reaction Inventories*. Austin, TX: Two Suns.

Nader, K., Fletcher, K., & Stuber, M. (2005). *The Traumatic Play Observation Scale (TPOS)*. Copyrighted observation measure.

Nader, K., Kriegler, J. A., Blake, D. D., & Pynoos, R. S. (1994). *Clinician Administered PTSD Scale, Child and Adolescent Version (CAPS-C)*. White River Junction, VT: National Center for PTSD.

Nader, K., Kriegler, J. A., Blake, D. D., Pynoos, R. S., Newman, E., & Weathers, F. (1996). *Clinician Administered PTSD Scale, Child and Adolescent Version (CAPS-C)*. White River Junction, VT: National Center for PTSD.

Nader, K., & Mello, C. (2001). Interactive trauma/grief focused therapy. In P. Lehmann & N. F. Coady (Eds.), *Theoretical perspectives for direct social work practice: A generalist-eclectic approach* (pp. 382–401). New York: Springer.

Nader, K., & Mello, C. (2002). Shootings & hostage takings. In A. M. La Greca, W. K. Silverman, E. M. Vernberg, & M. C. Roberts (Eds.), *Helping children cope with disasters and terrorism* (pp. 301–326). Washington, DC: APA Press.

Nader, K., & Muni, P. (2002). Individual crisis intervention. In S. Brock & P. Lazarus (Eds.), *Best practices in crisis prevention and intervention in the schools* (pp. 405–428). Bethesda, MD: National Association of School Psychologists.

Nader, K., Newman, E., Weathers, F., Kaloupek, D. G., Kriegler, J., & Blake, D. (2004). *Clinician-Administered PTSD Scale for Children and Adolescents (CAPS-CA)*. Los Angeles: Western Psychological Press.

Nader, K. & Prigerson, H. (2005). *Complicated Grief Assessment-Child, Parent or Caregiver Report* (CGA-C). A copyrighted scale.

Nader, K., Prigerson, H. & Maciejewski, P. (2005). *Complicated Grief Assessment (Child Version)-Long Form*. A copyrighted scale.

Nader, K., & Pynoos, R. (1989). *Study of the Child Posttraumatic Stress Disorder Inventory: Parent Interview*. Unpublished manuscript containing analysis of children exposed to a sniper attack using the Nader Parent Inventory.

Nader, K., & Pynoos, R. (1991). Play and drawing as tools for interviewing traumatized children. In C. Schaefer, K. Gitlin, & A. Sandgrund (Eds.), *Play, diagnosis and assessment* (pp. 375–389). New York: John Wiley.

Nader, K., & Pynoos, R. (1993). School disaster: Planning and initial interventions. *Journal of Social Behavior and Personality, 8*(5), 299–320.

Nader, K., Pynoos, R., Fairbanks, L., Al-Ajeel, M., & Al-Asfour, A. (1993). A preliminary study of PTSD and grief among the children of Kuwait following the Gulf crisis. *British Journal of Clinical Psychology, 32*, 407–416.

Nader, K., Pynoos, R., Fairbanks, L., & Frederick, C. (1990). Children's PTSD reactions one year after a sniper attack at their school. *American Journal of Psychiatry, 147*, 1526–1530.

Nader, K., & Stuber, M. (1992, October). Catastrophic events vs. catastrophic illness: A comparison of traumatized children. Workshop presented at the Annual Meeting of the International Society for Traumatic Stress Studies, Los Angeles.

Nader, K., & Stuber, M. (1993). *Three- to five-year-old Child Trauma Checklist*. ©Regents of University of California.

Nader, K., Stuber, M., & Pynoos, R. (1991). Post-traumatic stress reactions in preschool children with catastrophic illness: Assessment needs. *Comprehensive Mental Health Care, 1*(3), 223–239.

Naglieri, J. A., McNeish, T. J., & Bardos, A. N. (1991). *Draw-A-Person: Screening procedure for emotional disturbance*. Austin, TX: Pro-Ed.

National Center for Infants, Toddlers, and Families. (1994). *Diagnostic Classification 0–3*. Arlington, VA: Zero to Three.

National Council of Juvenile and Family Court Judges (NCFCJ) (1998). *Custody and visitation decision-making when there are allegations of domestic violence*. Reno, NV: Author. Available from NCFCJ, University of Nevada, P.O. Box 8970, Reno, NV 89507.

Naumov, A. I., & Puffer, S. M. (2000). Measuring Russian culture using Hofstede's Dimensions. *Applied Psychology, 49*(4), 709–718.

Neborsky, R. J. (2003). A clinical model for the comprehensive treatment of trauma using an affect experiencing—attachment theory approach. In M. Solomon & D. J. Siegel (Eds.), *Healing trauma* (pp. 282–321). New York: W. W. Norton.

Neisworth, J. T., Bagnato, S. J., Salvia, J., & Hunt, F. M. (1999). *TABS manual for the Temperament and Atypical Behavior Scale*. Baltimore: Brookes.

Nelson, B., Martin, R. P., Hodge, S., Havill, B., & Kamphaus, R. (1999). Modeling the prediction of elementary school adjustment from preschool temperament. *Personality and Individual Differences, 26*, 687–700.

Nesselroade, J. R. (1995). As the twig is bent, so grows the tree . . . sometimes. *Psychological Inquiry, 6*(4), 343–348.

Nesselroade, J. R. (2002). Elaborating the differential in differential psychology. *Multivariate Behavioral Research, 37*(4), 543–561.

Nesselroade, J. R., & McCollam, K. M. (2000). Putting the process in developmental processes. *International Journal of Behavioral Development, 24*(3), 295–300.

Neville, H., & Johnson, D. C. (1998). *Temperament tools.* Seattle, WA: The Parenting Press.

Newman, C. J. (1976). Children of disaster: Clinical observations at Buffalo Creek. *American Journal Psychiatry, 133*, 306–312.

Newman, E., Weathers, F., Nader, K., Kaloupek, D. G., Pynoos, R., Blake, D., & Kriegler, J. (1997). *Clinician-Administered PTSD Scale for Children and Adolescents (CAPS-AC) manual.* White River Junction, VT: National Center for PTSD.

Newman, E., Weathers, F., Nader, K., Kaloupek, D. G., Pynoos, R., Blake, D., & Kriegler, J. (2004). *Clinician-Administered PTSD Scale for Children and Adolescents (CAPS-C) manual.* Los Angeles: Western Psychological Press.

Nigro, G. N., & Wolpow, S. I. (2004). Interviewing young children with props: Prior experience matters. *Applied Cognitive Psychology, 18*, 549–565.

Nijenhuis, E., Spinhoven, P., Vanderlinden, J., van Dyck, R., & van der Hart, O. (1998). Somatoform dissociative symptoms as related to animal defensive reactions to predatory imminence and injury. *Journal of Abnormal Psychology, 107*(1), 63–73.

Nijenhuis, E., van der Hart, O., & Steele, K. (2002). The emerging psychobiology of trauma-related dissociation and dissociative disorders. In H. D'Haenen, J. den Boer, & P. Willner (Eds.), *Biological psychiatry* (pp. 1079–1098). New York: John Wiley & Sons.

Niolon, R. (2003). *House Tree Person drawings.* Retrieved May 17, 2005, from http://www.therapeuticchild.ca/children_drawings/tree_test_house_drawings.htm

North, C. S., & Pfefferbaum, B. (2002). Research on the mental health effects of terrorism. *Journal of the American Medical Association, 288*(5), 633–636.

Nova. (2005). Thematic Apperception Test. Retrieved May 10, 2005, from http://eps.nova.edu/~epphelp/TAT/html

Nowicki, S., Jr. (2005). *A manual for the Children's (or Adults') Nowicki Strickland Locus of Control Scale.* Unpublished manuscript, Department of Psychology, Emory University, Atlanta.

Nowicki, S., Jr., & Strickland, B. R. (1973). A Locus of Control Scale for Children. *Journal of Consulting and Clinical Psychology, 40*, 148–154.

Oakland, T. (2001, November). Different countries: Different types. Paper presented at a meeting of the Myers-Briggs Lunch Group held at the Center for Applications of Psychological Type, Inc., Gainesville, FL.

Oakland, T., Glutting, J. J., & Horton, C. B. (1996). *Student Styles Questionnaire: Star qualities in learning, relating, and working.* San Antonio, TX: The Psychological Corporation, Harcourt Brace.

Ochberg, F. (2002). A primer on interviewing victims. In M. B. Williams & J. F. Sommer (Eds.), *Simple and complex post-traumatic stress disorder* (pp. 351–360). New York: Haworth Press.

Ochberg, F., & Soskis, D. (1982). Planning for the future: Means and ends. In F. Ochberg & D. Soskis (Eds.), *Victims of terrorism* (pp. 173–190). Boulder, CO: Westview Press.

O'Donnell, W., & Warren, W. L. (in press). *Overeating Questionnaire: Manual*. Los Angeles: Western Psychological Services.

Ogawa, J. R., Sroufe, L. A., Weinfield, N. S., Carlson, E. A., & Egeland, B. (1997). Development and the fragmented self: Longitudinal study of dissociative symptomatology in a nonclinical sample. *Development and Psychopathology, 9*, 855–879.

Ollendick, T. H. (1983). Reliability and validity of the Revised Fear Survey Schedule for Children (FSSC-R), *Behavior Research and Therapy, 21*, 685–692.

Otis, G. D., & Louks, J. L. (1997). Rebelliousness and psychological distress in a sample of introverted veterans. *Journal of Psychological Type, 40*, 20–30.

Otto, M. W., McNally, R. J., Pollack, M. H., Chen, E., & Rosenbaum, J. F. (1994). Hemispheric laterality and memory bias for threat in anxiety disorders. *Journal of abnormal psychology, 103*(4), 828–831.

Oyserman, D., Coon, H. M., & Kemmelmeier, M. (2002). Rethinking individualism and collectivism: Evaluation of theoretical assumptions and meta-analyses. *Psychological Bulletin, 128*, 3–72.

Ozolins, A. R., & Stenstrom, U. (2003). Validation of health locus of control patterns in Swedish adolescents. *Adolescence, 38*(152), 651–657.

Panksepp, J. (1986). The anatomy of emotions. In R. Plutchik & H. Kellerman (Eds.), *Emotion: Theory, research and experience: Vol. 3. Biological foundations of emotions* (pp. 91–124). San Diego, CA: Academic Press.

Park, J. (1996, January). The universality of the MBTI, cultural ideal types and falsification issues in Korea. Paper presented at the Psychological Type and Culture—East and West: A Multicultural Research Symposium, University of Hawaii at Manoa, Hawaii.

Parkes, J. (2000). The interaction of assessment format and examinees' perceptions of control. *Educational Research, 42*(2), 175–182.

Parson, E. R. (1997). Post-Traumatic Child Therapy (P-TCT): Assessment and treatment factors in clinic work with inner-city children exposed to community violence. *Journal of Interpersonal Violence, 12*, 172–194.

Parson, E. R. (1999). Post-Trauma Child Therapy (P-TCT) with inner city children and adolescents. An unpublished description.

Paunovic, N. (1998). Cognitive factors is the maintenance of PTSD. *Scandinavian Journal of Behavior therapy, 27*, 167–178.

Pasquini, P., Liotti, G., Mazzotti, E., Fassone, G., & Picardi, A. (2002). Risk factors in the early family life of patients suffering from dissociative disorders. *Acta Psychiatrica Scandinavia, 105*, 110–116.

Patterson, G. R. (1982). *Coercive family process*. Eugene, OR: Castalia Press.

Pearlman, L. A. (2001). Treatment of persons with complex PTSD and other trauma-related disruptions of the self. In J. P. Wilson, M. Friedman, & J. Lindy (Eds.), *Treating psychological trauma and PTSD* (pp. 205–236). New York: Guilford Press.

Pelcovitz, D., van der Kolk, B., Roth, S., Kaplan, S., Mandel, F., & Resick, P. (1997). Development of a criteria set and a Structured Interview for Disorders of Extreme Stress (SIDES). *Journal of Traumatic Stress, 10*(1), 3–16.

Pellegrini, A. D. (1995). *School recess and playground behavior*. Albany, NY: SUNY Press.

Pellegrini, A. D. (2001). Practitioner review: The role of direct observation in the assessment of young children. *Journal of Child Psychology and Psychiatry, 42*(7), 861–869.

Pellegrini, A. D. (2003). Perceptions and functions of play and real fighting in early adolescence. *Child Development, 74*(5), 1522–1533.

Pellegrini, A. D., & Smith, P. K. (1998). Physical activity play: The nature and function of a neglected aspect of play. *Child Development, 69*(3), 577–598.

Perilla, J. L., Norris, F. H., & Lavizzo, E. A. (2002). Ethnicity, culture, and disaster response: Identifying and explaining ethnic differences in PTSD six months after Hurricane Andrew. *Journal of Social and Clinical Psychology, 21*, 20–45.

Perry, B. D. (1995, May). Evolution of symptoms following traumatic events in children. *Proceedings of the 148th Annual Meeting of the American Psychiatric Association*, Miami.

Perry, B. D. (1997). Incubated in terror: Neurodevelopmental factors in the "Cycle of Violence." In J. Osofsky (Ed.), *Children, youth and violence: The search for solutions* (pp. 124–148). New York: Guilford Press. Retrieved February 4, 2005, from http://www.childtrauma.org/CTAMATERIALS/incubated.asp

Perry, B. D. (1999). Memories of fear: How the brain stores and retrieves physiologic states, feelings, behaviors and thoughts from traumatic events. The Child Trauma Academy version of a chapter originally appearing in J. Goodwin & R. Attias (Eds.), *Splintered reflections: Images of the body in trauma*. New York: Basic Books. Retrieved February 4, 2005, from http://www.childtrauma. org/CTAMATERIALS/memories.asp

Perry, B. D. (2006). Applying principles of neurodevelopment to clinical work with maltreated and traumatized children. In N. B. Webb (Ed.), *Working with traumatized youth in child welfare* (pp. 27–52). New York: Guilford Press.

Perry, B. D., Pollard, R., Blakely, T., Baker, W., & Vigilante, D. (1995). Childhood trauma, the neurobiology of adaptation and "use-dependent" development of the brain: How "states" become "traits." *Infant Mental Health Journal, 16*(4), 271–291. Retrieved February 5, 2005, from http://www.childtrauma.org/ CTAMATERIALS/states_traits.asp

Peters, M., Jancke, L, Staiger, J. F., Schlaug, G., Huang, Y., & Steinmetz, H. (1998). Unsolved problems in comparing brain sizes in homo sapiens. *Brain and Cognition, 37*, 254–285.

Peterson, C., & Seligman, M. E. P. (1983). Learned helplessness and victimization. *Journal of Social Issues, 39*, 103–116.

Peterson, L. W., & Hardin, M. (1997). *Children in distress: A guide for screening children's art*. New York: W. W. Norton.

Peterson, L. W., Hardin, M., & Nitsch, M. J. (1995). The use of children's drawings in the evaluation and treatment of child sexual, emotional and physical abuse. *Archives of Family Medicine, 4*, 445–452.

Pettit, G. S., Laird, R. D., Dodge, K. A., Bates, J. E., & Criss, M. M. (2001). Antecedents and behavior-problem outcomes of parental monitoring and psychological control in early adolescence. *Child Development, 72*(2), 583–598.

Pfefferbaum, B., Nixon, S. J., Tucker, P. M., Tivis, R. D., Moore, V. L., Gurwitch, R. H., Pynoos, R. S., & Geis, H. K. (1999). Posttraumatic stress responses in bereaved children after the Oklahoma City bombing. *Journal of the American Academy of Child and Adolescent Psychiatry, 38*(11), 1372–1379.

Phan, T., & Silove, D. M. (1997). The influence of culture on psychiatric assessment: The Vietnamese refugee. *Psychiatric Services, 48*(1), 86–90.

Piaget, J. (1952). *The origins of intelligence in children*. New York: International Universities Press.

Piaget, J. (1962). *Play, dreams and imitation in childhood*. New York: Norton.

Pica, M., Beere, D., Lovinger, S., & Dush, D. (2001). The responses of dissociative patients on the thematic apperception test. *Journal of Clinical Psychology, 57*(7), 847–864.

Piers, E. V. (1977). Children's self-esteem, level of esteem certainty, and responsibility for success and failure. *Journal of Genetic Psychology, 130*, 295–304.

Piers, E. V. (1996). *Piers-Harris Children's Self-Concept Scale: Manual*. Los Angeles: Western Psychological Services.

Piers, E. V., & Harris, D. B. (1964). Age and other correlates of self-concept in children. *Journal of Educational Psychology, 55*(2), 91–95.

Piers, E. V., & Herzberg, D. S. (2002). *Piers-Harris Children's Self-Concept Scale: Manual* (2nd ed.). Los Angeles: Western Psychological Services.

Pinderhughes, E. (1998). Black genealogy revisited: Restorying an African American family. In M. McGoldrick (Ed.), *Re-visioning family therapy* (pp. 177–199). New York: Guilford Press.

Pole, N., Best, S. R., Metzler, T., & Marmar, C. R. (2005). Why are Hispanics at greater risk for PTSD? *Cultural Diversity and Ethnic Minority Psychology, 11*(2), 144–161.

Poole, D. A., & Lamb, M. E. (1998). *Investigative interviews of children: A guide for helping professionals*. Washington, DC: American Psychological Association.

Poole, D. A., & Lindsay, D. S. (2001). Children's eyewitness reports after exposure to misinformation from parents. *Journal of Experimental Psychology: Applied, 7*(1), 27–50.

Praver, F., DiGiuseppe, R., Pelcovitz, D., Mandel, F., & Gaines, R. (2000). A preliminary study of a cartoon measure for children's reactions to chronic trauma. *Child Maltreatment, 5*(3), 273–285.

Presley, R., & Martin, R. P. (1994). Toward a structure of preschool temperament: Factor structure of the Temperament Assessment Battery for Children. *Journal of Personality, 62*(3), 415–448.

Pretzlik, U., & Hindley, P. (1993, August). Assessment of coping strategies in young children. Paper presented at the VI European Conference on Developmental Psychology, Bonn, Germany.

Price, J. M., & Lento, J. (2001). The nature of child and adolescent vulnerability. In R. E. Ingram & J. M. Price (Eds.), *Vulnerability to psychopathology: Risk across the lifespan* (pp. 20–38). New York: Guilford Press.

Prigerson, H., Bierhals, A., Kasl, S., Reynolds, C., Shear, M., Day, N., Beery, L. C., Newsom, J. T., & Jacobs, S. (1997). Traumatic grief as a risk factor for mental and physical morbidity. *American Journal of Psychiatry, 154*, 616–623.

Prigerson, H., Bierhals, A., Kasl, S., Reynolds, C., Shear, M., Newsom, J., & Jacobs, S. (1996). Complicated grief as a disorder distinct from bereavement-related depression and anxiety: A replication study. *American Journal of Psychiatry, 153*, 1484–1486.

Prigerson, H., Bridge, J., Maciejewski, P., Beery, L., Rosenheck, R., Jacobs, S., Bierhals, A., Kupfer, D., & Brent, D. (1999). Influence of traumatic grief on suicidal ideation among young adults. *American Journal of Psychiatry, 156*, 1994–1995.

Prigerson, H.D. & Maciejewski, P. (2005) A Call for Sound Empirical Testing and Evaluation o Criteria for Complicated Grief Proposed for DSM-V. *Journal of Death & Dying, 52*(1), 9.

Prigerson, H., Nader, K. & Maciejewski, P. (2005). *Complicated Grief Assessment Interview (Child Version)-Short Form.* A copyighted scale.

Prigerson, H. G., Maciejewski, P. K., Reynolds, C. F., III, Bierhals, A. J., Newsom, J. T., Fasiczka, A., Frank, E., Doman, J., & Miller, M. (1995). The Inventory of Complicated Grief: A scale to measure certain maladaptive symptoms of loss. *Psychiatry Research, 59,* 65–79.

Prigerson, H.G. & Vanderwerker, L.C. (2005). *Journal of Death & Dying, 52*(1), 91.

Punamaki, R., Quota, S., & El-Sarraj, E. (2001). Resiliency factors predicting psychological adjustment after political violence among Palestinian children. *International Journal of Behavioral Development, 25*(3), 256–267.

Putnam, F. W. (1985). Pieces of the mind: Recognizing the psychological effects of abuse. *Justice for Children, 1,* 6–7.

Putnam, F. W. (1988). *Child Dissociative Checklist.* Bethesda, MD: National Institute of Mental Health (NIMH). Obtain from Frank Putnam, M.D.; Frank. Putnam@chmcc.org (see Putnam, 1990).

Putnam, F. W. (1990). *Child Dissociative Checklist.* Obtain from Frank Putnam, M.D.; Frank.Putnam@chmcc.org. (The instrument is also published as a part of Putnam, Helmers, & Trickett, 1993, and in Putnam & Peterson, 1994).

Putnam, F. W. (1997). *Dissociation in children and adolescents: A developmental perspective.* New York: Guilford Press.

Putnam, F. W. (1998). Trauma models of the effects of childhood maltreatment. *Journal of Aggression, Maltreatment, & Trauma, 2,* 51–66.

Putnam, F. W., Helmers, K., Horowitz, L. A., & Trickett, P. K. (1995). Hypnotizability and dissociativity in sexually abused girls. *Child Abuse and Neglect, 19*(5), 645–655.

Putnam, F. W., Helmers, K., & Trickett, P. K. (1993). Development, reliability and validity of a child dissociation scale. *Child Abuse and Neglect, 17,* 731–741.

Putnam, F. W., & Peterson, G. (1994). Further validation of the Child Dissociative Checklist. *Dissociation, 7*(4), 204–211.

Putnam, S. P., Ellis, L. K., & Rothbart, M. K. (2001). The structure of temperament from infancy through adolescence. In A. Eliasz & A. Angleitner (Eds.), *Advances in research on temperament* (pp. 165–182). Lengerich, Germany: Pabst Science.

Pynoos, R., & Eth, S. (1985). Children traumatized by witnessing acts of personal violence. In S. Eth & R. Pynoos (Ed.), *Posttraumatic stress in children.* Washington, DC: American Psychiatric Association Press.

Pynoos, R., & Eth, S. (1986). Witness to violence: The child interview. *Journal of the American Academy of Child Psychiatry, 25*(3), 306–319.

Pynoos, R., Frederick, C., Nader, K., Arroyo, W., Eth, S., Nunez, W., Steinberg, A., & Fairbanks, L. (1987). Life threat and posttraumatic stress in school age children. *Archives of General Psychiatry, 44,* 1057–1063.

Pynoos, R., Goenjian, A., Tashjian, M., Karakashian, M., Manjikian, R., Manoukian, G., Steinberg, A., & Fairbanks, L. A. (1993). Post-traumatic stress reactions in children after the 1988 Armenian earthquake. *British Journal of Psychiatry, 163,* 239–247.

Pynoos, R., & Nader, K. (1988). Psychological first aid and treatment approach for children exposed to community violence: Research implications. *Journal of Traumatic Stress, 1*(4), 445–473.

Pynoos, R., & Nader, K. (1989). Children's memory and proximity to violence. *Journal of the American Academy of Child and Adolescent Psychiatry, 28*(2), 236–241.

Pynoos, R., & Nader, K. (1993). Issues in the treatment of posttraumatic stress disorder in children and adolescents. In J. Wilson & B. Raphael (Eds.), *The international handbook of traumatic stress syndromes* (pp. 535–539). New York: Plenum Press.

Pynoos, R., Nader, K., & March, J. (1991). Posttraumatic stress disorder in children and adolescents. In J. Weiner (Ed.), *Comprehensive textbook of child & adolescent psychiatry* (pp. 339–348). Washington, DC: American Psychiatric Association Press.

Pynoos, R., Rodriguez, N., Steinberg, A., Stuber, M., & Frederick, C. (1998). *UCLA PTSD Index for DSM-IV.* Copyrighted scale.

Quenk, N. (1985). Conflicts in function development. *MBTI (Meyers Briggs Type Indicator) NEWS, 7*(2), 6–7.

Quiggle, N. L., Garber, J., Panak, W. F., & Dodge, K. A. (1992). Social information processing in aggressive and depressed children. *Child Development, 63,* 1305–1320.

Rabalais, A. E., Ruggiero, J. K., & Scotti, J. R. (2002). Multicultural issues in the response of children to disasters. In A. M. La Greca, W. K. Silverman, E. M. Vernberg, & M. C. Roberts (Eds.), *Helping children cope with disasters and terrorism.* Washington, DC: APA Press.

Radke-Yarrow, M., Cummings, E. M., Kuczynski, L., & Chapman, M. (1985). Patterns of attachment in two- and three-year-olds in normal families and families with parental depression, *Child Development, 56,* 884–893.

Raphael, B., & Wilson, J. (Eds.). (2001). *Psychological debriefing: Theory, practice and evidence.* Cambridge, UK: Cambridge University Press.

Rawdon, R. M. (1994). *Listening: The art of advocacy.* Retrieved March 18, 2005, from http://library.lp.findlaw.com/articles/file/00372/001690/title/Subject/topic/Civil%20Procedure_Jury/filename/civilprocedure_2_83

Rea, C. D. (1994). *Comparisons of patterns of traumatic stress symptoms in adolescents with and without overt behavior difficulties.* Doctoral dissertation, College of Education, Temple University, Philadelphia.

Realmuto, G. M., Masten, A., Carole, L. F., Hubbard, J., Groteluschen, A., & Chun, B. (1992). Adolescent survivors of massive childhood trauma in Cambodia: Life events and current symptoms. *Journal of Traumatic Stress, 5*(4), 589–599.

Regehr, C. (2001). Cognitive-behavioral theory. In P. Lehman & N. F. Coady (Eds.), *Theoretical perspectives for direct social work practice: A generalist-eclectic approach* (pp. 165–182). New York: Springer.

Reich, W. (2000). Diagnostic Interview for Children and Adolescents (DICA). *Journal of the American Academy of Child and Adolescent Psychiatry, 39,* 59–66.

Reich, W., & Earls, F. (1987). Rules for making psychiatric diagnoses in children on the basis of multiple sources of information: Preliminary strategies. *Journal of Abnormal Child Psychology, 15*(4), 601–616.

Reich, W., & Earls, F. (1990). Interviewing children by telephone: Preliminary results. *Comprehensive Psychiatry, 31*(3), 211–215.

Reich, W., Herjanic, B., Welner, Z., & Gandhy, P. R. (1982). Development of a structured psychiatric interview for children: Agreement of diagnosis comparing child and parent interviews. *Journal of Abnormal Child Psychology, 10,* 325–335.

Reich, W., & Kaplan, L. (1994). The effects of psychiatric and psychosocial interviews on children. *Comprehensive Psychiatry, 3,* 50–53.

Reich, W., Neuman, R. J., Volk, H. E., Joyner, C. A., & Todd, R. D. (in press). Comorbidity between ADHD and symptoms of bipolar disorder in a community sample of children and adolescents. *Twin Research and Human Genetics.*

Reich, W., & Todd, R. D. (2002a). *Missouri Assessment of Genetics Interview for Children.* St. Louis: Washington University School of Medicine.

Reich, W., & Todd, R. D. (2002b). *Missouri Assessment of Genetics Interview for Children specifications manual.* St. Louis: Washington University School of Medicine.

Reich, W., Todd, R. D., Joyner, C. A., Neuman, R. J., & Heath, A. C. (2003). Reliability and stability of mothers' reports about their pregnancies with twins. *Twin Research and Human Genetics, 6,* 85–88.

Renouf, A. G., & Harter, S. (1990). Low self-worth and anger as components of the depressive experience in young adolescents. *Development and Psychopathology, 2,* 293–310.

Reynolds, C. R., & Kamphaus, R. W. (1992). *Behavior Assessment System for Children manual.* Circle Pines, MN: American Guidance Service.

Reynolds, C. R., & Kamphaus, R. W. (1998). *Behavior Assessment System for Children manual.* Circle Pines, MN: American Guidance Service.

Reynolds, C. R., & Richmond, B.O. (1978). What I Think and Feel: A revised measure of children's manifest anxiety. *Journal of Abnormal Child Psychology, 6*(2), 271–280.

Reynolds, C. R., & Richmond, B. O. (2000). *Revised Children's Manifest Anxiety Scale manual.* Los Angeles: Western Psychological Services.

Richters, J. E., & Martinez, P. (1990). Things I have Seen and Heard. A structured interview for assessing young children's violence exposure. Unpublished measure, National Institute of Mental Health, Bethesda, MD.

Richters, J. E., & Martinez, P. (1991). Community violence project: Children as victims or witnesses to violence. *Psychiatry, 56,* 7–21.

Richters, J. E., & Martinez, P. (1993). The NIMH Community Violence Project: I. Children as victims of and witnesses to violence. *Psychiatry: Interpersonal & Biological Processes, 56*(1), 7–21.

Roberts, B. W., & Del Vecchio, W. F. (2000). The rank-order consistency of personality from childhood to old age: A quantitative review of longitudinal studies. *Psychological Bulletin, 126,* 3–25.

Roberts, B. W., & Helson, R. (1997). Changes in culture, changes in personality: The influence of individualism in a longitudinal study of women. *Journal of Personality and Social Psychology, 72,* 641–651.

Roberts, G.E. (2005). *Roberts-2.* Los Angeles, CA: Western Psychological Services.

Roberts, G. E. (1994). *Interpretive handbook for the Roberts Apperception Test for Children.* Los Angeles: Western Psychological Services.

Roberts, G. E. & Gruber, C. (2005). *Roberts-2, manual.* Los Angeles: Western Psychological Services.

Roberts, M. W. (2001). Clinic observations of structured parent-child interaction designed to evaluate externalizing disorders. *Psychological Assessment, 13*(1), 46–58.

Roche, D. N., Runtz, M. G., & Hunter, M. A. (1999). Adult attachment: A mediator between child sexual abuse and later psychological adjustment. *Journal of Interpersonal Violence, 14*(2), 184–207.

Rodriguez, N. (2001, December). Youth PTSD Assessment: Psychometric investigation of PTSD self-report instruments. Paper presented at the 17th Annual ISTSS Meeting, New Orleans.

Roemer, L., Orsillo, S. M., Borkovec, T. D., & Litz, B. T. (1998). Emotional response at the time of a potentially traumatizing event and PTSD symptomatology: A preliminary retrospective analysis of the DSM-IV Criterion A-2. *Journal of Behavior Therapy and Experimental Psychiatry, 29*(2), 123–130.

Rosen, K. S., & Burke, P. B. (1999). Multiple attachment relationships within families: Mothers and fathers with two young children. *Developmental Psychology, 35*(2), 436–444.

Rosen, K. S., & Rothbaum, F. (1993). Quality of parental caregiving and security of attachment. *Developmental Psychology, 29*(2), 358–367.

Rosenberg, M. (1965). *Society and the adolescent self-image.* Middletown, CT: Wesleyan University Press.

Rosenbloom, D. J., & Williams, M. B. (2002). Life after trauma: Finding hope by challenging your beliefs and meeting your needs. In M. B. Williams & J. F. Sommer (Eds.), *Simple and complex post-traumatic stress disorder: Strategies for comprehensive treatment in clinical practice* (pp. 119–133). Binghamton, NY: Haworth Press.

Rossi, E. (1993). *The psychobiology of mind-body healing: New concepts of therapeutic hypnosis* (Rev. ed.). New York: W. W. Norton.

Rotenberg, K. J., & Cerda, C. (1994). Racially based trust expectancies of Native American and Caucasian children. *Journal of Social Psychology, 134*(5), 621–631.

Rotenberg, K. J., & Morgan, C. J. (1995). Development of a scale to measure individual differences in children's trust value basis of friendship. *Journal of Genetic Psychology, 156*(4), 489–502.

Roth, S., Newman, E., Pelcovitz, D., van der Kolk, B., & Mandel, F. S. (1997). Complex PTSD in victims exposed to sexual and physical abuse: Results from the DSM-IV Field Trial for posttraumatic stress disorder. *Journal of Traumatic Stress, 10*(4), 539–555.

Rothbart, M. K. (2001). Temperament and human development. In N. Eisenberg, (Ed.), *The international encyclopedia of the social and behavioral sciences* (pp. 15586–15591). Amsterdam: Elsevier.

Rothbart, M. K., Ahadi, S. A., Hershey, K. L., & Fisher, P. (2001). Investigations of temperament at three to seven years: The Children's Behavior Questionnaire. *Child Development, 72*(5), 1394–1408.

Rothbart, M. K., & Bates, J. E. (1998). Temperament. In W. Damon (Series Ed.) & N. Eisenberg (Vol. Ed.), *Handbook of child psychology: Vol. 3. Social, emotional, and personality development* (5th ed., pp. 105–176). New York: Wiley.

Rothbart, M. K., Chew, K., & Gartstein, M. A. (2001). Assessment of temperament in early development. In L. Singer & P. S. Zeskind (Eds.), Biobehavioral assessment of the infant (pp. 190–208). New York: Guilford Press.

Rothbart, M. K., & Gartstein, M. A. (2000). *Child Behavior Questionnaire. A parent-report personality questionnaire for children ages 3–8.* Eugene: University of Oregon.

Rothbaum, F., Rosen, K., Ujiie, T., & Uchida, N. (2002). Family systems, theory, attachment theory, and culture. *Family Process, 41*(3), 328–350.

Rotter, J., & Rafferty, J. (1950). *The manual for the Rotter Incomplete Sentences Blank.* New York: Psychological Corporation.

Rousseau, C., & Drapeau, A. (1998). The impact of culture on the transmission of trauma: Refugees' stories and silence embodied in their children's lives. In Y. Danieli (Ed.), *An international handbook of multigenerational legacies of trauma* (pp. 465–486). New York: Plenum Press.

Rubin, K. H. (1989). *The Play Observation Scale (POS).* Waterloo, Ontario, Canada: University of Waterloo.

Rubin, K. H., Burgess, K. B., Kennedy, A. E., & Stewart, S. L. (2003). Social withdrawal in childhood. In E. J. Mash & R. A. Barkley (Eds.), *Child psychopathology* (2nd ed., pp. 372–406). New York: Guilford Press.

Ruchkin, V. V., Schwab-Stone, M., Koposov, R., Vermeiren, R., & Steiner, H. (2002). Violence exposure, posttraumatic stress, and personality in juvenile delinquents. *Journal of the American Academy of Child and Adolescent Psychiatry, 41*(3), 322–329.

Rutter, M. (1997). Clinical implications of attachment concepts: Retrospective and prospective. In L. Atkinson & K. Zucker (Eds.), *Attachment and psychopathology* (pp. 17–46). New York: Guilford Press.

Rutter, M. (2003). Commentary: Causal processes leading to antisocial behavior. *Developmental Psychology, 39*(2), 372–378.

Rutter, M., & Graham, P. (1967). A Children's Behavior Questionnaire for completion by teachers: Preliminary findings. *Journal of Child Psychology and Psychiatry, 8,* 1–11.

Rutter, M., & O'Connor, T. G. (1999). Implications of attachment theory for child care policies. In J. Cassidy & P. R. Shaver (Eds.), *Handbook of attachment: Theory, research, and clinical applications* (pp. 823–844). New York: Guilford Press.

Ruzek, J., & Watson, P. (2001). Early intervention to prevent PTSD and other trauma-related problems. *PTSD Research Quarterly, 12*(4), 1–7.

Sack W., Seeley, J., & Clarke, G. (1997). Does PTSD transcend cultural barriers? A study from the Khmer Adolescent Refugee Project. *Journal of the American Academy of Child and Adolescent Psychiatry, 36,* 49–54.

Sahelian, R. (2005). Serotonin. Retrieved June 25, 2005, from http://www.raysahelian.com/serotonin.html

Saigh, P. A., Yasik, A. E., Sack, W. H., & Koplewicz, H. S. (1999). Child-adolescent posttraumatic stress disorder: Prevalence, risk factors, and comorbidity. In P. A. Saigh & J. D. Bremner (Eds.), *Posttraumatic stress disorder* (pp. 18–43). Needham Heights, MA: Allyn & Bacon.

Santtila, P., Korkmana, J., & Sandnabba, N. K. (2004). Effects of interview phase, repeated interviewing, presence of a support person, and anatomically detailed dolls on child sexual abuse interviews. *Psychology, Crime & Law, 10*(1), 21–35.

Sapolsky, R. M. (1998). Biology and human behavior: The neurological origins of individuality [Videotape series]. Chantilly, VA: The Teaching Company.

Sapolsky, R. M. (2000). Glucocorticoids and hippocampal atrophy in neuropsychiatric disorders. *Archives of General Psychiatry, 57*, 925–935.

Saunders, D. G. (1998). Child custody and visitation decisions in domestic violence cases: Legal trends, research findings, and recommendations. Retrieved March 8, 2005, from http://www.vaw.umn.edu/documents/vawnet/custody/custody.html

Saxe, G. (2005). Risk factors for acute stress disorder in children with burns. *Journal of Trauma & Dissociation, 6*(2), 37–49.

Saylor, C., & Deroma, V. (2002). Assessment of children and adolescents exposed to disaster. In A. M. La Greca, W. K. Silverman, E. M. Vernberg, & M. C. Roberts (Eds.), *Helping children cope with disasters and terrorism* (pp. 35–53). Washington, DC: APA Press.

Scheeringa, M. S., Peebles, C. D., Cook, C. A., & Zeanah, C. H. (2001). Toward establishing procedural, criterion, and discriminant validity for PTSD in early childhood. *Journal of the American Academy of Child and Adolescent Psychiatry, 40*(1), 52–60.

Scheeringa, M. S., & Zeanah, C. H. (1994). PTSD Semi-Structured Interview and Observational Record for Infants and Young Children, Version 1.2. Semistructured interview.

Scheeringa, M. S., & Zeanah, C. H. (1995). Symptom expression and trauma variables in children under 48 months of age. *Infant Mental Health Journal, 16*, 259–270.

Scheeringa, M. S., & Zeanah, C. H. (2001) A relational perspective on PTSD in early childhood. *Journal of Traumatic Stress, 14*(4), 799–815.

Scheeringa, M. S., & Zeanah, C. H. (2005). PTSD Semi-Structured Interview and Observational Record for Infants and Young Children, Version 1.4. Semistructured interview.

Scheeringa, M. S., Zeanah, C., Drell, M., & Larrieu, J. (1995). Two approaches to the diagnosis of posttraumatic stress disorder in infancy and early childhood. *Journal of the American Academy of Child & Adolescent Psychiatry, 34*(2), 191–200.

Scheeringa, M. S., Zeanah, C. H., Myers, L., & Putnam, F. (2003). New findings on alternative criteria for PTSD in preschool children. *Journal of the American Academy of Child & Adolescent Psychiatry, 42*(5), 561–570.

Scheeringa, M. S., Zeanah, C. H., Myers, L., & Putnam, F. (2004). Heart period and variability findings in preschool children with posttraumatic stress symptoms. *Journal of the American Academy of Child & Adolescent Psychiatry, 55*, 685–691.

Scheeringa, M. S., Zeanah, C. H., Myers, L., & Putnam, F. (2005). Predictive validity in a prospective follow-up of PTSD in preschool children. *Journal of the American Academy of Child & Adolescent Psychiatry, 44*(9), 899–906.

Scheff, T. (1997). Deconstructing rage. Retrieved September 17, 2003, from http://www.soc.ucsb.edu/faculty/scheff/7.html

Schippell, P. L., Vasey, M. W., Cravens-Brown, L. M., & Bretveld, R. A. (2003). Suppressed attention to rejection, ridicule, and failure cues: A unique correlate of reactive but not proactive aggression in youth. *Journal of Clinical Child and Adolescent Psychology, 32*(1), 40–55.

Schiraldi, G. R. (2000). *The post-traumatic stress disorder sourcebook*. Los Angeles: Lowell House.

Schlenger, W. E., Caddell, J. M., Ebert, L., Jordan, B. K., Rourke, K. M., Wilson, D., Thalji, L., Dennis, M., Fairbank, J. A., & Kulka, R. A. (2002). Psychological reactions to terrorist attacks: Findings from the National Study of Americans' Reactions to September 11. *Journal of American Medical Association, 288,* 581–588.

Schmidt, L. A., & Fox, N. A. (2002). Individual differences in childhood shyness. In D. Cervone & W. Mischel (Eds.), *Advances in personality science* (pp. 83–105). New York: Guilford Press.

Schneider, M. L., Moore, C. F., & Kraemer, G. W. (2003). On the relevance of prenatal stress to developmental psychopathology. In D. Cicchetti & E. Walker (Eds.), *Neurodevelopmental mechanisms in psychopathology* (pp. 155–186). New York: Cambridge University Press.

Schneider-Rosen, K., Braunwald, K. G., Carlson, V., & Cicchetti, D. (1985). Current perspectives in attachment theory: Illustration from the study of maltreated infants. *Monographs of the Society for Research in Child Development, 50*(1-2, Series No. 209), 194–210.

Schnurr, P., & Jankowski, M. K. (1999). Physical health and post-traumatic stress disorder: Review and synthesis. *Seminars in Clinical Neuropsychiatry, 4*(4), 295–304.

Schore, A. N. (1994). *Affect regulation and the origin of the self: The neurobiology of emotional development.* Mahwah, New Jersey: Erlbaum.

Schore, A. N. (1996). The experience-dependent maturation of a regulatory system in the orbitofrontal cortex and the origin of developmental psychopathology: Social-environmental risk factors. *Pediatrics, 79,* 343–350.

Schore, A. N. (2001). The effects of early relational trauma on right brain development, affect regulation, and infant mental health. *Infant Mental Health Journal, 22,* 201–269.

Schore, A. N. (2003). Early relational trauma, disorganized attachment, and the development of a predisposition to violence. In M. Solomon & D. J. Siegel (Eds.), *Healing trauma* (pp. 107–167). New York: W. W. Norton.

Schultz, L. (1989). The social worker as an expert witness in suspected child abuse cases: A primer for beginners. Retrieved March 18, 2005, from http://www.ipt-forensics.com/journal/volume1/j1_2_4.htm

Schuster, M. A., Stein, B. D., Jaycox, L. H., Collins, R. L., Marshall, G. N., Elliott, M. N., Zhou, A. J., Kanouse, D. E., Morrison, J. L., & Berry, S. H. (2001). A national survey of stress reaction after the September 11, 2001 terrorist attacks. *New England Journal of Medicine, 345*(20), 1507–1512.

Schwartz, D., Dodge, K. A., & Coie, J. D. (1993). The emergence of chronic peer victimization in boys' play groups. *Child Development, 64*(6), 1755–1772.

Schwarz, E. D., & Kowalski, J. M. (1991). Malignant memories: PTSD in children and adults after a school shooting. *Journal of the American Academy of Child and Adolescent Psychiatry, 30*(6), 936–944.

Schwarz, E. D., & Kowalski, J. M. (1992). Malignant memories: Reluctance to utilize mental health services after a disaster. *Journal of Nervous and Mental Disease, 180*(12), 767–772.

Schwarzwald, J., Weisenberg, M., Waysman, M., Solomon, Z., & Klingman, A. (1993). Stress reaction of school-age children to the bombardment by SCUD missiles. *Journal of Abnormal Psychology, 102*(3), pp. 404–410.

Seals, D., & Young, J. (2003). Bullying and victimization: Prevalence and relationship to gender, grade level, ethnicity, self-esteem, and depression. *Adolescence, 38*(152), 735–747.

Self-Brown, S., LeBlanc, M., & Kelley, M. L. (2004). Effects of violence exposure and daily stressors on psychological outcomes in urban adolescents. *Journal of Traumatic Stress, 17*(6), 519–527.

Setterberg, S., Bird, H., Gould, M., Shaffer, D., & Fisher, P. Nonclinician Children's Global Assessment Scale. An adaptation of the Children's Global Assessment Scale. [Available in Bird, 1999].

Shaffer, D., Fisher, P., & Lucas, C. (1999). Respondent-based interviews. In D. Shaffer, C. Lucas, & J. Richters (Eds.), *Diagnostic assessment in child and adolescent psychopathology* (pp. 3–33). New York: Guilford Press.

Shaffer, D., Gould, M., Bird, H., & Fisher, P. (1983). *Children's Global Assessment Scale (C-GAS).* [Available in Bird, 1999; Shaffer et al., 1983].

Shaffer, D., Gould, M. S., Brasic, J., Ambrosini, P., Fisher, P., Bird, H., & Aluwahlia, S. (1983). A Children's Global Assessment Scale (CGAS). *Archives of General Psychiatry, 40*, 2228–2231.

Shannon, M. P., Lonigan, C. J., Finch, A. J., Jr., & Taylor, C. M. (1994). Children exposed to disaster: I. Epidemiology of posttraumatic stress symptoms and symptom profiles. *Journal of the American Academy of Child and Adolescent Psychiatry, 33*(1), 80–93.

Shapiro, F., & Maxfield, L. (2003). EMDR and information processing in psychotherapy treatment: Personal development and global implications. In M. Solomon & D. J. Siegel (Eds.), *Healing trauma* (pp. 196–220). New York: W. W. Norton.

Shapiro, J. (2000). *Attitudes Toward Guns and Violence Questionnaire: Manual.* Los Angeles: Western Psychological Services.

Shaw, J. A. (1997). Posttraumatic stress disorder: Acute and long-term responses to trauma and disaster. In C. S. Fullerton & R. J. Ursano (Eds.), *Children of the storm: A study of school children and Hurricane Andrew* (pp. 123–143). Washington, DC: American Psychiatric Press.

Shiang, J. (2000). Considering cultural beliefs and behaviors in the study of suicide. In R. Maris, S. Canetto, J. McIntosh, & M. Silverman (Eds.), *Review of suicidology* (pp. 226–241). New York: Guilford Press.

Shiang, J., Kjellander, C., Huang, K., & Bogumill, S. (1998). Developing cultural competency in clinical practice: Treatment considerations for Chinese cultural groups in the U.S. *Clinical Psychology: Science and Practice, 5*, 182–209.

Shiner, R. L., Tellegen, A., & Masten, A. S. (2001). Exploring personality across childhood into adulthood: Can one describe and predict a moving target? *Psychological Inquiry, 12*(2), 96–100.

Shoal, G. D., Giancola, P. R., & Kirillova , G. P. (2003). Salivary cortisol, personality, and aggressive behavior in adolescent boys: A 5-year longitudinal study. *Journal of the American Academy of Child and Adolescent Psychiatry, 42*(9), 1101–1107.

Showers, C. J. (2002). Integration and compartmentalization: A model of self-structure and self-change. In D. Cervone & W. Mischel (Eds.), *Advances in personality science* (pp. 271–289). New York: Guilford Press.

Siegel, D. J. (1996). Cognition, memory and dissociation. *Child and Adolescent Psychiatric Clinics of North America, 5*(2), 509–536.

Siegel, D. J. (1999). *The developing mind: How relationships and the brain interact to shape who we are.* New York: Guilford Press.

Siegel, D. J. (2003). An interpersonal neurobiology of psychotherapy: The developing mind and the resolution of trauma. In M. Solomon & D. J. Siegel (Eds.), *Healing trauma* (pp. 1–56). New York: W. W. Norton.

Silberg, J. L. (1996). *The dissociative child: Diagnosis, treatment, and management.* Baltimore: Sidran Press.

Silberg, J. L. (Ed.). (1998a). *The dissociative child: Afterword.* Baltimore: Sidran Press. Retrieved May 24, 2005, from http://www.sidran.org/sidcafter.html

Silberg, J. L. (Ed.). (1998b). *The dissociative child: Diagnosis, treatment, and management* (Second Edition). Baltimore: Sidran Press.

Silberg, J. L. (2004). The treatment of dissociation in sexually abused children from a family/attachment perspective. *Psychotherapy: Theory, Research, Practice, Training, 41*(4), 487–495.

Silberstein, S. D. (2001). Shared mechanisms and comorbidities in neurologic and psychiatric disorders. *Headache: The Journal of Head & Face Pain, 41*(s1), 11–17.

Silva, R. R., Cloitre, M., Davis, L., Levitt, J., Gomez, S., Ngai, I., & Brown, E. (2003). Early intervention with traumatized children. *Psychiatric Quarterly, 74*(4), 333–347.

Silver, R. C., Holman, E. A., McIntosh, D. N., Poulin, M., & Gil-Rivas, V. (2002). Nationwide longitudinal study of psychological responses to September 11. *Journal of American Medical Association, 288*(10), 1235–1244.

Silverman, A. B., Reinherz, H. Z., & Giaconia, R. M. (1996). The long-term sequelae of child and adolescent abuse: A longitudinal community study. *Child Abuse & Neglect, 20*(8), 709–723.

Silverman, G. K., Jacobs, S. C., Kasl, S. V., Shear, M. K., Maciejewski, P. K., Noaghiul, F. S., & Prigerson, H. G. (2000). Quality of life impairments associated with diagnostic criteria for traumatic grief. *Psychological Medicine, 30,* 857–862.

Silverman, W. K., & La Greca, A. M. (2002). Children experiencing disasters: Definitions, reactions, and predictors of outcomes. In A. M. La Greca, W. K. Silverman, E. M. Vernberg, & M. C. Roberts (Eds.), *Helping children cope with disasters and terrorism* (pp. 11–34). Washington, DC: APA Press.

Simmons, R. (2002). *Odd girl out.* New York: Harcourt.

Simmons, R. L., & Johnson, C. (1998). Intergeneration transmission of domestic violence. In Y. Danieli, *International handbook of multigenerational legacies of trauma* (pp. 553–570). New York: Plenum Press.

Singer, L. M., Burkowski, M., & Walters, E. (1985). Mother-infant attachment in adoptive families. *Child Development, 56,* 1543–1551.

Singer, M. I., Anglen, T. M., Song, L. Y., & Lunghofer, L. (1995). Adolescents' exposure to violence and associated symptoms of psychological trauma. *Journal of American Medical Association, 273*(6), 477–482.

Slade, A. (1999). Attachment theory and research: Implications for the theory and practice of individual psychotherapy with adults. In J. Cassidy & P. R. Shaver (Eds.), *Handbook of attachment: Theory, research, and clinical applications* (pp. 575–594). New York: Guilford Press.

Smith, S. R., & Carlson, E. B. (1996). Reliability and validity of the Adolescent Dissociative Experiences Scale. *Dissociation: Progress in the Dissociative Disorders, 9*(2), 125–129.

Soeters, J. L. (1996). Culture and conflict: An application of Hofstede's theory to the conflict in the former Yugoslavia. *Journal of Peace Psychology, 2*(3), 233–244.

Solnit, A. J. (1987). A psychoanalytic view of play. *The Psychoanalytic Study of the Child, 42,* 205–219.

Solomon, J., & George, C. (1999). The measurement of attachment security in infancy and childhood. In J. Cassidy & P. R. Shaver (Eds.), *Handbook of attachment: Theory, research, and clinical applications* (pp. 287–316). New York: Guilford Press.

Solomon, M., & Siegel, D. J. (Eds.). (2003). *Healing trauma.* New York: W. W. Norton.

Spielberger, C. D. (1972). Anxiety as an emotional state. In C. D. Spielberger (Ed.), *Anxiety: Current trends in theory and research* (p. 23–49). New York: Academic Press.

Spielberger, C. D. (1973). *Preliminary manual for the State-Trait Anxiety Inventory for Children ("How I Feel Questionnaire").* Palo Alto, CA: Consulting Psychologists Press.

Spirito, A., Stark, L. J., & Williams, C. (1988). Development of a brief coping checklist for use with pediatric populations. *Journal of Pediatric Psychology, 130,* 555–574.

Spitzmueller, W. R. (1991). *Cross-validation of two inventories for children referred to an outpatient clinic for sexual abuse assessment.* Unpublished doctoral dissertation, Minnesota School of Professional Psychology, Minneapolis.

Stallard, P., Velleman, R., Langsford, J., & Baldwin, S. (2001). Coping and psychological distress in children involved in road traffic accidents. *British Journal of Clinical Psychology, 40,* 197–208.

Stamm, B. H. (1999). Conceptualizing death and trauma. In C. R. Figley (Ed.), *Traumatology of grieving: Conceptual, theoretical, and treatment foundations* (pp. 3–21). Philadelphia: Brunner/Mazel.

Stamm, B. H., & Stamm, H. E. (1999). Trauma and loss in Native North America: An ethnocultural perspective. In K. Nader, N. Dubrow, & B. Stamm (Eds.), *Honoring differences: Cultural issues in the treatment of trauma and loss* (pp. 49–75). Philadelphia: Taylor & Francis.

Starkman, M. N., Giodani, B., Gebarski, S. S., Berent, S., Schork, M. A., & Schteingart, D. E. (1999). Decrease in cortisol reverses human hippocampal atrophy following treatment of Cushing's disease. *Biological Psychiatry, 46,* 1595–1602.

Stegge, H., & Ferguson, T. J. (1990). *Child-Child Attribution and Reaction Survey (C-CARS).* Logan: Utah State University.

Stein, N., Wade, E., & Liwag, M. D. (1996). A theoretical approach to understanding and remembering harmful events. In M. Stein, P. A. Ornstein, B. Tversky, & C. J. Brainerd (Eds.), *Memory for everyday and emotional events* (pp. 15–48). Hillsdale, NJ: Erlbaum.

Stein, P. T., & Kendall, J. (2004). *Psychological trauma and the developing brain: Neurologically based interventions for troubled children.* New York: Haworth Press.

Sternberg, K. J., Lamb, M. E., Greenbaum, C., Cicchetti, D., Dawud, S., Cortes, R. M., Krispin, O., & Lorey, F. (1993). Effects of domestic violence on children's behavior problems and depression. *Developmental Psychology, 29*(1), 44–52.

Stilwell, B. M., Galvin, M., & Kopta, S. M. (1991). Conceptualization of conscience in normal children and adolescents, ages 5 to 17. *Journal of the American Academy of Child and Adolescent Psychiatry, 30*(1), 16–21.

Street, A. E., Gibson, L. E., & Holohan, D. R. (2005). Impact of childhood traumatic events, trauma-related guilt, and avoidant coping strategies on PTSD symptoms in female survivors of domestic violence. *Journal of Traumatic Stress, 18*(3), 245–252.

Strelau, J. (1995). Temperament risk factor: The contribution of temperament to the consequences of the state of stress. In S. E. Hobfoll & M. W. de Vries (Eds.), *Extreme stress and communities: Impact and intervention* (pp. 63–81). Dordrecht, Netherlands: Kluwer Academic Publishers.

Stuber, M. L., & Nader, K. (1995). Psychiatric sequelae in adolescent bone mar- row transplantation survivors: Implications for psychotherapy. *The Journal of Psychotherapy Practice and Research, 4*(1), 30–42.

Stuber, M. L., Nader, K., & Pynoos, R. (1997). The violence of despair: Consultation to a Head Start program following the Los Angeles Uprising of 1992. *Community Mental Health Journal, 33*(3), 235–241.

Stuber, M. L., Nader, K., Yasuda, P., Pynoos, R., & Cohen, S. (1991). Stress responses after pediatric bone marrow transplantation: Preliminary results of a pro- spective longitudinal study. *Journal of the American Academy of Child and Ado- lescent Psychiatry, 30*(6), 952–957.

Styron, T., & Janoff-Bulman, R. (1997). Childhood attachment and abuse: Long- term effects on adult attachment, depression, and conflict resolution. *Child Abuse & Neglect, 21*(10), 1015–1023.

Suldo, S., & Huebner, E. S. (2004). Does life satisfaction moderate the effects of stressful life events on psychopathological behavior in adolescence? *School Psychology Quarterly, 19*, 93–105.

Suomi, S. J. (1995). Influence of Bowlby's attachment theory on research on nonhu- man primate biobehavioral development. In S. Goldberg, R. Muir, & J. Kerr (Eds.), *Attachment theory: Social, developmental and clinical perspectives* (pp. 185–201). Hillsdale, NJ: Analytic Press.

Suomi, S. J. (2002). Parents, peers, and the process of socialization in primates. In J. Borkowski & S. Ramey (Eds.), *Parenting and the child's world: Influences on academic, intellectual, and social-emotional development* (pp. 265–279). Mahwah, NJ: Lawrence Erlbaum Associates.

Suomi, S. J., & Levine, S. (1998). Psychobiology of intergenerational effects of trauma. In Y. Danieli (Ed.), *International handbook of multigenerational legacies of trauma* (pp. 623–637). New York: Plenum Press.

Susman-Stillman, A., Kalkose, M., Egeland, B., & Waldman, I. (1996). Infant tem- perament and maternal sensitivity as predictors of attachment security. *Infant Behavior & Development, 19*(1), 33–47.

Sutton, J. (2004). Understanding dissociation and its relationship to self-injury and childhood trauma. *Counselling & Psychotherapy Journal, 15*(3), 24–27.

Sutton, S. K. (2002). Incentive and threat reactivity. In D. Cervone & W. Mischel (Eds.), *Advances in Personality Science* (pp. 127–150). New York: Guilford Press.

Swenson, C. C., Saylor, C. F., Powell, M. P., Stokes, S. J., Foster, K.Y., & Belter, R. W. (1996). Impact of a natural disaster on preschool children: Adjustment 14 months after a hurricane. *American Journal of Orthopsychiatry, 66*, 122–130.

Swiss, S., & Giller, J. E. (1993). Rape as a crime of war: A medical perspective. *Jour- nal of the American Medical Association, 270*(5), 612–615.

Sykes, G., & Matza, D. (1957). Techniques of neutralization: A theory of delin- quency. *American Sociological Review, 22*, 664–670.

Tangney, J. P. (1990). Assessing individual differences in proneness to shame and guilt: Development of the Self-Conscious Affect and Attribution Inventory. *Journal of Personality and Social Psychology, 59*, 102–111.

Tangney, J. P. (1996). Conceptual and methodological issues in the assessment of shame and guilt. *Behaviour Research and Therapy, 34*(9), 741–754.

Tangney, J. P., Miller, R. S., Flicker, L., & Barlow, D. H. (1996). Are shame, guilt, and embarrassment distinct emotions? *Journal of Personality and Social Psychology, 70*(6), 1256–1269.

Tangney, J. P., Niedenthal, P. M., Covert, M. V., & Barlow, D. H. (1998). Are shame and guilt related to distinct self-discrepancies? A test of Higgins' 1987 hypotheses. *Journal of Personality and Social Psychology, 75*(1), 256–268.

Tangney, J. P., Wagner, P., Burggraf, S. A., Gramzow, R., & Fletcher, C. (1990). *The Test of Self-Conscious Affect for Children (TOSCA-C).* Fairfax, VA: George Mason University.

Tangney, J. P., Wagner, P., Fletcher, C., & Gramzow, R. (1992). Shamed into anger: The relation of shame and guilt to anger and self-reported aggression. *Journal of Personality and Social Psychology, 62*(4), 669–675.

Tangney, J. P., Wagner, P., Gavlas, J., & Gramzow, R. (1991). *The Test of Self-Conscious Affect for Adolescents (TOSCA-A).* Fairfax, VA: George Mason University.

Taylor, J. A. (1951). The relationship of anxiety to the conditioned eyelid response. *Journal of Experimental Psychology, 41*(2), 81–92.

Teerikangas, O. M., Aronen, E. T., Martin, R. P., & Huttunen, M. O. (1998). Effects of infant temperament and early intervention on the psychiatric symptoms of adolescents. *Journal of the American Academy of Child and Adolescent Psychiatry, 37*(10), 1070–1076.

Tellegen, A., & Waller, N. G. (1992). *Exploring personality through test construction: Development of the Multidimensional Personality Questionnaire (MPQ).* Unpublished manuscript, University of Minnesota, Minneapolis.

Terr, L. (1979). Children of Chowchilla: Study of psychic trauma. *The Psychoanalytic Study of the Child, 34,* 547–623.

Terr, L. (1981a). Forbidden games: Post-traumatic child's play. *Journal of American Academy of Child Psychiatry, 20,* 741–760.

Terr, L. (1981b). Psychic trauma in children: Observations following the Chowchilla school-bus kidnapping. *American Journal of Psychiatry, 138*(1), 14–19.

Terr, L. (1983a). Chowchilla revisited: The effects of psychic trauma four years after a school-bus kidnapping. *American Journal of Psychiatry, 140,* 1542–1550.

Terr, L. (1983b). Life attitudes, dreams and psychic trauma in a group of normal children. *Journal of American Academy of Child Psychiatry, 22,* 221–230.

Terr, L. (1985). Remembered images and trauma: A psychology of the supernatural. *Psychoanalytic Study of the Child, 40,* 493–533.

Terr, L. (1989). Treating psychic trauma in children: A preliminary discussion. *Journal of Traumatic Stress, 2*(1), 3–20.

Terr, L. (1991). Childhood traumas: An outline and overview. *American Journal of Psychiatry, 148,* 10–20.

Terr, L. (1994). *Unchained memories: True stories of traumatic memories, lost and found.* New York: Basic Books.

Terry, T., & Huebner, E. S. (1995). The relationship between self-concept and life satisfaction in children. *Social Indicators Research, 35,* 39–52.

Thomas, A., & Chess, S. (1977). *Temperament and development.* New York: Bruner/Mazel.

Thomas, P. M. (2005). Dissociation and internal models of protection: Psychotherapy with child abuse survivors. *Psychotherapy: Theory, Research, Practice, Training, 42*(1), 20–36.

Thompson, R. A. (1991). Attachment theory and research. In M. Lewis (Ed.), *Child and adolescent psychiatry: A comprehensive textbook* (pp. 100–108). Baltimore: Williams & Wilkins.

Thompson, R. A. (1999). Early attachment and later development. In J. Cassidy & P. R. Shaver (Eds.), *Handbook of attachment* (pp. 265–286). New York: Guilford Press.

Tinnen, L., Bills, L., & Gantt, L. (2002). Short-term treatment of simple and complex PTSD. In M. B. Williams, & J. Sommer (Eds.), *Simple and complex posttraumatic stress disorder* (pp. 99–118). New York: Haworth Maltreatment and Trauma Press.

Todd, R. D., Joyner, C. A., Heath, A.C., Neuman, R. J., & Reich, W. (2003). Reliability and stability of a semi-structured DSM-IV interview designed for family studies. *Journal of the American Academy of Child and Adolescent Psychiatry, 42*(12), 1460–1468.

Tomkins, S. S. (1979). Script theory: Differential magnification of affects. In H. E. Howe, Jr. & R. A. Dienstbier (Eds.), *Nebraska Symposium on Motivation* (Vol. 26, pp. 201–236). Lincoln: University of Nebraska Press.

Ton-That, N. (1998). Post-traumatic stress disorder in Asian refugees. *Psychiatry and Clinical Neurosciences, 52 (Supplement)*, S377-S379.

Triandis, H., Kashima, Y., Shimada, E., & Villareal, M. (1986). Acculturation indices as a means of confirming cultural differences. *International Journal of Psychology, 21*, 43–70.

Trickett, P. K., Noll, J. G., Reiffman, A., & Putnam, F. W. (2001). Variants of intrafamilial sexual abuse experience: Implications for short- and long-term development. *Develop and Psychopathology, 13*, 1001–1019.

Tully, M. (1999). Lifting our voices: African American cultural responses to trauma and loss. In K. Nader, N. Dubrow, & B. Stamm (Eds.), *Honoring differences: Cultural issues in the treatment of trauma and loss* (pp. 23–48). Philadelphia: Taylor & Francis.

Twenge, J. M. (2000). The age of anxiety? Birth cohort change in anxiety and neuroticism, 1952–1993. *Journal of Personality and Social Psychology, 79*, 1007–1021.

Twenge, J. M. (2002). Birth cohort, social change, and personality. In D. Cervone & W. Mischel (Eds.), *Advances in personality science* (pp. 196–218). New York: Guilford Press.

Twenge, J. M., & Campbell, W. K. (2001). Age and birth cohort differences in self-esteem: A cross-temporal meta-analysis. *Personality and Social Psychology Review, 5*(4), 321–344.

Udwin, O., Boyle, S., Yule, W., Bolton, D., & O'Ryan, D. (2000). Risk factors for long-term psychological effects of a disaster experienced in adolescence: Predictors of posttraumatic stress disorder. *Journal of Child Psychology and Psychiatry, 41*(8), 969–979.

Ullman, S. E. (1997). Attributions, world assumptions, and recovery from sexual assault. *Journal of Child Sexual Abuse, 6*(1), 1–19.

Underwager, R., & Wakefield, H. (1993). Misuse of psychological tests in forensic settings: Some horrible examples. *American Journal of Forensic Psychology, 11*(1). Retrieved March 8, 2005, from http://www.ipt-forensics.com/library/misuse.htm

van der Kolk, B. & Courtois, C. (2005). Editorial comments: Complex developmental trauma. *Journal of Traumatic Stress, 18*(5), 385–388.

van der Kolk, B., Roth, S. Pelcovitz, D., Sunday, S., Spinazzola, J. (2005). Disorders of Extreme Stress: The empirical foundation for a complex adaptation to trauma. *Journal of Traumatic Stress, 18*(5), 389–399.

van der Kolk, B. A. (2003). Posttraumatic stress disorder and the nature of trauma. In M. Solomon & D. J. Siegel (Eds.), *Healing trauma* (pp. 168–195). New York: W. W. Norton.

van der Kolk, B. A., & Pelcovitz, D. (1999). Clinical applications of the Structured Interview for Disorders of Extreme Stress (SIDES). *National Center for PTSD Clinical Quarterly, 8*(2), 1 and 23–26.

van der Kolk, B. A., Roth, S., Pelcovitz, D., & Mandel, F. S. (1992). *Disorders of extreme stress: Results from the DSM-IV field trials for PTSD.* Unpublished manuscript.

van der Kolk, B. A., & Sapporta, J. (1991). The biological response to psychic trauma: Mechanisms and treatment of intrusion and numbing. *Anxiety Research, 4*, 199–212.

van Lieshout, C. F. M. (2000). Lifespan personality development: Self-organising goal-oriented agents and developmental outcome. *International Journal of Behavioral Development, 24*(3), 276–288.

Vasey, M. W., Dalgleish, T., & Silverman, W. K. (2003). Research on information-processing factors in child and adolescent psychopathology: A critical commentary. *Journal of Clinical Child and Adolescent Psychology, 32*(1), 81–93.

Vassallo, P. (2002). Reporting for results: Creating a checklist. *ETC: A Review of General Semantics, 59*(3), 317–329.

Velez-Ibanez, C. G., & Parra, C. G. (1999). Trauma issues and social modalities concerning mental health concepts and practices among Mexicans of the southwest United States with reference to other Latino groups. In K. Nader, N. Dubrow, & B. Stamm (Eds.), *Honoring differences: Cultural issues in the treatment of trauma and loss* (pp. 76–97). Philadelphia: Taylor & Francis.

Vernberg, E. M., La Greca, A. M., Silverman, W. K., & Prinstein, M. J. (1996). Prediction of posttraumatic stress symptoms in children after Hurricane Andrew. *Journal of Abnormal Psychology, 105*, 237–248.

Verrier, N. N. (1993). *The primal wound: Understanding the adopted child.* Baltimore: Gateway Press.

Vila, G., Porche, L., & Mouren-Simeoni, M. (1999). An 18-month longitudinal study of posttraumatic disorders in children who were taken hostage in their school. *Psychosomatic Medicine, 61*, 746–754.

Vinokur, A., Oksenberg, L., & Cannell, C. F. (1979). Effects of feedback and reinforcement on the report of health information. In C. F. Cannell, L. Oksenberg, & J. M. Converse (Eds.), *Experiments in interviewing techniques: Field experiments in health reporting* (pp. 1971–1977). Ann Arbor: Survey Research Center, University of Michigan.

Vitulano, L. A., & Tebes, J. K. (1991). Child and adolescent behavior therapy. In M. Lewis (Ed.), *Child and adolescent psychiatry: A comprehensive textbook* (pp. 812–831). Baltimore: Williams & Wilkins.

Volkan, V. D. (2001). September 11 and societal regression. *Mind and Human Interaction, 12*, 196–216.

Waizer, J., Dorin, A., Stoller, E., & Laird, R. (2005). Community-based interventions in New York City after 9/11: A provider's perspective. In Y. Danieli, D. Brom, & J. Sills (Eds.), *The trauma of terrorism: Sharing knowledge and shared care* (pp. 499–512). New York: Haworth Press.

Wallace, J., Yorgin, P. D., Carolan, R., Moore, H., Sanchez, J., Belson, A., Yorgin, L., Major, C., Granucci, L., Alexander, S., & Arrington, D. (2004). The use of art therapy to detect depression and post-traumatic stress disorder in pediatric and young adult renal transplant recipients. *Pediatric Transplantation, 8*(1), 52–59.

Waller, N. G., Putnam, F. W., & Carlson, E. B. (1996). Types of dissociation and dissociative types. *Psychological Methods, 1,* 300–321.

Wandersman, L. P. (1998). Psychological evaluations in child maltreatment cases. Retrieved March 8, 2005, from http://childlaw.sc.edu/frmPublications/psycholgocialeveal_114200441025.pdf

Warren, A. R., & Lane, P. (1995). Effects of timing and type of questioning on eyewitness accuracy and suggestibility. In M. S. Zaragoza, J. R. Graham, G. C. N. Hall, R. Hirschman, & Y. S. Ben-Porath (Eds.), *Memory and testimony in the child witness* (pp. 44–60). Thousand Oaks, CA: Sage.

Waschbusch, D. A., Pelham, W.E., Jennings, J. R., Greiner, A. R., Tarter, R. E., & Moss, H. B. (2002). Reactive aggression in boys with disruptive behavior disorders: Behavior, physiology, and affect. *Journal of Abnormal Child Psychology, 30*(6), 641–656.

Waterman, A. H., Blades, M., & Spencer, C. P. (2001). Interviewing children and adults: The effect of question format on the tendency to speculate. *Applied Cognitive Psychology, 15,* 1–11.

Waterman, A. H., Blades, M., & Spencer, C. P. (2004). Indicating when you do not know the answer: The effect of question format and interviewer knowledge on children's "don't know" responses. *British Journal of Developmental Psychology, 22*(3), 335–348.

Waters, E. (1987). *The Attachment Behavior Q-set (Revision 3.0).* Unpublished manuscript. Stony Brook: State University of New York.

Watson, M. F. (1998). African American sibling relationships. In M. McGoldrick (Ed.), *Re-visioning family therapy* (pp. 282–294). New York: Guilford Press.

Weathers, F., Keane, T., King, L., & King, D. (1997). Psychometric theory in the development of posttraumatic stress disorder assessment tools. In J. P. Wilson & T. M. Keane (Eds.), *Assessing psychological trauma and PTSD* (1st ed., pp. 98–135). New York: Guilford Press.

Webb, N. B. (Ed.). (2002a). *Helping bereaved children* (2nd ed.). New York: Guilford Press.

Webb, N. B. (2002b). September 11, 2001. In N. B. Webb (Ed.), *Helping bereaved children* (2nd ed., pp. 365–384). New York: Guilford Press.

Webb, N. B. (Ed.). (2004). *Mass trauma, stress, and loss: Helping children and families cope.* New York: Guilford Press.

Wechsler, D. (2001). *Wechsler Individual Achievement Test, 2nd ed. (WIAT-II).* San Antonio, TX: The Psychological Corporation. [The Psychological Corporation, 19500 Bulverde Road, San Antonion, TX 78529, 1-800-972-1726].

Wechsler, D. (2002). *Wechsler Preschool and Primary Scale of Intelligence (WPPSI-III)* (3rd ed.). San Antonio, TX: Harcourt Assessment.

Wechsler, D. (2003). *Wechsler Intelligence Scale for Children (WISC-IV)* (4th ed.). San Antonio, TX: Harcourt Assessment.

Wechsler, D. (2004). *Wechsler Adult Intelligence Scale (WAIS-IV)*. San Antonio, TX: Harcourt Assessment.

Weems, C., Saltzman, K., & Reiss, A. (2003). A prospective test of the association between hyperarousal and emotional numbing in youth with a history of traumatic stress. *Journal of Clinical Child and Adolescent Psychology, 32*, 166–171.

Weine, S. (2001). From war zone to contact zone: Culture and refugee mental health services. *Journal of American Medical Association, 285*(9), 1214.

Weinfield, N. S., Sroufe, L. A., Egeland, B., & Carlson, E. A. (1999). The nature of individual differences in infant-caregiver attachment. In J. Cassidy & P. R. Shaver (Eds.), *Handbook of attachment* (pp. 68–88). New York: Guilford Press.

Weinstein, D., Staffelbach, D., & Biaggio, M. (2000). Attention-deficit hyperactivity disorder and posttraumatic stress disorder: Differential diagnosis in childhood sexual abuse. *Clinical Psychology Review, 20*(3), 359–378.

Weissman, M., Wichkramaratne, P., Warner, V., John, K., Prusoff, B., Merikangas, K., & Gammon, D. (1987). Assessing psychiatric disorders in children. *Archives of General Psychiatry, 44*, 747–753.

Weisz, J. R., & Sigman, M. (1993). Parent reports of behavioral and emotional problems among children in Kenya, Thailand, and the United States. *Child Development, 64*, 98–109.

Weisz, J. R., & Suwanlert, S. (1987). Epidemiology of behavioral and emotional problems among Thai and American children: Parent reports for ages 6 to 11. *Journal of the American Academy of Child & Adolescent Psychiatry, 26*, 890–897.

Werry, J. S. (1991). Brain and behavior. In M. Lewis (Ed.), *Child and adolescent psychiatry: A comprehensive textbook* (pp. 76–86). Baltimore: Williams & Wilkins.

West, M., Adam, K., Spreng, S., & Rose, S. (2001). Attachment disorganization and dissociative symptoms in clinically treated adolescents. *Canadian Journal of Psychiatry, 46*(7), 627–631.

Westerlund, B., & Johnson, C. (1989). DMT defenses and the experience of dreaming in children 12 to 13 years old. *Psychological Research Bulletin, 29*(6), 1–23.

Westermeyer, J. (1987). Cultural factors in clinical assessment. *Journal of Consulting and Clinical Psychology, 55*(4), 471–478.

Westermeyer, J. (1990). Working with an interpreter in psychiatric assessment and treatment. *Journal of Nervous and Mental Disease, 178*(12), 745–749.

Westermeyer, J., & Uecker, J. (1997). Predictors of hostility in a group of relocated refugees. *Cultural Diversity and Mental Health, 3*(1), 53–60.

Whealin, J. M., & Jackson, J. L. (2002). Childhood unwanted sexual attention and young women's present self-concept. *Journal of Interpersonal Violence, 17*(8), 854–871.

Wherry, J. N., Jolly, J. B., Feldman, J., Adam, B., & Manjanatha, S. (1994). The Child Dissociative Checklist: Preliminary findings of a screening instrument. *Child Abuse and Neglect, 3*, 51–66.

White, C. R., Wallace, J., & Huffman, L. C. (2004). Use of drawings to identify thought impairment among students with emotional and behavioral disorders: An exploratory study. *Art Therapy Journal of the American Art Therapy Association, 21*(4), 210–218.

White, S., Halpin, B. M., Strom, G. A., & Santilli, G. (1988). Behavioral comparisons of young sexually abused, neglected, and nonreferred children. *Journal of Clinical Child Psychology, 17*(1), 53–61.

Wiedemann, J., & Greenwald, R. (2000, November). Child trauma assessment with the CROPS and PROPS: Construct validity in a German translation. Symposium conducted at the annual meeting of the International Society for Traumatic Stress Studies, San Antonio, TX.

Williams, J. M. G., & Broadbent, K. (1986). Autobiographical memory in suicide attempters. *Journal of Abnormal Psychology, 95,* 144–149.

Williams, M. B. (1994). Intervention with child victims of trauma in the school setting. In M. B. Williams & J. F. Sommer (Eds.), *Handbook of post-traumatic therapy* (pp. 69–77). Westport, CT: Greenwood Press.

Williams, M. B. (In press). *Trauma and the internatiionally adopted child.* New York: Routledge.

Williams, M. B., & Sommer, J. F. (Eds.). (2002). *Simple and complex posttraumatic stress disorder.* New York: Haworth Maltreatment and Trauma Press.

Wilsey, D. D. (2004). Ethical obligation of child abuse prosecutors and allied professionals: Understanding the interconnection. *American Prosecutors Research Institute Newsletter, 17*(1) 1–3. Retrieved March 18, 2005, from www.ndaa.apri. org/publications/newsletter/update_volume_17_number_1_2004.html

Wilson, J. P. (2004a). PTSD and complex PTSD: Symptoms, syndromes, and diagnoses. In J. P. Wilson & T. M. Keane (Eds.), *Assessing psychological trauma and PTSD* (2nd ed., pp. 7–44). New York: Guilford Press.

Wilson, J. P. (2004b). The broken spirit: Post-traumatic damage to the self. In J. P. Wilson & B. Drozdek (Eds.), *Broken spirits: Treating traumatized asylum seekers, refugees, war and torture victims* (pp. 107–155). New York: Brunner-Routledge Press.

Wilson, J. P., Friedman, M., & Lindy, J. (Eds.). (2001). *Treating psychological trauma and PTSD.* New York: Guilford Press.

Wilson, J. P., & Moran, T. A. (2004). Forensic/clinical assessment of psychological trauma and PTSD in legal setting. In J. Wilson & T. Keane (Eds.), *Assessing psychological trauma & PTSD* (2nd ed., pp. 603–636). New York: Guilford Press.

Wilson, J. P., & Thomas, R. B. (2004). *Empathy in the treatment of trauma and PTSD.* New York: Brunner-Routledge.

Winje, D., & Ulvik, A. (1998). Long-term outcome of trauma in children: The psychological consequences of a bus accident. *Journal of Child Psychology and Psychiatry and Allied Disciplines, 39*(5), 635–642.

Winnicot, D. W. (1971). *Therapeutic consultations in child psychiatry.* New York: Basic Books.

Winston, F. K., Kassam-Adams, N., Garcia-Espana, F., Ittenbach, R., & Cnaan, A. (2003). Screening for risk of persistent posttraumatic stress in injured children and their parents. *JAMA: Journal of the American Medical Association, 290*(5), 643–649.

Witkin, S. J. (2005). Assessing developmental level when representing foster care children. *Human Rights: Journal of the Section of Individual Rights & Responsibilities, 32*(1), 8.

Wolfe, V. V., & Birt, J. H. (1993). The Children's Peritraumatic Experiences Questionnaire. Unpublished assessment instrument, Child and Adolescent Centre, London Health Sciences Centre, London, Ontario, Canada.

Wolfe, V. V., & Birt, J. H. (1997). Child sexual abuse. In E. J. Mash & L. G. Terdal (Eds.), *Behavioral assessment of childhood disorders* (3rd ed., pp. 569–626). New York: Guilford Press.

Wolfe, V. V., & Birt, J. H. (2002a). *The Children's Impact of Traumatic Events Scale-Revised (CITES-R): Scale structure, internal consistency, discriminant validity, and PTSD diagnostic patterns.* Manuscript submitted for publication.

Wolfe, V. V., & Birt, J. H. (2002b). *The Children's Peritraumatic Experiences Questionnaire: A measure to assess DSM-IV PTSD Criterion A2.* Manuscript submitted for publication.

Wolfe, V. V., & Gentile, C. (1991). Children's Impact of Traumatic Events Scale, Revised (CITES-R). Measure of childhood traumatic reactions.

Wolfe, V. V., & Gentile, C. (2003). Children's Impact of Traumatic Events Scale-2, Revised (CITES-2). Measure of childhood traumatic reactions. Available from Vicky Veitch Wolfe, Ph.D., Child & Adolescent Centre, 346 South Street, London Health Sciences Centre, London, Ontario, Canada N6A 4G5, or wolfev@lhsc.on.ca.

Wolfe, V. V., Gentile, C., & Bourdeau, P. (1987). History of Victimization Form. Unpublished assessment instrument, Child and Adolescent Centre, London Health Sciences Centre, London, Ontario, Canada.

Wolfe, V. V., Gentile, C., Michienzi, T., Sas, L., & Wolfe, D. A. (1991). The Children's Impact of Traumatic Events Scale: A measure of post-sexual-abuse PTSD symptoms. *Behavioral Assessment, 13*(4), 359–383.

Wolfe, V. V., Wolfe, D. A., Gentile, C., & Larose, L. (1986). Children's Impact of Traumatic Events Scale (CITES). Copyrighted instrument.

Wood, J., Foy, D. W., Goguen, C. A., Pynoos, R., & James, C. B. (2002). Violence exposure and PTSD among delinquent girls. In R. Greenwald (Ed.), *Trauma and juvenile delinquency: Theory, research, and interventions* (pp. 109–126). New York: Haworth Press.

World Health Organization (WHO). (1992). *The ICD-10 classification of mental and behavioral disorders: Clinical descriptions and diagnostic guidelines.* Geneva, Switzerland: Author.

Wyman, P. A. (2003). Emerging perspectives on context specificity of children's adaptation and resilience. In S. S. Luthar (Ed.), *Resilience and vulnerability: Adaptation in the context of childhood adversities* (pp. 293–317). New York: Cambridge University Press.

Yates, T. M., Egeland, B., & Sroufe, A. (2003). Rethinking resilience: A developmental process perspective. In S. S. Luthar (Ed.), *Resilience and vulnerability: Adaptation in the context of childhood adversities* (pp. 243–266). New York: Cambridge University Press.

Yee, P. L., Pierce, G. R., Ptacek, J. T., & Modzelesky, K. L. (2003). Learned helplessness attributional style and examination performance: Enhancement effects are not necessarily moderated by prior failure. *Anxiety, Stress & Coping, 16*(4), 359–373.

Yellin, C., Atwood, G., Melnick, S., & Lyons-Ruth, K. (2003). *Expanding the concept of unresolved mental states: Hostile/helpless states of mind on the adult attachment interview link maternal trauma to infant disorganization.* Manuscript submitted for publication.

Yoo, B., & Donthu, N. (2002). Review of the book *Culture's consequences. Journal of Marketing Research, 39*(3), 388–339.

Yule, W., Bolton, D., Udwin, O., Boyle, S., O'Ryan, D., & Nurrish, J. (2000). The long-term psychological effects of a disaster experienced in adolescence: I: The incidence and course of PTSD. *Journal of Child Psychology & Psychiatry & Allied Disciplines, 41,* 503–511.

Yule, W., Udwin, O., & Bolton, D. (2002). Mass transportation disasters. In A. M. La Greca, W. K. Silverman, E. M. Vernberg, & M. C. Roberts (Eds.), *Helping children cope with disasters and terrorism* (pp. 223–239). Washington, DC: APA Press.

Zahn, B. S. (1994). *Stress symptoms in 11-16-year-old victims of child sexual abuse.* Doctoral dissertation, College of Education, Temple University, Philadelphia.

Zalsman, G., Netanel, R., Fischel, T., Freudenstein, O., Landau, E., Orbach, I., Weizman, A., Pfeffer, C. R., & Apter, A. (2000). Human figure drawings in the evaluation of severe adolescent suicidal behavior. *Journal of the American Academy of Child & Adolescent Psychiatry, 39*(8), 1024–1031.

Zeanah, C. H., Jr. (Ed.). (2000). *Handbook of infant mental health* (2nd ed.). New York: Guilford Press.

Zeanah, C. H., Boris, N. W., & Scheeringa, M. S. (1997). Psychopathology in infancy. *Journal of Child Psychology and Psychiatry, 38,* 81–99.

Zhang, Y., Kohnstamm, G., Slotboom, A., Elphick, E., & Cheung, P. C. (2002). Chinese and Dutch parents' perceptions of their children's personality. *Journal of Genetic Psychology, 163*(2), 165–178.

Author Index

Subject Index

A

AAI, *see* Scales or assessment methods by name

Abandonment, 156, 182, 183, 194, 363, 399

Abnormal, *behavior, development*, 57, 178
brain/neurochemistry, 1, 35, 41, 47, 50
candor, 223

Abuse, *see also* Domestic violence; Emotional abuse; Molestation; Neglect; Sexual abuse; Substance abuse; Trauma types
adults with history of, 9, 42, 50
adoption, and, 182
aggression, and, 9, 78, 124, 324, 332
assessment, 355, 371, 372, 379, 382, 391
  art, 287, 288, 289, 293, table 12.1 (294), 295
  difficulties, chapter 4, 100
  exposure/intensity, 255, table 10.1 (256–259), 260–263
  information processing, 338–341
  measures (general information), 266, 267, 272
  observation, 323, 323–324
  parent report, 308–310, 313
  projective, 297–302
  PTSD and other symptoms, 244, table 11.1 (274–276), 278–279

attachment, and, 73, 195, 202, 203, 206, 210, 211, 212, 350
brain and neurobiology, 25, 42, 43, 50, 51–52, 56, 57, 73
case examples, 5, 86, 140, 194, 225, 395
complex trauma, and, 22, 24
dissociation, and, 341, 343, 344, 347, 350, 353, 354
domestic violence, and, 398
duration/frequency, 11–12, 22, 52, 83, 131, 243, 244, 245, 252, 260
elicitation of, 10
forensic issues, chapters 9 and 16, 391, 392, 393, 394, 400
gender, 51, 147-148
helplessness or vulnerability, and, 71, 195
humiliation, and, 71, 374
information processing, and, *biases, expectations, interpretations*, 78, 82, 334–338, 339
intensity, *severity*, 50, 83, 131, 203, 244, 245, 247, 260, 353
interviewing, chapter 9, 221–222, 225, 228, 235–238, 382
media, and, 242
medication abuse, *see* Substance abuse
memory, and, 231
nonabuse, 51, 83, 245, 262, 266, 268, 288, 298, 340, 399
onset, 50, 52, 100, 353–354